MANAGING ORGANIZATIONAL BEHAVIOR

MANAGING ORGANIZATIONAL BEHAVIOR

Ramon J. Aldag
Graduate School of Business
University of Wisconsin—Madison

Arthur P. Brief
Graduate School of Business
New York University

WEST PUBLISHING COMPANY
St. Paul New York Los Angeles San Francisco

Cover photo

© Phillip Harrington

The photo shows a very small section of printed circuitry on a computer chip used in an electronic organ.

Photo Credits

20, Bob Gaylord. **31,** Bob Gaylord. **51,** Jeffery P. Grosscup. **78,** Charles L. Farrow. **96,** Charles L. Farrow. **122,** Bob Gaylord. **159,** Bob Gaylord. **234,** Bob Gaylord. **276,** Bob Gaylord. **351,** Bob Gaylord. **375,** Bob Gaylord. **460,** Charles L. Farrow.

50 West Kellogg Boulevard
P.O. Box 3526
St. Paul, Minnesota 55165

Printed in the United States of America

Library of Congress Cataloging in Publication Data

Main entry under title:

Managing organizational behavior.

Bibliography: p.
Includes index.
1. Management—Addresses, essays, lectures.
2. Organizational behavior—Addresses, essays, lectures. I. Aldag, Ramon J., 1945-
II. Brief, Arthur P., 1946
HD31.M2942 658 80-26293
ISBN 0-8299-0306-2

DEDICATION

To Holly Jellinek
and Kay Brief

Contents

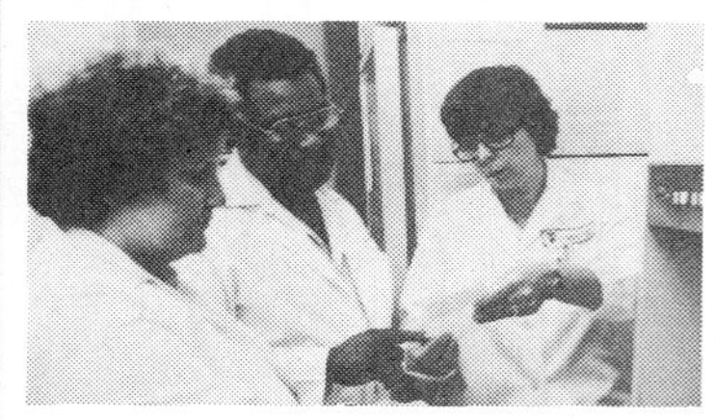

STRIKE
LOCAL UNION 120
I.B. of T.C.W.H. of A.
SAINT PAUL

Preface

We have found teaching and doing research in organizational behavior to be fascinating endeavors. However, we have also observed that our enthusiasm did not always infect our students, especially those at the introductory levels. Not wanting to attribute this state of affairs to our classroom performances, we naturally assumed that is was, at least in part, a function of the textbooks we were using.

After surveying the available options, we decided to write an introductory textbook that would try to (1) reflect the current state of knowledge, (2) demonstrate to the student the practical significance of the organizational literature, and (3) be enjoyable reading. We felt that if these three aims could be achieved we would have gone a long way toward providing a book that would stimulate the level of student interest in organizational behavior that the subject matter deserves. Ultimately, we hope our book will encourage students to try to learn more about the discipline and, of course, to apply their knowledge on the job.

In this book, we have tried to capture the essence of what it is that managers must accomplish to be successful. In doing so, we have rejected the view that there is something inappropriate about straightforward language, occasional humor, and the like. We feel that such devices as appropriate cartoons, engrossing examples, and evidence of "real-world" relevance enhance student interest without in any way compromising scholarly integrity. Further, we have made no attempt to impress the reader with unnecessarily heavy referencing. Rather, we have chosen to try to concisely summarize and interpret material relating to specific issues.

About a quarter of the text is composed of readings. Those readings are drawn not from sources which are heavily research oriented but from journals and texts which attempt to explain and note the relevance of specific issues and controversies. Readings are included simply because they are felt to be appropriate, timely, informative, and interesting. We also feel that the differing styles of the various authors add to the readability of the text. Readings are fully integrated into the text and are treated as chapters.

This book, like all professional efforts, reflects the influences of our teachers and colleagues. We would particularly like to express our gratitude to Larry Cummings, Andre Delbecq, Alan Filley, Dalton McFarland, Winston Oberg, Donald Schwab, Henry Tosi and Harold Wein. We would also like to thank our peers who commented on earlier drafts of the book. They include Arthur Bedeian, Lloyd Baird, Donald Hellriegel, James Quick, Laurie Larwood and John Slocum. Finally, we are indebted to the secretarial staff of the Business Schools of the University of Wisconsin-Madison and the University of Iowa for their assistance.

Ramon J. Aldag
Madison, Wisconsin

Arthur P. Brief
New York, New York

MANAGING ORGANIZATIONAL BEHAVIOR

SECTION I

Management And Organizational Behavior

The purpose of this section is to introduce organizational behavior to the reader and to describe how the remainder of the book is organized. First, we will identify the various roles a manager plays, and then we will discuss the importance of applying organizational behavior knowledge to those roles. Next, we will analyze the nature of organizational behavior as an applied science. The section ends with an overview of the remainder of the book.

KEY TERMS

MANAGERIAL ROLES
- Figurehead role
- Leader role
- Liaison role
- Monitor role
- Disseminator role
- Spokesman role
- Entrepreneur role
- Disturbance-handler role
- Resource-handler role
- Negotiator role

ORGANIZATIONAL BEHAVIOR
SCIENTIFIC METHOD
SPHERES OF MANAGERIAL ACTIVITY

OBJECTIVES

1. To describe what managers do on their jobs
2. To describe what organizational behavior is
3. To describe how the application of organizational behavior knowledge can contribute to the effective performance of managerial roles
4. To describe the organization of the book

CHAPTER

1

The Manager's Job: Folklore and Fact*

SOME FOLKLORE AND FACTS ABOUT MANAGERIAL WORK

There are four myths about the manager's job that do not bear up under careful scrutiny of the facts.

1. *Folklore: The manager is a reflective, systematic planner.* The evidence on this issue is overwhelming, but not a shred of it supports this statement.

Fact: Study after study has shown that managers work at an unrelenting pace, that their activities are characterized by brevity, variety, and discontinuity and that they are strongly oriented to action and dislike reflective activities.

2. *Folklore: The effective manager has no regular duties to perform.* Managers are constantly being told to spend more time planning and delegating, and less time seeing customers and engaging in negotiations. These are not, after all, the true tasks of the manager. To use the popular analogy, the good manager, like the good conductor, carefully orchestrates everything in advance, then sits back to enjoy the fruits of his labor, responding occasionally to an unforeseeable exception.

But here again the pleasant abstraction just does not seem to hold up. We had better take a closer look at those activities managers feel compelled to engage in before we arbitrarily define them away.

Fact: In addition to handling exceptions, managerial work involves performing a number of regular duties, including ritual and

*Abridged from Henry Mintzberg, "The Manager's Job: Folklore and Fact," *Harvard Business Review*, July-August 1975, *ceremony, negotiations, and processing of soft information that links the organization with its environment.*

3. *Folklore: The senior manager needs aggregated information, which a formal management information system best provides.* Not too long ago, the words *total information system* were everywhere in the management literature. In keeping with the classical view of the manager as that individual perched on the apex of a regulated, hierarchical system, the literature's manager was to receive all his important information from a giant, comprehensive MIS.

But lately, as it has become increasingly evident that these giant MIS systems are not working—that managers are simply not using them—the enthusiasm has waned. A look at how managers actually process information makes the reason quite clear. Managers have five media at their command—documents, telephone calls, scheduled and unscheduled meetings, and observational tours.

Fact: Managers strongly favor the verbal media—namely, telephone calls and meetings.

4. *Folklore: Management is, or at least is quickly becoming, a science and a profession.* By almost any definitions of *science* and *profession*, this statement is false. Brief observation of any manager will quickly lay to rest the notion that managers practice a science. A science involves the enaction of systematic, analytically determined procedures or programs. If we do not even know what procedures managers use, how can we prescribe them by scientific analysis? And how can we call management a profession if we cannot specify what managers are to learn? For after all, a profession involves "knowledge of some department of learning or science" (*Random House Dictionary*).

Fact: The managers' programs—to schedule time, process information, make decisions, and so on—remain locked deep inside their brains. Thus, to describe these programs, we rely on words like *judgment* and *intuition*, seldom stopping to realize that they are merely labels for our ignorance.

Considering the facts about managerial work, we can see that the manager's job is enormously complicated and difficult. The manager is overburdened with obligations; yet he cannot easily delegate his tasks. As a result, he is driven to overwork and is forced to do many tasks superficially. Brevity, fragmentation, and verbal communication characterize his work. Yet these are the very characteristics of managerial work that have impeded scientific attempts to improve it. As a result, the management scientist has concentrated his efforts on the specialized functions of the organization, where he could more easily analyze the procedures and quantify the relevant information.

But the pressures of the manager's job are becoming worse. Where before he needed only to respond to owners and directors, now he finds that subordinates with democratic norms continually reduce his freedom to issue unexplained orders, and a growing number of outside influences (consumer groups, government agencies, and so on) expect his attention. And the manager has had nowhere to turn for help. The first step in providing the manager with some help is to find out what his job really is.

BACK TO A BASIC DESCRIPTION OF MANAGERIAL WORK

Now let us try to put some of the pieces of this puzzle together. I define the manager as that person in charge of an organization or one of its subunits. Besides chief executive officers, this definition would include vice presidents, bishops, foremen, hockey coaches, and prime ministers. Can all of these people have anything in common? Indeed they can. For an important starting point, all are vested with formal authority over an organizational unit. From formal authority comes status, which leads to various interpersonal relations, and from these comes access to information. Information, in turn, enables the manager to make decisions and strategies for his unit.

The manager's job can be described in terms of various "roles," or organized sets of behaviors identified with a position. My description, shown in Figure 1-1, comprises ten roles. As we shall see, formal authority gives rise to the three interpersonal roles, which in turn give rise to the three informational roles; these two sets of roles enable the manager to play the four decisional roles.

Interpersonal roles

Three of the manager's roles arise directly from his formal authority and involve basic interpersonal relationships.

Figurehead role. First is the *figurehead* role. By virtue of his position as head of an organizational unit, every manager must perform some duties of a ceremonial nature. The president greets the touring dignitaries, the foreman attends the wedding of a lathe operator, and the sales manager takes an important customer to lunch.

Duties that involve interpersonal roles may sometimes be routine, involving little serious communication and no important decision making. Nevertheless, they are important to the smooth functioning of an organization and cannot be ignored by the manager.

Leader role. Because he is in charge of an organizational unit, the manager is responsible for the work of the people of that unit. His actions in this regard constitute the *leader* role. Some of this actions involve leadership directly—for example, in most organizations the manager is normally responsible for hiring and training his own staff.

In addition, there is the indirect exercise of the leader role. Every manager must motivate and encourage his employees, somehow reconciling their individual needs with the goals of the organization. In virtually every contact the manager has with his employees, subordinates seeking leadership clues probe his actions: "Does he approve?" "How would he like the report to turn out?" "Is he more interested in market share than high profits?"

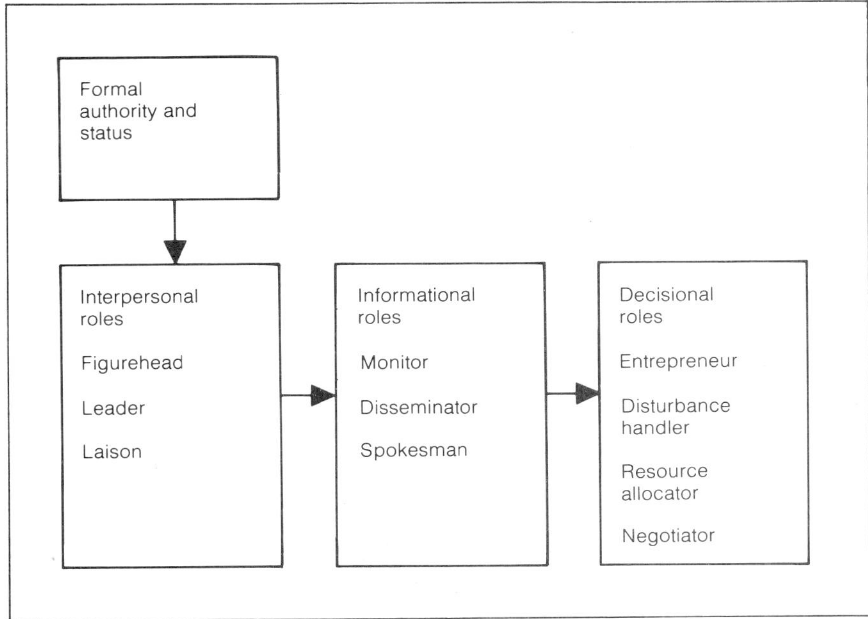

FIGURE 1-1

The influence of the manager is most clearly seen in the leader role. Formal authority vests him with great potential power; leadership determines in large part how much of it he will realize.

Liason role. The literature of management has always recognized the leader role, particularly those aspects of it related to motivation. In comparison, until recently it has hardly mentioned the *liaison* role, in which the manager makes contacts outside his vertical chain of command. This is remarkable in light of the finding of virtually every study of managerial work that managers spend as much time with peers and other people outside their units as they do with their own subordinates—and, surprisingly, very little time with their own superiors.

As we shall see shortly, the manager cultivates such contacts largely to find information. In effect, the liaison role is devoted to building up the manager's own external information system —informal, private, verbal, but nevertheless, effective.

Informational roles

By virtue of his interpersonal contacts, both with his subordinates and with his network of contacts, the manager emerges as the nerve center of his organizational unit. He may not know everything, but he typically knows more than any member of his staff.

Monitor role. As *monitor,* the manager perpetually scans his environment for information, interrogates his liaison contacts and his subordinates, and receives unsolicited information, much of it as a result of the network of personal contacts he has developed. Remember that a good part of the information the manager collects in his monitor role arrives in verbal form, often as gossip, hearsay, and speculation. By virtue of his contacts, the manager has a natural advantage in collecting this soft information for his organization.

Disseminator role. He must share and distribute much of this information. Information he gleans from outside personal contacts may be needed within his organization. In his *disseminator* role, the manager passes some of his privileged information directly to his subordinates, who would otherwise have no access to it. When his subordinates lack easy contact with one another, the manager will sometimes pass information from one to another.

Spokesman role. In his *spokesman* role, the manager sends some of his information to people outside his unit—a president makes a speech to lobby for an organization cause, or a foreman suggests a product modification to a supplier. In addition, as part of his role as spokesman, every manager must inform and satisfy the influential people who control his organizational unit. For the foreman, this may simply involve keeping the plant manager informed about the flow of work through the shop.

The president of a large corporation, however, may spend a great amount of his time dealing with a host of influences. Directors and shareholders must be advised about financial performance; consumer groups must be assured that the organization is fulfilling its social responsibilities; and government officials must be satisfied that the organization is abiding by the law.

Decisional roles

Information is not, of course, an end in itself; it is the basic input to decision making. One thing is clear in the study of managerial work: the manager plays the major role in his unit's decision-making system. As its formal authority, only he can commit the unit to important new courses of action; and as its nerve center, only he has full and current information to make the set of decisions that determines the unit's strategy. Four roles describe the manager as decision-maker.

Entrepreneur role. As *entrepreneur*, the manager seeks to improve his unit, to adapt it to changing conditions in the environment. In his monitor role, the president is constantly on the lookout for new ideas. When a good one appears, he initiates a development project that he may supervise himself or delegate to an employee (perhaps with the stipulation that he must approve the final proposal).

There are two interesting features about these development projects at the chief executive level. First, these projects do not involve single decisions or even unified clusters of decisions. Rather,

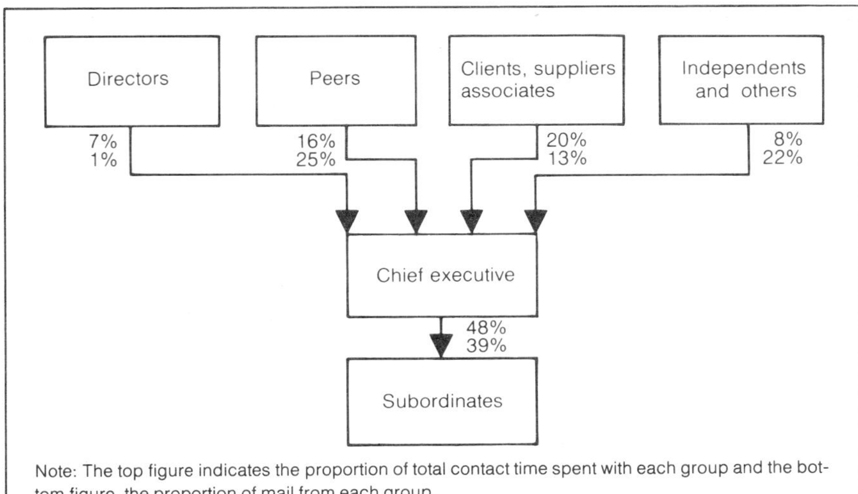

FIGURE 1-2
The Chief Executive's Contacts

they emerge as a series of small decisions and actions sequenced over time. Apparently, the chief executive prolongs each project so that he can fit it bit by bit into his busy, disjointed schedule and so that he can gradually come to comprehend the issue, it it is a complex one.

Second, the chief executives I studied supervised as many as 50 of these projects at the same time. Some projects entailed new products or processes; others involved public relations campaigns, improvement of the cash position, reorganization of a weak department, resolution of a morale problem in a foreign division, integration of computer operations, various acquisitions at different stages of development, and so on.

The chief executive appears to maintain a kind of inventory of the development projects that he himself supervises—projects that are at various stages of development, some active and some in limbo. Like a juggler, he keeps a number of projects in the air; periodically, one comes down, is given a new burst of energy, and is sent back into orbit. At various intervals, he puts new projects on-stream and discards old ones.

Disturbance handler. While the entrepreneur role describes the manager as the voluntary initiator of change, the *disturbance handler* role depicts the manager involuntarily responding to pressures. Here change is beyond the manager's control. He must act because the pressures of the situation are too severe to be ignored: strike looms, a major-customer has gone bankrupt, or a supplier reneges on his contract.

In effect, every manager must spend a good part of his time responding to high-pressure disturbances. No organization can be so well run, so standardized, that it has considered every contingency in the uncertain environment in advance. Disturbances arise not only because poor managers ignore situations until they reach crisis proportions, but also because good managers cannot possibly anticipate all the consequences of the actions they take.

Resource allocator. The third decisional role is that of *resource allocator.* To the manager falls the responsibility of deciding who will get what in his organizational unit. Perhaps the most important resource the manager allocates is his own time. Access to the manager constitutes exposure to the unit's nerve center and decision-maker. The manager is also charged with designing his unit's structure, that pattern of formal relationships that determines how work is to be divided and coordinated.

Also, in his role as resource allocator, the manager authorizes the important decisions of his unit before they are implemented. By retaining this power, the manager can ensure that decisions are interrelated; all must pass through a single brain. To fragment this power is to encourage discontinuous decision making and a disjointed strategy.

Negotiator role. The final decisional role is that of *negotiator.* Studies of managerial work at all levels indicate that managers spend considerable time in negotiations: the president of the football team is called in to work out a contract with the holdout superstar; the corporation president leads his company's contingent to negotiate a new strike issue; the foreman argues a grievance problem to its conclusion with the shop steward. As Leonard Sayles puts it, negotiations are a "way of life" for the sophisticated manager.

These negotiations are duties of the manager's job; perhaps routine, they are not to be shirked. They are an integral part of his job, for only he has the authority to commit organizational resources in "real time," and only he has the nerve center information that important negotiations require.

The integrated job

It should be clear by now that the ten roles I have been describing are not easily separable. In the terminology of the psychologist, they form a gestalt, an integrated whole. No role can be pulled out of the framework and the job be left intact. For example, a manager without liaison contacts lacks external information. As a result, he can neither disseminate the information his employees need nor make decisions that adequately reflect external conditions. (In fact, this is a problem for the new person in a managerial position, since he cannot make effective decisions until he has built up his network of contacts.)

To say that the ten roles form a gestalt is not to say that all managers give equal attention to each role. In fact, I found in my review of the various research studies that

—sales managers seem to spend relatively more of their time in the interpersonal roles, presumably a reflection of the extrovert nature of the marketing activity;

—production managers give relatively more attention to the decisional roles, presumably a reflection of their concern with efficient work flow;

—staff managers spend the most time in the informational roles, since they are experts who manage departments that advise other parts of the organization.

Nevertheless, in all cases the interpersonal, informational, and decisional roles remain inseparable.

CHAPTER 2

What Is Organizational Behavior?

So you want to be a successful manager. Maybe, you want the power, prestige, money, and satisfaction that may result from doing your job right and moving up the organizational ladder. The logical question to ask yourself is, "How do I get to be a good manager?" According to Henry Mintzberg (1975), who studied the chief executive officers of a consulting firm, a technology company, a hospital, a consumer goods company, and a school system, the way to become a good manager is to develop a number of important skills—"developing peer relationships, carrying out negotiations, motivating subordinates, resolving conflicts, establishing information networks and subsequently disseminating information, making decisions in conditions of extreme ambiguity, and allocating resources" (p. 61). Each of these skills requires the manager to know something about how people think, feel, and act in different circumstances.

Knowing something about people, however, is not enough. The successful manager has the ability to translate "people knowledge" into programs of action. For example, Susie, the accounting supervisor in the business office of a large manufacturing plant, once took a psychology course in interpersonal communications. Yet Susie finds it very difficult to constructively criticize a new bookkeeper who really needs counseling. Susie feels she learned a lot in her communications course, but she doesn't know how to apply her "textbook knowledge" to actually counseling an underachieving employee. In other words, Susie has some "people knowledge," but she doesn't know how to translate it into a course of action.

The basic sources of information about how and why people think, feel, and act the way they do come from the social sciences —anthropology, economics, history, political science, psychology, and sociology. The academic discipline principally concerned with translating basic social science knowledge into programs of managerial action is *organizational behavior*. Yes, organizational behavior is an academic discipline and, as such, encompasses a lot of "textbook knowledge." But organizational behavior is different from the other social sciences. Students of organizational behavior are concerned with developing theories that can be applied to the practice of management. Other social sciences are largely concerned with building basic, rather than applied, theories. Thus, the answer to the question "How do I get to be a good manager?" is, in part, "Learn something about organizational behavior." The purpose of this book is to help you in that learning process.

ORGANIZATIONAL BEHAVIOR DEFINED

We have already noted that organizational behavior is a branch of the social sciences concerned with the study of people's thoughts, feelings, and actions at work. Formally, organizational behavior can be defined as *a branch of the social sciences that seeks to build theories that can be applied to predicting, understanding, and controlling behavior in work organizations*. Let's look closely at the components of this definition. First, organizational behavior is a social science that seeks to build theories. This implies that if you really want to learn something about organizational behavior, you must become familiar with what a theory is and know how to separate good theories from bad theories.

The second part of the definition of organizational behavior states that the theories built are to be applied to predicting, understanding, and controlling behavior in work organizations. In other words, organizational behavior theories actually can be used by people in performing their jobs. Most people equate theory with useless ivory-tower abstractions. Not so with organizational behavior theory. A good organizational behavior theory is the manager's best guide to practice.

Before moving on, we probably should consider one word in particular—*controlling*. When someone starts talking about controlling someone else's behavior, the natural reaction is to think that the speaker is a devious manipulator. But the truth is, we don't think of ourselves that way at all. Our use of the word *controlling* merely reflects the belief that the manager's job involves getting things done through other people. Thus, the manager is concerned with influencing the behavior of other people. For example, what time someone arrives at work, how many units he or she produces, and the quality of those units are all legitimate concerns of the manager. The word *controlling*, as used in the definition of organizational behavior, refers to the responsibility of the manager to *influence* the job behaviors of those he or she supervises. If you feel better using *influencing* rather than *controlling*, please do.

THEORY AND RESEARCH IN ORGANIZATIONAL BEHAVIOR

Being a science, organizational behavior relies upon scientific methods to build, evaluate, and modify theories about behavior in work organizations. The *scientific method* attempts to produce information that is objective in the sense that it is certifiable and independent of a person's opinions or preferences. Thus, the scientific method involves (a) making predictions about the real world, (b) making observations in the real world to determine the accuracy of our predictions, and (c) using the results of our observations to explain relationships among objects, events, or persons in the real world.

We do not expect the reader to become a junior scientist; rather, our hope is that the reader will respect the scientific method as one way of *knowing*, in addition to relying on habit, intuition, or some other source of information. To aid you in gaining this respect, appendix I contains a more detailed discussion of theory and research in organizational behavior. If the scientific method is new to you, we urge you to study the material in the appendix carefully.

Design of book

We will not attempt to present one grand theory of how to manage —because there is none. Managers find themselves in many different spheres of activities; and, in each of the spheres, they perform one or more of the *roles* Mintzberg identified in the first chapter. At this time, it is not possible to link together systematically each sphere of activity and the roles which compose those spheres into a holistic, integrated framework that makes sense and could be used by the practicing manager. As our knowledge about behavior in work organizations increases, the presentation of such a model may become practical; but, for now, we feel the best approach is to address specific spheres of managerial activity and to help the manager better perform the roles found in those spheres.

The spheres of managerial activity we will discuss include (1) recruiting, selecting, and retaining employees; (2) fulfilling employee needs; (3) motivating employees; (4) making decisions; (5) leading; (6) managing work groups; (7) maintaining organizational vitality; and (8) career management. The boundaries between these spheres are not hard and fast. For example, motivating employees frequently involves making decisions and managing work groups. In addition, the activities that compose each sphere do not collectively represent everything managers do on their jobs. But the spheres selected represent the essential activities that constitute the human side of management. Finally, the managerial role or roles acted out in any particular sphere are likely to be found in several other spheres of activity. Thus, the aids we will present for developing role competencies in a given sphere will spill over into the activities in another realm of managerial activity.

The remainder of the book is organized into eight major sections, with the chapters in each section addressing one of the previously noted spheres of managerial activity. After we briefly describe the contents of each major section, you should have a better feel for where we are headed.

Recruiting, selecting, and retaining employees. This section contains three chapters. The first chapter discusses how people choose jobs and how organizations select people; the chapter concludes with a set of recommendations for selecting your own job. The second chapter in the section describes one employment interview technique that has been shown to reduce employee turnover. And the final chapter continues this theme with a more general discussion of how to build employee loyalty.

Fulfilling employee needs. In the first of the four chapters in this section, the results of a study of job satisfaction among a sample of younger workers are presented. The nature of human needs, their interrelationships, and how they might be satisfied at work are discussed in the second chapter. The third chapter addresses the importance of job satisfaction and what managers can do to increase it. In the final chapter, we will provide the means for answering the following three questions: When should job satisfaction be systematically assessed in a particular organization? How are levels of job satisfaction assessed? And what should be done with job satisfaction information once it has been collected?

Motivating employees. The six chapters in this section provide a basic framework for understanding the causes of employee performance, as well as suggestions for increasing performance levels. The first chapter examines three contemporary theories of employee motivation; collectively, these provide a powerful set of tools with which to understand, predict, and influence performance in organizations. The next chapter highlights a number of pitfalls associated with not linking rewards to desired behaviors. Money is the topic of the third chapter in the section, in which we will discuss how and when to use money to motivate and the roles of punishment and *behavior modification* in work organizations. Behavior modification as a management tool is further discussed in the next chapter. The fifth chapter introduces another motivational technique, *job enrichment*. And in the final chapter in the section we warn against viewing job enrichment as *the* solution to people problems in work organizations.

Making decisions. Collectively, the four chapters in this section address how to make better decisions. The first chapter zeros in on the manager as an individual decision maker, pointing out the imperfections of humans as decision makers and suggesting ways to improve decision-making skills. The next chapter, which serves as a transition to the topic of group decision making, highlights some interesting problems unique to groups. The third chapter elaborates upon our discussion of groups as problem-solving entities and provides specific strategies for improving group effectiveness. Creativity in organizations is the concern of the final chapter in the section; the "causes" of creativity are identified, and techniques to enhance creativity are described.

Leading. The two chapters in this section focus on the leadership activities of the manager. In the first chapter, leaders are viewed as power brokers, and the traits and styles of successful leaders are discussed. In addition, three situational theories of leadership are introduced, and a number of "substitutes" for leadership are identified. In the second chapter, how leaders can acquire power and use power in their jobs are examined.

Managing work groups. This section consists of four chapters that examine group processes and team building. In the first chapter, the notion of *status* is used to demonstrate how group structure affects group processes. The use of one "status symbol," clothing, is addressed in detail in the next chapter. The third chapter presents discussions of how work groups form and the concepts of group *cohesiveness* and *norms*. The final chapter offers the *management by group objectives* process as one means of achieving congruence between work group and organizational goals.

Maintaining organization vitality. The four chapters in this section focus on two ways to maintain a "healthy" organization, the successful resolutions of interpersonal conflicts, and organizational development. In the first chapter, sources of conflict, styles of dealing with conflict, and the outcomes of conflict are described in detail. Problem solving as a preferred conflict resolution strategy is advocated in the second chapter. In the third chapter, we define organizational development and describe a number of specific strategies. The detours and death traps associated with implementing change programs are pointed out in the final chapter.

Career management. The two chapters in this section are concerned with the management of your career and the implications of career management for organizations. The first chapter describes the stages of career development and offers a number of guidelines to ease movement through those stages. The second chapter focuses on what organizations can do to better utilize human resources through career planning.

The preceding descriptions should have demonstrated further what we mean by spheres of managerial activity and how we anticipate that this book will help you develop your skills in performing the roles found in those spheres. As you can see, the book covers a relatively large number of topics in organizational behavior. To help you get the most out of the material, we have provided several aids. Each major section begins with a brief overview of the material contained in the section, a list of key terms to look for in the section, and a list of learning objectives for the section. Also, each major section concludes with a set of discussion questions and a list of suggestions for additional readings.

SUMMARY

Organizational behavior is a branch of the social sciences that seeks to build theories that can be applied to predicting, understanding, and influencing behavior in work organizations. The person seeking to become a successful manager will find that organizational behavior theories can serve as a solid basis to guide managerial action.

Being a science, organizational behavior relies upon scientific methods to build, evaluate, and modify theories about behavior in work organizations. Appendix I provides a more detailed discussion of the use of scientific methods in organizational behavior.

DISCUSSION QUESTIONS

1. Why is it inappropriate to view managerial work solely in terms of organizing, planning, and controlling?

2. How can the science of organizational behavior contribute to the art of management?

3. Why is the description of the manager as the "nerve center" of his or her organizational unit accurate?

4. Why are the interpersonal, informational, and decisional roles of management inseparable?

5. How does organizational behavior differ from other social sciences? How is it similar?

6. Are managers "devious manipulators"? Why or why not?

7. How does the scientific method differ from other ways of knowing?

8. Why can't a grand theory of how to manage be presented?

SUGGESTIONS FOR ADVANCED READINGS

Behling, O., and Schriesheim, C. *Organizational Behavior: Theory, Research, and Application*. Boston: Allyn and Bacon, 1976, chapter 1.

Drucker, P. F. *Management: Tasks, Responsibilities, Practices*. New York: Harper and Row, 1974.

Dubin, R. "Theory Building in Applied Areas". In *Handbook of Industrial and Organizational Psychology*, edited by M. D. Dunnette. Chicago: Rand McNally, 1976.

Filley, A. C.; House, R. J.; and Kerr, S. *Managerial Process and Organizational Behavior*. Glenview Ill.: Scott, Foresman, 1976, chapters 2 and 3.

Mintzberg, H. *The Nature of Managerial Work*. New York: Harper and Row, 1973.

Scott, W. E., Jr. "The Development of Knowledge in Organizational Behavior and Human Performance." *Decision Sciences, 6, (1975): 142-65.*

Stone, E. *Research Methods in Organizational Behavior*. Santa Monica, Cal.: Goodyear Publishing Co., 1978.

The Scientific Method in Organizational Behavior

The following discussion of the scientific method in organizational behavior is provided for the reader with no prior exposure to the social sciences. The discussion is organized into three parts: (a) theory, (b) research, and (c) turning concepts into operational measures of variables.

THEORY

A theory is *a set of interrelated propositions*, and a proposition is *a statement that links two or more concepts.*[1] Finally, a concept is *a clearly defined phenomenon of substantive interest.* The following example should clarify these definitions.

The concepts of the theory are: effort—the number hours worked per week by a door-to-door salesperson; performance—the number of vacuum cleaners sold per week; and pay—the amount of money the salesperson earns per week. The theory's propositions are: The higher the level of effort, the higher the level of performance; and the higher the level of performance, the higher the level of pay. In other words, the theory simply says that salespersons who work harder sell more vacuum cleaners and, thus, make more money.

All of us walk around with literally dozens of theories about human behavior stored away in our heads. When we encounter a situation where a theory may apply, we pull it out from storage and use it to guide our actions in that situation. If we didn't have these theories to guide our behavior, we couldn't cope with the process of day-to-day living. Our personal theories of human behavior simplify and organize the overly complex world we live in. For example, assume you are a new vacuum cleaner salesperson interested in making a lot of money. The preceding theory tells you that the way to make that money is to knock on a lot of doors for a lot of hours.

The important question to ask about your theories of human behavior is whether or not they are good or bad theories. Regrettably, many managers never question the value of the theories they apply to supervising their employees. Unenlightened managers just assume that their theories are the best available and go about doing their jobs without ever knowing that a better way exists. As a student of organizational behavior, you are responsible for questioning not only your personal theories of human behavior but also the theories presented in this book. Ultimately, the enlightened student (and manager) must make a conscious and deliberate choice among the competing theories available for him or her.

How does one determine the value of a theory? Essentially, you must answer five questions. First, "Is the theory internally consistent?" In other words, is the theory logically structured? Basically, this question asks whether or not the propositions of the theory contradict themselves. Formally, one can answer the question of internal consistency by applying the principles of mathematical logic. On the other hand, one can frequently answer the question of internal consistency by applying a little common sense. For

[1] Our discussion of theory and research was, in part, drawn from Filley and House (1969).

instance, let's look again at the following theory. The higher the level of effort, the higher the level of performance; and the higher the level of performance, the higher the level of pay. Let's assume we add a third proposition to the theory: The higher the level of effort, the higher the level of pay. This proposition flows from the first two propositions and is consistent with them. If the third proposition was, however, the higher the level of effort, the lower the level of pay, it would be obvious to the thinking person that the theory is internally *in*consistent. In other words, the third proposition contradicts the first two propositions. In sum, the first thing to do in assessing the value of a theory is to determine whether or not the theory in and of itself makes sense. If it does, then you can proceed to the second question.

This question concerns the external consistency of the theory. In other words, is the theory consistent with real-world observations? For example, we can go to Ajax Vacuum Cleaner Company and measure how many hours the salespersons work per week and how many vacuum cleaners they sell per week. In addition, we can calculate the degree of association between effort and performance. Now, if we find that effort and performance are not associated, we can only conclude that our vacuum cleaner sales theory is a pretty bad one. It is not consistent with what really happens in the real world. Surprisingly, we have talked with dozens of managers who refuse to reject their pet theories of employee behavior even though they've been presented with information that clearly and simply shows the theories are not consistent with how employees actually behave. So remember to be open-minded enough to dismiss that externally *in*consistent theory and to search for a more sound managerial tool.

The third question to tackle in assessing the value of a theory concerns generalizability, the degree to which the theory is applicable to a variety of situations. A theory can be developed that allows us to predict perfectly the behavior of Frank, the bank teller; however, the theory doesn't work for Frank's coworker, Billy; or for Betty, the baker; or for Johnny, the candlestick maker; or for anyone else. Such a theory can be said to exhibit extremely limited generalizability. Why should you waste your time as a student learning a theory that is not applicable to a wide variety of jobs in an array of different organizations? You shouldn't. You must demand evidence that a theory works across a variety of situations.

The fourth question that should be answered in the process of selecting among competing theories is probably the easiest to deal with. It concerns the issue of parsimony. Assuming you have isolated two or more theories that exhibit comparable levels of internal consistency, external consistency, and generalizability, the criterion of parsimony requires that you select the least complex theory. Why concern yourself with a very sophisticated theory when a much simpler theory predicts behavior equally well? Unfortunately, in organizational behavior, one rarely has the opportunity to select among theories of equal quality. Most frequently, one theory stands out as superior.

The final question to answer in assessing the value of a theory is closely associated with the generalizability concept. The question is, "Can I use the theory?" Again, the reason you learn an organizational behavior theory is to help you become a better manager. So if a theory is internally consistent, externally consistent, generalizable, and parsimonious, but it concerns Frog behavior, you would waste your time as a student of organizational behavior if you learned the theory. Ideally, the practical significance of the theories presented to you in this book will be readily apparent.

In sum, if a theory is a) logically structured (internally consistent), b) consistent with real-world observations (externally consistent), c) applicable to a variety of situations, (generalizable), d) the simplest available (parsimonious), and e) of practical importance (usable), then you can safely conclude that the theory is worth learning. There are many other questions that could be asked in assessing the value of a theory; however, these tend to be beyond the scope of this book. Besides, the five questions presented are sufficient for our current purposes.

RESEARCH

As we have noted already, a good theory is externally consistent. And the way to establish external consistency is through research. The first step in the research process is to translate a theory's propositions into testable questions called *hypotheses.* The transformation of a proposition into an hypothesis essentially involves two things: a) developing measures of the theory's concepts and b) establishing a decision rule for determining whether or not the proposition is true. If you can't develop measures of the concept or establish a clear-cut decision rule, then you can't test the proposition. And if you can't test the proposition, you can't establish external consistency.

Some poorly written theories are so unclear and incomplete that it is impossible to develop measures of the theory's, concepts. For example, noted scholar, Jack, proposes: "The manifestation of endogenous needs by a worker is associated with the worker striving for personal accomplishments on the job." He proceeds to define endogenous needs as "those human needs which emanate from the person's subconscious." Now, do you know what an "endogenous need" is? If you don't know what something is, you can't develop a measure of it. So watch out for those big words that theorists sometimes neglect to clarify for us.

Developing a decision rule in forming hypotheses involves applying one's knowledge about statistical procedures. Because the use of statistics in research is beyond the boundaries of this book, you should consult a basic text in statistical inference if you have any questions about the statistical aspects of hypothesis testing.

There are at least four sources of information that can be used in determining whether or not a hypothesis is true or false: experience, qualitative research, associative research, and causal research. But most people rely only upon their experiences or the experiences of others to test an hypothesis. This is unfortunate because our experiences are commonly and unknowingly distorted and offer a limited basis for generalizing. To illustrate the distortion of experiences, turn the page and look quickly at the picture of the woman. Was she young-old, tall-short, fat-thin, pretty-ugly, sitting-standing, talking-writing? Check out your description of the picture with two of your classmates. No doubt, none of your initial descriptions was the same. Because all people are different, they all see the world somewhat differently. You can't trust someone's recollection of experiences to be a perfect representation of reality. Therefore, experiences offer a very limited basis for generalizing. Again, because all people are different, no two persons' experiences are exactly comparable. In similar situations, people will react to your personality, position, and appearance differently than those of any of your friends or family. In other words, your experiences in a given situation won't necessarily be the same as someone else's. Further, your experiences at one point in your life may not apply to what might happen to you at some future time. Furthermore, you shouldn't expect that the way your Uncle Bill manages his employees (his theory of leadership) will work for you on your job. Most forms of research offer a better means of testing an hypothesis than do your own or someone else's firsthand experiences.

One level of rigor above experiential evidence is qualitative research. The most common form of qualitative research is the case study, which is a written description of the experiences of one person, group, or organization during a given time. The style of the description is usually journalistic, and important concepts are rarely defined or measured. The types of case studies we refer to are frequently published in such magazines as *Business Week*, *Forbes* and *Fortune*. Recognized serious students of organizational behavior (so-called experts or authorities in the field) also frequently write case studies. The only difference between a case study and one's personal experiences is that the case study is prepared by an objective and trained observer. But even with a case study, we must place total faith in the ability of the author to collect the experiences of the subjects involved in the case and to interpret those experiences accurately. Without the precise definition and measurement of important concepts, the ability of any person to read someone else's experiences clearly is doubtful. Besides, a case study rarely can be duplicated and checked for accuracy, because it was researched and written in a given period of time under relatively unique circumstances. In sum, case studies and qualitative research in

general provide a better knowledge base than personal experiences, but they are still far from the ideal method of testing hypotheses. Some forms of case studies, however, are useful for purposes other than hypothesis testing. Case studies can sometimes serve as valuable sources of raw materials in the construction of a theory and can be used effectively in the classroom as a vehicle for developing specific managerial skills.

Associative research relies upon the precise definition and measurement of concepts and the collection of information from a relatively large number of subjects, compared to the one individual, group, or organization employed in the case study. Probably the most common form of associative research in organizational behavior is the survey. Here, the researcher goes into one or more organizations and measures two or more concepts relating to a large number of employees. Recall the test of our vacuum cleaner salesperson theory. We went into Ajax and measured levels of effort, performance, and pay across all the firm's salespersons. Then, we analyzed those measures to determine the degree of association between them. The survey uses measurement and analytic procedures that can readily be repeated in different places and at different times in order to check its accuracy.

Associative research offers a sound base for concluding two concepts are related; but it generally offers a weak base for making causal statements. A causal statement addresses the chicken-or-egg type of question. A causal statement specifies that a change in one thing produces a change in something else; for example, increasing an employee's job satisfaction causes the employee's productivity to increase. Survey research, however, usually takes the following form: the researcher goes into an organization and measures satisfaction and performance at the same time; the only safe conclusion that can be made from such a study is that satisfaction and performance are associated, not that satisfaction causes performance or the reverse, that high performance causes high job satisfaction. Causal research allows you to determine clearly what comes first, the chicken or the egg. The most frequent type of causal research is the experiment, a highly controlled study in which something is assumed to be changed by the independent variable. For example, in the first proposition of the vacuum cleaner salesperson theory, effort is the independent variable and performance is the dependent variable.

OPERATIONAL MEASURES OF VARIABLES

The operational measure of effort is how many hours per week the salesperson works; and the operational measure of performance is how many vacuum cleaners the salesperson sold per week. Turning theoretical concepts into operational measures of variables is an important part of the research process, as well as an important part of the manager's job. An operational measure is a measure that is useable. A yardstick, for example, is a useable measure of distance. A major part of a manager's job is to evaluate his or her subordinates; thus, the manager must develop operational measures of performance. A good operational measure must exhibit at least two characteristics: reliability and validity. Reliability refers to consistency of measurement while validity refers to accuracy of measurement. There are many types of reliability and validity, but, for simplicity, we will consider just one type of each characteristic.

Inter-rater reliability occurs when two or more persons use the same measurement instrument to gauge the identical thing and then arrive at the same measurement. For example, when two persons use the same yardstick to measure the length of a table and both report measuring the same length, we have inter-rater reliability. *Convergent validity* occurs when two different measurement instruments are used to gauge the identical thing and both instruments produce the same measurement. For example, when the length of a table is measured with a yardstick and a tape measure and both instruments measure the same amount —say, five feet—we have demonstrated that measures from the yardstick and the tape measure converge. If a yardstick exhibits inter-rater reliability and convergent validity, we can be more confident that the instrument provides a good measure of length. Likewise, if we can show that a measure of job performance has inter-rater reliability and convergent validity, the manager can feel somewhat secure that his or her performance evaluation tool is relatively accurate.

To repeat, there are several types of reliability and validity. The important point is that you shouldn't accept just any measure of performance. You should demand, rather, that the operational measure of any variable at least makes common sense to you. In academic jargon, that common sense is called *face validity*.

The purpose of this appendix was to help you gain a respect for the use of the scientific method in organizational behavior because that method provides the best way of separating good theories from bad. All managers are required to judge the utility of one theory or another. We hope that you are now somewhat better prepared to do so, too.

SECTION II

Recruiting, Selecting, And Retaining Employees

Even though personnel administrators are the recognized organizational specialists in performing membership maintenance activities, managers also find themselves involved in recruiting and selecting new employees and building employee loyalty. Thus, the purpose of this section is to present information that will aid managers in maintaining a dependable work force.

Successful work force maintenance requires managers to influence the jobs people choose. In other words, managers have to entice qualified persons into their organizations. An understanding of how people choose jobs should help managers persuade others to join their organization. The job choice process as seen from the job seeker's perspective, therefore, is the first topic in this section. Next, we will discuss the selection process from the organization's perspective. An understanding of how organizations choose people should help managers use more effectively the selection tools available to them.

Then, we will turn our attention to the employment interview, the most frequently used selection tool and one that can be used to build employee loyalty even before the new employee enters the organization. Finally, we will present other managerial strategies for building employee loyalty and point out some of the pitfalls associated with developing too high a level of loyalty.

KEY TERMS

OCCUPATIONAL CHOICE MODEL
- Fantasy stage
- Tentative stage
- Realistic stage

REALISTIC JOB PREVIEWS
LOYALTY
TURNOVER
ABSENTEEISM
INNOVATIVE BEHAVIOR
ORGANIZATIONAL REWARDS
- Membership rewards
- Instrumental rewards
- Intrinsic rewards

ORGANIZATION CLIMATE

OBJECTIVES

1. To describe a three-stage model of occupational choice
2. To identify individual characteristics that influence occupational choices
3. To describe how people choose among jobs
4. To describe how organizations choose people
5. To understand how to conduct a realistic job preview
6. To identify the positive and negative consequences of employee loyalty
7. To understand how to increase employee loyalty

CHAPTER

3

How People Choose Jobs

When you were a child, what did you want to be when you grew up? A doctor, lawyer, fire fighter, police officer, nurse, or Indian chief? Whatever your choice, your occupational aspirations probably weren't very realistic. In fact, your occupational aspirations were part of a *fantasy* world. According to Eli Ginzberg and his colleagues (Ginzberg, Ginzberg, Axelrod, and Herna, 1951), this make-believe world of children between the ages of six and eleven constitutes the first stage of a *three-stage model of occupational choice*.

Somewhere between the ages of eleven and sixteen, you probably entered the second stage of the choice process, the *tentative stage*. In this stage, people recognize that they must make some serious decision about their future occupation. The major thing a person thinks about during this stage is what type of occupation will best fit his or her interests, capabilities, and values. For example, the child may think: a) I really love playing baseball; b) I'm a pretty good second baseman; and c) I sure do admire professional baseball players. Therefore, I think I'll become a professional baseball player when I finish high school. Because most of the information the child uses is extremely subjective, the occupational choices made during the transition stage are not very realistic.

Around age seventeen, most people enter the third, or *realistic*, stage where they explore several possible occupational options, crystallize their preferences, and, finally, make an occupational choice. The realistic stage of the occupational choice process is characterized by the compromises that must be made between what a person wants and the available opportunities. The realistic stage does not complete itself overnight; in fact, for many people, it lasts for over a decade. So if you find yourself still exploring occupational options, don't be overly concerned. Many of your peers are doing the same thing.

The remainder of this chapter first examines a number of factors, such as socioeconomic status, race, and sex, that influence the occupational choice process. Next, we will consider a model of how people choose the type of organization they want to work for. Finally, we will touch upon the topic of how organizations select new employees.

WHAT MADE YOU WANT TO BECOME A MANAGER?

Most people reading this book have selected one or another aspect of management as their life's occupation. At each stage of the occupational choice process just described, several *individual characteristics influence the types of occupations a person considers* and, thus, the occupation that is ultimately selected. In other words, a number of things led you down the path to management as your life's work. Now, we will briefly consider some of these factors.[1]

A person's *interests, capabilities,* and *values* play a major role in the occupational choice process. For example, a person with a true interest in and love of the outdoors, as well as an ability to work with his or her hands, is more likely to consider a vocation in the construction industry than a person who detests outdoor activities and finds manual work difficult and a bore. Capabilities refer to a person's aptitudes, skills, and abilities. For instance, an individual with low manual dexterity who can type only twenty words per minute probably would not seriously consider a career as a clerk typist. One's value system can be characterized in many different ways. For example, George England (1967) has described two distinct types of value systems—the pragmatic and the ethical-moral. A person with a pragmatic value system determines whether or not to engage in a particular act principally by addressing the question, "Will engaging in the act help me become more successful?" A person with an ethical-moral value system determines whether or not to engage in a particular act principally by addressing the question, "Is the act ethically right or wrong?" England suggests that a person with a pragmatic value system might be attracted to a different group of occupations than a person with an ethical-moral value system.

Another obvious factor to consider is *sex*. During the fantasy stage of the occupational choice process, boys typically would not consider such female-dominated occupations as nursing, homemaking, and teaching at the primary level; in other words, boys limit the array of occupations they consider to those that they see are dominated by males. On the other hand, girls tend to limit the array of occupations they consider to those they see are dominated by females. In fact, boys and girls are commonly encouraged by their family, friends, and teachers not to consider occupations that are not "appropriate" for their sex.

---

[1]The following discussion is drawn, in part, from Schneider (1976).

Such sexual segregation of occupational considerations frequently continues into the transition and realistic stages. Some people argue, however, that the barriers that prohibited boys and girls from considering a complete array of occupations are beginning to crumble. If the Civil Rights Act of 1964 and related local, state, and federal laws prohibiting discrimination in employment on the basis of sex are rigidly enforced, eventually many of these barriers will, in fact, be destroyed. Nevertheless, some occupations in contemporary society are sexually segregated, and a person's sex still influences the occupations he or she considers.

A fifth factor influencing the occupational choice process is *race*. Like women, blacks and other nonwhite groups historically have found certain occupations closed to them. For example, a black child of the 1950s may have aspired to become a member of the management team of a *Fortune* 500 firm; but once the child explored this alternative, he would have discovered that these firms didn't employ many, if any, black management personnel. The black child would then have reasoned: "Why beat my head against a brick wall? I'll just try some other occupation where I have a real chance of succeeding." Today, as is the case with female occupational considerations, equal opportunity legislation and affirmative action programs are slowly broadening the array of occupational choices that minority group members may consider as realistic options.

Socioeconomic status refers to the relative position a person occupies on the social and economic ladder. A lower-class, poor person in the United States generally would not consider the same set of occupations that a person from a middle-class, middle-income family would explore. This is probably because of the limited occupational information available to the low-income person and because this person's estimates of occupational choices are limited.

The *type of community* a person grows up in is the seventh factor that influences the occupational choice process. People from rural areas frequently consider less prestigious occupations than do people from urban areas. That's because rural areas generally do not offer as rich a set of educational opportunities as do most urban areas, and the number of different kinds of occupations a rural person is exposed to is smaller than that found in an urban center.

Finally, an individual's level of *intelligence* is related somewhat to occupational choices. Most occupations require some minimal level of intelligence, which is different for different types of occupations.

The role of these eight factors is graphically summarized in figure 3-1. Note that while the eight factors do not represent an exhaustive list of those variables that influence the occupational choice process, they should show you how your occupational choice was shaped and modeled by a host of factors of which you may not have been aware.

Characteristics of managers

Let us assume that your chosen career is in the area of management. According to John Miner (1965), a person who wants to pursue a suc-

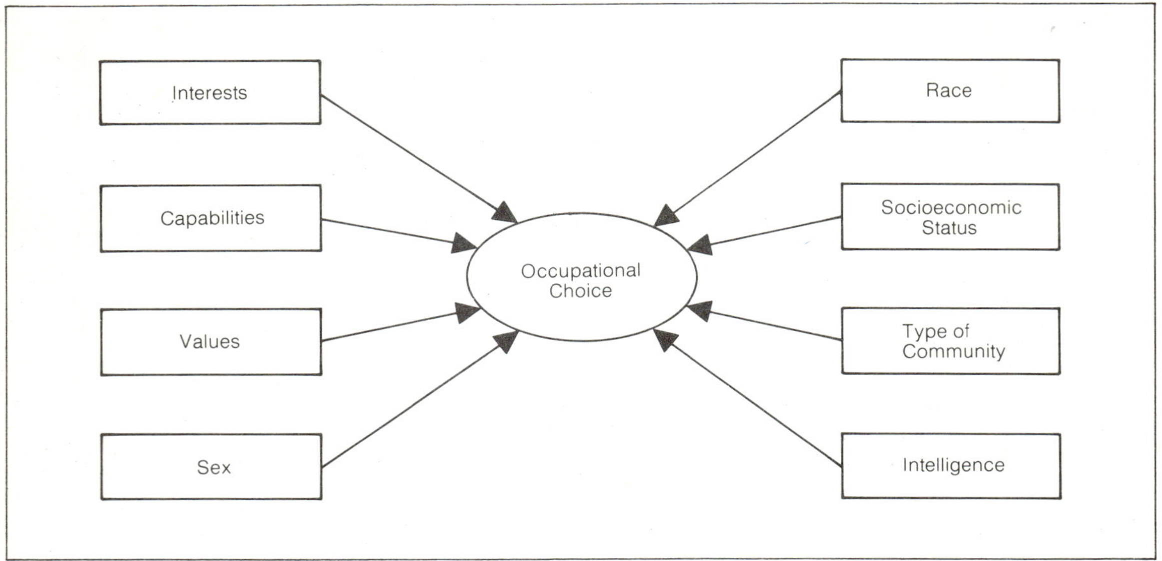

FIGURE 3-1
Factors Influencing Occupational Choice

cessful career in management should exhibit six characteristics: 1) favorable attitude toward authority; 2) desire to compete; 3) motivation to be assertive; 4) desire to exercise power; 5) desire to take center stage; and 6) a sense of responsibility toward performing routine tasks. These characteristics may not only lead to success within management but may have led you to select management as a career. The following interview with Larry Ross, former business executive, provides further insights into choosing management as an occupation.

LARRY ROSS*

I started in the corporate world, oh gosh—'42. After kicking around in the Depression, having all kinds of jobs and no formal education, I wasn't equipped to become an engineer, a lawyer, or a doctor. I gravitated to selling. Now they call it marketing. I grew up in various corporations. I became the executive vice president of a large corporation and then of an even larger one. Before I quit I became president and chief executive officer of another. All nationally known companies.

Sixty-eight, we sold out our corporation. There was enough money in the transaction where I didn't have to go back in business. I decided that I wasn't going to get involved in the corporate battle any more. It lost its excitement, its appeal. People often ask me, "Why weren't you in your own business? You'd probably have made a lot of money." I often ask it myself, I can't explain it, except. . .

*Reprinted by permission from "Working: People Talk About What They Do All Day and How They Feel About What They Do," Studs Terkel, pp. 53-540, O. Pantheon Books.

Most corporations I've been in, they were on the New York Stock Exchange with thousands and thousands of stockholders. The last one —whereas, I was the president and chief executive, I was always subject to the board of directors, who had pressure from the stockholders. I owned a portion of the business, but I wasn't in control. I don't know of any situation in the corporate world where an executive is completely free and sure of his job from moment to moment.

Corporations always have to be right. That's their face to the public. When things go bad, they have to protect themselves and fire somebody. "We had nothing to do with it. We had an executive that just screwed everything up." He's never really ever been his own boss.

The danger starts as soon as you become a district manager. You have men working for you and you have a boss above. You're caught in a squeeze. The squeeze progresses from station to station. I'll tell you what a squeeze is. You have the guys working for you that are shooting for your job. The guy you're working for is scared stiff you're gonna shove him out of his job. Everybody goes around and says, "The test of the true executive is that you have men working for you that can replace you, so you can move up." That's a lot of boloney. The manager is afraid of the bright young guy coming up.

Fear is always prevalent in the corporate structure. Even if you're a top man, even if you're hard, even if you do your job—by the slight flick of a finger, your boss can fire you. There's always the insecurity. You bungle a job. You're fearful of losing a big customer. You're fearful so many things will appear on your record, stand against you. You're always fearful of the big mistake. You've got to be careful when you go to corporation parties. Your wife, your children have to behave properly. You've got to fit in the mold. You've got to be on guard.

When I was president of this big corporation we lived in a small Ohio town, where the main plant was located. The corporation specified who you could socialize with, and on what level. (His wife interjects: "Who were the wives you could play bridge with.") The president's wife could do what she wants, as long as it's with dignity and grace. In a small town they didn't have to keep check on you. Everybody knew. There are certain sets of rules.

Not every corporation has that. The older the corporation, the longer it's been in a powerful position, the more rigid, the more conservative they are in their approach. Your swinging corporations are generally the new ones, the upstarts, the *nouveau riche*. But as they get older, like duPont, General Motors, General Electric, they became more rigid. I'd compare them to the old, old rich—the Rockefellers and the Mellons—that train their children how to handle money, how to conserve their money, and how to grow with their money. That's what happened to the older corporations. It's only when they get in trouble that they'll have a young upstart of a president come in and try to shake things up.

The executive is a lonely animal in the jungle who doesn't have a friend. Business is related to life. I think in our everyday living we're lonely. I have only a wife to talk to, but beyond that. . .When I talked business to her, I don't know whether she understood me. But that was unimportant. What's important is that I was able to talk out loud and hear myself—which is the function I serve as a consultant.

The executive who calls me usually knows the answer to his problem. He just has to have somebody to talk to and hear his decision out loud. If it sounds good when he speaks it out loud, then it's pretty good. As he's talking, he may suddenly realize his errors and he corrects them out loud. That's a great benefit wives provide for executives. She's listening and you know she's on your side. She's not gonna hurt you.

Gossip and rumor are always prevalent in a corporation. There's absolutely no secrets. I have always felt every office was wired. You come out of the board meeting and people in the office already know what's happened. I've tried many times to track down a rumor, but never could. I think people have been there so many years and have developed an ability to read reactions. From these reactions they make a good, educated guess. Gossip actually develops into fact.

It used to be a ploy for many minor executives to gain some information. "I heard that the district manager of California is being transferred to Seattle." he knows there's been talk going on about changing district managers. By using this ploy—"I know something" —he's making it clear to the person he's talking to that he's been in on it all along. So it's all right to tell him. Gossip is another way of building up importance within a person who starts the rumor. He's in, he's part of the inner circle. Again, we're back in the jungle. Every ploy, every trick is used to survive.

When you're gonna merge with a company or acquire another company, it's supposed to be top secret. You have to do something to stem the rumors because it might screw up the deal. Talk of the merger, the whole place is in a turmoil. It's like somebody saying there's a bomb in the building and we don't know where it is and when it's going to go off. There've been so many mergers where top executives are laid off, the accounting department is cut by sixty percent, the manufacturing is cut by twenty percent. I have yet to find anybody in a corporation who was so secure to honestly believe it couldn't happen to him.

They put on a front: "Oh, it can't happen to me. I'm too important." But deep down, they're scared stiff. The fear is there. You can smell it. You can see it on their faces. I'm not so sure you couldn't see it on my face many, many times during my climb up.

I always used to say—rough, tough Larry—I always said, "If you do a good job, I'll give you a great reward. You'll keep your job. " I'll have a sales contest and the men who make their quota will win a prize —they'll keep their jobs. I'm not saying there aren't executives who instill fear in their people. He's no different than anybody walking down the street. We're all subject to the same damn insecurities and neuroses —at every level. Competitiveness, that's the basis of it.

We will now leave behind the occupational choice process and consider the job choice process. We are not going to deal explicitly with the educational process that comes between the selection of an occupation and the choice of a job in that occupation. If you want more information about the occupational choice process, the vocational education process, and their interrelationships, you should contact a vocational or employment counselor. The college or university in your community probably can help you locate this resource person.

HOW PEOPLE CHOOSE JOBS

To some degree, your choice of an occupation determines the type of organization you want to work for and the type of position you want to occupy in that organization. But once you have selected an occupation, there is still considerable latitude in the job choice process. Jobs within the same occupation differ from one another in several ways. For example, the organizations where the job is located can differ in terms of *function, prestige,* and *climate.* Peter Blau and W. Richard Scott (1962) have identified four functionally different types of organizations: 1) *mutual-benefit associations,* whose primary function is to benefit their members (farm cooperatives, labor unions, and credit unions); 2) *business concerns,* whose primary function is to benefit their owners; 3) *service organizations,* whose primary function is to benefit their clients (hospitals, orphanages, and homes for the aged); and 4) *commonwealth organizations,* whose primary function is to benefit the public at large (most governmental agencies, such as police, fire, and sanitation departments). Many of the same occupations can be found in the four types of organizations. Thus, for example, a person who has chosen personnel management or man-

You should be aware that there are management opportunities outside business such as arts administration.

agerial accounting as an occupation has the option of selecting the type of organization in which he or she wishes to pursue a career.

Most persons contemplating management as an occupation tend to think solely in terms of their options in business concerns; however, the number of positions available in service and commonwealth organizations is greatly expanding. Indeed, specialized management education programs aimed at preparing people for positions in these types of organizations are commonplace today. For example, many major universities offer degree programs in public administration, health and hospital administration, education administration, and arts administration. It is important, then, not to ignore the options available outside of business concerns.

Organizations also differ in terms of their prestige. Harvard University's prestige may be extremely attractive to some professors, even though a job at Harvard may not be particularly attractive in other respects. (e.g., low pay, unattractive geographic location, or poor job security).

The climate of an organization refers to the organization's personality. Some organizations can be described as considerate, warm, and supportive, while others are indifferent, cold, and competitive. Some individuals will flourish in the former climate and others in the latter.

In addition to differences among jobs in terms of the organizations where they are located, job differences are apparent in several other ways. For instance, jobs can differ in terms of the *challenge and responsibility* they offer, the degree of *promotional opportunities* available, and the level of *security* provided. Some jobs offer a person a great deal of autonomy and variety and, thus, provide the person with responsibilities and challenges. Many jobs, however, can be characterized as monotonous and routine and are devoid of any meaningful responsibility and challenge. Compare the job of a police officer assigned to a low-crime area in a suburban neighborhood who is required to check in with the dispatch officer every hour with the job of a police officer assigned to a high-crime urban area who is required to report to the dispatch officer only at the beginning, and end of his or her tour of duty.

Some jobs are merely training grounds for bright, young potential executives; a successful person would be expected to be promoted out of this type of job in a few months. Other jobs offer no promotional opportunities. For instance, the person occupying the associate deanship at a university may know that the dean won't be retiring for years; this person obviously has a "dead-end" job.

Engineering jobs in the aircraft industry are notorious for their lack of security: when a project is completed, the engineers assigned to it are frequently dismissed. But engineers employed in other positions, particularly in governmental agencies, typically enjoy a much greater level of job security. Job security, like other job dimensions, varies among jobs.

The examples we have offered are only a few of the many ways that jobs differ. Pay, fringe benefits, coworkers, supervisors, and geographical location are some of the others. The important point is: *In the job choice process, the job seeker must evaluate a host of job dimensions.*

Job seekers as decision makers

A job seeker might be viewed as a rational decision-maker who asks three types of questions.[2] First, "What dimensions of a job are important to me?" As indicated, the importance of a job dimension differs among people. Some people would quickly choose a job that is challenging and responsible over one where the coworkers would be congenial and friendly. Others would prefer the friendly coworkers. The job search process frequently involves making these types of choices. It's unlikely that you will ever find a job that offers everything you are looking for. So you will have to make some difficult decisions. A good strategy to employ is to list all those things you want in a job and then to rate them in terms of their desirability.

The second type of question the rational job seeker asks in the search process is, "What is the probability that a particular job will provide a satisfactory level of a given job dimension?" The job seeker asks this question for each job being considered and for each important job dimension. Since the information available to a job seeker is not perfect, the job seeker is really making odds that a particular job will pay off in terms of the important dimensions.

Let's look at one job seeker's preferences. Table 3-1 lists the five dimensions that are desirable to him and his estimates of obtaining satisfactory levels of each dimension at three different organizations. In addition, the weighted desirability rating for each dimension of each job is shown. These weighted ratings reflect the desirability of a dimension tempered by the chances of actually obtaining a satisfactory level of the dimension from a particular job. The weighted ratings are calculated by multiplying the desirability rating of a given dimension times the corresponding probability of obtaining satisfactory levels of that dimension for a particular job. Finally, table 3-1 shows the total desirability rating for each job. These ratings are calculated simply by adding together the weighted desirability ratings for each job. The ratings can be interpreted as a measure of how important each job is to the job seeker.

The last type of question the job seeker asks concerns probability estimates: "What is the probability that I will be offered a particular job?" The job seeker may find the presidency of General Motors a very attractive job, but he or she knows that the probability of obtaining such a position is totally unrealistic. The rational job seeker adjusts the desirability of a job by the likelihood of being offered the job. One job seeker rated the desirability of three jobs as follows: Job A - 11.0, Job B - 10.1, and Job C - 5.6. He estimated the probability of being offered each job as follows: Job A - .9; Job B - .6, and Job C - .5. If we multiply each job desirability rating by the corresponding esti-

[2]The following discussion is drawn, in part, from Vroom (1964).

DIMENSION	IMPORTANCE RATING	PROBABILITIES OF OBTAINING SATISFACTORY LEVELS FOR EACH DIMENSION*			WEIGHTED IMPORTANCE RATING OF EACH DIMENSION**		
		Job A	Job B	Job C	Job A	Job B	Job C
Autonomy	5	.9	.7	.4	4.5	3.5	2.0
Pay	4	.8	.4	.4	3.2	1.6	1.6
Coworkers	3	.6	.9	.4	1.8	2.7	1.2
Prestige	2	.5	.7	.2	1.0	1.4	.4
Geographical location	1	.5	.9	.4	.5	.9	.4
Total Importance Rating***					11.0	10.1	5.6

*Probabilities are interpreted in terms of the chances in ten. For example, a .9 means that there are nine out of ten chances the job will provide satisfactory levels of the outcome.

**The weighted importance ratings are calculated by multiplying the importance rating times the probability estimates. For example, the 4.5 importance rating for Autonomy for Job A was calculated by multiplying 5 (the importance rating of Autonomy) times .9 (the probability estimate for autonomy for Job A).

***The total importance rating is calculated by adding together the weighted importance ratings for each job. For example, the weighted importance rating for Job A was calculated as follows: 4.5 + 3.2 + 1.8 + 1.0 + .5 = 11.0

TABLE 3-1
An Evaluation of Three Jobs

mates of being offered the job, we then have a rough notion of the realistic attractiveness of a job. The attractiveness scores for the three jobs our job seeker considered are: Job A - 9.90, Job B - 6.06, and Job C - 2.80. The obvious choice of a job, then, is Job A. Of course, the job seeker would only ask this last type of question if trying to get one job would, because of time constraints or other factors, prevent him or her from having any chance of getting the others. If that is not the case, the job seeker can largely ignore the likelihood of getting the job and simply apply first for the most desirable job, then for the next most desirable, and so on.

A number of studies have tested the job choice model just described. In most instances, researchers have found that, by asking job seekers these three types of questions, they are able to predict the actual job choices people make.[3] Figure 3-2 summarizes the job choice model.

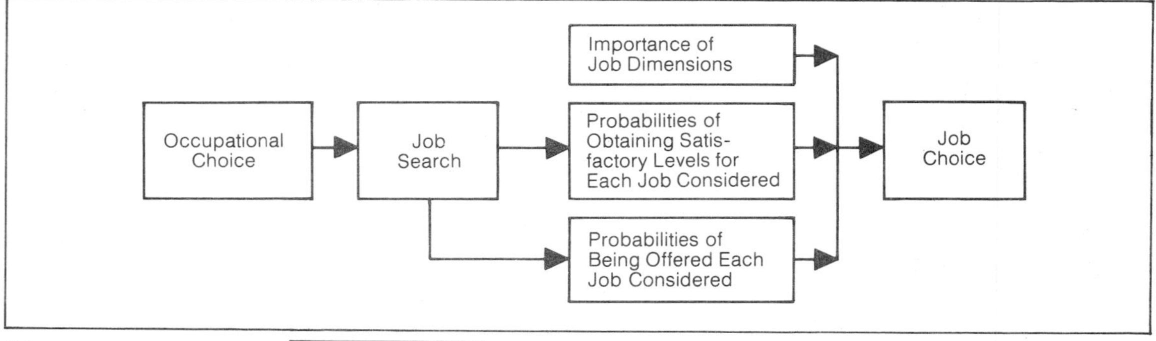

FIGURE 3-2
Job Choice Model

[3]See Wanous (1977) for a review of these studies.

FIGURE 3-3

"We'll be happy to put you on file, Mr. Bannister, but we don't have anything for an underling at the moment."

HOW ORGANIZATIONS SELECT NEW EMPLOYEES

Now that you know something about how a rational job seeker selects a job, let's examine the other side of the coin—how organizations select new employees. First, we will explore the use of *tests*, and then we will discuss the *interview*.

The objective of an organization's selection program is to identify those potential employees in the pool of available candidates most likely to excel on the job. One way of doing this is to administer one or more tests to all the applicants and then, on the basis of those test scores, to select the most promising person. Here, the organization assumes that the test scores can predict job performance.

Many people wrongly believe that employment testing is worthless and/or illegal. If a test's scores have been *shown* to be related to performance on a particular job, then that test is probably a useful and legal selection tool. Let's take a simple example. People applying for a typist position are required to take a typing test: over time, it has been demonstrated that scores on this typing test are, in fact, related to typing performance on the job; the typing test can then be used as an effective screening device. Most courts of law consider a test legal if it can be shown that test scores are predictive of performance. A test is considered illegal if a relationship between its scores and performance has not been demonstrated. Legal problems also arise if such relationships can't be shown to exist for some subgroup of workers, such as women or blacks, or they differ across subgroups. As an example of the latter difficulty, if men who score at least fifty on a particular test subsequently perform well on a job while women who score forty or above perform equally well, the test is unfair to women. So, either the test would have to be scrapped or different selection cut-off scores would have to be set for men and women. Incidentally, while such problems might tempt us to simply not use tests, these legal requirements hold for *all* selection devices.

Of course, many employment tests are not as clear-cut as typing ability tests. Organizations also use aptitude and other, more subjective types of tests. For example, the self-description inventory, developed by Edwin Ghiselli (1971), presumably measures such things as decisiveness, need for high financial rewards, and need for job security and has been used by organizations to select individuals for managerial positions. If it can be shown that the self-description inventory is, in fact, related to managerial performance, then it is as useful and legal as the typing test in its context.

Although they should, most organizations don't rely upon any formal testing procedures to help select new employees. Instead, the most frequently used selection tool is the highly subjective employment interview. Research has shown, however, that a) two or more interviewers who have interviewed the same person are likely to reach different conclusions about the employment potential of the interviewee; b) the information provided by an interviewee is not always as accurate as one might expect or like; and c) most interviewers are rather poor judges of the employment potential of job applicants.[4]

Employment interviews are also frequently used to "sell" the organization to the job applicant. In most instances, organizations try to convince the job applicant of the benefits of working for them. Superficially, this may seem like a good strategy to attract new employees; but recent research evidence shows that painting an overly rosy picture of an organization may, in the long run, reduce the loyalty of those job applicants who "bought a bill of goods" and accepted an offer from the organization. In the following chapter, John Wanous (1975) offers a useful set of guidelines to help organizations avoid the unrealistic job interview.

SUMMARY

The occupational choice process can be viewed as consisting of three stages—fantasy, tentative, and realistic. A number of factors, including a person's interests, capabilities, values, sex, race, socioeconomic status, and community, have been shown to influence occupational choices.

Once the occupational choice has been made, the process of choosing a job still remains. The rational job seeker ought to ask himself or herself three questions—"What dimensions of a job are important to me?;" "What is the probability that a particular job will provide a satisfactory level of a given job dimension?;" and "What is the probability that I will be offered a particular job?"

[4]See Mayfield (1964) and/or Schwab (1969) for reviews of these studies.

Even though organizations should use some form of testing in the selection of new employees, most rely upon the employment interview. It has been shown, however, that the interview process lacks inter-rater reliability; interviewees are not always completely honest and open; and interviewers are not particularly accurate in predicting the future job performance of applicants.

The following guidelines may be useful in helping you select your job.

1. If you're having difficulty zeroing in on an occupation, get some professional help from a competent vocational counselor.

2. Formalize your job search process. Make a list of what you realistically want out of a job and indicate the relative importance of each item on your list.

3. Plan your search for a job. Use as many avenues of search as are available. For example, contact potential employers directly, use your university placement service, check the want ads in your local paper and in several papers with a national circulation, and, possibly, contact a reputable public or private employment agency.

4. Go to a job interview with a list of important questions, and make sure they are answered. Ask specific questions about the dimensions of a job that are most important to you.

5. Put your best foot forward early in the interview. For example, show up for the interview on time and looking clean, neat, and professional.

6. Once you've collected all the information you can about your set of potential employers, give yourself time to consider your options seriously. You may want to ask your family, friends, and teachers for advice—but the ultimate decision is yours.

REFERENCES

Blau, P.M., and Scott, W.H. *Formal Organizations*. New York: The Free Press, 1961.

England, G.W. "Personal Value Systems of American Managers. *Academy of Management Journal, 10* (1967): 53-68.

Ghiselli, E.E. *Explorations in Managerial Talent*. Pacific Palisades, Cal.: Goodyear Publishing Co., 1971.

Ginzberg, E.; Ginzberg, J.W.; Axelrod, S.; and Herna, J.L. *Occupational Choice*. New York: Columbia University Press, 1951.

Mayfield, E.C. "The Selection Interview—A Re-evaluation of Published Research." *Personnel Psychology, 17* (1964):239-60.

Miner, J.B. *Studies in Management Education*. New York: Springer, 1965.

Schneider, B. *Staffing Organizations*. Pacific Palisades, Cal.: Goodyear Publishing Co., 1976.

Schwab, D.P. "Why Interview? A Critique." *Personnel Journal, 48* (1969): 129- .

Wanous, J.P. "Tell It Like It Is at Realistic Job Previews." *Personnel, 52* (1975): 50-60.

Wanous, J.P. "Organizational Entry: Newcomers Moving from Outside to Inside." *Psychological Bulletin, 84* (1977):601-18.

Vroom, V.H. *Work and Motivation*. New York: Wiley, 1964.

CHAPTER

4

Tell It Like It Is At Realistic Job Previews*

In analyzing the recruitment process, industrial psychologists traditionally have focused attention on how companies select new employees. More recently, however, organizational behaviorists have taken a hard look at how applicants choose one organization over others, and old assumptions about how new employees should be recruited are being questioned.

The traditional approach to recruitment and selection views the applicant as passive rather than active. An individual is typically selected for a job on the basis of tests, interviews, and background information. Almost completely ignored in the process is the organizational choice made by the applicant—how and why he showed up in the first place. To obtain a favorable selection ratio—that is, a large number of applications in relation to the number of job openings—companies sometimes present themselves to potential new employees in a more favorable light than the facts justify. In the end, this kind of policy can produce dysfunctional results, costly to both the organization and the employee.

Recent research suggests, however, that recruitment can be made more effective through the use of *realistic job previews* (RJP), an atypical, untraditional approach that stresses efforts to communicate—before an applicant's acceptance of a job offer—what organizational life will actually be like on the job. A study conducted by the author at Southern New England Telephone Company and related

*Reprinted by permission of the publisher, from John P. Wanous, "Tell It Like It Is At Realistic Job Previews," *Personnel*, July-August 1975, research by others at Prudential Insurance Company, the U.S. Military Academy, and Texas Instruments utilized the RJP approach to recruitment. Major findings from these studies show:

—Newly hired employees who received realistic job previews have greater job survival than those hired by traditional recruiting methods.

—Employees hired after RJPs indicate higher job satisfaction.

—An RJP can "set" the job expectations of new employees at realistic levels.

—RJPs do not reduce the flow of highly capable applicants.

WHY TRADITIONAL RECRUITMENT PRACTICES NEED REEXAMINATION

Traditional recruitment practice is characterized by its emphasis on having the organization "look good" to potential employees, usually to attract a large pool of job applicants so that a cream-of-the-crop selection may be made.

In selecting employees, most organizations try to match individual and organization. This usually means selection of those who the employer predicts will be good *performers*. Selection according to who also will be a good risk on turnover or absenteeism is sometimes considered, but this factor typically plays second fiddle to selection based on job performance predictions.

This approach deserves reexamination, however, because it has hidden costs and because of laws now controlling personnel selection and recruitment.

1. *Emphasis on expected job performance as the dominant—almost exclusive-criterion in selection overlooks possible turnover costs resulting from mismatches between the employee and the organization.* The forces influencing performance on the job and those influencing an individual to remain on the job have important distinctions. Job performance generally is considered to be influenced by an individual's abilities and his motivation, that is, his need to achieve. On the other hand, a person's tendency to remain in the organization is seen as a result of that person's need fulfillment, for example, satisfying his need for security, and resulting job satisfaction.

2. *In most organizations highest turnover occurs among newly hired employees—those in their first six months on the job.* Employees new to the job and organization have a higher turnover rate than those with more experience in the organization because they may simply be "testing out" the new environment to see if it suits their particular needs. And their "test" may be necessitated by the company's practice of overselling the attractiveness of jobs during the recruitment process.

Much research, spanning 40 years or more, shows that the higher the job satisfaction, the lower the turnover. But the relationship between job satisfaction and job performance is much less clearly understood and has been the focus of controversy over the years among both researchers and theorists in the field.

Selecting new employees on the basis of performance criteria thus will not necessarily result in long-tenure employees. In fact, it is not unusual to find that the best job performers are high-turnover employees because of the thrust of their upward mobility internally or in other organizations.

Careful attention must be paid, therefore, to the results desired in organizational recruitment and selection. For example, companies risk increased turnover problems if they elect to:

—Select new employees exclusively in terms of the company's interests rather than in terms of the balanced interests of both the company and the employee.

—Present the organization in overly attractive terms to encourage people to apply for jobs.

—Select new employees only on the basis of matching limited performance requirements to individual capabilities rather than on the basis of both performance and satisfaction requirements and capabilities.

Companies that cannot shift their personnel policies to recognize the interests of their employees may face personnel costs stemming from high turnover caused by mismatches between an individual's desires for human need satisfaction and the organization's capacity to fulfill these needs.

THE RJP: WHAT IS IT AND HOW DOES IT WORK?

A realistic job preview should be given to an applicant before the job offer has been accepted. It should try to communicate important information to the potential employee—especially information that is closely tied to employee satisfactions and dissatisfactions.

But just what is "reality," and how can it be designed into a job preview?

It must be understood that an RJP is not an indictment of a particular job nor does it exclude positive information. An RJP must be balanced to include important facets of a particular job (and the organization) that the typical employee experiences as satisfying and those that are commonly dissatisfying. The final balance between positive and negative characteristics will vary, depending on the nature of the job in question. Figure 4-1 illustrates RJP logic and the rationale underlying the research findings.

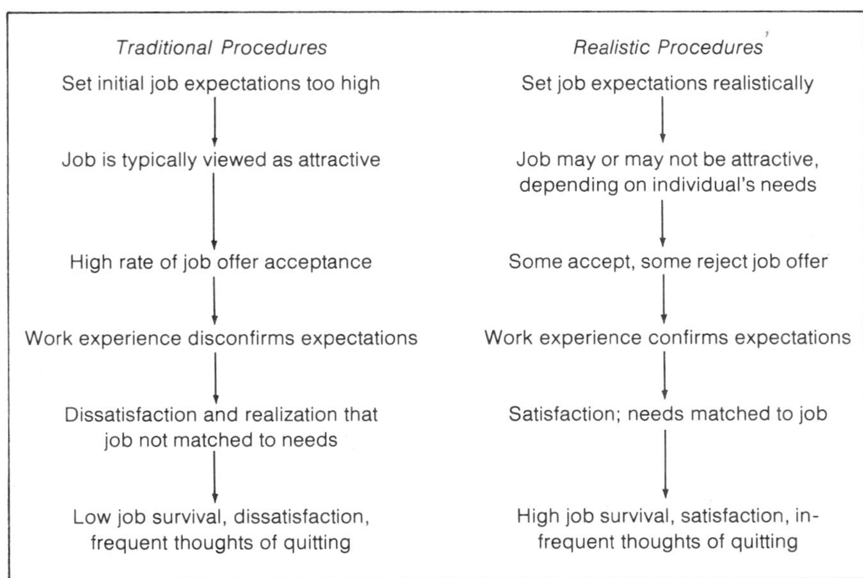

FIGURE 4-1
Typical Consequences of Job Preview Procedures

Impact of the traditional approach. The traditional job preview is not a homogeneous procedure. Organizations recruit new employees in a variety of ways, ranging from systematic attempts to "sell" the organization to the individual (via advertising techniques) to informal, unsystematic distribution of information given in the course of testing, interviewing, and selecting. Although there are wide degrees of conscious intent to sell an organization and widely varying methods for doing so, there is the common thread that an organization almost always presents itself attractively to outsiders who may become new employees.

Thus it often turns out that recruits have unrealistic initial expectations of what the job and the company are like. If these expectations, unrealistic as they may be, approach the recruit's personal preferences or desires, he is likely to conclude that the organization is an attractive place to work.

But what happens after a period of on-the-job experience? Typical reactions are disappointment and dissatisfaction because the initial expectations have not been realized. The employee probably will conclude the job is really not matched to his needs, and since this mismatch was not discovered until after work began, there is a good chance he may quit, or if the labor market is tight, he may stay on the job as a dissatisfied worker, think often about quitting, and be absent often.

Impact of a realistic preview. An RJP also "sets" the initial expectations of recruits, but in this case they are realistic expectations. To avoid pitfalls of the traditional preview, an RJP provides important job information—both positive and negative—completely and without bias. Thus when an individual compares his realistic expectations about the job and organization to his own desires, an appropriate organizational choice (or self-selection) can be made.

If the RJP has an impact on the individual's organizational choice, then those who actually go to work will tend to be better matched to the new environment than those recruited via the traditional procedure. This combination of "innoculating" the individual against disappointment and the more effective organizational choices typically results in greater job survival, higher job satisfaction, and fewer thoughts of quitting.

AN EXPERIMENT: RJP VS. THE TRADITIONAL

The author's study of RJP versus the traditional job preview involved a sample of about 80 female telephone operators at several employment offices of Southern New England Telephone Company.

Prior to the study, which covered a period of about nine months, the overall turnover rate for operators varied between 30 and 40 percent per year. But for operators in their first six months on the job, the rate often rose to 100 percent or higher.

To compare the effects of the two contrasting job preview approaches, the previews were presented to job candidates in the form of 15-minute films shown on portable units in each employment office. Figure 4-2 shows the sequence of events in this experiment for each job preview approach as well as the typical sequence used prior to the experiment. Applicants were assigned at random to the preview groups.

FIGURE 4-2
Selection Procedures for Operators

Preexperiment	*Realistic Experiment*	*Traditional Experiment*
Receptionist	Receptionist	Receptionist
Initial interview	Initial interview	Initial interview
	Questionnaire 1	*Questionnaire 1*
Testing, medical questionnaire	Testing, medical questionnaire	Testing, medical questionnaire
Application blank	Application blank	Application blank
Selection interview	Selection interview	Selection interview
	Realistic film	*Traditional film*
	Questionnaire 2	*Questionnaire 2*
Job visit	Job visit	Job visit
Training	Training	Training
Work experience	Work—1 month: *Questionnaire 3*	Work—1 month: *Questionnaire 3*
	Work—3 months: *Questionnaire 4*	Work—3 months: *Questionnaire 4*

The operator applicants also were asked to complete several questionnaires designed (1) to measure the impact of each preview on *initial expectations*, (2) to obtain a measurement of each individual's own *job preferences*, and (3) to assess *on-the-job satisfaction* and thoughts of quitting after some work experience.

The traditional preview film used in the experiment existed prior to the study. Dealing with the operator's job, it had been used in high school recruiting and in several other ways, but it never had been systematically applied as a job preview for all candidates on a regular basis.

Figure 4-3 shows some of the major differences between the preview films, but as a chart, it captures only part of the "flavor" of the sequences. Subjective impressions of company managers and colleagues of the author indicate that this RJP was about 60-40 negative in balance. Compared to the traditional preview film, this was quite a difference.

WHAT THE STUDY SHOWED

In terms of "job survival" (being on the job three months after starting to work), 62 percent of the realistic group of newly hired operators survived compared to 50 percent of the traditional group. This was similar to other research studies of the RJP concept.

FIGURE 4-3
Job Characteristics Emphasized by Each Job Preview Film

Overlap Between Films

1. Customers can be quite unfriendly at times
2. Work is fast paced
3. Some operators receive satisfaction from helping out customers
4. Action sequences of operators at work:
   a. emergency call
   b. "wise guy" calling operator
   c. credit card call
   d. overseas call
   e. directory assistance operators at work
   f. "nasty" customer calling operator
5. Dealing with others (customers, co-workers) is a large part of the job

Nonoverlap Characteristics

Realistic Film	*Traditional Film*
1. Lack of variety	1. Everyone seems happy at work
2. Job is routine; may become boring	2. Exciting work
3. Close supervision; little freedom	3. Important work
4. Limited opportunity to make friends	4. Challenging work
5. Receive criticism for bad performance, but no praise when deserved	
6. Challenging initially, but once learned is easy and not challenging	

For example, the first study of life insurance agents found a difference of 68 percent survival for the realistic group compared to 53 percent for the traditional after a period of five months. In a second study the difference was 71 percent vs. 57 percent survival over a six-month period.

The original West Point study found that 91 percent of the first-year cadets survived who received a realistic booklet before choosing to accept the appointment. Of those who received the traditional material from West Point, 80 percent survived the first year. A second West Point study analyzed the effects of an RJP booklet on voluntary resignations during the summer training period prior to the first year at West Point. Of those receiving the RJP, 94 percent survived as compared to only 88.5 percent of a control group, which had no such preview.

The study at Texas Instruments was not a job preview but an on-the-job first day indoctrination and did not report job survival data. But, in every case, to my knowledge, the RJP has increased job survival over traditional methods of recruitment.

In addition to higher job survival rates, members of the realistic group in the telephone study indicated higher job satisfaction after three months on the job and had thought much less about quitting after one month. The basis for these attitudes appears to be in the gap between expectations created by the traditional preview and the reality of being an operator.

Figure 4-4 charts a typical attitude pattern that emphasizes the sharp contrast between preview expectations and on-the-job reality for traditional and realistic groups.

Along with assessing the impact of an RJP on end-result variables, it was important to understand why an RJP "works." The questionnaire administered *before* job previews measured "naive, initial job expectations," but the results of the post-preview questionnaire

FIGURE 4-4
How Attitudes About Work Change

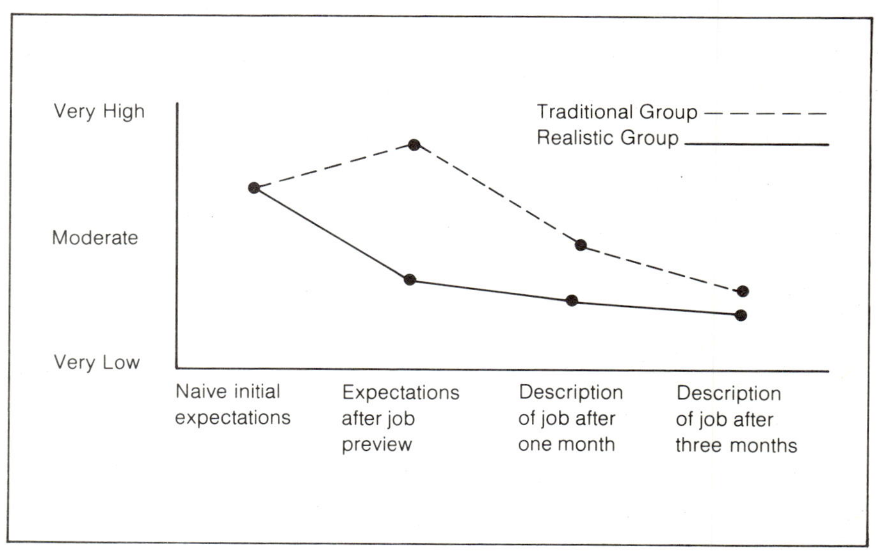

showed clearly that the expectations of those who received the traditional preview were raised, and the expectations of the RJP group were significantly lowered. For example, a sampling of the questionnaire tabulations shows that expectations particularly affected by RJPs included:

—Receiving praise for doing a good job.

—Having freedom to use one's own judgment.

—Making use of one's abilities and using one's own methods.

—Feelings of accomplishment from the job.

—Whether supervisors handle employees well.

The preview films did not touch all facets of the operator's job, just some of the most important. Thus some questions showed no differences between the two groups because the films included nothing pertaining to them. But while lowering certain expectations in comparison to the traditional job preview, the effect of realism was selective because it only affected expectations included in the previews and did not spill over to others.

Contrary to predictions, the realistic preview made no noticeable impact on actual job decisions; the effect of an RJP on applicants' organizational choices did not materialize. Only two out of about 80 applicants refused offers, and the fact that job-offer acceptances were not influenced could be one reason why job survival rates were not even further apart.

Two explanations seem reasonable. First, the study was conducted during a period of high and sharply increasing unemployment. Second, the job previews occurred "late" in the sequence of events in the recruitment and selection process. Each applicant involved in the study had made considerable personal effort to obtain a job—making trips to the employment office, taking tests and interviews, and so forth. Research data show that the more effort individuals put forth, the more attractive the object of their effort becomes. Thus it was quite possible that the operators hired had made some type of advance psychological commitment to accept if a job offer were made.

FUTURE USE OF REALISTIC JOB PREVIEWS

The results of the telephone operator study suggest the following guidelines for implementation of RJPs as an on-going personnel procedure.

Diagnose the situation. Before adopting an RJP policy, thoroughly diagnose the jobs to be considered for an RJP. Check on job-survival-rate data. Are the rates high or low? What is the rate pattern? How does it vary in relation to job experience?

If a job survival problem involving new employees is indicated, make a hard, objective assessment of job characteristics and other information given to recruits to ensure the validity of the data. For example, in identifying all facets of a particular job, a variety of data sources should be tapped. When diagnosing the nature of job information given to recruits, check all potential sources. Then compare these two assessments to determine whether any root problems can be corrected by using an RJP.

The medium may be the message. An effective RJP must realistically depict the important facets of a particular work environment. The study of telephone operators showed that the job visit portion of the recruitment and selection process did not fully communicate the job to an unfamiliar person. A short snatch of the action in an operator's workroom did not accurately reflect the long-term reactions of boredom and lack of autonomy that many operators experience.

Although the job visit was intended to be a realistic preview, it probably had the effect of enhancing the attractiveness of this job. In a film format the long-run reactions to this job were portrayed by experienced telephone operators who talked about them.

In contrast to the above example where the medium (film) turned out to affect the message, there are counter examples. The studies at Prudential and West Point used booklets effectively. The Texas Instruments' first-day "realistic orientation" used a small group of peers to set initial expectations and reduce first-day anxiety.

Use previews early rather than late. An RJP can function in two ways:

—As a "screening device" to help job candidates decide for themselves on their organizational choices.

—As an "innoculation" against disappointment with the realities of organizational life.

Early use of the RJP in the recruitment/selection/placement process could be difficult, however, because of the costs involved in adding it to standard personnel operating procedures. Thus it may be less expensive to wait until after the first few selection hurdles have thinned the list of applicants. In some situations there even may be a tradeoff between maximum influence on the organizational choice process and the costs of administration, as in the telephone operator study. In any case, whether used early or late, the effectiveness of an RJP to innoculate new employees against disappointment seems unimpaired.

High unemployment rates may affect outcomes. Because of the distinction between and RJP's effect on organizational choice versus its value as an innoculation, high unemployment may reduce the impact of an RJP on organizational choices. It has the same effect as that of an RJP administered too late, that is, after psychological commitment to accept a job offer as developed.

Is an RJP limited to a certain type of job? As we have seen, realistic previews have been used successfully on a variety of jobs in differing organizations. How far one can generalize from this is not completely clear. It seems reasonable, however, to assume that RJPs will be effective for a number of entry-level jobs—whether in white collar insurance sales or as a telephone operator. But in the end, each job situation must be analyzed to assess the potential usefulness of the RJP approach.

SUGGESTIONS FOR ADVANCED READING

Brayfield, A.H., and Crockett, W.H. "Employee Attitudes and Employee Performance." *Psychological Bulletin, 52,* (1955): 396-424.

Cronbach, L.J., and Gleser, G.C. *Psychological Tests and Personnel Decisions.* Urbana: University of Illinois Press, 1965.

Dunnette, M.D. *Personnel Selection and Placement.* Belmont, Cal.: Wadsworth Publishing, 1966.

Guion, R.M. *Personnel Testing.* New York: McGraw-Hill, 1965.

Hall, D.T. *Careers In Organizations.* Pacific Palisades, Cal.: Goodyear Pub. Co., 1976.

Hellriegel, D., and Slocum, J. "Organizational Climate: Measures, Research and Contingencies." *Academy of Management Journal, 17,* (1974): 255-80.

Herzberg, F.; Mausner, B.; Peterson, R.O.; and Capwell, D.F. *Job Attitudes: Review of Research and Opinion.* Pittsburgh: Psychological Services of Pittsburgh, 1957.

Holland, J.L. *Making Vocational Choices: A Theory of Careers.* Englewood Cliffs, N.J.: Prentice-Hall, 1973.

James, L.R., and Jones, A.P. "Organizational Climate: A Review of Theory and Research." *Psychological Bulletin, 81,* (1974): 1096-1112.

Porter, L.M., and Steers, R.M. "Organizational, Work, and Personal Factors in Employee Turnover and Absenteeism." *Psychological Bulletin, 80,* (1973): 151-76.

Price, J.L. *The Study of Turnover.* Ames, Iowa: Iowa State University Press, 1977.

Schuh, A. "The Predictability of Employee Tenure: A Review of the Literature." *Personnel Psychology, 20,* (1967): 133-52.

Steers, R.M. "Antecedents and Outcomes of Organizational Commitment." *Administrative Science Quarterly, 22* (1977): 46-56.

Super, D.E., and Bohn, M.J. *Occupational Psychology.* Belmont, Cal.: Brooks Cole, 1970.

Van Maanen, J., and Schein, E.H. "Career Development." In *Improving Life at Work,* edited by J.R. Hackman and J.L. Suttle. Santa Monica, Cal.: Goodyear Pub. Co., 1977, 30-95.

Vroom, W.H. *Work and Motivation.* New York: Wiley, 1964.

Wanous, J.P. "Organizational Entry: Newcomers Moving from Outside to Inside." *Psychological Bulletin, 84,* (1977): 601-18.

CHAPTER

5 Building Loyalty

According to the 1974 United States Bureau of Labor Statistics' study of employee turnover among the nation's manufacturing firms, approximately one out of every two workers left his or her employing organization during any given year. That statistic means that if you were managing 100 production-line employees, you would have to recruit and select 50 new employees a year to maintain your work force.

Employee turnover (or the movement of an employee out of an organization) costs many businesses and governmental agencies large sums of money year after year after year. In addition to the cost of recruiting and selecting a replacement, numerous other costs may be associated with a turnover. For example, the cost of training the replacement should be considered; and, more importantly, the cost associated with lost sales or productivity because the organization is understaffed may be astronomical. Yet few organizations seriously consider their cost of turnover or means of reducing it.

One way to reduce turnover is to build loyalty to the organization. A high level of loyalty (or commitment to the organization) also is associated with a low rate of *employee absenteeism*, which is another frequently ignored cost of labor. A number of other positive outcomes that may be attributed to employee loyalty are cooperative behavior, protection of the organization against a disaster, the formulation of creative solutions to organizational problems, and the dissemination of positive feedback about the organization to the community. Since none of these behaviors can really be programmed or mandated by an employer, they are best characterized as *innovative or spontaneous*.[1] Again, loyalty seems to be the key to such behaviors

[1]This notion is taken from Katz (1964).

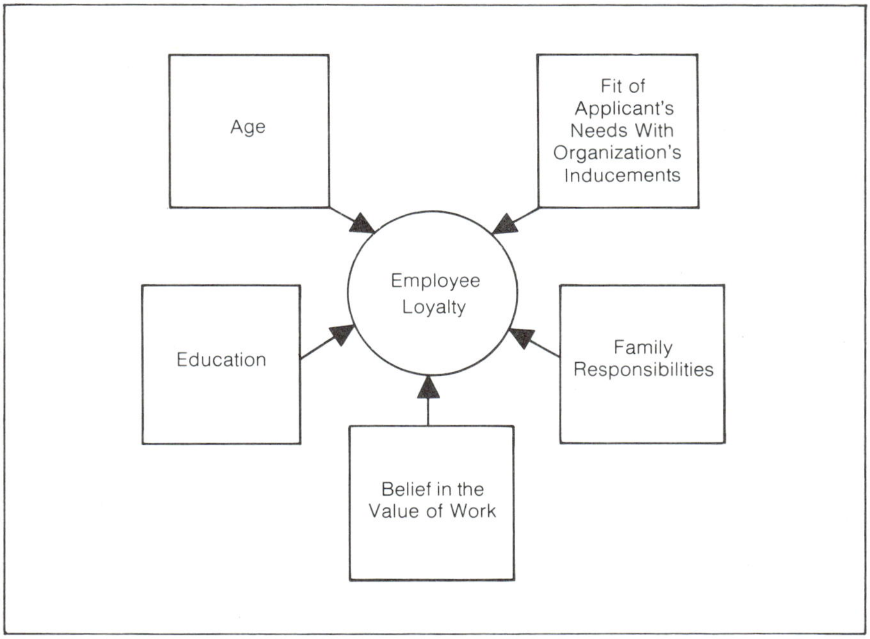

FIGURE 5-1
The Selection Process and Building Loyalty

as well as to increased attachment to the organization. The central question now becomes, "How does the manager develop in the employee this sense of loyalty so essential to the successful functioning of the organization?" Regrettably, the answer is not a simple one. At least three aspects of the organization must be examined—*selection procedures, reward structure,* and *the organization's climate and purpose.*

SELECTION PROCEDURES

As John Wanous (1975) noted in the previous chapter, the *realistic job preview* can serve two purposes. It can be both a *screening device* to help job applicants decide for themselves whether or not they would fit in the organization and an "*innoculation*" against disappointment in the realities of life in the organization. If a new employee is able to say, "I am pretty sure the organization offers what I want out of job" and "Working in the organization is awfully close to what I expected it to be like," that employee is a good candidate for a long-term, loyal period of employment. On the other hand, if the new employee has been hustled, intentionally or unintentionally, into the organization, that employee probably will be disillusioned and disappointed—a prime candidate for experiencing low levels of loyalty and for leaving the organization as soon as possible.

Obviously, the organization should not rely solely upon the applicant to self-select himself or herself out of a potentially undesirable situation. The organization should actively attempt to identify what the applicant wants out of a job and to determine if there is a good fit between the applicant's needs and what the organization has to offer. A firm job offer should be made when the potential contributions of the applicant and the inducements offered by the organization jibe. For example, a highly talented applicant is looking for a job with the opportunity to be promoted rapidly to a position with significantly more pay and responsibility; the organization is seeking to fill an entry-level position with an aggressive person who can be promoted in the near future. In this case, a job offer should be extended. But assume the job the organization has available is a dead end; if the talented, aggressive applicant is hired, he or she soon will become frustrated and possibly angry. Certainly, there would be no chance of building loyalty in this situation. Again, the organization should attempt to identify and select those applicants whose needs it has a good chance of fulfilling. An organization that can fulfill the needs of its employees is one that can develop a loyal work force.

During the selection process, attributes other than the applicant's desires should be examined. For example, a person's *age*, *education*, *family responsibilities*, and *belief in the value of work* are related to various aspects of loyalty.[2] Each of these attributes can be assessed in the selection process; and predictions can then be made about the likelihood of the applicant exhibiting loyalty to the organization once employed.

Older employees tend to be more loyal than their younger counterparts. Perhaps this is because the older worker feels that it is difficult to obtain employment elsewhere. The older worker is particularly interested in job security. Thus, the fact that the older job applicant is more likely to develop a strong sense of loyalty to the organization is a significant point in favor of hiring older people.

The more highly educated an employee, the less likely he or she is to exhibit a high level of organizational loyalty. One explanation for this is that education raises a person's expectations or aspirations. In many instances, these expectations turn out to be too high. And when a job fails to meet a person's expectations, the person frequently blames the organization rather than his or her unrealistic aspirations. Thus, the best selection strategy in terms of building loyalty is to identify the minimum level of education required for a given job and select people with that level of education. In other words, don't hire someone with a masters degree in business administration when a bachelors degree in the same field would do just as well.

Another employee attribute closely associated with education is *cosmopolitanism*.[3] A cosmopolitan identifies with groups of persons outside the organization and is strongly influenced by these groups. Conversely, a *local* identifies most closely with his or her employing organization and is influenced little by outside groups. Well-educated professionals tend to be labeled cosmopolitans. The following example will help to sharpen the distinction between a cosmopolitan and a local. Assume a retail organization employs two ac-

[2]Brief and Aldag (1980) provide a brief review of these studies.

[3]See Gouldner (1958) for a more detailed treatment of the term *cosmopolitan*.

Older employees tend to be more loyal than younger employees.

countants, Mary and Alice. Mary has a masters degree in business administration and is a certified public accountant (CPA). Alice has a bachelors degree in business administration and has never even thought of becoming a CPA. Mary strongly identifies with other CPAs, particularly those in public accounting firms. Her accounting practices conform to those prescribed by the American Institute of Certified Public Accountants, a professional association to which she belongs. On the other hand, Alice is not sure what the American Institute of Certified Public Accountants is; and her accounting practices closely follow those traditionally used by the retail firm. Mary would be happy practicing accounting almost any place that would allow her to exercise her professional judgement. Alice loves her current position. One can see that the highly educated, professional, cosmopolitan Mary is perhaps a less loyal employee than the local Alice. Which type of accountant would you want working for you?

The relationship between family responsibilities and loyalty is complex. Essentially, *family responsibilities* refer to the demands placed on the employee by his or her family. For instance, an employee whose household is comprised of a spouse and two pre-school-aged children would experience greater family responsibilities than would the single employee living alone. For female em-

Female

ployees, it appears that the greater the level of family responsibilities, the lower the level of loyalty to the organization. Even though an increasing number of women are entering the labor force and societal attitudes toward working mothers may be changing, the proposition reflects the notion that women still are experiencing a conflict between work and home demands, and home life remains paramount for most women. For men, on the other hand, there seems to be no consistent relationship between family responsibilities and organizational loyalty. This finding may reflect that men, traditionally the principal breadwinners in the family, are more able than women to cope with, or adjust to, the conflicts between home and work. We don't mean to imply that men are necessarily more successful at simultaneously playing the roles of parent and employee. Rather, they are probably more comfortable in playing both roles because that is what society has expected of them for so long. Nevertheless, the female job applicant with a strong sense of family responsibilities is not a likely candidate for developing as high a level of organizational loyalty as is the female applicant without such responsibilities.

For the manager concerned with selecting potentially loyal employees, a final applicant attribute to consider is belief in the value of work. Or, how important and central is work in the individual's life? People differ in the degrees to which work is central and important in their lives. A person with a strong belief in the value of work can be said to adhere to *Protestant Work Ethic ideals*, a term used frequently by sociologist Max Weber. Weber (1948) argues that the teachings of certain religions instruct their followers to pursue success vigorously in their chosen occupations. Table 5-1 presents four items commonly used to measure adherence to Protestant Work Ethic ideals. If during the selection process, an applicant reveals that she or he strongly believes in Protestant Work Ethic ideals, this individual is likely to be a loyal employee.

TABLE 5-1
A Measure of Belief in Protestant Work Ethic Ideals*

INSTRUCTIONS

The following four statements concern your attitudes toward *work in general.* You are to indicate the degree to which you agree or *dis*agree with each statement. Do this by circling the appropriate number following each statement, based on the scale below.

VERY UNTRUE	MOSTLY UNTRUE	SLIGHTLY UNTRUE	UNCERTAIN	SLIGHTLY TRUE	MODERATELY TRUE	VERY TRUE
1	2	3	4	5	6	7

1. Hard work makes a man a better person	1	2	3	4	5	6	7
2. Wasting time is as bad as wasting money	1	2	3	4	5	6	7
3. If all other things are equal, it is better to have a job with a lot of responsibility than one with little responsibility	1	2	3	4	5	6	7
4. A good indication of a man's worth is how well he does his job	1	2	3	4	5	6	7

*Adapted from Blood (1969)

As depicted in Figure 5-1, the fit between an applicant's needs and what the organization has to offer, as well as the applicant's age, education, family responsibilities, and belief in the value of work, all may be predictive of employee loyalty. But two cautions should be noted. First, most of the listed applicant attributes cannot be measured perfectly; nor can any one predict loyalty with certainty. Second, and equally important, there are a number of characteristics other than loyalty that are probably more relevant for selecting a new employee. For example, would you prefer a potentially loyal job applicant who lacked the necessary skills and abilities to perform well on the job to a person who might not exhibit great loyalty but who boasts an impressive set of appropriate skills and abilities? The attributes we have identified can be useful for selecting potentially loyal employees but, in no instance, should they be the sole or principal yardstick used to judge a job applicant.

REWARD STRUCTURE

More important than selecting new employees who are likely to be loyal is instilling loyalty in the current labor force. Organizational rewards are the principal vehicle for developing this sense of commitment.

One way to categorize organizational rewards would be *membership rewards, instrumental rewards,* and *intrinsic rewards.* Membership rewards are available to any employee who becomes a member of the organization. For example, various insurance benefits, paid vacation days, and across-the-board pay increases are types of membership rewards. An across-the-board pay increase is usually a fixed percentage increase in wages provided to all organizational members; a cost-of-living increase is an example. Increases in membership rewards tend to encourage loyalty because organizational membership per se becomes a vehicle for fulfilling the individual employee's needs. Furthermore, membership rewards typically increase for the individual worker the longer he or she remains with the organization. For instance, many organizations offer a two-week paid vacation to those persons employed less than five years and a three-week vacation to those persons employed between five and ten years. This method of distributing rewards clearly ties rewards to seniority and further encourages employees to remain loyal to the organization.

Instrumental rewards are earned through increased performance. Thus, high performers are rewarded more than low performers; and the needs of higher performers are more satisfied by instrumental rewards than are the needs of low performers. Instrumental rewards, therefore, lead to greater loyalty only for high-performing employees. For example, a small used-car firm employs two salespersons who are compensated on a straight commission basis; the commission rate is 10 percent of the retail value of the car. One salesperson averages $4,000 in sales per week; and the other, only $2,000. The sales-

FIGURE 5-2
Reward Structure and Building Loyalty

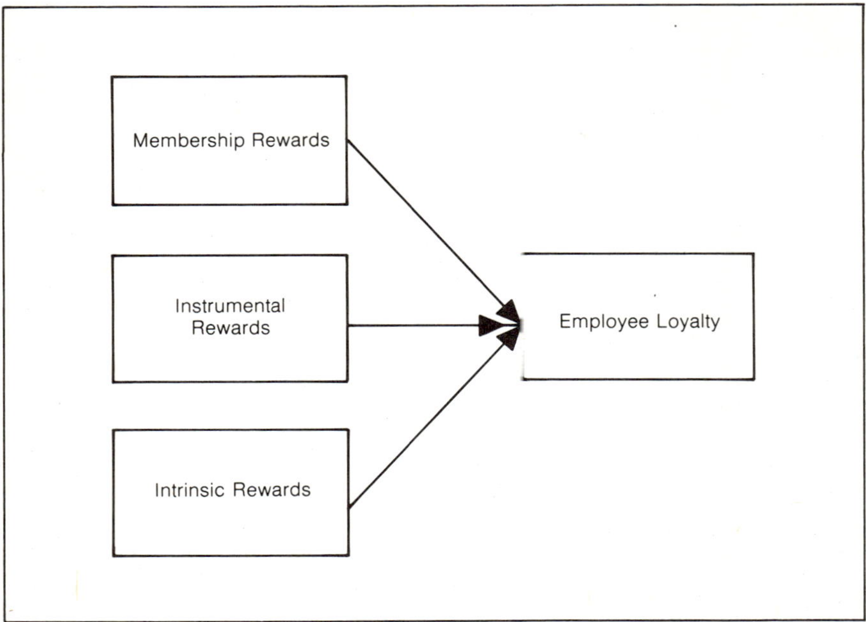

person earning an average of $400 per week is likely to be a more loyal employee than the employee earning an average of $200 per week.

Intrinsic rewards are derived directly from the actual work the employee performs. This implies that some types of work are more rewarding than other types. Jobs involving work that is challenging, responsible, and meaningful are more rewarding to the employee than are jobs involving work that is simple, routine, and unimportant. Organizations that can offer intrinsically rewarding jobs rather than monotonous and dull jobs are more likely to employ a loyal work force.

In sum, the more rewarding outcomes an organization can deliver to its members, the higher the level of organizational loyalty those members will experience. Figure 5-2 shows the three principal types of rewards—membership, instrumental, and intrinsic. Later, we will explore each of these reward types in detail. It is important to recognize that it is not only the *quantity* of rewards that determines loyalty. The *degree* to which the available rewards are judged by the employee to be fair and equitable also plays a major role in influencing levels of loyalty.

ORGANIZATIONAL CLIMATE AND PURPOSE

An organization's *climate* is simply its personality as seen by its members. As is the case with the personality of any individual, the climate of any organization consists of multiple dimensions.[4] Of particular relevance to the subject of employee loyalty is the *warmth and support* dimension of climate. This refers to the degree to which organizational members feel they are treated in a considerate fashion. Obviously, the more warmth and support an employee feels emanating from the organization, the more loyal he or she feels toward that organization.

Warmth and support comes from many sources in the organization. For example, employees can experience warmth and support from their coworkers and, if they occupy a supervisory position, from their subordinates. A manager can project consideration by being friendly and approachable, looking out for the welfare of his or her subordinates, and giving advance notice of any changes in the work environment.[5] From a managerial perspective, probably the most important source of warmth and support is the employee's boss.

An organization's *purpose*, like its climate, consists of multiple dimensions. Typically, an organization has no one single mission or dominant goal, but usually some overriding philosophy or ideology predominates. And these higher purposes frequently cause organizational members to exhibit extremely loyal behaviors. For instance, religious and political organizations throughout history have been able to call upon their members to engage in life-threatening acts.

FIGURE 5-3

"Dobbs, we've been through the executive roster ten times and decided you're the man for the job. How would you like to take a price-fixing rap?"

Reprinted by permission from W.M. Hamilton, *Anti-Social Register*, Chronicle Books, San Francisco, CA, ©1974.

[4]See Campbell, Dunnette, Lawler, and Weick (1970) for a discussion of these dimensions.

[5]See Chapter 20 or Stogdill (1974) for a complete discussion of this considerate leadership style.

FIGURE 5-4
Organization Climate and Purpose and Building Loyalty

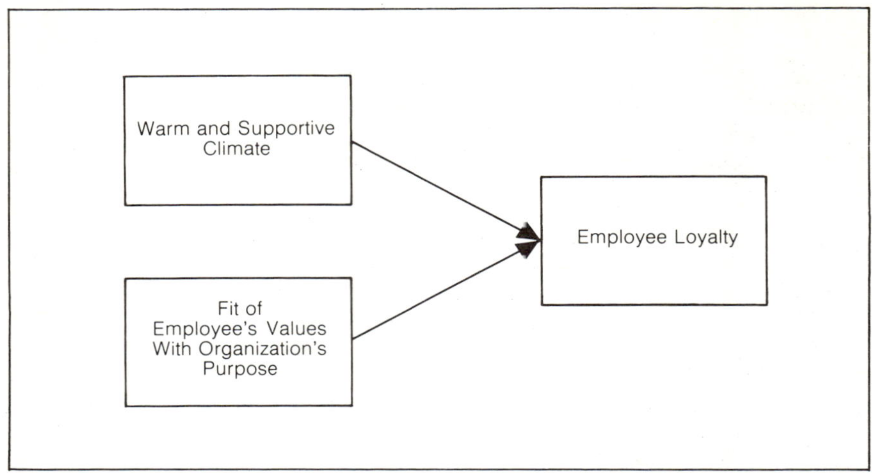

Think, for example, of the actions of the Christians in the Crusades of the eleventh century or the members of the Nazi party during World War II. Many modern organizations attempt to appeal to the basic values of their members in order to encourage them to engage in what are sometimes considered extreme acts of loyalty. The business executive who makes illegal corporate contributions to a political campaign and the union member who engages in strong-arm tactics to keep non-union members from crossing a picket line are examples of such excessive loyalty.

An organization's climate, particularly in terms of the warmth and support offered to its members, and an organization's purpose, in terms of its philosophy or ideology, can play important roles in determining employee loyalty. Of course, creating a considerate climate or establishing an appealing ideology is not an easy task. Nevertheless, the manager should not ignore these strategies as promising vehicles for building loyalty. See figure 5-4 for a summary of the role of climate and purpose.

IS LOYALTY ALWAYS DESIRED?

So far, we have discussed high levels of employee loyalty as though they are always desirable. But this is not really the case. In fact, there are at least four instances where high levels of loyalty can reduce organizational effectiveness. First, high levels of loyalty among low-performing employees may prove to be quite dysfunctional. This is particularly true if it is difficult to dismiss an employee or if there is a reluctance to do so. Ideally, the low performer and the disloyal employee will be the same person; thus, the low performer will voluntarily choose to leave the organization. The manager should encourage loyalty among high performers and discourage loyalty among those employees whose job performance is poor. One way to accomplish this distribution of loyalty is to ensure that high performers are rewarded more than low performers.

Second, high levels of loyalty may lead to the undesirable condition Irving Janis (1971) has labeled "groupthink." *Groupthink* refers to the situation where levels of loyalty are so high that weak ideas introduced by a group member are not critically evaluated and, therefore, not dismissed. When groupthink occurs, almost any proposal a group member introduces is accepted because it comes from the group. This is a particularly dangerous situation for top management teams. The management team can become so self-assured and loyal to the chief executive and the organization that it can no longer honestly and openly evaluate proposals generated from within. This inept decision making by the top management team can ruin the organization. Various decision-making and problem-solving strategies that can be used to overcome this problem are discussed in chapter 18.

Third, organizational loyalty can become so intense that is causes an employee to engage in an illegal act or an act considered immoral or unethical. Of course, such acts by an organization's members produce serious legal problems for the organization and also discredit the organization in the public's eye. Probably the best way to inhibit these undesirable acts is for top management to make it perfectly clear that illegal, immoral, or unethical acts by any employee on behalf of the organization will not be tolerated and will result in negative outcomes for the employee.

FIGURE 5-5

"In examining our books, Mr. Mathews promises to use generally accepted accounting principles, if you know what I mean."

Reprinted by permission from W.M. Hamilton, *Anti-Social Register,* Chronicle Books, San Francisco, CA, ©1974.

Finally, high levels of loyalty may cause an employee to commit organizational resources even in the face of certain loss. A classic example of such undesirable persistence was the escalation of the war in Vietnam by the United States government in spite of almost certain losses. Probably the best means of avoiding such persistence is to monitor closely the allocation of organizational resources and to create an environment where occasional failure is tolerated.

Even though loyalty leads to largely positive consequences for the organization, the preceding examples clearly demonstrate that excessive loyalty can be associated with dysfunctional outcomes. Thus, not only must a manager be concerned with the level of organizational loyalty among his or her employees, he or she must also consider the possible negative consequences of that loyalty.

SUMMARY

Increased organizational loyalty is associated with reduced employee turnover and absenteeism and increased cooperation, protection, creativity, self-development, and positive public relations efforts. Under adverse circumstances, however, increased loyalty can lead to a number of negative consequences, which management must guard against.

The manager can attempt to increase levels of loyalty by manipulating three aspects of the organization—selection procedures, reward structure, and the organization's climate and purpose. Regarding selection procedures, probably the most important applicant attribute to consider is the degree of fit between the applicant's needs and what the organization has to offer. The greater the fit, the more likely the applicant will become a loyal employee.

In terms of the organization's reward structure, the higher the levels of membership, instrumental, and intrinsic rewards, the higher the level of loyalty. Finally, the more warmth and support provided by the organization's climate and the more the organization's purpose meshes with the individual's values, the more loyalty that can be expected.

In conclusion, employee loyalty is an organizational asset to be managed, not left to chance. Both the level of loyalty and its consequences are the responsibility of management.

REFERENCES

Brief, A.P., and Aldag, R.J. "Antecedents of Organizational Commitment Among Hospital Nurses." *Sociology of Work and Occupations*, 1980, 1, 210-221.

Campbell, J.P.; Dunnette, M.D.; Lawler, E.E., III; and Weick, K.E. *Managerial Behavior, Performance, and Effectiveness.* New York: McGraw-Hill, 1970.

Gouldner, A.W. "Cosmopolitans and Locals: Toward an Analysis of Latent Social Roles — I and II." *Administrative Science Quarterly 2,* (1958): 281-306, 444-80.

Janis I.L. "Groupthink." *Psychology Today*, November 1971: 43-46.

Katz, D. "The Motivational Basis of Organizational Behavior." *Behavioral Science* 9, (1964): 131-46.

Stogdill, R.M. *Handbook of Leadership: A Survey of the Research.* New York: Free Press, 1974.

Wanous, J.P. "Tell It Like It Is at Realistic Job Previews." *Personnel* July-August 1975: 50-60.

Weber, M. *The Protestant Ethic and The Spirit of Capitalism.* Translated by T. Parsons. London: Allen and Unwin, 1948.

DISCUSSION QUESTIONS

1. Are you in the tentative or realistic stage of the occupational choice process? If you have selected a realistic occupational option, which individual characteristics influenced your decision? If you have not selected a realistic occupational option, where can you turn for help in the decision-making process?

2. Assuming you were a manager sent by your organization to a college campus to recruit persons with the potential to become successful managers, what individual characteristics would you look for in applicants? Where on campus (other than the business school) do you think you might find a sizable pool of persons exhibiting the appropriate characteristics?

3. What dimensions of a job are most important to you? What types of organizations are most likely to provide satisfactory levels of these dimensions?

4. From the employer's perspective, what characteristics should a selection test exhibit?

5. What is wrong with traditional recruitment practices?

6. How does the realistic job preview work?

7. How would you implement realistic job previews as an on-going personnel practice?

8. What are some positive *and* negative consequences of employee loyalty?

9. What is the association between family responsibilities and loyalty for men? For women? Why do you think we observe such sex differences?

10. If you had a choice between a cosmopolitan and a local-oriented employee, which would you choose? Why?

11. Identify a number of commonly used membership rewards. What is the disadvantage of using these rewards instead of instrumental rewards?

12. For each functional type of organization, identify one organization that uses its purpose to instill loyalty.

13. Assume you supervise fifty bookkeepers. During the last year, more than twenty of your staff have voluntarily quit, and you have found it difficult to recruit qualified personnel. Write a brief memo to your boss, suggesting a specific program to reduce this turnover.

SECTION III

Fulfilling Employee Needs

The purposes of this section are to provide a framework for understanding the role of employee needs in organizational behavior and to demonstrate what managers can do to satisfy their employees. First, we will discuss the results of a study of job satisfaction among a sample of younger workers. And then we will examine alternative theories of human needs. Third, the antecedents and consequences of job satisfaction are discussed. Finally, twenty questions concerning the use of job satisfaction measures are posed.

KEY TERMS

DISSATISFACTION
WORK VALUES
NEEDS
MOTIVATION
NEED-HIERARCHY THEORY
ERG THEORY
TWO FACTOR THEORY
ACHIEVEMENT-MOTIVATION THEORY
LOWER-ORDER NEEDS
HIGHER-ORDER NEEDS
DEFENSE MECHANISMS
WORK OUTCOMES
- Turnover
- Absenteeism
- Performance

LIFE SATISFACTION

OBJECTIVES

1. To explain the "satisfaction gap" of younger workers
2. To describe the distinction between satisfaction and motivation
3. To describe *and* evaluate various theories of human needs
4. To describe the need-satisfaction process
5. To specify the personal *and* organizational consequences of job satisfaction
6. To describe when and how to conduct a job-satisfaction survey

CHAPTER

The Now Generation Of Workers*

There is some reason to believe that the 22½ million full-time workers under age 30 produced by the communications revolution, Dr. Spock, and nearly 200 years of political democracy are less authoritarian[1] than past generations of young workers, yet are forced into even more frustrating work situations. Because of this, some experts go so far as to say that democratization of the workplace is inevitable.[2] Others believe this to be far from the truth. They say that our total society is hanging in the balance between democracy and repression. If the latter view is correct, the active choice of democracy in the workplace and the avoidance of a "final and active totalitarianism"[3] should be a major national concern. In either case, it should be useful to consider the characteristics and attitudes of young workers since they will provide much of the force and direction for change in the workplace during the 1970s.[4]

This chapter discusses the young work force, its composition, general levels of dissatisfaction, causes of dissatisfaction, work values, and the extent to which work expectations are realized. To keynote this discussion, we would suggest—based on the following table—that young workers do not seem to get much real fulfillment from their work. When asked the question "How often do you leave work with a good feeling that you have done something particularly well?" the following percentages of workers answered "very often":

*Abridged with permission of Macmillan Publishing Co., Inc. from *Where Have All The Robots Gone* by Harold L. Sheppard & Neal Herrick, pp. 113-121. Copyright © 1972 by The Free Press, a Division of the Macmillan Publishing Co.

Age Group	*Percentage Answering "Very Often"*
Under 20	23%
21-29	25%
30-44	38%
45-64	43%
65 and over	53%

People who rarely feel satisfied about doing something well at their jobs are probably not receiving one of the most important benefits work has to offer: the experience of achieving and growing on the job.

AN OBJECTIVE DESCRIPTION OF YOUNG WORKERS

Young workers 21-29 years of age know more, earn less, and tend to belong to unions. Very young workers, 16-20 years old, tend to be white, female, blue-collar, and non-union.

Education

Even very young workers, 16-20 years of age, had more formal education than those 45 or older. The age group which one would expect to far surpass the other in education—the 21-29 group—did have fewer members with less than a high school education. The percentage of its members with some college experience, however, was the same as for the 30-44 age group. The 45-and-older group, of course, had the least education.

Personal income

Three quarters of the very young workers earned less than $5000 per year. In each of the three older groups, the percentage of low earners was about the same (25-29 percent). The percentage of workers making more than $10,000, however, was larger in each successively older group, except that it dropped off significantly among workers over age 44.

Sex

The ever-increasing role of women in the labor force is underscored by the fact that, among very young workers 16-20 years of age, women outnumbered men by a ratio of 6 to 4. The percentage of women dropped sharply to 38 among the 21-29 year old workers, to 33 among workers in their middle years, and to 31 among older workers. Evidently, female participation in the labor force is no longer a case of "back-to-work" after child rearing. Higher percentages of women in their child-rearing years than in their after-child-rearing years are now active participants in the work force.

Race

Very young (16-20) and older (45+) blacks were under-represented among employed persons. In other words unemployment not only affects young blacks disproportionately but is almost equally hard on the older black worker.

Occupational status

"Grow old along with me, the best is yet to be . . ." Browning's words ring true when one sees that workers over age 44 were more than 10 times as likely to be self-employed as very young workers, and five times as likely as workers in their 20s. The chances of a worker's being self-employed increase steadily with age: 2 percent of workers 16-20 years of age was self-employed, 4 percent for those in their 20s, 13 percent for workers in their middle years, and 21 percent of workers age 45 and over. Since self-employed people are remarkably satisfied with their jobs, their concentration in the higher age brackets may help explain the fact that job satisfaction is similarly concentrated.

The percentage of white-collar workers steadily increases from 44 percent among very young workers to 50 percent for workers age 21-29, to 57 percent for workers in their middle years. Then, as with income, the older worker (age 45 and over) slips back a few rungs on the ladder; in this case, back to the 50 percent white-collar composition which also characterized young workers 21-29 years of age.

Union status

Very young workers were only half as likely to be unionized as workers over age 20. Perhaps, they find it difficult to gain entrance to the trade unions because of extreme youth, lack of a high school diploma, lack of training, and so on, and are obliged to take the poorer non-union jobs. Workers in their teens also tend to be less strongly attached to the labor force and often attend school or have other commitments which prevent them from seeking jobs in industries and occupations organized by unions.

WHO ARE THE DISSATISFIED YOUNG WORKERS?

With the exception of young workers who earned more than $10,000 per year, significantly more young workers than workers over 29 years of age expressed negative attitudes toward work. This was true regardless of race, sex, marital status, education, collar color, etc. However, young black workers were even more dissatisfied than their white brothers (37 percent expressed negative attitudes toward work as compared to 22 percent of young whites). Young workers with more than a high school education, females "under 30" and young workers making less than $5,000 per year represented other pockets of high dissatisfaction within a generally dissatisfied age group.

Race

In the two younger age groups, blacks were less satisfied than whites. Among older workers, the reverse is true. This suggests a greater generation gap among black workers than among white workers. It also supports the notion that, at least among black workers, young workers today are different from young workers of the past.

Education

Young workers with education beyond high school were somewhat more likely to report dissatisfaction than were those without any college. Slightly fewer workers in their middle years who had college experience reported work dissatisfaction and, among workers over age 44, the percentages are exactly identical.[5] Perhaps the more educated workers begin to achieve their goals during their middle years, while the less educated workers (with many of the same aspirations) begin to realize, as they enter their 30s, that their early goals were only fantasies.

Sex

In general, women workers were significantly more likely to report dissatisfaction than were male workers. This was true among all age groups, but the gap between men and women was least among young workers.[6]

Marital status

For the total work force, married people were significantly more satisfied with their jobs than were unmarrieds. This general trend persisted within the young worker group.[7]

Personal income

For the work force as a whole, income was a strong and statistically significant predictor of overall job satisfaction. However, young workers appear to be relatively indifferent to income levels. Workers over age 44 seem to share this indifference to some degree, but workers in their middle years were almost twice as likely to report dissatisfaction if they made less than $7500 per year.

The similarities among young workers were more impressive than the differences. In no subgroup of young workers identified in the sample did fewer than 21 percent express dissatisfaction—except the 41 workers age 29 and under who were earning $10,000 or more. Only 10 percent of these workers were dissatisfied. This contrasts with the fact that no middle-aged worker subgroup (ages 30-44) had more than 21 percent dissatisfied, and no older workers (ages 45 and over) had more than 15 percent.

It will become increasingly apparent throughout this chapter that, at least in terms of attitude, young workers are a more homogenous group than are their elders. Young workers with more education did tend to be somewhat less satisfied with their jobs. Socio-economic differences, however, seem to have far more pronounced effects on the job satisfaction of workers over age 29.

WHY ARE YOUNG WORKERS DISSATISFIED?

Early in the interview, all respondents were asked to rate 25 characteristics of work according to whether they considered these characteristics to be "very important," "somewhat important," "not too important," or "not at all important." Then, later on in the interview, they were asked whether the same characteristics were "very true," "somewhat true," "not too true," or "not at all true" of their jobs. For our purposes, the percentage of respondents in each age group who considered an aspect of work to be very important is taken as an index of that item's importance to the group under consideration, and the percentage of each group who reported it to be very true of their jobs is taken as an indication of the quality of the jobs held by that group. Where a larger percentage of respondents in an age group considered a specific work characteristic to be very important than reported it to be very true of their jobs, a "satisfaction gap" is assumed: we know for sure that some workers in that group felt they were being "shortchanged."

Work values

The labor force as a whole considered job content characteristics to be more important than the economic benefits derived from the job. The highest-ranked item among all age groups was interesting work.

Young workers placed even more importance than their elders on the nature of the work itself and far less on the comfort aspects of jobs (such as, transportation arrangements and whether or not one is asked to do excessive amounts of work).

We often suppose that young workers have a different set of work values than do their elders and, indeed, this appears to be quite true. But contrary to the suppositions of many older people, their values appear to be highly responsible. They placed substantially more importance on the interesting nature of the work, on their opportunity to develop their own special abilities, and on their chances for promotion. They were less concerned than their elders with being asked to do excessive amounts of work, whether or not their transportation arrangements were convenient, and whether their jobs allowed them to forget their personal problems. With regard to pay, job security, and fringe benefits, age seemed to make no difference: all age groups seemed to be equally interested in the economics of work. While most differences either increased or decreased steadily with age, the importance placed on the chance to make new friends at work was higher for young workers and for workers past age 44, but lower for workers in their middle years.

Work realities

If the worker's own view of his job is any yardstick, young workers have very bad jobs indeed!

The differences in work values described above were minor compared to the differences in the extent to which young workers believed certain desirable characteristics to be lacking in their jobs. For 19 of the 25 elements specified, young workers rated their jobs lower than did workers 30 and older.

The differences between workers in their middle years and older workers were not so great. Nonetheless—with regard to every element of work except "the chances for promotion being good" —workers over age 44 rated their jobs as high or higher than did workers in their middle years. The progression was fairly constant, ranging from low percentages of young workers who gave their jobs high ratings, to medium percentages among workers in their middle years. to high percentages among older workers.

The satisfaction gap

When the compounding effects of their higher work values and lower work realities are taken into account, the greater general dissatisfaction of the young worker can readily be understood. The expectation/reality discrepancy among young workers is most acutely felt in matters concerning the work itself.

In order to place in context the answers to the question, "Why are young workers dissatisfied?" it is first necessary to describe the principal dissatisfaction of middle-aged and older workers. Using the satisfaction gap[8] as a means of identifying the job features which cause dissatisfaction to large numbers of people, it would appear that most workers in their middle years and older workers had as much comfort as they desired in their jobs, had the resources they required to get their jobs done, were well satisfied with their personal work relationships, and had relatively little fault to find with the content of their jobs. They had two substantial areas of dissatisfaction, however. First, while few workers in those age groups considered chances for promotion to be very important, even fewer felt these chances to be very good. Second, older workers did place a very high premium on good pay. While a high percentage of them also believed they were getting very good pay, there were at least 20 percent who considered good pay to be "very important" but, at the same time, not "very true" of their jobs.

Young workers were also dissatisfied with their pay and with their chances for promotion. In fact, since they rated their jobs very low on these characteristics, far more workers under 30 had pay and promotion "satisfaction gaps" than did their elders. But their prime dissatisfaction centered around something quite different: the *work itself*. While the greatest satisfaction gap among workers over 30 had to do with pay, among younger workers it concerned their lack of opportunity for self-development. (The issue of pay placed second.) The third and fourth areas of greatest discrepancy among young workers (the interesting [or uninteresting] nature of their work, and their chance to do the things they believed they did best) also resulted from high values and low realities in job-content areas.

It is clear from this analysis of the 'satisfaction gaps' that the important difference between the dissatisfaction of young workers and that of their elders stems first, from the high value they placed on challenging work, and second, from the lack of challenge in the work they were actually required to perform.

WHAT CAN BE DONE?

The most significant and persistent differences in work attitudes and values (and, apparently, in actual work situations) are attributable to age. The young worker has different work values than do middle-aged and older workers. Since he also judges his actual situation more harshly than do workers in their middle years and older workers, with regard to many of the work characteristics he most values, there is apparently a general and pervasive discrepancy in the young worker's work life. This discrepancy differs from dissatisfactions in the work force as a whole, in that—while it includes a feeling of being underpaid—it is primarily directed at the work itself. Young workers place high values on interesting work, opportunities to develop and use their abilities, chances to do the things they do best, and chances for promotion. To a greater extent than older workers, they also view their jobs as lacking these opportunities. This creates a difficult and potentially destructive situation—a situation with implications which go far beyond the workplace itself.

One more observation: While young workers do not place any greater importance upon economic benefits than do their older co-workers, the actual benefits available to them are so far inferior that a serious discrepancy—particularly with regard to pay—also exists in this aspect of the young worker's world.

Having concluded that the younger worker is indeed a person of different values, feelings, and aspirations than his older counterpart, and having identified the most pronounced of these differences, at least two possible conclusions can be reached: (1) The structure of work should change to accommodate young people, or (2) young people should change to accommodate the structure of work. The latter is a popular notion among older folk. They recall their own accommodations (and those of their fathers), and feel it is only proper that the young people of today should change.

But this give rise to two questions: First, is a possibly pathological adaptation to sterile work actually desirable? Second, if it *is* desirable, are the young people of today willing to go that route? My answer to the first question is an emphatic no! The existence of deadening, numbing, and individually constraining work in the past is no argument for its continuation in the future.

The real potential for change in the 1970s depends far more on the answer to the second question. If young people are willing to adapt and to accept the values of the hierarchical work situation (seeking their place in it and striving to improve their situation step-by-step), we can be assured that little attention will be given to restructuring work. If, on the other hand, young people draw the line and demand that their unions reorder bargaining priorities and that their employers give them a voice in shaping their work lives, then (assuming that the specific forms which the demands take are constructive) we may see at long last an extension of our democratic principles to the workplace.

NOTES

1. See Harold Sheppard's findings in Chapter 7 of Sheppard & Herrick (1972) which report on young white blue-collar workers.

2. Warren G. Bennis, *Changing Organizations* (New York: McGraw-Hill Book Company, 1966), p. 32. However, Bennis appears to believe that the system is already becoming less hierarchical. He says, "our position is, in brief, that democracy is the only system which can successfully cope with the changing demands of contemporary civilization." He adds that the inevitability of democratization should not prevent us from "giving a little push here and there to the inevitable."

3. Marcus G. Raskin, *Being & Doing* (New York: Random House, 1971), p. xvi.

On the other hand, the collapse of liberal authoritarian structures where people are colonized tenderly can result in a final and active totalitarianism in which violence and magic are no longer mediated through education, consumer goods and dreams, but are stated as goals and the basis of life.

4. The data used in discussing these characteristics and attitudes were gathered by the Survey Research Center (SRC) of the University of Michigan under contract to the U.S. Department of Labor. The SRC survey was conducted in November and December of 1969, among a national probability sample of 1,533 employed persons 16 years of age and older who worked 20 hours a week or more.

5. It is noteworthy that the same pattern persists with regard to overall satisfaction with life, except that, during the middle years, a lack of higher education is associated with even higher life than job dissatisfaction, and, conversely, middle-years' workers with some college are extremely unlikely to report negative attitudes toward life in general. After age 45, as with negative attitudes toward work, the percentages of college and non-college people reporting negative attitudes toward life are identical.

6. A statistically significant difference between the general attitude of men and women within age groups was the fact that women in their middle years were twice as likely as men in that age group to report dissatisfactions with life in general.

7. The difference in life satisfaction between marrieds and unmarrieds was so great that it was highly significant even within age group.

Among young workers, unmarrieds were about twice as likely as marrieds to be dissatisfied with their lives. In the middle years, the likelihood of general dissatisfaction was about three times as great and, among workers over age 44, four times as great.

8. The difference between the percentages of workers who stated that a work element was "very important" to them and the percentage in that group who later indicated that it was "very true" of their jobs.

9. On the general topic of the limits and pathology of "adaptability," see René Dubos, "Man Over Adapting," *Psychology Today*, February 1971.

CHAPTER 7

Understanding Human Needs

In the preceding chapter by Harold Sheppard and Neal Herrick (1972), the level of job dissatisfaction younger workers experience was explained in terms of the gap between what they value in work and the realities of what work has to offer. What people value in work can be viewed in terms of their *needs*. The following examples further illustrate the importance of employees' needs.

Fred's subordinates were docked in pay when they missed work without a valid excuse. Despite this penalty, almost half of them weren't showing up on Fridays and Mondays. When Fred asked one of them, Sam, to justify his repeated absences, Sam flatly said, "I make enough in three or four days to do everything I want. Why should I work any more?" Fred shook his head in disgust and muttered something about the decline of employee motivation.

Claire had been a teller at her local credit union for the last four years. And they had been good years; the women in the office were friendly, exchanging jokes on the job and during breaks, sometimes playing cards at lunch time, and always getting together after work once or twice a week for shopping, dinner, or partying. Claire liked to interact with the people who came into the credit union, too. In view of her enthusiasm and outgoing, competent manner, nobody was surprised when Claire was promoted to become assistant accounts manager. With the promotion came a raise, a private glassed-in office, and more responsibility. But soon Claire began to feel separated from her old coworkers by more than a glass wall. They were reluctant to have lunch with her and began to find reasons why they were busy after hours. Claire seemed to lose interest in her work, making several minor but conspicuous and easily avoidable errors. Her superior, Lois, confronted her three months after the promotion. "Claire," she said, "I don't understand it. There's no question you deserved your promotion, but you're just not doing the kind of job we expected. Are you afraid of success?"

Employees of Local 216 of the United Fabricators Union struck against Federated Metalworks on October 13, 1979. They said their work was dehumanizing, that they were treated as robots, and that they were "mad as hell and weren't going to take it anymore." A spokesperson for Federated said in a press conference the next week, "We've done everything we can for these people. The factory has been cleaned up, wage increases have been well above the industry average, and our fringe benefit program is recognized as a model. The grievances presented by the UFU are simply a ploy to get us to give them unprecedented and completely unjustifiable pay increases."

These vignettes point up the frustration many managers face in trying to understand what makes employees "tick." It is often hard to figure out why employees behave the way they do and whether their stated demands reflect their true desires. Often, we don't learn what people want until there are signs that things are not going well. It's important, therefore, that we do all we can to understand the nature of employee motivation.

Figure 7-1 shows that when our needs are unsatisfied, we search for and attempt to attain goals that may satisfy them.

The figure highlights several important points.

1. The attempt to satisfy needs is called *motivation*. Motivation flows from *dissatisfaction*.

2. To figure out how to improve our employees' satisfaction levels, as well as to increase their motivation levels, we must learn about their need structures and about the degree to which their needs are currently satisfied.

3. Satisfaction and motivation, while related, are very different things. Employees may show various combinations of satisfaction and motivation. We have to keep the distinction between satisfaction and motivation clear in our minds.

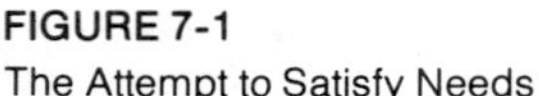
FIGURE 7-1
The Attempt to Satisfy Needs

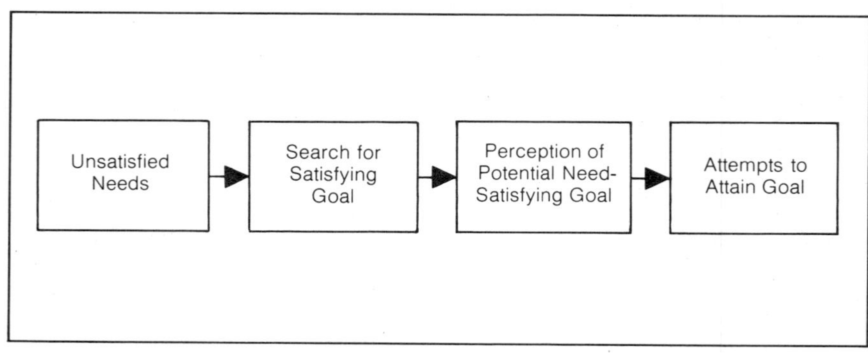

SOME THEORIES CONCERNING HUMAN NEEDS

Maslow's need hierarchy theory

Briefly summarized, Abraham Maslow, a humanistic psychologist, believed that:

1. Humans have five basic categories of needs:

   a. *Physiological.* These basic bodily needs include such things as food, water, sex, and air.

   b. *Security.* Needs for safety, absence from illness and pain, and stability would fall into this category.

   c. *Social or affiliation.* These would include the needs for belonging, interaction with others, friendship, and love.

   d. *Esteem.* This category contains needs both for respect and recognition from others and for personal feelings of accomplishment and self-worth.

   e. *Self-actualization.* These are the needs to become all that one is capable of becoming, to realize one's potential. They are desires for growth, for creativity and for constructive accomplishment.

2. A satisfied need is not a motivator. Once a need is satisfied, we aren't so concerned about it, and it becomes less important.

3. Needs are arranged in a hierarchy of "successive prepotency." That is, we first try to satisfy needs at the bottom of the hierarchy. Then, when they are fairly well satisfied, needs at the next higher level become most important, and so on. A *positive* relationship exists between the degree of satisfaction of needs at one level of the hierarchy and the degree of importance of needs at the next higher level.

Maslow's need-hierarchy theory has been widely accepted. The need categories, diagrammed in figure 7-2, seem to make intuitive sense, and we can all think of cases where the desire to satisfy our physiological needs made everything else seem unimportant. However, we can probably also think of a number of exceptions to Maslow's propositions. In fact, Maslow himself was concerned that people were uncritically accepting of his theory.

The studies that have examined Maslow's propositions have not been particularly supportive. The following three findings actually contradict portions of Maslow's theory.

1. Employee' needs don't really seem to fall into five distinct categories. Statistical procedures suggest that there are no more than two or three categories of needs.

FIGURE 7-2
The Need Hierarchy

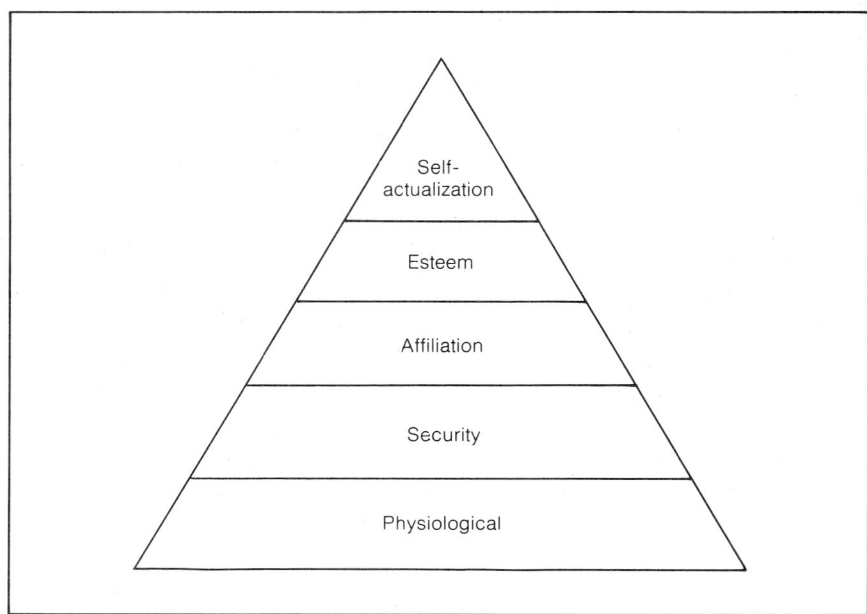

2. While need satisfaction and need importance are negatively related for physiological needs, they are apparently *positively* related for needs that Maslow placed high in his hierarchy. That is, as we are able to satisfy our needs for such things as food, liquids, and sex, they become temporarily less important to us. However, as we find that we're capable of achievement and the acceptance of responsibility, we may emphasize them even more.

3. Although we generally may place great importance on physiological needs when they aren't satisfied, we generally don't proceed up the hierarchy in an orderly fashion once they are satisfied. Instead, there appears to be no clear pattern concerning what needs will become most important once our physiological needs are satisfied.

Where does this leave us? Was Maslow's theorizing of no value? Clearly not. Maslow gave us a place to begin in our examination of need structures. He provided a set of propositions that could be tested and, if refuted, could lead to an improved theory of human needs. In fact, Clayton Alderfer developed a new theory called the existence-relatedness-growth (or ERG) theory, which revises Maslow's theory to make it more consistent with what we now know about human needs.

Alderfer's existence-relatedness-growth (ERG) theory

As we pointed out, studies have not confirmed the existence of the five distinct need categories Maslow hypothesized. Instead, there seems to be some overlap between the security, social, and physiological needs Maslow discussed. Also, the lines between esteem, social, and self-actualization needs are not entirely clear. With these findings in mind, Clayton Alderfer collapsed Maslow's five need categories into three sets.

1. *Existence needs.* These include all forms of material and physiological desires.

2. *Relatedness needs.* These include all needs that involve relationships with other people we care about. (Note that this could include anger and hostility, as well as friendship. Thus, the opposite of satisfaction of relatedness needs is emotional distance rather than hatred.)

3. *Growth needs.* These are all needs that involve persons making creative efforts on themselves and the environment.

Alderfer also revised Maslow's theory in three other ways.

1. He argued that the three need categories form a hierarchy only in the sense of decreasing concreteness. That is, as we move from a focus on existence to relatedness to growth needs, the ways we can satisfy those needs become increasingly abstract.

2. He recognized that, while increasing the level of satisfaction of our existence and relatedness needs may result in decreases in their importance to us, our growth needs become more important as we successfully satisfy them. That is, as we are able to be productive and creative, we look to higher growth goals and, in so doing, are again dissatisfied.

3. He reasoned that we are likely to try to first satisfy our most concrete needs and then to move on to more abstract needs. In this sense, Alderfer sounds somewhat like Maslow, suggesting a pattern of *satisfaction progression*—that is, as one need is satisfied, we progress to the next higher need. However, Alderfer also argued that, along with satisfaction progression, we can experience *frustration regression*. That is, if we can't satisfy needs at a given level of abstractness, we "drop back" and again focus on more concrete needs. Thus, if we are unable to satisfy our growth needs, we again focus on relatedness needs; we can go through cycles, moving from a focus on one need, then another, and then back again.

Alderfer's work reconciles recent research findings with earlier theorizing, and it gives us a sound way to categorize human needs and to think about the relationships between need categories. Before leaving the question of the nature of human needs, we should examine two other well-known theories that tell us something about the subject—Frederick Herzberg's two-factor theory and David McClelland's achievement motivation theory.

Herzberg's two-factor theory

While Frederick Herzberg didn't focus directly on the question of how needs might be categorized, he did feel that it was important to learn what things caused employees to be satisfied or dissatisfied at work. Given such information, we should be able to make inferences about the relative strengths of various needs.

To gain familiarity with this subject, Herzberg first interviewed 200 engineers and accountants in nine companies. Using the *critical incidents method*, he asked them to describe past work experiences that were "exceptionally good" or "exceptionally bad." After analyzing those interviews, Herzberg argued that there are two relatively distinct sets of factors in organizations. One set, which he called motivators or satisfiers, resulted in satisfaction when adequate; the other set of factors, which he called hygiene factors or dissatisfiers, caused dissatisfaction when deficient.

Employees could not, Herzberg argued, be made satisfied solely by improving hygiene factors, nor was the absence of satisfiers likely to dissatisfy them. For example, when Ted's pay was increased and his working area cleaned up and made more comfortable, he felt better about his job. Still, the routine work didn't "turn him on." When a researcher asked Andrea about her feelings about her job, she replied, "My pay is good, and I like the people I work with. I don't really get to do anything very challenging, and I sure can't brag about my job to my kids, but I guess I can't gripe." Table 7-1 shows some of the components of Herzberg's two categories.

Herzberg's well-known and widely accepted work obviously has important implications for organizations. It suggests that satisfaction and dissatisfaction, as shown in Figure 7-3, are not opposites. Rather, the opposite of satisfaction is no satisfaction, and the opposite of dissatisfaction is no dissatisfaction. As a result, some things can make us less dissatisfied but aren't capable of satisfying us, and vice versa. Further, Herzberg classes pay as a dissatisfier. The clear implication is that, once pay is raised to a level at which dissatisfaction is alleviated, further pay increases won't have much positive impact. In

TABLE 7-1
Herzberg's Motivators and Hygiene Factors

MOTIVATORS (SATISFIERS)	HYGIENE FACTORS (DISSATISFIERS)
Achievement	Pay
Challenging Job	Technical Supervision
Responsibility	Working Conditions
Growth	Work Rules and Company Policy
Advancement	Fringe Benefits
Recognition	Seniority Rights
Work Itself	

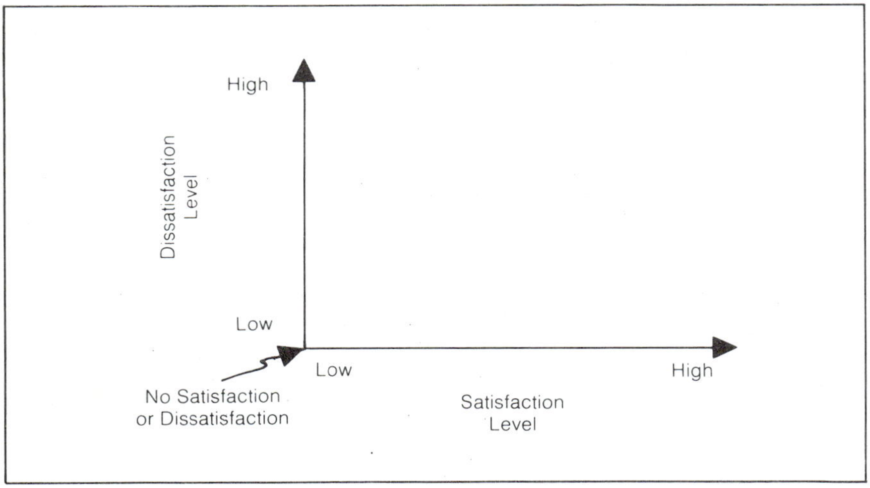

FIGURE 7-3
The Two-factor Theory's View of Satisfaction and Dissatisfaction

general, Herzberg argues that *intrinsic* rewards (those under the employee's control) influence satisfaction and motivation, while *extrinsic* rewards (those under the control of the supervisor or some person other than the employee) influence dissatisfaction and sap motivation.

As a result of Herzberg's work, firms have emphasized challenging work, autonomy, and the opportunity to exercise a variety of skills and to complete a "whole" job. Based on recent evidence, such an emphasis seems appropriate. That is, researchers have found that intrinsic rewards are important determinants of employees' reactions to work.

Unfortunately, while Herzberg's work has probably had a generally positive impact on organizations, his theory has at least three apparent flaws.

1. Herzberg implies that satisfaction and motivation are basically the same thing. However, we have seen that motivation is actually the result of *dissatisfaction*. Therefore, it is dangerous to draw conclusions about how we can motivate employees on the basis of what satisfies them. While satisfaction and motivation sometimes occur together, they often do not.

2. It appears that Herzberg's findings occur only when his particular critical-incidents methodology is used; recall that he asked employees to remember satisfying and dissatisfying events. It has been argued that his findings are exactly what we'd expect to see if employees wanted, consciously or subconsciously, to make themselves look good. That is, we would expect employees to attribute dissatisfaction to outside (extrinsic) things, while seeing themselves as responsible for good things. When methods other than the critical-incidents technique are used to test Herzberg's theory, the results are quite different.

According to Herzberg's theory, it would not be a stockbrokers's lucrative salary but the intrinsic rewards (challenging work, autonomy and skill required) which would make his or her job satisfying.

3. Herzberg's data can be reinterpreted in ways that challenge his contentions. For example, table 7-2 shows the number of times various things were cited as causing satisfaction or dissatisfaction in six studies reported by Herzberg. To class something as a "satisfier" or "dissatisfier," Herzberg looked at the *relative* number of times it caused satisfaction or dissatisfaction. For example, recognition was called a "satisfier" since about three-quarters of the time it was associated with satisfying events. On the other hand, relations with superiors were called a "dissatisfier" since they were generally associated with dissatisfying events. However, if we look again at table 7-2, we can see that, on an *absolute* basis, achievement and recognition were each given more often as causes for dissatisfaction than were such "dissatisfiers" as working conditions or relations with superiors or with peers. In fact, if we look at just the absolute number

TABLE 7-2
Frequency of Reports of "Satisfiers" and "Dissatisfiers" in Six Studies Reported by Herzberg

ITEM	TIMES MENTIONED AS SATISFYING	TIMES MENTIONED AS DISSATISFYING
Achievement	440	122
Recognition	309	110
Working Conditions	20	108
Relations with Superiors	15	59
Relations with Peers	9	57

of times something was mentioned as being related to a satisfying or dissatisfying event, we can see that intrinsics dominate *both* categories. Thus, Herzberg's classification scheme is suspect.

In addition, questions have been raised concerning possible biases of interviewers and other issues. In sum, these criticisms effectively refute Herzberg's contentions concerning the satisfying or dissatisfying roles of various things.

In spite of these problems, Herzberg has contributed considerably to the understanding and management of behavior in organizations. In particular, he has caused organizations to pay more attention to intrinsic rewards, which appear to be very important for most employees, both in terms of satisfaction and dissatisfaction.

McClelland's achievement motivation theory

David McClelland studied the achievement motive, which is the desire to perform in terms of a standard of excellence and to succeed in competitive situations. His studies focused on how this achievement motivation could be developed, on what characterized an individual who exhibited the achievement motive, and on the consequences of high achievement motivation, both for executives and for nations.

McClelland used a variety of interesting techniques to measure the degree to which an individual had high achievement motives. With one such technique, called a projective test, individuals are shown a series of pictures and are asked to write stories based on each picture. Figure 7-4 shows an excerpt from a projective test. Based on the number of achievement-oriented ideas in the stories —for example, thinking of ways to solve problems or anticipating the

FIGURE 7-4
A Projective Test to Measure Achievement Motivation*

Look at this picture for ten or fifteen seconds. Now write a brief but imaginative story suggested by the picture and by the following questions:

1. What is happening? Who is the man?
2. What has led up to this situation? That is, what has happened in the past?
3. What is the man thinking? What is wanted? By whom?
4. What will happen? What will be done?

*From McClelland (1962), p. 100.

consequences of success or failure—an overall achievement motivation score is calculated. McClelland recognized that such a technique wasn't really reliable enough to be used for such purposes as selection of individuals; but he felt that it was useful for measuring average differences between groups of people, such as lawyers and business executives. Using this technique, McClelland found that business managers in several different countries generally scored much higher than did professionals. He also found that there were major differences in average scores across countries. For example, the average score for professionals in the U.S. was twice as high as that of Italian professionals.

McClelland also measured levels of achievement motivation for various nations by looking at the number of achievement ideas per 100 lines in children's stories used in public school textbooks. He argued that whether the stories mainly focused on power, friendship, achievement, or other factors was a function of the spirit currently prevailing in the country. Further, he felt that national achievement levels were closely tied to achievement motivation as expressed in the literature.

> Normally, we found, a high level of concern for achievement is followed some 50 years or so later by a rapid rate of economic growth and prosperity. Such was certainly the case in ancient Greece and in Spain in the late Middle Ages. Furthermore, in both cases a decline in achievement concern was followed very soon after by a decline in economic welfare. (1962, p. 106)

McClelland also argued that individuals with high needs for achievement shared the following characteristics:

1. A strong desire for personal responsibility.
2. A desire for quick, concrete feedback concerning the results of their actions.
3. Intrinsic satisfaction from doing a job well. For them, the monetary and other material rewards associated with accomplishment are seen more as a kind of feedback concerning performance than as ends in themselves.
4. A tendency to set *moderate* achievement goals.

The last of these characteristics might seem surprising; that is, we might expect that an individual with a high need for achievement would set high goals. In fact, though, such individuals recognize that they could achieve very difficult goals only if they were lucky. Knowing this, they weigh the odds and choose a goal they think is likely to give them the best expected return, considering both the level of the return and the probability they will be able to get it.

McClelland reasoned that individuals with strong needs for achievement would be drawn to such occupations as sales, entrepreneurship, or promotion, where there are quick feedback and personal responsibility for results. He also felt that a high need for achievement would be important for success in such jobs but *not* in jobs such as research scientist, accountant, or personnel manager. He found, for example, that even Nobel-Prize-winning research scientists had only moderate levels of achievement motivation. To explain this, he pointed out that research scientists often wait years to learn whether their ideas are successful, and such a wait would be infuriating for an individual with high achievement needs as defined by McClelland.

Based on his studies, McClelland felt that achievement motivation was developed in childhood as a result of encouragement and reinforcement of autonomy and self-reliance by parents. However, he also felt that achievement motivation could be developed in adults. To do this, he felt it was necessary to get the individual to:

1. Speak the "language of achievement." The individual is encouraged to think, talk, act and perceive others as would a person with a high achievement motive. He or she is taught how to take moderate risks to maximize expected payoff and is shown how to code thoughts and fantasies to measure achievement needs.

2. Feel that he or she can and should change and focus on specific personal goals for change in the near future.

3. Develop an honest picture of himself or herself, and his or her desires and possibilities.

4. Feel emotionally supported by instructors and other group members in attempts at self change.

Using an approach that focuses on such factors, McClelland trained a group of sixteen American executives and subsequently found that they were promoted faster than similar individuals who had not been so trained. He also trained a large number of businessmen in Kakinada and Bombay, India, and found that their degree of unusual achievement activity (such as starting a new business, expanding an old business, sharply increasing profits, or diversifying) almost doubled, while the achievement activity of people who couldn't participate in the programs because of space constraints remained about the same. One participant even raised enough money to put up the tallest building in Bombay—the Everest Apartments.

HUMAN NEEDS: AN INTEGRATION

What then, do these four theories tell us about needs?

First, there appears to be an important distinction between what have been called "lower-order" and "higher-order" needs. Higher-order needs, such as Maslow's need for self-actualization, Alderfer's growth needs, McClelland's need for achievement, and those needs that would be satisfied by Herzberg's motivators, seem to be very important. In chapter 14, we will see how such needs seem to determine how employees will respond to job enrichment.

Also, higher-order needs behave differently from other needs. For example, while the importance of lower-order needs declines as they are satisfied, the ability to achieve our higher-order needs seems to increase their importance to us. While the neat sequence of need-importance prepotency Maslow hypothesized apparently doesn't exist, lower-order needs must be fairly well met before higher-order needs become important.

Third, the ideas the various authors present concerning higher-order needs are complementary. That is, Herzberg's findings show that such needs *are* crucial; McClelland's work gives us clues about *how* higher-order need strength is developed; and the theories of Maslow and Alderfer help to explain *when* such needs will become salient.

But this is not to imply that only higher-order needs are important. On the contrary, a key lesson of this chaper is that we all have our own particular, often complex need structures. By understanding the topic of motivation, by sensitively observing and carefully analyzing, and perhaps by directly measuring employee need strengths, managers should be able to better appraise such structures. Once they do so, they will have the potential both to improve the lot of the employee and to direct behaviors to benefit their organizations.

SUMMARY

In this chapter, we have seen that if we want to satisfy or motivate employees, we must understand their needs. Maslow's need hierarchy provided a useful first pass at specifying the nature of human needs and the relationships between need satisfaction and need importance. Based on research findings and his own theorizing, Alderfer honed Maslow's need hierarchy to develop the existence-relatedness-growth theory. That theory collapsed Maslow's five need categories into three and recognized a more complex pattern of interrelationships among needs. While criticized on many grounds, Herzberg's two-factor theory has almost certainly had a beneficial impact on organizations; it emphasizes the importance of satisfaction of higher-order needs and has been useful in specifying particular job characteristics that may contribute to such satisfaction. Finally, McClelland's achievement motivation theory considers how achievement motivation may be developed, how individuals imbued with achievement motivation differ from others, and how achievement motivation can translate into personal, organizational, and even national consequences.

It would be helpful to have a general model to predict exactly which of Sandy's or Paul's needs are likely to be most important tomorrow or a week from Thursday. But apparently no such model currently exists. Instead, it is probably still necessary to measure directly the strengths of various needs of employees. And, as we will see in chapter 14, there are some seemingly valid and reliable measures of such need strength.

While the theories discussed here don't allow us to specify confidently how we can best try to satisfy and/or motivate each employee, they do give us ways to think about important categories of needs and the relationships between them. Thus, when we try to measure the strengths of various needs, we at least know what categories of needs should concern us. Again, the theories we have described in this chapter should make us be especially careful to differentiate clearly between higher-order and lower-order needs.

Taken together, such theories provide useful information about the nature of human needs, their interrelationships, and potential sources for their satisfaction. Following the next two chapters, which deal with satisfaction and its measurement, we will see how such information can be used to help motivate employees.

REFERENCES

McClelland, D.C. "Business Drive and National Achievement." *Harvard Business Review 40* (1962): 99-112.

Maslow, A.H. "A Theory of Human Motivation." *Psychological Review 50* (1943): 370-96.

CHAPTER 8

The Satisfied Employee

It is difficult to say how many people are really satisfied with their jobs. National surveys conducted over the past twenty years have shown the percentage of employees who described themselves as being satisfied or very satisfied with their jobs has increased from about 80 percent in 1958 to about 90 percent in 1964. Since then, that figure has stayed around 90 percent.[1] However, a recent national survey of its readers by *Psychology Today* examined, among other things, how satisfied people were with their jobs and whether they felt "trapped" in them.[2] Less than 18 percent of the respondents indicated they could "strongly agree" with a statement that they were satisfied with their jobs. About 26 percent expressed some level of disagreement with that statement. Further, almost as many people agreed that they felt trapped by their jobs as those who disagreed. Since the readers of *Psychology Today* have relatively high incomes and high-status jobs, it would seem likely that the actual percentage of employees in the United States who are dissatisfied with and feel trapped by their work is higher than this study suggests. What are the consequences of this? What can be done about it?

Because most people spend almost half of their waking lives at work, only the most callous employers would suggest that worker satisfaction is unimportant. In fact, more and more emphasis is being placed on attempts to satisfy workers' needs.

There are at least two major reasons why organizations might be concerned with employee job satisfaction. First, high satisfaction is important in itself. Second, it has often been argued that satisfaction is related to a variety of organizationally relevant outcomes. For ex-

[1] U.S. Department of Labor (1974).

[2] Renwick, Lawler, and the *Psychology Today* staff (1978).

ample, most of us have heard it said that "a happy employee is a productive employee." This would suggest that high job satisfaction should cause high productivity. On the other hand, it has also been said that "what's good for the company is good for the worker." This seems to imply that if we improve productivity, satisfaction will naturally follow. It's important to explore evidence relating to such contentions. That is, how does satisfaction relate to such important outcomes as turnover, absenteeism, and performance? Further, if such relationships do exist, what is the cause and what is the effect in each case? Finally, how does this sort of information help us to manage behavior successfully in organizations? There are actually a number of reasons why we should take a close look at the relation of job satisfaction to other variables.

First, many of the ways by which we may try to increase employee satisfaction—by raising pay, for instance, or changing the nature of the job—may be very costly. Even if we are willing to accept higher costs in order to satisfy our employees, we should at least ask what kinds of benefits we might get to help offset such costs. In fact, we may need just that kind of information if we are to "sell" the benefits of increased employee job satisfaction to others in the organization who insist that we should focus only on dollars and cents.

Second, there are a number of ways we may attempt to raise worker satisfaction. Some of those ways may also result in high productivity, low turnover, and so on, while others may not. Consequently, it is important that we really understand the mechanisms that link satisfaction to other outcomes.

Finally, we want to see how job satisfaction affects an employee's whole existence. Imagine that you are a manager and someone says to you: "What's important is that the employee be satisfied with his or her life *in total*. You might do things to increase the employees' job satisfaction that would actually make their overall lives *less* satisfying. For instance, you might make jobs so interesting to your employees that they would be satisfied with them, even though salary increases were smaller and less frequent than on other jobs. If that situation produces squabbles at home over financial problems, have you really helped the employees? And what have you done for their families?"

While we might like to sidestep such questions by saying that we shouldn't delve into employees' private lives, to do so is to ignore a critical issue. If we do things that, no matter how good our intentions, have a net negative impact on the employee, we have to admit failure. We can't just consider job satisfaction in isolation. Instead, we must look at how job satisfaction relates to the rest of the employee's work and nonwork life.

THE QUALITY OF WORK LIFE

A further, and currently well-publicized, reason for understanding employee satisfaction is a rapidly developing interest in the *quality of work life*, a term that various people use in many different ways. To some, it refers to such things as worker participation in decision making, to the "humanizing" of work, or to the full utilization and development of human capabilities. To others, it concerns making working conditions more healthy and tolerable and distributing more equitably the organization's resources, including income.

In 1973, Richard E. Walton provided a list of categories, briefly summarized here, to be used to analyze and assess the phenomenon of quality of work life.

1. Adequate and fair compensation
2. Safe and healthy environment
3. Development of human capacities
4. Growth and security—the opportunity to maintain and expand capabilities, to use those capabilities in future work assignments, and to advance in organizational or career terms
5. Social integration—the opportunity to achieve personal identity and self-esteem
6. Constitutionalism—the degree to which a worker has rights and can protect those rights
7. The total life space—the extent to which a person's work has a balanced role in his or her life, not demanding so much time, effort, or other inputs to severely disrupt leisure and family time
8. Social relevance—the degree to which the worker views what the organization does as socially responsible and, therefore, sees his or her own work as being of social value

Common to the views of quality of work life cited here and to the specific categories Walton presented is a focus on the satisfaction of needs, whether for security, growth, meaningful work, interaction with others, achievement, or whatever. It may well be that the term *quality of work life* will be a popular rallying call in the 1980s, on the tongues of labor leaders, academicians, politicians, business persons and others. If that is to be the case, it is imperative that we understand employee satisfaction.

WHAT IS JOB SATISFACTION?

In chapter 7, we discussed the nature of employee needs and considered the relationships between need satisfaction and need importance. Now, we might ask, "Is need satisfaction the same thing as job satisfaction? If not, how are they related?" In fact, people who have examined employee satisfaction often have not clearly distinguished between, or carefully related, satisfaction of specific needs (such as existence, relatedness, and growth needs), satisfaction with specific work outcomes (such as pay, supervision, coworkers, and so on), and overall satisfaction with work or with life.

Some work outcomes, such as pay, may help to satisfy a wide variety of needs. So it is possible that we might be able to satisfy most, or all, of our needs even though we might find certain work-related factors—such as coworkers—to be somewhat unsatisfactory. Overall job satisfaction is a function of satisfaction with the various aspects of work, weighted by the relative importance of those aspects to the particular employee. Thus, an employee may somehow satisfy all of his or her needs without really being satisfied with some parts of the job; also, the job may be satisfactory in all respects without fully satisfying all of the employee's needs. The selection by Karlene Roberts and Frederick Savage that follows this chapter discusses, among other things, some of the ways employees' need satisfaction and job satisfaction have been measured.

The need-satisfaction process

We noted earlier that it is important to learn how satisfaction is associated with other work-related and nonwork-related variables. To begin to understand that association, it might be useful to consider the simplified picture of the need-satisfaction process shown in figure 8-1. That figure, which elaborates on figure 7-1, shows that an unsatisfied need causes us to search for some way to satisfy it. Eventually, we may see some way to satisfy the need and may attempt to do so.

For example, Janet has unsatisfied needs for the respect of others. She decides that one way to gain such respect is to be promoted to the top hierarchical levels of her firm. She subsequently does all she can to get promoted. If Janet is able to achieve her goal, the level of satisfaction of her esteem needs will probably increase. On the other hand, if she is frustrated in her attempts to be promoted, at least three things might happen. One possibility is that Janet might simply look for some other way to gain the respect of others; for instance, she might try to assume a leadership role in community affairs. Another possibility is that Janet might seek a more easily attainable goal than before; that is, she might lower her *level of aspiration*. And, finally, because of repeated frustration, Janet might eventually resort to using *defense mechanisms*. Defense mechanisms are reactions to frustration, attempts to somehow alleviate the negative consequences of an inability to satisfy needs.

There are many alternative defense mechanisms. To learn what sorts of defense mechanisms might result from frustration at work, we should ask, "How could dissatisfied employees reduce tensions resulting from repeated inability to achieve need-satisfying goals?" The following is a list of some possible answers.

1. They could take out their frustration elsewhere. For example, an employee who has a bad day at the office may relieve tension by going home and yelling at her husband. This is called *displacement*.

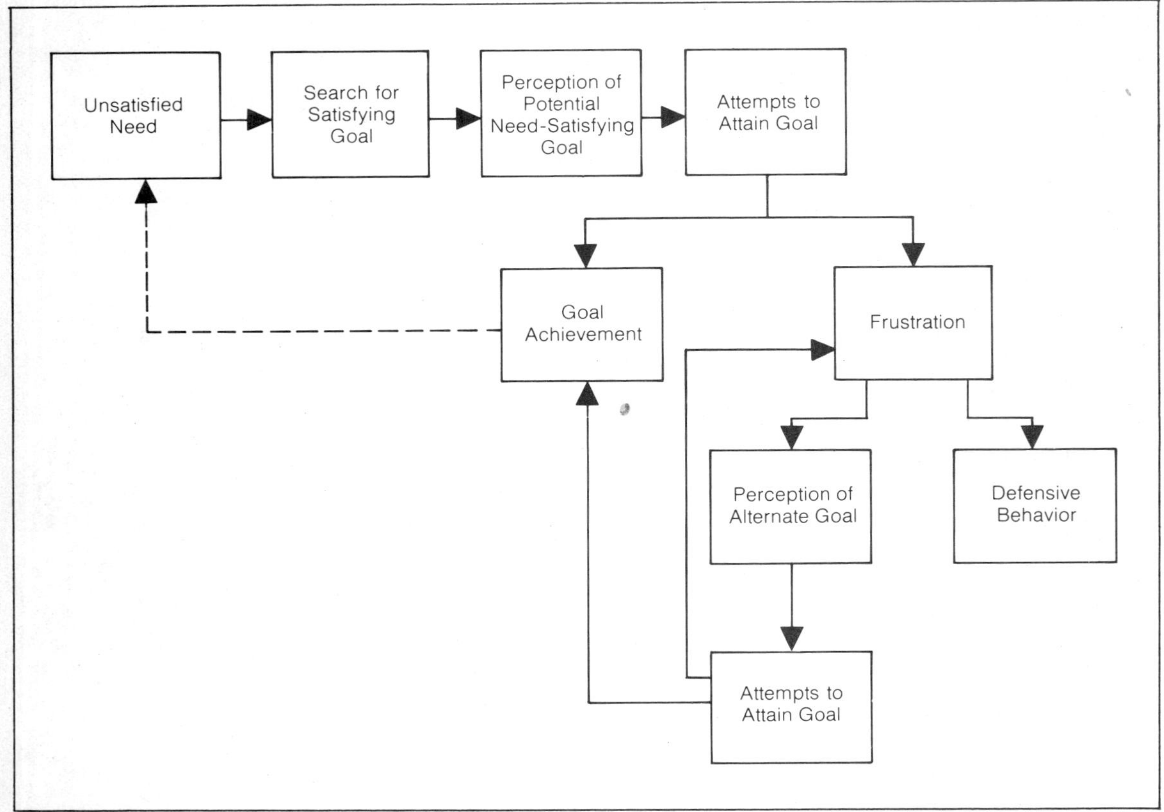

FIGURE 8-1
The Need Satisfaction Process

2. They could become less concerned about their work, thereby reducing the importance of any failure at work. That is, they may become *apathetic*.

3. They could strike back at the source of their frustration. For instance, they might make negative comments about the company, join with others in slowing down on the job, or even resort to strikes or sabotage.

4. They could mentally "leave" the source of frustration by daydreaming or fantasizing while on the job.

5. They could physically leave the source of frustration by being absent from work or by quitting.

These possibilities generally suggest that employee dissatisfaction may have negative consequences for the organization as well as for the employee. Given such possibilities, let's briefly review recent evidence concerning the relationships of job satisfaction to certain work outcomes.

Relationships of job satisfaction to work outcomes

Satisfaction and turnover.[3] All major reviews of research into the relationship of job satisfaction to turnover show that relationship to be strongly negative. That is, dissatisfied employees are much more likely to leave the firm than are satisfied employees. Further, many studies of such employees as clerical workers, life insurance agents, retail store employees, and operatives have shown that satisfaction levels can be used successfully to *predict* subsequent turnover. Thus, it appears that job dissatisfaction and turnover are not only related but that dissatisfaction causes turnover.

Satisfaction and absenteeism. While the results are not as strong as with turnover, studies generally find that dissatisfied workers have higher rates of absenteeism than do satisfied workers. For example, one study of female clerical workers in a regional office of a national insurance company found that satisfaction levels of employees measured one year significantly predicted frequency of absences the next year.[4] So it seems that dissatisfied workers are, in fact, more likely to leave the organization, temporarily or permanently, than are satisfied workers.

Satisfaction and performance. For quite a while, it was generally accepted that satisfied employees would be highly motivated and perform well. In fact, theorist Frederick Herzberg used the terms *satisfier* and *motivator* interchangeably. However, actual studies of the relationship between satisfaction and performance don't support such a viewpoint. One early review of those studies concluded that ". . . there is little evidence that employee attitudes of the type usually measured in morale surveys bear any simple—or, for that matter, appreciable—relationship to performance on the job."[5] Another review of twenty studies showed that only about 2 percent of variations in performance levels were related to variations in satisfaction levels.[6] Yet another review found positive relationships between satisfaction and performance in only about half the studies considered.[7] More recent studies have yielded similar results, concluding that high satisfaction apparently does not result in high performance. Actually, this is not too surprising. There are many ways we could satisfy employees—by, say, shortening the work day to four hours—that might hurt performance. On the other hand, some studies have shown that performance levels of employees at one point in time may be useful in predicting *later* satisfaction levels. Let's explore the implications of such findings.

---

[3]See Porter and Steers (1973) for a discussion of several factors relating to absenteeism and turnover.
[4]Waters and Roach (1971).
[5]Brayfield and Crockett (1955).
[6]Vroom (1964).
[7]Herzberg, Mausner, Peterson, and Capwell (1957).

Implications for the management of organizational behavior

We have seen that employee dissatisfaction may result in such undesirable outcomes for the organization as absenteeism and turnover and that it might be expected also to lead to employee apathy, daydreaming, and negativism. We have also seen that there is no necessary relationship between job satisfaction and performance. That relationship may be positive, negative, or absent, depending upon other factors. It now seems reasonable to ask, "What are those other factors? What are their roles?"

A study by David Cherrington, H. Joseph Reitz, and William Scott helps answer these questions.[8] They reasoned that employees' job satisfaction is probably largely a function of the amount of rewards those employees receive. On the other hand (consistent with the discussion of expectancy theory presented in chapter 10 and of learning theory presented in chapter 12), performance levels probably depend more upon whether employees feel that rewards are tied to good performance. Depending, then, on who gets rewarded and whether or not rewards are linked to performance, it is likely that any combination of satisfaction and performance could result.

To test this, Cherrington *et. al.* hired workers to score aptitude tests. While some workers performed at high levels and others at low levels, bonuses were randomly given to half the high performers and half the low performers. As expected, those workers given the bonus were most satisfied. Also, workers who received a bonus that was consistent with their performance in the first period (that is, high performers who got a bonus or low performers who didn't) performed at the highest levels in the second period. In fact, the highest performers in the second period were the *low* performers who didn't get a bonus in the first period. This strongly suggests that the nature of the organization's reward system may influence the relationship between performance and job satisfaction.

Figure 8-2 illustrates this possibility. Employees perform at some level and subsequently get—or don't get—a variety of rewards (pay, praise, feelings of accomplishment, and so on). They then compare those rewards to the rewards they feel they should get on the basis of their contributions to the organization. If employees feel that they are getting what they deserve, they will probably be satisfied. On the other hand, if they feel that, relative to others they see in the organization and elsewhere, they aren't getting what their contributions warrant, dissatisfaction is likely.

Now, let's consider two hypothetical situations.

Situation A. Employees at Clothes Encounters make robot costumes. Some employees produce far more and better costumes than do others, but everyone is paid the same. As a result, relatively low-performing employees are quite satisfied with their pay levels,

---

[8]Cherrington, Reitz, and Scott (1971).

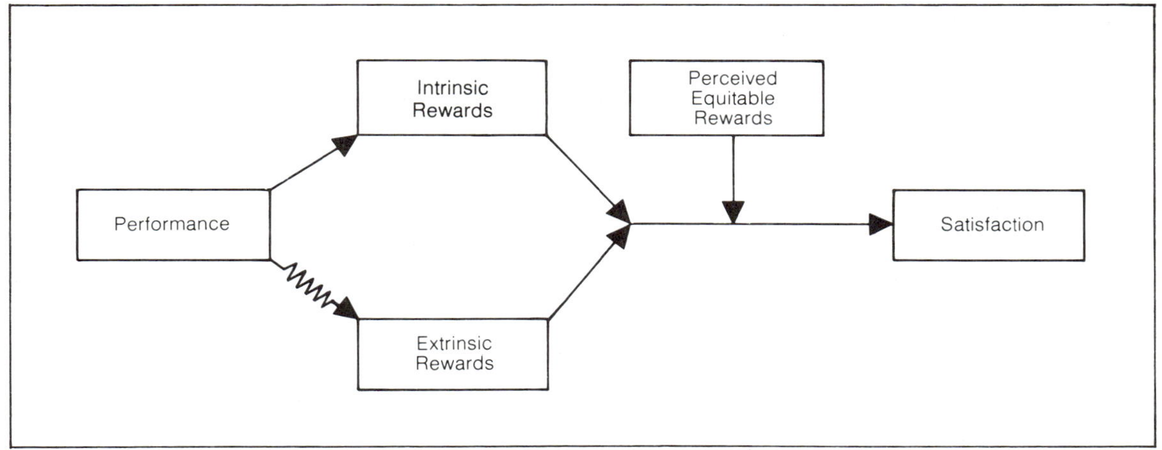

*From Gene Dalton, Paul Lawrence, and Larry Greiner, *Organizational Change and Development* (Homewood, Il.: Richard D. Irwin, 1970), p. 222. ©1970 by Richard D. Irwin, Inc.

FIGURE 8-2
How Rewards Influence the Satisfaction-Performance Relationship*

while high-performing employees feel they are not getting what they deserve and are thus dissatisfied. A *negative* relationship between job satisfaction and performance exists among the employees of Clothes Encounters. Low performers are satisfied; high performers are dissatisfied. Also, because of their dissatisfaction, the high-performing workers are more likely to leave the organization than are their low-performing colleagues.

Situation B. At Star Wears, employees make Wookie costumes and are rewarded on the basis of the quality and quantity of their output. As a result, high performers are well paid and satisfied, while low performers grumble that they cannot live on their earnings. Thus, those low performers are relatively more likely to leave the organization (probably in search of a company like Clothes Encounters) than are high performers. At Star Wears, there is a *positive* correlation between job satisfaction and performance.

These situations highlight an important point: While there is no *necessary* relationship between job satisfaction and performance, that does not mean we wouldn't like to see a positive relationship between them in our company. In fact, if we tailor our reward system so that high performance is adequately rewarded, we should see a positive relationship between job satisfaction and performance. Such a relationship is a good clue that our reward system is working properly. And it generally restricts turnover and absenteeism to low-performing employees.

In chapter 10, we will consider *expectancy theory,* which looks at this issue of proper design of reward systems in more detail. For now, we should remember that while job satisfaction and performance do not have to be positively related, we would like to find such a relationship in our firm. If we don't, we should take a close look at the design of our reward system.

SOME OTHER THINGS RELATED TO JOB SATISFACTION

Job satisfaction, besides being important in itself, is associated with such organizationally relevant outcomes as absenteeism and turnover and to a number of defense mechanisms. We have also seen that it is important that we maintain a positive relationship between job satisfaction and job performance among our employees. Given this evidence of the pervasive role of job satisfaction, let's consider how job satisfaction is related to a number of other variables.

Job satisfaction and organizational structure[9]

It is difficult to assess the impacts of various characteristics of organizational structure on job satisfaction. For one thing, many such characteristics tend to occur together. As an example, larger firms generally also have larger subunits, more hierarchical levels, and so on, than do smaller firms; consequently, it is difficult to determine the relative roles of organizational size, subunit size, and organization "height." Also, people "self select" into particular types of jobs and organizations. So if people who are naturally hard to satisfy tend to pick firms with certain characteristics, it may be extremely difficult to sort out the effects of individual differences and organizational characteristics.

However, we can probably draw the following tentative conclusions based on the research to date.

1. Employees at higher organizational levels are generally more satisfied than are those at lower levels.

2. Employees in line positions—that is, those in the direct "chain of command" from the top to the bottom of the organizational hierarchy—are regularly seen to be more satisfied than those in staff positions—positions that support line positions.

3. Employees in large subunits are less satisfied and exhibit higher turnover and absenteeism than do those in small subunits.

4. While employees in large organizations tend to show lower levels of satisfaction than those in small organizations, such findings may be misleading since differences in size of subunits and other factors generally have not been controlled.

5. It seems that "tall" organizations—with many hierarchical levels and relatively few people at each level—satisfy existence and relatedness needs better than do "flat" organizations. On the other hand, "flat" organizations satisfy growth needs better.

6. Reactions of employees to decentralization of authority and related factors are, to some extent, a function of individual differences, which will be discussed in chapter 14, "What Job Enrichment Is All About."

[9]Much of this section is based on Berger and Cummings (1979).

JOB SATISFACTION AND OCCUPATIONAL AND DEMOGRAPHIC CHARACTERISTICS

The relationships of job satisfaction to various occupational and demographic characteristics are interesting and sometimes surprising.

1. Men and women don't differ much in their average job-satisfaction levels. Surveys conducted during this decade sometimes show men to be slightly more satisfied—and sometimes show just the opposite. Differences in satisfaction with the job between the sexes are rarely more than two or three percentage points.[10]

2. Both age and years of work experience tend to be positively related to job satisfaction. For example, table 8-1 presents average job-satisfaction scores for employees in various age categories. However, Donald Schwab and Herbert Heneman (1977) have argued that such findings may be somewhat confounded by the fact that older workers generally also have more experience in the organization. In particular, they found that when experience was controlled, age was positively related to satisfaction with intrinsic outcomes but *not* to satisfaction with extrinsic outcomes. Also, the relationship of age to satisfaction in their study (and in two previous studies that also controlled for experience) was stronger for males than for females.

3. As Philip Ash (1972) has noted, until very recently there has been a "color-blind constraint" on industrial psychological research. As such, relatively few studies have explored the relationship of race to job satisfaction. However, national surveys conducted since 1962 consistently show that a larger percentage of whites than of blacks consider themselves to be satisfied workers.[11] Further, Ash (1972) found whites to be more satisfied with their jobs than blacks, even when sex and occupation were controlled for.

TABLE 8-1
Average Job Satisfaction Levels for Various Age Groups

AGE	JOB SATISFACTION*
16-20 (N=175)	-41
21-29 (N=584)	-27
30-44 (N=657)	10
45-54 (N=443)	9
55 or older (N=292)	23

*A higher numerical score indicates greater job satisfaction. The mean of this measure was -2; its standard deviation was 84.

SOURCE: *Job Satisfaction: Is There a Trend?* Manpower Research Monograph No. 30, U.S. Department of Labor, Manpower Administration, 1974, p. 12. Data taken from: R. P. Quinn and L. J. Shepard, *The 1972-73 Quality of Employment Survey: Descriptive Statistics, with Comparison Data from the 1969-70 Survey of Working Conditions* (Ann Arbor, Mich.: Survey Research Center, 1974).

[10]U.S. Department of Labor (1974).

[11]U.S. Department of Labor (1974). Also, Weaver (1974) reported similar findings for a national sample.

4. Interestingly, surveys show that workers with either relatively little education (eight years or less) or quite a bit of education (a college degree or more) are more satisfied with their jobs than are workers with an intermediate amount of schooling.[12]

5. Not surprisingly, job satisfaction varies substantially with occupation. Table 8-2 shows that average job satisfaction levels are highest for professional and technical workers and lowest for nonfarm laborers.

Satisfaction and stress

People whose jobs make them feel tense and anxious are certainly less satisfied with their jobs than are those employed in a more stressfree work environment. What working conditions cause a work environment to become stressful? Two of the most frequently identified antecedents of job stress are role conflict and role ambiguity.

Role conflict. This occurs when employees are required to engage in activities that run counter to their own expectations or when another person or persons place competing demands on their time and energies.

TABLE 8-2
Average Job Satisfaction Levels for Various Occupational Groups

OCCUPATIONAL GROUP*	MEAN JOB SATISFACTION†
Professional and technical (N=323)	25
Managers, officials, and proprietors (N=319)	19
Sales (N=112)	11
Craftsmen and foremen (N=270)	8
Service workers, except private household (N=238)	-11
Clerical (N=364)	-14
Operatives (N=379)	-35
Nonfarm laborers (N=72)	-42

*The following categories have been omitted due to small numbers of cases: farmers and farm managers, farm laborers, and private household workers.
†Mean values are based on a twenty-eight-question measure of overall job satisfaction. A higher numerical score indicates greater job satisfaction. The mean of this measure in 1973 was -2; its standard deviation was 84.
SOURCE: *Job Satisfaction: Is There a Trend?* Manpower Research Monograph No. 30, U.S. Department of Labor, Manpower Administration, 1974, p. 10. Data taken from: R.P. Quinn and L.J. Shepard, *The 1972-73 Quality of Employment Survey: Descriptive Statistics, with Comparison Data from the 1969-70 Survey of Working Conditions* (Ann Arbor, Mich.: Survey Research Center, 1974).

[12]U.S. Department of Labor (1974).

Role conflict is found in several forms. (1) Inter-sender role conflict—A single role sender demands incompatible behaviors from the employee. For example, the president of one company expects the vice president of manufacturing to increase production by 2 percent *and* reduce the labor force by 1 to ½ percent during the next quarter. (2) Inter-sender role conflict—Two or more role senders demand incompatible behaviors from the employee. For example, a personnel director is expected to hire only the most eminently qualified engineers, while, at the same time, she feels pressured to hire only members of particular race and sex subgroups. (3) Person-role conflict—The employee is expected to engage in behaviors that are incompatible with his or her own expectations. For example, an employee seriously concerned with product quality is expected to sacrifice that quality in order to meet production schedules. (4) Inter-role conflict—The pressures stemming from one role an individual occupies are incompatible with the pressures stemming from a different role he or she also occupies. For example, as a member of the capital budgeting committee, a manager is responsible for reducing capital expenditures; and, as corporate transportation manager, he desperately wants to update his equipment. A busy manager who must also find time to perform adequately in her roles as wife and mother also exemplifies inter-role conflict. (5) Role overload—The employee is expected to engage in two or more behaviors within a time period too short to accommodate the multiple behaviors. For example, a salesperson is expected to meet with an important client Monday morning in San Francisco and another customer early Monday afternoon in New York.[13]

Role ambiguity. This lack of role clarity also is found in several forms: (a) employees lack clear information about what people expect them to accomplish; (b) employees know what outcomes people expect but don't know how to meet those ends; and (c) employees don't know what personal costs or benefits are associated with meeting particular expectations. We should point out here that at least some minimal levels of role conflict and role ambiguity are inherently present in many, if not most, types of jobs. The successful management of stress, therefore, involves reducing it where possible and then coping with a realistic level of stress, not in totally eliminating its sources.

The pertinent question now becomes, "What can managers do to help their subordinates deal with the stresses inherent in their jobs?" There are several possible answers. For example, establishing a goal-setting program that produces a set of measurable objectives the organization expects employees to achieve will reduce the stresses the employees experience by directly influencing the employees' levels of role ambiguity. Such a set of well-defined goals clarifies to the employees what people expect from them. Second, a sensible performance-appraisal system also reduces job stress by further clar-

[13]For a further discussion of the forms of role conflict, see Kahn, Wolfe, Quinn, Snoek, and Rosenthal (1964).

Salespeople generally have relatively low levels of role ambiguity. Since they usually have well-defined sales quotas, it is easy to gauge how they've performed; they also have *very* formalized reward systems based on sales.

ifying the expectations placed on the employee. Finally, implementing a formalized reward system helps to clarify the personal costs or benefits associated with meeting particular expectations; thus, this practice may also contribute to reduce job stress. Again, goal-setting programs and performance appraisal and reward systems are examples of sound managerial practices that reduce job stress and, therefore, increase job satisfaction.

JOB SATISFACTION AND LIFE SATISFACTION

Earlier we said that companies should be concerned with how satisfied employees are with their lives in total, not just with their jobs. If we as managers do something that makes our employees more satisfied with their jobs but less satisfied with their total lives, our contribution is questionable. We should, therefore, ask how job satisfaction and life satisfaction are related.

There are various possibilities. For example, job satisfaction may "spill over" into overall life satisfaction. That is, workers who are happy with their jobs may also be happy with their lives. Or there may be a *compensatory* relationship: workers who are dissatisfied at work find satisfaction elsewhere in their lives. Finally, workers may be so satisfied with and involved in their work that their overall life satisfaction suffers; perhaps we could call this an *opiate* effect.

This issue has not really received the amount of careful examination it deserves. However, what little research has been done seems to support the "spill-over" idea. For example, one study of auto workers found that those employees who were dissatisfied with work also tended to be dissatisfied with their lives.[14] Another study focused on first-level supervisors in two departments of a chemical plant:[15] supervisors in one department had low job satisfaction, as well as low satisfaction with life and leisure; in the other department, supervisors were more satisfied with their jobs, as well as with other aspects of life. Again, this supports the idea of a "spill-over" from satisfaction with the job to satisfaction with life in general.[16]

Such findings are encouraging. They suggest that if we as managers can raise our employees' levels of job satisfaction, we may also improve their overall satisfaction with life.

SUMMARY

In this chapter, we have seen that job satisfaction is important, both in itself and how it relates to other variables. By increasing job satisfaction of the employee, we can also reduce absenteeism and turnover and a number of the undesirable responses. Also, a positive relationship of job satisfaction to performance among our employees suggests that our reward system is working properly and that turnover and absenteeism will be largely restricted to our low performers.

We have also seen that certain characteristics of the organization, such as subunit size, are associated with satisfaction, as are various characteristics of the employee, such as age. Finally, some evidence indicates that increasing job satisfaction is also likely to reduce stress and increase satisfaction with life in general.

The following reading, by Karlene Roberts and Frederick Savage, presents a series of questions that can be asked to determine whether a company should consider using a job-satisfaction survey, what specific job-satisfaction measures might be useful, and the probable consequences of conducting such a survey.

[14]Kornhauser (1965).

[15]Iris and Barrett (1972).

[16]See Kavanagh and Halpern (1977) for more on this issue.

REFERENCES

Ash, P., "Job Satisfaction Differences among Women of different Ethnic Groups. *Journal of Vocational Behavior* 2 (1972): 492-507.

Berger, C.J., and Cummings, L.L. "Organizational Structure, Attitudes, and Behaviors." In *Research in Organizational Behavior*, edited by B.M. Staw, vol. 1. Greenwich, Conn: JAI Press, 1979.

Brayfield, A.H., and Crockett, W.H. "Employee Attitudes and Employee Performance. *Psychological Bulletin* 52 (1955): 396-424.

Cherrington, D.J; Reitz, H.J; and Scott, W.E., Jr. "Effects of Contingent and Non-contingent Reward on the Relationship Between Satisfaction and Task Performance." *Journal of Applied Psychology* 55 (1971): 531-36.

Herzberg, F.; Mausner, B.; Peterson, R.D.; and Capwell, D.F. *Job Attitudes: Review of Research and Opinion.* Pittsburgh: Psychological Service of Pittsburgh, 1957.

Iris, B., and Barrett, G.V. Some Relations between Job and Life Satisfaction and Job Importance. *Journal of Applied Psychology* 56 (1972): 301-04.

Kahn, R.; Wolfe, D.; Quinn, R.; Snoek, J.; and Rosenthal, R. *Organizational Stress: Studies in Role Conflict and Ambiguity.* New York: Wiley, 1964.

Kavanagh, M.J., and Halpern, M. "The Impact of Job Level and Sex Differences on the Relationship between Life and Job Satisfaction." *Academy of Management Journal* 20 (1977): 66-73.

Kornhauser, A.W. *Mental Health of the Industrial Worker.* New York: Wiley, 1965.

Porter, L.W., and Lawler, E.E. "Properties of Organization Structure in Relation to Job Attitudes and Job Behavior." *Psychological Bulletin* 64 (1965): 23-51.

Porter, L.W., and Lawler, E.E. *Managerial Attitudes and Performance.* Homewood, Ill.: Irwin-Dorsey, 1968.

Porter, L.W., and Steers, R.M. "Organizational, Work, and Personal Factors in Employee Turnover and Absenteeism." *Psychological Bulletin* 80 (1973): 151-76.

Quinn, R.P., and Shepard, L.J. *The 1972-73 Quality of Employment Survey: Descriptive Statistics, with Comparison Data from the 1969-70 Survey of Working Conditions.* Ann Arbor, Mich.: Survey Research Center, 1974.

Renwick, P.A., and Lawler, E.E. "What You Really Want from Your Job." *Psychology Today* 11 (12) (1978): 53-58, 60, 62-65, 118.

Roberts, K.H., and Savage, F. "Twenty Questions: Utilizing Job Satisfaction Measures." *California Management Review* 15 (3) (1973): 21-28.

Schwab, D.P., and Heneman, H.G., III. "Age and Satisfaction with Dimensions of Work." *Journal of Vocational Behavior* 10 (1977): 212-20.

U.S. Department of Labor. *Job Satisfaction: Is There a Trend?* Manpower Research Monograph No. 30. Manpower Administration, 1974.

Vroom, V.H. *Work and Motivation.* New York: Wiley, 1964.

Walton, R.E. "Quality of Work Life: What Is It?" *Sloan Management Review* 15 (1973): 11-21.

Waters, L.K., and Roach, D. "Relationship between Job Attitudes and Two Forms of Withdrawal from the Work Situation." *Journal of Applied Psychology* 55 (1971): 92-94.

Weaver, C. "Negro-White Differences in Job Satisfaction." *Business Horizons* 17 (1974): 67-78.

CHAPTER

Twenty Questions: Utilizing Job Satisfaction Measures*

During the last decade the issue of employee job satisfaction has received considerable attention. There are several obvious reasons for measuring satisfaction.

There is a growing concern with the human as well as the physical assets of organizations. Among these human assets are the values employees hold about their employers and their jobs.

Some researchers and some managers believe that satisfaction contributes to job performance; that the dissatisfied employee will perform poorly.

There is ample evidence that satisfaction is negatively related to absenteeism and turnover, both of which are costly to organizations. Managers can better allocate their personnel resources if they understand the attitudes of their various groups of employees.

It is always a good idea for managers to know how their employees feel about their jobs. Our research shows that different kinds of employees in the same organization respond to their jobs with different attitudes and values.

Unfortunately, having information about employee satisfaction is futile unless the firm is willing to take positive steps where there is low morale. However, even where there is a commitment to action and a desire to collect reliable information about employee attitudes, there are at least two further problems. How does a manager know whether he should conduct a job satisfaction survey? And, if he does conduct one, how should he measure satisfaction?

To date, no one has attempted to present managers with an effective strategy for determining whether their companies should conduct attitude surveys, and there is no groundwork for selecting appropriate job satisfaction measures. To remedy this situation, we offer the following strategy, based primarily on our own research.

THE "TWENTY QUESTION" STRATEGY

At one time or another most of us have seen the television program "What's My Line?" As in the game, "Twenty Questions," the "What's My Line?" panel attempts to guess the occupation of a guest by asking a series of questions which can be answered "yes" or "no." After watching the program, most of us are amazed at how quickly the panel usually guesses the guest's occupation. On closer examination, we note that a skillful panel member first asks questions of a very general nature. As these are answered, he narrows his scope of interest, ignoring certain options and concentrating on increasingly specific questions to elicit the appropriate information. Arlene Francis' famous question, "Is it bigger than a bread-box?" illustrates the skillful use of a partition question to zero in on an individual's occupation.

This "Twenty Questions" strategy can be equally useful in deciding the cost-benefit trade-offs of conducting a job satisfaction survey. The more general questions force an examination of an individual's managerial goals and the goals of his company and force him to ask *if* conducting a job satisfaction survey will benefit the firm. If such a survey is recommended, the narrower questions will help determine how it might benefit the firm and how one should go about measuring job satisfaction. The economical questioning strategy helps conserve time and money.

To illustrate this strategy consider the following situation: The president of Barrow Company, a manufacturing firm with 1,000 employees, notices that the female clerical personnel are not doing their jobs well. This group is characterized by high absenteeism and turnover rates. To correct this situation he decides to restructure the clerical job so that each girl has more opportunity for growth and responsibility. After the jobs are restructured, however, job performance drops more, absenteeism and turnover increase another 15 percent per year.

Question no. 1: Should the manager conduct a job satisfaction survey?

Yes, if he is prepared to make some changes in those job facets which are particularly dissatisfying to his employees. Employees may think that in providing the manager, or an outsider who conducts the survey, with information about their job related feelings, they can expect some attempt to change those job facets related to attitudes.

In our example, the workers may value pay more than they value responsibility. A job satisfaction survey would probably have revealed this. A company's deteriorating organizational climate may well be a result of failing to consider this kind of need in restructuring jobs. If a job satisfaction survey had been conducted before the jobs were restructured, the situation of increased absenteeism and turnover might have been avoided. Our research, as well as that of many other authors, shows that different employee groups want different things from their jobs. Even if a survey indicated that girls wanted greater job responsibility, their participation in job restructuring might have been crucial to the effectiveness of such a change. By not directly participating in the change, employees can feel left out of decision processes directly affecting them, and they may sabotage efforts at change.

In situations similar to that in our example, job satisfaction surveys may help in two ways: first, they provide a means for employees to communicate their feelings to higher management and thus participate indirectly in job restructuring; second, questions concerned with the desirability of employee participation in decision-making can be a part of the survey—employees may or may not indicate a need for direct participation in such matters and management can act accordingly.

But what if the situation has gone as far as it has in our example? The jobs have already been changed. A job satisfaction survey still could be profitable. First, it will provide information on employee attitudes about the restructured jobs and can include questions about attitudes the employees had before the changes took place. Such information can furnish insight as to whether the restructured jobs caused the company's deteriorating organizational climate. (For the most convincing case to be made, however, job satisfaction information should have been collected both before and after the job restructuring.) Second, open-ended questions about future job changes considered by the company can be included in the survey. Finally, a job satisfaction survey will allow employees to participate in proposed changes by encouraging them to evaluate such changes. Again, none of this will benefit a company in which management is unwilling to act on the results of the survey. Thus, management philosophy may ultimately determine whether or not to conduct a job satisfaction survey.

Question no. 2: Could information about employee attitudes really be useful in improving a firm's organizational climate?

Yes. As evidenced from our example and the foregoing discussion, a job satisfaction survey might help managers make decisions related to improving organizational climate. Research has shown a positive relationship between job dissatisfaction and such components of organizational climate as accidents, grievance rate, absenteeism, and turnover.[1] By ascertaining those job factors associated with dis-

[1]V.H. Vroom, *Work and Motivation* (New York: Wiley, 1964), p. 186; C.L. Hulin, "Effects of Changes in Jobs Satisfaction Levels on Employee Turnover," *Journal of Applied Psychology* 52 (1968): 122-26; C.L. Hulin, "Job Satisfaction and Turnover in a Female Clerical Population," *Journal of Applied Psychology* 50 (1966): 280-85; and I.C. Ross and A.F. Zander. "Need Satisfaction and Employee Turnover," *Personnel Psychology* 10 (1957): 327-38.

satisfaction and working with employees to correct them, grievance rate, absenteeism, and turnover can be decreased. Because hiring and training personnel are expensive, reducing turnover rate alone might more than repay the cost of conducting a job satisfaction survey.

Job performance is also a facet of organizational climate. However, the relationship between satisfaction and performance is less clear than are the relationships we have just discussed. In the past it was thought that high satisfaction produces good performance. Research, however, has questioned this notion of causality.[2] It may be that high performance causes satisfaction, or that the two are unrelated. Obviously, it is fallacious to conduct a job satisfaction survey based on the single assumption that from knowing the degree to which an employee is satisfied, you can predict his performance. Other factors, such as employee expectations concerning their rewards and the value of these rewards to them, may contribute to both satisfaction and performance.[3] Your satisfaction survey might include a measure of how employees view their rewards. With this additional information you can look at both satisfaction and performance in relation to these rewards.

Question no. 3: If a job satisfaction survey were to be conducted, should more than one measure of satisfaction be used?

Yes. Too often managers rely on information obtained from only one estimate of job satisfaction. Yet all of our measures are imperfect. Any measure of this kind is subject to bias; but the kind of bias inherent in one instrument, say a questionnaire, is different from that inherent in another measure, perhaps another questionnaire.

Again, let's look at our example. If a job satisfaction survey had been done at any point in time and had included only questions about pay and supervision, management would have entirely missed obtaining any information about the feelings these girls associated with the amount of responsibility in their jobs. For a *complete* picture of employee attitudes, then results obtained from two or more instruments must be looked at, each with its independent sources of error, and each tapping different aspects of employee satisfaction. One measure may be concerned with employee feelings about pay and supervision, another with general attitudes toward the job. Using multiple measures improves the probability of measuring exactly what is intended. That is, it improves the validity of the assessment.

To see how this works, let's take the concept of job satisfaction and look at it a little more systematically, as in Figure 1. Assume that any measure of the concept contains some *error* (either it measures something other than job satisfaction or it measures nothing at all). If each of your measures is contaminated with different errors, or bias,

[2]V.H. Vroom, p. 186, and A.H. Brayfield and W.H. Crockett, "Employee Attitudes and Employee Performance," *Psychological Bulletin* 52 (1955): 396-424.

[3]V.H. Vroom, *op. cit.*, pp. 14-19; and L.W. Porter and E.E. Lawler, *Managerial Attitudes and Performance* (Homewood, Ill.: Irwin, 1968).

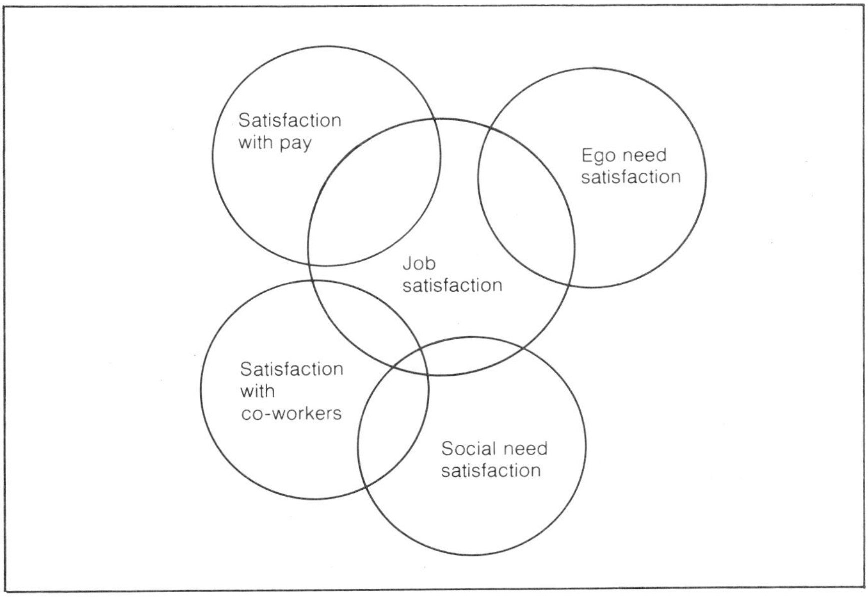

FIGURE 9-1
The Possible Relationship of Job Satisfaction to Various Measures of It

combining the measures should cancel out the effect of these random errors. Note the relationship, then, of the concept job satisfaction and the various paper and pencil measures of it.

The central circle represents the concept to be measured, job satisfaction, and the other circles are imperfect measures of that concept. Some parts of a measure (maybe particular questions on a questionnaire) may fail to overlap the concept at all (measurement error), and other parts of the measure are good indicators of job satisfaction. Some of these may overlap each other. For instance, in order to measure specific facets of job satisfaction, novel questions are designed. But they happen to measure some of the same and some different aspects of job satisfaction as the standardized instrument(s) also used.

Job satisfaction measures can be direct or indirect. Direct measures are those which ask employees in a straightforward way how satisfied they are. For example, employees are asked to check on a seven-point scale the degree to which they are satisfied with their work, or with their supervision. One problem in using such measures is that they may elicit answers employees think you want to hear. Indirect measures of job satisfaction get around this problem. These are measures of feelings acquired in ways other than by asking the people involved. They are often obtainable from data your company regularly collects. A manager might, for example, find that increased thievery is an indicator of employee dissatisfaction. Only if the relationship between direct measures of job satisfaction and such indirect designators of it as thievery can be established, should the less stable indicators be accepted as reflections of morale.

Our research has attempted to establish a relationship between employee satisfaction and some inexpensive, indirect indicators of it.

We have not yet met with success. We find it is better to ask employees directly how they feel about their jobs than to search futilely for such elusive indirect estimates. However, we know of one firm which noticed that employees in work units characterized by low satisfaction tended to lose work gloves more frequently than did workers in better satisfied units. By establishing a definite relationship between employee dissatisfaction with company policies (as measured in a straightforward manner) and glove loss rate, the company gained an easily accessible and inexpensive job satisfaction measure.

Finally, one cannot simply look informally at the answers to questions on the various instruments and expect to arrive at reasonable conclusions about employee job satisfaction. Nor can one look casually at some combination of direct and indirect measures for such conclusions. Instead, it is important that appropriate statistical techniques be used in the reduction and analyses of data. Both indirect and direct measures of job satisfaction are easily tallied for application of data analyses techniques which are relatively robust.

To recapitulate, to measure employee job satisfaction use more than one measure, each tapping a different aspect of satisfaction. Questionnaires are less expensive than interviews. Indirect measures, if they can be found, and only when they are shown to be related for a firm to the more stable direct measures, might offer quick cheap indicators of general employee morale. Once data are collected they should be coded and analyzed using appropriate statistical methods.

Question no. 4: Should a manager rely only on his own tailor-made job satisfaction questionnaire?

No. Unless the firm's workforce and organizational characteristics are particularly unique, standardized job satisfaction measures should be used. In our example, these characteristics were not sufficiently unusual to warrant the use of tailor-made measures.

Even when management decides to do a job satisfaction survey, the most frequent next step is for someone to design a set of questions they think will measure satisfaction. In doing this they have no history against which to evaluate the answers to their questions, and no information about the reliability and validity of their measures. Reliability asks whether the instrument measures whatever it measures consistently. Validity is concerned with how well the instrument measures what it is intended to measure. For instance, we ask the girls in our example: "Answer on a seven-point scale (from highly dissatisfied to highly satisfied), how happy are you with the kind of supervision you have?" We obtain a mean score for the group of four on this question. Does this mean our sample is any more or less satisfied than is any other group of workers? If we measure these employees' satisfaction with their supervision the same way tomorrow, will we get the same answer? And, does this question really elicit employees' feelings about their supervision? Standardized job satisfaction measures are available which are both relatively consistent and relatively valid. They should be used wherever possible and perhaps supplemented with other questions, the answers to which can be examined in relation to results of more stable measures.

In our example, it might be useful to compare employee job satisfaction with the morale of similar work groups. We know, for instance, that different aspects of their jobs contribute to satisfaction for males and females. The same holds true for urban and rural workers.[4] It would not be useful to compare our employees to some nondescript group. There is a great deal of information about age, sex, education, industry, and job function of the people who have responded to some instruments. In some cases there is even information about the communities in which these people work. All of these factors can be expected to influence job satisfaction. Where possible it is advisable to compare employee satisfaction to that of groups similar to them on these dimensions.

Question no. 5: In searching for appropriate standardized job satisfaction instruments, should all available instruments be examined?

No. Because of the sheer number of job satisfaction instruments available, the search should be restricted to only the major ones. In selecting any instrument for your package, the following questions should be asked:

What theoretical assumptions underlie the instrument? Instruments are based on different definitions of job satisfaction. Consequently, some may measure a concept of job satisfaction not appropriate to the needs.

Have adequate reliability and validity been demonstrated for the instrument?

Under what conditions should the instrument be used?

Some of the major instruments to be considered are the Job Description Index, the Brayfield-Rothe Index, the General Motors Faces Scale, the Porter Instrument, and the Minnesota Satisfaction Questionnaire.

Job description index: A job facet instrument[5]

One well-known authority describes the JDI as the most carefully constructed job satisfaction instrument in use today. The JDI taps five dimensions of job satisfaction: work itself, co-workers, supervision, pay, and opportunities for promotion. Instead of directly asking re-

[4]C.L. Hulin and M.R. Blood, "Job Enlargement, Individual Differences, and Worker Responses," *Psychological Bulletin* 69 (1968): 41-55; and P.C. Smith, L.M. Kendall, and C.L. Hulin, *The Measurement of Satisfaction in Work and Retirement* (Chicago: Rand McNally, 1969), p. 96.
[5]Smith, Kendall, and Hulin, ibid.

spondents to evaluate their satisfaction with each of these job facets, the JDI uses a list of adjectives from which respondents check those which describe their job situation. This format was selected so that people who are not very good readers or who are in a hurry to finish filling out the instrument can easily complete it. The JDI can be a very good instrument to use with employees like those in our example. To compare employees' scores on the five dimensions with those of other groups, an extensive amount of information available for groups characterized by different personal, community, and industrial variables can be examined.

Brayfield-Rothe Index: An explicit measure of overall job satisfaction[6]

Designed in 1951, this index is an explicit type of overall job satisfaction measure. That is, each of the 18 items in the questionnaire attempts to describe directly the respondent's overall job environment. By summing the respondent's score on each item, an overall index of job satisfaction is obtained. Although our research suggests that some of the items are out of date, the total score on the 18 items is reliable and is highly intercorrelated with other measures of job satisfaction. Very little information exists about the characteristics of people who have responded to this instrument.

General Motors Faces Scale: A projective measure of overall job satisfaction[7]

While the Brayfield-Rothe Index is an example of an explicit measure of job satisfaction, the GM Faces Scale is a projective technique. According to the scale's developer, some degree of error is inherent in all questionnaires which rely on words to represent feelings. This error is greatly magnified when the questionnaire is given to people with poor verbal ability. To solve this problem, Kunin developed an overall measure of job satisfaction (as opposed to a measure of satisfaction with various job facets) which utilizes a series of 11 faces to project job satisfaction. The faces "smile" or "frown" in different degrees, and the respondent checks that face which is most representative of how he feels about his job. A great deal of research, including ours, indicates that the Faces Scales is a fairly good measure of overall job satisfaction. Considerable information exists about the characteristics of the instrument respondents.

---

[6]A.H. Brayfield and H.F. Rothe, "An Index of Job Satisfaction," *Journal of Applied Psychology* 35 (1951): 307-11.

[7]T. Kunin, "The Construction of a New Type of Attitude Measure," *Personnel Psychology* 8 (1955): 65-77.

Porter Instrument: A measure of an employee's need structure[8]

This measure is based on a theory of job satisfaction which says that dissatisfaction occurs when actual rewards fail to meet what the employee perceives as equitable. To measure "perceived need deficiency" Porter developed a questionnaire based on four need categories. They are social needs, ego needs, esteem needs, and self-actualization needs. The instrument, then, emphasizes the employee's need structure rather than his satisfaction with individual job facets or his overall satisfaction with his job.

There are two problems involved in using this measure. First, respondents must be adept at abstract thinking. People with poor reading skills have great difficulty filling out this questionnaire. It may not be useful for groups such as the girls in our example and has been primarily used with managers. Second, our research indicates that the questionnaire may not measure the needs indicated.[9]

Minnesota Satisfaction Questionnaire: A measure of work adjustment[10]

Based on a theory of work adjustment, this job satisfaction instrument conceptually overlaps Porter's in some respects. Both instruments define job satisfaction as a function of how well an individual's work environment provides for his needs. The Minnesota Satisfaction Questionnaire comes in a long form and a short form. Each item in the long form refers to a reinforcer, some aspect of the individual's work environment which can fulfill a specific need. From these items, 20 scales were derived, based on such reinforcers as ability utilization and working conditions. The instrument has been extensively researched and is reliable. It also appears to tap those reinforcers it purports to measure. Furthermore, a great deal of information is available about the way various kinds of workers fill it out. Thus, it is possible to compare workers' responses on this instrument to those of other workers with similar or different characteristics.

Question no. 6: Are there more specific considerations to be made in selecting one or more of the above instruments?

Yes. Besides thinking about using measures of overall satisfaction and job facet satisfaction, one should consider the relative merits of job satisfaction instruments which emphasize employee need struc-

[8]L.W. Porter, "Job Attitudes in Management: I. Perceived Deficiencies in Need Fulfillment as a Function of Job Level," *Journal of Applied Psychology* 46 (1962): 375-84.

[9]K.H. Roberts, G.A. Walter, and R.E. Miles, "A Factor Analytic Study of Job Satisfaction Items Designed to Measure Maslow Need Categories," *Personnel Psychology* 24 (1971): 205-20.

[10]D. Weiss, R. Dawis, G. England, and L. Lofquist, *Manual for Minnesota Satisfaction Questionnaire*, Bulletin 45, (Minneapolis: University of Minnesota, Industrial Relations Center, 1967).

ture. To determine whether or not such needs as the opportunity for growth, friendship, and self-esteem are fulfilled, the instruments to use are those other than those used to investigate employee satisfaction with pay, promotion, and co-workers. The selection of overall, job facet, or need structure instruments depends on the goals.

Let's look back at our example. Before restructuring the jobs, the manager should have had information about employee needs. However, once the restructuring occurred, it may have been more useful to examine satisfaction with job facets. An instrument package, given both before and after job restructuring, containing overall job facet, and need structure measures would have filled the bill. This combination of instruments also meets the goals of a multi-method approach to measuring job satisfaction.

Question no. 7: Should only standardized measures of job satisfaction be utilized?

No. In really thinking about the uses to which information about employee morale can be put, specific questions not contained in any of the available instruments will suggest themselves. As implied in the answer to question four, these should be added to the package, but not substituted for it because there will be little evidence of reliability and validity for these questions.

Second, only by collecting information about respondents' personal characteristics, job functions, and so on, can job satisfaction be compared across groups and the comparisons understood. Third, in general, job satisfaction measures have been used in conjunction with interest in absenteeism, turnover, and other personnel behaviors. These data should be collected for each respondent's unit so that summaries of unit job satisfaction can be looked at in relation to summaries of unit personnel behaviors.

Question no. 8: If standardized job satisfaction measures are used, will the answers the employees give be specifically influenced by the firm's workforce characteristics and organizational structure?

Yes. Our research shows that such individual characteristics as education are related to the utility of various satisfaction instruments. Again, because of its conceptual complexity, the Porter Instrument cannot be answered adequately by poorly educated respondents. Other personnel variables such as employee race, and whether they work part-time or full-time may influence satisfaction. For a sample of 495 hospital employees at several job levels, we found significant differences in satisfaction level for whites and nonwhites as measured by the JDI, the Brayfield-Rothe items, and the GM Faces Scale. Not only do these racial groups differ in overall satisfaction, they respond to different aspects of their jobs. That it, their satisfaction patterns are different. The same is true for part-time versus full-time hospital employees.[11]

Organizational characteristics also contribute to job satisfaction. We found increased satisfaction associated with higher job level, increasing organizational flatness, and with whether hospitals are teaching or nonteaching facilities.[12] The job of the astute manager is to try to understand the separate contributions of individual, organizational, and job function variables to employee satisfaction, and to consider the useful changes in these characteristics it is possible for him to make. He should also be aware of the fact that differences in community characteristics influence the degree to which employees are satisfied.

CONCLUSION

Although the "Twenty Questions" strategy is somewhat structured and slightly artificial, it presents one effective way to determine whether a job satisfaction survey should be conducted, what measures should be used, and what outcomes can be expected. Of course, many of our questions are best answered "maybe," and management can always expend more resources for additional information about them where it is desired. The "Twenty Questions" strategy will merely force consideration of the costs and benefits associated with

FIGURE 9-2
Guide to Considerations Involved in Job Satisfaction Surveys

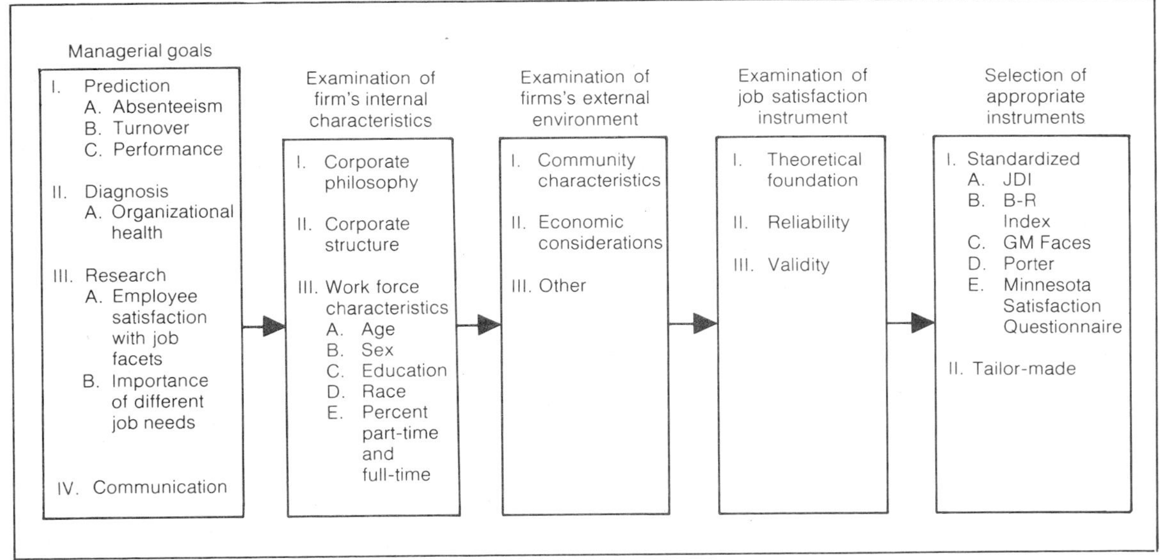

[11]C.A. O'Reilly and K.H. Roberts, "Job Satisfaction Among Whites and Non-Whites: A Cross-Cultural Approach," *Journal of Applied Psychology* 57 (1973): 295-99, and N. Logan, C.A. O'Reilly, and K.H. Roberts, "Job Satisfaction Among Part-Time and Full-Time Employees," *Journal of Vocational Behavior* 3 (1973): 33-43.

[12]N. Imparato, S. Sedeck, H.T. Baker, R.J. Day and K.H. Roberts. "An Exploratory Study of the Effects of Community and Organizational Characteristics on Job Satisfaction of Nursing Personnel" (in press).

job satisfaction surveys and provide the groundwork for selecting instruments.

We have discussed here the importance of asking a series of increasingly specific questions prior to advocating a job satisfaction survey. These questions are broadly concerned with managerial goals in conducting the survey, attention to corporate philosophy and structure, and the influence of employee characteristics and the external environment on job satisfaction. If a survey is to be conducted attention must be given to the selection of instruments by considering their theoretical bases, reliability and validity. Figure 2 provides a guide to the considerations involved in job satisfaction surveys.

SUGGESTIONS FOR ADVANCED READINGS

Alderfer, C.P. "An Empirical Test of a New Theory of Human Needs." *Organizational Behavior and Human Performance* 4, (1969): 142-75.

Alderfer, C.P. *Existence, Relatedness, and Growth.* New York: Free Press, 1972.

Campbell, J.P.; Dunnette, M.D.; Lawler, E.E.; and Weick, K.E. *Managerial Behavior, Performance, and Effectiveness.* New York: McGraw-Hill, 1970.

Hall, D.T., and Nougaim, K.E. "An Examination of Maslow's Need Hierarchy in an Organizational Setting." *Organizational Behavior and Human Performance* 3, (1968): 12-35.

Herzberg, F. *Work and the Nature of Man.* Cleveland: World, 1966.

Herzberg, F. *The Managerial Choice: To Be Efficient and to Be Human.* Homewood, Ill.: Dow Jones-Irwin, 1976.

House, R.J., and Wigdor, L. "Herzberg's Dual Factor Theory of Job Satisfaction and Motivation: A Review of Evidence and a Criticism." *Personnel Psychology* 20, (1967): 369-89.

Locke, E. "What Is Job Satisfaction?" *Organizational Behavior and Human Performance* 4, (1968): 309-36.

Locke, E. "The Nature and Causes of Job Satisfaction." In *Handbook of Industrial and Organizational Psychology*, edited by M. Dunnette, pp. 1297-1349. Chicago: Rand McNally, 1976.

McClelland, D.C.; Atkinson, J.W.; Clark R.A.; and Lowell, E.L. *The Achievement Motive.* New York: Appleton Century Crofts, 1953.

Maslow, A.H. *Motivation and Personality.* New York: Harper, 1954.

Organ, D.W. "A Reappraisal and Reinterpretation of the Satisfaction-Causes-Performance Hypothesis." *Academy of Management Review* 2, (1977): 46-53.

Robinson, J.; Athanasiou, E.; and Head, K. *Measures of Occupational Attitudes and Occupational Characteristics.* Ann Arbor: University of Mich.: Survey Research Center, 1969.

Schwab, D.P., and Cummings, L.L. "Theories of Performance and Satisfaction: A Review." *Industrial Relations* 9, (1970): 408-30.

Sheppard, H.L., and Herrick, N.Q. *Where Have All the Robots Gone?: Worker Dissatisfaction in the 70's.* New York: Free Press, 1972.

Wahba, M.A., and Bridwell, L.G. "Maslow Reconsidered: A Review of Research on the Need Hierarchy Theory." *Organizational Behavior and Human Performance* 15, (1976): 212-40.

DISCUSSION QUESTIONS

1. Can it be said that a "satisfaction gap" exists for younger workers? Why?

2. Are the needs of younger workers different from the needs of older workers? Are the jobs that younger workers occupy different from the jobs older workers occupy? What are the managerial implications of your answers?

3. What is the distinction between satisfaction and motivation?

4. Make a list of five things you want very much. Rank those things from most important to least important. Then indicate which of Alderfer's need categories each relates to. (Remember that some things may satisfy more than a single need.) What does the listing of desired things and their importance rankings tell you about your need structure?

5. Describe a case in which you experienced frustration regression.

6. List five things you hope to get out of a job. Classify each of those things as either an intrinsic or an extrinsic reward. Which set of rewards seems most important to you?

7. To what extent do you think you possess the characteristics of a person with strong need for achievement? Is high need for achievement likely to be important for success in the sort of job you would like? Why or why not?

8. Write down the names of five people you have worked with in the past, preferably on the same job. Rank them from most satisfied with their jobs to least satisfied. Then rank them from highest performing to lowest performing. Do the two sets of rankings differ much? Why or why not?

9. In one department of a particular university, teachers are required to distribute evaluation forms to students at the end of each term. Besides evaluating the examinations, text materials, and the teacher's performance in the class, the students are asked what grade they expect to receive. If they expect to get a high grade, their evaluations are subsequently lowered a bit, and vice versa. What do you think of the logic underlying such an adjustment? Do you agree with that logic?

10. Think about the students in your organizational behavior class. Which ones are the most dissatisfied with the class? What do you think causes their dissatisfaction? How do they show that dissatisfaction?

11. Under what conditions would you recommend to your boss *not* to conduct a job-satisfaction survey?

12. Humanistic *and* productivity reasons aside, why should you care about the job-satisfaction levels of your employees?

SECTION

Increasing Productivity

This section focuses on the central issue of performance in organizations. First, we will review a number of theories that will help you better understand employee performance and how to improve performance through proper design of reward systems. Next, we will consider the consequences of improperly designed reward systems and the relative merits of reliance on the "carrot"—rewards—or the "stick"—punishment. Following a discussion of operant theory as a management tool, we will discuss techniques of behavior modification and rules for the successful use of operant conditioning techniques. Finally, job enrichment is explained, its effects on employee attitudes and behaviors are considered, and the situations in which enrichment attempts may be successful are specified. Taken together, the chapters in this section provide a powerful set of tools to help improve employee performance and other important behaviors.

KEY TERMS

JOB ENRICHMENT
BLUE-COLLAR BLUES
JOB SIZE
HIGHER-ORDER NEED STRENGTH
CORE TASK DIMENSIONS
EXPECTANCY THEORY
INSTRUMENTALITY
VALENCE
EQUITY THEORY
GOAL SETTING
MANAGEMENT BY OBJECTIVES
OPERANT THEORY
BEHAVIOR MODIFICATION
CONTINGENCIES OF REINFORCEMENT

OBJECTIVES

1. To identify sets of factors that affect performance
2. To describe useful theories for predicting and understanding employee performance and other behaviors

3. To illustrate how improperly designed reward systems can result in undesirable behaviors
4. To show how money influences employee performance
5. To describe punishment and its consequences
6. To describe operant theory and how it can be used to modify employees' behaviors
7. To show why job content is important
8. To indicate the conditions under which job enrichment may be useful and the steps in a job enrichment attempt

CHAPTER 10

The Performance Puzzle

The standard of living to which we have become accustomed is largely due to the high productivity of U.S. industry. In absolute terms, the United States still fares extremely well when its productivity is compared with that of other nations. However, in terms of *growth* in productivity, the picture is less rosy. For instance, while the annual rates of productivity of France, Italy, West Germany, Denmark, and Japan increased more than 5 percent from 1967 to 1977, that of the United States increased only 2.3 percent. To some extent, this slow growth in productivity can be blamed on relatively low levels of investment in new technology. However, many observers are also concerned that employees' motivation to work hard has eroded. The question of how we can bolster the level of our employees' efforts is clearly important and extremely complex. For example, consider the following cases.

Ian supervised fourteen hourly paid production workers in a small firm. The workers each assembled entire Cheryl Tiegs dolls. They seemed to enjoy their jobs, constructing the dolls with loving care. However, they weren't producing nearly as many dolls as were the employees of certain competitors. Ian wondered what he might do to speed up the production of his staff.

Mike owned a small company that manufactured a fishing lure, Mike's Magic Minnow. His employees were capable and energetic, producing by far the highest number of lures per person-hour in the industry. The employees received thirty cents per lure and, in view of their high productivity levels, received very comfortable wages. In a moment of inspiration, Mike decided to increase his employees' pay per item—to fifty cents. That, he thought, should motivate them to produce even more. To his dismay, production levels dropped almost immediately. But Mike did notice that fewer lures were being returned because of flaws.

Sara had always told her subordinates exactly how much they were supposed to produce. She set high goals but felt that they were equitable and achievable. Lately, though, she began to wonder if she should change her style. Maybe if she gave her subordinates a free hand it would inspire them to do more than she would have asked. So when Sara's subordinates asked her what their production quotas were for the next month, she told them, "Just do your best. That's all I can ask." A few months after issuing these instructions, Sara realized that productivity was declining and wondered if her subordinates were exploiting their newfound freedom.

These cases illustrate the difficulties often associated with achieving and maintaining high levels of performance. In this chapter, we will consider three tools that should make that task a bit easier—*expectancy theory, equity theory,* and *goal setting.*

In chapter 7, we examined four *content* theories of motivation —Maslow's need hierarchy, Alderfer's ERG theory, Herzberg's two-factor theory, and McClelland's achievement motivation theory. These helped us understand the content of employees' need structures. The material in this chapter focuses on an important related issue: What is the *process* by which employees choose how they will behave? This is partly a function of needs, but, as we will see, it also depends on a number of other things.

EXPECTANCY THEORY

One aid to understanding the motivation process is called *expectancy theory.* Expectancy theory tries to explain that process by examining the links in the sequence from effort to ultimate rewards. For example, consider the following situations.

Bob is waiting for the bus to take him downtown to work. He's dreading the day. His job didn't seem too bad years ago, when he really needed the good salary it paid. Now, though, with his wife working and his children grown and away from home, money is not so important. The job doesn't seem to offer him anything he really wants anymore. No challenge. No chance for advancement. No esteem in the eyes of others. As he waits for the bus to work, he knows that he'll be waiting for the bus home all day.

Jane was excited when she took her new job. It seemed to offer ideal opportunities. If she performed well, there was a good chance for advancement, the potential to take on increased responsibility, and the prospect of sizable salary increases and bonuses. But now Jane is becoming more and more aware of the fact that her efforts are not resulting in improved performance. It almost seems that no matter what she does, her performance ratings remain the same. She asks herself if her efforts were misguided. Were other factors that she couldn't pinpoint fouling things up? She begins to wonder if her efforts were worthwhile.

Upon coming to her new job, Mary was quickly approached by her new coworkers. They explained to her that nobody was fired in this company, regardless of their performance. They pointed out that salary increases and other benefits were strictly tied to seniority. Even if she could perform so well as to stand the world on its ear, it wouldn't make a nickel difference in her paycheck or anyplace else. In short, Mary's coworkers told her that she might as well relax.

How motivated do you think Bob, Jane, and Mary would be to do their jobs well? Probably not very. In each case, a key element required for motivation is missing. What is needed for an individual to be motivated to try to do a good job? It would seem that, by exerting effort, an individual should at least get some kind of reward or avoid negative consequences.

The requirements for motivation

Figure 10-1 shows that there are two key links in the sequence from effort to rewards. First, there is the link between effort and performance. Second, there is the link between performance and rewards. This implies that three things are necessary if employees are going to be motivated to do a good job.

First, they have to *want* what the job offers. Second, they have to *think* that those things are somehow tied to performance. Third, they have to *believe* that trying harder will really improve their performance. If any of those three elements is missing, we'd expect motivation to be low. To return to our examples, Bob didn't see his job as offering anything he really wanted; Jane couldn't see how her effort influenced her performance; and Mary was told that performance was unrelated to outcomes. In each case, it seems unlikely that any more than minimal effort would be exerted.

The three elements we've just considered form the basis of expectancy theory. Expectancy theory assumes that employees want to maximize their welfare. Models in many areas of business—such as marketing, economics, and finance—make this same assumption. But, as we will see in chapter 16, this assumption often isn't justified. People do many things that don't really lead to optimal solutions: sometimes they act without fully weighing the consequences of their behaviors, sometimes they just seek a minimally acceptable solution, and so on. Expectancy theory advocates recognize this. They simply say, "Of course, people aren't completely rational, but let's focus on the part of behavior that *is* rational. Since it's probably impossible to predict irrational behavior, we might as well try to predict the predictable."

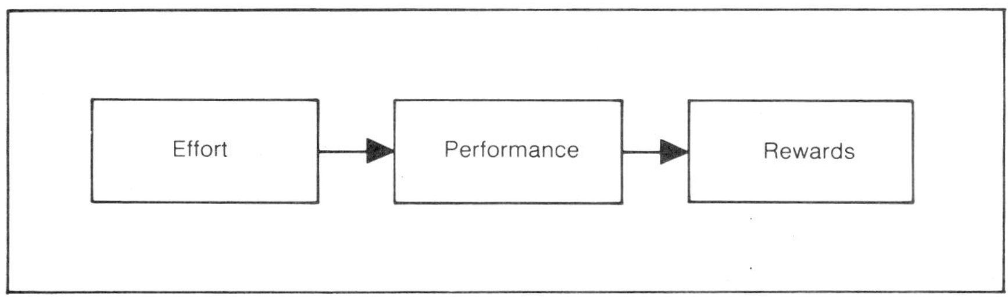

FIGURE 10-1
The Sequence from Effort to Rewards

Expectancy theory terminology

Figure 10-2 presents an expanded version of figure 10-1, along with some expectancy theory terms.

1. *First-order outcome.* This is the direct consequence of effort. In organizations, the first-order outcome generally focused upon is performance. However, the theory can be applied just as easily to other first-order outcomes, such as absenteeism or turnover.

2. *Second-order outcomes.* These are all the things, good or bad, that may result from performance (for instance, pay, promotions, approval by the boss, and so on).

3. *Expectancy.* This is the perceived linkage between effort and the first-order outcome. For instance, if Sam doesn't think he can do any better, no matter how hard he tries, his expectancy is low. Expectancy is generally expressed as a probability or a correlation.

4. *Instrumentalities.* These are the perceived linkages between the first-order outcome and the various second-order outcomes. If, for example, Karen thinks her salary is closely tied to her performance, the instrumentality of performance for the attainment of salary is high. Instrumentalities are also generally expressed as probabilities or correlations.

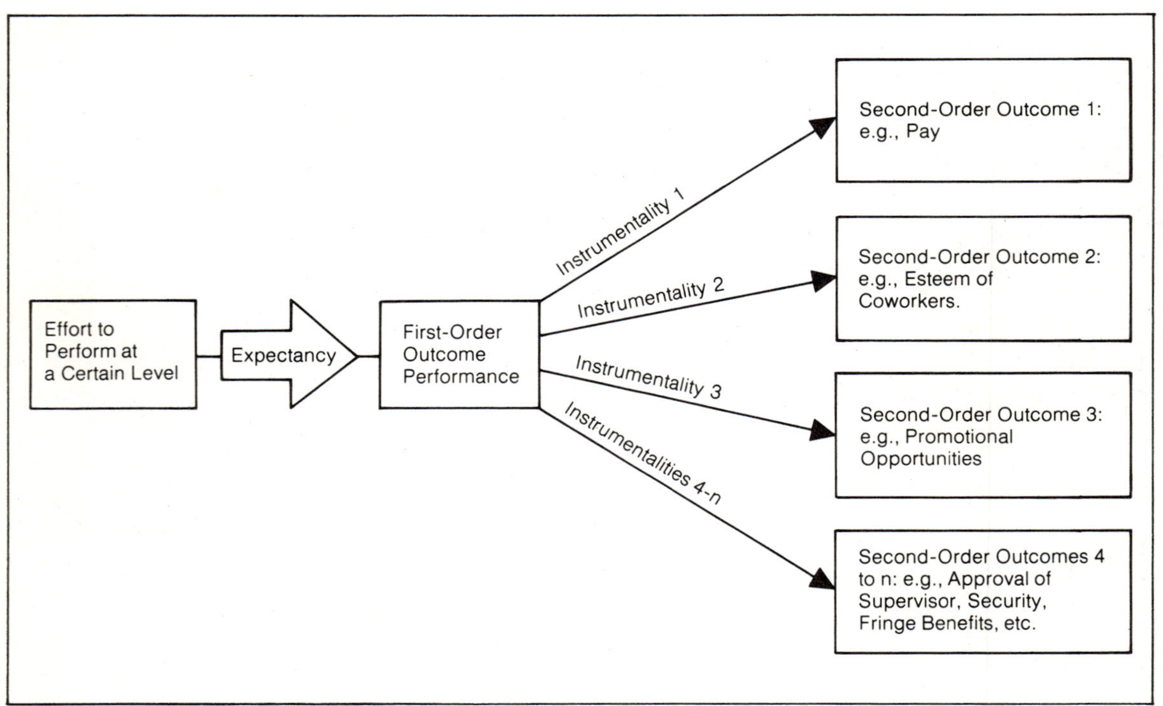

FIGURE 10-2
The Element of Expectancy Theory

5. *Valence*. This is the value of an outcome. It is the employee's anticipated level of satisfaction with an outcome. The valences of second-order outcomes are simply the values of such things as pay, promotional opportunities, esteem of coworkers, and so on. The valence of the first-order outcome, performance, depends on the valences of second-order outcomes and the perceived instrumentality of the first-order outcome for the attainment of each second-order outcome. In particular, the valence of the first-order outcome is an expected value—the sum of the products of second-order outcomes and the instrumentalities of the first-order outcome for the attainment of those second-order outcomes. That is, for the case where performance is the first-order outcome that we're concerned about:

$$\text{Valence of Peformance} = \sum_{i=1}^{n} \text{Valence of Second Order Outcome i} \times \text{Instrumentality of Performance for the Attainment of Second Order Outcome i}$$

6. *Force to perform, or effort*. As shown in figure 10-3, the degree to which an employee exerts effort to perform at a particular level depends upon the valence of the first-order outcome and the expectancy that effort will result in the first-order outcome. In particular:

$$\text{Effort to Perform at a Given Level} = \text{Expectancy} \times \text{Valence of Performance at a Given Level}$$

Expectancy theory basically argues that people will consider the consequences of performing at various levels. And people will aim at the level that results in the highest force to perform. In determining those effort or force levels, the employee's perceptions, not necessarily the actual situation, are relevant.

An example of expectancy theory use

Generally, employees can be directly surveyed, using questionnaires, to learn how much they value certain second-order outcomes

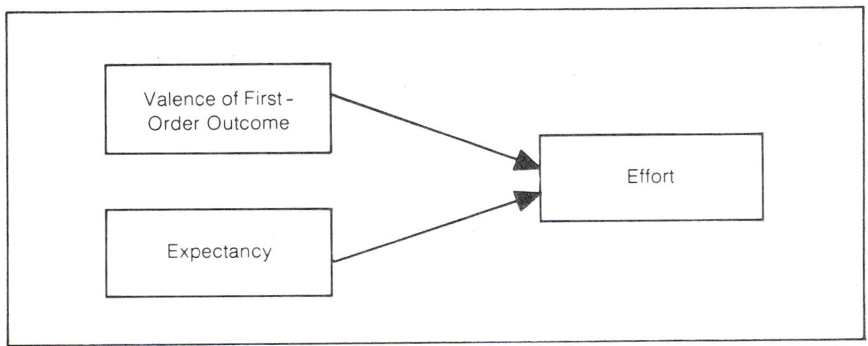

FIGURE 10-3
The Determinants of Effort to Perform at a Given Level

and how they view the linkages between effort and performance and between performance and second-order outcomes. Suppose a survey shows that the valences a particular employee attaches to second-order outcomes are as follows:

Second-order Outcome	*Valence*
Pay	10
Supervisory Approval	5
Peer Group Approval	10
Intrinsic Rewards	5
All Others	0

Clearly, pay and peer group approval are very important to this employee, while supervisory approval and intrinsic rewards are only moderately important.

Suppose we also find that the employee perceives increased performance to have the following instrumentalities for the attainment of the preceding second-order outcomes:

Second-order Outcome	*Instrumentality*
Pay	.3
Supervisory Approval	.2
Peer Group Approval	-.8
Intrinsic Rewards	.5

These instrumentalities suggest that pay, supervisory approval, and intrinsic rewards are seen as positively related to higher performance, while peer group *dis*approval is seen as likely if performance is increased.

Finally, suppose that expectancy = .5; that is, the worker perceives a moderate positive linkage between effort and performance.

Then:

$$\text{Valence of Performance} = \sum_{i=1}^{4} \text{Valence of Second Order Outcome } i \times \text{Instrumentality of Performance for the Attainment of Second Order Outcome } i$$

$$= 10 \times .3 + 5 \times .2 + 10 \times (-.8) + 5 \times .5$$

$$= -1.5$$

And:

$$\text{Force to Perform (Effort)} = \text{Valence of Performance} \times \text{Expectancy}$$

$$= -1.5 \times .5 = -.75$$

What does this tell us? What does a force to perform score of −.75 mean? For one thing, the *sign* of the number is important. In this case, the negative sign shows that higher performance has a negative value to the employee. As a result, there is really no reason to expect the employee to try to improve his or her performance. To interpret what the *magnitude* of the number means, we need a basis for comparison.

How does this number compare with that of other employees in the department? With the average employee in the firm? How do the scores of employees in this department compare with those of others in the firm? How have scores changed over time? Finally, the components of the overall effort score are important in themselves. For example, the valences tell us what is, and is not, important to the employee. In this case, to offer rewards other than those four identified as positively valent wouldn't really influence motivation levels. Further, the instrumentalities are revealing. We learn in this case, for instance, that pay and supervisory approval are seen as having only relatively weak links to performance. If the company thinks it is closely tying pay to performance and has told supervisors to reinforce good performance with praise, such findings should be upsetting. Perhaps just as important, the instrumentality of $-.8$ of performance for the attainment of peer group approval suggests that strong group norms favor rate restriction. The expectancy of .5 illustrates that the employee may doubt that increasing effort will really lead to heightened performance.

The linkage of effort to performance

So far, we have described expectancy theory as a way to predict employee effort or motivation to perform. We have said that motivation depends on expectancy and the valence of performance. To expand expectancy theory to predict performance, we have to consider some additional variables. Figure 10-4 shows that performance depends not only on motivation but also on ability, situational constraints, and role perceptions. That is:

1. If an individual lacks ability, motivation won't help much. Regardless of motivation and rich fantasy lives, certain individuals could never be successful brain surgeons.

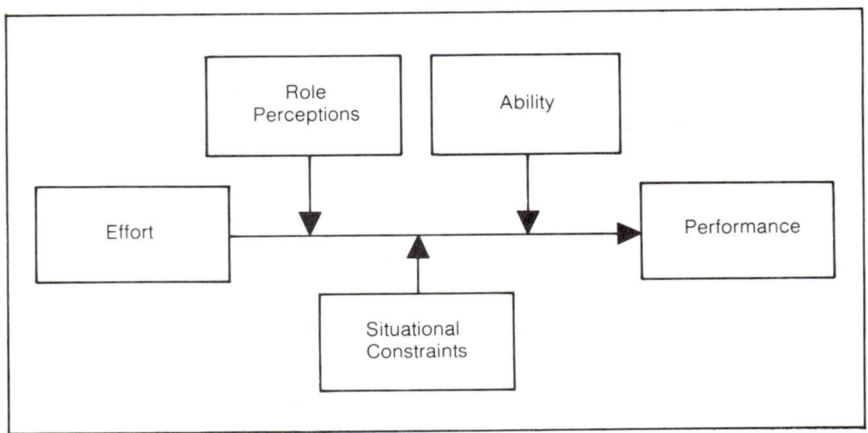

FIGURE 10-4
The Linkage of Effort to Performance

On an assembly line, situational factors may overwhelm motivation. One worker may be able to work quickly, but he may be unable to live up to his potential because others on the same line are slow.

2. In some cases, situational factors may overwhelm motivation. For example, Fred, a worker on an assembly line, could dance on the line if he wanted to, but the line wouldn't speed up.

3. Employees often don't know what their superiors expect them to do. If Lena works hard to maximize the *quality* of her output but the boss wants *quantity*, her performance will almost certainly be rated low.

A more complete model

Figure 10-5 presents a model that includes the various factors we've considered and elaborates upon them. That figure combines figures 10-3, 10-4, and 8-2. It also adds two feedback loops—from satisfaction to valence of performance and from performance to expectancy. That is, as our needs are satisfied, their importance changes. (See the discussion of Alderfer's ERG theory in chapter 7.) Also, as we are able to perform successfully at a particular level, our expectancy perceptions are likely to increase, and vice versa.

The predictive power of expectancy theory

Expectancy theory does not precisely predict employees' responses. After all, people are not completely rational. Also, of course, the instruments used to measure employees' valences of outcomes, instrumentality perceptions, and expectancy perceptions aren't perfect, so it is unreasonable to expect them to predict perfectly. Re-

FIGURE 10-5 A Model of Employee Behavior

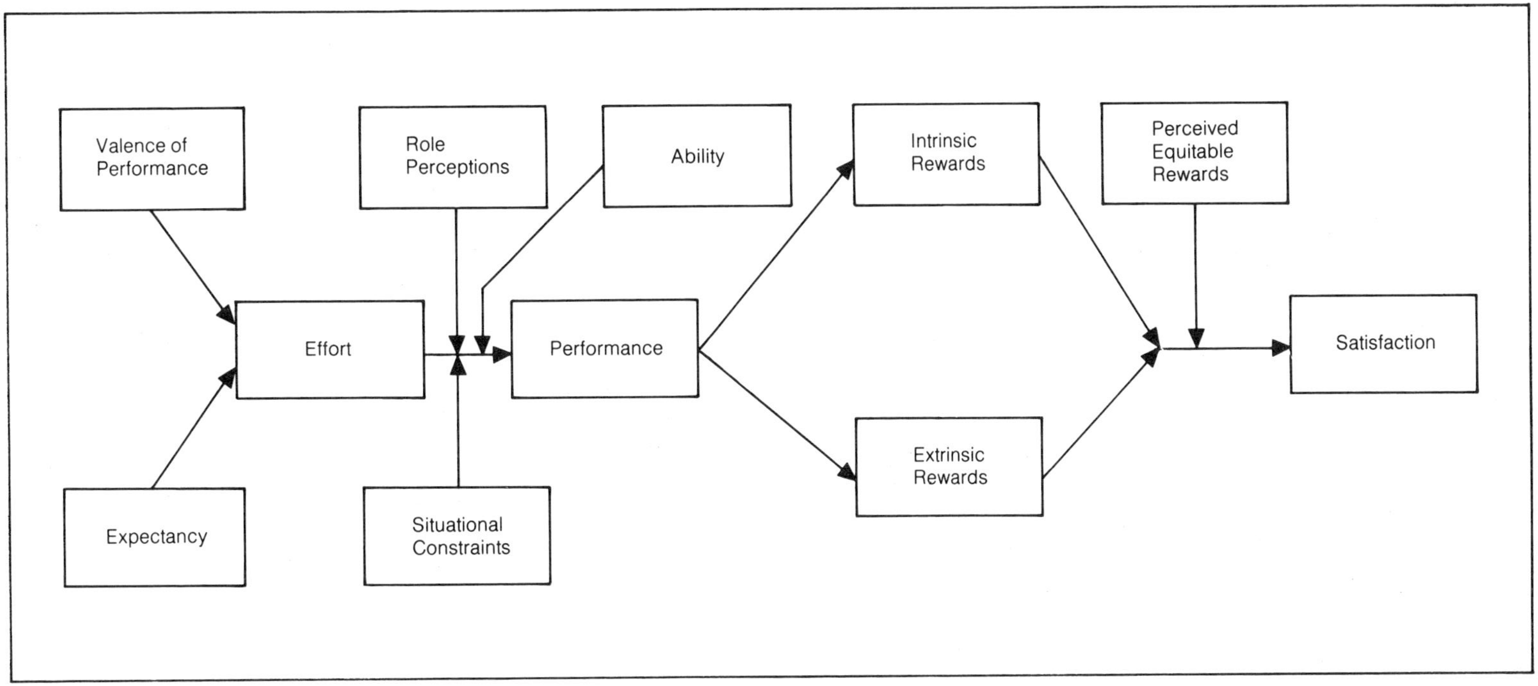

Based on Porter and Lawler (1968)

views of expectancy studies show that the expectancy model can predict about 25 percent of the variance in workers' satisfaction and about 10 percent of the variance in their performance. Perhaps that doesn't seem like much, but any tool that can explain a meaningful proportion of employees' behaviors is extremely useful.

The lessons of expectancy theory

Perhaps more important, expectancy theory provides valuable guidelines for managers who want to increase their subordinates' motivation to perform. In particular, they can increase subordinates' expectancy perceptions by explaining carefully how the job should be done; by offering training programs, setting clear goals, and defining jobs accurately; and perhaps by trying to bolster subordinates' confidence. They can increase instrumentality perceptions by making sure that the reward system is properly designed—that is, it contains rewards the employees value and links them to performance—is adhered to, and is explained clearly to subordinates. It's probably more difficult to directly influence valences. However, it's possible that managers, by their behaviors, may affect the degree to which supervisory approval is valent to employees. For example, if Bob's boss acts in such a way that Bob really respects him, Bob may be very concerned about what his boss thinks of him. Also, the expectancy model makes it clear that managers must understand the values their subordinates attach to outcomes. Since there are likely to be many differences among individuals in the valences that are attached to outcomes, it's probably useful to try to measure what employees want; we'll discuss this point in more detail in chapter 14, "What Job Enrichment Is All About." The *path-goal* theory of leadership, to be discussed in Chapter 20, "Leadership in Organizations," is based on expectancy theory and spells out in more detail what managers can do to raise subordinates' motivation levels.

EQUITY THEORY

The model we considered in figure 10-4 showed that employees' satisfaction with rewards is a function both of the nature and amount of rewards received and of the employees' perceptions of equitable rewards. But what is meant by equitable rewards? And what are the consequences of perceived inequity? Equity theory, which addresses these questions, is one member of a family of theories that argue that people want somehow to maintain balance. Equity theory focuses specifically on the balance of the inputs individuals make to the outcomes they receive. While equity theory has been applied to a wide variety of relationships—philanthropist-recipient, exploiter-victim, employer-employee, and those among intimates—we will limit our focus to the work setting.[1]

[1]See Walster et al. (1978) for a thorough review of evidence relating to each of these areas.

Why behave equitably?

Equity theory argues that people want to maintain *distributive fairness*, a state that exists when someone thinks people are getting the outcomes they deserve. There is considerable evidence to support the contention that people generally try to maintain distributive fairness for at least the following reasons.[2]

1. When the observed situation is different from the situation felt to be fair, an unpleasant state of tension may develop. Restoration of distributive fairness can reduce that tension.

2. Some people may try to be fair because they think others will reward them for being fair.

3. Behaving fairly may bolster a person's self-esteem.

4. It's comforting to believe that people get what they deserve. By giving people what we think they deserve, we strengthen that belief.

The determination of equity

But how do people decide whether outcomes are equitable? J. Stacy Adams (1965) has proposed the following equation for an equitable relationship (based on the writings of Aristotle).[3]

$$\frac{O_p}{I_p} = \frac{O_o}{I_o}$$

where:

O_p is the person's perception of the outcomes he or she is receiving.

I_p is the person's perception of his or her inputs.

O_o is the person's perception of the outcomes some comparison person (or comparison *other*) is receiving.

I_o is the person's perceptions o the inputs of the comparison other.

The equation says that equity exists when a person feels the ratio of his or her outcomes to his or her inputs is equal to that of the comparison other. That is, neither gets more or less—relative to the other—than he or she deserves. If the ratios are not equal, the situation is seen to be inequitable. Figure 10-6 shows the conditions for equity and inequity. For example, Bob, Jane, and Paul all started on the job at the same time with about the same qualifications. Bob knows he hasn't done as well as Jane but thinks he has clearly outperformed Paul. Thus, he felt that his input fell between those of Jane and Paul. When salary increases were announced, he learned that Jane got a

[2]This listing is drawn from Leventhal (1976b).

[3]There are some more sophisticated equity formulations—for instance, see Walster et al. (1978). However, this simple formulation is perfectly adequate in most cases.

FIGURE 10-6
Situations of Inequity and Equity

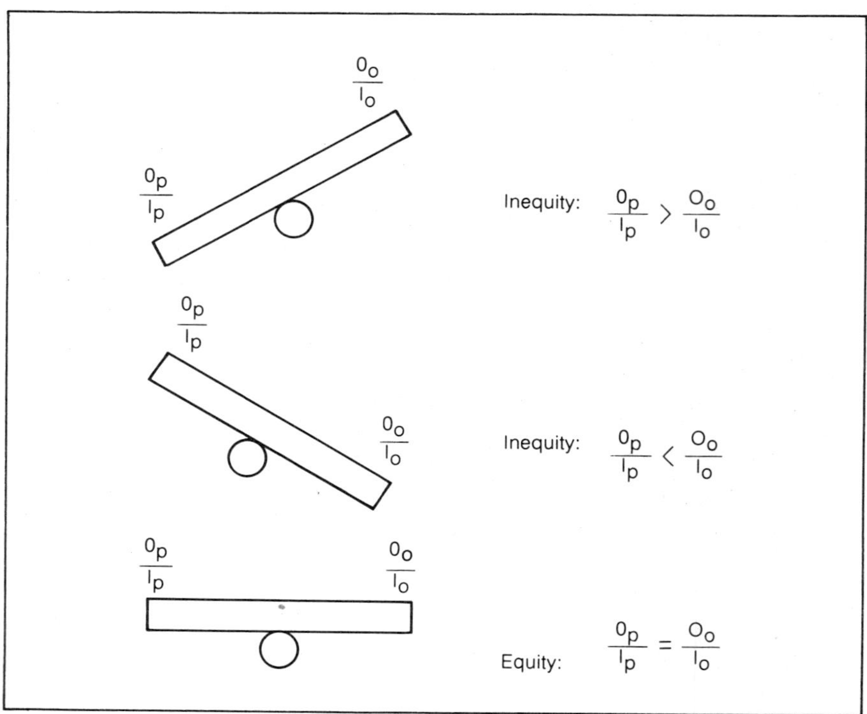

bit more than he did, and Paul got the same. Since Bob felt Jane's inputs were greater than his, he didn't begrudge her somewhat greater outcomes (though he did vow that he would outperform her next year). What irked him was that he and Paul had been rewarded the same. Bob felt that just wasn't fair.

We should stress here that it is the person's *perceptions* that are relevant. While the real situation may influence those perceptions, it is otherwise irrelevant. Also, the comparison other may be a particular individual (such as a coworker, a neighbor, or a friend), a number of people (such as workers on another job), some abstract combination of people, or even the perceiving person at an earlier point in time.

Inputs and outcomes

Table 10-1 presents a listing of some possible inputs and outcomes that employees may consider. We say "possible" because different people may be concerned with very different inputs and outcomes. Also, it is even possible that some people will treat as inputs things that others think of as outcomes. For instance, Paul says, "I have to work on my own, and the company is lucky to get someone like me who can do all the things this job demands. But at least the pay is good." On the other hand, Donna recently told her friend, "I know I'm not getting much money on my job, but I get to work on my own and I can do all kinds of things." What Paul thinks of as inputs, Donna

TABLE 10-1
Some Possible Inputs and Outcomes

INPUTS	OUTCOMES
Seniority	Pay
Age	Promotional Opportunities
Effort	Job Status
Performance	Job Interest
Social Class	Approval by Supervisors
Time	Esteem of Coworkers
Dedication to the Organization	Dangerous Working Conditions
Education	Monotony
Sex	Praise
Intelligence	Job Insecurity
Provision of Needed Tools	Fringe Benefits
Appearance	Fatigue

views as outcomes, and vice versa. So it is important, as we suggested earlier, to try to find out what it is that employees want, as well as what they think they're contributing. Table 10-1 also highlights one other important point: some outcomes may be viewed negatively. For example, most employees would regard dangerous working conditions, job insecurity, and monotony as negative outcomes.

In a work setting, both employers and employees may be concerned about equity. Let's consider this issue from both points of view.

Why do employers care about fairness?

There are a variety of specific reasons why employers may want to treat their employees fairly. For example:[4]

1. They may be committed to abstract ideals of equity and justice.

2. They may want to conform to business-world norms. For instance, people in business generally agree that employees who do better work should get more rewards.

3. They may want to attract superior workers to the company and weed out inferior ones. We said in chapter 8 that, by properly tying rewards to performance, a positive association between satisfaction and performance would result. Since satisfaction is negatively related to turnover, such an association means that high performers probably will be attracted to and stay with the organization, while low performers will leave.

4. They may want to motivate workers to produce. As we said in our discussion of expectancy theory, tying rewards to performance increases instrumentality perceptions and, as a result, motivation to perform well.

[4]This listing is drawn from Leventhal (1976a).

5. They may want to avoid conflict. Allocation schemes that are considered unfair are likely to lead to trouble.

Do employees care about fairness?

There's not much doubt that employees are distressed when they feel they are being treated unfairly. Almost two decades ago, Elliott Jaques (1961) found that British factory workers showed signs of unease both when they were underpaid *and* when they were overpaid. More recently, Robert Pritchard and his colleagues (1972) carried out an experiment in which they hired men to work for "their" day-labor firm. A day or so after the men were promised a specified salary, they were told that the recruitment flyer had been incorrect and that the error either could or could not be rectified. So some workers were overpaid, others were underpaid, and still others were treated equitably. It was found that the equitably treated men were more satisfied than were *either* those who were underpaid or overpaid.

Restoring equity

If individuals feel their situations are inequitable, they may try to restore equity in any number of ways. For instance, suppose that Janet feels underpaid compared to her coworker, Liz. She could try to restore equity by:

1. Raising her own outcomes (perhaps by demanding and getting a raise, or even by theft)

2. Lowering her inputs (by slowing down on the job, for instance, withholding important information, or stopping unpaid overtime work)

3. Perceptually distorting her inputs or outputs or those of Liz (For example, Janet might tell herself that she was getting a lot of things out of the job she hadn't considered before. Or she might downgrade her own abilities. Also, she could re-evaluate Liz's inputs and/or outcomes.)

4. Leaving the situation (That is, Janet could quit, apply for a transfer, be absent from work, or withdraw psychologically.)

5. Acting on Liz (For instance, Janet could try to talk Liz into raising her inputs, could try to convince Liz's boss that she was overpaid, or could do things to make Liz leave her job.)

6. Changing her comparison other (That is, Janet might begin to compare her situation with that of another of her coworkers, Bob, rather than with that of Liz.)

People really do use each of these mechanisms to restore equity, though to varying degrees.[5] For instance, a variety of field studies and

---

[5]See Walster *et. al.* (1978) for a review of studies relating to the restoration of equity.

		Basis of Inequity	
		Underpayment	Overpayment
Basis Of Pay	Hourly	Produce Less and/or Lower Quality Work	Produce More and/or Higher Quality Work
	Piece Rate	Produce More and/or Lower Quality Work	Produce Less and/or Higher Quality Work

FIGURE 10-7
Possible Changes in Inputs to Reduce Perceived Inequity

laboratory experiments have shown that individuals withdraw from tasks when they are inequitably treated—even, in some cases, when they are overpaid. And there is substantial support for the idea that people change their perceptions to restore equity. Underpaid individuals often perceive that they have made relatively low inputs and begin to see themselves as less qualified than others. Some of them also exaggerate their outcomes, rating their jobs as far more interesting than others do.

Probably, through, the findings that have drawn most interest are those relating to actual changes in inputs as a result of inequity. J. Stacy Adams and William Rosenbaum (1962) reasoned that employees' reactions would depend upon whether they were underpaid or overpaid *and* whether they were paid on an hourly basis or for each unit of output. Figure 10-7 shows what input changes would help restore equity in each of those four situations.

These findings suggest that sometimes underpaid employees will reduce their output, and sometimes they will raise it. Sometimes overpaid workers will increase their output, and sometimes, surprisingly, they will actually reduce it. The evidence relating to actual changes in inputs as a result of inequity is remarkable both in its volume and degree of controversy. This is partly because it is extremely difficult to make people feel overpaid or underpaid without also manipulating other things, such as their self-esteem, feelings of job security, perceptions of production demands, and so on. And it may be that those other things influence inputs instead of, or as well as, perceived inequity. Nevertheless, it does seem that most workers try to restore equity by altering their inputs. Of twenty-two studies involving hourly workers, almost 70 percent at least partially supported Adams' predictions. And more than 85 percent of studies focusing on piece rate workers gave partial or full support to those predictions.[6]

As we suggested earlier, one problem in trying to interpret studies of equity theory is that if there is no change in behavior in an apparently inequitable situation, the theory is not necessarily refuted.

[6]Walster, *et. al.* (1978).

That is, perceptual adjustments may have occurred. J. Stacy Adams (1965) provided the following set of propositions (slightly reworded here) concerning how people choose from among alternative ways to reduce inequity.

1. They will try to maximize valued outcomes. For example, if Bob can restore equity by either getting a raise or somehow cutting down on the rewards of his comparison person, Sam, Bob probably will try for the raise.

2. They will minimize increasing inputs that are difficult or costly to change.

3. They will resist real or perceived changes in inputs or outcomes that are central to their self-concept and self-esteem.

4. They will be more resistant to changing perceptions about their own outcomes and inputs than about their comparison person's outcomes and inputs.

5. They will leave the inequitable situation only when the magnitude of inequity is great and other means of reducing it are unavailable. Partial withdrawal, such as absenteeism, will occur more frequently and under lower conditions of inequity.

6. They will be reluctant to change their comparison persons. For example, ever since Herb has been on the faculty at the university, he has compared his performance and pay to Frank's. If he now began to weigh them against Jack's, he really wouldn't feel as though he had as good an idea of whether he was being treated right.

What is fair?[7]

Equity theory assumes that distributive fairness is based on somehow equating contributions (inputs) with outcomes. That is, it assumes that the *contributions rule* is used. However, as Gerald Leventhal (1976b) pointed out, there are other ways people may decide what is fair. For example, some may feel it is fair to give people what they need (the *needs rule*). Others may think that fairness results only when everyone gets the same amount (the *equality rule*). Tina, who thinks scholarships should be awarded partly on the basis of need, disagrees sharply with Hank, who advocates relying solely on evidence of probable academic achievement.

A number of things apparently affect the extent to which people apply these various rules. Some of those factors are general, influencing the weights of all the justice rules in the same way. Others are specific, either affecting the weight of only one rule or affecting the various rules in different ways.

Some things that influence the weights given to all the rules are:

[7]This section is drawn from Leventhal (1976b).

1. *Self-interest.* People are likely to assign higher weight to rules that favor them. Sam, who is broke, favors the needs rule. Jack, a high performer, argues for the contributions role.

2. *Conformity.* People conform to other peoples' beliefs and behaviors. So if all of Tim's friends regularly apply the equality rule, Tim probably will, too.

3. *Availability of relevant information.* People will avoid using a particular rule if they don't think they have enough information to apply it. So, for example, if Bonnie doesn't know what her subordinates need, she's not likely to try to apply the needs rule.

The following are some things that affect the weights of specific rules.

1. When it is important for high performers to maintain their productivity, the contributions rule will probably be weighted heavily.

2. The more a person likes or feels responsible for the receivers' welfare, the more the needs rule is likely to be applied.

3. When a person interacts with receivers whose demands are overwhelming, he or she will probably reduce involvement with them and pay little attention to their needs. So when Tom's subordinates all continue to ask for raises that he can't possibly grant, he finally tunes them out.

4. Equal outcomes tend to foster harmony and solidarity. When it is important to prevent conflict among group members, the equality rule will probably be emphasized.

5. The equality rule is easier to apply than the others: it is much simpler to give everyone the same size slice of the pie than to try to figure out what each has contributed. Young children and people with limited cognitive capacity often follow the equality rule. Also, people often resort to the equality rule when it's hard to assess contributions or needs.

Walster *et al.* (1978) argue that because some people apply the equality rule rather than the contributions rule doesn't necessarily refute equity theory. They suggest that people applying the equality rule think that only one input—the person's humanity—matters. Since all people have equal humanity, they all deserve equal outcomes.

Procedural fairness

Distributive fairness is concerned with whether receivers deserve their outcomes. But people are often also concerned with *procedural fairness*—that is, with whether the procedures used to allocate outcomes are fair. If procedures don't seem to be fair, people understandably will also question the distribution of rewards. On the other hand, even when they haven't fared well in terms of reward allocation, people generally are satisfied if they think the allocation process was fair. For example, one of the authors is the chairperson of an admissions committee for a graduate program. One unpleasant but unavoidable chore associated with that position is the need to explain to rejected applicants why they weren't accepted. In such cases, an attempt is made to fully explain the process the committee members go through in making their decisions and the factors they consider—undergraduate grade-point average, entrance exam scores, grades in particular types of classes, previous work experience, outside activities, and so on. Once the process is explained and the average ratings on each dimension of students accepted to the program are presented, the rejected applicant generally is satisfied that he or she has been treated fairly. Happily, such a process also lets such rejected applicants know what they need to do to improve their credentials in the hope of later getting into the program—some retake their entrance exams, some get additional work experience, some take more courses in specific areas.

The particular procedures that people think are fair depend upon a number of factors. For one, people feel procedures are more fair when they favor their interests. Also, people think procedures are more fair when they have some personal control over the allocation process. Further, a procedure is likely to be considered unfair if it uses questionable means to obtain information about receivers' behaviors (such as the use of hidden cameras), or if the evaluations of receivers seem to be based on unreliable or irrelevant information (such as faulty performance appraisals).

There is evidence, albeit somewhat conflicting, to suggest that when people feel that both distributions of outcomes and procedures for distribution are unfair, they may exert more effort to restore distributive justice than when they believe procedures are fair. Therefore, it is important to consider not just the outcomes of the allocation process but also the nature of that process.

GOAL SETTING

It appears that an additional (though related) determinant of employees' performance is the set of goals they pursue. Edwin Locke is a leading advocate of the view that conscious goals influence subsequent performance. For example, he has written:

> A cardinal attribute of the behavior of living organisms is goal-directedness. It may be observed at all levels of life: in the assimilation of food by an amoeba, in the root growth of a tree or plant, in the stalking of prey by a wild animal, and in the activities of a scientist in a laboratory. (1969, p. 991)

Evidence concerning the impact of goal setting

Richard Steers and Lyman Porter (1974) have reviewed research relating to six attributes of goals: goal specificity, participation in goal setting, feedback on goal progress, peer competition for goal attainment, goal difficulty and goal acceptance. Let's briefly review the evidence concerning the impacts of those attributes.[8]

Goal specificity. Both field investigations and laboratory experiments provide strong and generally consistent evidence that it is better to set clear and specific goals than just to say, "Do your best." When a runner is circling a track and yells to her coach, "How much farther do I have to go?," she doesn't want to hear, "Just do your best!" In one study of the impact of goal specification, subjects were assigned to either a "low motivation" or a "high motivation" group based on their performance, ability and attitude ratings. The low-motivation group was given highly specific task goals, while the high-motivation group was told to "do your best." The low-motivation group soon caught up to the high-motivation group in both performance and positive attitudes toward the task.[9]

Participation in goal setting. In general, participation seems to increase understanding and acceptance of a goal. On the other hand, the impact of participation on performance depends upon a number of situational and personality characteristics. There is some evidence, though, that when people participate in the goal-setting process, they may set more difficult goals than they would have had set for them. Thus, to the extent that difficult goals lead to higher performance, participation may help.

Feedback on goal progress. It has been argued that giving employees feedback about how well they are doing serves two functions. It helps them keep their behavior on track, and it stimulates them to greater effort. In fact, though, the relationship between feedback and performance is quite complex. For instance, it seems that when employees get feedback about their performance, they set personal improvement goals. It could be argued, then, that it is the higher goals that are set in response to feedback, rather than the feedback itself, that is important.[10] Also, it appears that feedback is more important for some people than for others. For example, one study showed that, while feedback was positively related to effort and performance for people who had high needs for achievement, affiliation, and independence, it was unrelated to those variables for others.[11]

---

[8] This section is drawn largely from Steers and Porter (1974).

[9] Bryan and Locke (1967).

[10] For instance, see Locke et al. (1968).

[11] Steers (1973).

Peer competition for goal attainment. If employees compete with one another to meet goals, we might expect that they would try harder than otherwise. Perhaps this is because competition is stimulating in itself and because employees know that if they are in a competitive situation, their productivity might be compared with that of their competitors. However, it seems that the situation is a bit more complicted than this. For one thing, when the tasks employees are working on are somehow interdependent, competition may be harmful. Also, there is reason to believe that, as employees compete to maximize the quantity of their output, quality may suffer. Finally, it seems that competition has much more impact on performance when employees are seeking slices of a "fixed pie"—such as the case where there is one winner or where a specific reward is to be distributed—than otherwise.

Goal difficulty. Some writers have reasoned that, within reasonable limits, setting difficult goals should increase the challenge presented by those goals and, as a result, the degree of effort exerted to try to reach them. Of course, impossible goals would probably simply result in frustration and resignation rather than heightened effort. Studies generally show that high goals lead to high performance. For instance, one early study found that setting a goal of improving performance by 25 percent per day resulted in faster improvement than did an improvement goal of only 5 percent.[12]

It is important that the employees for whom the goals are set accept them. If not, goal difficulty doesn't make much difference. Also, individuals probably simultaneously pursue a variety of goals. If one of those goals is made extremely difficult, employees may deemphasize it in favor of other, more easily reachable goals. Again, we have to make sure that goals are within reasonable reach. Finally, there is some evidence that people who are given difficult goals engage in more problem analysis and creative behavior than do those with simpler goals. In many cases, such analysis and creativity could be very useful.

Goal acceptance. This refers to the degree to which individuals agree with and accept their task goals. We said earlier that goal difficulty doesn't seem to make much difference unless goals are accepted. In general, then, it may well be that goal acceptance will determine whether or not other goal attributes will have an impact on employee responses. Also, studies have clearly shown that it is dangerous simply to assume that employees will accept the goals that have been set.

This brief summary indicates that several goal attributes may be important, though their relationships to employee responses may be complex, and many personal and situational factors may play a role. Also, of course, many of the goal-setting actions we may take would affect a number of goal attributes. One notable example came to light

[12] Mace (1935).

when Gary Latham and James Baldes (1975) conducted a field experiment in the logging industry. Trucks carrying logs from the woods to the mill varied in the number of trees they hauled from one time to the next since the trees differed in size. As a result, considerable judgment entered into the decision of what was a full load. However, analyses indicated that trucks were carrying an average of only about 60 percent of their legal net weight. Eventually, the researchers, management and the union decided that a goal of 94 percent of legal net weight was difficult but reachable, and the drivers, who were responsible for loading the trucks were assigned this 94 percent goal. After about a month, performance increased from the initial 60 percent to about 80 percent of capacity, then dipped to 70 percent for another month, and then rose to 90 percent, where it remained for the next six months. A variety of changes in goal attributes may have led to these results, which company accountants estimated resulted in savings equivalent to the purchase of a quarter of a million dollars worth of new trucks alone. Goals were specific, they were more difficult than in the past, and there was reason to believe that they had been accepted.

Management by objectives

One well-known technique that involves goal setting is *management by objectives* (MBO). MBO relies on the superior and subordinate setting specific goals. According to Walter Wikstrom: "(1) The clearer the idea one has of what it is one is trying to accomplish, the greater the chances of accomplishing it; and (2) progress can only be measured in terms of what one is trying to make progress toward." (1968, p. 2)

MBO is based upon the following four steps.

1. Goals are defined for the employee. The employee should be actively involved in this goal setting, either by suggesting goals or, at the very least, by discussing the goals with the superior and approving them. To the greatest extent possible, the goals should be tangible and specific.

2. The employee carries out the objectives established.

3. Performance is evaluated against the goals that were established. Reasons for failure to meet goals are discussed.

4. New goals are established for the next time period.

One reason for the appeal of MBO is that it combines a number of characteristics that should lead to desirable outcomes. For instance:

1. MBO forces planning.

2. Feedback is built into the process. While managers may be reluctant to give feedback to employees about their personal characteristics, discussion of the sorts of concrete goals set in MBO is easier.

3. The process guarantees that the subordinate and superior agree on what the subordinate is supposed to do.

4. MBO recognizes individual differences among employees and allows for the setting of individualized goals.

5. The subordinate's participation in the goal-setting process is likely to improve his or her understanding and acceptance of the goal.

6. Specific goals are set. As we have already indicated, it appears that when subordinates participate in the process, the goals set are generally more difficult than if the superior imposed them. This should also improve performance.

7. MBO is a control mechanism, allowing deviations of actual performance from goals to be regularly and systematically evaluated.

Despite these advantages, however, the following problems associated with MBO may severely limit its usefulness in many situations.

1. Goal setting may be difficult in some cases.

2. Fixed goals may build rigidity into the system. That is, the employee may continue to pursue the goals that were set despite markedly changed circumstances.

3. Managers often complain that MBO is time-consuming and involves a lot of paper work.

4. Since MBO focuses on concrete, quantifiable goals, less quantifiable criteria may be sacrificed. For example, MBO has been accused of rewarding productivity at the expense of creativity.

5. Some studies show the favorable impact of MBO to deteriorate over time.

6. It takes a lot of time—perhaps three to five years—to implement an MBO program properly and fully.

Expectancy theory, equity theory, and goal setting: Some links

The three sets of theories presented in this chapter are complementary as well as intimately related. For example, consider the following links between goal setting and expectancy theory:

1. Setting precise goals should let the employee know what is expected of him or her, clarifying role perceptions and thereby increasing expectancy.

2. Setting specific goals and making rewards contingent on their accomplishment should strengthen instrumentality perceptions.

3. If an employee is involved in the goal-setting process, he or she may be more ego involved in goal attainment than otherwise. As a re-

sult, goal attainment may increase in valence when employees participate in goal setting.

Thus, goal setting may influence each of the three expectancy theory motivational components—valences, expectancy, and instrumentalities.

Also, we have seen that elements of expectancy theory are useful in understanding how people decide what is fair. For example:

1. Employers may try to be equitable—that is, to tie rewards to contributions or, in expectancy theory terms, to maximize the instrumentality of performance for the attainment of rewards—in order to attract superior performers to the company and weed out inferior ones.

2. Employers may try to be equitable (again, to tie rewards to performance or to maximize the instrumentality of performance for the attainment of rewards) in order to motivate workers to produce.

3. In order to maximize instrumentalities of performance for the attainment of rewards, employers may apply the contributions rule rather than the needs rule or the equality rule.

SUMMARY

In this chapter, we have considered three approaches to examining the important topic of performance in organizations—expectancy theory, equity theory, and goal setting.

Expectancy theory assumes that employees try to maximize their welfare. It argues that three elements must be present if an employee is to be motivated to perform. First, outcomes that are important to the employee must be present. Second, the employee must see those outcomes as being linked to performance. Finally, he or she must feel that effort really affects performance. Expectancy theory has some predictive ability and provides useful guidelines for the design of reward systems, leader behavior, and other issues central to the effective management of behavior in organizations.

Equity theory reasons that individuals think people should get what they deserve. It argues that the fairness of a situation depends on the ratio of outcomes to inputs. When that ratio is thought to be unjust, employees may take any of a wide variety of actions to restore equity. Interestingly, equity theory suggests that, in some situations, giving employees more pay may actually reduce output. There is considerable evidence to support the contention that employees do try to restore equity. However, it is possible that, in some cases, alternatives to the contributions rule, such as the needs rule or the equality rule, may be applied. Also, the fairness of procedures for distribution, as well as the actual distribution of outcomes, may be important.

Conscious goals that employees set are apparently important determinants of their behavior. In particular, it seems that specific, difficult goals are better than vague, easy goals. While the roles of feedback on goal progress, participation in goal setting, and peer competition for goal attainment are complex, each of these goal attributes is important for some people in some situations. Finally, if goals are not accepted, they probably won't have much impact on responses. Management by objectives is a technique that explicitly incorporates goal setting. While MBO possesses a number of important features, it is not without problems.

Taken together, the topics in this chapter provide a powerful set of tools with which to understand, predict, and influence performance in organizations. And, if used properly, they will help management meet employees' needs more effectively.

In the chapter that follows, Steve Kerr provides a number of examples of the consequences of failure to tie rewards to desired behaviors. Keep this chapter—especially the discussion of expectancy theory—in mind when you consider those examples.

REFERENCES

Adams, J.S. "Inequity in Social Exchange." In *Advances in Experimental Social Psychology*, vol. 2, edited by L. Berkowitz. New York: Academic, 1965.

Adams, J.S., and Rosenbaum, W.E. "The Relationship of Worker Productivity to Cognitive Dissonance about Wage Inequities." *Journal of Applied Psychology 46* (1962): 161-64.

Bryan, J.F., and Locke, E.A. "Goal Setting As a Means of Increasing Motivation." *Journal of Applied Psychology 51* (1967) 274-77.

Jaques, E. *Equitable Payment*. New York: Wiley, 1961.

Latham, G.P., and Baldes, J.J. "The 'Practical Significance' of Locke's Theory of Goal Setting." *Journal of Applied Psychology 60* (1975): 122-24.

Leventhal, G.S. "The Distribution of Rewards and Resources in Groups and Organizations." In *Advances in Experimental Social Psychology*, vol. 9, edited by L. Berkowitz and E. Walster. New York, Academic Press, 1976a.

Leventhal, G.S. "Fairness in Social Relationships." In *Contemporary Topics in Social Psychology*, edited by J. Thibaut, J.T. Spence, and R. Carson. Morristown, N.J.: General Learning Press, 1976b.

Locke, E.A. "Toward a Theory of Task Motivation and Incentives." *Organizational Behavior and Human Performance 3* (1968): 157-89.

Locke, E.A. "Purpose without Consciousness: A Contradiction." *Psychological Reports 25* (1969): 991-1009.

Locke, E.A. "The Ubiquity of the Technique of Goal Setting in Theories of and Approaches to Employee Motivation." *Academy of Management Review 3* (1978): 594-601.

Locke, E.A.; Cartledge, N.; and Koeppel, J. "Motivational Effects of Knowledge of Results: A Goal Setting Phenomenon?" *Psychological Bulletin 70* (1968): 474-85.

Mace, C.A. *Incentives: Some Experimental Studies*, reprint 72. London: Industrial Health Research Board, 1935.

McGregor, D. *The Human Side of Enterprise*. New York: McGraw-Hill, 1960.

Porter, L.W., and Lawler, E.E. *Managerial Attitudes and Performance*. Homewood, Ill.: Dorsey-Irwin 1968.

Pritchard, R.D.; Dunnette, M.D.; and Jorgenson, D.O. "Effects of Perceptions of Equity and Inequity on Worker Performance and Satisfaction." *Journal of Applied Psychology Monograph* 56 (1972): 75-94.

Steers, R.M. "Task Goals, Individual Need Strengths, and Supervisory Performance." Unpublished doctoral dissertation, Graduate School of Administration, University of California, Irvine, 1973.

Steers, R.M., and Porter, L.W. "The Role of Task-Goal Attributes in Employee Performance." *Psychological Bulletin* 81 (1974): 434-52.

Tornow, W.W. "The Development and Application of an Input-Outcome Moderator Test on the Perception and Reduction of Inequity." *Organizational Behavior and Human Performance* 6 (1971): 614-38.

Vroom, V.H. *Work and Motivation.* New York: Wiley, 1964.

Walster, E.; Walster, G.W.; and Berscheid, E. *Equity: Theory and Research.* (Boston: Allyn and Bacon, 1978.

Wikstrom, W.S. *Managing by—and with—Objectives.* New York: National Industrial Conference Board, 1968.

SUGGESTIONS FOR ADVANCED READINGS

Adams, J.S. "Inequity in Social Exchange." In *Advances in Experimental Social Psychology,* vol. 2, edited by L. Berkowitz. New York: Academic, 1965.

Heneman, H.H., III, and Schwab, D.P. "An Evaluation of Research on Expectancy Theory Predictions of Employee Performance." *Psychological Bulletin* 78 (1972): 1-9.

House, R.J.; Shapiro, H.J.; and Wahba, M.A. "Expectancy Theory As a Predictor of Work Behavior and Attitude: A Re-evaluation of Empirical Evidence." *Decision Sciences* 5 (1974): 481-506.

Leventhal, G.S. "Fairness in Social Relationships." In *Contemporary Topics in Social Psychology,* edited by J. Thibaut, J.T. Spence, and R. Carson. Morristown, N.J.: General Learning Press, 1976.

Locke, E.A. "Toward a Theory of Task Motivation and Incentives." *Organizational Behavior and Human Performance* 3 (1968): 157-89.

Steers, R.M., and Porter, L.W. "The Role of Task-Goal Attributes in Employee Performance." *Psychological Bulletin* 81 (1974): 434-52.

Vroom, V.H. *Work and Motivation.* New York: Wiley, 1964.

Walster, E.; Walster, G.W.; and Berscheid, E. *Equity: Theory and Research.* Boston: Allyn and Bacon, Inc., 1978.

CHAPTER

11

On The Folly Of Rewarding A, While Hoping For B*

Whether dealing with monkeys, rats, or human beings, it is hardly controversial to state that most organisms seek information concerning what activities are rewarded, and then seek to do (or at least pretend to do) those things, often to the virtual exclusion of activities not rewarded. The extent to which this occurs of course will depend on the perceived attractiveness of the rewards offered, but neither operant nor expectancy theorists would quarrel with the essence of this notion.

Nevertheless, numerous examples exist of reward systems that are fouled up in that behaviors which are rewarded are those which the rewarder is trying to *discourage*, while the behavior he desires is not being rewarded at all.

In an effort to understand and explain this phenomenon, this paper presents examples from society, from organizations in general, and from profit-making firms in particular. Data from a manufacturing company and information from an insurance firm are examined to demonstrate the consequences of such reward systems for the organizations involved, and possible reasons why such reward systems continue to exist are considered.

SOCIETAL EXAMPLES

Politics

Official goals are "purposely vague and general and do not indicate . . . the host of decisions that must be made among alternative ways of

*Reprinted with permission of the publisher and author from Steven Kerr, "On The Folly of Rewarding A, While Hoping for B," *Academy of Management Journal* 1975, 18, pp. 769-783.

achieving official goals and the priority of multiple goals . . ." (8, p. 66). They usually may be relied on to offend absolutely no one, and in this sense can be considered high-acceptance, low-quality goals. An example might be "build better schools." Operative goals are higher in quality but lower in acceptance, since they specify where the money will come from, what alternative goals will be ignored, etc.

The American citizenry supposedly wants its candidates for public office to set forth operative goals, making their proposed programs "perfectly clear," specifying sources and uses of funds, etc. However, since operative goals are lower in acceptance, and since aspirants to public office need acceptance (from at least 50.1 percent of the people), most politicians prefer to speak only of official goals, at least until after the election. They of course would agree to speak at the operative level if "punished" for not doing so. The electorate could do this by refusing to support candidates who do not speak at the operative level.

Instead, however, the American voter typically punishes (withholds support from) candidates who frankly discuss where the money will come from, rewards politicians who speak only of official goals, but hopes that candidates (despite the reward system) will discuss the issues operatively. It is academic whether it was moral for Nixon, for example, to refuse to discuss his 1968 "secret plan" to end the Vietnam war, his 1972 operative goals concerning the lifting of price controls, the reshuffling of his cabinet, etc. The point is that the reward system made such refusal rational.

It seems worth mentioning that no manuscript can adequately define what is "moral" and what is not. However, examination of costs and benefits, combined with knowledge of what motivates a particular individual, often will suffice to determine what for him is "rational."[1] If the reward system is so designed that it is irrational to be moral, this does not necessarily mean that immorality will result. But is this not asking for trouble?

War

If some oversimplification may be permitted, let it be assumed that the primary goal of the organization (Pentagon, Luftwaffe, or whatever) is to win. Let it be assumed further that the primary goal of most individuals on the front lines is to get home alive. Then there appears to be an important conflict in goals—personally rational behavior by those at the bottom will endanger goal attainment by those at the top.

But not necessarily! It depends on how the reward system is set up. The Vietnam war was indeed a study of disobedience and rebellion, with terms such as "fragging" (killing one's own commanding

[1]In Simon's (10, pp. 76-77) terms, a decision is "subjectively rational" if it maximizes an individual's valued outcomes so far as his knowledge permits. A decision is "personally rational" if it is oriented toward the individual's goals.

officer) and "search and evade" becoming part of the military vocabulary. The difference in subordinates' acceptance of authority between World War II and Vietnam is reported to be considerable, and veterans of the Second World War often have been quoted as being outraged at the mutinous actions of many American soldiers in Vietnam.

Consider, however, some critical diferences in the reward system in use during the two conflicts. What did the GI in World War II want? To go home. And when did he get to go home? When the war was won! If he disobeyed the orders to clean out the trenches and take the hills, the war would not be won and he would not go home. Furthermore, what were his chances of attaining his goal (getting home alive) if he obeyed the orders compared to his chances if he did not? What is being suggested is that the rational soldier in World War II, *whether patriotic or not,* probably found it expedient to obey.

Consider the reward system in use in Vietnam. What did the man at the bottom want? To go home. And when did he get to go home? When his tour of duty was over! This was the case *whether or not* the war was won. Furthermore, concerning the relative chance of getting home alive by obeying orders compared to the chance if they were disobeyed, it is worth noting that a mutineer in Vietnam was far more likely to be assigned rest and rehabilitation (on the assumption that fatigue was the cause) than he was to suffer any negative consequence.

In his description of the "zone of indifference," Barnard stated that "a person can and will accept a communication as authoritative only when . . . at the time of his decision, he believes it to be compatible with his personal interests as a whole" (1, p. 165). In light of the reward system used in Vietnam, would it not have been personally irrational for some orders to have been obeyed? Was not the military implementing a system which *rewarded* disobedience, while *hoping* that soldiers (despite the reward system) would obey orders?

Medicine

Theoretically, a physician can make either of two types of error, and intuitively one seems as bad as the other. A doctor can pronounce a patient sick when he is actually well, thus causing him needless anxiety and expense, curtailment of enjoyable foods and activities, and even physical danger by subjecting him to needless medication and surgery. Alternately, a doctor can label a sick person well, and thus avoid treating what may be a serious, even fatal ailment. It might be natural to conclude that physicians seek to minimize both types of error.

Such a conclusion would be wrong.[2] It is estimated that numerous Americans are presently afflicted with iatrogenic (physician *caused*)

---

[2]In one study (4) of 14,867 films for signs of tuberculosis, 1,216 positive readings turned out to be clinically negative; only 24 negative readings proved clinically active, a ratio of 50 to 1.

illnesses (9). This occurs when the doctor is approached by someone complaining of a few stray symptoms. The doctor classifies and organizes these symptoms, gives them a name, and obligingly tells the patient what further symptoms may be expected. This information often acts as a self-fulfilling prophecy, with the result that from that day on the patient for all practical purposes is sick.

Why does this happen? Why are physicians so reluctant to sustain a type 2 error (pronouncing a sick person well) that they will tolerate many type 1 errors? Again, a look at the reward system is needed. The punishments for a type 2 error are real: guilt, embarrassment, and the threat of lawsuit and scandal. On the other hand, a type 1 error (labeling a well person sick) "is sometimes seen as sound clinical practice, indicating a healthy conservative approach to medicine" (9, p. 69). Type 1 errors also are likely to generate increased income and a stream of steady customers who, being well in a limited physiological sense, will not embarrass the doctor by dying abruptly.

Fellow physicians and the general public therefore are really *rewarding* type 1 errors and at the same time *hoping* fervently that doctors will try not to make them.

GENERAL ORGANIZATIONAL EXAMPLES

Rehabilitation centers and orphanages

In terms of the prime beneficiary classification (2, p. 42) organizations such as these are supposed to exist for the "public-in-contract," that is, clients. The orphanage therefore theoretically is interested in placing as many children as possible in good homes. However, often orphanages surround themselves with so many rules concerning adoption that it is nearly impossible to pry a child out of the place. Orphanages may deny adoption unless the applicants are a married couple, both of the same religion as the child, without a history of emotional or vocational instability, with a specified minimum income and a private room for the child, etc.

If the primary goal is to place children in good homes, then the rules ought to constitute means toward that goal. Goal displacement results when these "means become ends-in-themselves that displace the original goals" (2, p. 229).

To some extent these rules are required by law. But the influence of the reward system on the orphanage's management should not be ignored. Consider, for example, that the:

1. Number of children enrolled often is the most important determinant of the size of the allocated budget.

2. Number of children under the director's care also will affect the size of his staff.

3. Total organizational size will determine largely the director's prestige at the annual conventions, in the community, etc.

Therefore, to the extent that staff size, total budget, and personal prestige are valued by the orphanage's executive personnel, it becomes rational for them to make it difficult for children to be adopted. After all, who wants to be the director of the small orphanage in the state?

If the reward system errs in the opposite direction, paying off only for placements, extensive goal displacement again is likely to result. A common example of vocational rehabilitation in many states, for example, consists of placing someone in a job for which he has little interest and few qualifications, for two months or so, and then "rehabilitating" him again in another position. Such behavior is quite consistent with the prevailing reward system, which pays off for the number of individuals placed in any position for 60 days or more. Rehabilitation counselors also confess to competing with one another to place relatively skilled clients, sometimes ignoring persons with few skills who would be harder to place. Extensively disabled clients find that counselors often prefer to work with those whose disabilities are less severe.[3]

Universities

Society *hopes* that teachers will not neglect their teaching responsibilities but *rewards* them almost entirely for research and publications. This is most true at the large and prestigious universities. Clichés such as "good research and good teaching go together" notwithstanding, professors often find that they must choose between teaching and research-oriented activities when allocating their time. Rewards for good teaching usually are limited to outstanding teacher awards, which are given to only a small percentage of good teachers and which usually bestow little money and fleeting prestige. Punishments for poor teaching also are rare.

Rewards for research and publications, on the other hand, and punishments for failure to accomplish these, are commonly administered by universities at which teachers are employed. Furthermore, publication-oriented resumés usually will be well received at other universities, whereas teaching credentials, harder to document and quantify, are much less transferable. Consequently it is rational for university teachers to concentrate on research, even if to the detriment of teaching and at the expense of their students.

By the same token, it is rational for students to act based upon the goal displacement which has occurred within universities concerning what they are rewarded for. If it is assumed that a primary goal of a university is to transfer knowledge from teacher to student, then grades become identifiable as a means toward that goal, serving as motivational, control, and feedback devices to expedite the knowledge transfer. Instead, however, the grades themselves have become much more important for entrance to graduate school, successful em-

[3]Personal interviews conducted 1972-73.

ployment, tuition refunds, parental respect, etc., than the knowledge or lack of knowledge they are supposed to signify.

It therefore should come as no surprise that information has surfaced in recent years concerning fraternity files for examinations, term-paper writing services, organized cheating at the service academies, and the like. Such activities constitute a personally rational response to a reward system which pays off for grades rather than knowledge.

BUSINESS-RELATED EXAMPLES

Ecology

Assume that the president of XYZ Corporation is confronted with the following alternatives:

1. Spend $11 million for antipollution equipment to keep from poisoning fish in the river adjacent to the plant; or

2. Do nothing, in violation of the law, and assume a one in ten chance of being caught, with a resultant $1 million fine plus the necessity of buying the equipment.

Under this not unrealistic set of choices it requires no linear program to determine that XYZ Corporation can maximize its probabilities by flouting the law. Add the fact that XYZ's president is probably being rewarded (by creditors, stockholders, and other salient parts of his task environment) according to criteria totally unrelated to the number of fish poisoned, and his probable course of action becomes clear.

Evaluation of training

It is axiomatic that those who care about a firm's well-being should insist that the organization get fair value for its expenditures. Yet it is commonly known that firms seldom bother to evaluate a new GRID, MBO, job enrichment program, or whatever, to see if the company is getting its money's worth. Why? Certainly it is not because people have not pointed out that this situation exists; numerous practitioner-oriented articles are written each year to just this point.

The individuals (whether in personnel, manpower planning, or wherever) who normally would be responsible for conducting such evaluations are the same ones often charged with introducing the change effort in the first place. Having convinced top management to spend the money, they usually are quite animated afterwards in collecting arigorous vignettes and anecdotes about how successful the program was. The last thing many desire is formal, systematic, and revealing evaluation. Although members of top management may actually *hope* for such systematic evaluation, their reward systems continue to *reward* ignorance in this area. And if the personnel department abdicates its responsibility, who is to step into the breach? The change agent himself? Hardly! He is likely to be too busy collecting anecdotal "evidence" of his own, for use with his next client.

Miscellaneous

Many additional examples could be cited of systems which in fact are rewarding behaviors other than those supposedly desired by the rewarder. A few of these are described briefly below.

Most coaches disdain to discuss individual accomplishments, preferring to speak of teamwork, proper attitude, and a one-for-all spirit. Usually, however, rewards are distributed according to individual performance. The college basketball player who feeds his teammates instead of shooting will not compile impressive scoring statistics and is less likely to be drafted by the pros. The ballplayer who hits to right field to advance the runners will win neither the batting nor home run titles, and will be offered smaller raises. It therefore is rational for players to think of themselves first, and the team second.

In business organizations where rewards are dispensed for unit performance or for individual goals achieved, without regard for overall effectiveness, similar attitudes often are observed. Under most Management by Objectives (MBO) systems, goals in areas where quantification is difficult often go unspecified. The organization therefore often is in a position where it *hopes* for employee effort in the areas of team building, interpersonal relations, creativity, etc., but it formally *rewards* none of these. In cases where promotions and raises are formally tied to MBO, the system itself contains a paradox in that it "asks employees to set challenging, risky goals, only to face smaller paychecks and possibly damaged careers if these goals are not accomplished" (5, p. 40).

It is *hoped* that administrators will pay attention to long-run costs and opportunities and will institute programs which will bear fruit later on. However, many organizational reward systems pay off for short-run sales and earnings only. Under such circumstances it is personally rational for officials to sacrifice long-term growth and profit (by selling off equipment and property, or by stifling research and development) for short-term advantages. This probably is most pertinent in the public sector, with the result that many public officials are unwilling to implement programs which will not show benefits by election time.

As a final, clear-cut example of a fouled-up reward system, consider the cost-plus contract or its next of kin, the allocation for next year's budget as a direct function of this year's expenditures. It probably is conceivable that those who award such budgets and contracts really hope for economy and prudence in spending. It is obvious, however, that adopting the proverb "to him who spends shall more be given," rewards not economy, but spending itself.

TWO COMPANIES' EXPERIENCES

A manufacturing organization

A midwest manufacturer of industrial goods had been troubled for some time by aspects of its organizational climate it believed dysfunctional. For research purposes, inteviews were conducted with many employees and a questionnaire was administered on a company-wide basis, including plants and offices in several American and Canadian locations. The company strongly encouraged employee participation in the survey, and made available time and space during the workday for completion of the instrument. All employees in attendance during the day of the survey completed the questionnaire. All instruments were collected directly by the researcher, who personally administered each session. Since no one employed by the firm handled the questionnaires, and since respondent names were not asked for, it seems likely that the pledge of anonymity given was believed.

A modified version of the Expect Approval scale (7) was included as part of the questionnaire. The instrument asked respondents to indicate the degree of approval or disapproval they could expect if they performed each of the described actions. A seven-point Likert scale was used, with 1 indicating that the action would probably bring strong disapproval and 7 signifying likely strong approval.

Although normative data for this scale from studies of other organizations are unavailable, it is possible to examine fruitfully the data obtained from this survey in several ways. First, it may be worth noting that the questionnaire data corresponded closely to information gathered through interviews. Furthermore, as can be seen from the results summarized in Table 1, sizable differences between various work units, and between employees at different job levels within the same work unit, were obtained. This suggests that response bias effects (social desirability in particular loomed as a potential concern) are not likely to be severe.

Most importantly, comparisons between scores obtained on the Expect Approval scale and a statement of problems which were the reason for the survey revealed that the same behaviors which managers in each division thought dysfunctional were those which lower level employees claimed were rewarded. As compared to job levels 1 to 8 in Division B (see Table 1), those in Division A claimed a much higher acceptance by management of "conforming" activities. Between 31 and 37 percent of Division A employees at levels 1-8 stated that going along with the majority, agreeing with the boss, and staying on everyone's good side brought approval; only once (level 5-8 responses to one of the three items) did a majority suggest that such actions would generate disapproval.

Furthermore, responses from Division A workers at levels 1-4 indicate that behaviors geared toward risk avoidance were as likely to be rewarded as to be punished. Only at job levels 9 and above was it

TABLE 11-1 Summary of Two Divisions' Data Relevant to Conforming and Risk-Avoidance Behaviors (extent to which subjects expect approval)

DIMENSION	ITEM	DIVISION AND SAMPLE	TOTAL RESPONSES	PERCENTAGE OF WORKERS RESPONDING		
				1, 2, OR 3 (DISAPPROVAL)	4	5, 6, OR 7 (APPROVAL)
Risk avoidance	Making a risky decision based on the best information available at the time, but which turns out wrong.	A, levels 1-4 (lowest)	127	61	25	14
		A, levels 5-8	172	46	31	23
		A, levels 9 and above	17	41	30	30
		B, levels 1-4 (lowest)	31	58	26	16
		B, levels 5-8	19	42	42	16
		B, levels 9 and above	10	50	20	30
Risk	Setting extremely high and challenging standards and goals, and then narrowly failing to make them.	A, levels 1-4	122	47	28	25
		A, levels 5-8	168	33	26	41
		A, levels 9+	17	24	6	70
		B, levels 1-4	31	48	23	29
		B, levels 5-8	18	17	33	50
		B, levels 9+	10	30	0	70

(Table 11-1 continued)

DIMENSION	ITEM	DIVISION AND SAMPLE	TOTAL RESPONSES	PERCENTAGE OF WORKERS RESPONDING		
				1, 2, OR 3 (DISAPPROVAL)	4	5, 6, OR 7 (APPROVAL)
	Setting goals which are extremely easy to make and then making them.	A, levels 1-4	124	35	30	35
		A, levels 5-8	171	47	27	26
		A, levels 9+	17	70	24	6
		B, levels 1-4	31	58	26	16
		B, levels 5-8	19	63	16	21
		B, levels 9+	10	80	0	20
	Being a "yes man" and always agreeing with the boss.	A, levels 1-4	126	46	17	37
		A, levels 5-8	180	54	14	31
		A, levels 9+	17	88	12	0
		B, levels 1-4	32	53	28	19
		B, levels 5-8	19	68	21	11
		B, levels 9+	10	80	10	10

(Table 11-1 continued)

DIMENSION	ITEM	DIVISION AND SAMPLE	TOTAL RESPONSES	PERCENTAGE OF WORKERS RESPONDING		
				1, 2, OR 3 (DISAPPROVAL)	4	5, 6, OR 7 (APPROVAL)
	Always going along with the majority.	A, levels 1-4	125	40	25	35
		A, levels 5-8	173	47	21	32
		A, levels 9+	17	70	12	18
		B, levels 1-4	31	61	23	16
		B, levels 5-8	19	68	11	21
		B, levels 9+	10	80	10	10
	Being careful to stay on the good side of everyone. so that everyone agrees that you are a great guy.	A, levels 1-4	124	45	18	37
		A, levels 5-8	173	45	22	33
		A, levels 9+	17	64	6	30
		B, levels 1-4	31	54	23	23
		B, levels 5-8	19	73	11	16
		B, levels 9+	10	80	10	10

apparent that the reward system was positively reinforcing behaviors desired by top management. Overall, the same "tendencies toward conservatism and apple-polishing at the lower levels" which divisional management had complained about during the interviews were those claimed by subordinates to be the most rational course of action in light of the existing reward system. Management apparently was not getting the behaviors it was *hoping* for, but it certainly was getting the behaviors it was perceived by subordinates to be *rewarding*.

An insurance firm

The Group Health Claims Division of a large eastern insurance company provides another rich illustration of a reward system which reinforces behaviors not desired by top management.

Attempting to measure and reward accuracy in paying surgical claims, the firm systematically keeps track of the number of returned checks and letters of complaint received from policyholders. However, underpayments are likely to provoke cries of outrage from the insured, while overpayments often are accepted in courteous silence. Since it often is impossible to tell from the physician's statement which of two surgical procedures, with different allowable benefits, was performed, and since writing for clarifications will interfere with other standards used by the firm concerning "percentage of claims paid within two days of receipt," the new hire in more than one claims section is soon acquainted with the informal norm: "When in doubt, pay it out!"

The situation would be even worse were it not for the fact that other features of the firm's reward system tend to neutralize those described. For example, annual "merit" increases are given to all employees, in one of the following three amounts:

1. If the worker is "outstanding" (a select category, into which no more than two employees per section may be placed): 5 percent

2. If the worker is "above average" (normally all workers not "outstanding" are so rated): 4 percent

3. If the worker commits gross acts of negligence and irresponsibility for which he might be discharged in many other companies: 3 percent.

Now, since *(a)* the difference between the 5 percent theoretically attainable through hard work and the 4 percent attainable merely by living until the review date is small and *(b)* since insurance firms seldom dispense much of a salary increase in cash (rather, the worker's insurance benefits increase, causing him to be further overinsured), many employees are rather indifferent to the possibility of obtaining the extra one percent reward and therefore tend to ignore the norm concerning indiscriminant payments.

However, most employees are not indifferent to the rule which states that, should absences or latenesses total three or more in any six-month period, the entire 4 or 5 percent due at the next "merit" review must be forfeited. In this sense the firm may be described as *hoping* for performance, while *rewarding* attendance. What it gets, of course, is attendance. (If the absence-lateness rule appears to the reader to be stringent, it really is not. The company counts "times" rather than "days" absent, and a ten-day absence therefore counts the same as one lasting two days. A worker in danger of accumulating a third absence within six months merely has to remain ill (away from work) during his second absence until his first absence is more than six months old. The limiting factor is that at some point his salary ceases, and his sickness benefits take over. This usually is sufficient to get the younger workers to return, but for those with 20 or more years' service, the company provides sickness benefits of 90 percent of normal salary, tax-free! Therefore . . . .)

CAUSES

Extremely diverse instances of systems which reward behavior A although the rewarder apparently hopes for behavior B have been given. These are useful to illustrate the breadth and magnitude of the phenomenon, but the diversity increases the difficulty of determining commonalities and establishing causes. However, four general factors may be pertinent to an explanation of why fouled-up reward systems seem to be so prevalant.

Fascination with an "objective" criterion

It has been mentioned elsewhere that:

> Most "objective" measures of productivity are objective only in that their subjective elements are *(a)* determined in advance, rather than coming into play at the time of the formal evaluation, and *(b)* well concealed on the rating instrument itself. Thus industrial firms seeking to devise objective rating systems first decide, in an arbitrary manner, what dimensions are to be rated, . . . usually including some items having little to do with organizational effectiveness while excluding others that do. Only then does Personnel Division churn out official-looking documents on which all dimensions chosen to be rated are assigned point values, categories, or whatever. (6, p. 92)

Nonetheless, many individuals seek to establish simple, quantifiable standards against which to measure and reward performance. Such efforts may be successful in highly predictable areas within an organization, but are likely to cause goal displacement when applied anywhere else. Overconcern with attendance and lateness in the insurance firm and with number of people placed in the vocational rehabilitation division may have been largely responsible for the problems described in those organizations.

Overemphasis on highly visible behaviors

Difficulties often stem from the fact that some parts of the task are highly visible while other parts are not. For example, publications are easier to demonstrate than teaching, and scoring baskets and hitting home runs are more readily observable than feeding teammates and advancing base runners. Similarly, the adverse consequences of pronouncing a sick person well are more visible than those sustained by labeling a well person sick. Team-building and creativity are other examples of behaviors which may not be rewarded simply because they are hard to observe.

Hypocrisy

In some of the instances described the rewarder may have been getting the desired behavior, notwithstanding claims that the behavior was not desired. This may be true, for example, of management's attitude toward apple-polishing in the manufacturing firm (a behavior which subordinates felt was rewarded, despite management's avowed dislike of the practice). This also may explain politicians' unwillingness to revise the penalties for disobedience of ecology laws, and the failure of top management to devise reward systems which would cause systematic evaluation of training and development programs.

Emphasis on morality or equity rather than efficiency

Some consideration of other factors prevents the establishment of a system which rewards behaviors desired by the rewarder. The felt obligation of many Americans to vote for one candidate or another, for example, may impair their ability to withhold support from politicians who refuse to discuss the issues. Similarly, the concern for spreading the risks and costs of wartime military service may outweigh the advantage to be obtained by committing personnel to combat until the war is over.

It should be noted that only with respect to the first two causes are reward systems really paying off for other than desired behaviors. In the case of the third and fourth causes the system is rewarding behaviors desired by the rewarder, and the systems are fouled up only from the standpoints of those who believe the rewarder's public statements (cause 3), or those who seek to maximize efficiency rather than other outcomes (cause 4).

CONCLUSIONS

Modern organization theory requires a recognition that the members of organizations and society possess divergent goals and motives. It therefore is unlikely that managers and their subordinates will seek the same outcomes. Three possible remedies for this potential problem are suggested.

Selection

It is theoretically possible for organizations to employ only those individuals whose goals and motives are wholly consonant with those of management. In such cases the same behaviors judged by subordinates to be rational would be perceived by management as desirable. State-of-the-art reviews of selection techniques, however, provide scant grounds for hope that such an approach would be successful (for example, see 12.).

Training

Another theoretical alternative is for the organization to admit those employees whose goals are not consonant with those of management and then, though training, socialization, or whatever, alter employee goals to make them consonant. However, research on the effectiveness of such training programs, though limited, provides further grounds for pessimism (for example, see 3).

Altering the reward system

What would have been the result if:

1. Nixon had been assured by his advisors that he could not win reelection except by discussing the issues in detail?

2. Physicians' conduct was subjected to regular examination by review boards for type 1 errors (calling healthy people ill) and to penalties (fines, censure, etc.) for errors of either type?

3. The President of XYZ Corporation had to choose between *(a)* spending $11 million for antipollution equipment, and *(b)* incurring a 50-50 chance of going to jail for five years?

Managers who complain that their workers are not motivated might do well to consider the possibility that they have installed reward systems which are paying off for behaviors other than those they are seeking. This, in part, is what happened in Vietnam, and this is what regularly frustrates societal efforts to bring about honest politicians, civic-minded managers, etc. This certainly is what happened in both the manufacturing and the insurance companies.

A first step for such managers might be to find out what behaviors currently are being rewarded. Perhaps an instrument similar to that used in the manufacturing firm could be useful for this purpose. Chances are excellent that these managers will be surprised by what they find—that their firms are not rewarding what they assume they are. In fact, such undesirable behavior by organizational members as they have observed may be explained larely by the reward systems in use.

This is not to say that all organizational behavior is determined by formal rewards and punishments. Certainly it is true that in the absence of formal reinforcement some soldiers will be patriotic, some presidents will be ecology-minded, and some orphanage directors will care about children. The point, however, is that in such cases the rewarder is not *causing* the behaviors desired but is only a fortunate bystander. For an organization to *act* upon its members, the formal reward system should positively reinforce desired behaviors, not constitute an obstacle to be overcome.

It might be wise to underscore the obvious fact that there is nothing really new in what has been said. In both theory and practice these matters have been mentioned before. Thus in many states Good Samaritan laws have been installed to protect doctors who stop to assist a stricken motorist. In states without such laws it is commonplace for doctors to refuse to stop, for fear of involvement in a subsequent lawsuit. In college basketball additional penalties have been instituted against players who foul their opponents deliberately. It has long been argued by Milton Friedman and others that penalties should be altered so as to make it irrational to disobey the ecology laws, and so on.

By altering the reward system the organization escapes the necessity of selecting only desirable people or of trying to alter undesirable ones. In Skinnerian terms (as described in 11, p. 704), "As for responsibility and goodness—as commonly defined—no one . . . would want or need them. They refer to a man's behaving well despite the absence of positive reinforcement that is obviously sufficient to explain it. Where such reinforcement exists, 'no one needs goodness.' "

REFERENCES

1. Barnard, Chester I. *The functions of the executive.* Cambridge, Mass.: Harvard University Press, 1964.

2. Blau, Peter M., & Scott, W. Richard. *Formal organizations.* San Francisco: Chandler, 1962.

3. Fiedler, Fred E. Predicting the effects of leadership training and experience from the contingency model. *Journal of Applied Psychology,* 1972, *56,* 114-119.

4. Garland, L.H. Studies of the accuracy of diagnostic procedures. *American Journal Roentgenological, Radium Therapy Nuclear Medicine,* 1959, *82,* 25-38.

5. Kerr, Steven. Some modifications in MBO as an OD strategy. *Academy of Management Proceedings,* 1973, pp. 39-42.

6. Kerr, Steven. What price objectivity? *American Sociologist,* 1973, *8,* 92-93.

7. Litwin, G.H., & Stringer, R.A., Jr. *Motivation and organizational climate,* Boston: Harvard University Press, 1968.

8. Perrow, Charles. The analysis of goals in complex organizations. In A. Etzioni (Ed.), *Readings on Modern Organizations.* Englewood Cliffs, N.J.: Prentice-Hall, 1969.

9. Scheff, Thomas J. Decision rules, types of error, and their consequences in medical diagnosis. In F. Massarik & P. Ratoosh (Eds.), *Mathematical Explorations in Behavioral Science.* Homewood, Ill.: Irwin, 1965.

10. Simon, Herbert A. *Administrative behavior.* New York: Free Press, 1957.

11. Swanson, G.E. Review symposium: Beyond freedom and dignity. *American Journal of Sociology,* 1972, *78,* 702-705.

12. Webster, E. *Decision making in the employment interview.* Montreal: Industrial Relations Center, McGill University, 1964.

CHAPTER 12

Using The Carrot Or The Stick?

Many managers act as though they believe that the cost of labor is a necessary evil associated with operating an organization. Indeed, labor costs for most organizations are absolutely staggering, as the data presented in table 12-1 indicate. But when it comes to discussing or doing something about the cost of labor, most managers tend to be somewhat narrow-minded. The prevalent notion seems to be "Hold down labor cost, regardless of the cost." Such thinking frequently becomes apparent at the collective bargaining table. Management focuses all its energy on negotiating the smallest possible wage increase while ignoring the question of how wages ought to be distributed.

As we noted in the preceding two chapters, an employee's motivation to produce is largely determined by the link between job performance and the outcomes that are valued. If the employee sees improved job performance as the avenue to earning more money, then the employee is likely to be motivated to increase his or her productivity. On the other hand, if the employee feels that pay increases are not linked to performance (for example, are determined by seniority), then money probably won't exhibit any motivational properties. Thus, to negotiate with a union for a minimum wage increase without negotiating the bases for earning the increase in wages is foolhardy.

This chapter begins by examining more closely the use of rewards (the "carrot") as a motivational device. Next, we will consider an alternative to rewards, punishment (the "stick"). Finally, we will introduce a theoretical model, *operant learning theory,* that offers a sound framework for the manager to use in designing effective compensation systems.

FIRM	LABOR COST (IN MILLIONS)	COST OF GOODS SOLD (IN MILLIONS)	LABOR COST/ COST OF GOODS SOLD
American Motors Corp.	$55.9	$212.2	26.5%
Boeing Aircraft Co.	122.2	356.4	32.3
Campbell Soup Co.	34.5	117.6	29.3
Chrysler Corp.	274.0	1099.0	24.9
Deere, Inc.	102.0	222.0	45.9
Exxon	269.4	3098.2	8.7
General Motors Corp.	1214.6	3110.0	39.1
McGraw-Hill, Inc.	15.5	26.2	59.0

TABLE 12-1
Selected Labor Costs and Costs of Goods Sold

MONEY AS A MOTIVATOR

Money may be viewed as an instrument for satisfying a variety of human needs. Because money is valued by the vast majority of people, it can be used effectively to motivate specific job behaviors. Surprisingly, though, the notion that money can be a motivator runs counter to some well-known theories of motivation. For instance, Herzberg (1968), in his two-factor theory, explicitly argues that money is not a motivator; because of Herzberg's position toward money and for a number of other reasons discussed in chapter 7, we should view the two-factor theory with some skepticism.

Given that money can motivate, what is the most effective way to use money to improve employee performance? According to the expectancy theory framework (discussed in chapter 10), the most important rule to follow in designing a compensation system is to insure that pay is tied to performance. For money to motivate, the employee must feel that performing at a higher level will earn him or her more pay. There are many techniques for linking pay to performance. Broadly speaking, one can group these techniques into three categories: individual, group, and organizational.[1]

Individual pay plans

Individual pay plans determine the level of an employee's pay partly on the basis of that employee's level of job performance. Salespersons who earn a commission on their sales, factory workers who are paid an incentive for producing above some standard, and professional employees who can earn year-end merit or bonus payments for their exceptional performance are all examples of persons working under an individual pay plan. Obviously, the installation of an individual pay plan requires an accurate measure of individual performance. But such measures aren't always so easy to achieve. For instance, take three scientists jointly working together in the same labo-

[1]The material to follow is drawn in part from Lawler (1971).

ratory on developing new personal care products. How would you separate and measure the contribution of each scientist to the discovery of a perfumed nasal decongestant? When they are feasible, however, individual pay plans work much better than group or organizational pay plans because employees perceive a much greater degree of association between their job performance and their pay and are, therefore, more motivated.

Group pay plans

Group pay plans determine the level of an employee's pay partly on the basis of the performance of the work group to which he or she belongs. Take, for example, our three research scientists. The vice president of research and development determines that the group should receive a bonus of $12,000 for its discovery, and each scientist should receive $4,000 as his or her share. This would constitute a group incentive. Group pay plans are becoming more and more prevalent in industry as the use of teams and autonomous work groups becomes more common. Because group plans somewhat blur the link between individual performance and pay, however, they should be used only in a limited number of situations. If either or both of the following conditions are met, then a group pay plan would be advisable:

1. Individual performance cannot be separated from group performance.
2. Cooperation among group members is imperative.

If the outputs of each group member become the inputs for the other group members,[2] then the need for cooperation would typically meet the level where a group compensation plan is warranted. An example of a work group with such interdependencies would be a unit consisting of people responsible for both production *and* maintenance. The output of the maintenance personnel is an input for production personnel in the form of usable production equipment; and the output (or by-product) of the production personnel is an input for maintenance in the form of equipment that needs servicing. Again, the work group must contain both production and maintenance personnel. If the group consisted only of production people or only maintenance people, the need for cooperation would be greatly reduced.

If there is a great need for cooperation among group members but individual performance can be separated from group performance, then the manager may want to use a combination of individual and group-pay plans. Individual performance in terms of the quantity and quality of units produced could be directly compensated; and

[2]Thompson (1967) has labeled this type of group-member interdependence "reciprocal interdependence."

group members, in addition, could share in a group bonus that depends upon group output. Such a pay scheme would simultaneously motivate individual productivity and encourage cooperation among group members.

Organizational pay plans

Organizational pay plans determine the level of en employee's pay partly on the basis of the performance of the entire organization or a major subunit of the organization. The most frequently talked-about type of organizational pay plan is profit sharing. When the profits of a major subunit, rather than the profits of the entire organization, are used to determine the share (or incentive pay) for the members of that subunit, the subunit is often called a *profit center*. For example, an international electrical contracting firm is organized into several geographical regions: each region is treated as a profit center; and the compensation of each regional manager is, in large part, a function of his or her subunit's profits.

The major problem with organizational pay plans is that the employee rarely has direct control over any meaningful portion of the organization's or subunit's performance. Thus, as is frequently the case with group pay plans, the employee sees no clear-cut link between his or her efforts and the rewards he or she receives. Therefore, the motivational potential of most organizational pay plans is dubious. For instance, after completing a number of years of service, the sales personnel of a large retail organization are allowed to par-

When a team of research scientists are working to solve the same problem, it is often difficult to judge individual performances and a group pay plan may be advisable.

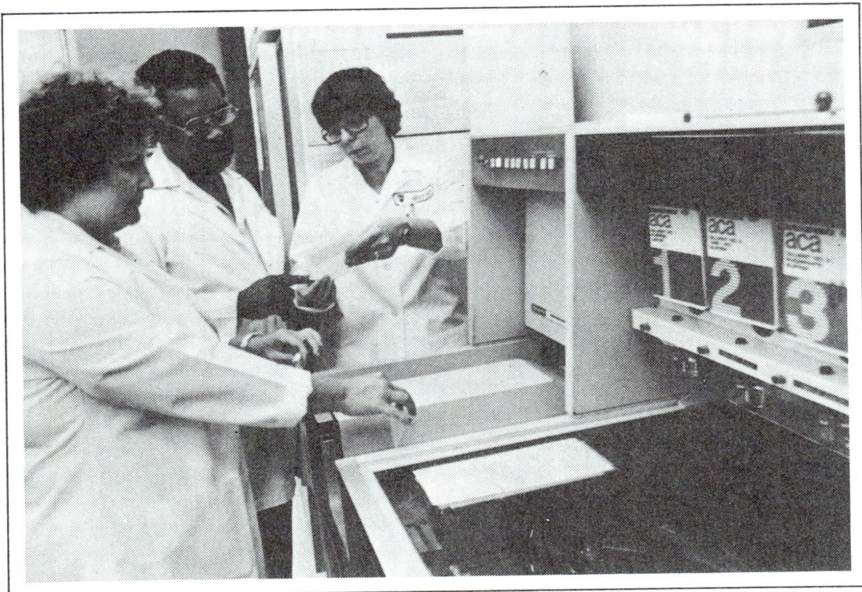

ticipate in the firm's profit-sharing plan. It is doubtful, however, that a sales clerk working in the hardware department of the firm's Iowa City outlet will see any meaningful association between his sales volume and the $90,000,000 in profits of the firm that are the basis for determining his level of incentive pay. In particular, the sales clerk may recognize that his contribution to organizational performance is constrained by the general level of consumer demand for hardware in his local area, the number of competitors in the town, the product mix purchased by the store's buyer, and the location of the hardware department relative to the flow of traffic through the store, as well as a host of other factors essentially beyond his control.

A counterargument in favor of organizational pay plans, particularly for the managers of profit centers, is that even though the employee does not have complete control over organizational performance, he or she is responsible for that performance; and the profit center manager is held accountable for his or her organization's or subunit's productivity, cost effectiveness, and/or profits. If some standard of performance—based upon, say, a reasonable estimate of projected profits—is used to determine the level of incentive pay (rather than simply using the absolute level of performance), then this counterargument would seem to be reasonable. The standard of performance used would take into consideration constraints on performance we discussed earlier.

Individual pay plans are recommended

In the last analysis, individual pay plans are recommended over group or organizational pay plans for most employees for two reasons.

1. Individual pay plans have a greater motivational potential than either group or organizational pay plans because individual pay plans more closely tie pay to individual performance. Employees who see improved job performance as the avenue to earning more money are more motivated than are those who do not see a clear-cut link between their performance and their pay.

2. Employees who work under an individual pay plan are generally more satisfied with their pay than are those working under a group or organizational plan.

In addition, under an individual plan, low-performing employees earn less money than high-performing employees, are relatively dissatisfied with their lower level of pay, and are, therefore, more likely to leave the organization voluntarily. Thus, individual pay plans center on job dissatisfaction and turnover among the organization's weakest group of employees, and that is exactly where a good manager wants them centered. Employees are generally happier with individual pay plans because they feel they are being treated equitably by the organization. People who feel they are getting as much out of their jobs as they are putting into them and who also feel others are being treated in the same fashion will report being equitably treated. Conversely, people who think they are getting less out of their jobs than they are putting into them or who feel others are getting a bigger payoff for the same amount of inputs will report being unfairly treated. As we pointed out earlier, J. Stacy Adams has developed a theoretical model around these notions, demonstrating that feelings of inequity generate tension within the employee, and this tension may drive the employee to alter his or her inputs to the job.

Potential problems with individual pay plans

Even though individual pay plans are the recommended approach to employee compensation, the manager should be aware of some of the problems individual pay plans may generate and how to cope with these problems. First, the pool of money available to a group of employees in many organizations is a fixed sum and *not* dependent upon the group's performance. This is not typically a problem for production-line employees working under a piece-rate system, for salespersons working under a commission system, or for other groups of employees who draw their incentive pay from a pool of money that expands with performance. But for employees working under a merit pay plan, for example, where the pool of money available for individual pay incentives is fixed by some formal budgetary process excessive competition may arise for a greater share of this fixed pool.

For example, Professor Newton is a distinguished member of State University's physics department. Her annual pay raise is partially determined by the number and quality of scholarly journal articles she publishes during the year. For the current year, the state legislature, which controls the university budget, has appropriated enough funds to allow for an average pay increase of 6 percent. Thus, for Professor Newton's department of ten faculty members and a payroll of $200,000, $12,000 are available to the department's chairperson to divide among the ten faculty members for their annual raises. Professor Newton knows that the more her colleagues publish, the less merit pay is available to her; so she is cautious about how much she assists and cooperates with her colleagues to boost their publication records. Thus, you can see how individual pay plans that draw from a fixed pool of money can diminish group effort and generate harmful levels of competition among employees vying for a larger share of the pool.

A manager can combat this competition in two ways. He or she can plead for a budgetary process that allows for his or her subordinate's job performance to be the major factor determining the pool of incentive pay available. Or he or she can specify that cooperation with one's peers is one dimension of performance that will be used to ascertain an employee's incentive pay. Clearly, neither solution is ideal; but, given the politics of most budgetary processes, the latter solution generally will prove to be the most useful.

Second, even though the manager *actually* has installed an equitable individual pay plan—that is, performance is accurately measured and the level of rewards matches the contribution of the employee—employees may not *perceive* the pay plan to be fair. If the employee does not have faith in how performance is measured or in how dollar increases are tied to performance, the employee's trust in management will diminish. Management can solve this problem by behaving honestly and openly. This means removing the veil of secrecy surrounding many compensation systems. Managers should communicate, directly and repeatedly, to their employees how, when, and by whom performance is measured. Also, they should explain why these procedures are used. Having employees participate in the development of their own performance appraisal systems is a good way to ensure that this information is clearly communicated. In addition, managers should tell employees how these appraisals are translated into dollars. Finally and without violating the privacy of any individual employee, managers should openly specify the performance ratings achieved by their employees and the pay increases those ratings earned. Presumably, the only reason a manager is not candid about a compensation system is fear that the system will not be perceived as equitable. But, in fact, employees are much more comfortable with open, rather than secret, pay plans, assuming, of course, that the pay plan is fair.

The third problem an individual pay plan may generate is increased administrative cost. Simply, it costs more to measure, record, and compensate individual performance than it does to give everybody the same percentage pay increase. These increased costs can't be avoided. Rather, the manager must ensure that the administrative cost of an individual pay plan doesn't outweigh the motivational benefits it generates. The best way to do this is to keep paper work down to a minimum. Don't generate a lot of useless forms for bookkeeping purposes; and, if a large enough number of employees are covered by the plan, consider a computer for information storage and retrieval.

Since individual pay plans motivate employees to engage in those job behaviors that are rewarded, it is crucial to specify which dimensions of performance will be used to determine an employee's pay increment. In other words, employees under an individual pay plan will direct their efforts to those aspects of their jobs for which they are financially rewarded, and they will tend to ignore those activities with no personal payoff.

For example, Tom, a property insurance salesperson, works under a straight commission plan whereby his pay is solely a function of how many dollars in premiums he generates. Because this pay plan ignores the risk associated with the policies he writes, most of the business Tom generates for the firm tends to be from neighborhoods with high risks of fire, theft, and vandalism. Of course, the firm's underwriting department rejects a lot of Tom's business. All in all, however, the policies Tom has written for the firm have been costly in terms of the losses they have incurred. If Tom was compensated on the basis of how many premium dollars he generates *and* how few claims his clients file, then his sales strategy would most assuredly take into account the risk factor. Managers, therefore, must try to gauge and reward most of those job behaviors that contribute to organizational effectiveness. Of course, rare and unpredictable behaviors can't be formally included in the system, but these infrequent behaviors can be rewarded on an *ad hoc* basis.

Fifth, individual pay plans require managers to provide each of their subordinates with information regarding their performance. The weakest form of this type of feedback is the employee's paycheck. In other words, the only solid information some employees receive from their superiors about the level of their performance is conveyed by the size of their paycheck. But a paycheck doesn't tell an employee what he or she is doing well on the job or in what areas improvement is needed. Face-to-face interaction between superior and subordinate is required to communicate this essential type of information. Many managers avoid such interactions because they dislike looking someone in the eye and saying boldly that performance is below par or because they assume good performers know they are good and don't need to be told. Numerous research studies clearly show that most subordinates are not really aware of what their superiors think of them.[3] So the effective administration of individual pay plans requires managers to "tell it like it is" to their subordinates. Thus, managers who fear performance feedback sessions with their subordinates must take the necessary steps to overcome this apprehension. Probably the first thing managers should do is build up confidence in their ability to counsel underachieving employees. M. Jane Kay (1977), manager of employee relations at Detroit Edison, provides a useful overview of the employee counseling process. For example, she suggests putting the employee at ease by establishing a pleasant atmosphere. Convey interest and attention by using such phrases as "I see," "I understand," "Tell me more," or by nodding and smiling. Don't rush in during pauses; instead, use them to indicate that you want the employee to continue talking. Kay and other experienced counselers provide many useful suggestions to the manager inexperienced in employee counseling, a skill that is closely related to administering an individual pay plan.

The final problem managers must face in establishing an individual pay plan is determining how much of a pay increase to award for a given level of performance. Too large an increase is a waste of the organization's financial resources and too small an increase won't foster motivation and may induce undesirable levels of inequity. Let's assume that the manager of a merit pay plan has evaluated her ten subordinates and gauged these evaluations on a 100-point scale, such as that shown in table 12-2: 0 represents very poor performance; 25, poor; 50, average; 75, above average; and 100, outstanding. The manager decides that the poor performances of employees A

[3]See Brief, Aldag, and VanSell (1977) for a discussion of this literature.

TABLE 12-2
Hypothetical Evaluations and Merit Pay Increases

EMPLOYEE	EVALUATION	MERIT PAY INCREASE*
A	16	0%
B	24	0
C	49	5
D	50	5
E	51	5
F	53	5
G	71	10
H	72	10
I	74	10
J	92	20

*Given as a percent of current pay

and B do not deserve any merit pay increase. The average performances of employees C, D, E, and F should earn them a low increase of 5 percent. Employees G, H, and I will receive 10 percent increases. And employee J clearly has earned a 20 percent increase for her outstanding performance. Did the manager do the right thing? This is a difficult question to answer. If she previously has given similar percentage pay increases for similar levels of performance *and* these increases have produced the motivational effects she wanted, then she probably has done the right thing.

If employees know what to expect for their performances and if, over the long haul, the pay increases distributed tended to encourage low performers to increase their efforts and high performers to maintain their output, then a manager can be satisfied that he or she has done an adequate job in allocating rewards. In other words, consistency and close monitoring of the effects of pay are the only ways to ensure that an individual pay plan is being properly administered. It is important to remember, however, that higher performers should receive greater increases than low performers and that these differences in rewards should be meaningful to the employee.

In sum, individual pay plans work because they provide managers with a tool for effectively directing the behavior of their subordinates. Such pay plans can, however, present a host of problems; but the informed and sensitive manager can, with care, avoid or overcome these problems.

PUNISHMENT: WHAT IS IT ALL ABOUT?

Sam, an industrial salesperson, works for a firm that compensates its salespersons on a straight commission basis. For every dollar in sales revenue Sam generates, he earns ten cents. Last year Sam sold $200,000 of goods and earned $20,000. Was Sam punished by not earning $25,000 because he did not sell $250,000 worth of goods? Of course not; however, some people view withholding an unearned reward as a form of punishment. For example, a manager who chooses not to award a merit pay increase to an employee may think he or she is punishing that employee; and, in fact, under certain circumstances, the employee may feel he or she is being punished. A more positive and accurate view would be that the employee had not *earned* the merit increase. Employees who feel punished for not receiving an unearned pay increase are those who historically have received a pay increase *regardless* of their performance. They have become used to being rewarded merely for being a member of the organization. Thus, to prevent an employee from feeling he or she was punished when an unearned reward was withheld, the employee must be made aware, through the consistent actions of management, that rewards are earned for specific job behaviors and are not just doled out at random.

If punishment is not withholding an unearned reward, then what is it? *Punishment* is an outcome following an undesired job behavior that should cause the employee to reduce the occurrence of that behavior. At a minimum, punishment causes the employee to feel some level of discomfort. The most frequently used form of punishment in work organizations is verbal abuse by the employee's immediate superior. For example, a manager yells at, threatens, or otherwise insults an employee who is late to work or who makes an error on an important project or whose productivity is below par.

Does punishment work? In other words, can a manager reduce the occurrence of undesired job behavior by verbally abusing his or her subordinates? The answer to this difficult question is yes if the manager provides close supervision and continuously monitors his or her subordinates. The answer is no if the manager cannot continuously observe the activities of his or her subordinates. In other words, the use of punishment produces public compliance but not private acceptance of the manager's authority. Managers who frequently use punishment generally can expect their subordinates to follow their orders only when they are present and only when their subordinates think they will get caught if they violate the manager's rules. Thus, for the managers whose style is not to provide close supervision or who cannot physically be present on an ongoing basis, the use of verbal punishment is neither advisable nor effective.

Furthermore, heavy reliance on punishment embitters the employee. This embitterment has two negative consequences. First, an employee who is not satisfied with his or her supervisor and who has other employment opportunities is likely to leave the organization. Second, the manager who is personally disliked by his or her subordinates because of reliance on punishment will find it difficult to use verbal praise as a reward for good performance. For example, Florence is a staff nurse for a large community hospital. Her boss, Minnie, constantly yells at her for the slightest deviation from hospital procedures. To Florence's surprise, Minnie one day pats Florence on the back and tells her how proud she is of the way she handled a particularly difficult patient. Florence's understandable response to this unusual verbal praise is "So what?" Florence finds it very difficult to care what Minnie thinks of her performance because Minnie's punishing style has caused Florence to lose all respect for her supervisor.

Finally, many managers find it difficult to punish their subordinates overtly. It is just not part of their psychological make-up to be openly abusive of anyone. So if punishment only leads to public compliance, embitters the employee, and makes the supervisor feel uncomfortable, why should a manager adopt a punishing style? The obvious answer is that he or she shouldn't. But this does not mean that the use of punishment has no place in work organizations. Of course, certain very serious employee behaviors (e.g., theft) warrant strong deterrent action by management.

The use of punishment prevails in many areas of our society. Think, for instance, of parent-child, husband-wife, and employee-employer relationships. Therefore, it is not easy to devise alternatives to the use of punishment. Essentially, it is a matter of choosing between the use of punishment or rewards. If a manager considers a specific behavior undesirable, he or she probably will opt for the use of punishment. On the other hand, if the manager interprets the same behavioral problem as the lack of a desirable response on the part of the employee, he or she probably will offer some reward to change the employee's behavior.

For example, a large governmental agency provides its employees with one day of paid sick-leave per month. Approximately 300 of the agency's 500 employees choose to take their sick leave each and every month. The agency director realizes that many of his employees view the agency's sick-leave policy as an add-on to their vacation. Furthermore, the average sick-day costs the agency $50 in salary and fringe benefits, for a total annual cost of $180,000 in taxpayer dollars. The director can regard unwarranted sick-leave as undesired behavior, or he can view the employee being on the job each and every workday as a desirable behavior. If he views the former situation as undesired behavior, he probably will establish some form of punishment for those employees caught abusing their sick-leave privileges. Conversely, if he says, "I need to do something to encourage each of my employees to be at work as expected," he most likely will establish a system to reward good attendance.

Many persons respond negatively to rewarding a behavior such as attendance. They say, "An employee is supposed to show up for work every day and shouldn't get anything extra for doing something we're all supposed to do." These people are imposing their personal values on the management of the organization—a hard thing not to do. However, the manager who wants to honorably discharge his or her responsibilities to the organization will ask, "How can I best enhance the effectiveness of this organization?" Going back to the governmental agency example, the director correctly chose to reward attendance rather than merely to punish absenteeism. He installed a system whereby each employee who did not miss a day of work during the month earned the chance to win a day and a half off from work with pay. Each month, twenty-five chance holders were randomly selected as winners. The program cost the agency $22,500 per year and cut sick-leave costs by $90,000; thus, the director saved the organization $67,500 a year.

In sum, using rewards to encourage desired employee behaviors is generally a more advisable strategy than using punishment to reduce undesired behaviors. Clearly, the use of rewards generally requires a degree of creativity on the part of the manager. Operant theory, which we will discuss next, can provide a wealth of suggestions to managers who want to capitalize on the use of rewards in their organizations.

OPERANT THEORY: AN EFFECTIVE MANAGEMENT TOOL

All the motivational theories that we have discussed so far rely upon the thoughts, feelings, and emotions of the employee to explain job performance. Operant theory does not. Operant theorists largely ignore the internal workings of people; instead, they examine the behavior of persons and the interactions between persons and their environments for keys to influencing an employee's job performance. More precisely, operant theorists argue that the consequences of an employee's behavior determine the likelihood of that behavior occurring in the future. Thus, examination of a behavior and its consequences without probing the mind of the worker is felt to be sufficient to identify how the manager might go about gaining control over the behavior.

Certain types of consequences or contingencies (for example, positive reinforcement or escape learning) can be used to increase the occurrence of a desired behavior; and other types of contingencies (for example, extinction or punishment) can be used to decrease the occurrence of an undesired behavior. In the following chapter, Hamner and Hamner will discuss various types of contingencies and how they can be and have been used in work organizations. The remainder of this discussion will focus on some obstacles managers frequently encounter when using operant techniques.

The most frequently talked-about application of operant techniques in work organizations is *behavior modification*. The essential steps in implementing a behavior modification program include (1) identifying and specifying the target behavior and when that behavior occurs, (2) identifying the environmental consequences of the target behavior, and (3) modifying those consequences according to the principles of operant theory in order to change the target behavior in the desired manner. The biggest problem a manager may encounter in attempting to implement a behavior modification program is the charge that the use of behavior modification is somehow unethical. This condemnation stems from at least three sources.

First, numerous newspaper and magazine articles have appeared recently about the supposed misuses of behavior modification in our nation's prisons and mental institutions. Some of these stories are grounded in fact; others reflect the uninformed biases of their authors. Nevertheless, behavior modification is a frequently used strategy to change the so-called deviant behaviors of institutionalized persons. Thus, some "normal" persons think of behavior modification as a tool to deal with "sick" people and not as something applicable to healthy members of work organizations. It is also true, however, that behavior modification is now being used to tackle a host of normal, everyday problems we all encounter. For example, Nathan H. Azrin and Richard M. Foxx (1974) recently wrote a book, titled *Toilet Training in Less Than a Day*, in which they spell out a behavior modification program for toilet training toddlers. The program was developed for use with institutionalized retarded persons, but Azrin and Foxx report the results of a study conducted to evaluate the program among 200 noninstitutionalized children. The average child was trained in *less than four hours* to use the toilet without assistance or a reminder. A result like this is absolutely astonishing to any parent who has been through the toilet-training ordeal and serves to demonstrate how useful behavior modification techniques can be when applied to so-called normal populations.

The second reason some people consider the use of behavior modification to be unethical is rooted in the works of the eminent Harvard psychologist, B.F. Skinner. Skinner is an outspoken advocate of the application of operant principles and has written numerous works on the subject. In his book *Beyond Freedom and Dignity*, he argues that because the use of the concepts of "freedom" and "dignity" are dysfunctional for society, their use should be curtailed. As you can imagine, such a position, particularly among humanists, has generated a lot of controversy, as well as criticism of Skinner and operant theory. Few critics, however, have closely examined the logic behind Skinner's position. Essentially, Skinner believes that behavior is regulated by its environmental consequences and, as such, is controlled. Believing that one is truly free prohibits close investigation of one's environment in order to identify those environmental consequences that actually control behavior. Without identifying these consequences, one cannot take the steps necessary to gain a higher level of personal autonomy.

A final reason people oppose behavior modification programs concerns the issue of bribery. As is the case with most individual pay plans, some persons view the positive reinforcement of a desired employee behavior as a form of bribery and, therefore, as unethical. In reality, however, compensating an employee for effectively performing his or her organizational role is just plain good management.

Besides being labeled "unethical," because of his or her advocacy of behavior modification, a manager may face other obstacles when implementing a behavior modification program. These involve specifying and measuring the employee behaviors desired, as well as gaining control over the consequences of those behaviors. These problems, however, are encountered in implementing virtually any effective reward system and are hardly unique to behavior modification.

SUMMARY

Money can serve as a vehicle for satisfying a variety of employee needs, including existence, relatedness, and growth needs. Money, therefore, is valued by most employees for a number of different reasons and, when appropriately used, can motivate effective job performance.

The appropriate use of money requires that it be directly linked to job performance. Individual, group, and organizational pay plans are different ways of tying pay to performance. Because individual pay plans tie an employee's pay more closely to his or her performance, they generally are recommended over either group or organizational pay plans. Group pay plans are advisable, however, when individual performance cannot be separated from group performance and/or when cooperation among group members is imperative. In general, organizational pay plans are not recommended.

Individual pay plans, however, are not trouble-free. They can (1) generate harmful levels of competition among employees, (2) lower employee trust in management, (3) increase administrative costs, (4) cause employees to ignore those aspects of their jobs not directly compensated, (5) require managers to feed back negative information to their subordinates, and (6) require managers to determine the appropriate level of pay for a given level of performance. The manager can and must cope with each of these potential difficulties.

Punishment is an outcome following an undesired job behavior that causes the employee to reduce the occurrence of that behavior. Punishment produces public compliance with but not private acceptance of the manager's authority. Punishment embitters the employee who is punished. Many managers find it difficult to punish their subordinates overtly. For these reasons, heavy reliance on the use of punishment is not recommended.

Operant theory largely ignores the internal workings of people; rather, the behavior of persons and the interactions between persons and their environments are considered the keys to influencing an employee's job performance. Behavior modification, an application of operant theory to change employee behavior, often encounters resistance. This resistance is due to the negative coverage behavior modification has received in the popular press, misinterpretations of the works of the noted operant theorist, B.F. Skinner, and the view that behavior modification is a form of bribery. The well-informed manager can overcome each of these charges, however. The following chapter explains how work organizations can use behavior modification successfully.

REFERENCES

Adams, J.S. "Inequity in Social Exchange." In *Advances in Experimental Social Psychology*, edited by L. Berkowitz. New York: Academic Press, 1965.

Alderfer, C.P. *Existence, Relatedness, and Growth*. New York: Free Press, 1972.

Azrin, N.H., and Foxx, R.M. *Toilet Training in Less Than a Day*. New

York: Simon and Schuster, 1974.

Brief, A.P.; Aldag, R.J.; and VanSell, M. "Moderators of the Relationships between Self and Superior Evaluations of Job Performance." *Journal of Occupational Psychology 50* (1977): 129-34.

Herzberg, F. "One More Time: How Do You Motivate Employees?" *Harvard Business Review 46* (1968): 53-62.

Kay, M. Jane. "Employee Counseling." In *Training and Development*, edited by D. Yoder and H.G. Heneman, Jr. Washington, D.C.: Bureau of National Affairs, Inc., 1977.

Lawler, E.E., III. *Pay and Organizational Effectiveness*. New York: McGraw-Hill, 1971.

Skinner, B.F. *Beyond Freedom and Dignity*. New York: Alfred A. Knopf, 1971.

Thompson, J.D. *Organizations in Action*. New York: McGraw-Hill, 1967.

SUGGESTIONS FOR ADVANCED READINGS

Belcher, D.W. *Compensation Administration*. Englewood Cliffs, N.J.: Prentice-Hall, 1974.

Hamner, W.C. "Reinforcement Theory and Contingency Management in Organizational Settings." In *Organizational Behavior and Management: A Contingency Approach*. edited by H.L. Tosi and W.C. Hamner. Chicago: St. Clair Press, 1974.

Jaques, E. *Equitable Payment*. New York: Wiley, 1961.

Lawler, E.E., III. "Equity Theory As a Predictor of Productivity and Work Quality." *Psychological Bulletin 70* (1968): 596-610

Luthans, F., and Kreitner, R. *Organizational Behavior Modification*. Glenview, Ill.: Scott, Foresman, 1975.

Nord, W. "Beyond the Teaching Machine: The Neglected Area of Operant Conditioning in the Theory and Practice of Management." *Organizational Behavior and Human Performance 4* (1969): 375-401.

Patchen, M. *The Choice of Wage Comparisons*. Englewood Cliffs, N.J.: Prentice-Hall, 1961.

Skinner, B.F. "Behaviorism at Fifty." *Science 134* (1963a): 566-602.

Skinner, B.F. "Operant Behavior." *American Psychologist 18* (1963b): 503-515.

Skinner, B.F. *Contingencies of Reinforcement*. New York: Appleton-Century-Crofts, 1969.

Skinner, B.F. *About Behaviorism*. New York: Alfred A Knopf. 1974.

CHAPTER 13

Behavior Modification On The Bottom Line*

It may be easy to say *what* a manager does. Telling *how* he influences the behavior of the employee in the direction of task accomplishment is far more difficult to comprehend and describe. The purpose of this article is to describe and spell out the determinants of employee productivity or performance from a reinforcement theory point of view, and to show how managing the contingencies of positive reinforcement in organizational settings leads to successful management. We hope these descriptions will enable the manager to understand how his or her behavior affects the behavior of subordinates and to see that, in many cases, a worker's failure to perform a task properly is a direct outcome of the manager's own behavior. The employee has failed to perform because the manager has failed to motivate.

MANAGING THE CONTINGENCIES OF REINFORCEMENT

The interrelationship among three components—work environment, task performance, and consequences of reinforcements—are known as the contingencies of reinforcement. The reward that is contingent upon good performance in a given work situation (environment) acts as a motivator for future performance. The manager controls the *work environment* (Where am I going? What are the goals? Is the leader supportive? Is this a pleasant place to work?), the *task assignment* (How will I get there? What behavior is desired? What is

*Reprinted, by permission of the publisher, from W. Clay Hamner, and Ellen P. Hamner, "Behavior Modification on The Bottom Line," *Organizational Dynamics*, Spring 1976, © 1976 by AMACOM, a division of American Management Associations.

considered appropriate performance?), and the *consequences* of job performance (How will I know when I've reached the desired goal? Is the feedback relevant and timely? Is my pay based upon my performance?). By shaping these three components of behavior so that all are positive, the manager can go a long way toward creating a work climate that supports high productivity.

ARRANGING THE CONTINGENCIES OF REINFORCEMENT

Someone who expects to influence behavior must be able to manipulate the consequences of behavior. Whether managers realize it or not, they constantly shape the behavior of their subordinates by the way they utilize the rewards at their disposal. Employers intuitively use rewards all the time—but their efforts often produce limited results because the methods are used improperly, inconsistently, or inefficiently. In many instances employees are given rewards that are not conditional or contingent on the behavior the manager wishes to promote. Even when they are, long delays often intervene between the occurrence of the desired behavior and its intended consequences. Special privileges, activities, and rewards are often furnished according to length of service rather than performance requirements. In many cases, positive reinforcers are inadvertently made contingent upon the wrong kind of behavior. In short, intuition provides a poor guide to motivation.

A primary reason managers fail to "motivate" workers to perform in the desired manner is their failure to understand the power of the contingencies of reinforcement over the employee. The laws or principles for arranging the contingencies to condition behavior are not hard to understand; if properly applied, they constitute powerful managerial tools that can be used for increasing supervisory effectiveness.

Conditioning is the process by which behavior is modified through manipulation of the contingencies of behavior. To understand how this works, we will first look at various kinds of arrangements of the contingencies: *positive reinforcement* conditioning, *escape* conditioning, *extinction* conditioning, and *punishment* conditioning. The differences among these kinds of contingencies depend on the consequences that result from the behavioral act. Positive reinforcement and avoidance learning are methods of strengthening desired behavior, while extinction and punishment are methods of weakening undesired behavior.

Positive reinforcement

According to B.F. Skinner, a positive reinforcer or reward is a stimulus that, when added to a situation, strengthens the probability of the response in that situation. Behavior that appears to lead to a positive consequence tends to be repeated, while behavior that appears to lead to a negative consequence tends not be repeated.

Once it has been determined that a specific consequence has reward value to a work group, we can use it to increase that group's performance. Thus the first step in the successful application of reinforcement procedures is to select reinforcers that are sufficiently powerful and durable to establish and strengthen desired behavior. These could include such things as an interesting work assignment, the chance to use one's mind, seeing the results of one's work, good pay, recognition for a job well done, promotion, freedom to decide how to do a job, and so on.

The second step is to design the contingencies in such a way that the reinforcing events are made contingent on the desired level of performance. This is the rule of reinforcement most often violated. Rewards *must* result from performance—and the better an employee's performance is, the greater his or her rewards should be.

Unless a manager is willing to discriminate among employees on the basis of their performance levels, the effectiveness of his or her power over the employee is nil. For example, Edward E. Lawler III, a leading researcher on pay and performance, has noted that one of the major reasons managers are unhappy with their salary system is that they do not perceive the relationship between how hard they work (productivity) and how much thay earn. In a survey of 600 managers, Lawler found virtually no relationship between their pay and their rated level of performance.

The third step is to design the contingencies in such a way that a reliable procedure for eliciting or inducing the desired response patterns is established; when desired responses rarely occur, there are few opportunities to influence behavior through contingency management. Training programs, goal-setting programs and similar efforts should be undertaken to let workers know what is expected of them. If the criterion for reinforcement is unclear, unspecified or set too high, most—if not all—of the worker's responses go unrewarded; eventually his or her efforts will be extinguished.

Escape conditioning

The second kind of contingency arrangement available to the manager is called escape or avoidance conditioning. Just as with positive reinforcement, this is a method of strengthening desired behavior. A contingency arrangement in which an individual's performance can terminate a noxious environment is called escape learning. When behavior can prevent the onset of a noxious stimulus, the procedure is called avoidance learning.

An employee is given an unpleasant task assignment, for example, with the promise that when he completes it, he can move on (escape) to a more pleasant job. Or a manager is such an unpleasant person to be around that the employees work when he is present in order to "avoid" him.

Let's note the distinction between strengthening behavior through positive reinforcement techniques and doing so through avoidance learning techniques. In one case, the individual works hard to gain the consequences from the environment (provided by the manager in most cases) that result from good work, and in the second case, the individual works hard to avoid the negative aspects of the environment itself (again, the manager is the source). In both cases the same behavior is strengthened over the short run. In escape learning, however, the manager is more process-oriented; he or she must be present in order to elicit the desired level of performance. Under positive reinforcement, however, the manager is outcome-oriented and does not have to be physically present at all times in order to maintain the desired level of performance.

Extinction

When positive reinforcement for a learned or previously conditioned response is withheld, individuals will still continue to exhibit that behavior for an extended period of time. With repeated nonreinforcement, however, the behavior decreases and eventually disappears. This decline in response rate as a result of nonrewarded repetition of a task is defined as *extinction*.

This method, when combined with a positive reinforcement method, is the procedure of behavior modification recommended by Skinner. It leads to the fewest negative side effects. Using the two methods together allows employees to get the rewards they desire and allows the organization to eliminate the undesired behavior.

Punishment

Punishment is the most controversial method of behavior modification. Punishment is defined as presenting an aversive or noxious consequence contingent upon a response, or removing a positive consequence contingent upon a response. The Law of Effect operates here, too: As rewards strengthen behavior, punishment weakens it. Notice carefully the difference between withholding rewards in the punishment process and withholding rewards in the extinction process. In the extinction process, we withhold rewards for behavior that has previously been rewarded because the behavior was previously desired. In punishment, we withhold a reward because the behavior is undesired, has never been associated with the reward before, and is plainly an undesirable consequence.

RULES FOR USING OPERANT CONDITIONING TECHNIQUES

Rule 1. Don't give the same level of reward to all

Differentiate rewards based on performance in relation to defined objectives or standards. We know that people compare their performance with the performance of their peers to determine how well they are doing and that they compare their rewards with peer rewards to determine how to evaluate theirs. Some managers may think that the fairest compensation system is one in which everyone in the same job classification gets the same pay, but employees want differentiation as evidence of how important their services are to the organization. Managers who reward all people at the same level are simply encouraging, at most, only average performance. Behavior leading to high performance is being extinguished (ignored), while average and poor performance are being strengthened by means of positive reinforcement.

Rule 2. Failure to respond to behavior has reinforcing consequences

Managers who find the job of differentiating between workers so unpleasant or so difficult that they fail to respond to their behavior must recognize that failure to respond is itself a form of response that, in turn, modifies behavior. Superiors are bound to shape the behavior of their subordinates by the way in which they utilize the rewards at their disposal. Therefore, managers must be careful that they examine the consequences on performance of their nonactions as well as their actions.

Rule 3. Tell a person what behavior gets reinforced

By making clear to a worker the contingencies of reinforcement, a manager may actually be increasing his individual freedom. The employee who has a standard against which to measure his job will have a built-in feedback system that allows him or her to make judgments about his or her own level of performance. The awarding of reinforcements in an organization where workers' goals are specified will be associated with worker performance, not supervisory bias. The assumption is, of course, that the supervisor rates the employee accurately and then reinforces the employee according to his ratings. If the supervisor fails to rate accurately or administer rewards based on performance, then the worker will be forced to search for the "true" contingencies—that is, what behavior he or she should display in order to get rewarded (ingratiation? loyalty? positive attitude?).

Rule 4. Tell a person what he or she is doing wrong

As a general rule, very few people find failure rewarding. One assumption of behavior conditioning therefore is that a worker wants to be rewarded for positive accomplishments. A supervisor should never use extinction or punishment as the sole method for modifying behavior—but if one of these is used judiciously in conjunction with positive reinforcement techniques, such combined procedures can hasten the change process. If the supervisor fails to specify why a reward is being withheld, the employee may associate the withholding of the reward with past desired behavior instead of the behavior that the supervisor is trying to extinguish. Thus the supervisor extinguishes good performance while having no effect on the undesired behavior.

Rule 5. Don't punish in front of others

The reason for this rule is quite simple. The punishment (for example, a reprimand) should be enough to extinguish the undesired behavior. By administering the punishment in front of the work group, the worker is doubly punished; he also "loses face." This additional punishment may lead to negative side-effects in three ways. First, the worker whose self-image is damaged may feel that he must retaliate in order to protect himself. Therefore, the supervisor has actually increased undesired responses. Second, the work group may associate the punishment with another behavior of the worker and, through "avoidance learning" techniques, may modify their own behavior in ways not intended by the supervisor. Third, the work group is also being punished—in the sense that observing a member of their team being reprimanded is unpleasant to most people. This may result in lowered performance of the total work group.

Rule 6. Make the consequences equal to the behavior

In other words, don't cheat the worker out of his just rewards. If he is a good worker, tell him. Many supervisors find it very difficult to praise an employee. Others find it very difficult to counsel an employee about what he is doing wrong. When a manager fails to use these reinforcement tools, he is actually reducing his effectiveness. Overrewarding a worker may make him feel guilty and certainly reinforces his current performance level. If the performance level is lower than that of others who get the same reward, he has no reason to increase his output. When a worker is underrewarded, he becomes angry with the system. His behavior is being extinguished and the company may be forcing the good employee (underrewarded) to seek employment elsewhere while encouraging the poor employee (overrewarded) to stay on.

SETTING UP A POSITIVE REINFORCEMENT PROGRAM IN INDUSTRY

Many organizations are setting up formal motivational programs in an attempt to use the principles of positive reinforcement to increase employee productivity.

A positive reinforcement approach to management differs from traditional motivational theories in two basic ways. First, as noted above, a positive reinforcement program calls for the maximum use of reinforcement and the minimum use of punishment. Punishment tends to leave the individual feeling controlled and coerced. Second, a positive reinforcement program avoids psychological probing into the worker's attitudes as a possible cause of behavior. Instead, the work situation itself is analyzed, with the focus on the reward contingencies that cause a worker to act the way in which he does.

A positive reinforcement program, therefore, is results-oriented rather than process-oriented. Geary A. Rummler, president of Praxis

Corporation, a management consultant firm, claims that the motivational theories of such behavioral scientists as Herzberg and Maslow, which stress workers' psychological needs, are impractical. "They can't be made operative. While they help classify a problem, a positive reinforcement program leads to solutions."

Stages in program development

Positive reinforcement programs currently used in industry generally involve at least four stages. The *first stage,* according to Edward J. Feeney, formerly vice-president, systems, of Emery Air Freight Corporation, is to define the behavioral aspects of performance and do a performance audit. This step is potentially one of the most difficult, since some companies do not have a formal performance evaluation program, especially for nonmanagerial employees, and those that do have a program often rate the employee's behavior on nonjob related measures (such as friendliness, loyalty, cooperation, overall attitude, and so on). But once these behavioral aspects are defined, the task of convincing managers that improvement is needed and of persuading them to cooperate with such a program is simplified. Feeney asserts, "Most managers genuinely think that operations in their bailiwick are doing well; a performance audit that proves they're not comes as a real and unpleasant surprise."

The *second stage* in developing a working positive reinforcement program is to develop and set specific goals for each worker. Failure to specify concrete behavioral goals is a major reason many programs do not work. Goals should be expressed in such terms as "decreased employee turnover" or "schedules met" rather than only in terms of "better identification with the company" or "increased job satisfaction." The goals set, therefore, should be in the same terms as those defined in the performance audit, goals that specifically relate to the task at hand. Goals should be reasonable—that is, set somewhere between "where you are" (as spelled out in the performance audit) and some ideal.

While it is important for the manager to set goals, it is also important for the employee to accept them. An approach that tends to build in goal acceptance is to allow employees to work with management in setting work goals. According to John C. Emery, president of Emery Air Freight Corporation, the use of a participatory management technique to enlist the ideas of those performing the job not only results in their acceptance of goals, but also stimulates them to come up with goals.

The *third stage* in a positive reinforcement program is to allow the employee to keep a record of his or her own work. This process of self-feedback maintains a continuous schedule of reinforcement for the worker and helps him obtain intrinsic reinforcement from the task itself. Where employees can total their own results, they can see whether they are meeting their goals and whether they are improving over their previous performance level (as measured in the performance audit stage). In other words, the worker has two chances of being successful—either by beating his previous record or by beating both his previous record and his established goal. E.D. Grady, general manager—operator services for Michigan Bell, maintains that the manager should set up the work environment in such a way that people have a chance to succeed. One way to do this, he says, is to "shorten the success interval." Grady says, "If you're looking for success, keep shortening the interval of measurement so you can get a greater chance of success which you can latch on to for positive reinforcements." Instead of setting monthly or quarterly goals, for example, set weekly or daily goals.

The *fourth stage*—the most important step in a positive reinforcement program—is one that separates it from all other motivation plans. The supervisor looks at the self-feedback report of the employee and/or other indications of performance (sales records, for example) and then praises the positive aspects of the employee's performance (as determined by the performance audit and subsequent goal setting). This extrinsic reinforcement should strengthen the desired performance, while the withholding of praise for substandard performance should give the employee incentive to improve that performance level. Since the worker already knows the areas of his or her deficiencies, there is no reason for the supervisor to criticize the employee. In other words, negative feedback is self-induced, whereas positive feedback comes from both internal and external sources.

As noted previously, this approach to feedback follows the teachings of B.F. Skinner, who believes that use of positive reinforcement leads to a greater feeling of self-control, while the avoidance of negative reinforcement keeps the individual from feeling controlled or coerced. Skinner says, "You can get the same effect if the supervisor simply discovers things being done right and says something like 'Good, I see you're doing it the way that works best.' "

While the feedback initially used in step four of the positive reinforcement program is praise, it is important to note that other forms of reinforcement can have the same effect. M.W. Warren, the director of organization and management development at the Questor Corporation, says that the five "reinforcers" he find most effective are (1) money (but only when it is a consequence of a specific performance and when the relation to the performance is known); (2) praise or recognition; (3) freedom to choose one's own activity; (4) opportunity to see oneself become better, more important, or more useful; and (5) power to influence both co-workers and management. Warren states, "By building these reinforcers into programs at various facilities, Questor is getting results." The need for using more than praise after the positive reinforcement program has proved effective is discussed by Skinner.

> It does not cost the company anything to use praise rather than blame, but if the company then makes a great deal more money that way, the worker may seem to be getting gypped. However, the welfare of the worker depends on the welfare of the company, and if the company is smart enough

to distribute some of the fruits of positive reinforcement in the form of higher wages and better fringe benefits, everybody gains from the supervisor's use of positive reinforcements. (*Organizational Dynamics*, Winter, 1973, p. 35.)

EARLY RESULTS OF POSITIVE REINFORCEMENT PROGRAMS IN ORGANIZATIONS, 1969-1973

Companies that claimed to be implementing and using positive reinforcement programs such as the one described above include Emery Air Freight, Michigan Bell Telephone, Questor Corporation. Cole National Company in Cleveland, Ford Motor Company, American Can, Upjohn, United Air Lines, Warner-Lambert, Addressograph-Multigraph, Allis-Chalmers, Bethlehem Steel, Chase Manhattan Bank, IBM, IT&T, Proctor and Gamble, PPG Industries, Standard Oil of Ohio, Westinghouse, and Wheeling-Pittsburgh Steel Corporation (see *Business Week*, December 18, 1971 and December 2, 1972). Because such programs are relatively new in industrial settings (most have begun since 1968), few statements of their relative effectiveness have been reported. In the Winter 1973 issue of *Organizational Dynamics* (p. 49), it was stated that "there's little objective evidence available, and what evidence there is abounds in caveats—the technique will work under the proper circumstances, the parameters of which are usually not easily apparent."

In the area of employee training, Northern Systems Company, General Electric Corporation, and Emery Air Freight claim that positive reinforcement has improved the speed and efficiency of their training program. In their programmed learning program, the Northern Systems Company structures the feedback system in such a way that the trainee receives positive feedback only when he demonstrates correct performance at the tool station. The absence of feedback is experienced by the trainee when he fails to perform correctly. Therefore, through positive reinforcements, he quickly perceives that correct behaviors obtain for him the satisfaction of his needs, and that incorrect behaviors do not. Emery has designed a similar program for sales trainees. *Business Week* reported the success of the program by saying:

> It is a carefully engineered, step-by-step program, with frequent feedback questions and answers to let the salesman know how he is doing. The course contrasts with movies and lectures in which, Feeney says, the salesman is unable to gauge what he has learned. The aim is to get the customer on each sales call to take some kind of action indicating that he will use Emery services. Significantly, in 1968, the first full year after the new course was launched, sales jumped from $62.4 million to $79.8 million, a gain of 27.8 percent compared with an 11.3 percent rise the year before.

Since 1969, Emery has instituted a positive reinforcement program for all of its employees and credits the program with direct savings to the company of over $3 million in the first three years and indirectly with pushing 1973 sales over the $160 million mark. While Emery Air Freight is and remains the biggest success story for a positive reinforcement program to date, other companies also claim improvements as a result of initiating similar programs. At Michigan Bell's Detroit office, 2,000 employees in 1973 participated in a positive reinforcement program. Michigan Bell credits the program with reducing absenteeism from 11 percent to 6.5 percent in one group, from 75 percent to 4.5 percent in another group, and from 3.3 percent to 2.6 percent for all employees. In addition, the program has resulted in the correct completion of reports on time 90 percent of the time as compared with 20 percent of the time before the program's implementation. The Wheeling-Pittsburgh Steel Corporation credits its feedback program with saving $200,000 a month in scrap costs.

In an attempt to reduce the number of employees who constantly violated plant rules, General Motors implemented a plan in one plant that gave employees opportunities to improve or clear their records by going through varying periods of time without committing further shop violations. They credit this positive reinforcement plan with reducing the number of punitive actions for shop-rule infractions by two-thirds from 1969 to 1972 and the number of production-standard grievances by 70 percent during the same period.

While there was a great deal of interest in applying behavior modification in industrial settings after the successes of Emery Air Freight and others who followed suit were made known in 1971, the critics of this approach to worker motivation predicted that it would be short-lived. Any success would owe more to a "Hawthorne Effect" (the positive consequences of paying special attention to employees) than to any real long-term increase in productivity and/or worker satisfaction. The critics pointed out—quite legitimately, we might add—that most of the claims were testimonial in nature and that the length of experience between 1969-1973 was too short to allow enough data to accumulate to determine the true successes of positive reinforcement in improving morale and productivity. With this in mind, we surveyed ten organizations, all of which currently use a behavior modification approach, to see if the "fad" created by Emery Air Freight had died or had persisted and extended its gains.

Specifically, we were interested in knowing (1) how many employees were covered; (2) the kinds of employees covered; (3) specific goals (stages 1 & 2); (4) frequency of self-feedback (stage 3); (5) the kinds of reinforcers used (stage 4); and (6) results of the program. A summary of companies surveyed and the information gained are shown in Figure 13-1.

CURRENT RESULTS OF POSITIVE REINFORCEMENT PROGRAMS IN ORGANIZATIONS

The ten organizations surveyed included Emery Air Freight, Michigan Bell—Operator Services, Michigan Bell—Maintenance Services,

Connecticut General Life Insurance Company, General Electric, Standard Oil of Ohio, Weyerhaeuser, City of Detroit, B.F. Goodrich Chemical Company, and ACDC Electronics. In our interviews with each of the managers, we tried to determine both the successes and the failures they attributed to the use of behavior modification or positive reinforcement techniques. We were also interested in whether the managers saw this as a fad or as a legitimate management technique for improving the productivity and quality of work life among employees.

Emery air freight

Figure 13-1 shows Emery Air Freight still using positive reinforcement as a motivational tool. John C. Emery commented: "Positive reinforcement, always linked to feedback systems, plays a central role in performance improvement at Emery Air Freight. *All* managers and supervisors are being trained via self-instructional, programmed instruction texts—one on reinforcement and one on feedback. No formal off-the-job training is needed. Once he has studied the texts, the supervisor is encouraged immediately to apply the learning to the performance area for which he is responsible."

Paul F. Hammond, Emery's manager of system performance and the person currently in charge of the positive reinforcement program, said that there are a considerable number of company areas in which quantifiable success has been attained over the last six or seven years. Apart from the well-publicized container savings illustration (results of which stood at $600,000 gross savings in 1970 and over $2,000,000 in 1975), several other recent success stories were noted by Emery and Hammond. They include:

—Standards for customer service on the telephone had been set up and service was running 60 to 70 percent of standard. A program very heavily involved with feedback and reinforcement was introduced a few years ago and increased performance to 90 percent of objectives within three months—a level that has been maintained ever since.

—Several offices have installed a program in which specified planned reinforcements are provided when targeted levels of shipment volume are requested by Emery customers. All offices have increased revenue substantially; one office doubled the number of export shipments handled, and another averages an additional $60,000 of revenue per month.

—A program of measuring dimensions of certain lightweight shipments to rate them by volume rather than weight uses reinforcement and feedback extensively. All measures have increased dramatically since its inception five years ago, not the least of which is an increase in revenue from $400,000 per year to well over $2,000,000 per year.

FIGURE 13-1 Results of Positive Reinforcement and Similar Behavior Modification Programs in Organizations in 1976

ORGANIZATION & PERSON SURVEYED	LENGTH OF PROGRAM	NUMBER OF EMPLOYEES COVERED/ TOTAL EMPLOYEES	TYPE OF EMPLOYEES	SPECIFIC GOALS	FREQUENCY OF FEEDBACK	REINFORCERS USED	RESULTS
EMERY AIR FREIGHT John C. Emery, Jr., *President* Paul F. Hammond, *Manager—Systems Performance*	1969-1976	500/2800	Entire workforce	(a) Increase productivity (b) Improve quality of service	Immediate to monthly, depending on task	Previously only praise and recognition; others now being introduced	Cost savings can be directly attributed to the program
MICHIGAN BELL—OPERATOR SERVICES E.D. Grady, *General Manager—Operator Services*	1972-1976	2000/5500	Employees at all levels in operator services	(a) Decrease turnover & absenteeism (b) Increase productivity (c) Improve union-management relations	(a) Lower level—weekly & daily (b) Higher level—monthly & quarterly	(a) Praise & recognition (b) Opportunity to see oneself become better	(a) Attendance performance has improved by 50% (b) Productivity and efficiency has continued to be above standard in areas where positive reinforcement (PR) is used
MICHIGAN BELL—MAINTENANCE SERVICES Donald E. Burwell, *Division Superintendent, Maintenance & Supplies* Dr. W. Clay Hamner *Consultant*	1974-1976	220/5500	Maintenance workers, mechanics & first & second level supervisors	Improve (a) productivity (b) quality (c) safety (d) customer employee relations	Daily, weekly, and quarterly	(a) Self-feedback (b) Supervisory feedback	(a) Cost efficiency increase (b) Safety improved (c) Service improved (d) No change in absenteeism (e) Satisfaction with superior & co-workers improved (f) Satisfaction with pay decreased
CONNECTICUT GENERAL LIFE INSURANCE CO. Donald D. Illig, *Director of Personnel Administration*	1941-1976	3000/13,500	Clerical employees & first-line supervisors	(a) Decrease absenteeism (b) Decrease lateness	Immediate	(a) Self-feedback (b) System-feedback (c) Earned time off	(a) Chronic absenteeism & lateness has been drastically reduced (b) Some divisions refuse to use PR because it is "outdated"

(Figure 13-1 continued)

ORGANIZATION & PERSON SURVEYED	LENGTH OF PROGRAM	NUMBER OF EMPLOYEES COVERED/ TOTAL EMPLOYEES	TYPE OF EMPLOYEES	SPECIFIC GOALS	FREQUENCY OF FEEDBACK	REINFORCERS USED	RESULTS
GENERAL ELECTRIC[1] Melvin Sorcher, *Ph.D.*, formerly *Director of Personnel Research* Now *Director of Management Development, Richardson-Merrell, Inc.*	1973-1976	1000	Employees at all levels	(a) Meet EEO objectives (b) Decrease absenteeism & turnover (c) Improve training (d) Increase productivity	Immediate—uses modeling & role playing as training tools to teach interpersonal exchanges & behavior requirements	Social reinforcers (praise, rewards, & constructive feedback)	(a) Cost savings can be directly attributed to the program (b) Productivity has increased (c) Worked extremely well in training minority groups and raising their self esteem (d) Direct labor cost decreased
STANDARD OIL OF OHIO T.E. Standings, *Ph.D., Manager of Psychological Services*	1974	28	Supervisors	Increase supervisor competence	Weekly over 5 weeks (25-hour) training period	Feedback	(a) Improved supervisory ability to give feedback judiciously (b) Discontinued because of lack of overall success
WEYERHAEUSER COMPANY Gary P. Latham, *Ph.D., Manager of Human Resource Research*	1974-1976	500/40,000	Clerical, production (tree planters) & middle-level management & scientists	(a) To teach managers to minimize criticism & to maximize praise (b) To teach managers to make rewards contingent on specified performance levels & (c) To use optimal schedule to increase productivity	Immediate—daily & quarterly	(a) Pay (b) Praise & recognition	(a) Using money, obtained 33% increase in productivity with one group of workers, an 18% increase with a second group, and an 8% decrease in a third group (b) Currently experimenting with goal setting & praise and /or money at various levels in organization (c) With a lottery-type bonus, the cultural & religious values of workers must be taken into account

(Figure 13-1 continued)

ORGANIZATION & PERSON SURVEYED	LENGTH OF PROGRAM	NUMBER OF EMPLOYEES COVERED/ TOTAL EMPLOYEES	TYPE OF EMPLOYEES	SPECIFIC GOALS	FREQUENCY OF FEEDBACK	REINFORCERS USED	RESULTS
CITY OF DETROIT GARBAGE COLLECTORS[2]	1973-1975	1122/1930	Garbage collectors	(a) Reduction in paid man-hour per ton (b) Reduction in overtime (c) 90% of routes completed by standard (d) Effectiveness (quality)	Daily & quarterly based on formula negotiated by city & sanitation union	Bonus (profit sharing) & praise	(a) Citizen complaints declined significantly (b) City saved $1,654,000 first year after bonus paid (c) Worker bonus = $307,000 first year or $350 annually per man (d) Union somewhat dissatisfied with productivity measure and is pushing for more bonus to employee (c) 1975 results not yet available
B.F. GOODRICH CHEMICAL CO. Donald J. Barnicki, *Production Manager*	1972-1976	100/420	Manufacturing employees at all levels	(a) Better meeting of schedules (b) Increase productivity	Weekly	Praise & recognition; freedom to choose one's own activity	Production has increased over 300%
ACDC ELECTRONICS DIVISION OF EMERSON ELECTRONICS Edward J. Feeney, *Consultant*	1974-1976	350/350	All levels	(a) 96% attendance (b) 90% engineering specifications met (c) Daily production objectives met 95 % of time (d) Cost reduced by 10%	Daily & weekly feedback from foreman to company president	Positive feedback	(a) Profit up 25% over forecast (b) $550,000 cost reduction on $10 M sales (c) Return of 1900% on investment including consultant fees (d) Turnaround time on repairs went from 30 to 10 days (e) Attendance is now 98.2% (from 93.5%)

[1]Similar programs are now being implemented at Richardson-Merrell under the direction of Dr. Sorcher and at AT&T under the direction of Douglas W. Bray, Ph.D., director of management selection and development, along with several other smaller organizations (see A. P. Goldstein, Ph.D. & Melvin Sorcher, Ph. D., *Changing Supervisor Behavior*, Pergamon Press, 1974).

[2]From *Improving Municipal Productivity: The Detroit Refuse Incentive Plan*, The National Commission on Productivity, April, 1974.

While this latest information indicates that positive reinforcement is more than a fad at Emery Air Freight, Emery pointed out that a major flaw in the program had to be overcome. He said, "Inasmuch as praise is the most readily available no-cost reinforcer, it tends to be the reinforcer used most frequently. However, the result has been to *dull* its effect as a reinforcer through its sheer repetition, even to risk making praise an *irritant* to the receiver." To counter this potential difficulty, Emery managers and supervisors have been taught and encouraged to expand their reinforcers beyond praise. Among the recommended reinforcers have been formal recognition such as a public letter or a letter home, being given a more enjoyable task after completing a less enjoyable one, invitations to business luncheons or meetings, delegating responsibility and decision making, and tying such requests as special time off or any other deviation from normal procedure to performance. Thus it seems that Skinner's prediction made in 1973 about the need for using more than praise after the reinforcement program has been around for a while has been vindicated at Emery Air Freight.

Michigan Bell—operator service

The operator services division is still actively using positive reinforcement feedback as a motivational tool. E.D. Grady, general manager for Operator Services said, "We have found through experience that when standards and feedback are not provided, workers generally feel their performance is at about the 95 percent level. When the performance is then compared with clearly defined standards, it is usually found to meet only the 50th percentile in performance. It has been our experience, over the past ten years, that when standards are set and feedback provided in a positive manner, performance will reach very high levels—perhaps in the upper 90th percentile in a very short period of time.... We have also found that when positive reinforcement is discontinued, performance returns to levels that existed prior to the establishment of feedback." Grady said that while he was not able at this time to put a specific dollar appraisal on the cost savings from using a positive reinforcement program, the savings were continuing to increase and the program was being expanded.

In one recent experiment, Michigan Bell found that when goal setting and positive reinforcement were used in a low-productivity inner-city operator group, service promptness (time to answer call) went from 94 to 99 percent of standard, average work time per call (time taken to give information) decreased from 60 units of work time to 43 units of work time, the percentage of work time completed within ideal limits went from 50 to 93 percent of ideal time (standard was 80 percent of ideal), and the percentage of time operators made proper use of references went from 80 to 94 percent. This led to an overall productivity index score for these operators that was significantly higher than that found in the control group where positive reinforcement was not being used, even though the control group of operators had previously (six months earlier) been one of the highest producing units.

Michigan Bell—maintenance services

Donald E. Burwell, Division Superintendent of Maintenance and Services at Michigan Bell, established a goal-setting and positive reinforcement program in early 1974. He said, "After assignment to my present area of responsibility in January, I found that my new department of 220 employees (maintenance, mechanics, and janitorial services), including managers, possessed generally good morale. However, I soon became aware that 1973 performances were generally lower than the 1973 objectives. In some cases objectives were either ambiguous or nonexistent."

With the help of a consultant, Burwell overcame the problem by establishing a four-step positive reinforcement program similar to the one described earlier in this article. As a result, the 1974 year-end results showed significant improvements over the 1973 base-year averages in all areas, including safety (from 75.6 to 89.0), service (from 76.4 to 83.0), cost performance/hour (from 27.9 to 21.2, indexed), attendance (from 4.7 to 4.0) and worker satisfaction and cooperation (3.01 to 3.51 on a scale of 5), and worker satisfaction with the supervisors (2.88 to 3.70, also on a scale of five). 1975 figures reflect continuing success.

While Burwell is extremely pleased with the results of this program to date, he adds a word of caution to other managers thinking of implementing such a program: "I would advise against accepting any one method, including positive reinforcement, as a panacea for all the negative performance trends that confront managers. On the other hand, positive reinforcement has aided substantially in performance improvement for marketing, production, and service operators. Nevertheless, the manager needs to know when the positive effects of the reinforcement program have begun to plateau and what steps he should consider taking to maintain his positive performance trends."

Connecticut General Life Insurance Company

The Director of Personnel Administration at Connecticut General Life Insurance Company, Donald D. Illig, stated that Connecticut General has been using positive reinforcement in the form of an attendance bonus system for 25 years with over 3,200 clerical employees. Employees receive one extra day off for each ten weeks of perfect attendance. The results have been outstanding. Chronic absenteeism and lateness have been drastically reduced, and the employees are very happy with the system. Illig noted, however, that, "Our property and casualty company, with less than half the number of clerical employees countrywide, has not had an attendance-bonus system . . . and wants no part of it. At the crux of the problem is an anti-Skinnerian feeling, which looks at positive reinforcement—and thus an attendance-bonus system—as being overly manipulative and old-fashioned in light of current theories of motivation."

General Electric

A unique program of behavior modification has been introduced quite successfully at General Electric as well as several other organizations by Melvin Sorcher, formerly director of personnel research at G.E. The behavior modification program used at G.E. involves using positive reinforcement and feedback in training employees. While the first program centered primarily on teaching male supervisors how to interact and communicate with minority and female employees and on teaching minority and female employees how to become successful by improving their self-images, subsequent programs focused on the relationship between supervisors and employees in general. By using a reinforcement technique known as behavior modeling, Sorcher goes beyond the traditional positive reinforcement ("PR") program. The employee is shown a videotape of a model (someone with his own characteristics—that is, male or female, black or white, subordinate or superior) who is performing in a correct or desired manner. Then, through the process of role playing, the employee is encouraged to act in the successful or desired manner shown on the film (that is, he is asked to model the behavior). Positive reinforcement is given when the goal of successful display of this behavior is made in the role-playing session.

Sorcher notes that this method has been successfully used with over 1,000 G.E. supervisors. As a result, productivity has increased, the self-esteem of hard-core employees has increased, and EEO objectives are being met. He says, "The positive results have been the gratifying changes or improvements that have occurred, especially improvements that increase over time as opposed to the usual erosion of effort after most training programs have passed their peak. ... On the negative side, some people and organizations are calling their training 'behavior modeling' when it does not fit the criteria originally defined for such a program. For example, some programs not only neglect self-esteem as a component, but show little evidence of how to shape new behaviors.... Regarding the more general area of behavior modification and positive reinforcement, there is still a need for better research. There's not a lot taking place at present, which is unfortunate because on the surface these processes seem to have a lot of validity."

Standard Oil of Ohio

T.E. Standings, manager of psychological services at SOHIO, tried a training program similar to the one used by Sorcher at General Electric. After 28 supervisors had completed five weeks of training, Standings disbanded the program even though there were some short-term successes. He said, "My feelings at this point are that reinforcement cannot be taught at a conceptual level in a brief period of time. (Of course, the same comments can no doubt be made about Theory Y, MBO, and TA.) I see two alternatives: (1) Identify common problem situations, structure an appropriate reinforcement response for the supervisor, and teach the response through the behavioral model, or (2) alter reinforcement contingencies affecting defined behaviors through direct alternatives in procedural and/or informational systems without going through the supervisor directly."

Weyerhaeuser Company

Whereas Emery Air Freight has the longest history with applied reinforcement theory, Weyerhaeuser probably has the most experience with controlled experiments using goal setting and PR techniques. The Human Resource Research Center at Weyerhaeuser, under the direction of G.P. Latham, is actively seeking ways to improve the productivity of all levels of employees using the goal-setting, PR feedback technique.

According to Dr. Latham, "The purpose of our positive reinforcement program is threefold: (1) To teach managers to embrace the philosopy that 'the glass is half-full rather than half-empty.' In other words, our objective is to teach managers to minimize criticism (which is often self-defeating since it can fixate the employee's attention on ineffective job behavior and thus reinforce it) and to maximize praise and hence fixate both their and the employee's attention on effective job behavior. (2) To teach managers that praise by itself may increase job satisfaction, but that it will have little or no effect on productivity unless it is made contingent upon specified job behaviors. Telling an employee that he is doing a good job in no way conveys to him what he is doing correctly. Such blanket praise can inadvertently reinforce the very things that the employee is doing in a mediocre way. (3) To teach managers to determine the optimum schedule for administering a reinforcer—be it praise, a smile, or money in the employee's pocket."

Weyerhaeuser has found that by using money as a reinforcer (that it, as a bonus over and above the worker's hourly rate), they obtained a 33 percent increase in productivity with one group of workers, an 18 percent increase in productivity with a second group of workers, and an 8 percent decrease in productivity with a third group of workers. Latham says, "These findings point out the need to measure and document the effectiveness of any human resource program. The results obtained in one industrial setting cannot necessarily be expected in another setting."

Latham notes that because of its current success with PR, Weyerhaeuser is currently applying reinforcement principles with tree planters in the rural South as well as with engineers and scientists at their corporate headquarters. In the latter case, they are comparing different forms of goal setting (assigned, participative, and a generalized goal of "do your best") with three different forms of reinforcement (praise or private recognition from a supervisor, public recognition in terms of a citation for excellence, and a monetary reward). Latham adds, "The purpose of the program is to motivate scientists to attain excellence. Excellence is defined in terms of the frequency with which an individual displays specific behaviors that have been identified by the engineers/scientists themselves as making the difference between success and failure in fulfilling the requirements of their job."

City of Detroit, garbage collectors

In December 1972, the City of Detroit instituted a unique productivity bonus system for sanitation workers engaged in refuse collection. The plan, which provides for sharing the savings for productivity improvement efforts, was designed to save money for the city while rewarding workers for increased efficiency. The city's Labor Relations Bureau negotiated the productivity contract with the two unions concerned with refuse collection: The American Federation of State, County and Municipal Employees (AFSCME), representing sanitation laborers (loaders), and the Teamsters Union, representing drivers. The two agreements took effect on July 1, 1973.

The bonus system was based on savings gained in productivity (reductions in paid man-hours per ton of refuse collected, reduction in the total hours of overtime, percentage of routes completed on schedule, and effectiveness or cleanliness). A bonus pool was established and the sanitation laborers share 50-50 in the pool with the city —each worker's portion being determined by the number of hours worked under the productivity bonus pool, exclusive of overtime.

By any measure, this program was a success. Citizen complaints decreased dramatically. During 1974, the city saved $1,654,000 after the bonus of $307,000 ($350 per man) was paid. The bonus system is still in effect, but the unions are currently disputing with the city the question of what constitutes a fair day's work. Both unions involved have expressed doubts about the accuracy of the data used to compute the productivity index or, to be more precise, how the data are gathered and the index and bonus computed. Given this expected prenegotiation tactic by the unions, the city and the customers both agree that the plan has worked.

B.F. Goodrich Chemical Company

In 1972, one of the production sections in the B.F. Goodrich Chemical plant in Avon Lake, Ohio, as measured by standard accounting procedures, was failing. At that time, Donald J. Barnicki, the production manager, introduced a positive reinforcement program that included goal setting and feedback about scheduling, targets, costs, and problem areas. This program gave the information directly to the foremen on a once-a-week basis. In addition, daily meetings were held to discuss problems and describe how each group was doing. For the first time the foremen and their employees were told about costs that were incurred by their group. Charts were published that showed area achievements in terms of sales, cost, and productivity as compared with targets. Films were made that showed top management what the employees were doing, and these films were shown to the workers so they would know what management was being told.

According to Barnicki, this program of positive reinforcement turned the plant around. "Our productivity has increased 300 percent over the past five years. Costs are down. We had our best startup time in 1976 and passed our daily production level from last year the second day after we returned from the holidays."

ACDC Electronics

Edward J. Feeney, of Emery Air Freight fame, now heads a consulting firm that works with such firms as General Electric, Xerox, Braniff Airways, and General Atomic in the area of positive reinforcement programs. One of Mr. Feeney's current clients is the ACDC Electronics Company (a division of Emerson Electronics). After establishing a program that incorporated the four-step approach outlined earlier in this article, the ACDC Company experienced a profit increase of 25 percent over the forecast; a $550,000 cost reduction on $10 million in sales; a return of 1,900 percent on investment, including consultant fees; a reduction in turnaround time on repairs from 30 to 10 days; and a significant increase in attendance.

According to Ken Kilpatrick, ACDC President, "The results were as dramatic as those that Feeney had described. We found our output increased 30-40 percent almost immediately and has stayed at that high level for well over a year." The results were not accomplished, however, without initial problems, according to Feeney. "With some managers there were problems of inertia, disbelief, lack of time to implement, interest, difficulty in defining output for hard-to-measure areas, setting standards, measuring past performance, estimating economic payoffs, and failure to apply all feedback or reinforcement principles." Nevertheless, after positive results began to surface and initial problems were overcome, the ACDC management became enthused about the program.

CONCLUSION

This article has attempted to explain how reinforcement theory can be applied in organizational settings. We have argued that the arrangement of the contingencies of reinforcement is crucial in influencing behavior. Different ways of arranging these contingencies were explained, followed by a recommendation that the use of positive reinforcement combined with oral explanations of incorrect behaviors, when applied correctly, is an underestimated and powerful tool of management. The correct application includes three conditions: *First*, reinforcers must be selected that are sufficiently powerful and durable to establish and strengthen behavior; *second*, the manager must design the contingencies in such a way that the reinforcing events are made contingent on the desired level of performance; *third*, the program must be designed in such a way that it is possible to establish a reliable training procedure for inducing the desired response patterns.

To meet these three conditions for effective contingency management, many firms have set up a formal positive reinforcement motivational program. These include firms such as Emery Air Freight, Michigan Bell, Standard Oil of Ohio, General Electric, and B.F. Goodrich, among others. Typically, these firms employ a four-stage approach in designing their programs: (1) A performance audit is conducted in order to determine what performance patterns are desired and to measure the current levels of that performance; (2) specific and reasonable goals are set for each worker; (3) each employee is generally instructed to keep a record of his or her own work; and (4) positive aspects of the employee's performance are positively reinforced by the supervisor. Under this four-stage program, the employee has two chances of being successful—he can beat his previous level of performance or he can beat that plus his own goal. Also under this system, negative feedback routinely comes only from the employee (since he knows when he failed to meet the objective), whereas positive feedback comes from both the employee and his supervisor.

While we noted that many firms have credited this approach with improving morale and increasing profits, several points of concern and potential shortcomings of this approach should also be cited. Many people claim that you cannot teach reinforcement principles to lower-level managers very easily and unless you get managers to understand the principles, you certainly risk misusing these tools. Poorly designed reward systems can interfere with the development of spontaneity and creativity. Reinforcement systems that are deceptive and manipulative are an insult to employees.

One way in which a positive reinforcement program based solely on praise can be deceptive and manipulative occurs when productivity continues to increase month after month and year after year, and the company's profits increase as well, but employee salaries do not reflect their contributions. This seems obviously unethical and contradictory. It is unethical because the workers are being exploited and praise by itself will not have any long-term effect on performance. Emery Air Freight, for example, has begun to experience this backlash effect. It is contradictory because the manager is saying he believes in the principle of making intangible rewards contingent on performance but at the same time refuses to make the tangible monetary reward contingent on performance. Often the excuse given is that "our employees are unionized." Well, this is not always the case. Many firms that are without unions, such as Emery, refuse to pay on performance. Many other firms with unions have a contingent bonus plan. Skinner in 1969 warned managers that a poorly designed monetary reward system may actually reduce performance. The employee should be a willing party to the influence attempt, with both parties benefitting from the relationship.

Peter Drucker's concern is different. He worries that perhaps positive reinforcers may be misused by management to the detriment of the economy. He says, "The carrot of material rewards has not, like the stick of fear, lost its potency. On the contrary, it has become so potent that it threatens to destroy the earth's finite resources if it does not first destroy more economies through inflation that reflects rising expectations." In other words, positive reinforcement can be too effective as used by firms concerned solely with their own personal gains.

Skinner in an interview in *Organizational Dynamics* stated that a feedback system alone may not be enough. He recommended that the organization should design feedback and incentive systems in such a way that the dual objective of getting things done and making work enjoyable is met. He says what must be accomplished, and what he believes is currently lacking, is an effective training program for managers. "In the not-too-distant future, however, a new breed of industrial managers may be able to apply the principles of operant conditioning effectively."

We have evidence in at least a few organizational settings that Skinner's hopes are on the way to realization, that a new breed of industrial managers are indeed applying the principles of operant conditioning effectively.

SELECTED BIBLIOGRAPHY

For an understandable view of Skinner's basic ideas in his own words, see B.F. Skinner's *Contingencies of Reinforcement* (Appleton-Century-Crofts, 1969) and Carl R. Rogers and B.F. Skinner's "Some Issues Concerning the Control of Human Behavior" (*Science*, 1965, Vol. 24, pp. 1057-1066). For Skinner's views on the applications of his ideas in industry see "An Interview with B.F. Skinner (*Organizational Dynamics*, Winter 1973, pp. 31-40).

For an account of Skinner's ideas in action, see the same issue of *Organizational Dynamics* (pp. 41-50) and "Where Skinner's Theories Work" (*Business Week*, December 2, 1972, pp. 64-69).

An article highly critical of the application of Skinner's ideas in industry is W.F. Whyte's "Pigeons, Persons and Piece Rates" (*Psychology Today*, April 1972, pp. 67-68). For a more sympathetic and more systematic treatment see W. R. Nord's "Beyond the Teaching Machine: The Neglected Area of Operant Conditioning in The Theory and Practice of Management,"(*Organizational Behavior and Human Performance*, 1969, No. 4, pp. 375-401).

For previous comments on behavior modification by the author, see W. Clay Hamner's "Reinforcement Theory and Contingency Management" in L. Tosi and W. Clay Hamner, eds., *Organizational Behavior and Management: A Contingency Approach* (St. Clair Press, 1974, pp. 188-204) and W. Clay Hamner's "Worker Motivation Programs: Importance of Climate Structure and Performance Consequences" in W. Clay Hamner and Frank L. Schmidt's *Contemporary Problems in Personnel* (St. Clair Press, 1974, pp. 280-308).

Last, the best discussion of the general subject of pay and performance is Edward E. Lawler III's *Pay and Organizational Effectiveness* (McGraw-Hill, 1971).

CHAPTER

14

What Job Enrichment Is All About

Consider the case of Peter Porter. Peter has spent the last twelve years as a pickle packer, stuffing eleven pickles into each of eight jars a minute. Sometimes, if the last pickle won't properly pack, Peter pares off the perverse portion. Otherwise, Peter is completely controlled by the pickle pace. About a month ago, Peter's pal Paul started a new business—the production of biodegradable textbooks. Paul figures this will cut down on stale knowledge pollution and stimulate sales of new textbooks, thereby appealing both to conservationists and publishers. He has offered Peter a job as vice president for advertising. Peter knows he would have a lot of freedom on the job, could exercise some unused skills, and would finally have a job title he could brag about. But the job somehow seems less than secure, and the pay level will depend on how well the new idea is accepted. Peter Porter is puzzled. He is faced with the hard choice of whether to keep a job with good pay, security, and pleasant pickle-packing peers or to give it all up for the chance to do different, possibly exciting and challenging things. In short, he is asking himself, "What do I really want from a job?"

This is a question almost all of us ask ourselves at one time or another. It would be nice to have a job that was perfect in all respects but, as suggested in figure 14-1, it's probably unrealistic to expect such perfection. Instead, like Peter, we generally have to make trade-offs. What do you want *your* next job to be like?

Figure 14-2 presents a scale describing a series of pairs of jobs. Fill out the scale. Later, we'll discuss how the scale is scored and what your score says about your job preferences.

More and more, it seems that everyone is clamoring for the redesign of work, arguing that what employees want are meaningful, challenging, "large" jobs. Many firms in the United States have tried

FIGURE 14-1
The Quest for the Perfect Job

to provide such jobs, in some cases giving employees responsibility for the planning and control of work as well as its execution.

In a number of countries, including West Germany, Sweden, Norway, and Austria, things have progressed even further than in the United States. Companies in such countries are now forced by law to have large numbers of employee representatives on their governing boards. Because both workers and management determine what the company will do, this is called *codetermination.*[1] As an example of this, over thirty U.S. multinational companies doing business in Germany are subject to a new codetermination law that requires employees to have equal representation with shareholders on the supervisory board (something like our board of directors). Also, a new European Company Law gives companies doing business in more than one European country the option to become "European companies" rather than to register under existing national laws. Under the law, the supervisory board of the company would have to include at least one-third employees' representatives.[2]

While codetermination increases workers' involvement in top-level corporate decisions, there are other laws that affect more directly the employee's job itself. For example, some of the requirements of a new Working Environment Act laid before the Norwegian Parliament in December of 1976 are as follows:[3]

> **General Requirements**
> ...Employees shall be afforded opportunities for personal development and the maintenance and development of their skills.
>
> **Job Design**
> Full account shall be taken of the need for employee self-determination and maintenance of skills in the planning of work and design of jobs.

---

[1]See Agthe (1977) and Kühne (1976) for discussions of codetermination.
[2]Garson (1977) and Kühne (1976) discuss this law.
[3]See Gustavsen (1977) for a discussion of this act.

FIGURE 14-2 A Measure of Job Preferences

Instructions

People differ in what they like and dislike in their jobs. Listed below are twelve pairs of jobs. For each pair, you are to indicate which job you would prefer. Assume that everything else about the jobs is the same—pay attention only to the characteristics actually listed for each pair of jobs.

If you would prefer the job in the left-hand column (Column A), indicate *how much* you prefer it by putting a check mark in a blank to the left of the "neutral" point. If you prefer the job in the right-hand column (Column B), check one of the blanks to the right of "neutral." Check the "neutral" blank *only* if you find the two jobs equally attractive or unattractive. Try to use the "neutral" blank rarely.

COLUMN A				COLUMN B
1. A job which offers little or no challenge.	Strongly prefer A	Neutral	Strongly prefer B	A job which requires you to be completely isolated from co-workers.
2. A job where the pay is very good	Strongly prefer A	Neutral	Strongly prefer B	A job where there is considerable opportunity to be creative and innovative.
3. A job where your are often required to make important decisions.	Strongly prefer A	Neutral	Strongly prefer B	A job with many pleasant people to work with.
4. A job with little security in a somewhat unstable organization.	Strongly prefer A	Neutral	Strongly prefer B	A job in which you have little or no opportunity to participate in decisions which affect your work.
5. A job in which greater responsibility is given to those who do the best work.	Strongly prefer A	Neutral	Strongly prefer B	A job in which greater responsibility is given to loyal employees who have the most seniority.

(Figure 14-2 continued on next page)

(Figure 14-2 continued)

COLUMN A		COLUMN B
6. A job with a supervisor who sometimes is highly critical.	Strongly prefer A — Neutral — Strongly prefer B	A job which does not require you to use much of your talent.
7. A very routine job.	Strongly prefer A — Neutral — Strongly prefer B	A job where your co-workers are not very friendly.
8. A job with a supervisor who respects you and treats you fairly.	Strongly prefer A — Strongly prefer B	A job which provides constant opportunities for you to learn new and interesting things.
9. A job where you have a real chance to develop yourself personally.	Strongly prefer A — Neutral — Strongly prefer B	A job with excellent vacations and fringe benefits.
10. A job where there is a real chance you could be laid off.	Strongly prefer A — Neutral — Strongly prefer B	A job with very little chance to do challenging work.
11. A job with little freedom and independence to do your work in the way you think best.	Strongly prefer A — Neutral — Strongly prefer B	A job where the working conditions are poor.
12. A job with very satisfying team-work	Strongly prefer A — Neutral — Strongly prefer B	A job which allows you to use your skills and abilities to the fullest extent.

Reprinted with permission of the authors from Hackman, J.R., and Oldham, G.R., *The Job Diagnostic Survey: An Instrument for the Diagnosis of Jobs and the Evaluation of Job Redesign Projects.* Technical Report No. 4, Department of Administrative Sciences, Yale University, May 1974.

Monotonous, repetitive work and machine or assembly-line work that does not permit alteration of pace shall be avoided.

Jobs shall be so designed as to allow some possibility for variation, for contact with other workers, for interdependence between their constituent elements, and for information and feedback to the employees concerning production requirements and performance.

Planning and Control Systems

Employees or their representatives shall be kept informed about planning and control systems, including any changes in such systems. They shall be given the necessary training to understand the systems adopted and shall have the right to influence their design.

ADVANTAGES OF SPECIALIZATION

Clearly employees are being given greater opportunities to perform what were traditionally considered managerial functions. In fact, it is easy to forget in the midst of cries to enlarge the employee's role that early theorists saw a simplified, routine, nonchallenging job as ideal in most cases. For example, Frederick Taylor argued that we should try to find the "one best way" to perform a job. That "one best way" generally resulted in jobs being simplified, with workers performing only a few activities. While it is now popular to criticize Taylor for his emphasis on work simplification, he simply felt that such an approach was in the best interests of everyone. Among the advantages its advocates cite for specialization are:

1. The worker should be better able to perform the task and should consider it easier.

2. Time won't be lost moving from one work step to another.

3. The use of specialized machinery will be encouraged.

4. If employees are absent or leave the organization, it will be easier to replace them.

5. Especially in the case of the assembly line, the worker will adjust to the required pace and be drawn along by "traction."

Reactions to specialization

Despite these apparent advantages, there have been a number of negative reactions to simplification of the job. For instance, it has been argued that such simplification is dehumanizing and, thus, morally wrong and that it results in negative consequences for both the employee and the organization. The model underlying that argument

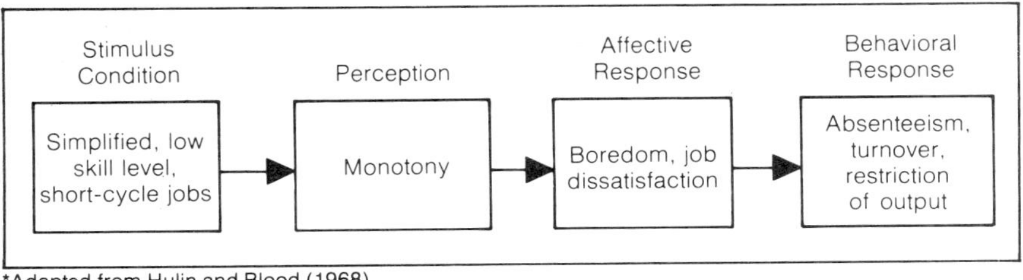

*Adapted from Hulin and Blood (1968)

FIGURE 14-3 The Behavioral Consequences of Work Simplification and Standardization* is presented in figure 14-3. Such an argument is reflected in the ad shown in figure 14-4; the ad views job enrichment as a way to avoid what has come to be known as the "blue-collar blues."

We all recognize that jobs differ substantially in their potential to induce boredom. One scene in a film showing workers on a number of assembly lines showed a pair of workers standing on opposite

FIGURE 14-4

Bored people build bad cars. That's why we're doing away with the assembly line.

For years, the assembly line did a lot of good. It made it easier to manufacture a product, increased production, and made costly products less expensive.

But today, the assembly line seems to be doing more harm than good. The quality of products has suffered, because working on an assembly line is monotonous. And boring. And after a while, people begin to not care anymore.

So, at Saab, we're replacing the assembly line with assembly teams. Small groups of just three or four people who see a job through from start to finish. It's meant less absenteeism and less turnover, so more experienced people are on the job. People who are more involved. People who care more. Which means you get a car that's built better.

We're building our new 2-liter engines this way. And the doors to our Saab 99. And we're planning to use this same system to build other parts of our car as well.

So, eventually, the Saab you buy may be built entirely by assembly teams. To give you the best engineered, best built car we can.

Saab. It's what a car should be.

There are more than 300 Saab dealers nationwide. For the name and address of the one nearest you call 800-243-6000 toll free. In Connecticut, call 1-800-882-6500.

The assembly line has a lot of advantages, but it also has many disadvantages. It's monotonous. And boring. And bored people build bad cars.

This ad tells the reader that, at least as far as Saab is concerned, the disadvantages far outweigh the advantages. So we're doing away with the assembly line.

sides of a conveyor belt. As metal sheets came to the end of the line, the workers each grabbed a side of the sheet and carried it to a nearby box. The film's commentator stated, "The following year, the employee on the left was replaced by a small rubber wheel." Can you imagine a job so boring that it could be performed by a small rubber wheel? How would it feel to go home to your family and tell them that you'd been replaced by a wheel?

Researchers at the Institute for Social Research at the University of Michigan interviewed over 2,000 workers in twenty-three different jobs and developed boredom ratings for each job. An average boredom rating was 100. The rankings and ratings of the jobs are shown in table 14-1. While it probably would be impossible to make an assembly-line worker's job as stimulating as that of a physician, the table shows that simply letting an assembler pace his or her own work might substantially reduce boredom.

INCREASING JOB SIZE

In response to arguments that "small" jobs lead to negative consequences, it was reasoned that the size of employees' jobs should be increased. There are two major dimensions to job size—job depth and job scope (or range). Job depth is the degree to which employees are able to influence their work environments and to carry out planning and control functions. Job scope is a measure of the number of

TABLE 14-1
Typical Jobs Rated According to Boredom

Job	Boredom Rating
1. Assembler (work paced by machine)	207
2. Relief worker on assembly line	175
3. Forklift-truck driver	170
4. Machine tender	169
5. Assembler (working at own pace)	160
6. Monitor of continuous-flow goods	122
7. Accountant	107
8. Engineer	100
9. (tie). Tool and die maker	96
9. (tie). Computer programmer	96
11. Electronic technician	87
12. Delivery service courier	86
13. Blue-collar supervisor	85
14. White-collar supervisor	72
15. (tie). Scientist	66
15. (tie). Administrator	66
17. Train dispatcher	64
18. Policeman	63
19. Air traffic controller (large airport)	59
20. Air traffic controller (small airport)	52
21. Professor with administrative duties	51
22. Professor	49
23. Physician	48

different activities the employee peforms, regardless of their content. Increases in job depth are usually called *job enrichment*, while increases in job scope are generally called *job enlargement*. (Sometimes, the term job enlargement is used to refer to any increase in job size. In such cases, increases in job depth are called vertical job enlargement, while increases in job scope are called horizontal job enlargement.) While many changes made in jobs would involve altering both job scope and job depth, it is important to realize that they are independent dimensions. Figure 14-5 shows that some jobs may actually have high scope but low depth or vice versa. Similarly, we might be able to increase one of these dimensions while leaving alone, or even decreasing, the other.

The following advantages have been cited for increased job scope:

1. Particular muscles of the employee will be less fatigued.
2. The employee will be able to complete a larger portion of the work, thus having a greater feeling of accomplishment.
3. The employee may have an opportunity to exercise a wider variety of skills.
4. Flexibility may be increased. For example, it may be easier to shut down a few work benches than an entire assembly line.

The arguments in favor of increasing job depth (that is, for job enrichment) generally rest on psychological considerations. Advocates of job enrichment claim that simple, repetitive jobs frustrate the em-

FIGURE 14-5
Jobs Varying in Job Depth and/or Scope*

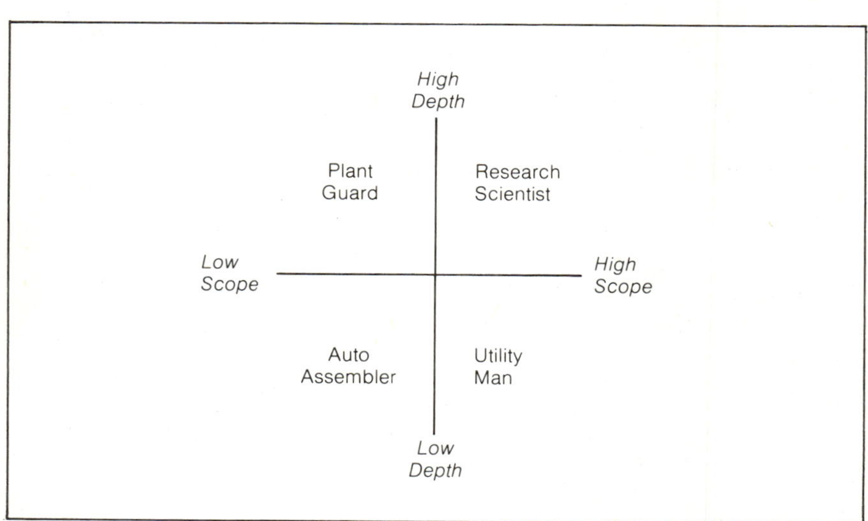

*From *Managerial Process and Organizational Behavior*, Second Edition, by Alan C. Filley, Robert J. House, and Steven Kerr. Copyright © 1976, 1969 by Scott, Foresman and Company. Reprinted by permission.

ployee. Chris Argyris has written about a maturity drive frustration cycle, shown in figure 14-6. He reasons that people have drives toward maturity. However, the characteristics of bureaucratic organizations frustrate those maturity drives. As a result, employees seek alternative outlets for satisfaction of such drives. Many of those alternative outlets may be harmful to the organization. For example, employees might slow down production or purposely make errors until conditions were improved. In response to such harmful actions, the organization tightens its rules and regulations, further constraining the employee, and the cycle is reinforced. Thus, Argyris argues that it is important to let the employee engage in challenging, meaningful, autonomous work.

M. Scott Myers has said that one key assumption underlying work simplification is that there are two distinct categories of people. One category, called managers, is responsible and highly motivated while the other, called workers, must be told exactly what to do and then closely watched. Consequently, as shown in figure 14-7, workers are relegated to "doing," while managers are responsible for deciding how things should be done, seeing that workers do them, and checking on whether they were done properly. What we need, Myers has argued, is to "make every employee a manager." As shown in figure 14-8, this would involve letting employees plan and control, as well as execute, their work. That is, their jobs should be enriched.

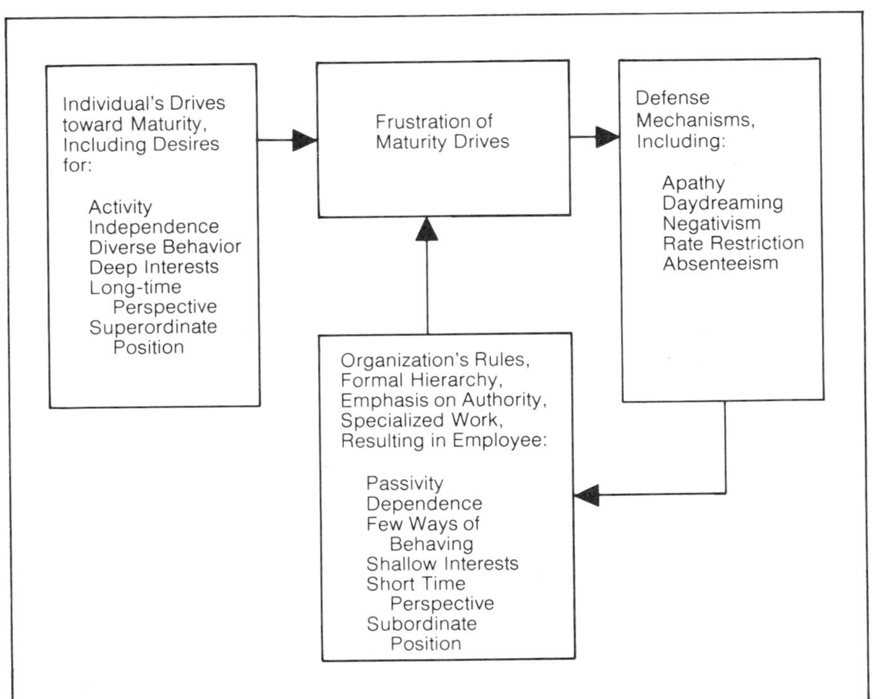

FIGURE 14-6
The Argyris Maturity Drive Frustration Cycle*

*_Integrating the Individual and the Organization,_ C. Argyris, Copyright © 1964, John Wiley and Sons, Inc. Reprinted by permission of John Wiley and Sons, Inc.

FIGURE 14-7
The Dichotomy between Workers and Managers*

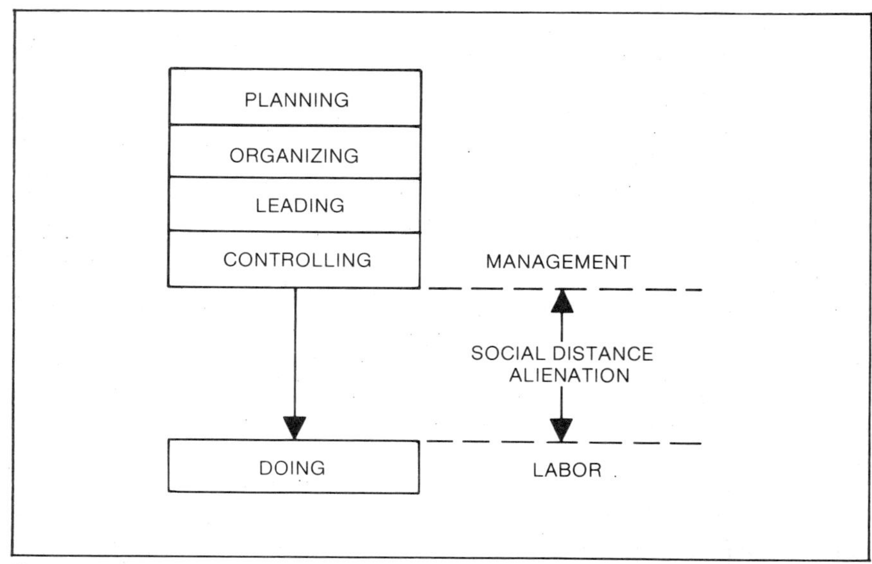

*Reprinted with permission of the publisher from *Every Employee a Manager* by M.S. Myers, p. 70. Copyright © 1970 by McGraw-Hill Inc., New York, N.Y.

FIGURE 14-8
"Making Every Employee a Manager"*

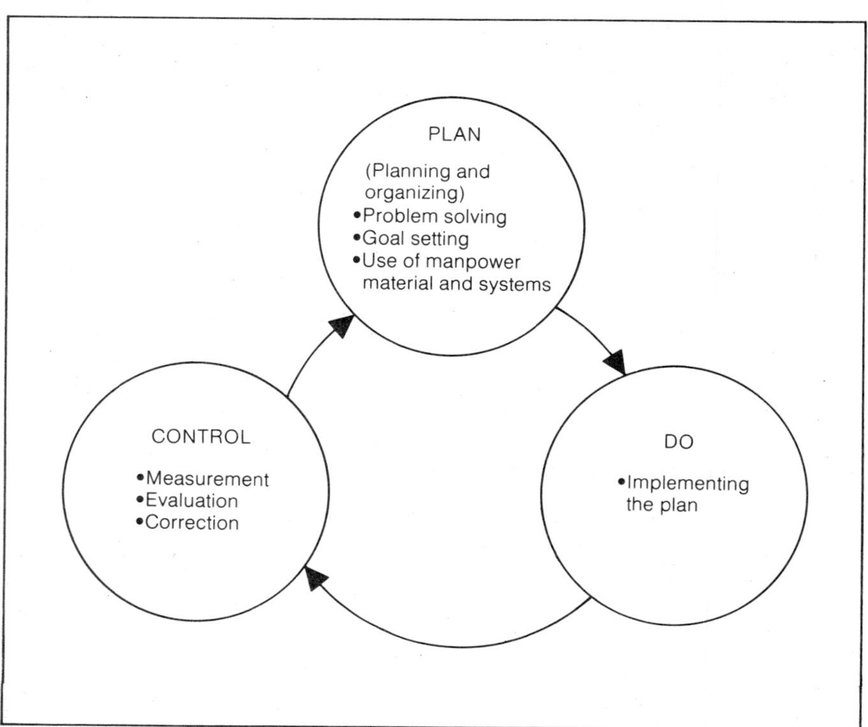

*Reprinted with permission of the publisher from *Every Employee a Manager* by M. S. Myers, p. 70. Copyright © 1970 by McGraw-Hill Inc., New York, N.Y.

Evidence concerning increased job size

Literally hundreds of studies have examined the effectiveness of increasing job scope and/or depth. Briefly summarized, the predominant findings are as follows:

1. Increases in job scope, without increased job depth, generally don't help either the employee or the organization. Herzberg has said, in reference to such findings, that if you tell employees who have been washing knives that they can now wash both knives and forks, they're not likely to get very excited.

2. Increases in job depth are generally associated with:

   a. Increased satisfaction

   b. Decreased turnover

   c. Decreased absenteeism

   d. Improved work quality

   e. Little change in work quantity

In considering these findings, we have to keep several things in mind. First, not all employees respond in the same ways to increases in job depth. Second, there are many dimensions to job depth. It is important to determine exactly what they are, how they fit together, and how they individually and jointly influence various outcomes. Third, job redesign doesn't take place in a vacuum. It must be worked into an existing organization structure and technology with continuing personnel. The impacts of such things on the probable success of a job redesign attempt have to be considered. Finally, any time evidence is reviewed concerning the effectiveness of some technique, it is important to realize that various individuals or firms may have implemented the technique very differently. Thus, it is important to ask what steps should be taken to implement job enrichment properly. We will consider these four issues in turn.

INDIVIDUAL DIFFERENCES IN RESPONSES TO JOB DESIGN

It seems obvious that not all employees want the same things from their jobs. Thus, it is unreasonable to expect that every employee will prefer an enriched job. For instance, Studs Terkel (1972), in his book *Working*, interviews a former radio-show "quiz kid" who says he likes his job in a greenhouse because it allows his mind to be relaxed all day long. What may not be so clear, though, is exactly how we can tell before the job redesign takes place who is likely to respond favorably and who probably will not. A large number of variables have been considered as possible determinants of the ways employees might respond to particular job characteristics. Among these are how urbanized the area was where the employee grew up, the extent to which the employee accepts Protestant Work Ethic ideals, the "higher order need strength" of the employee, and the employee's age and sex.

How urbanized the area was where the individual grew up was the first variable researchers thought might determine how employees would respond to an enriched job. Charles Hulin and Milton Blood (1968) argued that blue-collar workers who grew up in urbanized areas would probably not want challenging, responsible jobs because they probably hadn't developed middle-class work values (that is, Protestant Work Ethic ideals). As we mentioned earlier, people adhering to the ideals of the Protestant Work Ethic see hard work as a reflection of personal worth, think that wasting time is bad, and so on.

However, most recent research shows that it is generally not possible to predict accurately how employees will respond to job enrichment, either by considering where they grew up or by measuring directly the strength of their adherence to Protestant Work Ethic ideals. While variables such as adherence to Protestant Work Ethic ideals might be useful in determining how someone will respond to work *in general*, they apparently are less useful in predicting how that person will react to particular types of job changes.

Instead, it is best to measure directly whether or not someone wants the sorts of things found in an enriched job. Since those sorts of things (such as responsibility, autonomy, and challenge) may be used to satisfy what are the top needs on Maslow's hierarchy, the strength of a person's desire for such things is generally called "higher-order need strength." At the beginning of this chapter, you indicated your preference for one or the other of a number of pairs of jobs. The scale you filled out to indicate those preferences measures the strength of an employee's higher-order needs. The scoring key for that scale and an explanation of the meaning of your score are provided in Figure 14-9.

Calculate your score. There is nothing "good" or "bad" about a high or low score. Instead, high scores suggest that you would like an enriched job, while low scores show that you are more concerned with job security, good pay, and friendly coworkers than with challenge, responsibility, and autonomy. Considerable evidence shows that people who have relatively high scores on this scale do, in fact, react more favorably to enriched job characteristics than do those with low scores. Think seriously about your score. If it is in the 60s or above, you are likely to be happy in a complex, challenging job; if it is in the 40s or below, such a job may not be for you.

Two other variables—age and sex—have been considered possible influences on the way people might respond to enriched job characteristics. For instance, it seems that dissatisfaction with routine, simple jobs usually is thought to be confined to young, well-educated employees. It is generally suggested that older employees, brought up during harder economic times, basically want good pay and secure jobs. However, there is really no good evidence to support such a contention. For example, we examined two samples of employees

Figure 14-9
How To Assess
Your Job Preferences

To find your "higher-order need strength" score:

1. First, for each of the twelve items, give a number to the space you checked. If you checked the space that is farthest left, score a one. Score a two for the space next to that, and so on, until a check in the farthest right space would get a score of seven.
2. Add up your scores for items 1, 2, 7, 8, 11 and 12. Call the sum of these X.
3. Add up your scores for items 3, 4, 5, 6, 9 and 10. Call the sum of these Y.
4. Your "higher-order need strength" score is 48+X−Y.

Your score can range from 12 to 84. The higher your score, the more you prefer a job that offers such things as challenge and autonomy to one that gives such things as good pay, secure working conditions, and friendly coworkers.

We have administered this scale to a number of groups of employees, whose average scores are presented here. By comparing your score to those averages, you can get some feel for the relative strength of your "higher-order needs."

Sample	Average Score
Nursing Aides	56.2
Correctional Employees	53.6
Manufacturing Employees	48.4
Hospital Janitorial Employees	47.2
Police Officers	55.2

—one from a manufacturing firm and the other from a public sector agency—and found few significant differences between the ways younger and older workers responded to perceptions of task dimensions.[4]

For some time, many researchers argued that women are more concerned with social aspects of jobs than are men, while men are relatively more interested in pay, advancement, and freedom on the job. Such arguments would imply that men might respond well to job enrichment, while women might see the changes as unnecessary and as disrupting current social relationships. However, there are a couple of problems with such a conclusion. For one thing, some of the differences between what men and women previously said they wanted from their jobs were probably due to the different ways boys and girls were raised. That is, boys grew up thinking they would have to be the breadwinners of their families, while girls were taught that they would be the families' social leaders, maintaining the homes and caring for the children. One recent study looked at the sorts of gifts that toy salespersons recommended for boys and girls. Most (whether male or female) suggested things like dolls for girls and tools or guns for boys, even when they were told the gifts should be "different." When one salesperson was asked to suggest gifts for a

[4]Aldag and Brief (1975)

brother and sister who regularly played together, he recommended a tool kit for the boy so that he could make a dollhouse for the girl.[5] However, as traditional sex-role stereotypes change, boys and girls probably won't be raised with such rigid expectations.

Also, women in the past may have shown more concern for social relationships on the job simply because they were in jobs that required lots of contact with other people. For example, Ruth's job as a receptionist requires that she constantly interact with clients of the firm for which she works. Jane, a nurse, spends almost all her time with patients, doctors, or other nurses. It's not too surprising that women in such positions as receptionist, secretary, or nurse would be concerned about the quality of social interactions.

Interestingly, the results of a recent study we conducted showed that, when men and women in the *same* occupation were surveyed, they ranked the things they wanted from their jobs almost identically.[6] So while a female nurse may want different things than would a male executive, probably male and female executives want rather similar things. As sex-role stereotypes change and more women move into the work force and into traditionally male-dominated jobs, differences between the preferences for job outcomes of males and females will probably shrink or disappear.

In summary, it's probably unwise to try to predict how people will respond to job enrichment on the basis of such things as their age, sex, or where they grew up. Instead, it's best to measure directly the strength of their higher-order needs.

THE DIMENSIONS OF JOB DEPTH

It is one thing just to talk in general terms about enriching the job and quite another actually to make specific changes. What are the important characteristics of the job itself? What specific things should we try to change?

Arthur Turner and Paul Lawrence (1965) took a major step toward answering these questions by attempting to identify a specific set of task attributes that would affect employees' responses. More recently, J. Richard Hackman and Edward Lawler (1971) slightly modified the set of attributes discussed by Turner and Lawrence and came up with the following four *core task dimensions* and two *interpersonal dimensions:*

Core Task Dimensions

1. Skill variety—The degree to which a job requires employees to perform a wide range of operations in their work and/or the degree

[5]Kutner, N. G. and Levinson, R. M., "The Toy Salesperson: A Voice for Change in Sex Role Stereotypes?" *Sex Roles*: 4(1), 1978, pp. 1-7.
[6]See Brief, Rose and Aldag (1977)

to which employees must use a variety of equipment and procedures in their work

2. Autonomy—The extent to which employees have a major say in scheduling their work, selecting the equipment they will use, and deciding on procedures to be followed

3. Task Identity—The extent to which employees do an entire or whole piece of work and can clearly identify the result of their efforts

4. Feedback—The degree to which employees receive information as they are working that reveals how well they are performing on the job

Interpersonal Dimensions

1. Dealing with Others—The degree to which a job requires employees to deal with other people (either customers, other company employees, or both) to complete the work

2. Friendship Opportunities—The degree to which a job allows employees to talk with one another on the job and to establish informal relationships with other employees at work

Later, Hackman and his associates added another core task dimension, task significance, defined as "the extent to which the job has a substantial impact on the lives and work of other people." A scale to measure perceptions of the dimensions is called the job diagnostic survey. Sample items for each of the dimensions are presented in table 14-2. Think about some job you now hold or have held in the past (perhaps even a job around the house). Take a minute to respond to the items in table 14-2 for that job and sum up your re-

TABLE 14-2
Selected Items to Measure Task Dimensions*

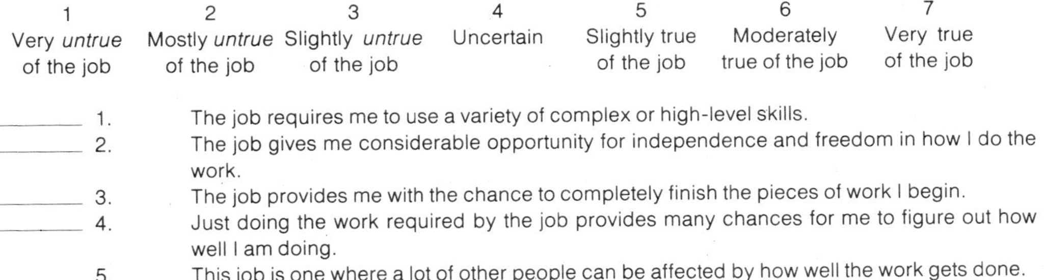

Listed below are a number of statements which might (or might not) describe your job. You are to indicate the degree to which each statement is an accurate description of the job on which you work. Do this by writing the appropriate number in the left-hand margin, based on the scale below.

Please make your descriptions as *objectively* and *factually accurate* as possible, without regard for whether you like or dislike your job.

1	2	3	4	5	6	7
Very *untrue* of the job	Mostly *untrue* of the job	Slightly *untrue* of the job	Uncertain	Slightly true of the job	Moderately true of the job	Very true of the job

_______ 1. The job requires me to use a variety of complex or high-level skills.
_______ 2. The job gives me considerable opportunity for independence and freedom in how I do the work.
_______ 3. The job provides me with the chance to completely finish the pieces of work I begin.
_______ 4. Just doing the work required by the job provides many chances for me to figure out how well I am doing.
_______ 5. This job is one where a lot of other people can be affected by how well the work gets done.

*Adapted from Hackman and Oldham (1974)

sponses. A total score above 20 shows you see the job as being above neutral in terms of enriched characteristics. (The five questions tap skill variety, autonomy, task identity, feedback, and task significance respectively.)

These or similar task characteristics are currently being used in most studies relating to job design. While there is some question about whether employees really view all jobs precisely in terms of these specific dimensions, they do at least provide a means for approaching the issue of job characteristics. Studies show that each of these dimensions is generally significantly related to satisfaction with work but *not* necessarily to performance.

However, if we think in terms of expectancy theory, the generally disappointing findings concerning the impact of job enrichment on performance aren't very surprising. While variety, autonomy, and the other core task dimensions may be positively *valent* outcomes to employees, they probably won't have much impact on performance unless good performance is seen as being *instrumental* in getting those outcomes. Most job enrichment programs simply try to increase levels of the core task dimensions for everyone, regardless of his or her performance. So while they are likely to satisfy employees, they probably won't get them to perform especially well.

J. Richard Hackman and Greg Oldham (1974) have argued that perceptions of the core task dimensions fit together according to the formula shown in figure 14-10 to determine the overall "Motivating Potential Score" of the job. Since the formula involves multiplying scores, a very low score on any dimension will lead to a low overall score. This implies that if a perceived task dimension, such as autonomy or feedback, remains at a very low level, improving other dimensions won't do much to increase the employee's motivation. However, recent studies suggest that there is really no good evidence to support such a model. Instead, it seems that increasing the level of any of the perceived task dimensions will help. It is probably most appropriate just to add up the perceived task dimension scores to get an overall score.

It should be stressed that we've been discussing employees' *perceptions* of their jobs. Some people argue that if we are going to pre-

FIGURE 14-10
One View of How the Core Task Dimensions Fit Together*

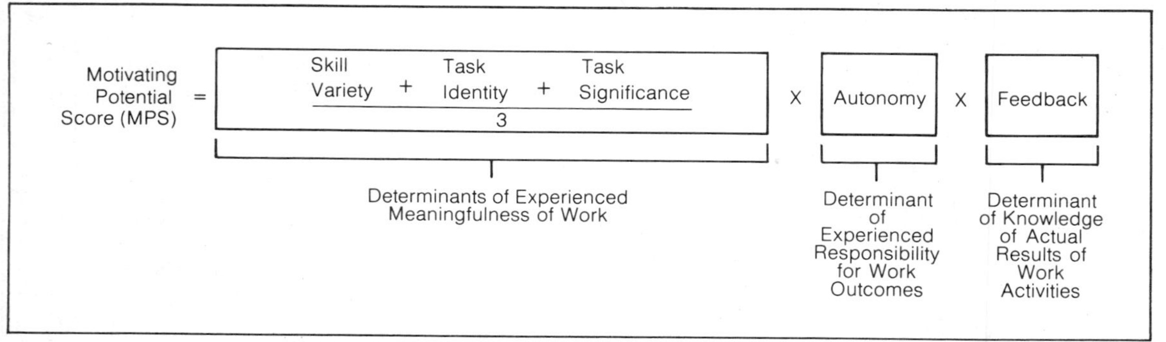

*Adapted from Hackman and Oldham (1974)

dict how employees will respond, and if we hope to influence those responses, we have to examine those perceptions. That is, people behave on the basis of the way they *think* things are. If a pedestrian thinks a traffic light is green, he or she will probably cross the street, regardless of the actual color of the light. On the other hand, job redesign programs must directly change actual job characteristics, not employees' perceptions. The catch is that different people sometimes perceive the same job in different ways. For example, Gene Stone (1976) asked students to perform a simple assembly task. While the task was exactly the same for all students, the way the students perceived its variety, autonomy, task identity, and feedback depended on their ages and personalities. As one example, older students felt the jobs offered significantly more skill variety and feedback, but less task identity, than did younger students. It's clear, then, that along with learning about how employees perceive their current and desired jobs, we also have to examine the links between actual job characteristics and the employees' perceptions of those characteristics. That is, job enrichment should not be implemented without checking on how objective job characteristics are perceived.

THE CONDITIONS FOR SUCCESSFUL JOB ENRICHMENT

As we said earlier, job enrichment doesn't take place in a vacuum. Instead, it takes place in organizations with existing structures, technologies, reward systems, and personnel. Each of those things may affect the probability of success of enrichment attempts. We've already seen that such attempts should be most successful if employees have strong higher-order needs. Some other questions we should ask before trying job enrichment are:

1. What are the current levels of the core task dimensions? If employees already think their jobs have enough variety, autonomy, and so on, further increases may not help and may even cause problems. It's not enough simply to assume a job is boring to the employee because it looks boring to us. Instead, we must check the perceptions of the specific people whose jobs we are thinking of changing.

2. Are employees satisfied with other aspects of the organizational reward system, such as pay? If employees are unhappy with pay and other extrinsic rewards, they probably won't respond very well to job enrichment.

3. Is it really feasible to enrich the jobs very much? This complex question can really only be answered by thoroughly analyzing the particular situation. However, there are a couple of general guidelines. For one, it is generally easier to design enriched jobs from scratch in a new company or subunit than to change long-standing patterns of behavior. Also, some types of technologies (the way inputs are changed into outputs) present special obstacles to job en-

richment. For example, it is very difficult—though, of course, not impossible—to change jobs in subunits that have assembly-line type technologies.

4. How would enriched jobs blend in with the rest of the organization? In some cases, if we redesign a set of jobs, they might become an enriched oasis in an otherwise bureaucratic desert. In such instances, the people on those enriched jobs probably won't be very happy. Instead, it's generally best to "fit" the job to the overall structure of the organization. Employees on enriched jobs in very bureaucratic organizations are likely to be confused by conflicting messages "sent" from the job and the rest of the organization. For instance, Bob's job has just been redesigned to give him more autonomy and feedback concerning performance. He knows, though, that most employees in the organization are closely supervised and that they don't have any idea of how well they're doing until they're punished. He wonders if the apparent autonomy and feedback on his job are just a ploy of some kind and, even if they're not, how long they're likely to last.

Implementation of job enrichment

If the answers to the preceding questions indicate that job enrichment will probably be successful, a job-redesign task force made up of management and labor representatives should take the following steps. It should:

1. Identify the actual activities currently performed in the target jobs.

2. Examine the relationships between those activities and the employees' perceptions of the core task dimensions.

3. Specify a detailed job redesign plan, based largely on the findings in the first steps.

4. Test the plan on a small scale.

5. If the small-scale test is successful, apply the plan to the whole set of jobs to be redesigned.

Arguments against job enrichment

It would be misleading not to point out that a lot of people still argue against job enrichment. We have already reviewed some of the bases for their arguments. For instance, some people may not want enriched jobs, it may be hard to enrich certain jobs, and there are certain advantages to specialization. Some other arguments against job enrichment are as follows.

1. Emphasis on employee dissatisfaction and on terms such as the "blue-collar blues" represents a fad exploited by behavioral scien-

tists. For instance, in 1973 Leonard Woodcock, then president of the United Auto Workers, said that academics were writing "elitist nonsense." "Sure, work is dull and monotonous," he told a UAW production workers' conference, "but if it's useful, the people who do it are entitled to be honored and not degraded, which is what's going on in this day and time."[7]

2. Much of the blame for worker dissatisfaction, which has been attributed to the lack of opportunity to obtain intrinsic rewards, is really the result of other factors, such as work speed-ups.

3. Management's goal should be to raise worker satisfaction in total, not just on the job. Satisfying work may require pay cuts or reduce the rate of pay increases. If those reductions interfere with the opportunity to achieve satisfaction off the job, the employee's total life satisfaction may decrease. Thus, it may be wrong to treat the employee as if his or her existence ended at the plant door.

4. Only a certain amount can be done in any given company. To enrich one employee's job means that another's must be made more trivial.

5. It may be possible to delegate responsibility, but competence can't be shifted so easily. Many employees simply do not currently have, and are unlikely to be willing or able to acquire, necessary competencies.

6. Emphasis on employee dissatisfaction is a way of shifting blame for declining productivity from management to the worker.

7. If jobs are enriched, employees will expect to get paid more to perform those jobs because of their greater skill requirements and the increased flexibility that such enrichment may provide the organization.

Some of these points should be taken seriously. For example, it is important to ask whether job redesign will affect pay demands. Also, as suggested earlier, we have to be sure that dissatisfaction is really due to boring work rather than other things. Finally, we can't just assume that the worker's life takes place entirely at work. Instead, we should think about how job changes may affect the worker's total life satisfaction.

On the other hand, some of the preceding arguments are debatable. For example, it's true that workers deserve respect, no matter how routine their jobs. However, that is no excuse for not giving them the chance to do more interesting and challenging things. Also, there is evidence that organizations *as a whole* differ in the total amount of control that is exercised. So it is not necessarily true that enriching one job means making another job less meaningful.

[7] "Issue of boredom distorted, Woodcock says," *Detroit Free Press*, February, 1973.

Alternatives to job enrichment

As a result of such arguments, a number of alternatives to job enrichment have been suggested. Some people have reasoned, for example, that attempts should be made to remove the human element from routine jobs through automation. Others have suggested that workers should be given increased extrinsic rewards, which they could use to try to satisfy higher-order needs off the job. It has even been argued that heavy taxes should be placed on assembly lines and other boredom-inducing technology so that alternative technologies would be economically advantageous.

Stephen Robbins (1976) offers one provocative alternative in the following passage.

> If we accept that employees are dissatisfied and desire work that is more active and autonomous, what do we do if the vast majority of our jobs simply do not lend themselves to allowing their incumbents more activity and autonomy? It has been suggested that a more drastic and realistic solution to alienation be considered—organizational psychopharmacology, the use of drugs to influence behavior in the work environment...The argument is that we live in a drug-oriented society. Americans alone spend in excess of $30 billion annually for chemicals that alter their consciousness, awareness, or mood...In view of the fact that we are a drug-oriented society, it seems entirely apropos to at least consider the case for bringing chemicals into the work environment...Truck drivers, air controllers, athletes, and military personnel are all known to be heavy amphetamine users...Stimulants such as Ritalin are used daily by more than a quarter of a million schoolchildren in North America who suffer from hyperactivity...The drug relieves boredom, yet does not affect the ability to solve problems and does not alter judgment. (p. 335-337)

Robbins notes that, while there are ethical questions associated with the use of drugs in organizations to manage behavior, "...such programs, when offered to employees on a voluntary basis, represent only an extension of medical services now offered through many organizations, just as the concept of organizational psychopharmacology represents an extension of the realities of organizational life" (p. 338).

SUMMARY

In this chapter, we have looked at the issue of job design. We've seen that, despite some apparent advantages of specialization, there is a trend toward giving employees more say in how to plan and control their work. While some countries have gone so far as to pass laws placing employees on the governing boards of their companies, most changes in the United States have been restricted to altering employees' jobs directly.

Job size can be changed by manipulating job scope and/or job depth. While increases only in job scope don't seem to help much, it appears that increasing job depth (that is, enriching the job) may produce a variety of desirable outcomes for both the employee and the organization. However, we must remember a number of things. For one, not everyone wants an enriched job. Second, when it comes to actually changing the job, it's important to know precisely how specific objective job characteristics relate to employee perceptions of such job dimensions as skill variety, task identity, task significance, feedback, and autonomy. Third, job redesign must be viewed in the context of the surrounding organization; some types of organizational structures and technologies make it difficult to enrich jobs and also make it unlikely that enrichment will produce desirable outcomes. Finally, proper implementation of the redesign attempt is crucial.

While some people aren't convinced that it is a good idea to try to enrich jobs, they seem to be a shrinking minority. In the following reading, David Sirota discusses a number of successes of job enrichment but also points out some causes for skepticism. His observations reinforce our contention: job enrichment is not a panacea, but, if used properly in appropriate situations, it can improve employee attitudes, work quality, and other important outcomes.

REFERENCES

Agthe, K.E. "Mitbestimmung: Report on a Social Experiment." *Business Horizons 20 (1)* (1977): 5-14.

Aldag, R.J., and Brief, A.P. "Age and Reactions to Task Characteristics." *Industrial Gerontology 2* (1975): 223-29.

Argyris, C. *Integrating the Individual and the Organization.* New York: Wiley, 1964.

Brief, A.P.; Rose, G.L.; and Aldag, R.J. "Sex differences in Work Attitudes Revisited." *Journal of Applied Psychology 62* (1977): 645-46.

Filley, A.C.; House, R.J.; and Kerr, S. *Managerial Process and Organizational Behavior.* Glenview, Ill.: Scott, Foresman, 1976.

Garson, G.D. "The Codetermination Model of Workers' Participation: Where Is It Leading?" *Sloan Management Review 19* (1977): 63-78.

Gustavsen, G. "A Legislative Approach to Job Reform in Norway." *International Labor Review 115* (1977): 263-76.

Hackman, J.R., and Lawler, E.E., III. "Employee Reactions to Job Characteristics." *Journal of Applied Psychology Monograph 55* (1971): 259-86.

Hackman, J.R., and Oldham, G.R. *The Job Diagnostic Survey: An Instrument for the Diagnosis of Jobs and the Evaluation of Job Redesign Projects.* Technical Report No. 4, Department of Administrative Sciences, Yale University, May 1974.

Hulin, C.L., and Blood, M.R. "Job Enlargement, Individual Differences, and Worker Responses." *Psychological Bulletin 69* (1968): 41-55.

"Issue of Boredom Distorted, Woodcock Says." *Detroit Free Press*, Feb. 17, 1973, p. 1.

Kuhne, R.J. "Co-determination: A Statutory Re-structuring of the Organization." *Columbia Journal of World Business 11(2)* (1976): 17-25.

Myers, M.S. *Every Employee a Manager.* New York: McGraw-Hill, 1970.

Robbins, S.P. *The Administrative Process.* Englewood Cliffs, N. J.: Prentice-Hall, 1976.

Stone, E.F. "Some Personality Correlates of Perceptions of and Reactions to Task Characteristics. Working paper, Purdue University, 1977.

Terkel, S. *Working*. New York: Pantheon Books, 1972.

Turner, A.N., and Lawrence, P.R. *Industrial Jobs and the Worker: An Investigation of Response to Task Attributes*. Boston: Harvard University Press, 1965.

CHAPTER 15

Job Enrichment—Another Management Fad?*

Over the last several years there has been an enormous amount of publicity about job enrichment and about the problems it is designed to overcome: the boring and demotivating work so much of our work-force presumably is required to perform. Much of the current interest in the content of work stems from a few highly publicized industrial relations incidents such as the strikes by General Motors workers that began in the Lordstown, Ohio, plant and spread to 13 plants throughout the country. In these occurrences the disaffection and antagonism of workers were widely believed to have been caused by dull and "dehumanizing" work (the so-called blue-collar blues) rather than the more traditional bread-and-butter labor relations issues.

Thus, in a recent *Life* magazine cover story titled "Bored On The Job," the correspondent concludes that ". . . the striker who walked out of Lordstown last spring to protest working conditions *is a* symbol of a new factor which has hit the auto plants hardest and is spreading through American industry: job boredom."[1]

Job content has even been the subject of a recent Congressional investigation. Senator Edward M. Kennedy, opening the hearings of a subcommittee on Worker Alienation, commented: ". . . the key element in the productivity equation is the worker and the noneconomic needs of the worker have been forgotten. Too many young workers are finding their jobs a place of confinement and frustration. And we should not be surprised that our lack of concern is producing a class

*Reprinted with permission of the publisher from D. Sirota, "Job Enrichment—Another Management Fad?" *Conference Board Record*, vol. 10, no. 4, (April 1973), pp. 40-45. Copyright © 1973 Conference Board, Inc., New York, N.Y.

[1]*Life*, September 1, 1972. p. 31.

of angry and rebellious workers. . . . Few people in America have ever heard of Lordstown, where auto workers have tied up lines more than once to protest the robotlike monotony of a 36-second interval assembly process."[2]

The concern about job content has stimulated a plethora of ideas for the "humanization of work." The proposed solutions range from the relatively conventional (e.g., a further shortening of the work-week), to suggestions for fundamental revisions in the way work is organized and performed. In the latter category the idea that has by far gained the greatest currency is "job enrichment." Based on the theories of Frederick Herzberg,[3] job enrichment is essentially an attempt to put back into work opportunity for real achievement—and thus satisfaction and motivation. This is accomplished by systematically giving an employee:

—greater responsibility,

—greater autonomy in carrying out his responsibility,

—increased "closure" (doing the "whole thing").

—more immediate feedback as to how well he has done.

—more recognition for doing a job well.

Numerous descriptions of enrichment projects have been published. Perhaps the most well-known of these are the experiments performed during the 1960's at American Telephone & Telegraph, especially the one among correspondents in the Stockholder Relations Department. As described by Herzberg, ". . . almost all indexes of performance and job attitudes [of these correspondents] were low and exit interviews confirmed that the challenge of the job existed only as words."[4] Among the more significant enrichment changes adopted were those in which the correspondents' responsibilities were raised by giving them tasks previously performed only by supervision. For example, subject matter experts were appointed within the unit to answer specialized questions (all such questions had previously been handled by the supervisor); each correspondent was made responsible for the quality of her own letters (this had been the responsibility of the supervisor and verifier); verification of the more experienced correspondents' letters was reduced from 100% to 10%: and the correspondents now signed their own letters (previously the supervisor signed all letters).

Strikingly successful results were reported from this experiment at AT&T, including significant improvements in quality and quantity

[2]E.M. Kennedy, In *Hearings Before the Subcommittee on Unemployment, Manpower and Poverty* (Washington, U.S. Government Printing Office, 1972), p. 8.

[3]F. Herzberg, B. Mausner, and B. Snyderman, *The Motivation To Work* (New York, John Wiley & Sons. Inc., 1959).

[4]F. Herzberg, "One More Time: How Do You Motivate Employees?" *Harvard Business Review*. January-February. 1968. pp. 53-62.

of work and job attitudes, and significant reductions in absenteeism and turnover. These gains were not observed in a control group doing similar work but in which enrichment changes had not been introduced.[5]

The favorable—sometimes spectacular—results asserted for job enrichment projects have received extensive publicity. While much of the original experimentation with the technique was done at AT&T —18 of the 19 projects undertaken there were reported as "successful" (9 "outstandingly successful")—similar achievements have been reported in companies such as Texas Instruments, Maytag, Motorola, and IBM. The published results have been almost uniformly favorable, with improvements claimed on just about every conceivable dimension of organization effectiveness, ranging from work quality and productivity to labor-management cooperation and harmony.

Given these generally enthusiastic reports—coupled with the public concern about issues such as the "blue-collar blues"—it is not surprising that job enrichment would soon come to be sold throughout our country as *the* solution to our industrial relations ills. Thus, the president of the consulting firm most active in job enrichment application can write (under the heading "The Need for Job Enrichment Is Urgent"): "The recent explosions in several large plants are an indication of what is to come at other locations. Young workers, trapped in dull, monotonous, routine jobs, will not continue to perform as management desires. They will slow down production, sabotage the plant, and eventually walk off the job. . . . Managements have been completely blind to these basic problems . . . *Job enrichment* seems to hold the solution to these extensive problems . . . The 1970's will demand the best from management. Learning how to redesign work and actually installing the new design requires hard, rigorous efforts. We have no choice but to go this route. Any other effort will be too costly!"[6]

SKEPTICISM

The upsurge in interest in job content problems—and the job enrichment solution—has not been devoid of controversy. While gaining less public attention than the advocates of urgent change, those skeptical of the import of the problem are numerous.

One locus of the dispute has been academia, where many industrial psychologists have attacked job enrichment, and Herzberg's theory on which it is based, on methodological and theoretical grounds. These arguments, however, are often akin to medieval church disputes (especially the incomprehensible language in which

[5]For a complete review of AT&T's job enrichment projects, see R.N. Ford, *Motivation Through the Work Itself* (New York, American Management Association, 1969).

[6]R. Walters. "The Need for Job Enrichment is Urgent." *Industrial Engineering*, July 1972. pp. 14-16.

they tend to be couched) and need not greatly concern the manager searching for practical guidance.[7]

The other major source of controversy is of considerable importance to management. This is the attack on enrichment (as indeed upon much of behavioral science) waged by the more traditional segments of the management and industrial engineering communities. One of the most eloquent expressions of this view is that of Mitchell Fein, an industrial engineering consultant, who argues in various papers that the assumptions underlying enrichment theory (e.g., that people *want* challenging, responsible work) apply to but a small proportion (he thinks about 15%) of the blue- and white-collar worker populations.[8]

Fein further asserts that the job content issue, and its supposedly dire consequences, are largely myths: "From my discussions with workers, managers and union leaders, I find no evidence that the recent disruptions in the GM factories were caused by the content of the job. This issue is a figment of journalists' and sociologists' imaginations."[9]

Our own investigation of the automobile factory disputes strongly supports Fein's interpretation of these events. The key reason for the workers' militancy in these plants was their view that the company was engaged in a *speedup*—certainly not a new issue in the history of labor-management conflict. The General Motors Assembly Division, in its desire to cut manufacturing costs and thus improve GM's competitive posture, increased employee workloads, enforced penalties (such as disciplinary layoffs) for failure to meet performance standards, and generally increased the closeness with which the workers were supervised. It is against *these* measures that the workers rebelled.

Irving Bluestone, UAW vice president in charge of the GM department, speaks of the GM Assembly Division as coming in with ". . . a heavy hand . . . a real sledge hammer."[10] and as being on ". . . a constant treadmill of elevating efficiency and cutting unit costs."[11] Richard C. Gerstenberg, chairman of General Motors, has asserted that ". . . the causes of the Lordstown strike were not new or peculiar to that plant; they involved familiar disputes about standards."[12] And *The Wall Street Journal*, in its review of the matter, concluded that it

---

[7]For a comprehensive review of academic research and opinion in this area, see R.J. House, and L.A. Wigdor, "Herzberg's Dual-Factor Theory of Job Satisfaction and Motivation: A Review of The Evidence and A Criticism." *Personnel Psychology*. Winter 1967, pp. 367-389.

[8]See Mitchell Fein. "The Real Needs and Goals of Blue Collar Workers." *The RECORD*, February 1973, p. 26.

[9]M. Fein, "Manufacturing Management," Address to American Management Association Seminar, September 22, 1972.

[10]Quoted in *The Wall Street Journal*, October 17, 1972.

[11]Quoted in *The New York Times*, April 16, 1972.

[12]R.C. Gerstenberg, "Danger in Public Misconception," Address before the Tax Foundation in New York City, December 6, 1972.

was the efficiency moves that were "... at the root of the ... wave of strikes that has disrupted 13 GM plants."[13]

The industrial relations incidents in the automobile industry thus come not from any new worker demands about job content, but rather are continuations of age-old labor-management controversies about job *pace*. Given this evidence—coupled with the skepticism naturally raised by the marketing of panacealike solutions—it is relevant to ask: Is all of this concern about job content "for real?" In other words, is job enrichment just another of those behavioral science fads that will soon reach a peak in popularity and then rapidly decline? Or, are we witnessing a truly important change in management outlook and practice—one that will persevere because, despite certain bloated claims and propoganda, there are genuine organizational needs that this technique does indeed serve?[14]

WHAT JOB ENRICHMENT DOES DO

Numerous reports of job enrichment projects have been published, and, as expected, some diversity can be found in the meaning of this activity for various practitioners. However, despite these differences, *in every case we have reviewed the essential effect of the job enrichment effort has been to raise the skill demands that a job places on its occupant.* Whether called "growth," or "achievement," or "challenge," or "responsibility," or "fulfillment," or "actualizing," or all of these; whether obtained by moving tasks into a job from "before" operations, or from "after" operations, or from the supervisor, or from an entirely different department, or from all of these —the core mission of these projects has been to break down barriers that impede an organization from fully exploiting its human resources. The specific problem, therefore, that job enrichment is geared to ameliorate is *manpower underutilization* and, more precisely, the underutilization of *talent* (as opposed to the more conventional management concern with the underutilization of workers' time).

There is no gainsaying the severity of the talent underutilizaton problem in much of industry and, therefore, the importance of techniques designed to help solve it. In the name of efficiency, a good deal of the work in factories and offices has been structured to be performed by rote with minimal judgmental demands—that is, for monkeys or machines, rather than for normal human beings. The theory is that the fragmentation of work into its simplest components

[13]L.G. O'Donnel, "A Day's Work," *The Wall Street Journal*, December 6, 1972.

[14]The author has long been active in the introduction of job enrichment in a number of companies but does not view it as a solution for all, most, or even more than one of our industrial relations ills. A disservice has been done to the approach by overstated claims as to its applicability; it does, however, have utility—for a limited, albeit important, class of problems.

cuts costs by reducing training time and time spent in the exercise of judgment.

The difficulty with the theory is that, unhappily, normal human beings are usually hired to fill these jobs. The wastage in both skill and motivational energy (sapped by frustration and sheer boredom) is enormous.

Observations about underutilization and its effects are far from new. Even Adam Smith, a strong advocate of work specialization as a precondition of efficiency, asserted that ". . . the man whose life is spent performing a few simple operations . . . becomes as stupid and ignorant as it is possible for a human creature to become." And Karl Marx, ordinarily considered a rigid economic determinist, wrote extensively about the *psychological* consequences of industrialization: "They [the capitalists] mutilate the laborer into a fragment of a man, degrade him to the level of an appendage of a machine, destroy every remnant of charm in his work, and turn it into a hated toil. They estrange him from the intellectual potentialities of the labor process."

In recent times, but still 15 years before the current clamor about job content (and "new values," "new generation," etc.), Robert Guest[15] wrote: ". . . the theory and practice of over-specialization . . . is based on a very narrow conception of what really motivates people to put out their best effort . . . Management [must] take a fresh look at the intrinsic nature of work itself . . . the meaning of work to the individual. We have equated specialization with productivity and just about denuded work of any real value in and of itself other than the pay envelope." Guest quotes Peter Drucker, writing in 1950, as pointing out the ". . . essential flaw in these [traditional] efficiency methods." namely, that ". . . the worker is put to use as a poorly designed, one purpose machine tool, but repetition and uniformity are two qualities in which human beings are weakest. In everything but the ability to judge and coordinate, machines can perform better than men."

Guest's plea is for a sympathetic view by management of ". . . a new idea . . . that is beginning to take hold," namely, "job enlargement" through which a much more complete use of human talent —and therefore meaning and motivation—can be restored to work. His description of job enlargement is in all fundamental respects identical to what has now come to be termed job enrichment.

WHAT JOB ENRICHMENT DOES NOT DO

Despite the importance of the job content problem, it must be recognized that it is neither universal, (there are many challenging and fulfilling jobs) nor, where it does exist, necessarily the only serious problem that a company's management must face. On this latter point

[15]R.H. Guest, "Job Enlargement—A Revolution in Job Design." *Personnel Administration*. March-April, 1957. pp. 9-16.

we know of no instance in which underutilization has been the precipitating factor in serious industrial relations disputes—such as those which bring on unionization, the election of militant union leaderships, or work stoppages. These conflicts—as in the GM incidents discussed earlier—have invariably been the consequences of disagreements about *equity* (work standards, pay, violations of seniority rules, etc.), not job content. We have yet to see picket signs demanding less boring work.

Here, then, are some example of ills for which enrichment is *not* a solution:

—Dissatisfaction with pay. (Enrichment can even aggravate this problem by increasing the discrepancy between what the individual gives and what he gets from the organization.)

—Employment insecurity. (This concern, too, can be worsened because of the task combinations and eliminations enrichment so frequently entails.)

—Dissatisfaction with fringe benefits.

—Various obstacles to getting the work done, such as poor tooling and materials, or inadequate clerical and administrative support.

—Technical incompetence, (Job *de*-enrichment may be the appropriate answer here.)

Unfortunately, as we have indicated, job enrichment is being sold today as a panacea for just about every business ill. This is dangerous nonsense.

The answer, then, to our question: Is job enrichment "for real"? obviously depends on the answer to a further question: In what situation is it being applied? *Job enrichment has applicability in those situations where talent underutilization (because of job content) is a key organization problem, and where, further, there are not complicating factors such as serious pay dissatisfaction or job insecurity.* When limited to these conditions, we find the claims made for the usefulness of enrichment to be hardly exaggerated at all. The technique can then have a major and beneficial impact on management practice and effectiveness.

THE NEED FOR DIAGNOSIS

Our argument is simple: Apply enrichment where it makes sense. This brings us logically to the need to determine just what the problems in a company are before deciding whether job enrichment (or any other technique) can be of value. Our recommendation as to diagnostic method is also simple: *The best way to find out what is happening is to go directly to the people to whom it is happening—the employees themselves.* In other words: Ask! Not only are employees the most knowledgable sources of information about their own situ-

TABLE 15-1
"How Much of Your Work Could be Handled by a Person Having Less Experience or Training?

	% RESPONDING "A GREAT DEAL" OR "QUITE A BIT"
Production Workers	46
Plant-Support	30
Engineers	24
Managers	15

tations (for example, they know better than anyone else whether they *are* being underutilized), but we find they are also motivated to report their condition truthfully (they don't *want* to be underutilized).

A variety of techniques can be used for asking employees the right questions in the right way.[16] In our case, these have ranged from nondirective group interviews to highly structured opinion questionnaires. Such methods can produce rather precise pictures of the problems of companies, including the severity of the problems, their probable causes, and exactly where in the organization they reside.

Here is one small example of diagnostic data, dealing specifically with the underutilization issue. We asked employees in a questionnaire: "How much of your work could be handled by a person having less experience or training?" The results in one company, from 16,000 manufacturing employees divided into four occupational categories, are shown in Table 15-1. As can be seen, the lower the occupational level, the greater the feeling of underutilization. This is to be expected, given the decrease in judgmental demands management makes of workers as we descend the occupational hierarchy.

The importance of diagnosing precisely what the problems are —and where they are—is reinforced by the following data obtained from the same four occupations, but now on a question dealing with compensation: "How would you rate your pay considering what you could get for the same kind of work in other companies?" The percentages responding favorably ("Very good" or "Good") to this question are presented in Table 15-2.

The degree of satisfaction with pay of these various occupations bears little relation to their underutilization attitudes. This is a very

TABLE 15-2
"How Would You Rate Your Pay Considering What You Could Get for the Same Kind of Work in Other Companies?

	% RESPONDING "VERY GOOD" OR "GOOD"
Production Workers	74
Plant-Support	76
Engineers	35
Managers	39

[16]See D. Sirota and A.D. Wolfson, "Pragmatic Approach to People Problems," *Harvard Business Review*, January-February, 1973, pp. 120-128.

common occurrence: It is rare that our diagnoses of large population segments reveal attitudes which are either consistently low or consistently high. Groups vary greatly in their satisfactions and dissatisfactions—and the solutions chosen must reflect these differences.

These diagnostic methods have an additional important advantage: they make moot the perennial debate as to the importance to workers of economic versus social-psychological goals. We say, let's not argue, let's get away from the finely spun theories and the quasi-theological disputations; in other words, let's stop talking to each other and start talking to the *workers:* Let's ask *them* what *they* want. Management practices, to the extent that they are based on assumptions about employee goals and satisfactions, can then be built on the firm foundation of concrete empirical evidence.

DIAGNOSIS LEADS TO APPLICATION

Extensive enrichment work has been done in the company in which the attitude data previously shown were collected. Because the diagnosis revealed the most widespread job content problem to be among production ("Direct") workers in these plants—in some departments perceived under-utilization exceeded 80%—initial enrichment work was begun there. Here are two examples of the many Direct enrichment projects and their results.

—**Case A.** *Type of work:* Assembly of office equipment.

Enrichment changes made: Seventeen separate operations combined into five "whole jobs" (combinations done by the five major mechanisms of the machine).

Results: 1. Easier to identify source of quality errors (know who built what mechanism). 2. Significant improvement in work quality. 3. Significant improvement in employee attitudes towards job.

—**Case B.** *Type of work:* Entire production area of electronics assembly plant.

Enrichment changes made: Movement of "Indirect" work into production jobs, e.g., production workers given responsibility for preventative maintenance, investigation and solution of quality problems, maintenance of process documentation, and departmental in-process inventory control (ordering, expediting, and location of parts).

Results: 1. Significant improvement in productivity. 2. Significant improvement in work quality. 3. Reduction in labor force (handled through normal attrition). 4. Reduction in space requirements. 5. Significant improvement in employee attitudes towards job.

While the attitude data showed the most widespread under-utilization to be in the Direct departments, there was considerable variation in the white-collar—"Indirect"—areas. Some of these departments did have severe job content problems and the company has since initiated enrichment work there. For example:

—**Case C.** *Type of work:* Documentation clerk.

Enrichment changes made: 1. Each clerk made responsible for all three major tasks: pulling and filing, copying, and distributing documents (previously, tasks divided among the clerks). 2. Clerks given new responsibility, document inspection. 3. Clerks permitted to perform touch-ups when they think it desirable. 4. Clerks allowed to contact their "client" functions directly (previously, all contact was through their manager).

Results: 1. Although workload increased, number of clerks and overtime were reduced (surpluses handled through normal attrition). 2. One-day service on routine requests provided (previously, three days). 3. Instant service provided on special requests (completely new). 4. Documents improved because of inspection and touch-up. 5. Significant improvement in job attitudes (several requests-for-transfer withdrawn by employees).

SO FAR, SO GOOD

Our experience thus far in the application of job enrichment has been extremely encouraging. Significant changes have been made in the design of work and substantial improvements achieved in terms of both job performance and job satisfaction. More than 100 enrichment projects have been undertaken since this work was begun in the company.[17]

Despite these successes, however, we would warn against any overgeneralization from them to situations in which job enrichment has nothing to offer. This technique is not *the* solution to the "people" problems of industry, but rather one of many that needs to be applied with thought and care. Even more important, there ought to be good evidence that the ailment under treatment is really one for which job enrichment is the appropriate medication.

DISCUSSION QUESTIONS

1. Analyze each of the vignettes presented in the beginning of the section in terms of expectancy theory, equity theory, and/or goal setting.

2. Think of a situation in which someone you know had apparently not been motivated to perform a certain task at a satisfactory level. Analyze the situation in an expectancy theory framework.

[17]A description of the total job enrichment strategy employed in this company (including methods of training internal job enrichment practitioners) may be found in two articles by the author and A.D. Wolfson: "Job Enrichment: The Obstacles," and "Job Enrichment: Surmounting the Obstacles," in *Personnel*, May-June, 1972 and July-August 1972, respectively.

3. Consider a case in which you felt that some outcome or set of outcomes that you received—pay, praise, a grade, or whatever—was unfair; analyze that case in terms of equity theory.

4. Consider the three rules of distributive fairness suggested by Leventhal. Describe cases where you used each of these rules. What sorts of things caused you to emphasize each rule in each situation?

5. List four goals you recently have set for yourself (quitting or cutting down on smoking, meeting more people, learning certain disco steps, getting a particular grade, or whatever). Classify those goals in terms of the degree to which you feel they were specific, difficult, and competitive. Also indicate the amount and nature of the feedback you got concerning progress toward your goals. In each case, do you think the goals helped? Why or why not? Discuss how the characteristics of the goals may have contributed to the success or failure of your efforts.

6. You supervise twenty-five unionized employees. The collective bargaining agreement under which your employees work is in the process of being renegotiated. The union has asked for a 15 percent across-the-board pay increase. Write a memo to your boss detailing your reactions to that request.

7. We have said that people with differing levels of higher-order need strength (HONS) respond differently to enriched job characteristics. Suppose that women are found to exhibit lower levels of HONS than do men. What might be some legal and ethical implications of assigning people to jobs on the basis of their HONS scores?

8. Some people argue that if employees say they don't want their jobs to be enriched, their wishes should be honored. Others argue that such employees have probably never had enriched jobs, will never psychologically "grow" unless they experience such jobs, and, therefore, should be placed on enriched jobs to see if they would learn to like them. Which viewpoint do you agree with? Why?

9. To what extent to you agree with each of the following statements? Why?

a. If it turns out that a company can't enrich jobs because of cost considerations, the government should provide subsidies to help.

b. Voluntary use of drugs to reduce boredom at work should be allowed.

c. Assembly lines should be outlawed or at least heavily taxed.

d. Some people simply aren't capable of accepting responsibility.

e. All employees should be given enriched jobs.

10. Compare your "higher-order need strength" score with those of your classmates. Do your relative scores seem consistant with the sorts of future jobs you are seeking?

11. Select any three of the arguments against job enrichment presented in chapter 14 and critically assess each.

12. Do you feel that recent concern about job content is genuine? How widespread do you feel the situations are for which job enrichment would seem appropriate?

SECTION

V

Making Good Decisions

Solving problems, sometimes by individuals and sometimes by groups, is central to all behavior in organizations. When individuals try to solve problems, they face a variety of difficulties. Bringing together a number of people to seek a solution makes things better in some ways and worse in others. This section explores the many factors that influence decision making—especially those that lead to difficulties—and presents techniques and structures that should be useful in improving decisions in organizations.

First, we will discuss individual decision making and consider pitfalls in the decision-making process and their organizational implications. Then we will examine alternatives to the use of human decision makers and suggest ways to improve individual decision making, including normative decision-making techniques. Finally, an appendix presents models for decision making under a variety of different conditions.

Next, we will consider group problem solving. Potential advantages and disadvantages of use of groups for problem solving purposes are reviewed, the appropriate situations for the use of groups are considered, and issues relating to optimal group size and spatial arrangements of group members are examined. Finally, we will present group processes aimed at capturing group advantages while minimizing the problems often associated with groups.

As the chapters on individual and group decision making point out, the vital first step in the problem-solving process—the generation of a number of useful alternatives—is often virtually ignored, sometimes with damaging consequences. The final chapter explores the issue of creativity—the generation of new and useful alternatives. Creative behavior is discussed, stages in the creative process are considered, and alternative views of the sources of creativity are summarized. Next, we will show that creative ability can be validly measured. After discussing variables that seem to be related to creative behavior, we will present specific techniques and structures to enhance creativity.

KEY TERMS

HEURISTICS
SATISFICING
COGNITIVE DISSONANCE
CLINICAL-ACTUARIAL CONTROVERSY
MAN VERSUS MODELS OF MAN CONTROVERSY
NORMATIVE DECISION MAKING
DESCRIPTIVE DECISION MAKING
DECISION MATRIX
SCREENING APPROACH
SCORING APPROACH
DECISION MAKING UNDER:
- Certainty
- Risk
- Uncertainty
- Conflict

SOCIAL FACILITATION EFFECT
RISKY SHIFT PHENOMENON
PROBLEM SOLVING STAGES:
- Orientation
- Evaluation
- Control

NOMINAL GROUP TECHNIQUE
DELPHI PROCESS
PERSONAL SPACE
COACTING GROUP
CREATIVE BEHAVIOR
STAGES OF CREATIVE PROCESS
REMOTE ASSOCIATES TEST
TORRANCE TESTS OF CREATIVE THINKING
GORDON TECHNIQUE
SYNECTICS
BRAINSTORMING
RETRODUCTION
SELF-INTERROGATION

OBJECTIVES

1. To stress the importance of decision making in organizations
2. To help explain how decisions are made and why they are often less than optimal
3. To examine alternatives to the use of human decision makers
4. To show how individuals can make better decisions
5. To indicate the benefits and problems associated with the use of groups for problem solving.
6. To show how to determine whether to use a group in a problem-solving situation
7. To describe why group size, spatial arrangements, and member heterogeneity are important
8. To illustrate promising new group processes
9. To explain creativity, its sources and measurement
10. To describe specific techniques and structures to enhance creative behavior

CHAPTER

16

Individual Decision Making

Janet has been concerned about some decisions Fred, her subordinate, made recently. While she couldn't say that they were *bad* decisions, Janet had the nagging feeling that they could have been a lot better. When confronted by Janet, Fred argued that all his decisions had been "good enough," meeting all the requirements of the situation. Jane wasn't sure how to respond.

Tomorrow morning, Jim Long, director of personnel, is to recommend to the executive vice-president whom to hire as the department head of data processing. It is well past midnight, and Jim still hasn't made a decision. He keeps re-reading the files of the three most likely candidates and pondering each candidate's strengths and weaknesses. The candidates differ in terms of their past managerial experience, level of appropriate education, and quality of references provided. Jim can't determine how much weight to give each of these characteristics in making his choice. For example, one candidate has five years of experience as a data processing supervisor and holds a master's degree in computer sciences from a prestigious school. However, one of her past employers wrote a rather damning letter of recommendation. Jim doesn't know whether or not to discount this negative information in light of the applicant's other qualifications. Jim is afraid he faces a sleepless night.

Linda had learned that her boss, Al, would be transferred to another location in less than a year. Linda also knew that, in all likelihood, either she or her coworker, Bob, would be promoted to fill his vacancy. Linda felt that she could either pursue the promotion aggressively or continue to behave as she had in the past. If she was aggressive, her chances of getting the promotion would probably be improved, *unless* Bob was also aggressive. Also, if Linda acted aggressively and didn't get the promotion, her relations with her probable new boss, Bob, would be extremely strained. She might even eventually have to look for work elsewhere. Linda had no idea whether Bob would seek the promotion aggressively and wondered what she should do.

With her new business still financially strapped, Althea was concerned about the decisions that her subordinates might make. It wasn't that they were incompetent. To the contrary, they all had the sort of training and experience she felt lucky to find in employees who were willing to work for a young, untested firm. Still, she knew that, given the same information, they would probably make very different decisions. Some would seek high gain. Some would avoid risks at all costs. Althea wanted her subordinates to be cautious, of course, but not *too* cautious. How could she tell what sorts of decisions they might make?

What do motivation and loyalty and productivity and other organization behavior topics we've discussed have in common? Some people would argue that one important way they are similar is that they all involve decision making. In fact, some people have gone so far as to declare that the decision is the basic building block of organizational behavior, somewhat like the atom in the physical sciences. We make decisions about how hard to work, about whether to stay in the organization, about how much to tell the boss, and so on. The sum of all those decisions determines behavior in organizations. So if we are really going to understand, predict, or influence organizational behavior, we have to understand decision making.

Further, of course, how well managers make decisions is a major determinant of the salary increases they will get, their promotion potential, the satisfaction of their subordinates, and so on. Consequently, decision making is clearly important both from the organization's point of view and that of the individual manager.

Organizations are becoming more aware of the importance of decision making. Many are sending their employees to special programs to learn decision-making techniques or are bringing in consultants to give training programs. DuPont, Pillsbury, General Electric, and many other major organizations use sophisticated decision-making techniques extensively. And there are now journals, such as *Decision Sciences*, and professional organizations, such as the American Institute for Decision Sciences that focus primarily upon decision making in organizations.

It is useful to differentiate between *descriptive* and *prescriptive*, or *normative*, aspects of decision making. Descriptive decision analysis is concerned with how people *do* make decisions. *Prescriptive* or *normative* decision analysis focuses on how people *should* make decisions. We will first consider how decisions actually are made and then discuss some techniques to improve decision making in organizations.

STUDYING INDIVIDUAL DECISION-MAKING

There have been many different approaches to study of individual decision making. Some studies have considered how characteristics of the decision maker—such as age, intelligence, motivation, interests, and personality characteristics—are related to such variables as decision accuracy, time to reach a decision, confidence in the decision, riskiness of the decision, and so on.[1] Others have looked at such things as how time and other constraints influence the decision-making process.[2]

Still other studies have focused directly on the question of how the decision maker uses information to arrive at a decision. One way this has been done is to look at the decision makers' choices and the characteristics of the alternatives they accepted and rejected and use statistical techniques to figure out how those characteristics were weighted. Another approach is to have the decision makers voice their thoughts as they go through the decision-making process. Still other approaches are to watch decision makers' eye movements as they examine alternatives or to consider the order in which they select pieces of information from a board that contains various kinds of information about a number of alternatives.

We will refer to many of these studies at relevant points in this chapter. As we will see, one recurring finding is that individuals generally make decisions that are of less than optimal quality.

PITFALLS IN THE DECISION-MAKING PROCESS

To help understand why individuals often make imperfect decisions, it might be useful to consider the sequence of steps shown in figure 16-1. That figure outlines the steps from the point at which information is initially acquired to the point at which a decision is actually made to the time when the consequences of that decision have been evaluated and stored in memory for future reference. The figure also shows some of the many places in the sequence where individual, group, and organizational factors may have some impact.

In an ideal situation:

1. All the information we would need would be available in a convenient form;

2. Our perceptual sensors (sight, hearing, smell, touch, and taste) would accurately and completely pick up signals that we need while filtering out unnecessary signals;

[1]For instance, see Taylor and Dunnette (1974).
[2]For Instance see Wright (1974).

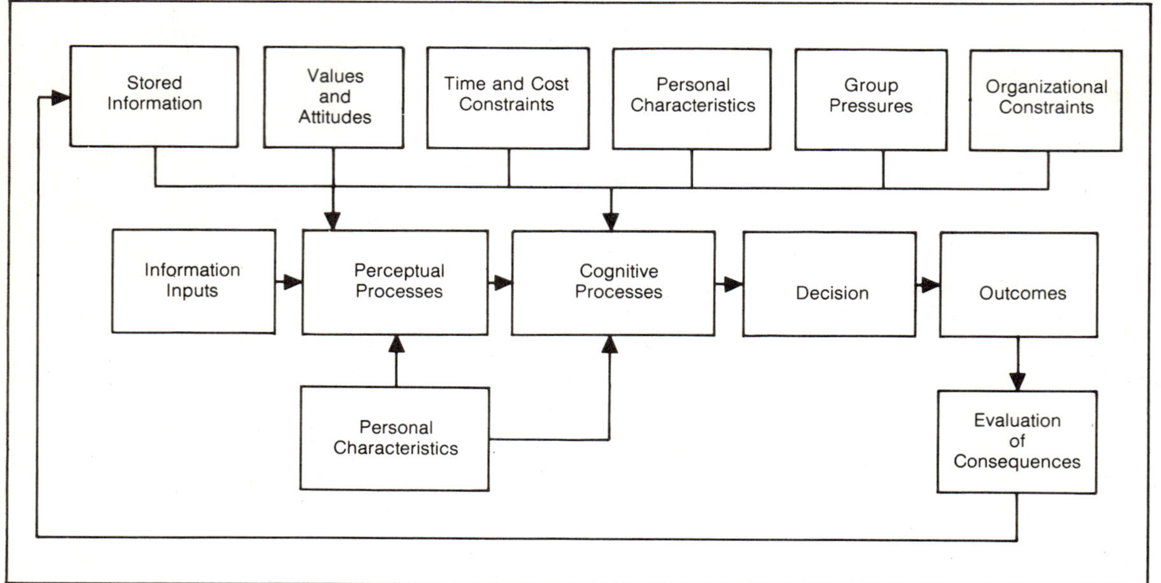

FIGURE 16-1
Some Influences on Individual Decision Making

3. Our cognitive (mental) processes would efficiently process information in such a way as to arrive at an optimal decision; and

4. We would objectively evaluate and store the consequences of the decision.

In fact, though, difficulties may occur at each stage of the process.

Information inputs

In real-life decision-making situations, we may be forced to make decisions on the basis of less good information than we would like. For example, we may not really be aware of all the alternatives available to us, we may not know what things may happen after we have made our decision that could influence how good it is, we may not really know what all the outcomes of our decision will be, and so on. Generally, if the environment in which we're operating is complex and rapidly changing, our difficulties in getting good information may increase. Also, some individuals make decisions on the basis of less information than do others. For example, there is some evidence that people who are risk takers acquire less information before making decisions than do people who are risk averse.[3] Also, dogmatic individuals (people who authoritatively assert their views and doggedly stick to them) have been shown to search less for information before making a decision than do others.[4]

[3]Taylor and Dunnette (1974).
[4]Long and Ziller (1965).

Clearly, if we don't have enough good information to begin with, the quality of our ultimate decision will suffer. On the other hand, there may also be cases where we have too *much* information, much of it probably irrelevant to the decision we're trying to make. What we need is to get the right information in a manageable form.

Perceptual processes

For a number of reasons, our perceptual processes might cause us to make ineffective decisions. For one thing, we have *selective* perception. Only a little of the information that impacts on us gets through our perceptual filters. Unfortunately, that filtering process is biased. That is, we tend to perceive what we're ready to perceive ("I'll see it when I believe it"). As an example, in one study, executives from various departments in a large manufacturing firm were asked to consider a case concerning a steel company and to then write a brief statement about the most important problem facing that company.[5] As shown in table 16-1, almost all sales executives mentioned sales as the primary problem area, while almost all production employees saw organizational problems as most important.

Also, perception is *subjective*. That is, our perceptions tend to be distorted in ways that make them more consistent with our prior attitudes and beliefs. Thus, two different decision makers may perceive the same raw data in very different ways.

Taken together, selective and subjective perceptions may seriously distort the decision maker's view of the world, possibly resulting in poor decisions.

TABLE 16-1
Evidence of Selective Perception in Problem Definition*

		NUMBER OF EXECUTIVES WHO MENTIONED		
Department	Number of Executives	Sales	Organization Structure	Human Relations
Sales	6	5	1	0
Production	5	1	4	0
Accounting	4	3	0	0
Miscellaneous	8	1	3	3
Total	23	10	8	3

*Adapted from Dearborn and Simon (1958)

[5]Dearborn and Simon (1958).

Cognitive processes

Humans are restricted by a number of cognitive limitations. For example:[6]

1. We have a short-term memory with a capacity for only a few symbols.

2. We generally aren't able to perform in our heads the sorts of calculations that would be needed to come up with a really optimal solution.

3. We find decision making uncomfortable. When we make a nontrivial decision, we are often faced with nagging doubts about whether our choice was correct, especially since our rejected alternatives probably had some good characteristics and our accepted alternative may have had some relative weaknesses. This leads us to what is called *cognitive dissonance*. Cognitive dissonance means that we

People have a tendency to put things in classes of which they seem representative. Because women in executive positions are a relatively recent development, many people have trouble thinking of women as executives and, as a consequence, they may be passed over for important positions.

[6]See Simon and Newell (1971) for an expanded discussion of such limitations.

have various cognitions (thoughts) that somehow clash with one another. (For instance, "I've chosen Bob for a position, but in some ways Mary is better," or, "I've purchased a Pinto, but a Chevette is less likely to explode.")

These cognitive limitations and others cause us to do a number of things. For example, because we have limited memory capacity and limited computational abilities, we often use *heuristics*. The term heuristic is derived from a Greek word meaning "to limit search." One heuristic is called *satisficing*, which means taking the first acceptable alternative instead of looking for the best possible solution. James March and Herbert Simon (1958) have compared satisficing to taking the *first* needle you find in a haystack instead of waiting to find the *sharpest* needle. For example, Janet selects as her secretary the first person who can type fifty words a minute instead of testing all applicants and choosing the fastest.

Another simplifying heuristic is simply to ignore much of the information about each alternative and make a decision on the basis of only two or three characteristics, even though we think others might be important. For instance, members of a selection committee, faced with volumes of information concerning job applicants, may focus only on past experience, age, or even physical attractiveness, virtually ignoring everything else. Yet another heuristic is to consider sequentially a series of hurdles and eliminate any alternatives that don't meet those hurdles. (We'll discuss this further in appendix A.)

One other important heuristic, called *representativeness*, refers to the tendency to place something in a class if it seems representative at the class. For instance, if someone seems quite representative of (that is, similar to) a librarian, we're liable to think he or she is a librarian, despite the fact that there are relatively few librarians. This could have serious consequences in organizations. For example, because women have not traditionally been executives, they do not "look like" executives to many people, and, as a result, they may be passed over for important promotions.

There is considerable evidence to indicate that we do use heuristics.[8] Also, it seems that we are often unaware of using such simplifying devices and, in general, that we really don't have a very good idea of how we use information. As one example, a number of employment interviewers were asked to indicate how much they weighted each of five factors, such as typing speed, shorthand speed, and years of experience, when selecting secretaries.[9] They were then asked to rate a large number of hypothetical applicants. Analyses of their ratings showed that the weights they actually gave the various characteristics were quite different from those they thought they were using. Also, it turned out that many of the disagreements among the various interviewers were caused not by differences in the ways

[8]For instance, see Glueck (1974) and Tversky and Kahneman (1974).

[9]Valenzi and Andrews (1973).

they felt they *should* weight the various characteristics but by differences in the ways they actually *did* weight them. This suggests that, even though people may be in complete agreement on a point, errors in the ways they process information may lead to disagreement.

Some other consequences of our cognitive limitations are as follows:

1. We exhibit *conservatism* in the way we process information. That is, when we get new information, we don't revise our prior opinions as much as we should. So if Bob has the initial impression that women can't be good managers, he may retain that impression even after he's been presented with considerable evidence to the contrary.

2. Because decision making is uncomfortable, we often delay our commitment to a particular alternative. That is, we *procrastinate*.

3. To try to reduce the tension caused by cognitive dissonance, we may seek out information that confirms our choice and avoid information that challenges it. For instance, if we buy a Ford, we may then read Ford ads and avoid ads for rival autos. As a result, we're likely to think our decision was better than it actually was. This causes us to store distorted information that may unfavorably affect our future decisions.

4. Since our search processes are inefficient, we tend simply to revise currently available alternatives rather than come up with really new ones. Because this revision is an incremental process in which we first change one thing a bit and then another, this is called *incrementalizing*.

Group influences

Groups exert a number of pressures on decision makers that can influence the nature and quality of their decisions. For example, groups exert pressures for conformity to group norms, they generally cause decisions to be riskier than would otherwise be the case, and they may slow down the decision process. We will consider each of these factors in more detail in chapter 18, "Group Problem Solving."

Organizational influence

A number of organizational factors influence the way we make decisions. One important factor is the nature of the organizational reward system. For instance, if we, as managers, feel that the company penalizes losses more than it rewards gains, we will tend to avoid alternatives that have some possibility of loss, even though the potential gains might be substantial.

Ralph Swalm (1966) examined the risk preferences of about 100 managers. While he found some managers to be risk takers, the great majority clearly tried to avoid risky alternatives. Generally, if an alternative had any possibility of resulting in a loss, the managers saw it as extremely undesirable. Also, the managers became much less consistent in their statements when they were forced to consider losses, suggesting that they were less rational in such a situation than when considering gains. These are important findings. If managers avoid potentially good opportunities because there is some slight chance for loss, the organization will suffer.

Time and cost constraints

It is easy to think of cases in which we simply haven't had the time or resources to make a really good decision. As such, it may seem unnecessary even to mention this point. If we don't have sufficient time or money, we may not be able to get necessary information, to properly implement our decision, and so on. But what may not be so obvious is that such constraints may also influence the fundamental nature of our decision processes. For example, when faced with time constraints, we tend to rely increasingly on heuristics, considering only a few characteristics of alternatives.[10] Also, we tend in such situations to focus on negative information, looking for reasons to reject alternatives.[11]

There is some evidence that certain individuals work better under time constraints than do others. For example, dogmatic individuals (who we previously said search for relatively little information before making a decision) may outperform others when under severe time constraints, but not do so well in other cases.[12] That is, because dogmatic types are accustomed to making decisions with limited data, they do relatively well when there is no time to acquire substantial information. In other cases, their hasty decision making is apparently costly.

ALTERNATIVES TO THE USE OF HUMAN DECISION MAKERS

In view of all these difficulties, we might be tempted just to toss our hands in the air and say, "Forget it. If humans have such problems making decisions, maybe it's best just to flip a coin. Or, maybe we can get a computer to make the decisions." In fact, such a viewpoint is fairly widely held.

The clinical-actuarial controversy

Many writers have argued that whenever possible, we should use a statistical model to choose the best alternative (an *actuarial* approach) instead of using a human decision maker (a *clinical* approach). For instance, Sam, the personnel manager of Security Insurance, faced the problem of selecting insurance agents. In the past,

---

[10,11]Wright (1974).

[12]See Long and Ziller (1965).

agents had been chosen through an intensive interview process. However, poor performance and high turnover of agents signalled the need for a different selection procedure. Also, Sam had been reading some disturbing things about problems associated with interviews. He wanted to find a way to take into consideration all the factors that seemed to be important—years of previous experience, past sales records, education, and so on—and to come up with a less subjective ranking of job candidates. To do this, Sam asked a company statistician to go back to the files of past agents and learn which of their characteristics had been statistically related to high performance. He was then able to apply the resultant equation to characteristics of new applicants to get a good initial estimate of their probable success. He now had a more objective and defensible selection tool.

The controversy of whether to use a statistical model, which finds the maximum relationship between a number of predictor variables and some criterion, or to use a human decision maker is called the *clinical-actuarial* controversy. In fact, substantial evidence suggests that, in many cases, such actuarial models do much better than human decision makers.[13]

The man versus model-of-man controversy

It has also been suggested that, instead of using either a human decision maker or a model that maximizes the relationship between a criterion and various predictor variables, we should build a model of how the human decision maker has acted in the past and use that model to make future decisions. The question of whether to use a human decision maker or a model of that human decision maker is called the *man versus model-of-man* controversy.[14] For example, George had been elated when he was promoted to his current position because it offered the opportunity to make important decisions on a daily basis. As it turned out, though, there was too *much* opportunity to make decisions, and they were taking all his time. And, while the decisions were certainly important enough, they often seemed terribly routine. Day after day, George looked at the same sorts of factors in making his choices. In most cases, things were so clear-cut that a choice was fairly obvious. George had thought about delegating responsibility for most of the decisions but decided against it; routine or not, these should be *his* decisions, determined by his own particular criteria. The solution to George's problem, suggested a consultant, was to develop a model-of-George. By looking at past decisions George had made and the characteristics of accepted and rejected alternatives, it was possible to develop a statistical model that would behave essentially like George. Of course, George didn't just let the model take over. He still looked at marginal cases or

[13]For instance, see Goldberg (1970).

[14]For instance, see Goldberg (1970). Libby (1976a, b), Goldberg (1976), and Smith (1968).

those that were somehow unusual. But, even in those situations where the model-of-George made the choice, George was confident that his preferences were being respected.

One argument in favor of use of models-of-man is that they actually perform better than the human they model since they are completely reliable. That is, unlike a human, if they are given the same information on two different days, they will make the same decisions rather than being influenced by moods, distractions, and so on. Another advantage cited for use of models-of-man is that they free the human decision maker's time for performing more important tasks. Also, once the model is derived, it can be used to train novice decision makers and may also provide useful self-insight for the individual who was modeled.

However, there are some arguments against use of such models. For example, will people accept a decision made by a model as readily as they will accept an "expert" judgment? Also, what are the ethical implications of using such models for making decisions? That is, is it ethical to use a model at all? If a model is used, do we have an obligation to tell people who are affected by the decision that it was reached by use of a model? On the other hand, is it ethical *not* to use a model if we have evidence that it works better than a human decision maker?

IMPROVING INDIVIDUAL DECISION MAKING

While it sometimes may be possible to let computers choose from among alternatives, such an approach is probably cost effective only in the case of important decisions that will be made many times. Also, of course, we don't want to move managers completely out of decision-making roles. Because the bulk of hard decisions in organizations will remain with human decision makers, it is important to ask how individual decision making can be improved.

There are a number of things individuals can do to try to improve their decision making in organizations. For example, they can:

1. Ask if this is, in fact, a decision that is best made by an individual or whether a group process would be preferable.

2. Simply be aware of the potential problems involved in decision making. Conscious attention to such pitfalls may help prevent them.

3. Attempt to gain self-insight about characteristics relevant to decision making, such as risk-taking propensity, dogmatism, and cognitive complexity. Scales to measure each of these dimensions and many others are readily available.

4. Try to proceed systematically through the decision-making process. For example, decision makers who take the time to search for a number of alternatives and then to evaluate them carefully prior to

making a choice generally outperform those who focus almost entirely on the choice step.

5. Try to take actions to insure that the information they receive from subordinates and others is as complete as necessary and unbiased.

6. Try to make sure that their communications to those who must implement the decision or are affected by it are clear and forceful.

Also, decision makers can use a number of techniques to help offset their weaknesses. These would include techniques to:

1. Generate a large number of alternatives, as well as other necessary information

2. Display available alternatives and information

3. Prevent incrementalizing and procrastination

4. Prevent conservatism in information processing. Such techniques for this final purpose, primarily statistical, are described in most basic statistics texts.

NORMATIVE DECISION-MAKING TECHNIQUES

Yet another way decision makers can improve their choices is by applying normative models. As we said before, normative approaches focus on how people *should* make decisions as opposed to how they *do* make decisions. The appropriate models will depend on whether the decision is made in a situation of *certainty, risk, uncertainty,* or *conflict.* To understand the differences between these situations, it will be useful to consider a *decision matrix.* A decision matrix is simply one way of displaying the sorts of information we need in order to make an optimal decision. To determine this, we must answer the following questions.

1. What *alternatives* do we have?

2. What *states of nature* (or events) might occur after we make our choice that will influence the quality of our choice?

3. What are the respective *probabilities* of the various states of nature?

4. What *outcomes* would result from various combinations of alternatives and states of nature?

5. What are the *utilities* (that is, levels of satisfactoriness) of each of those outcomes?

For example, consider the case, shown in figure 16-2, of an executive making a decision about expanding plant capacity. The *alternatives* under review might be (a) no expansion, (b) 25 percent expansion, (c) 50 percent expansion, and (d) 100 percent expansion.

	States of Nature				
	Sharply Declining Economy	Slightly Declining Economy	Unchanged Economy	Slightly Improving Economy	Sharply Improving Economy
Alternatives	p=.2	p=.2	p=.3	p=.2	p=.1
No Expansion	50	60	75	50	0
25% Expansion	35	55	70	80	50
50% Expansion	25	50	60	70	75
100% Expansion	0	25	50	75	100

FIGURE 16-2
Sample Decision Matrix

The relevant *states of nature* that would occur after his or her choice was made might include the rate of growth of the national economy (which could perhaps be roughly classified as sharply declining, slightly declining, unchanged, slightly improving, and sharply improving). Associated with each possible state of nature is a *probability* that it will occur. For instance, the probability of slight economic growth might be .2. Finally, for every combination of a particular degree of plant expansion and of economic growth, certain outcomes (measured perhaps in terms of sales or earnings) and their corresponding *utilities* to the organization can be identified. In figure 16-2, the cells in the matrix show the utilities (levels of satisfactoriness) of the various outcomes. For instance, the best possible outcome, given a utility of 100, would occur if the plant was expanded by 100 percent and the economy sharply improved. On the other hand, failure to expand in the event of a sharply improving economy or 100 percent expansion in the face of a sharply declining economy would be the worst outcomes, given utilities of zero.

The sorts of information we need to make an optimal decision aren't always available. However, a number of techniques can help us get that information. For example, in later chapters we'll consider various processes that are useful in generating a large number of good alternatives and other parts of the decision matrix.

The decision situation is one of *certainty* if we know exactly which state of nature is going to occur. For example, if the states of nature are various weather conditions (perhaps rain, snow, sunshine, and tornado) and we are certain that it will rain, we have a decision under certainty. On the other hand, if we know the probabilities of the various states of nature (such as .5 for rain, .1 for snow, .39 for sunshine, and .01 for tornado), we are faced with a decision under *risk*. If we don't know anything at all about which state of nature will occur—that is, we can't even attach crude probabilities to them—the decision is one under *uncertainty*. Finally, if the states of nature are the actions of a competitor rather than of an uncaring environment, we have the case of a decision under *conflict*.

SUMMARY

Decision making is crucial for both the organization and the individual manager. Unfortunately, numerous studies show that humans are less than perfect decision makers. Some causes for that imperfection include inadequate information, perceptual difficulties, cognitive limitations, group pressures, organizational influences, and time and cost constraints.

In response to evidence of human limitations, some writers have argued that human decision makers should be replaced either by actuarial models or by models of the human decision maker. There is, in fact, considerable evidence that such models may actually outperform humans in some situations and may offer a number of other advantages.

However, humans undoubtedly will continue to make most decisions in organizations. Individuals can do a variety of things to improve their decision making, including using normative models. Which model is appropriate depends upon whether the decision is made in a situation of certainty, risk, uncertainty, or conflict.

REFERENCES

Dearborn, D.C., and Simon, H.A. "Selective Perception: A Note on the Departmental Identifications of Executives." In *Psychology in Administration*, edited by T.W. Costello and S.S. Zalkind, pp. 49-52. Englewood Cliffs, N.J.: Prentice-Hall, 1963.

Einhorn, H.J. "Use of Nonlinear, Noncompensatory Models as a Function of Task and Amount of Information." *Organizational Behavior and Human Performance 6* (1971): 1-27.

Glueck, W.F. "Decision Making: Organization Choice." *Personnel Psychology 27* (1974): 77-93.

Goldberg, L.R. "Man Versus Model of Man: A Rationale, Plus Some Evidence, for a Method of Improving on Clinical Inferences." *Psychological Bulletin 73* (1970): 422-32.

Goldberg, L.R. "Just How Conflicting Is the Evidence? *Organizational Behavior and Human Performance 16* (1976): 13-22.

Huber, G.P. "Methods for Quantifying Subjective Probabilities and Multi-attribute Utilities." *Decision Sciences 5* (1974): 430-58.

Huber, G.P. *Managerial Decision Making*. Glenview Ill.: Scott, Foresman, 1980.

Keeney, R.L. "Energy Policy and Value Tradeoffs." International Institute for Applied Systems Analysis Research Memorandum. Schloss Laxenburg, Austria, 1975.

Libby, R. "Man Versus Model of Man: Some Conflicting Evidence. *Organizational Behavior and Human Performance 16* (1976a): 1-12.

Libby, R. "Man Versus Model of Man: The Need for a Nonlinear Model." *Organizational Behavior and Human Performance 16* (1976b): 23-26.

Long, B.H., and Ziller, R.C. "Dogmatism and Predecisional Information Search." *Journal of Applied Psychology 49* (1965): 376-78.

March, J.G., and Simon, H.A. *Organizations*. New York: Wiley, 1958.

Payne, J.W. "Task Complexity and Contingent Processing in Decision Making: An Information Search and Protocol Analysis. *Organizational Behavior and Human Performance 16* (1976): 366-87.

Simon, H.A., and Newell, A. "Human Problem Solving: The State of the Theory in 1970." *American Psychologist 26* (1971): 145-59.

Smith, R.D. "Heuristic Simulation of Psychological Decision Processes." *Journal of Applied Psychology 52* (1968): 325-30.

Swalm, R.O. "Utility theory—Insights into Risk Taking." *Harvard Business Review 44* (Nov.-Dec. 1966): 123-36.

Taylor, R.N., and Dunnette, M.D. "Relative Contribution of Decision-Maker Attributes to Decision Processes." *Organizational Behavior and Human Performance 12* (1974): 286-98.

Tversky, A., and Kahneman, D. "Judgment under Uncertainty: Heuristics and Biases." *Science 185* (1974): 1124-31.

Valenzi, E., and Andrews, I.R. "Individual Differences in the Decision Process of Employment Interviewers." *Journal of Applied Psychology 58* (1973): 49-53.

Williams, J.D. *The Compleat Strategyst.* New York: McGraw-Hill, 1966.

Wright, P. "The Harassed Decision Maker: Time Pressures, Distractions, and the Use of Evidence." *Journal of Applied Psychology 59* (1974): 555-61.

SUGGESTIONS FOR ADVANCED READINGS

Feldman, J. and Kanter, H.E. "Organizational Decision Making." In *Handbook of Organizations,* (edited by J.G. March.) Chicago: Rand McNally, 1965.

Huber, G.P. *Managerial Decision Making.* Glenview Ill.: Scott, Foresman, 1980.

Simon, H. and Newell, A. "Human Probelm Solving: The State of the Theory in 1970." *American Psychologist 26* (1971): 145-59.

Swalm, R.O. "Utility Theory—Insights into Risk Taking." *Harvard Business Review 44* (1966): 123-36.

Taylor, R.N. "Psychological Determinants of Bounded Rationality: Implications for Decision-Making Strategies." *Decision Sciences* 6 (1975): 409-29.

Taylor, R.N., and Dunnette, M.D. "Relative Contribution of Decision-Maker Attributes to Decision Processes." *Organizational Behavior and Human Performance 12* (1974): 286-98.

Tversky, A. and Kahneman, D. Judgment under Uncertainty: Heuristics and Biases." *Science 185* (1974): 1124-31.

Williams, J.D. *The Compleat Strategyst.* New York: McGraw-Hill, 1966.

Models for Decision Making

DECISION MAKING UNDER CERTAINTY

In the case of decision making under certainty, things are pretty straightforward. That is, since we know which state of nature will occur, we can simply choose the alternative with the highest utility for that state of nature. For example, if we know it is going to rain, we will probably wear a raincoat. If we know there is going to be an oil embargo, we will probably purchase a small car instead of a gas guzzler.

Of course, one problem is deciding on the utilities of various alternatives. If alternatives differ in terms of just one attribute, such as cost or expected return or color, there are fairly simple techniques available to calculate their corresponding utilities and, thus, to determine the best alternative.[1] On the other hand, the things we must choose between often differ in terms of several attributes. For example, various jobs may differ in terms of salary offers, promotion potential, geographical location, prestige, and so on. Various products may differ in terms of such characteristics as price, quality, and color. How can we choose among alternatives that differ in so many ways? As another example, consider table A-1 which depicts some of the various factors an energy policy maker from Wisconsin considered in choosing from among alternative sources of energy. Those factors include such things as probable loss of human lives, radioactive waste, SO_2 pollution, and electricity generated. How can we trade off electricity with pollution? How many kilowatts of electricity are equivalent to a human life?

In fact, there are at least two primary ways to choose from among alternatives differing in terms of their ratings on a number of attributes.

1. Screening Approaches—With these, we systematically screen out alternatives that don't meet various constraints or hurdles that we impose. We generally would start by screening out alternatives that are unsatisfactory in terms of the attribute we consider to be most important, then those that are unsatisfactory in terms of the second most important attribute, and so on. (We alluded to such approaches in the discussion of simplifying heuristics.)
2. Scoring Approaches—With these, we give a weight to each attribute, score each alternative on each attribute, and then some-

TABLE A-1
Selected Data Concerning Energy Alternatives*

Attribute	Measure	LEVEL Best	Worst
X_1 = fatalities	deaths	100	700
X_5 = SO_2 pollution	10^6 tons	5	80
X_7 = thermal energy needed	10^{12} kwh (thermal)	3	6
X_8 = radioactive waste	metric tons	0	200
X_{11} = electricity generated	10^{12} kwh (electric)	3	0.5

*From Keeney (1975)

[1]See, for instance Swalm (1966).

how combine those weights and scores to get an overall score for each alternative.

As an example of a screening approach, consider the bicycles in table A-2. Suppose that we consider price to be the most important attribute, then weight, then handling precision, then shifting ease and precision, and so on. Suppose further that we decide we would like the bicycle we choose to:

1. Cost under $200,
2. Weigh under thirty pounds, and
3. Have a handling precision rating above 5.

By first applying the cost constraint, we would screen out the Fuji, leaving the Nishiki, Schwinn, and Iverson. By applying the weight constraint, we would screen out the Schwinn and Iverson, leaving the Nishiki as our first choice by the process of elimination. This approach—where we consider one attribute at a time—is called *elimination*. Another screening approach is called *satisficing*. With satisficing, we would first look at the Nishiki. If the Nishiki met all of our constraints, we would accept it and not look at other alternatives. If it didn't, we would next consider the Schwinn, and so on. Since the satisfacing approach leads to choosing the first acceptable alternative, the order in which alternatives are presented is clearly important. Such is not the case with the elimination approach.

If we were to use a scoring approach to choose from among the bicycles, we somehow would have to determine the weight we want to attach to each characteristic and then decide how to combine all that information in order to reach an overall score. Obviously, we would choose the bicycle with the highest score. The overall model we would put together for each individual decision maker is called a *multiattribute utility model*. While we don't have the space here to describe the techniques used to derive such models, they are fully explained elsewhere.[2]

Suppose that the following model was derived for our bicycle example, where the X_i's refer to the characteristics shown in table A-2:

TABLE A-2
Characteristics of Various Bicycles*

BICYCLE CHARACTERISTICS						
Model	X_1 Weight (Pounds)	X_2 Price (Dollars)	X_3 Overall Bearing Quality (0-10)	X_4 Wet Braking (% of Dry)	X_5 Handling Precision (0-10)	X_6 Shifting Ease and Precision (0-10)
Nishiki 585 International	28.5	166	6	20	7	10
Schwinn Continental 324	37	150	5	20	6	2
Iverson Grand Sport 9754	36.5	90	1	30	5	4
Fuji Road Racer S105	28	215	7	60	7	10

*Adapted from *Consumer Reports*

[2]For instance, see Huber (1980) for a thorough discussion of derivation of such models, including examples.

$$\text{Utility} = 5X_3 + X_4 + 2X_5 + X_6 - X_1 - X_2/4$$

This equation tells us that the overall utility of each bicycle is a linear combination of its scores on the various characteristics. Characteristics 3 through 6 have positive signs, telling us that they are desirable. Characteristics 1 and 2 have negative signs, showing that we would like them to be as low as possible. To get the overall utility for each bicycle, we simply plug in the scores from table A-2. For the Nishiki, for instance, the utility would be:

$$\text{Utility} = (5 \times 6) + 20 + (2 \times 7) + 10 - 28.5 - (166/4) = 4.0$$

Similar calculations for the other bicycles show that the utilities for Schwinn, Iverson, and Fuji are −15.5, −5, and 37.25 respectively. The absolute scores don't mean much. What is important is how one score compares to another. That is, which bicycle has the highest overall utility? In this case, the Fuji is the clear choice.

We can see here one of the important differences between screening and scoring approaches. With a screening approach, one unsatisfactory characteristic will eliminate an alternative, no matter how good it is in other ways. Scoring approaches let good characteristics compensate for the bad. So while the Fuji was eliminated by the screening approach because of its price, the fact that it did well in all other categories made it the distinct first choice by the scoring approach. An interesting finding concerning such models is that different people combine information in considerably different ways.[3] Also, the same people tend to combine information differently for different tasks.[4] It is important, therefore, that we do not make unfounded assumptions about how people use information. For instance, we can't just assume that overall job satisfaction is simply the sum of the satisfactions with various job characteristics.

DECISION MAKING UNDER RISK

In the case of decision making under risk, we don't know what state of nature will occur, but we do at least know the probabilities of various states of nature. In such a case, the appropriate criterion is to choose the alternative with the highest *expected utility*. To get the expected utility for an alternative, we multiply the utility of each outcome associated with an alternative by the probability of the corresponding state of nature and add up those products. For example, consider the following situation:

Carol is trying to decide which of two crops to plant, A or B. Success of crop A depends largely on average temperature during the growing season. If average temperature is below normal (p = .3), value of the crop will be $100. If average temperature is normal (p = .4), value of the crop will be $175. When average temperature is above normal (p = .3), value of the crop should be $80.

Success of crop B, a sensitive potato variety, depends solely on precipitation levels. If they are normal or above (p = .6), the crop will be successful with a value of $150. If they are below normal, the potatoes will dry up. In such a case, the potatoes can only be sold as imitation pet rocks, with a value of $20.

Which crop should Carol plant?

To properly answer this question, we first would have to determine the utility to Carol of different amounts of money. In the absence of that information, we must

[3] For example, see Payne (1976)

[4] See Einhorn (1971) on this point.

assume that Carol's utility function for money is linear—that is, each additional dollar has the same utility as the dollar before it. Making that assumption, we can compare the expected dollar values of the two alternative crops:

Crop A: .3 x 100 + .4 x 175 + .3 x 80 = $124

Crop B: .6 x 150 + .4 x 20 = $98

Thus, Carol should plant crop A to maximize expected value.

In some cases, we lack really good objective probabilities (such as the probability of getting a head on the flip of a fair coin); instead, we have to estimate those probabilities. Since those estimates are somewhat subjective, they are called *subjective probabilities*. There are a number of ways available to help us get good subjective probabilities.[5] Once we have those subjective probabilities, we can use them just as we would use objective probabilities. That is, we would find the *subjective expected utility* for each alternative and choose the alternative with the highest value. Expectancy theory, which we discussed earlier, is a subjective expected utility maximizing model.

DECISION MAKING UNDER UNCERTAINTY

In the case of decision making under uncertainty, we don't know anything at all about the respective probabilities of the various states of nature. We don't even feel confident in saying that any one state of nature is more or less likely than any other. This uncomfortable situation requires the decision maker to make an essentially arbitrary application of one of a number of criteria. Each of those criteria violates at least one of a series of "postulates of rationality," which describe rational behavior. So we will say in advance: Where possible, don't make decisions under uncertainty. Instead, do all you can somehow to come up with probabilities of states of nature, either subjective or objective.

Assuming, though, that there is no way to get such probabilities, there are several criteria that can be applied. Some are based on observations of how people actually do seem to make choices in uncertain situations. To understand those criteria, consider figure A-1 which shows a situation where the decision maker must choose among four alternatives and where three states of nature may

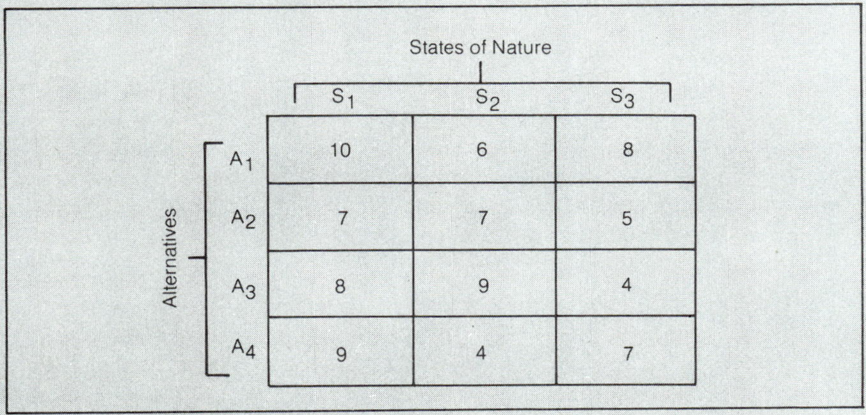

	S_1	S_2	S_3
A_1	10	6	8
A_2	7	7	5
A_3	8	9	4
A_4	9	4	7

FIGURE A-1
Decision Making under Uncertainty Example

[5] For instance, see Huber (1974).

occur. The numbers in the cells of the matrix are the values to the decision maker of the various possible outcomes. For example, if the decision maker chooses alternative 3 and state of nature 2 occurs, the value of the corresponding outcome will be 9.

One thing we can see immediately is that the values for alternative 1 are always better than those for alternative 4. So alternative 4 is said to be *dominated* by alternative 1. When one alternative is dominated by another, it can be eliminated from consideration. No matter what criterion is applied, it will lose.

Of the several criteria that can be applied to the remaining alternatives, the following four are the best known:

1. The maximax criterion (or criterion of optimism) basically says, "Assume that the best that can happen will happen. So choose the alternative with the biggest possible return". In this case, alternative 1 would be chosen since it has the greatest possible value (10) compared to a maximum of 7 for alternative 2 and 9 for alternative 3. Clearly, this criterion is unrealistically optimistic.
2. The maximin criterion (or criterion of pessimism) says, "Assume that, no matter what alternative you pick, things will go wrong. Assume that for each alternative, the worst possible state of nature will occur. Choose the alternative with the greatest minimum return". For our example, the minimums for the alternatives are 6, 5, and 4 respectively. Thus, alternative 1 should be chosen. (If we're talking about losses rather than returns, we want to minimize the maximum loss, so we apply the minimax criterion).
3. The Laplace criterion (or criterion of rationality or criterion of insufficient reason) simply says, "If you really can't say anything at all about the probabilities of various states of nature, the reasonable thing to do is to assume they're equal. If you have any reason to believe they're not equal, you should use that information to come up with subjective probabilities". In the case of our example, there are three states of nature, so we would assume that the probabilities of each are $1/3$. Thus, the expected utilities of each would be 8, $6\frac{1}{3}$, and 7 respectively, indicating that alternative 1 should be chosen.
4. The Savage criterion (or criterion of minimax regret) says that what people really want to do is not maximize return but rather minimize the extent to which they may regret their choice. So we should choose the alternative with the lowest possible maximum regret. To do this, we have to transform the original decision matrix into a *regret* matrix. For instance, in the situation we are considering, the decision maker might ask, "How sorry would I be if I chose alternative 3 and state of nature 1 occurred?" The answer is that he or she would have two units of regret since alternative 1 in that case would have led to a value of 10, as opposed to the value of 8 for alternative 3. To get the regret matrix, then, we subtract each number in a column from the best number in the column. The resulting matrix for this example is shown in figure A-2. In this case, the maximum possible regrets for the alternatives are 3, 3, and 4, respectively. As a result, either alternatives 1 or 2 should be chosen. Basically, application of the Savage criterion means never having to say you're sorry.

Some of these criteria seem more intuitively appealing than others. However, we should again stress that each of the criteria is, in fact, some-

FIGURE A-2
Regret Matrix

Alternatives	S_1	S_2	S_3	Maximum Possible Regret
A_1	0	3	0	3
A_2	3	2	3	3
A_3	2	0	4	4

(States of Nature: S_1, S_2, S_3)

how flawed. In this case, we were lucky. That is, each of the criteria indicated that A_1 was better than, or at least as good as, any other alternative. But this happy coincidence doesn't generally occur. In most cases, two or more alternatives are preferred by the various criteria. Thus, the decision maker must either choose the alternative suggested by the largest number of criteria or simply pick a number from a hat. So, as we said earlier, if there is any way we can do so, we should try to avoid the situation of decision making under uncertainty, the various criteria for which are summarized in table A-3.

DECISION MAKING UNDER CONFLICT

Up to this point, we have considered the case of decision makers acting in an environment that was indifferent to them. That is, while the decision makers may have had some trouble in learning about the probabilities of various potential states of nature, they at least could feel confident that nature was not "out to get them." There are cases, though, where such an assumption is unwarranted. For example, suppose that the states of nature were, instead, the actions of a competitor. In such an instance, we not only could probably not attach probabilities to various potential actions but we could be pretty sure that the competitor was, in fact, "out to get us." Especially in cases where there is a relatively fixed amount of gains to be divided by the competitors, our competition probably will try to minimize our returns.

At one level, the competitor might be some rival organization fighting with our firm for shares of a fixed market. Within the firm, the competitor might be the head of another department, in conflict with our department for shares of the cor-

TABLE A-3
Criteria for Decision Making under Uncertainty

CRITERION	
Maximax (or criterion of optimism)	Choose alternative corresponding to the best outcome in the decision matrix.
Maximin (or criterion of pessimism)	Choose alternative with the largest minimum return.
Laplace (or criterion of rationality or criterion of insufficient reason)	Assume states of nature are equally likely and treat the problem as one under risk.
Minimax regret (or Savage criterion)	Determine regret levels. Choose the alternative with the lowest possible regret.

porate budget, or even another individual vying with us for promotion to a single higher-level position. *Game theory* is an approach used to determine what strategies each competitor should choose in order to do as well as possible in the face of competition.[6] It allows each competitor to decide which of his or her alternative strategies to play (or, perhaps, what *mix* of strategies to play over time) and also to figure out how much he or she can expect to lose or gain by competing.

In the case of decision making under conflict, game theory argues that each competitor should adopt a strategy to do as well as possible in the face of an adversary who is trying to minimize his or her well-being. That is, each competitor should adopt a maximin strategy (if gains are being considered) or a minimax strategy (if losses are being considered).

We can't explore the mechanics of game theory in the space available, but we can say that calculations may lead to one of two situations:

1. A situation in which it is found that each player should play the same strategy each time the game is played. This is called playing a *pure strategy*.
2. A situation in which it is determined that a player or players should vary the strategy played from one time to the next. This is called playing a *mixed strategy*. For instance, it might be determined that the optimal mixed strategy for a competitor is to play strategy 1 three times for every one time that strategy 2 is played.

A problem that occurs in a situation calling for a mixed strategy is determining *when* to play each strategy. For instance, even though the competitor knows that he or she should play strategy 1 three times for every one time that strategy 2 is played, the question still remains of how to mix up those three and one times. The competitor can't just play the first strategy three times and then the second once, because his or her adversary would quickly catch onto this and retaliate. On the other hand, the competitor might try randomly to play strategy 1 three times, on the average, for every one time that strategy 2 is played.

However, we have already indicated that humans are, in many ways, inferior to computers. More depressingly, we are even in some ways inferior to the simple flip of a coin. That is, we can't even act *randomly* when we would like to. Instead, we show *patterning behavior*. For example, assume that heads and tails are equally likely outcomes of the flip of a fair coin. Consider the following sequences of outcomes:

Sequence A: HHHHHHHH

Sequence B: TTHTHTHH

Which sequence seems most likely to occur by chance? Many people would pick sequence B; it seems reasonable that a mixture of tails and heads is more likely to occur randomly than a sequence of all heads. In fact, though, each sequence is equally probable and would be expected to occur once in every 256 series of tosses. That is, any *particular* sequence of heads and tails is just as likely as a string of all heads.

So we can't count on ourselves to act randomly, because we'll probably avoid long "runs" of the same outcome. Instead, in cases where random behavior is required, we should rely on true random-number generating devices. For example, if we need a .5 probability for the occurrence of each of two outcomes, we can flip a coin; heads can represent the occurrence of the first out-

[6]See Williams (1966) for a thorough and interesting examination of game theory.

DECISION SITUATIONS	CHARACTERISTICS	APPROPRIATE CRITERIA	SUITABLE TOOLS
Certainty	State of nature which will occur is known	Maximize Utility	Utility Models, Multi-attribute Utility Models, Decision Structure Tables
Risk	Probabilities of states of nature are known	Maximize Expected Utility	Decision Trees, Decision Matrices
Uncertainty	Probabilities of states of nature are unknown	Various (See table 16-4)	Decision Matrices
Conflict	States of nature are actions of a competitor	Maximize Minimum Return	Game Theory

TABLE A-4
Summary of Normative Models

come and tails of the other. If we need a probability of one-sixth for an outcome, we can pick a number from one to six and toss a die to see if that number comes up. If we want a probability of one-quarter, we can choose a particular fifteen-second interval on our watch and then see whether the second hand is or is not in that interval.

Table A-4 summarizes the various decision situations we've considered, their characteristics, appropriate criteria to be applied, and suitable tools.

CHAPTER

17

Groupthink*

"How could we have been so stupid?" President John F. Kennedy asked after he and a close group of advisors had blundered into the Bay of Pigs invasion. For the last two years I have been studying that question, as it applies not only to the Bay of Pigs decision makers but also to those who led the United States into such other major fiascos as the failure to be prepared for the attack on Pearl Harbor, the Korean War stalemate, and the escalation of the Vietnam War.

Stupidity certainly is not the explanation. The men who participated in making the Bay of Pigs decision, for instance, comprised one of the greatest arrays of intellectual talent in the history of American Government—Dean Rusk, Robert McNamara, Douglas Dillon, Robert Kennedy, McGeorge Bundy, Arthur Schlesinger Jr., Allen Dulles, and others.

It also seemed to me that explanations were incomplete if they concentrated only on disturbances in the behavior of each individual within a decision-making body: temporary emotional states of elation, fear, or anger that reduce a man's mental efficiency, for example, or chronic blind spots arising from a man's social prejudices or idiosyncratic biases.

I preferred to broaden the picture by looking at the fiascos from the standpoint of group dynamics as it has been explored over the past three decades, first by the great social psychologist Kurt Lewin and later in many experimental situations by myself and other behavioral scientists. My conclusion after poring over hundreds of relevant documents—historical reports about formal group meetings and informal conversations among the members—is that the groups that committed the fiascos were victims of what I call "groupthink."

*Reprinted from Irving L. Janis, "Groupthink," *Psychology Today*. Copyright © 1971 Ziff-Davis Publishing Company.

"GROUPY"

In each case study, I was surprised to discover the extent to which each group displayed the typical phenomena of social conformity that are regularly encountered in studies of group dynamics among ordinary citizens. For example, some of the phenomena appear to be completely in line with findings from social-psychological experiments showing that powerful social pressures are brought to bear by the members of a cohesive group whenever a dissident begins to voice his objections to a group consensus. Other phenomena are reminiscent of the shared illusions observed in encounter groups and friendship cliques when the members simultaneously reach a peak of "groupy" feelings.

Above all, there are numerous indications pointing to the development of group norms that bolster morale at the expense of critical thinking. One of the most common norms appears to be that of remaining loyal to the group by sticking with the policies to which the group has already committed itself, even when those policies are obviously working out badly and have unintended consequences that disturb the conscience of each member. This is one of the key characteristics of groupthink.

1984

I use the term *groupthink* as a quick and easy way to refer to the mode of thinking that persons engage in when *concurrence seeking* becomes so dominant in a cohesive ingroup that it tends to override realistic appraisal of alternative courses of action. Groupthink is a term of the same order as the words in the newspeak vocabulary George Orwell used in his dismaying world of *1984*. In that context, groupthink takes on an invidious connotation. Exactly such a connotation is intended, since the term refers to a deterioration in mental efficiency, reality testing, and moral judgments as a result of group pressures.

The symptoms of groupthink arise when the members of decision-making groups become motivated to avoid being too harsh in their judgments of their leaders' or their colleagues' ideas. They adopt a soft line of criticism, even in their own thinking. At their meetings, all the members are amiable and seek complete concurrence on every important issue, with no bickering or conflict to spoil the cozy, "we-feeling" atmosphere.

KILL

Paradoxically, soft-headed groups are often hard-hearted when it comes to dealing with outgroups or enemies. They find it relatively easy to resort to dehumanizing solutions—they will readily authorize bombing attacks that kill large numbers of civilians in the name of the noble cause of persuading an unfriendly government to negotiate at the peace table. They are unlikely to pursue the more difficult and controversial issues that arise when alternatives to a harsh military solution come up for discussion. Nor are they inclined to raise ethical issues that carry the implication that *this fine group of ours, with its humanitarianism and its high-minded principles, might be capable of adopting a course of action that is inhumane and immoral.*

NORMS

There is evidence from a number of social-psychological studies that as the members of a group feel more accepted by the others, which is a central feature of increased group cohesiveness, they display less overt conformity to group norms. Thus we would expect that the more cohesive a group becomes, the less the members will feel constrained to censor what they say out of fear of being socially punished for antagonizing the leader or any of their fellow members.

In contrast, the groupthink type of conformity tends to increase as group cohesiveness increases. Groupthink involves nondeliberate suppression of critical thoughts as a result of internalization of the group's norms, which is quite different from deliberate suppression on the basis of external threats of social punishment. The more cohesive the group, the greater the inner compulsion on the part of each member to avoid creating disunity, which inclines him to believe in the soundness of whatever proposals are promoted by the leader or by a majority of the group's members.

In a cohesive group, the danger is not so much that each individual will fail to reveal his objections to what the others propose but that he will think the proposal is a good one, without attempting to carry out a careful, critical scrutiny of the pros and cons of the alternatives. When groupthink becomes dominant, there also is considerable suppression of deviant thoughts, but it takes the form of each person's deciding that his misgivings are not relevant and should be set aside, that the benefit of the doubt regarding any lingering uncertainties should be given to the group consensus.

STRESS

I do not mean to imply that all cohesive groups necessarily suffer from groupthink. All ingroups may have a mild tendency toward groupthink, displaying one or another of the symptoms from time to time, but it need not be so dominant as to influence the quality of the group's final decision. Neither do I mean to imply that there is anything necessarily inefficient or harmful about group decisions in general. On the contrary, a group whose members have properly defined roles, with traditions concerning the procedures to follow in pursuing a critical inquiry, probably is capable of making better decisions than any individual group member working alone.

The problem is that the advantages of having decisions made by groups are often lost because of powerful psychological pressures that arise when the members work closely together, share the same set of values, and, above all, face a crisis situation that puts everyone under intense stress.

The main principle of groupthink, which I offer in the spirit of Parkinson's Law, is this: *The more amiability and esprit de corps there is among the members of a policy-making ingroup, the greater the danger that independent critical thinking will be replaced by groupthink, which is likely to result in irrational and dehumanizing actions directed against outgroups.*

SYMPTOMS

In my studies of high-level governmental decision makers, both civilian and military, I have found eight main symptoms of groupthink.

1. Invulnerability

Most or all of the members of the ingroup share an *illusion* of invulnerability that provides for them some degree of reassurance about obvious dangers and leads them to become overoptimistic and willing to take extraordinary risks. It also causes them to fail to respond to clear warnings of danger.

The Kennedy ingroup, which uncritically accepted the Central Intelligence Agency's disastrous Bay of Pigs plan, operated on the false assumption that they could keep secret the fact that the United States was responsible for the invasion of Cuba. Even after news of the plan began to leak out, their belief remained unshaken. They failed even to consider the danger that awaited them: a worldwide revulsion against the U.S.

A similar attitude appeared among the members of President Lyndon B. Johnson's ingroup, the "Tuesday Cabinet," which kept escalating the Vietnam War despite repeated setbacks and failures. "There was a belief," Bill Moyers commented after he resigned, "that if we indicated a willingness to use our power, they *the North Vietnamese* would get the message and back away from an all-out confrontation. . . . There was a confidence—it was never bragged about, it was just there—that when the chips were really down, the other people would fold."

A most poignant example of an illusion of invulnerability involves the ingroup around Admiral H.E. Kimmel, which failed to prepare for the possibility of a Japanese attack on Pearl Harbor despite repeated warnings. Informed by his intelligence chief that radio contact with Japanese aircraft carriers had been lost, Kimmel joked about it: "What, you don't know where the carriers are? Do you mean to say that they could be rounding Diamond Head (at Honolulu) and you wouldn't know it?" The carriers were in fact moving full-steam toward Kimmel's command post at the time. Laughing together about a danger signal, which labels it as a purely laughing matter, is a characteristic manifestation of groupthink.

2. Rationale

As we see, victims of groupthink ignore warnings; they also collectively construct rationalizations in order to discount warnings and other forms of negative feedback that, taken seriously, might lead the group members to reconsider their assumptions each time they recommit themselves to past decisions. Why did the Johnson ingroup avoid reconsidering its escalation policy when time and again the expectations on which they based their decisions turned out to be wrong? James C. Thompson Jr., a Harvard historian who spent five years as an observing participant in both the State Department and the White House, tells us that the policymakers avoided critical discussion of their prior decisions and continually invented new rationalizations so that they could sincerely recommit themselves to defeating the North Vietnamese.

In the fall of 1964, before the bombing of North Vietnam began, some of the policymakers predicted that six weeks of air strikes would induce the North Vietnamese to seek peace talks. When someone asked, "What if they don't?" the answer was that another four weeks certainly would do the trick.

Later, after each setback, the ingroup agreed that by investing just a bit more effort (by stepping up the bomb tonnage a bit, for instance), their course of action would prove to be right. *The Pentagon Papers* bear out these observations.

In *The Limits of Intervention,* Townsend Hoopes, who was acting Secretary of the Air Force under Johnson, says that Walt W. Rostow in particular showed a remarkable capacity for what has been called "instant rationalization." According to Hoopes, Rostow buttressed the group's optimism about being on the road to victory by culling selected scraps of evidence from news reports or, if necessary, by inventing "plausible" forecasts that had no basis in evidence at all.

Admiral Kimmel's group rationalized away their warnings, too. Right up to December 7, 1941, they convinced themselves that the Japanese would never dare attempt a full-scale surprise assault against Hawaii because Japan's leaders would realize that it would precipitate an all-out war which the United States would surely win. They made no attempt to look at the situation through the eyes of the Japanese leaders—another manifestation of groupthink.

3. Morality

Victims of groupthink believe unquestioningly in the inherent morality of their ingroup; this belief inclines the members to ignore the ethical or moral consequences of their decisions.

Evidence that this symptom is at work usually is of a negative kind —the things that are left unsaid in group meetings. At least two influential persons had doubts about the morality of the Bay of Pigs adventure. One of them, Arthur Schlesinger, Jr., presented his strong objections in a memorandum to President Kennedy and Secretary of State Rusk but suppressed them when he attended meetings of the Kennedy team. The other, Senator J. William Fulbright, was not a member of the group, but the President invited him to express his misgivings in a speech to the policymakers. However, when Fulbright finished speaking the President moved on to other agenda items without asking for reactions of the group.

David Kraslow and Stuart H. Loory, in *The Secret Search for Peace in Vietnam*, report that during 1966 President Johnson's ingroup was concerned primarily with selecting bomb targets in North Vietnam. They based their selections on four factors—the military advantage, the risk to American aircraft and pilots, the danger of forcing other countries into the fighting, and the danger of heavy civilian casualties. At their regular Tuesday luncheons, they weighed these factors the way schoolteachers grade examination papers, averaging them out. Though evidence on this point is scant, I suspect that the group's ritualistic adherence to a standardized procedure induced the members to the feel morally justified in their destructive way of dealing with the Vietnamese people—after all, the danger of heavy civilian casualties from U.S. air strikes was taken into account on their checklists.

4. Stereotypes

Victims of groupthink hold stereotyped views of the leaders of enemy groups: they are so evil that genuine attempts at negotiating differences with them are unwarranted, or they are too weak or too stupid to deal effectively with whatever attempts the ingroup makes to defeat their purposes, no matter how risky the attempts are.

Kennedy's groupthinkers believed that Premier Fidel Castro's air force was so ineffectual that obsolete B-26s could knock it out completely in a surprise attack before the invasion began. They also believed that Castro's army was so weak that a small Cuban-exile brigade could establish a well-protected beachhead at the Bay of Pigs. In addition, they believed that Castro was not smart enough to put down any possible internal uprisings in support of the exiles. They were wrong on all three assumptions. Though much of the blame was attributable to faulty intelligence, the point is that none of Kennedy's advisers even questioned the CIA planners about these assumptions.

The Johnson advisers' sloganistic thinking about "the Communist apparatus" that was "working all around the world" (as Dean Rusk put it) led them to overlook the powerful nationalistic strivings of the North Vietnamese government and its efforts to ward off Chinese domination. The crudest of all stereotypes used by Johnson's inner circle to justify their policies was the domino theory ("If we don't stop the Reds in South Vietnam, tomorrow they will be in Hawaii and next week they will be in San Francisco," Johnson once said). The group so firmly accepted this stereotype that it became almost impossible for any advisor to introduce a more sophisticated viewpoint.

In the documents on Pearl Harbor, it is clear to see that the Navy commanders stationed in Hawaii had a naive image of Japan as a midget that would not dare to strike a blow against a powerful giant.

5. Pressure

Victims of groupthink apply direct pressure to any individual who momentarily expresses doubts about any of the group's shared illusions or who questions the validity of the arguments supporting a policy alternative favored by the majority. This gambit reinforces the concurrence-seeking norm that loyal members are expected to maintain.

President Kennedy probably was more active than anyone else in raising skeptical questions during the Bay of Pigs meetings, and yet he seems to have encouraged the group's docile, uncritical acceptance of defective arguments in favor of the CIA's plan. At every meeting, he allowed the CIA representatives to dominate the discussion. He permitted them to give their immediate refutations in response to each tentative doubt that one of the others expressed, instead of asking whether anyone shared the doubt or wanted to pursue the implications of the new worrisome issue that had just been raised. And at the most crucial meeting, when he was calling on each member to give his vote for or against the plan, he did not call on Arthur Schlesinger, the one man there who was known by the President to have serious misgivings.

Historian Thomson informs us that whenever a member of Johnson's ingroup began to express doubts, the group used subtle social pressures to "domesticate" him. To start with, the dissenter was made to feel at home, provided that he lived up to two restrictions: (1) that he did not voice his doubts to outsiders, which would play into the hands of the opposition; and (2) that he kept his criticisms within the bounds of acceptable deviation, which meant not challenging any of the fundamental assumptions that went into the group's prior commitments. One such "domesticated dissenter" was Bill Moyers. When Moyers arrived at a meeting, Thomson tells us, the President greeted him with, "Well, here comes Mr. Stop-the-Bombing."

6. Self-Censorship

Victims of groupthink avoid deviating from what appears to be group consensus; they keep silent about their misgivings and even minimize to themselves the importance of their doubts.

As we have seen, Schlesinger was not at all hesitant about presenting his strong objections to the Bay of Pigs plan in a memorandum to the President and the Secretary of State. But he became keenly aware of his tendency to suppress objections at the White House meetings. "In the months after the Bay of Pigs I bitterly reproached myself for having kept so silent during those crucial discussions in the cabinet room," Schlesinger writes in *A Thousand Days.* "I can only explain my failure to do more than raise a few timid questions by reporting that one's impulse to blow the whistle on this nonsense was simply undone by the circumstances of the discussion."

7. Unanimity

Victims of groupthink share an *illusion* of unanimity within the group concerning almost all judgments expressed by members who speak in favor of the majority view. This symptom results partly from the preceding one, whose effects are augmented by the false assumption that any individual who remains silent during any part of the discussion is in full accord with what the others are saying.

When a group of persons who respect each other's opinions arrives at a unanimous view, each member is likely to feel that the belief must be true. This reliance on consensual validation within the group tends to replace individual critical thinking and reality testing, unless there are clear-cut disagreements among the members. In contemplating a course of action such as the invasion of Cuba, it is painful for the members to confront disagreements within their group, particularly if it becomes apparent that there are widely divergent views about whether the preferred course of action is too risky to undertake at all. Such disagreements are likely to arouse anxieties about making a serious error. Once the sense of unanimity is shattered, the members no longer can feel complacently confident about the decision they are inclined to make. Each man must then face the annoying realization that there are troublesome uncertainties and he must diligently seek out the best information he can get in order to decide for himself exactly how serious the risks might be. This is one of the unpleasant consequences of being in a group of hardheaded, critical thinkers.

To avoid such an unpleasant state, the members often become inclined, without quite realizing it, to prevent latent disagreements from surfacing when they are about to initiate a risky course of action. The group leader and the members support each other in playing up the areas of convergence in their thinking, at the expense of fully exploring divergencies that might reveal unsettled issues.

"Our meetings took place in a curious atmosphere of assumed consensus," Schlesinger writes. His additional comments clearly show that, curiously, the consensus was an illusion—an illusion that could be maintained only because the major participants did not reveal their own reasoning or discuss their idiosyncratic assumptions and vague reservations. Evidence from several sources makes it clear that even the three principals—President Kennedy, Rusk and McNamara—had widely differing assumptions abut the invasion plan.

8. Mindguards

Victims of groupthink sometimes appoint themselves as mindguards to protect the leader and fellow members from adverse information that might break the complacency they shared about the effectiveness and morality of past decisions. At a large birthday party for his wife, Attorney General Robert F. Kennedy, who had been constantly informed about the Cuban invasion plan, took Schlesinger aside and asked him why he was opposed. Kennedy listened coldly and said, "You may be right or you may be wrong, but the President has made his mind up. Don't push it any further. Now is the time for everyone to help him all they can."

Rusk also functioned as a highly effective mindguard by failing to transmit to the group the strong objections of three "outsiders" who had learned of the invasion plan—Undersecretary of State Chester Bowles, USIA Director Edward R. Murrow, and Rusk's intelligence chief, Roger Hilsman. Had Rusk done so, their warnings might have reinforced Schlesinger's memorandum and jolted some of Kennedy's ingroup, if not the President himself, into reconsidering the decision.

PRODUCTS

When a group of executives frequently displays most or all of these interrelated symptoms, a detailed study of their deliberations is likely to reveal a number of immediate consequences. These consequences are, in effect, products of poor decision-making practices because they lead to inadequate solutions to the problems under discussion.

First, the group limits its discussions to a few alternative courses of action (often only two) without an initial survey of all the alternatives that might be worthy of consideration.

Second, the group fails to reexamine the course of action initially preferred by the majority after they learn of risks and drawbacks they had not considered originally.

Third, the members spend little or no time discussing whether there are non-obvious gains they may have overlooked or ways of reducing the seemingly prohibitive costs that made rejected alternatives appear undesirable to them.

Fourth, members make little or no attempt to obtain information from experts within their own organizations who might be able to supply more precise estimates of potential losses and gains.

Fifth, members show positive interest in facts and opinions that support their preferred policy; they tend to ignore facts and opinions that do not.

Sixth, members spend little time deliberating about how the chosen policy might be hindered by bureaucratic inertia, sabotaged by political opponents, or temporarily derailed by common accidents. Consequently, they fail to work out contingency plans to cope with foreseeable setbacks that could endanger the overall success of their chosen course.

SUPPORT

The search for an explanation of why groupthink occurs has led me through a quagmire of complicated theoretical issues in the murky area of human motivation. My belief, based on recent social psychological research, is that we can best understand the various symptoms of groupthink as a mutual effort among the group members to maintain self-esteem and emotional equanimity by providing social support to each other, especially at times when they share responsibility for making vital decisions.

Even when no important decision is pending, the typical administrator will begin to doubt the wisdom and morality of his past decisions each time he receives information about setbacks, particularly if the information is accompanied by negative feedback from prominent men who originally had been his supporters. It should not be surprising, therefore, to find that individual members strive to develop unanimity and esprit de corps that will help bolster each other's morale, to create an optimistic outlook about the success of pending decisions, and to reaffirm the positive value of past policies to which all of them are committed.

PRIDE

Shared illusions of invulnerability, for example, can reduce anxiety about taking risks. Rationalizations help members believe that the risks are really not so bad after all. The assumption of inherent morality helps the members to avoid feelings of shame or guilt. Negative stereotypes function as stress-reducing devices to enhance a sense of moral righteousness as well as pride in a lofty mission.

The mutual enhancement of self-esteem and morale may have functional value in enabling the members to maintain their capacity to take action, but it has maladaptive consequences insofar as concurrence-seeking tendencies interfere with critical, rational capacities and lead to serious errors of judgment.

While I have limited my study to decision-making bodies in Government, groupthinking symptoms appear in business, industry and any other field where small, cohesive groups make the decisions. It is vital, then, for all sorts of people—and especially group leaders—to know what steps they can take to prevent groupthink.

REMEDIES

To counterpoint my case studies of the major fiascos, I have also investigated two highly successful group enterprises, the formulation of the Marshall Plan in the Truman Administration and the handling of the Cuban missile crisis by President Kennedy and his advisers. I have found it instructive to examine the steps Kennedy took to change his group's decision-making processes. These changes ensured that the mistakes made by his Bay of Pigs ingroup were not repeated by the missile-crisis ingroup, even though the membership of both groups was essentially the same.

The following recommendations for preventing groupthink incorporate many of the good practices I discovered to be characteristic of the Marshall Plan and missile-crisis groups:

1. The leader of a policy-forming group should assign the role of critical evaluation to each member, encouraging the group to give high priority to open airing of objections and doubts. This practice needs to be reinforced by the leader's acceptance of criticism of his own judgments in order to discourage members from soft-pedaling their disagreements and from allowing their striving for concurrence to inhibit critical thinking.

2. When the key members of a hierarchy assign a policy-planning mission to any group within their organization, they should adopt an impartial stance instead of stating preferences and expectations at the beginning. This will encourage open inquiry and impartial probing of a wide range of policy alternatives.

3. The organization routinely should set up several outside policy-planning and evaluation groups to work on the same policy question, each deliberating under a different leader. This can prevent the insulation of an ingroup.

4. At intervals before the group reaches a final consensus, the leader should require each member to discuss the group's deliberations with associates in his own unit of the organization—assuming that those associates can be trusted to adhere to the same security regulations that govern the policy-makers—and then to report back their reactions to the group.

5. The group should invite one or more outside experts to each meeting on a staggered basis and encourage the experts to challenge the views of the core members.

6. At every general meeting of the group, whenever the agenda calls for an evaluation of policy alternatives, at least one member should play devil's advocate, functioning as a good lawyer in challenging the testimony of those who advocate the majority position.

7. Whenever the policy issue involves relations with a rival nation or organization, the group should devote a sizable block of time, perhaps an entire session, to a survey of all warning signals from the rivals and should write alternative scenarios on the rivals' intentions.

8. When the group is surveying policy alternatives for feasibility and effectiveness, it should from time to time divide into two or more subgroups to meet separately, under different chairmen, and then come back together to hammer out differences.

9. After reaching a preliminary consensus about what seems to be the best policy, the group should hold a "second-chance" meeting at

which every member expresses as vividly as he can all his residual doubts, and rethinks the entire issue before making a definitive choice.

HOW

These recommendations have their disadvantages. To encourage the open airing of objections, for instance, might lead to prolonged and costly debates when a rapidly growing crisis requires immediate solution. It also could cause rejection, depression and anger. A leader's failure to set a norm might create cleavage between leader and members that could develop into a disruptive power struggle if the leader looks on the emerging consensus as anathema. Setting up outside evaluation groups might increase the risk of security leakage. Still, inventive executives who know their way around the organizational maze probably can figure out how to apply one or another of the prescriptions successfully, without harmful side effects.

They also could benefit from the advice of outside experts in the administrative and behavioral sciences. Though these experts have much to offer, they have had few chances to work on policy-making machinery within large organizations. As matters now stand, executives innovate only when they need new procedures to avoid repeating serious errors that have deflated their self-images.

In this era of atomic warheads, urban disorganization and ecocatastrophes, it seems to me that policymakers should collaborate with behavioral scientists and give top priority to preventing groupthink and its attendant fiascos.

CHAPTER 18

Group Problem Solving

At committee meetings, when E.X. Dutton talked, people listened. The trouble was, they did nothing *but* listen. In the firm for thirty years and with close ties to the president and other top executives, E.X. struck fear in the hearts of most employees. Even when his statements were clearly pure nonsense, other committee members simply lowered their heads and doodled. On the rare occasions when someone did challenge one of E.X.'s comments, he or she would immediately be the object of a personal attack. In such cases, the other committee members would remain silent, once again lower their heads, and continue doodling.

After the meeting had dragged into its fourth hour, Janina wondered, "Do these people like to hear themselves talk? Don't they have anything better to do with their time? Don't they have hobbies, a garden to tend, a family to see?" Janina couldn't understand how apparently intelligent individuals could spend hours of their time every week in pointless, directionless, seemingly endless meetings. It was as if the meetings were a company ritual, sacred and unchallengable. They went off on any of a number of unchartable tangents. The stated purpose of each meeting was briefly addressed and quickly forgotten.

It seems reasonable to expect that we could improve problem solving by simply bringing more minds to bear on an issue. But, as these two vignettes and the previous reading by Irving Janis illustrate, there are a number of problems with interacting groups. For instance, Janis pointed out such potential difficulties as reluctance of members to contribute, pressures for conformity, and overly risky decisions. While the examples Janis used primarily were related to international affairs, they illustrate exactly the same things often seen in typical business organizations. Clearly, there is more to having a successful group process than just bringing people together.

Fortunately, there seem to be some good ways to decide whether a group-decision process should be used and, if so, how it can be most successfully implemented. This chapter will consider four important questions concerning group problem solving:

1. What are relevant potential advantages of using groups for problem solving, difficulties often associated with group problem solving, and other relevant differences between groups and individuals for problem-solving purposes?
2. For any given problem situation, how can we decide whether a group or individual decision process would be most appropriate?
3. How are size, spatial arrangements, and heterogeneity of group members relevant?
4. Are there group processes that capture the advantages of groups while minimizing problems often associated with groups?

GROUPS VERSUS INDIVIDUALS FOR DECISION-MAKING PURPOSES[1]

There are a number of relevant differences between individuals and groups, some of which would seem to suggest that groups should have the potential to make better decisions, others of which highlight problems with interacting groups, and still others that could be viewed as advantages in one situation but as disadvantages in another. However, before we can talk about relative advantages and disadvantages of groups for decision-making purposes, we first must ask what we want to accomplish in the problem-solving process.

We have to consider at least two major criteria. They are *quality* of the solution and *acceptability* of the solution to those who will be affected by it and/or must implement it. While the two criteria may, in some cases, be closely related, in others they may be independent or even in conflict. Ideally, a decision would be both of high quality and acceptability. But even the highest quality decision, if resented or misunderstood by those affected by it, would be poorly received and would meet with problems in implementation. Beyond these two key criteria are a number of other things we may also want to consider as "second level" criteria. That is, if we know that two or more decisions of equal quality and acceptability can be reached in any of a number of different ways, we may want some way to "break the tie." For instance, we may simply want to use the fastest method. Or we may want to use the approach that will give the largest number of

[1]Much of this discussion is drawn from Maier (1967) and Van de Ven and Delbecq (1971).

people practice in decision making in order to further their managerial development. The following listing of relevant differences between individuals and groups focuses on the key criteria of decision quality and acceptability.

It should be noted that we now are considering *interacting* groups, the kinds of groups where members are free to talk to or to communicate with one another in various other ways. The opposite of an interacting group is a *coacting* or *nominal* group, where people are working together on a task but not interacting in any way. For example, when you and your classmates are taking an exam, you form a coacting group: you are in the same place working on a task but not, we hope, interacting. Later in this chapter, we will discuss coacting groups.

Group advantages

Groups have at least four major advantages over individuals.

1. Groups have the potential for many more inputs concerning possible alternatives and concerning evaluation of those alternatives.

2. In most cases, participation in the problem-solving process increases understanding and acceptance of the final decision.

3. Working in the presence of other individuals increases our activation levels. This heightened arousal in groups settings is called *social facilitation effect.*

4. By having a large number of people make inputs, biases may be offset, and the unreliability of individuals' decisions may be reduced.

Potential problems associated with interacting groups

A number of factors prevent many groups from realizing their potential.

1. Some members may be reluctant to make inputs because they think they may sound stupid, because they think they may somehow be punished if they say something offensive to other group members, or because they feel that others in the group are of higher status and should be deferred to.

2. Some members may simply be unable to make inputs because one or a few dominant or stubborn individuals are doing all the talking.

3. The group may focus on one or two suggested alternatives, begin to evaluate them, and never come up with other ideas. That is, they may exhibit *focus effect.*

4. Group members may be more concerned with winning an argument and having their own way than with achieving the group's goals.

In sum, these potential problems can negate most of the potential benefits of groups. Because some members don't make inputs, we lose those inputs, and those members probably won't feel that they have truly participated. Because only a few people make most inputs, we lose the statistical benefits of a dampening of biases and unreliability. Finally, because the group focuses on one or two alternatives, the group advantage of being able to generate a large number of alternatives is never realized. Relating to this point are three key phases in group problem solving:

1. Orientation. In this phase, the group members come up with alternatives and with information relevant to those alternatives.

2. Evaluation. Here, the group members evaluate the alternatives.

3. Control. In this phase, the group members actually choose among alternatives.

The following example illustrates one problem inherent in group interaction. Shortly after the meeting was called to order, Bob, the chairperson, raised the vital question of how the company could counter the threat posed by the substantial gains in market share by its major competitor. Doug immediately suggested an all-out advertising campaign, saturating the media. Fred countered with the idea that a more selective campaign, aimed at carefully chosen market segments, would be more cost effective. Sides were quickly drawn, and the merits of the two views were debated for over two hours. Finally, the majority of committee members opted for Fred's approach. When Bob later presented the solution to his boss, her immediate response was: "I agree that Fred's approach is superior to Doug's, but there are surely many other viable alternatives, most of them having nothing to do with advertising. I have to think that some of them would have avoided the flaws in Fred's proposal." Taken aback for a moment, Bob had to admit that the committee had never gotten beyond the two initial alternatives.

This vignette demonstrates that a group that moves too quickly out of the orientation phase is unlikely to find a truly optimal solution.

Other relevant differences between individuals and groups

Three other differences, which may be advantageous in one case but disadvantageous in another, are as follows.

1. Groups take more time to make a decision. This is certainly true if we consider the total person-hours used. But it is also true if we just look at the time taken from the start to the finish of the problem-solving process. While, in many cases, this would be disadvantageous, there are some instances where time constraints aren't important or where, in fact, we may be afraid that a decision made too quickly could be deficient.

2. Groups exert pressure on their members to conform to group norms. Norms are basically unwritten rules or laws that groups develop. If a group has norms that the organization feels are desirable —such as a norm that all its members should work hard—then pressures for conformity are likely to be beneficial to the organization. On the other hand, if the norms are for such things as rate restriction or disruption, such conformity pressures are clearly undesirable.

3. For most types of problems that are relevant to organizations, groups make riskier decisions than do individuals. This is called the "risky shift" phenomenon since individual risk preferences shift in the risky direction after group interaction. Whether such a shift is desirable depends on the risk preferences of the organization and the current levels of risk taking of its members.

Now that we have seen some important ways in which groups and individuals differ, it seems reasonable to ask, "So what good does it do us to know that groups are better than individuals in some ways and worse in others? How does it fit together?" There are at least three answers to these questions. First, simple awareness of such potential group problems as focus effect and dominating personality types can help us to try consciously to avoid them. Second, we can use the information to help decide when to use a group process and when to rely on an individual decision maker. Finally, we can use the information to try to find group processes that capture potential group advantages while avoiding the corresponding pitfalls.

The decision of whether to use a group problem-solving process

In this section, we will examine a model that tries systematically to determine relevant characteristics of the decision situation; these, along with the sorts of information just detailed, determine whether a group or individual process is most appropriate. Developed by Victor Vroom and his associates, the model consists of a set of questions about the situation, each of which the manager must answer with a yes or no. On the basis of answers to the sequence of questions shown in figure 18-1, certain decision styles are rejected as inappropriate. After the entire series of questions has been answered, one or more styles will remain that meet all requirements in terms of quality and acceptability. The choice among those remaining styles is then made

FIGURE 18-1
Steps in Deciding Whether to Use a Group or Individual Process

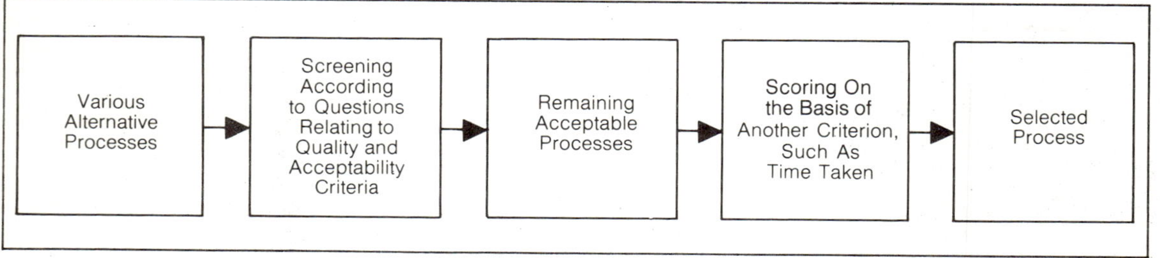

on the basis of some other criterion, such as how long it takes to use the process. The specific alternative styles Vroom considers are shown in table 18-1. They range from AI, a completely autocratic, individual decision, to GII, a pure group decision.

We should point out that, while the model speaks of "superiors" and "subordinates," the terms "individual" and "others" could be substituted. That is, the model is generally applicable and is not restricted to superior-subordinate relations.

The specific problem attributes and corresponding questions considered in the model are shown in table 18-2.

The model itself, which somewhat resembles a complex tree, is presented in figure 18-2. Try to follow one or two of its branches; the number at the end of each branch tells the problem type. Table 18-3 shows the appropriate methods for each problem type. The letter following the number at the end of each branch of the tree indicates the quickest acceptable method for the particular problem type. For example, the number at the end of the very top branch of the tree indicates that the problem type is 1. Table 18-3 shows that any of the methods is appropriate for such a problem type since it has no quality or acceptability requirements. Since a completely autocratic, individual decision style (AI) is fastest, it is listed after the number 1 at the end of the top branch.

TABLE 18-1
Alternative Decision Styles in the Vroom and Yetton Model*

AI	You solve the problem or make the decision yourself, using information available to you at that time.
AII	You obtain the necessary information from your subordinate(s), then decide on the solution to the problem yourself. You may or may not tell your subordinates what the problem is in getting the information from them. The role played by your subordinates in making the decision is clearly one of providing the necessary information to you, rather than generating or evaluating alternative solutions.
CI	You share the problem with relevant subordinates individually, getting their ideas and suggestions without bringing them together as a group. Then *you* make the decision that may or may not reflect your subordinates' influence.
CII	You share the problem with your subordinates as a group, collectively obtaining their ideas and suggestions. Then *you* make the decision that may or may not reflect your subordinates' influence.
GII	You share a problem with your subordinates as a group. Together you generate and evaluate alternatives and attempt to reach agreement (consensus) on a solution. Your role is much like that of chairman. You do not try to influence the group to adopt "your" solution and you are willing to accept and implement any solution that has the support of the entire group.

*Reprinted, by permission of the publisher, from V.H. Vroom, "A New Look at Managerial Decision Making," *Organizational Dynamics,* Spring 1973, © 1973 by AMACOM, a division of American Management Associations, p. 67.

To see how Vroom's model works, let's consider the following case.*

You are president of a small but growing midwestern bank, with its head office in the state's capital and branches in several nearby market towns. The location and type of business are factors that contribute to the emphasis on traditional and conservative banking practices at all levels.

When you bought the bank five years ago, it was in poor financial shape. Under your leadership, much progress has been made. This progress has been achieved while the economy has moved into a mild recession, and as a result, your prestige among your bank managers is very high. Your success, which you are inclined to attribute principally to good luck and to a few timely decisions on your part, has, in your judgment, one unfortunate by-product. It has caused your subordinates to look to you for leadership and guidance in decision making beyond what you consider necessary. You have no doubts about the fundamental capabilities of these men but wish that they were not quite so willing to accede to your judgment.

You have recently acquired funds to permit opening a new branch. Your problem is to decide on a suitable location. You believe that there is no "magic formula" by which it is possible to select an optimal site. The choice will be made by a combination of some simple commonsense criteria and "what feels right." You have asked your managers to keep their eyes open for commerical real estate sites that might be suitable. Their knowledge about the communities in which they operate should be extremely useful in making a wise choice.

Their support is important because the success of the new branch will be highly dependent on your managers' willingness to supply staff and technical assistance during its early days. Your bank is small enough for everyone to feel like a part of a team, and you feel that this has been and will be critical to the bank's prosperity.

The success of this project will benefit everybody. Directly, they will reap the personal and business advantages of being part of a successful and expanding business.

To choose an appropriate decision style, you must answer the seven diagnostic questions presented in table 18-2. First, it's clear that there is a quality requirement in this case: success of the new branch is at stake. Second, you don't currently have all the information you'll need; your subordinates' inputs concerning the communities within which they operate are important. Third, the problem is not structured; instead, you have to rely on common sense and "what feels right." Fourth, acceptance by subordinates is critical; their willingness to supply staff and technical assistance could make or break the new branch. Fifth, your subordinates look to you for guidance and

*This case is drawn from Vroom and Jago (1974)

PROBLEM ATTRIBUTES	DIAGNOSTIC QUESTIONS
A. The importance of the quality of the decision.	Is there a quality requirement such that one solution is likely to be more rational than another?
B. The extent to which the leader possesses sufficient information/expertise to make a high-quality decision by himself.	Do I have sufficient information to make a high-quality decision?
C. The extent to which the problem is structured.	Is the problem structured?
D. The extent to which acceptance or commitment on the part of subordinates is critical to the effective implementation of the decision.	Is acceptance of the decision by subordinates critical to effective implementation?
E. The prior probability that the leader's autocratic decision will receive acceptance by subordinates.	If you were to make the decision by yourself, is it reasonably certain that it would be accepted by your subordinates?
F. The extent to which subordinates are motivated to attain the organizational goals as represented in the objectives explicit in the statement of the problem.	Do subordinates share the organizational goals to be obtained in solving this problem?
G. The extent to which subordinates are likely to be in conflict over preferred solutions.	Is conflict among subordinates likely in preferred solutions?

*Reprinted, by permission of the publisher, from V.H. Vroom, "A New Look at Managerial Decision Making," *Organizational Dynamics,* Spring 1973, © 1973 by AMACOM, a division of American Management Associations, p. 69. All rights reserved.

TABLE 18-2
Problem Attributes and Questions in the Vroom and Yetton Model*

leadership in decision making (even more than you would like), so they will almost definitely accept your decision. Sixth, your subordinates share the organization's goals, so success of the project will benefit everybody. Finally, the subordinates are not likely to be in conflict over preferred solutions since the selection of the most profitable site will help them all.

The answers to the seven diagnostic questions are, respectively: Yes, no, no, yes, yes, yes, and no. Following the appropriate branches in figure 18-2 (you can see that we didn't even have to ask the last questions), we are told that the problem type is 11 (where table 18-3 tells us either style CII or GII is appropriate) and that the fastest of those types (shown at the end of the branch in figure 18-2) is CII.

Incidentally, Vroom reports that a "black box" the size of a hand calculator has been developed, with switches labeled with the series of questions. For any problem situation, the manager just sets each

FIGURE 18-2 The Vroom and Yetton Model*

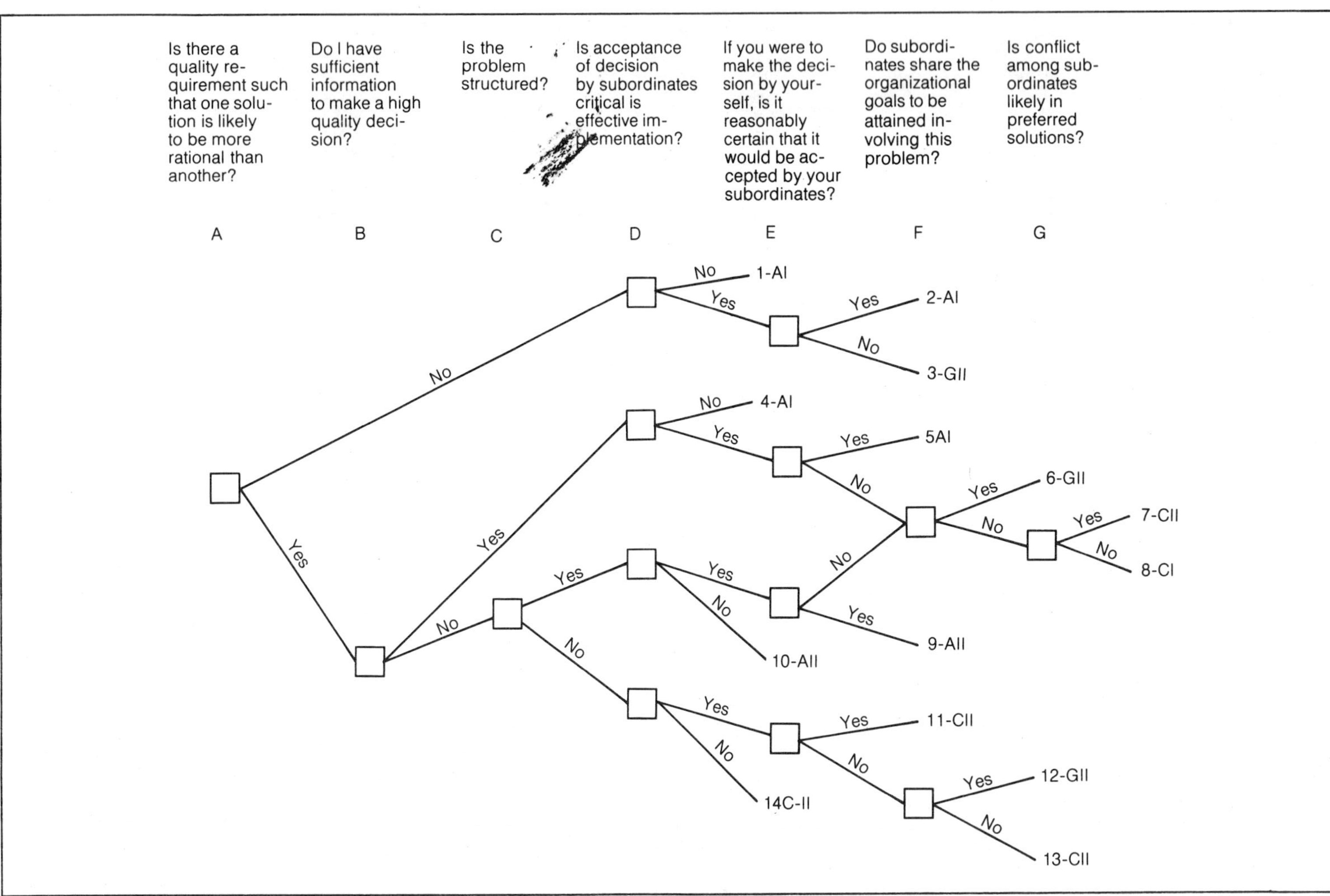

*Reprinted, by permission of the publisher, from V.H. Vroom, "A New Look at Managerial Decision Making," *Organizational Dynamics*, Spring 1973, © 1973 by AMACOM, a division of American Management Associations, p. 70.

TABLE 18-3
Appropriate Decision Styles for Each Problem Type*

PROBLEM TYPE	ACCEPTABLE METHODS
1	AI, AII, CI, CII, GII
2	AI, AII, CI, CII, GII
3	GII
4	AI, AII, CI, CII, GII**
5	AI, AII, CI, CII, GII**
6	GII
7	CII
8	CI, CII
9	AII, CI, CII, GII**
10	AII, CI, CII, GII**
11	CII, GII**
12	GII
13	CII
14	CII, GII

*Reprinted, by permission of the publisher, from V.H. Vroom, "A New Look at Managerial Decision Making." *Organizational Dynamics,* Spring 1973, © 1973 by AMACOM, a division of American Management Associations, p. 71. All rights reserved.

**Within the feasible set only when the answer to question F is yes.

switch in the "yes" or "no" position, pushes a button, and lights representing appropriate styles are illuminated.

The Vroom model can be a useful teaching device. That is, managers can compare the decision styles they would use, or have used, with those styles the model would suggest are "correct." By looking at the ways their choices of decision styles differ from those of the model, managers perhaps can gain self-insight and learn what important factors they have failed to consider. But the model is certainly not "perfect." Undoubtedly, other variables should be considered in some cases. Also, some of the situational factors that the model takes as given, such as the existence of conflict among group members over the preferred solution, should perhaps be viewed as subject to change; that is, it may be better to try to reduce such conflict than to accept it and choose a process consistent with it. Certainly, then, the model should be treated as a guide, as a tool for the decision maker, rather than as a substitute for judgment. As Vroom says in defending the model, "The criterion for social utility is not perfection but improvement over present practice." (1973, p. 80)

Vroom and his colleagues have studied thousands of managers to learn whether the decision styles they choose are consistent with the model and, if not, specifically how they differ. Using both the managers' recall of the decisions they have made in actual situations and the managers' choices of decision processes for standardized cases, Vroom found that:

1. Managers' choices were consistent with those of the model in far more cases than would have occurred by chance. However, they

were somehow inconsistent with the model in about one-third of the cases.

2. In their choice of styles, managers more often violated acceptability criteria than quality criteria.

3. While some managers were a bit more "autocratic" or "democratic" than others, the situation was a much greater determinant of the selected style than were managerial predispositions.

4. Managers were less flexible in their choice of styles than the model indicates they should be.

Such findings suggest that managers do seem to consider important variables when choosing between group and individual decision styles and that, while there are differences among managers in the styles they prefer, the impact of such differences is small compared to that of the situation. Further, the findings show that managers give less emphasis to the acceptability of their decisions to those affected by them than they should. Finally, the finding that managers don't vary their styles as much across situations as they should has important implications for leadership; an important leadership characteristic might be the extent to which the leader is flexible, varying style with situation. (Of course, as shown in figure 18-3, the leader may sometimes find that group members rebel against use of a certain style.)

FIGURE 18-3
Group Members May Reject the Style Chosen by the Leader

Recently, Vroom and Arthur Jago (1978) conducted a study to see whether behavior in accordance with the model was related to success. They asked managers to think of two decision-making situations in which they had been involved. The managers were told that they should select one situation that had worked out well from the organizational standpoint and one that was unsuccessful. Then the managers' reports of the behaviors they had used in these situations were compared with those prescribed by the model. Vroom and Jago found that of those cases where the managers' behaviors coincided with the model's prescription, 68 percent were successful. On the other hand, when managers had behaved in ways that were inconsistent with the model's choices, only 22 percent were successful.

ORGANIZING INTERACTING GROUPS

In this section, we will consider the questions of optimal group size, the composition of groups, and spatial arrangements.

Group size

There is, of course, no one single size that is best for all groups, regardless of their task, composition, criteria for choice, and so on. However, we can make some general statements about the problems associated with small and large groups.[2]

The smallest group—the *dyad*—faces a number of peculiar problems. For one thing, if either of its two members gets upset and leaves the group, the group task will not be achieved. Thus, each member has potential "veto power." Also, in cases of disagreement, the members can't refer to group norms or to majority consensus and can't expect another group member to step in and mediate the disagreement. As a result, dyads are characterized by high rates of tension and anxiety, reluctance to give opinions, and either high levels of antagonism or conscious attempts to prevent latent antagonism from surfacing.

In three-person groups—triads—there is a tendency for two persons to form a coalition against the third. Further, anyone on the "short end" of a decision in a triad is by definition an isolate and is likely to feel resentful.

Four-person groups may be split by a frustrating two-to-two deadlock. Also, in groups of this size or smaller, interactions tend to be personalized. Individuals feel tied to their statements and find it hard to change their opinions without losing face.

On the other hand, there are a number of problems associated with large groups. For example:

1. As size increases, the number of potential interactions grows sharply, increasing coordination problems.

[2]Much of this discussion is drawn from Shull, Delbecq, and Cummings (1970) and Cummings, Huber and Arendt (1974).

In three-person decision-making groups or triads, a two against one situation tends to develop and the odd-man-out may feel resentful.

2. As groups get larger, each person has less chance to make inputs.

3. In large groups, some members just sit back and keep quiet.

4. In groups larger than six or seven, we have difficulty thinking of members as individuals.

5. Dominant members tend to become increasingly aggressive in large groups.

6. Because of coordination difficulties, there are increased tendencies in large groups to centralize communication flows.

Based on the preceding problems related to very small and very large groups is the premise that a group of five individuals is probably optimal. In a group of five:

1. A strict deadlock isn't possible.

2. The group tends, in cases of disagreement, to split into a majority of three and a minority of two. Thus, holding a minority opinion generally doesn't isolate an individual.

3. The group is small enough to let all members play an active role but large enough to let members shift their opinions and roles. In fact, empirical evidence, as summarized in table 18-4, generally shows that decision quality and member satisfaction are higher in groups of five or six than in larger or smaller groups. On the other hand, if a wide range of inputs is desired, a large group is probably

MAXIMIZED AT SMALL SIZES (<5)	MAXIMIZED AT SIZE 5 OR 6	MAXIMIZED AT LARGE SIZES (>6)
Member Participation	Decision Quality	Range of Member Inputs
Consensus	Member Satisfaction	

TABLE 18-4
Summary of Empirical Evidence Relating to the Impact of Group Size

preferable. Or, if consensus and members' feelings of participation are crucial, very small groups may be best.

Variety of composition of group members

The question of how varied we should try to make the composition of a group is complex. People who are very different from one another have a great deal of difficulty communicating adequately. On the other hand, if we need a variety of inputs, it may be necessary to assemble a mix of dissimilar types. In general, it is probably best to rely on common sense in putting the group together. If the problem under consideration requires expertise of only one specific type, the problems associated with having a heterogeneous group probably overcome any benefits inherent in variety. But if a particular mix of skills is needed to handle the task, individuals providing that mix should be brought together. And if very creative solutions are sought, it may be best to build variety into the group composition.

Spatial arrangements

The way group members are physically arranged in the meeting area can influence communication flows, perceptions of who the group leader is, status perceptions, and feelings of discomfort. At least three aspects of physical arrangement are important.

First, we consider the space immediately around our bodies as almost a part of us, as our "personal space." If people come within our personal space, we may move, shift our positions, or show our discomfort in other ways. In our culture, we prefer not to conduct business with others at a distance of less than about four feet. In other cultures, the comfortable distance for business interactions may be substantially more or less. For example, Arabs generally prefer to interact at much closer range than we do.

Second, when people who feel they possess high status enter a group meeting, they tend to place themselves in positions that reflect that status level. For example, when people enter a meeting room that has a long, rectangular table, those with highest status tend to sit at the ends of the table. In general, high-status people seek positions that, like the ends of a long table, offer the most eye contact with other group members. Also, if people are randomly arranged in a meeting place, those who end up in positions offering the most eye contact with others tend to have the most communications directed toward them, to be perceived as having the highest status, and to be viewed as the group leaders. Thus, the relative eye contacts of people at the meeting can have very important consequences.

Finally, figure 18-4 shows that the way people seat themselves around a table tends to depend on their expectations about the nature of the task they're about to undertake. For example, if they anticipate an adversary situation, they tend to sit across the table from their expected opponents. Or, if they think the task is to be cooperative, they are likely to sit side by side. Whether this is due to our cultural expectations about various types of tasks, to the fact that certain tasks can be carried out best by particular arrangements, or to other factors isn't really clear, but such tendencies definitely do exist. Also, while there is less evidence concerning this point, it seems likely that if people are arranged in certain ways, those arrangements may influence the likelihood that they will compete or cooperate. For example, people seated "nose to nose" across a table are probably more likely to adopt an adversary pose than if they were seated side by side.

In sum, the spatial arrangements of group members would seem to be important enough not to be left to chance.[3] Instead, we should be aware of the possible impacts of distance between members, their relative degrees of eye contact, and their patterns of positioning around a meeting table.

FIGURE 18-4
Most Likely Seating Arrangements for Various Tasks*

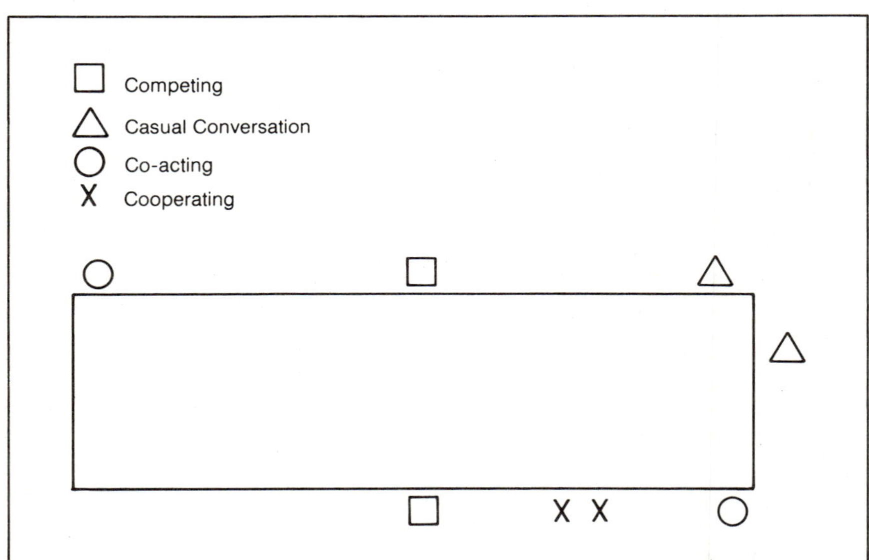

*Based on data from Sommer (1969).

[3]For a good discussion of the role of physical arrangements, see Filley (1975).

ALTERNATIVE GROUP PROCESSES

The discussion of group decision making has, to this point, focused on interacting groups. It would seem that we could capture many of the advantages of groups while minimizing problems if we simply didn't allow group members to interact, at least during certain phases of the problem-solving process. In this section, we consider two group decision processes that allow only limited interactions among members —the nominal group technique and the Delphi process.

The nominal group technique

Earlier we indicated that the opposite of an interacting group is a nominal or coacting group, characterized by individual silent effort in a group setting. As an example, a group leader simply might present a specific problem to the group members and then ask them to write down a number of possible solutions to the problem. Van de Ven and Delbecq (1971) presented some of the relative advantages of nominal versus interacting groups:

1. Evaluation is avoided while alternative solutions are being generated. This prevents focus effect and reduces the danger that the search for alternatives will end too soon.

2. Each individual has time to search for solutions and is forced to record his or her ideas. Thus, minority opinions are expressed, and everyone makes an input.

3. The search process is proactive rather than simply reactive. That is, group members must come up with their own original ideas rather than just responding to or building upon the ideas of others.

4. Strong personality types cannot dominate the process.

5. Since ideas are expressed in writing, there is a greater feeling of commitment and a greater sense of permanence than spoken expression produces.

Thus, use of a nominal group should reduce many of the problems associated with interacting groups while still reaping such potential group advantages as a large number of inputs, feelings of participation, and social facilitation effect. Further, the advantages of a nominal group relative to an interacting group become greater as groups get larger and more varied in composition. Since large, heterogeneous groups offer the greatest potential for the generation of many distinct alternatives, the advantages of nominal groups would appear to be greatest precisely when group processes should be most beneficial. It would also seem that a nominal group would be useful at the point where a final group decision must be made (in the *control* phase of the process). That is, by use of a silent, secret voting or ranking procedure, the chances that people will be afraid to make what they truly believe is the best choice will be reduced.

So are interacting groups worthless? Not really. For example, interacting groups allow group members to synthesize and evaluate alternative solutions, to elaborate upon and modify solutions, and to work toward a consensus. That is, interacting groups would seem to be especially desirable during the *evaluation* phase of the decision process.

It would be nice to have the best of both worlds, and that is just what the nominal group technique tries to give us. In particular, the above discussion would suggest that whether an interacting or nominal group process is best depends on the current stage in the problem-solving process. As table 18-5 shows, it would be ideal if we could shift from a nominal to an interacting group and back again during that process. In fact, the nominal group technique switches between interacting and nominal groups in exactly that way; perhaps it is misnamed since it doesn't rely solely on use of a nominal group. The specific steps of the nominal group technique are presented in table 18-6.

Finally, we offer an example of use of the nominal group technique (NGT). The six top-level officers of a major pharmaceutical firm had, in response to considerable press coverage, spent several meetings fruitlessly debating the appropriate goals of a company in an industry so directly responsible for public well-being. Upon the advice of a consultant, the chief executive officer decided to try the NGT. She asked the consultant to direct the next meeting. At that meeting, the consultant first asked the officers each to take twenty minutes to list what they felt to be five appropriate primary goals of the firm. Then, the officers read off the goals in round-robin fashion, and the consultant wrote them on flip-charts. After duplicate goals were crossed off, the merits of the remaining alternatives were considered in order. Following the discussion, the consultant asked the officers to list the five goals they now felt to be most appropriate and to rank them from 5 (most important) to 1 (fifth most important). The subsequent rankings were averaged to provide an overall goal ranking. While some officers clearly were less satisfied than others with the final ranking, all agreed that the process had been fair and orderly and that alternative viewpoints had been fully expressed. The CEO was pleased to have a concrete, neatly specified ranking of goals with which to guide the firm and a well-reasoned set of arguments with which to explain their rationale to outside parties.

TABLE 18-5
Optimal Group Processes for Various States in the Problem-Solving Process

PROBLEM-SOLVING STAGE	OPTIMAL GROUP PROCESS
Orientation	Nominal
Evaluation	Interacting
Control	Nominal

TABLE 18-6
Stages in the Nominal Group Technique*

1. Members of the group (called the "target group") are selected and brought together.
2. If the group is very large, it is broken down into subgroups of eight members or less.
3. The group leader presents a specific question.
4. Individual members silently and independently write down their ideas.
5. Each group member (one at a time, in turn, around the table) presents one of his or her ideas to the group without discussion. The ideas are summarized and written on a blackboard or sheet of paper on the wall.
6. After all individuals have presented their ideas, there is a discussion of the recorded ideas for the purposes of clarification and evaluation.
7. The meeting ends with a silent independent voting on priorities by individuals through a rank ordering or rating procedure. The "group decision" is the pooled outcome of the individual votes.

*Reprinted with permission of the publisher and the authors from A.H. Van de Ven and A.L. Debecq, "The Effectiveness of Nominal, Delphi, and Interacting Group Decision Making Processes," *Academy of Management Journal* vol. 17(4), 1974, p. 606. Copyright © 1974 by Academy of Management Journal.

The NGT is now widely used, generally with considerable success. Studies show it to be at least as good as, and generally better than, an interacting group for purposes of generating a large number of alternatives, minimizing errors, and satisfying group members.

The Delphi process

It was clear enough to Howard whom he needed in order to address the problem he faced. He needed, for starters, technicians, forecasters, statisticians, and practitioners. Also, Howard knew the problem would require the inputs of experts in at least five specific content areas. What was not so clear to Howard was how he could ever get all these people together. And, given the limited resources his company provided, he saw no way he could even begin to pay them for the expenses they would incur in attending such a meeting or for the loss of their time.

Many times, we would like to involve a number of people in problem solving, but we find that it is either unfeasible or inadvisable to bring them together. For example[4]:

1. The individuals may be widely scattered geographically.

[4]This listing is largely drawn from Turoff (1971).

2. They may have time constraints that prevent them from getting together.

3. They may want to remain anonymous.

4. They may not get along well with one another.

5. The problem may be so broad as to require many diverse inputs.

In such cases, the Delphi process, developed by Norman Dalkey and his associates at the RAND Corporation, may be useful. Initially, the process was used to forecast technological developments. However, the Delphi process, which takes its name from the Oracle of Delphi, is now used for a variety of purposes beyond forecasting. Murray Turoff lists the following applications:

1. Examining the significance of historical events

2. Gathering current and historical data

3. Putting together the structure of a model

4. Delineating the pros and cons associated with potential decision or policy options

5. Developing causal relationships in complex economic or social phenomena

6. Clarifying human interactions through role-playing concepts

While there are a number of variants of Delphi, it basically relies upon individuals completing and returning by mail a series of questionnaires. Figure 18-5 shows the steps in the process. The hope is that, after a series of iterations, the participants will arrive at some kind of agreement. In fact, though, any of a variety of approaches may be used to come up with a final choice. Responses might be averaged, some participants' choices might be weighted more heavily than others, and so on.

There are clearly some cases where a process like Delphi would be necessary. However, there are a few problems associated with the Delphi process:

1. It takes weeks or months to complete even a few iterations of the process.

2. If participants aren't very highly motivated, they may fail to fill out their questionnaires or may send them in late, delaying the whole process.

3. Participants may miss the opportunity to engage in face-to-face problem solving.

4. Participants may dislike the absence of verbal clarification of any questions they may have.

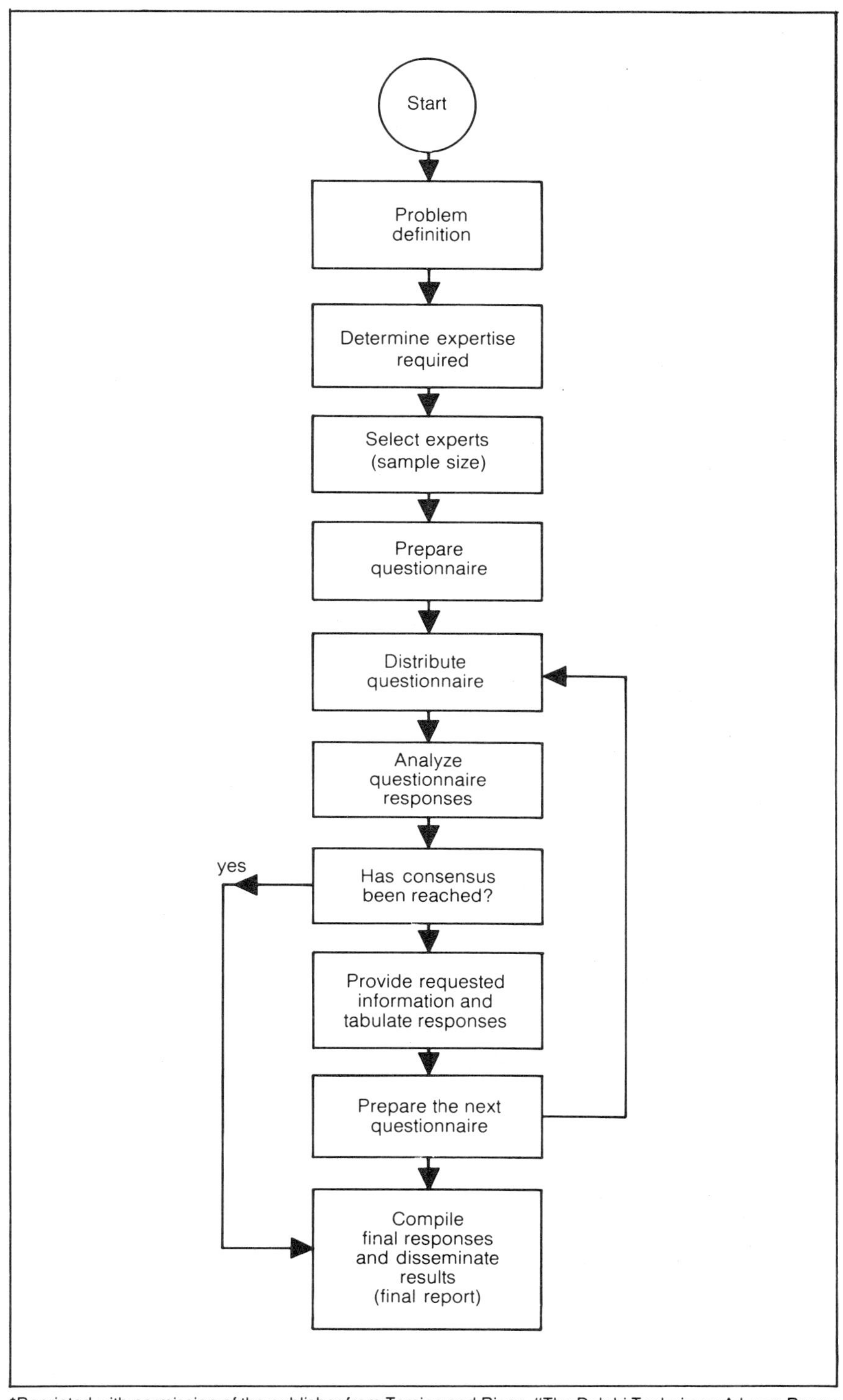

FIGURE 18-5
Steps in the Delphi Process*

*Reprinted with permission of the publisher from Tersine and Riggs, "The Delphi Technique: A Long-Range Planning Tool," *Business Horizons,* April 1976, p. 53. Copyright ©, 1976, by the Foundation for the School of Business at Indiana University.

However, like the nominal group technique, the Delphi process forces proactive search and written expression and provides a clearly structured process where participants can see progress. Also, the anonymity of participants should reduce harmful conformity pressures. The Delphi process has been shown to outperform an interacting group for such purposes as fact finding and determining the accuracy of sets of facts.[5]

SUMMARY

In this chapter, we have considered the use of groups for problem-solving purposes. We've seen that groups have a number of important potential advantages relative to individuals but that certain pitfalls related to interacting groups may reduce or overcome such benefits. With this in mind, we have provided three suggestions.

1. Be aware of and attentive to such potential group problems as focus effect, dominance by strong personality types, and so on, and consciously seek to minimize them by properly controlling the group process.[6]

2. By considering a number of characteristics of the particular decision situation, try to determine whether a group or individual process is most appropriate. For this purpose, the model developed by Vroom and his colleagues should be useful.

3. Consider a group decision process that incorporates group advantages while avoiding many of the difficulties common to interacting groups. Two such processes are the nominal group technique and the Delphi process.

Also, we've seen that consideration of the impacts of group size, variety of group membership, and member spatial arrangements on group effectiveness may be useful.

Thus, we don't have to settle for the undesirable characteristics of "groupthink," which Irving Janis discussed in the previous reading. Instead, by being conscious of the guidelines just offered, we should be able to reach decisions that are of high quality, are acceptable to those affected by them, and perhaps even help in achieving some other goal, such as increased subordinate development or minimization of time consumption.

We aren't through with groups yet. Since one potential advantage of groups is that they may generate a large number of unique ideas and a great amount of information to bear on such ideas, it would seem that groups might be useful in situations demanding creativity. We will discuss creativity and consider techniques for its enhancement in the next chapter.

---

[5]See Van de Ven and Delbecq (1974) for a discussion of studies relating to the nominal group technique and Delphi process.

[6]For a discussion of ways to plan, organize, staff, direct and control problem-solving groups, see Huber (1979).

REFERENCES

Cummings, L.L.; Huber, G.P.; and Arendt, E. "Effects of Size and Spatial Arrangements on Group Decision Making," *Academy of Management Journal 17* (1974): 460-75.

Filley, A.C. *Interpersonal Conflict Resolution*, Glenview, Ill.: Scott, Foresman, 1975.

Huber, G.P. *Decision Making*, Glenview, Ill.: Scott, Foresman, 1979.

Janis, I.L. "Groupthink." *Psychology Today*, 5 [6] (1971): 43-46 and 74-76.

Maier, N.R.F. "Assets and Liabilities in Group Problem Solving: The Need for an Integrative Function," *Psychological Review 74* (1967): 239-49.

Shull, F.A.; Delbecq, A.L.; and Cummings, L.L. *Organizational Decision Making*. New York: McGraw-Hill, 1970.

Sommer, R. *Personal Space: The Behavioral Basis of Design*. Englewood Cliffs, N.J.: Prentice-Hall, 1969.

Turoff, M. "Delphi and Its Potential Impact on Information Systems." *AFIPS—Conference Proceedings 39* (1971): 317-26.

Van de Ven, A.H., and Delbecq, A.L. "Nominal Versus Interacting Groups for Committee Decision-Making Effectiveness." *Academy of Management Journal 14* (1971): 203-12.

Van de Ven, A.H., and Delbecq, A.L. "The Effectiveness of Nominal, Delphi, and Interacting Group Processes." *Academy of Management Journal 17* (1974): 605-21.

Vroom, V.H. "A New Look at Managerial Decision Making." *Organizational Dynamics* (Spring 1973): 66-80.

Vroom, V.H., and Jago, A.G. "Decision Making As a Social Process: Normative and Descriptive Models of Leader Behavior." *Decision Sciences 5* (1974): 743-69.

Vroom, V.H., and Jago, A.G. "On the Validity of the Vroom-Yetton Model." *Journal of Applied Psychology 63* (1978): 151-62.

SUGGESTIONS FOR ADVANCED READINGS

Clark, R.D., III. "Group-induced Shift Toward Risk: A Critical Appraisal." *Psychological Bulletin 76* (1971): 251-70.

Delbecq, A.L.; Van de Ven, A.H.; and Gustafson, D. *Group Techniques for Program Planning*, Glenview, Ill.: Scott, Foresman, 1975.

Shaw, M.E., and Costanzo, P.R. *Theories of Social Psychology*. New York: McGraw-Hill, 1970.

Vroom, V.H., and Jago, A.G. "Decision Making as a Social Process: Normative and Descriptive Models of Leader Behavior." *Decision Sciences 5* (1974): 743-69.

CHAPTER 19

Creativity In Organizations

As the incoming vice president for research and development of Interwest, Incorporated, Ingrid was responsible for assembling a team that would come up with ideas for new products. Ingrid was free to draw from anywhere within the organization and, if necessary, to recruit elsewhere. As much as she relished her new position, Ingrid now found it to be distinctly uncomfortable. She knew she wanted to find creative people and, more important, to put together a creative team. Beyond that, though, she felt lost. What sorts of people should she pick? Should she seek some kind of optimal *mix*?

Success of Tanya's company, Energy Alternatives, was intimately linked to the ability of her employees to generate unique, dollar-saving approaches to the design of energy systems for commercial properties. While her company had initially done very well, the competition moving into the field was quickly making things tougher and tougher. Tanya was concerned that her employees weren't stretching their imaginations. Instead, they seemed content simply to tinker with systems they had designed in the past. Tanya wondered what she should do.

When John was growing up in the 1950s and 60s, he never imagined that he would be a businessman, the owner of a thriving firm that manufactured stereo equipment. In those days, the very word *business* had seemed vulgar to him. Now, in his unexpected new role, he was vehement in his arguments that his firm wouldn't become a "typical, bureaucratic, uncaring" place. He wanted it to be stimulating, challenging, concerned, alive. He pictured it as a company where people's minds would be free and aware, where they could reach their creative potential. But John, who had never felt the need to learn about organizations, had no idea how to guide the company in the directions he envisioned.

These scenarios suggest the common need in organizations to select people, techniques, or structures to enhance creativity. Creativity should not be thought of as something that is important only to artists and con men. Instead, the generation of a large number of unique alternatives is a vital first step in the problem-solving process, whether the problem be the design of a new reward system, the choice of an organization structure, or the selection of a competitive strategy. With organizational environments rapidly becoming more complex, turbulent, and uncertain, the need for creative response is increasingly crucial.

So it is not surprising that more and more organizations are realizing that they must often be concerned with creativity as well as productivity. This realization reflects a general mushrooming of interest in the topic of creativity since about 1950. Alex Osborn reported as early as 1964 that over 100,000 businesspeople had taken at least one course in creativity enhancement in the previous decade and that methods of creativity enhancement were taught at over 200 colleges and universities. J.P. Guilford (1970) reported that, in 1965, almost 100 articles relating to creativity were published, as opposed to five to ten per year in the interval from 1925 to 1950. There is now an entire journal—the *Journal of Creative Behavior*—devoted to theoretical and empirical examinations of creativity. Charles Schulz has written that his most popular *Peanuts* cartoon of all time, shown in figure 19-1, was one essentially relating to creativity.

FIGURE 19-1

In this chapter, we will consider a number of key issues related to creativity. What *is* creative behavior? What are the stages in the creative process? What are the sources of creativity? Can creative ability be measured? What are some correlates of creative behavior? Is creativity always good? If we decide we want to enhance creative behavior, what techniques are available? Finally, how might we design a creative organization?

CREATIVE BEHAVIOR

We will define *creative behavior* as behavior that results in discovering new and better means to accomplish our purposes. In a way, this seems like a debatable definition. Who is to say what is better? However, unless we accept such a definition, we are left in the uncomfortable position of having to classify any new idea, no matter how ridiculous, as creative. To resolve this problem, Sarnoff Mednick distinguishes between originality and creativity. He writes, "... 7,363,474 is quite an original answer to the problem 'How much is 12 + 12?' However, it is only when conditions are such that this answer is useful that we can also call it creative." (1962, p. 221)

We should be careful to distinguish at this point between creative ability and creative behavior or performance. As we saw in our discussion of expectancy theory, performance is a function not only of ability but also of effort and of situational factors. Thus, people may have innate creative ability but never show creative behavior, either because they are unmotivated or because of the setting in which they exist. For example, one experiment demonstrated that students who were told they would get extra points if they could improve their creativity test scores showed significantly greater improvement than did others who weren't promised such a bonus.[1] Later in this chapter, we will discuss situational factors that influence creative behavior, as well as specific techniques aimed at improving that behavior. For now, we should simply remember that creative ability won't always translate into creative behavior.

STAGES IN THE CREATIVE PROCESS

We should also recognize that there is more to creativity than the cry of "Eureka!" after a sudden inspiration. Instead, it seems that such insight is just one of a number of stages in the creative process. Graham Wallas (1962) called those stages preparation, incubation, insight, and verification.

Preparation includes the job of seeking out and putting together the sorts of information and other raw materials needed to form the foundation for any insightful breakthrough. The discoverers of the

[1] Halpin and Halpin (1973)

DNA double-helix could never have made their important advance without a thorough knowledge of relevant scientific materials. *Incubation* is a stage at which the individual does not consciously think about the problem at hand; instead, he or she relaxes, perhaps focusing on other activities. *Insight* is the "Eureka," stage, the sudden, often unexpected moment of inspiration. Finally, *verification* involves the sometimes tedious job of rigorously backing up the insight, proving that space is, in fact, curved or that gold really does replace its weight in water.

Numerous creative individuals have presented descriptions of their discoveries that closely parallel the stages Wallas suggested. Further, researchers have found that the process steps Wallas proposed are evident in experimental studies of creativity, though not necessarily in the order he suggested. This implies that it is not enough for someone just to sit back and wait for an inspiration to strike. Instead, it seems that careful consideration of a problem must precede such insights. Again, creative behavior is a function not just of ability but also of effort and the situation.

THE SOURCES OF CREATIVITY

Creativity is a fascinating and elusive thing. Consider, for instance, the following contrasting views on the sources of creativity.

—*Cesare Lombroso* (1895), late nineteenth-century psychiatrist: Creativity is a sign of mental illness. Men of genius show such "signs of degeneration" as shortness, rickets, pallor, emaciation, lesions of the head, stammering, precocity, sterility, left-handedness, and originality.

—*Abraham Maslow* (1969): Creativity and the concept of the healthy, self-actualized individual are intimately linked. There is within the human being ". . . a pressure (among other pressures) toward full individuality and identity, toward seeing the truth rather than being blind, toward being creative, toward being good, and a lot else, . . .) (1959, p. 126).

—*B.F. Skinner* (1972): The act of creation can be explained according to strict learning theory principles. (See chapters 12 & 13 for a discussion of such principles.) "It is not prior purpose, intention, or act of will which accounts for novel behavior; it is the "contingencies of reinforcement." (1972).

—*J.P. Guilford* (1967): Individuals have 120 different and independent intellectual abilities. Each of those abilities consists of applying one of five mental *operations* to manipulate one of four *contents* to yield one of six *products* (5 x 4 x 6 = 120). Operations are things we do with the information we receive; for example, one operation is memory. Contents are the types of information we receive—for instance, symbolic information or semantic information. Products are the forms information takes as we process it; for example, we might classify the information or find relationships between pieces of information. Abilities especially relevant to creativity fall into two categories. One category consists of *divergent-production* abilities. Divergent production is an operation in which available information is used to generate new ideas in order to get quantity and variety. The other relevant category relates to the products known as *transformations*. Such transformations involve revising what we already experience or know, thus producing new forms and patterns.

—*John Curtis Gowan* (1977): The variance in creativity across individuals can best be accounted for by the concept of "psychological openness" to preconscious sources. "We theorize that the collective preconscious is best compared to the terminal of a giant computer which is in another realm, outside time and space, and contains an infinity of potentialities; all are real in that realm but only one will eventuate in our dimension. Under conditions of relaxation, meditation, incubation, and the like, messages in the form of images manifest in the printout of that cosmic computer and collator." (1977, p. 79).

There may be a bit of truth in each of the views. Part of the allure of the topic of creativity is that such markedly differing opinions could be conceived and presented.

THE MEASUREMENT OF CREATIVE ABILITY

In cases where creativity is needed, it would be nice to know in advance whether or not various individuals would be able to meet such a requirement. A great number of tests try to measure creative ability.[2] Gary Davis compares the proliferation of such tests to "a beer-can-littering scramble up the hillside" (1975, p. 75). Rather than try to survey the hillside, we will consider two of the best-known tests of creative ability.

The Remote Associates Test

Sarnoff Mednick developed the Remote Associates Test (RAT) on the basis of his theory of the creative process. He saw the creative thinking process as ". . . the forming of associative elements into new combinations which either meet specified requirements or are in some way useful. The more mutually remote the elements of the new combination, the more creative the process or solution." (1962, p. 221). To measure the extent to which people are able to bring together things only remotely associated with each other, Mednick developed a series of thirty sets of three words. The subject is required to find a

[2]For instance, see Davis (1971) and Kaltsounis (1971, 1972).

fourth word that somehow links the other words. Examples Mednick provided include:[3]

rat	blue	cottage
surprise	line	birthday
wheel	electric	high
out	dog	cat[4]

The subject's score on the test is the number of linking words he or she gets right within forty minutes.

While the RAT is quite popular, it has been criticized on a number of grounds. For instance, the test taps just one of many creative abilities. Also, scores on the test are apparently largely a function of verbal intelligence as well as creativity. And, since there are "right" and "wrong" answers for each set, it is possible that some truly creative links would be scored as incorrect.

The Torrance Tests of Creative Thinking[5]

One well-known set of tests that measures a number of aspects of creativity was developed by an educational psychologist, E. Paul Torrance. The Torrance Tests of Creative Thinking attempt to tap several of the individual's creative abilities. The exact forms of the tests depend upon who (children, nurses, salespersons, and so on) will be taking them. A few of the tests are:

1. The Ask-and-Guess Test. Subjects are shown a picture and asked "What is happening? What can you tell for sure? What do you need to know to understand what is happening, what caused it to happen, and what will be the result?"

2. The Product Improvement Task. Subjects must suggest ways to change a product to somehow make it better. For example, they may be asked to think of how to alter a stuffed animal so that it will be more interesting for children to play with.

3. The Just Suppose Test. The subject is asked to "just suppose" some unusual situation happened and to think of the consequences. For example, "Just suppose when it was raining, all the rain drops stood still in the air and wouldn't move—and they were solid."

Considerable evidence suggests that tests such as the Torrance Tests of Creative Thinking are valid. For example, scores on the Torrance tests have been found to predict creative behavior of students

[3]Mednick (1962).
[4]The answers to these sample items are cheese, party, chair or wire, and house.
[5]Much of this section is based on Torrance (1965).

of various ages and of teachers.[6] On the basis of such tests, it is now generally agreed that most people have substantial creative potential. As we've indicated previously, whether or not that potential is realized depends on effort and the situation.

SOME CORRELATES OF CREATIVE BEHAVIOR

If we were to look for creatively behaving individuals, what sorts of characteristics should we seek? Briefly summarized, evidence concerning individual differences suggests the following:

1. While people with high IQ's may show almost any level of creative performance, those with low IQ's are likely to exhibit low creativity levels.

2. Creative individuals generally value independence, have a wide range of interests, enjoy aesthetic expressions, have high aspiration levels, and are nonauthoritarian and nondogmatic.[7]

3. In our society, girls after the fourth grade regularly outscore boys on some figural creativity tests and all verbal creativity tests.[8]

4. Creativity appears to peak at age thirty to forty across a wide range of occupations, though many exceptions can be cited.[9]

5. Such family background measures as family wealth, birth order, whether the family was intact or broken, and whether the childhood was marked by sickness or good health generally are not consistently related to creative behavior.[10] However, individuals exhibiting creative behavior generally feel that they were given the opportunity to act responsibly early in life and see their families as being socially or intellectually superior.

Other studies of creative behaviors indicate that:

1. Individuals who show high levels of creative behavior are more likely to leave the organizations of which they are members than are others. For example, they have relatively high dropout rates from college[11] and a large number of job changes.[12]

2. Creatively behaving individuals seem to be both conformists and nonconformists, depending on how central the issue is to their

[6]See Cropley (1972) and Torrance (1972)
[7]See Barron (1968), Scott (1965) and Steiner (1965)
[8]Torrance and Aliotti (1969)
[9]Lehman (1953)
[10]Christie (1970)
[11]Heist (1968)
[12]Torrance (1971)

creative lives.[13] In particular, such people apparently resist pressure for conformity that they feel would interfere with their creative work but are willing to conform to norms that would have little bearing on their creative performance.

COSTS OF CREATIVITY

It may seem from the preceding discussion that it is always desirable to try to find especially creative individuals and to develop creativity in the organization. But such an attitude would ignore the very real costs of creativity. For example:

1. Time spent on creativity detracts from time available for other purposes.

2. As noted previously, creatively behaving individuals exhibit high levels of turnover. If we have invested a substantial amount of money in a particular project, especially of a developmental nature, it would be costly—and perhaps disastrous—if creative individuals associated with that project left to join one of our competitors.

3. Things aren't quite so secure in an organization stressing creativity as in one focusing more on efficiency and productivity. For some people, this lack of comfortable predictability may be distressing.

So, as with most things in life, creativity involves trade-offs. We have to ask whether the need for enhanced creative behavior in our organization more than balances anticipated costs. In view of the relatively low priority many organizations have placed on creativity in the past and of increasing pressures for organizations to be able to adapt to change, the answer to this question often will be affirmative.

TECHNIQUES TO ENHANCE CREATIVITY

Evidence indicates that creative output can be enhanced by the use of training in appropriate techniques. For example, Sidney Parnes and Eugene Brunelle (1967) reviewed forty studies and found that 90 percent reported some success in improving ability through training.

A tremendous number of techniques to try to increase creative output have been proposed. We discussed two of those methods—the Delphi process and the nominal group technique—in chapter 18. Rather than simply list other techniques, we will briefly describe five of the most popular—the Gordon Technique, Synectics, brainstorming, retroduction, and self-interrogation.

[13]See Raia and Osipow (1970) for one study on this subject.

Gordon technique

As we noted earlier, when we would like to have a truly new and unique idea, it is frustrating to see people *incrementalize*—that is, just take the best idea currently available and try incrementally to improve it. One way to avoid this problem might be simply to *not tell* those people that they are trying to, say, build a better mousetrap. Instead, we might simply tell them that their task is to discover a better way to capture. That is, we might tell them the *function* of the device they're trying to develop. This focus on function is the essence of the Gordon technique, developed by William J.J. Gordon. With the Gordon technique, only the leader knows exactly what the group is working on. Because group members try to come up with ways to perform a function, incrementalizing should be sharply reduced.

Synectics[14]

William Gordon also developed Synectics. Gordon writes, "The word *synectics*, from the Greek, means the joining together of different and apparently irrelevant elements. Synectics theory applies to the integration of diverse individuals into a problem-stating, problem-solving group." (1961, p. 3)

Synectics tries to make the strange familiar and make the familiar strange. Making the strange familiar involves careful analysis, gathering any necessary information concerning the problem. Making the familiar strange allows us to get a new perspective from which to view the world. To do this, Synectics relies on the use of four types of analogy.

1. *Personal Analogy.* This requires psychological identification with essential parts of the problem. As an example, a Synectics group was faced with the problem of inventing a new and practical constant-speed mechanism. They had to figure out how to run a shaft at speeds varying from 400 to 4000 rpm so that the power take-off end of the shaft would always turn at 400 rpm. To do this, each member of the group metaphorically entered the box and attempted to use his or her own body to get the required constant speed. Eventually, an efficient and economical model was developed based on the members' experiences "in" the box.

2. *Direct Analogy.* This involves looking for parallel facts, knowledge, or technology in a different domain from the one being worked on. To illustrate this, Gordon recalls the words of Alexander Graham Bell:

> "It struck me that the bones of the human ear were very massive, indeed, as compared with the delicate thin membrane that operated them, and the thought occurred that if a membrane so delicate could move bones relatively so massive, why should not a thicker and stouter piece of membrane move my piece of steel. And the telephone was conceived."

[14]This section is largely drawn from Gordon (1961).

Gordon also describes how a Synectics group was faced with the problem of inventing a dispenser that could be used with such products as glue and nail polish. The dispenser was to be in one piece, without a top to be removed and replaced with each use. The mouth of the dispenser would have to be opened for dispensing and closed tightly after each use. The group members considered various analogies in nature and finally designed a dispenser, based on one member's childhood experiences on a farm, modeled after the anal sphincter of a horse.

3. *Symbolic Analogy.* This involves the use of objective and impersonal images to describe the problem. For example, a Synectics group was presented with the problem of inventing a jacking mechanism that would fit into a box not bigger than four by four inches and be able to extend out and up three feet and support four tons. There were a number of false starts before one group member thought of the Indian rope trick. A model built on the basis of the symbolic analogy of the Indian rope trick satisfied the requirements of the problem.

4. *Fantasy Analogy.* Basically, fantasy analogy requires the individual to ask, "How in my wildest fantasies can I get this thing to happen?" For instance, Gordon tells of how a Synectics group was faced with the problem of inventing a vapor-proof closure for space suits. They finally solved the problem by designing a spring mechanism based on the fantasy analogy of tiny trained insects closing the opening.

Gordon (1972) reports that, as of 1971, more than 200 businesses in the United States and elsewhere had invested over $100,000,000 in the Synectics technique and that materials developed by Synectics Education Systems had influenced more than 10,000 classrooms.

Brainstorming

As described by Alex Osborn, brainstorming means ". . . using the brain to storm a creative problem . . . commando fashion, with each stormer attacking the same objective." The idea behind brainstorming is to create a situation where group members will toss out a large number of ideas without fear of negative evaluations. Osborn's four rules for brainstorming are:

1. No one should criticize anyone else's ideas.

2. Participants should say anything that comes to their minds. The wilder the idea, the better.

3. Participants should generate as many ideas as possible.

4. In addition to providing their own ideas, participants should try to improve upon or combine the ideas of others.

The brainstorming group generally consists of six to twelve individuals. Since it is desirable to analyze the problem from different points of view, it is helpful to have members from a variety of backgrounds.

Brainstorming was very popular in the 1950s but then fell from favor after the results of an experiment conducted by Donald Taylor and his colleagues at Yale University were published in 1958.[15] The experiment demonstrated that individuals working alone could come up with more unique ideas than could a brainstorming group. When Marvin Dunnette and his colleagues at the University of Minnesota repeated and improved upon the Taylor experiment in 1963 and got the same results, enthusiasm for brainstorming was further dampened.[16]

However, Thomas Bouchard (1971) has argued that such findings have been misinterpreted. For one thing, he pointed out that such results focus only on the number of unique ideas generated, not on how acceptable they are to the group members. As we saw in chapter 18, group problem solving increases the acceptability of decisions. Also, Bouchard demonstrated that simply by using a sequencing procedure —where each individual in the group speaks in sequence with an idea or says "pass" if he or she has no idea—rather than letting interaction go unchecked, group performance in terms of number of ideas generated was similar to that of pooled individual performance. Thus, brainstorming may hold considerably more promise than has been recently suggested.

Retroduction[17]

Our beliefs and actions are, in large part, a function of the assumptions we make about the way things are. If we assume that the earth is flat, we probably won't consider the consequences of sailing around it. While our assumptions may generally be correct, they are wrong often enough that it may be useful to challenge them. Also, we may even sometimes get useful insights by building on novel but incorrect assumptions. Retroduction involves changing an assumption. For example, Einstein revised Newton's assumption that space was flat to the assumption that space is curved and developed a new perspective on time and space. Retroduction techniques involve asking things like "what if?" or "suppose."

One retroduction technique is to say, "Suppose x were y." For example, groups might brainstorm by saying, "Suppose elephants were birds." Another technique is to pair strange and familiar concepts (such as electronics and jewelry). Yet another is to ask, "What if?" For instance, "What if the speed of light could be varied? What if gravity could be turned on and off?"

---

[15]Taylor, Berry, and Block (1958).
[16]Dunnette, Campbell, and Jastad.
[17]This section is largely drawn from Olmo (1977).

For example, Tim might say, "I've always felt that Sam's motivation for working late was simply to make a good impression on me in hopes of a promotion. What if it's really because he enjoys his work and is concerned about the productivity of the department? What would be the implications if that were the case? How can I check on the validity of my past assumption?" Or Meg might think, "My image of Don has been that of a competitor for the same sorts of promotions I'd like. If I were to assume, instead, that we could really help each other get ahead, how would it change the way I should behave? What might be the sorts of consequences?" By changing our assumptions about such things as people's motivation to work, the nature of our subordinates' probable responses to structure or rewards, appropriate behaviors in particular situations, and so on, our knowledge of organizational behavior, of suitable management techniques, and perhaps of life in general might be considerably enhanced.

Self-interrogation

Alex Osborn has pointed out that systematic self-questioning can often generate a great number of alternatives. In particular, Osborn provides a summary of the kinds of self-interrogation that can lead to ideas by somehow altering currently available alternatives. (1953, p. 284). For example, can you:

1. Put to other uses? New ways to use as is? Other uses if modified?

2. Adapt? What else is like this? What other idea does this suggest? Does past offer parallel? What could I copy? Whom could I emulate?

3. Minify? What to subtract? Smaller? Condensed? Miniature? Lower? Shorter? Lighter? Omit? Streamline? Split up? Understate?

4. Substitute? Who else instead? What else instead? Other ingredient? Other material? Other process? Other power? Other place? Other approach? Other tone of voice?

5. Combine? How about a blend, an alloy, an assortment, an ensemble? Combine units? Combine purposes? Combine appeals? Combine ideas?

Osborn cites many concrete examples of the effectiveness of such questioning. For example, he notes that use of the questioning technique during World War II brought about better thinking in the operations of arsenals, motor-maintenance shops, and other war-production installations. In fifty installations in which this method was applied, 6,000,000 man-hours per year were saved. The question, "In what other products could my materials be used?," led to George Washington Carver's enumeration of more than 300 articles in which peanuts could be used. Similarly, fiberglass was a result of the question, "To what uses could glass thread be put?" Osborn cites everything from tapered roller bearings to bubbling Christmas-tree lights to Spic and Span to freeze-dried foods to the sewing machine to be the results of questioning techniques.

TABLE 19-1
Some Characteristics of the Creative Organization

Some Characteristics of the Creative Organization
Open channels of communication
Encouragement of contact with outside sources
Idea units absolved of other responsibilities
Heterogeneous personnel policy
Investment in basic research
Decentralized; diversified
Risk-taking ethos
Not run as a "tight ship"
Separation of creative from productive functions
"Creators" are provided with a stable, secure environment

Drawn from Steiner (1965).

THE CREATIVE ORGANIZATION

We've now discussed a number of potentially useful techniques to enhance creativity. However, we might also ask, "What other things should the organization do to raise creativity levels? How should it be structured? How should it be run?" Unfortunately, there is not a great deal of hard data available to help answer such questions. However, by looking at characteristics of creatively behaving individuals and of their apparent preferences, some writers have attempted to paint a picture of the "creative organization." One such organization, depicted by George Steiner, is described in part in table 19-1.

Such an organization is typically described as fairly "loose," free flowing, and adaptive. This type of organization also is described as "organic," since it is similar in many ways to a living organism.

SUMMARY AND CONCLUSIONS

For most organizations, creativity will probably become increasingly important, but such creativity won't materialize spontaneously. Instead, creative behavior is a function of effort and setting as well as ability. Thorough preparation is a necessary first step in the creative process.

A number of approaches have been taken to understand the "causes" of creativity. They range from physiological to behaviorist to ability oriented to almost extrasensory. Each of those approaches may have some merit.

Creative ability apparently can be reliably and validly measured. The best measures are those, such as the Torrance Tests of Creative Ability, that recognize there are a number of facets to creativity and try to tap several of those facets. Partly on the basis of administration of such tests, it is now generally agreed that most people have substantial creative ability.

Creatively behaving individuals value independence, have high aspiration levels, and prefer a relatively complex situation. However, beyond a certain IQ threshold, creativity is not necessarily related to intelligence. Creativity is apparently related to sex, age, and a restricted number of family background measures. Further, creatively behaving individuals are relatively likely to resist pressures for conformity to norms that they feel will interfere with their creative efforts and are somewhat likely to leave their host organizations. As might be suggested by such relationships, creativity exacts a price. An organization stressing creativity may have to pay in terms of time taken from productive endeavors, in high turnover, and in a less "comfortable" climate.

Research findings consistently show that creative behavior can be sharply enhanced. A number of specific techniques are useful for that purpose. Further, appropriate organization design may foster creativity. Such a design would seem to be relatively "loose," characterized by open communications, a risk-taking atmosphere, a diverse mixture of personnel, and an emphasis on basic research.

REFERENCES

Barron, F. "The Psychology of Creativity." In *New Directions in Psychology II*, New York: Holt, Rinehart and Winston, 1965.

Barron, F. "The Dream of Art and Poetry." *Psychology Today*, 2(12), (1968): 18-23.

Bouchard, T.J. "Whatever Happened to Brainstorming?" *Industry Week* (Aug. 2, 1971): 26-27.

Christie, T. "Environmental Factors in Creativity." *Journal of Creative Behavior* 4 (1970): 13-31.

Cropley, A.J. "A Five-Year Longitudinal Study of the Validity of Creativity Tests." *Developmental Psychology* 6 (1972): 119-24.

Davis, G.A. "Instruments Useful in Studying Creative Behavior and Creative Talent." *Journal of Creative Behavior* 5 (1971): 162-65.

Dunnette, M.D.; Campbell, J.; and Jostad, K. "Effect of Group Participation on Brainstorming Effectiveness for Two Industrial Samples." *Journal of Applied Psychology* 47 (1963): 30-37.

Gordon, W.J.J. *Synectics*. New York: Harper and Row, 1961.

Gordon, W.J.J. "On Being Explicit about Creative Process." *Journal of Creative Behavior* 6 (1972): 295-300.

Gowan, J.C. "Some New Thoughts on the Development of Creativity." *Journal of Creative Behavior* 11 (1977): 77-90.

Guilford, J.P. *The Nature of Human Intelligence*. New York: McGraw Hill, 1967.

Guilford, J.P. "Creativity: Retrospect and Prospect." *Journal of Creative Behavior* 4 (1970): 149-68.

Halpin, G., and Halpin, G. "The Effect of Motivation on Creative Thinking Abilities." *Journal of Creative Behavior* 7 (1973): 51-53.

Heist, P.O. "Creative Students: College Transients." In *The Creative College Student: An Unmet Challenge*. San Francisco: Jossey-Bass, 1968.

Kaltsounis, B. "Instruments Useful in Studying Creative Behavior and Creative Talent." *Journal of Creative Behavior* 5 (1971): 117-26.

Kaltsounis, B. "Additional Instruments Useful in Studying Creative Behavior and Creative Talent." *Journal of Creative Behavior* 6 (1972): 268-74.

Lehman, H.C. *Age and Achievement*. Princeton, N.J.: Princeton University Press, 1953.

Lombroso, C. *The Man of Genius*.

London: Charles Scribner's Sons, 1895.

Maslow, A.H., ed. *New Knowledge in Human Values*. Chicago: Henry Regnery, 1959.

Mednick, S.A. "The Associative Basis of the Creative Process," *Psychological Review 69* (1962): 220-32.

Olmo, B. "Retroduction: The Key to Creativity." *Journal of Creative Behavior 11* (1977): 216, 221.

Osborn, A.F. *Applied Imagination*. New York: Charles Scribner's Sons, 1953.

Osborn, A.F. *The Creative Education Movement*. Buffalo, N.Y.: Creative Education Foundation, 1964.

Parnes, S.J., and Brunelle, E.A. "The Literature of Creativity: Part I." *Journal of Creative Behavior 1* (1967): 52-109.

Raia, J.R., and Osipow, S.H. "Creative Thinking Ability and Susceptibility to Persuasion." *Journal of Social Psychology 28* (1970): 181-86.

Scott, W.E., Jr. "The Creative Individual." *Academy of Management Journal 8* (1965): 211-19.

Skinner, B.F. "A Lecture on 'Having' a Poem." In *B.F. Skinner, Cumulative Record: A Selection of Papers*, 3rd ed. Englewood Cliffs, N.J.: Prentice Hall, 1972.

Steiner, G.A. ed. *The Creative Organization*. Chicago: University of Chicago Press, 1965.

Taylor, D.W.; Berry, P.C.; and Block, C.H. "Does Group Participation When Using Brainstorming Facilitate or Inhibit Creative Thinking?" *Administrative Science Quarterly 3* (1958): 23-47.

Torrance, E.P. "Scientific Views of Creativity and Factors Affecting Its Growth." *Daedalus 94* (1965): 663-81.

Torrance, E.P. "Is Bias against Job Changing Bias against Giftedness?" *Gifted Child Quarterly 15* (1971): 244-48.

Torrance, E.P. "Predictive Validity of 'Bonus' Scoring for Combinations on Repeated Figures Tests of Creative Thinking." *Journal of Psychology 81* (1972): 167-71.

Torrance, E.P., and Aliotti, N.C. "Sex Differences in Levels of Performance and Test-Retest Reliability on the Torrance Tests of Creative Thinking Ability." *Journal of Creative Behavior 3* (1969): 52-57.

Wallas, G. *The Art of Thought*. New York: Harcourt Brace Jovanovich, 1926.

SUGGESTIONS FOR ADVANCED READINGS

Gordon, W.J.J. *Synectics*. New York: Harper and Row, 1961.

Guilford, J.P. *The Nature of Human Intelligence*. New York: McGraw-Hill, 1967.

Journal of Creative Behavior. (Skim a few issues.)

Osborn, A.F. *Applied Imagination*. New York: Charles Scribner's Sons, 1953.

Rothenberg, A., and Hausman, C.R., eds. *The Creativity Question*. Durham, N.C.: Duke University Press, 1976.

DISCUSSION QUESTIONS

1. Think of an important choice you made between two or more alternatives that differed in a number of ways. How did you make that choice? Would you say the process you used was more like a screening approach or a scoring approach?

2. What do you think of the idea of replacing human decision makers with statistical models? What do you feel are implications of such a development? Would you want important decisions affecting your welfare to be made by a statistical model? Why or why not?

3. Given the following decision matrix, which alternative should be chosen according to the:

—a. Maximax criterion?

—b. Maximin criterion?

—c. Laplace criterion?

—d. Savage criterion?

		States of Nature			
		1	2	3	4
	1	10	8	0	6
Alternatives	2	7	7	7	7
	3	5	8	10	9

4. Bob is considering investing his $1000 in one of two ways. One alternative he is considering is to invest in a new invention, solar-power skateboards. If the invention succeeds (Bob figures the probability of this is .4), total returns should be $3,000. If it fails, Bob expects to salvage only about $250.

The other alternative is to invest in a new dog food developed by his neighbor. The dog food, shaped like spaghetti and aimed at the French poodle market, would be called "Poodles' Noodles." Bob figures this idea should be a big hit, with total returns of $5000, unless there is an epidemic of poodle blight. If rumors of ensuing poodle blight are valid—Bob sees the probability of this as .5—Bob's investment will be a total loss.

Assuming that Bob's utility function for money is linear, what investment should he make, if any?

5. Consider each of the following cases:*

Case I: You are general foreman in charge of a large gang laying an oil pipeline and have to estimate your expected rate of progress in order to schedule material deliveries to the next field site.

You know the nature of the terrain you will be traveling and have the historical data needed to compute the mean and variance in the rate of speed over that type of terrain. Given these two variables, it is a simple matter to calculate the earliest and

---

*Reprinted, by permission of the publisher, from V.H. Vroom, "A New Look at Managerial Decision Making," *Organizational Dynamics*, Spring 1973, ©1973 by AMACOM, a division of American Management Associations, pp. 72-74. All rights reserved.

latest times at which materials and support facilities will be needed at the next site. It is important that your estimate be reasonably accurate. Underestimates result in idle foremen and workers, and an overestimate results in tying up materials for a period of time before they are to be used.

Progress has been good, and your five foremen and other members of the gang stand to receive substantial bonuses if the project is completed ahead of schedule.

Case II: You are on the division manager's staff and work on a wide variety of problems of both an administrative and technical nature. You have been given the assignment of developing a standard method to be used in each of the five plants in the division for manually reading equipment registers, recording the readings, and transmitting the scorings to a centralized information system.

Until now, there has been a high error rate in the reading and/or transmittal of the data. Some locations have considerably higher error rates than others, and the methods used to record and transmit the data vary among plants. It is probable, therefore, that part of the error variance is a function of specific local conditions rather than anything else, and this will complicate the establishment of any system common to all plants. You have the information on error rates but no information on the local practices that generate these errors or on the local conditions that necessitate the different practices.

Everyone would benefit from an improvement in the quality of the data; it is used in a number of important decisions. Your contacts with the plants are through the quality-control supervisors who are responsible for collecting the data. They are a conscientious group committed to doing their jobs well; but are highly sensitive to interference on the part of higher management in their own operations. Any solution that does not receive the active support of the various plant supervisors is unlikely to reduce the error rate significantly.

For each case:

a. First indicate which of the five alternative decision styles used by Vroom you would normally be inclined to use.

b. Then answer each of the diagnostic questions in the Vroom and Yetton model and use those answers to find which styles are in the feasible set and which is the quickest feasible solution.

c. Was the style you initially chose in the feasible set? If not, in what way did your choice differ from that of the model?

6. Bob's boss sometimes called him in for advice on departmental problems and sometimes left him completely in the dark. Bob's coworkers had expressed the same feelings: they really didn't know when they would be asked to make contributions. Sometimes they

were asked to spend time on problems they didn't really care about or know anything about. In other cases, they didn't get a chance to make any inputs, even in decisions that were crucial to them. So Bob was anxious to tell his boss about a new tool he had learned about in his night class—the Vroom and Yetton model. However, Bob's boss responded to his suggestion by saying, "I'd be the laughingstock of the company if people knew I used something like that. I'm supposed to know, on the basis of my training and experience, when and to what extent I should involve subordinates in decision making. There's no way I'm going to get caught leaning on some fancy academic tree to do my job." How do you think Bob should respond to his boss?

7. One criticism of the Vroom and Yetton model is that it takes certain situational characteristics as given and then chooses an appropriate style in view of those characteristics. Some argue that it would be better to change the situation than to just accept things the way they are. Which of the questions in the model do you think take for granted things that might better be changed?

8. John, the head of a small research and development firm, has said, "If I have three people around when I have to solve a problem, I'll use them—or four or five or six if they're available. I think we should involve as many people as possible." How would you respond? What might John's approach accomplish? What might be the costs of such an approach?

9. When the company's consultant suggested use of the NGT, Ursula said, "I'm not going to be forced into some artificial process. If I want to say what I think about some idea, I'll say it. I'm not going to have my comments about important organizational issues compartmentalized by some outsider." As the consultant, how would you respond?

10. Think of a case in which you came up with a unique idea. How did you go about it? Did you seem to go through the stages Wallas described?

11. In this section, we described some characteristics of a "creative organization." Would you like to work in such an organization? What might be some problems with such a structure? Can you envision situations in which such a structure would not be appropriate?

12. Think of people whom you consider to be really creative. Do they share any common characteristics? If so, do you think such characteristics are likely to be found among most creative individuals?

13. We presented several views of the sources of creativity. To what extent do you agree or disagree with each of those views? Why?

14. Which of the creativity enhancement techniques that were reviewed do you feel would be most useful to organizations? Least useful? On what sorts of dimensions do the techniques differ?

SECTION

Becoming A Successful Leader

From time to time, all of us assume leadership roles, perhaps on a formal basis but often informally. In this section, we consider a number of important issues relating to leadership. We first look at what a leader does and the sorts of things that give a leader power to carry out those functions. Then, we will review various attempts to identify traits or behaviors of successful leaders, always stressing the need to consider the particular situation. Next, we will examine three well-known sitational approaches to leadership effectiveness. Surprisingly, leadership may not always be especially important since various things may neutralize its impact. In general, though, we argue that leadership does make a difference in organizations. The section ends with an examination of how leaders can acquire and use power in their jobs.

KEY TERMS

LEADERSHIP
INFLUENCE
POWER
BASES OF POWER
- Legitimate
- Reward
- Coercive
- Referent
- Expert

FORMAL LEADER
INFORMAL LEADER
TRAIT
THEORY X
THEORY Y
SELF-DESCRIPTION INVENTORY
AUTOCRATIC STYLE
DEMOCRATIC STYLE
CONSIDERATION
INITIATING STRUCTURE
MANAGERIAL GRID
LPC
PATH-GOAL THEORY
SUBSTITUTES FOR LEADERSHIP

OBJECTIVES

1. To consider the functions of a leader
2. To examine a leader's bases of power
3. To see how traits and behaviors of leaders are related to such outcomes as subordinate satisfaction and performance
4. To examine specific situational theories of leadership effectiveness
5. To consider substitutes for leadership
6. To see how leaders can get and effectively use power

CHAPTER

20

Leadership In Organizations

Paul sipped a beer and thought about how his day at work had gone. He was upset that his boss had criticized him in front of other employees for not working fast enough. He almost wished that he had just told him where to get off. Still, he had thought, his boss is the one who hands out the raises and decides who gets canned. Anyway, John, one of Paul's coworkers, had been there to calm him down. John told Paul to cool off, that the boss was just having a bad day. Paul and most of his friends really respected John and followed his advice. He always seemed to have things under control. So Paul had tried his best to calm down, concentrate on his work, and increase his output. Even now, though, finishing his beer, he half regretted the fact that he hadn't stood up to his boss.

Chester Barnard (1938) defined leadership as the ability of one person to influence the behavior of another. *Influence* refers to the exertion of force on another person to change certain attitudes or behaviors. *Power* is generally defined as *potential influence.* That is, one person has power over another if he or she has the potential to exert force on that person.

In the little scenario that opened this chapter, Paul clearly was influenced by both his boss and John. Each of them somehow did things that changed his behavior. The boss got him to speed up. John got him to cool down and concentrate on his work rather than seethe about the boss. So Paul's boss and John were both, in a sense, assuming leadership roles relative to Paul. While the boss is Paul's *formal* leader, John is an *informal* leader.

Later, we'll discuss some sources of power that leaders can draw upon. Based on the example we've just considered, we can see that those sources may be quite varied. Paul obeyed the orders of his boss because his boss controlled rewards and punishments. He followed John's advice out of respect.

Most of our focus in this chapter will be on formal leaders. However, it should be remembered that leadership isn't restricted to the one person formally designated as the group leader. Many people may assume leadership functions. Therefore, to focus only on the formal leader would not be appropriate.

There are many reasons why we might want to consider leadership in organizations. For example, Barbara Karmel has written that:

> . . . the practitioner wants to know how to *train* and *evaluate* a leader; the behavioral scientist asks how to *know* a leader when you see one; the student asks how to *be* a leader; and society asks, "Where have all the leaders gone?" (1978, p. 478)

While each of these questions is important, we'll focus primarily on what is known about the important issue of how to be a sucessful leader.

FUNCTIONS OF THE FORMAL LEADER

We've said that leadership involves the exertion of influence over others. Before we consider the question of the bases of the leader's potential influence, let's look briefly at what formal leaders do. To varying degrees, a formal leader performs a wide variety of functions, among which are the following ten[1]:

1. Serves as a source of information and experience, often possessing special skills that others need

2. Is the point of official contact with other parts of the organization, acting as a representative of group members and channeling outgoing and incoming messages

3. Controls internal relations, influencing group structure and sometimes serving as the hub of communications and group dynamics

4. Gives out rewards and punishments or makes or approves recommendations concerning them

5. Serves as a model for the behavior of other members

6. Is the symbol of the group

7. Acts as a substitute for individual responsibility, giving formal approval to acts of subordinates

8. Often has a major impact on the norms, beliefs, and values of the group

9. Sometimes acts as a "father [or mother] figure," the focus of individual identification and personal emotional feelings

[1]This listing is adapted from Krech, Crutchfield, and Ballachey (1962).

10. Must often serve as a scapegoat, the target of criticism when things go wrong

Based on this listing of functions, we can get a pretty good fix on the ways a leader is able to influence others. Let's consider some bases of power.

BASES OF POWER

John French and Bertram Raven (1960) have identified five bases of power:

1. *Legitimate power* results when one individual feels that he or she "ought" to act in ways that another individual suggests. That is, such suggestions are seen as legitimate. Legitimate power may be:

   a. *Culturally specified.* That is, in some cultures it is felt that, for instance, the requests of people of certain ages, intelligence levels, castes, or particular physical characteristics should be deferred to.

   b. *Due to acceptance of the social structure.* For example, if employees think the organization's hierarchy is legitimate, they are likely to accept the fact that individuals at higher levels should be able to tell them what to do.

   c. *Designated by a legitimizing agent.* That is, if one individual is seen as having legitimate power, he or she may pass on that power to someone else. For example, a company president may appoint an assistant. Or, in our society, the populace may pass legitimate power on to a particular individual by election.

2. *Reward power* is based on the ability to influence the rewards that others receive. Thus, Dan has reward power over Sarah if he can decide what raise she should get or if he can make an input to that decision.

3. *Coercive power* is based on the ability to influence the punishments that others receive. Sally's boss, Jane, who can fire her, has coercive power over Sally.

4. *Referent power* is derived from some identification that one person has with another. By identification, we mean a feeling of oneness or a desire for such an identity. For example, Bob says, "I am like Tom so I'll act like Tom." Or Hank says, "I want to be like Joe Namath, so I'll do the sorts of things that Joe Namath does." So, if Hank goes out and buys panty hose and a butter-up corn popper, we have some evidence that Joe Namath has referent power over Hank.

5. *Expert power* is based on one person's perception that another has certain needed skills, knowledge, or abilities. For instance, you probably obey your doctor's instructions since you feel that he or she knows more about medicine than you do.

Two other relevant terms need to be defined. The *domain of power* refers to the number of individuals over whom someone can exert influence. The *range of power* refers to the number of different areas in which one person can influence another. The various bases of power probably differ substantially in terms of range. For instance, expert power is probably relatively restricted in range, while referent power has broad range (as evidenced by Joe Namath's ability to sell us butter-up corn poppers.)

To some extent, the degree to which leaders rely on these various bases of power probably depends upon the sorts of assumptions they make about the people they are trying to influence. For example, Douglas McGregor (1960) has named two differing sets of beliefs about human behavior "Theory X" and "Theory Y." Theory X is based on the belief that people generally dislike work and responsibility but feel that they must work to get money and other extrinsic rewards. As a result, they must be closely supervised and threatened with punishment if we are going to get them to produce. Theory Y, on the other hand, is based on the assumption that people like work and are capable of self-direction and self-control. It also assumes that people can learn to seek and accept responsibility and can show creativity in attacking organizational problems. While McGregor's classification scheme illustrates two extreme viewpoints, it does seem clear that leaders leaning toward one extreme or the other are likely to depend on different bases of power. A Theory X viewpoint would probably result in reliance largely upon reward, coercive, and legitimate power. A Theory Y orientation would lead to greater emphasis on expert and referent power.

The issue of power will be considered in more detail in the next chapter.

BECOMING A LEADER VERSUS BECOMING A SUCCESSFUL LEADER

We have now seen some of the things that leaders do and some of the bases of power they can use to get them done. But how do successful leaders differ from those who are unsuccessful? Do they have different characteristics? Do they behave differently?

At this point, we should be careful to distinguish between the question of who is likely to *become* a leader and that of who is likely to become a *successful* leader. While we will focus on the second of these questions, let's briefly consider the first. It does appear that certain characteristics of individuals can be used to predict their relative probabilities of being selected for leadership positions.[2] For instance, your chances of gaining a leadership position are improved if you:

1. Are tall

[2]For example, see Stogdill (1948) and Powell (1969).

2. Are of high socioeconomic status (though this doesn't seem to be as important as it once was)

3. Are intelligent, exhibiting superior judgment, decisiveness, knowledge, and fluency of speech

4. Exhibit interpersonal skills, such as participation in a wide range of activities, cooperation, and effective interaction with a variety of people

5. Have high needs for achievement and responsibility

Let's now consider some approaches to finding how successful leaders differ from others.

TRAIT APPROACHES

The earliest approach to the study of leadership was to try to determine which characteristics, or traits, successful leaders possessed. Traits are characteristics of individuals that seem to account for their behaviors. As one example of a trait approach, Tom Mahoney, Tom Jerdee, and Al Nash (1961) studied 468 managers in thirteen Minnesota companies. They found leadership success, measured in terms of an effectiveness rating assigned by high-level managers, to be positively related to intelligence, education, high risk preferences, desire for independence, and other variables.

While it is tempting to try to isolate such characteristics, it is also frustrating. In fact, most reviews of studies relating to leadership traits have been pessimistic.[3] For instance, Charles Bird (1940) concluded his survey of the literature by pointing out that of all those traits that one study or another had shown to be related to leadership or success, only 5 percent showed up in four or more studies. Also, Launor Carter and Mary Nixon (1949) showed that some high-school students emerged as leaders on one type of task, while others turned out to be the leaders for different tasks. It seems clear, then, that situational factors might dictate the characteristics a leader needs.

One possible exception to these generally disappointing results is the work of Edwin Ghiselli. Ghiselli set out to isolate traits that were relevant to managerial success. In a series of studies, he developed and validated a scale called the *self-description inventory*. The scale requires people to check one or the other of a series of sixty-four pairs of responses; for instance, one pair is sincere or calm and another is stubborn or cold. In some cases, they are asked to check the response that best describes them; in others, that which least describes them. The self-description inventory measures thirteen abilities, personality characteristics, and motivations. By considering the relationships between employees' scores on each of these traits and their success on the job, Ghiselli concluded that the thirteen traits had sub-

[3]For instance, see Jenkins (1947), Stogdill (1948), and Gibb (1954).

FIGURE 20-1
The Relative Importance of the Thirteen Traits to Managerial Talent*

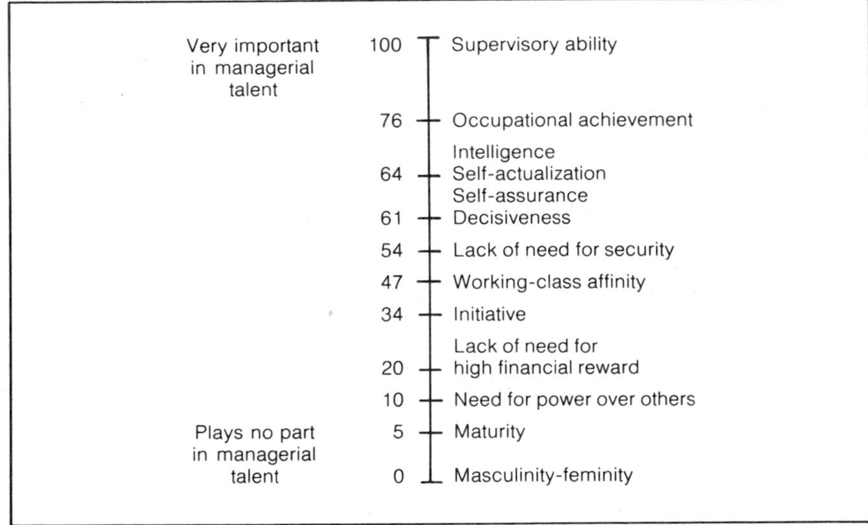

*From *Explorations in Managerial Talent*, by E.E. Ghiselli, (p. 165). Copyright ©1971 by Goodyear Publishing Co. Reprinted by permission.

stantially different degrees of importance for success as a manager. For example, figure 20-1, shows that, while the trait of supervisory ability was found to be of primary importance, other traits—such as need for power over others and masculinity-femininity—played only minor roles.[4]

In sum, most trait appoaches to the study of leadership have been disappointing since they generally have not been able to find characteristics that were consistently related to success across a variety of situations. While Ghiselli's work seems more promising, it will have to be tested more widely before his conclusions concerning the importance of particular traits can be confidently accepted. Also, it seems clear that certain of the traits Ghiselli considered would be more important in some situations than in others.

Figure 20-2 illustrates another criticism of trait approaches. Even if traits related to success as a leader can be isolated, the usefulness of such findings would be restricted. That is, while it might be possible to use that information for selection purposes, it is difficult—if not impossible—to change people's traits. So, since it is probably easier to alter behavior than traits, it might be better to try to find things that successful leaders *do* than things that describe the way they *are*.

DEMOCRATIC AND AUTOCRATIC STYLES

One early approach to examining the differences between how successful and unsuccessful leaders behaved considered the extent to

[4]For positive evidence concerning Ghiselli's work, see Fiedler and Meumese (1963) and Korman (1968).

FIGURE 20-2

which leaders are *autocratic* or *democratic.* Autocratic leaders are those who make decisions themselves, without inputs from subordinates. At the other extreme, democratic leaders let subordinates actively participate in decision making. Thus, autocratic and democratic leaders differ on a single dimension—the degree to which they delegate decision-making authority. We stress this point because there is sometimes a tendency to equate democratic with sensitivity and caring and autocratic with callousness and lack of concern for subordinates' welfare. But a little reflection should dispel such ideas. For instance, Carl's subordinates consider him to be a "benevolent autocrat." They don't doubt that he wants to do what's best for them, but they wish he would let them take care of themselves. On the other hand, Phil is upset that his boss never seems willing to make decisions on his own. Whenever Phil asks him a question, he replies, "I'll leave that up to you." Phil thinks his boss is just evading responsibility.

Findings relating to these styles are somewhat mixed.[5] It does seem that more democratic approaches are consistently related to subordinate satisfaction. However, the relationships of democratic style to productivity, while generally positive, have often been low or unclear. And it seems that the extent to which a democratic style is appropriate depends upon the task to be performed and, to some extent, on the personalities of subordinates. For instance, when tasks are routine and repetitive, letting subordinates participate in decision making seems to be ineffective. In such cases, participation is apparently viewed as relatively meaningless since, as Filley, House, and Kerr (1976) noted, ". . . there is little to participate about." (p. 226). Also, the effects of participation seem to be most favorable when subordinates are intelligent and, perhaps, when they have strong needs for independence. The Vroom and Yetton normative leadership model, discussed later in this chapter and in more detail

[5]See Filley, House and Kerr (1967) for a review of these studies.

A democratic style of leadership is most appropriate when the subordinates are intelligent, well-educated and exhibit a high need for independence.

in chapter 19, considers the sorts of situational factors that influence the impact of participation.

Finally, figure 20-3 makes a point that we will stress again later. That is, it could be that subordinates' actions determine leader behaviors instead of, or as well as, vice versa.

CONSIDERATION AND INITIATING STRUCTURE

As we indicated earlier, autocratic and democratic styles differ in terms of a single dimension—the degree of delegation of decision-making authority. Such a focus on just one dimension may seem extremely restricted. Instead, it would seem to be more promising to develop a fairly exhaustive list of the things that leaders do, see how those behaviors "cluster together," and examine how those clusters are related to subordinates' responses. This is precisely the approach taken in a major research program carried out at Ohio State University.

Researchers at Ohio State developed a scale, called the Leader Behavior Description Questionnaire, that asked subordinates to indicate the extent to which leaders engaged in particular behaviors. When the scale was administered to members of bomber crews, it was found that two independent underlying factors were most important in explaining crew members' responses. Those two dimensions were:

ANIMAL CRACKERS by Rog Bollen

FIGURE 20-3
The Influence of Subordinates' Behaviors on the Leader's Style

1. *Consideration*, defined as behaviors that are "indicative of friendship, mutual trust, respect, and warmth." (Halpin and Winer, 1957, p. 42)

2. *Initiating Structure*, defined as behaviors "which indicate that the aircraft commander . . . organizes and defines the relationship between himself and the members of the crew." (p. 42)

Figure 20-4 presents some sample items gauging consideration and initiating structure.

Many recent studies using the Leader Behavior Description Questionnaire in a great variety of settings consistently have found consideration and initiating structure to be key dimensions of perceived leader behavior.[6] Again, we should point out that these are independ-

Consideration:

He does personal favors for group members.
He finds time to listen to group members.
He backs up the members in their actions.
He treats all group members as his equals.
He puts suggestions made by the group into operation.

Initiating Structure:

He rules with an iron hand.
He criticizes poor work.
He assigns group members to particular tasks.
He schedules the work to be done.
He emphasizes the meeting of deadlines.

FIGURE 20-4
Sample Items to Measure Consideration and Initiating Structure

[6]See Filley, House, and Kerr (1976) for a review of these studies.

ent dimensions: a leader could be high on both, low on both, or high on one and low on the other.

In general, subordinates of leaders who are seen as being high on consideration tend to be satisfied and often exhibit relatively high productivity. However, there are a number of exceptions to these findings, and, as we'll see shortly, many other issues serve to cloud the picture. Initiating structure is often found to be negatively related to subordinate satisfaction, though again there are many exceptions.

To see *why* it is so hard to make any general statements about the impacts of consideration and initiating structure, we must explore at least three issues: 1) Is leader behavior a cause or a consequence of subordinates' responses? 2) Do consideration and initiating structure act separately, or do they somehow interact? 3) What situational factors may be relevant?

What causes what?

One problem in sorting out the roles of consideration and initiating structure is that, as we mentioned earlier, correlations merely tell us whether or not a pair of variables is related. They don't indicate what is causing what. So, even if we find that certain leader behaviors are correlated with an employee response, such as high productivity, we can't be sure that those behaviors caused the high productivity.

In fact, it could often be the case that subordinates' behaviors cause leader behavior, rather than vice versa. For example, if Bob feels that his subordinate, Larry, is a good performer, he may be more considerate of him and give him more autonomy than if he feels Larry is goofing off on the job. A variety of studies support this idea.

For example, Aaron Lowin and James Craig (1960) carried out an experiment in which subjects were led to believe they had been hired to supervise a "Job Corps trainee" who was typing letters. In fact, the "Job Corps trainee" was an experimental confederate, and the quality of the letters was experimentally varied. It was found that when the subjects felt the typist was not competent, they behaved less considerately, supervised more closely, and exhibited higher levels of initiating structure than when they thought the typist was competent.[7]

Another possibility is that the correlations between leader behavior and subordinate responses are spurious. A *spurious correlation* occurs when two variables are not related in any cause-and-effect fashion but move together since they're both causally related to another variable. That is, certain situational factors may cause leaders to behave in particular ways and cause subordinates to respond in particular ways. For example, it could be that on pleasant, sunny days subordinates perform at high levels, and leaders behave considerately. On overcast, depressing days, leaders may be less considerate, and subordinates may not perform well. While there is no

[7]Also, see Farris and Lim (1969) and Rosen (1969).

causal relationship between leader behavior and subordinate performance in such a case, a positive correlation would exist. Figure 20-5 summarizes these alternative possibilities.

The interaction of consideration and initiating structure

Also, most studies have considered the impacts of consideration and initiating structure separately. It could be that they somehow interact to affect subordinate responses. With this in mind, we studied how the satisfaction of 131 manufacturing employees was related to their superiors' behaviors. As shown in table 20-1, employees who felt their superiors were considerate were generally more satisfied than others. Interestingly, though, the impact of initiating structure depended upon how considerate the leader was felt to be. When the leader was seen as considerate, initiating structure was apparently viewed as helpful and was responded to favorably. When the leader was thought to be inconsiderate, initiating structure was seen as an intrusion and reacted to negatively.

FIGURE 20-5
Some Possible Links between Leader Behavior and Subordinate Performance

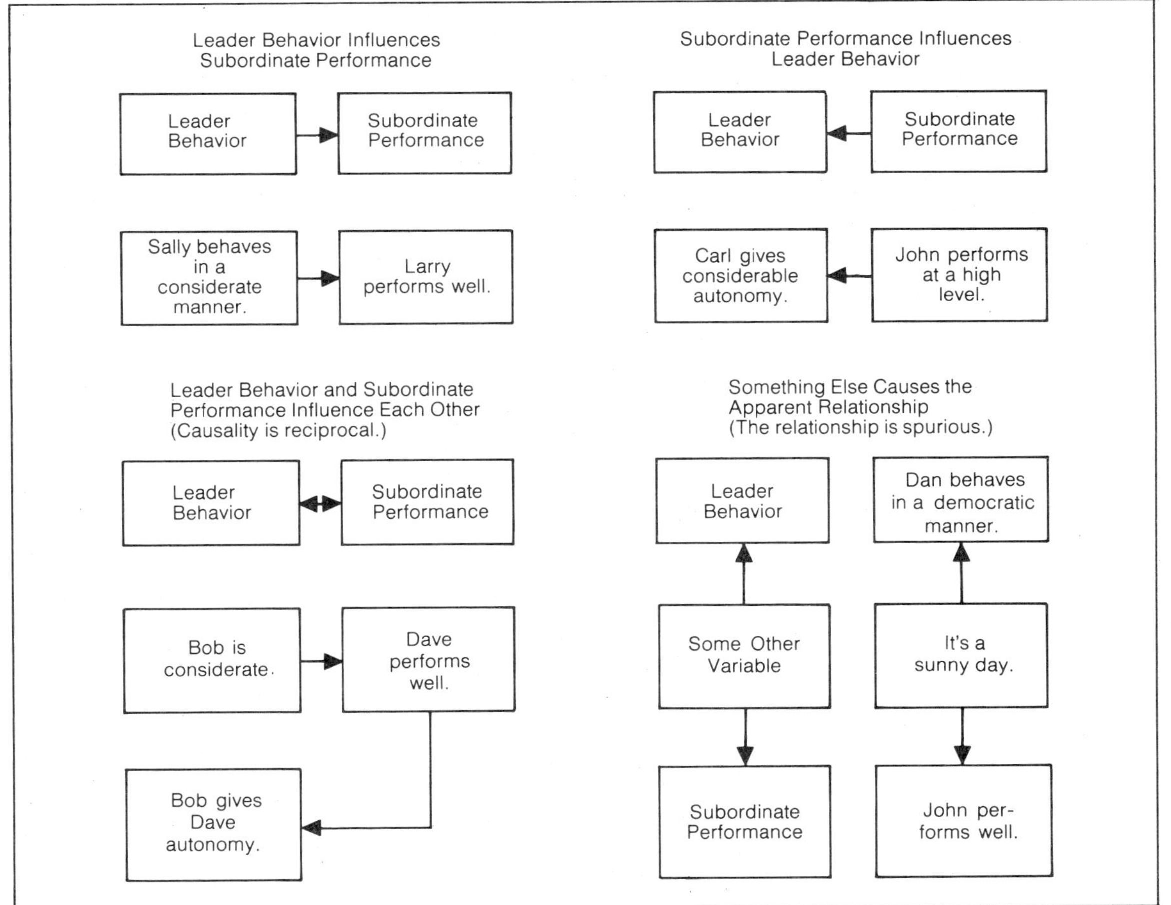

TABLE 20-1
General Job Satisfaction As a Function of Consideration and Initiating Structure*

		CONSIDERATION LOW	CONSIDERATION HIGH
INITIATING STRUCTURE	LOW	4.06	4.63
	HIGH	3.50	5.18

*From Brief and Aldag (1976)

Related to this viewpoint is the popular *managerial grid*, shown in figure 20-6. Developed by Robert Blake and Jane Srygly Mouton, the managerial grid has as its axes concern for people and concern for production. These are similar to consideration and initiating structure, respectively, except that they focus on attitudes rather than behaviors. It can be seen that, depending on the manager's degrees of concern for people and for production, he or she may fall into any of the eighty-one cells of the grid. Basically, Blake and Mouton argue that a nine, nine approach—with high concern for both people and production—is best and should be striven for.

Such an idea certainly seems reasonable and is consistent with the findings we have just discussed. However, the perspective of the grid is a bit simplistic. That is, it implies that the formally designated

FIGURE 20-6
The Managerial Grid*

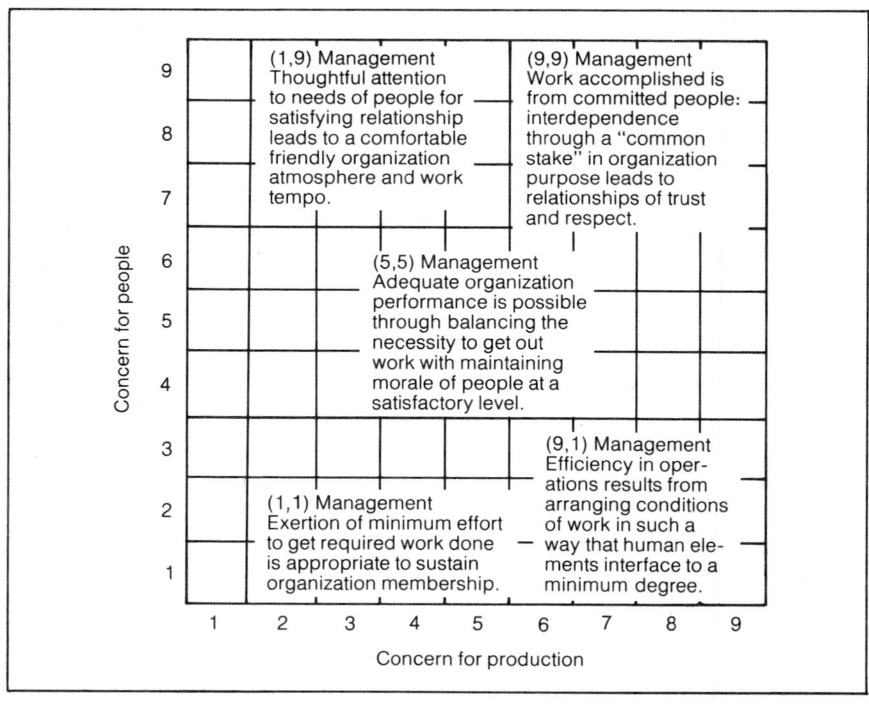

*The Managerial Grid figure from *The New Managerial Grid,* by Robert R. Blake and Jane Srygley Mouton. Houston: Gulf Publishing Company, Copyright ©1978, page 11. Reproduced with permission.

leader is the only one who has an impact on the satisfaction and performance of the group. In fact, other individuals may sometimes play important roles. Thus, in some cases it may be clearly undesirable for the formally designated leader to try to show both high consideration and high initiating structure. That is, subordinates may see some of those behaviors as redundant, or they may present challenges to informal leaders of the group. For instance, everyone in the shipping and receiving department at Allied Furniture thinks coworker Al is a great guy. He's always telling jokes, organizing parties, and generally keeping everyone is a good mood. Now, though, the new head of the department, Tom, has started acting like a social director, slapping everyone on the back, organizing outings, and plastering multi-colored posters all over the walls. Tom's behavior has clearly upset Al, and some of the employees are concerned that they may soon have to "choose sides" in this deceptively cheery struggle. Not surprisingly, a variety of studies have shown that it is not *always* best to adopt a "high-high" leadership style. Instead, as we'll see in the next sections, careful consideration has to be given to the situation, to the nature of subordinates, and to other variables.

One interesting finding that emerged from studies of this issue is that the leaders' superiors and subordinates appear to evaluate them in terms of different things. The leaders' superiors generally want them to be task oriented, to supervise closely, and to be decisive. On the other hand, most of the leaders' subordinates would prefer that they be considerate, not supervise closely, and be democratic in their decision-making processes. This puts the leaders in a touchy situation where they must try to satisfy conflicting expectations and remarks. They can partially resolve that conflict by showing high levels of both consideration and initiating structure. Again, though, there are some situations in which such behaviors will not produce favorable outcomes.

The impact of the situation

In fact, many situational factors must be considered when deciding which leader behaviors are most appropriate. For example, Steve Kerr and his colleagues (1974) have reviewed the literature relating to this topic and concluded that the following factors, among others, determine how particular leader behaviors will affect subordinates' satisfaction and performance.

1. *Pressure.* When time pressures, stress, task demands, or physical danger are present, leader initiating structure is viewed more favorably, and consideration may be less important than otherwise. For example, in times of national emergency, the populace generally seems more willing to accept a structuring, autocratic leader than in more placid times. After all, when you're charging up a hill in battle, you don't want a leader who says, "Hey guys, let's talk about our alternatives."

2. *Task-related satisfaction.* When jobs are not intrinsically satisfying, leader initiating structure seems to increase subordinate resentment and dissatisfaction but to increase performance. For instance, Sandy enjoys her work and wants to learn how to do it better, so she is glad to get instructions from her boss. On the other hand, Ken's job is so boring he just wants to get it over with. The last thing he wants is to have his supervisor give him instructions. Ken figures, "Why should I try to do any better? Why doesn't he just get off my back?" Also, the relationship between leader consideration and subordinate satisfaction and performance tends to be less positive when the task is intrinsically satisfying than otherwise. That is, with an unsatisfying task, it may seem crucial to have a supportive, friendly, comforting leader. But with an intrinsically satisfying task, such behaviors may seem less important.

3. *Subordinate need for information.* In situations where subordinates have low job knowledge, perhaps as a result of role ambiguity, initiating structure will probably be received favorably. For example, when we examined how police personnel responded to initiating structure,[8] we learned that the role of these public servants is ambiguous. Police officers generally are separated from their superiors, often have no idea what to expect upon arriving at an assignment, and can behave in any of several ways. In such a situation, initiating structure was reacted to very favorably. Subsequent analyses showed that initiating structure reduced role ambiguity, resulting in increased performance and, interestingly, in more favorable attitudes toward the citizenry.

4. *Subordinate expectations.* It seems that when leaders behave, in terms of consideration and initiating structure, as subordinates expect them to, the subordinates generally respond more favorably than when leader behaviors are unexpected.

In this section, we'll consider three approaches to the relevance of situational factors.

SITUATIONAL APPROACHES TO THE STUDY OF LEADERSHIP

Fiedler's contingency model

Fred Fiedler (1965) developed one early situational approach to the examination of leadership. Fiedler argues that, if we find that a particular leader behavior or style seems to "fit" a given situation, we have four options. We can

1. try to train the leader to behave appropriately,
2. select individuals who meet the situational requirements,

[8]Aldag and Brief (1978).

3. juggle managers around in the organization until they are in positions that fit their styles, or

4. change the situation.

Fiedler believes that the first three options—training, selection, and placement—don't work very well. Instead, he says, we should "engineer the job to fit the manager." He reasons that we should find how the effectiveness of particular styles is related to certain situational factors that we are able to manipulate. Once we have done that, we can change the situation to make it hospitable to any leader's particular style.

Fiedler's measure of the leader is unique. He uses a scale to assess how favorably or unfavorably the leader describes his or her least-preferred coworker (LPC). Figure 20-7 presents a few of the scale items. Essentially, Fiedler views a high LPC leader (that is, one who sees even a least-preferred coworker in relatively favorable terms) as being concerned with relationships and nondirective and a low LPC leader as task oriented and directing.

Fiedler also selected three situational factors, each of which he felt could be manipulated, and reflected on how favorable the situation was to the leader.

1. Leader-member relations—the degree to which group members trust and like the leader and are willing to follow his or her guidance

2. Task structure—the degree to which the task is spelled out step-by-step for the group and to which it can be done according to a detailed set of standard operating procedures

3. Leader position power—the power of the leadership position, as opposed to personal power (This would include reward power and coercive power, as well as the degree to which the leader's position is secure.)

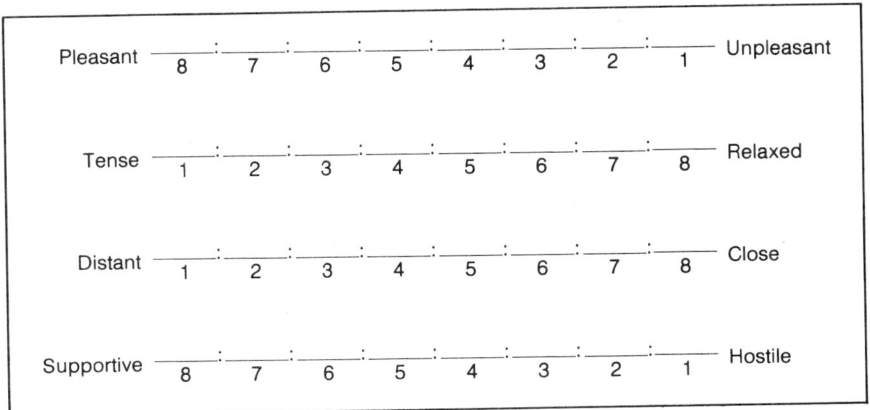

FIGURE 20-7
Sample Items from the LPC Scale

The most favorable situation for the leader, according to Fiedler, is one in which leader-member relations are positive, the task is highly structured, and the leader has substantial position power. By considering whether each of the situational factors was high or low in a particular case, the situation can be placed in one of eight octants, ranging from very favorable to very unfavorable.

Based on research involving over 800 groups in a wide variety of settings—everything from bombers to bowling alleys, from heavy-machinery plants to research labs—Fiedler concluded that the best LPC depended upon the situation. Figure 20-8 shows his representation of those findings. The vertical axis in the figure shows the correlation between the leader's LPC score and the performance of his or her group. (The correlation can range from +1, if the LPC score and performance always move in the same direction, through 0, if they're independent, and down to -1, if they always move in different directions.) The figure shows that in very favorable or very unfavorable situations, low LPC leaders do better than high LPC leaders. On the other hand, high LPC leaders do better than low LPC leaders when the situation is moderately favorable.

FIGURE 20-8
How Effective Leadership Varies with the Situation*

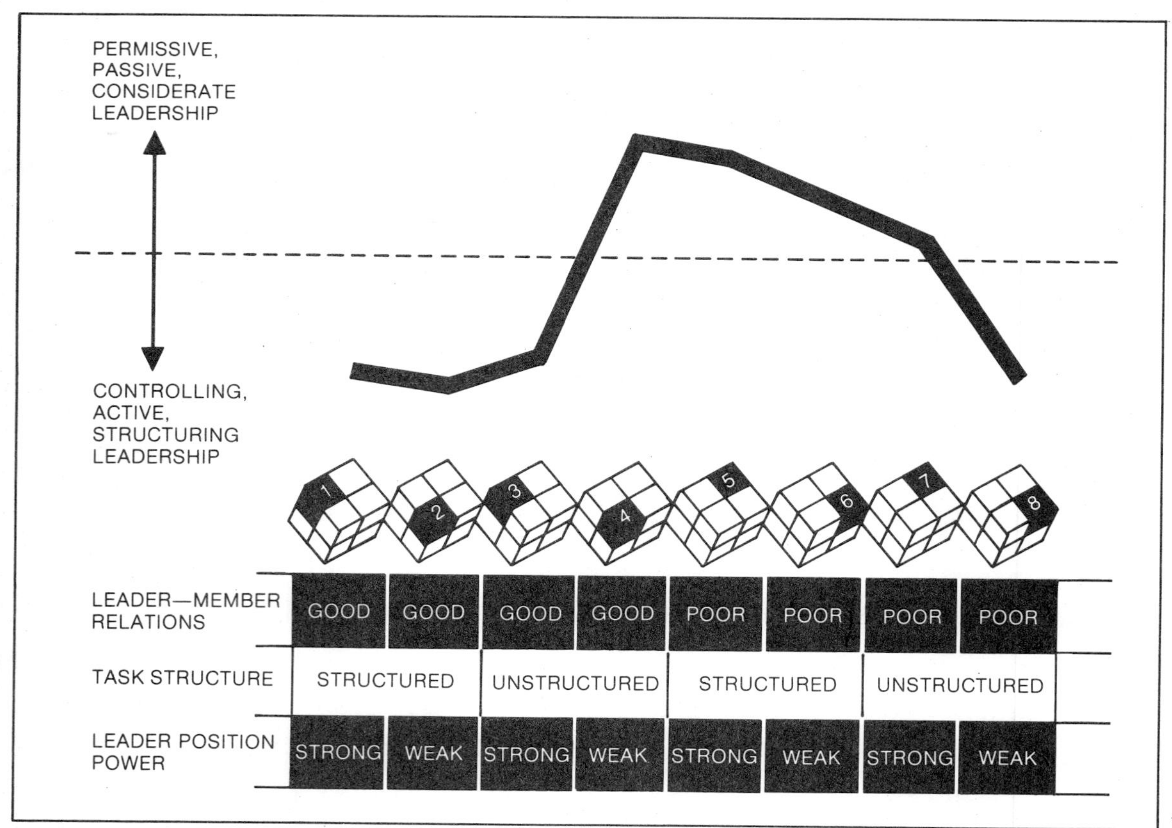

*Reprinted by permission of the Harvard Business Review. Exhibit from "Engineer the Job to Fit the Manager" by Fred E. Fiedler (September-October 1965).

Here, Fiedler argues that such findings make good sense.

> In very favorable conditions, where the leader has power, formal backing, and a relatively well-structured task, the group is ready to be directed on how to go about its task. Under a very unfavorable condition, however, the group will fall apart unless the leader's active intervention and control can keep the members on the job. In moderately unfavorable conditions, the accepted leader faces an ambiguous task, or his relations with group members are tenuous. Under these circumstances, a relationship-oriented, nondirective, permissive attitude may reduce member anxiety or intragroup conflict, and this enables the group to operate more effectively (i.e., the members would not feel threatened by the leader, and considerate, diplomatic leader behavior under these conditions may induce group members to cooperate) (1967, p. 165).

Fiedler's own training program, called LEADER MATCH, is based upon a self-paced programmed manual which trainees can complete on their own time in about five hours and which can be augmented by lectures, group discussions, or films. Basically, the manual explains Fiedler's contingency theory and instructs trainees on how to compute their LPC scores and scores on situational factors. It then suggests ways the trainees can alter their situations (in terms of leader-member relations, task structure, and position power) so that they match each trainee's style as measured by the LPC.

To the extent that Fiedler's arguments are valid, they have important implications. For example, they suggest that, since we can change the situation, we can focus our selection processes on finding talented individuals without being too concerned about their leadership styles. Also, not only can we de-emphasize certain types of training of leaders, but such training might actually be harmful. For example, training a leader in human relations skills might result in improved leader-member relations. But if that changes the situation so that it no longer fits the leader's LPC, performance of the leader's group could decline.

However, we must point out that Fiedler's work has been criticized for a number of reasons. For one, many of the studies used to develop figure 20-8 were based on findings that could have occurred by chance. Also, the theory assumes that the LPC is stable; if it is not, changing the situation might also change LPC. In fact, some evidence suggests that the leader's LPC may change over time. For example, it has been shown that people entering the military quickly found coworkers they liked less than anyone they had ever worked with before, thereby lowering their LPC scores. Further, many people are uncomfortable with the LPC since it is not really clear what the scale is measuring. Many other criticisms have been raised concerning Fiedler's methodology and interpretation of results.

In view of such criticisms, we must view Fiedler's arguments with caution. Nevertheless, the theory provides a useful way to consider leadership and does appear to have some predictive validity.[9] Also,

[9]For instance, see Chemers and Skrzypek (1972).

each of twelve studies of the effectiveness of the LEADER MATCH training program found that leaders who were trainees subsequently received significantly better performance ratings than did leaders in control groups.[10] At this point, it is probably best to think of this as an interesting and potentially useful approach, but one that needs further testing and more adequate explanation.

House's path-goal theory

Another situational approach is Robert House's (1971) path-goal theory of leader effectiveness, an extension and revision of the work of Martin Evans (1970). Basically, House follows an expectancy theory framework, as he and Terence Mitchell explain here:

> According to this theory, leaders are effective because of their impact on subordinates' motivation, ability to perform effectively, and satisfactions. The theory is called path-goal because its major concern is how the leader influences the subordinates' perceptions of their work goals, personal goals and paths to goal attainment. The theory suggests that a leader's behavior is motivating or satisfying to the degree that the behavior increases subordinate goal attainment and clarifies the paths to these goals (1974, p. 81).

In expectancy theory terms, the leader's motivational functions are to increase valences associated with work-goal attainment, the instrumentalities of work-goal attainment for the acquisition of desired personal outcomes, and the expectancy that effort will result in work-goal attainment.

The theory deals with four kinds of leader behavior.

1. *Directive leadership*, characterized by a leader who lets subordinates know what is expected of them and tells them how to do it. This is quite similar to what we referred to earlier as initiating structure.

2. *Supportive leadership*, characterized by a friendly and approachable leader who shows concern for the status, well-being, and needs of subordinates. This is quite similar to consideration.

3. *Participative leadership*, characterized by a leader who consults with subordinates and asks for their suggestions, which he or she seriously considers before making a decision.

4. *Achievement-oriented leadership*, characterized by a leader who sets challenging goals, expects subordinates to perform at their highest level, and shows confidence that subordinates will meet such expectations.

---

[10]Fiedler and Mahar, 1979.

The theory tries to explain how these four types of leadership affect the satisfaction of subordinates, their acceptance of the leader, and the extent to which they feel their effort will result in performance (expectancy) and that performance will lead to rewards (instrumentalities). The theory basically states that subordinates will see each style of leadership as acceptable, satisfying, and motivating to the extent that they see the behavior as either an immediate source of desired outcomes or as useful in leading to such outcomes in the future.

The theory considers two key contingency factors—the personal characteristics of subordinates and the sort of task that must be performed. For example, subordinates who do not feel they have the necessary ability to carry out their task will probably welcome directive leadership. For example, Al, who is new on the job, wants help, while Don, a seasoned employee who knows just about everything there is to know about his work, doesn't need or want directions.

An important characteristic of the task is the degree to which it is structured. For example, if the task is quite routine, any attempt by the leader to try to clarify paths and goals will probably be considered unnecessary. So Tom, whose job is completely specified step-by-step, gets upset when his boss is directive.

House (1971) has shown how the theory can be used to reconcile earlier, apparently contradictory findings and has conducted a series of studies that supported almost all the hypotheses derived from the theory.[11]

We should stress an important difference between the situational approaches Fiedler and House take. Fiedler's approach suggests that a leader should be put in a situation that fits his or her style. On the other hand, House, who reasons that it will be necessary to vary style with the situation, stresses the importance of flexibility on the part of the leader. The next approach we'll consider supports this viewpoint.

Vroom and Yetton's normative model

Victor Vroom and Philip Yetton (1973) provide a final situational approach to leadership. Their approach is prescriptive or normative rather than descriptive. That is, it specifies how leaders *should* behave rather than how they *do* behave. In chapter 19, where we considered the Vroom and Yetton model, we saw that:

1. The model argues that different styles—ranging from completely autocratic to very participative—are appropriate in different situations. Thus, it is important that leaders be flexible in choosing their behaviors.

2. Managers' actual behaviors tend to conform to the model. However, many managers choose styles inconsistent with those suggested by the model. Also, managers are less flexible in their choice of styles

[11]House and Mitchell (1974) also review a variety of studies supporting the theory.

than the model would recommend. Nevertheless, situational factors do play a major role in determining how managers behave.

3. Some evidence suggests that managers have better results when they behave as the model says they should than when they don't.

SUBSTITUTES FOR LEADERSHIP

The approaches we have just considered suggest that the situation may determine the appropriate style of leadership. Steve Kerr (1976) has gone a bit further, arguing that, in many cases, there may be "substitutes for leadership." He reasons that:

> Current theories and models of leadership have something . . . in common —a conviction that hierarchical leadership is always important. Even situational approaches to leadership share the assumption that while the *style* of leadership likely to be effective will vary according to the situation, *some* leadership style will be effective *regardless* of the situation.

As shown in table 20-2, Kerr stresses that there may be many cases when the leader's behaviors really don't make much difference. That is, characteristics of the subordinate, of the task, or of the organization may either take the place of the leader's behaviors or make it difficult for them to have much impact. For example, Bob has such a strong need for independence that he doesn't pay much attention to anything his boss does. And Mary's job is so routine and unambiguous that she hasn't needed directions from her superior in years. On the other hand, Janet finds her job to be so satisfying that her boss doesn't have to worry about keeping her happy; still, he often has to explain to her how to do certain things.

DOES LEADERSHIP REALLY MATTER?

It has become rather popular lately to argue that leadership really isn't very important. In a way, we have seen a complete swing of the pendulum on this issue. Early writers gave relatively little emphasis to leadership. Because they felt that workers would automatically behave as they were supposed to, leader influence wasn't seen as necessary and, as a result, wasn't seen as an especially important focus of study. More recently, as suggested by much of this chapter, considerable attention has been paid to the role of the leader. Now, however, some writers are arguing that there are many situations where leadership doesn't matter and, in general, that leaders are not as free to act as they once were.

For instance, Steve Kerr, in discussing "substitutes" and "neutralizers" of leadership, writes that one of the few things leadership approaches have in common is that they don't seem to be very useful in explaining how employees respond. Similarly, Warren Bennis (1976), writing mainly about top-level leaders in organizations, has argued

CHARACTERISTIC	WILL TEND TO NEUTRALIZE: RELATIONSHIP-ORIENTED SUPPORTIVE, CONSIDERATE LEADERSHIP	WILL TEND TO NEUTRALIZE: TASK-ORIENTED DIRECTIVE, STRUCTURING LEADERSHIP
OF THE SUBORDINATE		
1. Ability, Experience, Training, Knowledge		X
2. Need for Independence	X	X
3. "Professional" Orientation	X	X
4. Indifference toward Organizational Rewards	X	X
OF THE TASK		
5. Unambiguous and Routine		X
6. Standardized Methods		X
7. Provides Its Own Feedback Concerning Accomplishment		X
8. Intrinsically Satisfying	X	
OF THE ORGANIZATION		
9. Formalization (Explicit Plans, Goals, and Areas of Responsibility)		X
10. Inflexibility (Rigid, Unbending Rules and Procedures)		X
11. Closely Knit, Cohesive Work Groups	X	X
12. Highly Specified and Active Advisory and Staff Functions		X
13. Organizational Rewards Not within the Leader's Contract	X	X
14. Considerable Distance between Superior and Subordinate	X	X

*Adapted from Kerr and Jermier (1978)

TABLE 20-2
Substitutes for Leadership*

that they are currently so constrained by a variety of societal and organizational forces that they have little real power:

> Where have all the leaders gone? They're consulting, pleading, trotting here and there, temporizing, putting out fires, either avoiding or (more often) taking too much heat, and spending too much energy in doing both. They are peering at a landscape of "bottom lines" and ostentatiously taking the bus to work (with four bodyguards rather than the one chauffeur they might need if they drove) to demonstrate their commitment to energy conservation. They are money changers lost in a narrow orbit. They resign. They burn out. They decide not to run or serve. They read Buddhist economics, listen to prophets of decentralization, and then proceed to create new bureaucracies to stamp out old ones (1976, p. 13).

We think these views are a bit overstated. And this chapter has shown that certain leader behaviors, and perhaps some traits, do seem to make quite a difference in some situations. Also, Alan Filley and Ray Aldag (1979) have recently argued that leaders, especially in small organizations, play crucial roles in defining the organization's mission and the means by which it is accomplished. It is true that most studies show leader behavior to explain only about 10 or 15 percent of the variance in subordinates' responses. However, a 10 or 15 percent increase in performance can make a tremendous difference to the success of an organization. As we learn more about how to examine leadership and about how leadership and the situation interact, we will probably find stronger links between leadership and subordinate responses.

SUMMARY

We have seen that leadership involves an exertion of influence over others. The formally designated leader adopts a wide variety of roles and draws on a number of bases of power—reward, coercive, legitimate, expert, and referent—to carry them out. To some extent, the assumptions leaders make about the nature of their subordinates probably affect the degree to which they rely on those alternative power bases.

Some characteristics of individuals, such as height, interpersonal skills, and socioeconomic status, are useful in predicting who will become a leader. And a number of approaches have been taken to try to understand who is likely to be a *successful* leader.

Trait approaches, focusing on how characteristics of successful leaders differ from those of unsuccessful leaders, generally have been disappointing. It is difficult to find traits that are consistently important across situations, and it is hard to change people's traits even if we find they are important. However, some of Edwin Ghiselli's work in this area seems promising. As we understand more about important situational factors, trait approaches may prove to be more useful.

There has been a tremendous amount of research into the effects of democratic and autocratic leadership styles, the findings of which are generally mixed. It seems clear that characteristics of subordinates and of the task will influence the success of the use of participative or autocratic styles.

Close examination of a large number of leader behaviors and the ways they hang together has led to the isolation of consideration and initiating structure as important sets of behaviors. There is some question, though, of whether such behaviors cause subordinates to respond differently, or vice versa. Also, consideration and initiating structure may interact to affect employee responses. The impacts of these sets of behaviors probably depend on a number of situational factors, such as pressure, subordinate expectations, and subordinate need for information.

Three approaches that explicitly consider situational factors were reviewed. Fred Fiedler argues that we should change the situation to fit the leader. Conversely, Robert House, Victor Vroom, and Philip Yetton present models that suggest that leaders should vary their behaviors to fit the demands of the situation. This latter emphasis on the need for leader flexibility probably will get increasing attention.

In some cases, substitutes may exist for leadership. However, leadership is probably very important in most instances. As we learn more about how various situational factors interact with leader behaviors to affect subordinate responses, we should get a better understanding of this elusive topic.

REFERENCES

Aldag, R.J., and Brief, A.P. "Supervisory Style and Police Role Stress." *Journal of Police Science and Administration* 6 (1978): 362-67.

Barnard, C.I, *The Functions of the Executive*. Cambridge, Mass.: Harvard University Press, 1938.

Bennis, W. "Leadership: A Beleaguered Species?" *Organizational Dynamics 4(1)* (1976): 3-16.

Bird, C. *Social Psychology*. New York: Appleton-Century, 1940.

Blake, R.R., and Mouton, J.S. *The Managerial Grid*. Houston: Gulf Publishing Co., 1961.

Brief, A.P., and Aldag, R.J. "The Impact of Leader Behavior and Task Characteristics on Subordinate Job Satisfaction." *Proceedings of the Southeast AIDS Conference*. Columbia, S.C., 1976.

Brown, J.A. *The Social Psychology of Industry*. Baltimore: Penguin, 1954.

Carter, L.F., and Nixon, M. "An Investigation of the Relationship between Four Criteria of Leadership Ability for Three Different Tasks." *Journal of Psychology 23* (1949): 245-61.

Chemers, M.M., and Skrzypek, G.J. "An Experimental Test of the Contingency Model." *Journal of Personality and Social Psychology 24* (1972): 172-77.

Farris, G.F., and Lim, F.G. "Effects of Performance on Leadership, Cohesiveness, Influence, Satisfaction, and Subsequent Performance." *Journal of Applied Psychology 53* (1969): 490-99.

Fiedler, F.E. "Engineer the Job to Fit the Manager." *Harvard Business Review 43(5)* (1965): 115-22.

Fiedler, F.E. *A Theory of Leadership Effectiveness*. New York: McGraw-Hill, 1967.

Fiedler, F.E. "Personality, Motivational Systems, and Behavior of High and Low LPC Persons." *Human Relations 25* (1972): 391-412.

Fiedler, F.E., and Mahar, L. "The Effectiveness of Contingency Model Training: A Review of the Validation of LEADER MATCH," *Personnel Psychology 32* (1979): 45-62.

Fiedler, F., and Meuwese, W. "Leaders' Contribution to Task Performance in Cohesive and Noncohesive Groups." *Journal of Abnormal and Social Psychology 67* (1963): 83-87.

Filley, A.C., and Aldag, R.J. "Organizational Growth and Types: Lessons from Small Institutions." In *Research in Organizational Behavior*, edited by B.M. Staw and L.L. Cummings, vol. II. Greenwich, Conn.: JAI Press, 1979.

Filley, A.C.; House, R.J.; and Kerr, S. *Managerial Process and Organizational Behavior*, 2nd ed. Glenview, Ill.: Scott, Foresman, 1976.

French, J.R.P., and Raven, B. "The Bases of Social Power." In *Group Dynamics*, edited by D. Cartwright and A.F. Zander, 2nd ed. Evanston, Ill.: Row, Peterson, 1960.

Ghiselli, E.E. *Explorations in Managerial Talent*. Pacific Palisades, Cal.: Goodyear Pub. Co., 1971.

Gibb, C.A. "Leadership." In *Handbook of Social Psychology*, edited by G. Lindzey. Reading, Mass.: Addison-Wesley, 1954.

Halpin, A.W., and Winer, J.J. "A Factorial Study of the Leader Behavior Descriptions." In *Leader Behavior: Its Description and Measurement,* edited by R.M. Stogdill and A.E. Coons. Monograph No. 88. Columbus, Ohio: Ohio State University, Bureau of Business Research, 1957.

House, R.J. "A Path-Goal Theory of Leader Effectiveness." *Administrative Science Quarterly 16* (1971): 321-38.

House, R.J., and Mitchell, T.R. "Path-Goal Theory of Leadership." *Journal of Contemporary Business 3* (1974): 81-98.

Jenkins, W.O. "A Review of Leadership Studies with Particular Reference to Military Problems." *Psychological Bulletin 44* (1947): 54-79.

Karmel, B. "Leadership: A Challenge to Traditional Research Methods and Assumptions." *Academy of Management Review 3* (1978): 475-82.

Kerr, S. "Substitutes for Leadership." *Proceedings of the 8th Annual Conference of the American Institute for Decision Sciences 8* (1976): 150-52.

Kerr, S.; Schriesheim, C.; Murphy, C.J.; and Stogdill, R.M. "Toward a Contingency Theory of Leadership Based upon the Consideration and Initiating Structure Literature." *Organizational Behavior and Human Performance 12* (1974): 62-82.

Korman, A. "Task Success, Task Popularity, and Self-esteem as Influences on Task Liking." *Journal of Applied Psychology 52* (1968): 484-90.

Krech, D.; Crutchfield, R.S.; and Ballachey, E.L. *Individual in Society* New York: McGraw: McGraw-Hill, 1962.

Lowin, A., and Craig, J.R. "The Influence of Level of Performance on Managerial Style: An Experimental Object Lesson in the Ambiguity of Correlational Data." *Organizational Behavior and Human Performance 3* (1968): 440-58.

McGregor, D. *The Human Side of Enterprise.* New York; McGraw-Hill, 1960.

Mahoney, T.A.; Jerdee, T.H.; and Nash, A.N. *The Identification of Management Potential—A Research Approach to Management Development.* Dubuque: Wm. C. Brown Co., 1961.

Powell, R.M. *Race, Religion, and the Promotion of the American Executive.* Columbus; Ohio: Ohio State University, Bureau of Business Research, 1969.

Rosen, N. *Leadership Change and Group Dynamics: An Experiment.* Ithaca, N.Y.: Cornell University Press, 1969.

Stogdill, R.M. "Personal Factors Associated with Leadership: A Survey of the Literature." *Journal of Psychology 25* (1948): 35-71.

Vroom, V.H., and Jago, A.G. "On the Validity of the Vroom-Yetton Model." *Journal of Applied Psychology 63* (1978): 151-62.

Vroom, V.H., and Yetton, P.W. *Leadership and Decision Making.* Pittsburgh: University of Pittsburgh Press, 1973.

SUGGESTIONS FOR ADVANCED READINGS

Filley, A.C.; House, R.J.; and Kerr, S. *Managerial Process and Organizational Behavior,* 2nd ed., chapters 11 and 12. Glenview, Ill.: Scott, Foresman, 1976.

Schriesheim, C., and Kerr, S. "Theories and Measures of Leadership: A Critical Appraisal of Current and Future Directions." In *Leadership: The Cutting Edge,* edited by J. Hunt and L. Larson. Kent, Ohio: Kent State University Press, 1978.

Stogdill, R. *Handbook of Leadership: A Survey of Theory and Research.* New York: Free Press/Macmillan, 1974.

Vroom, V. "Leadership." In *Handbook of Industrial and Organizational Psychology*, edited by M. Dunnette. Chicago: Rand McNally, 1976.

Vroom, V., and Yetton, P.W. *Leadership and Decision Making.* Pittsburgh: University of Pittsburgh Press, 1973.

CHAPTER

21

Power, Dependence, And Effective Management*

Americans, as a rule, are not very comfortable with power or with its dynamics. We often distrust and question the motives of people who we think actively seek power. We have a certain fear of being manipulated. Even those people who think the dynamics of power are inevitable and needed often feel somewhat guilty when they themselves mobilize and use power. Simply put, the overall attitude and feeling toward power, which can easily be traced to the nation's very birth, is negative. In his enormously popular *Greening of America*, Charles Reich reflects the views of many when he writes. "It is not the misuse of power that is evil; the very existence of power is evil."[1]

One of the many consequences of this attitude is that power as a topic for rational study and dialogue has not received much attention, even in managerial circles. If the reader doubts this, all he or she need do is flip through some textbooks, journals, or advanced management course descriptions. The word *power* rarely appears.

This lack of attention to the subject of power merely adds to the already enormous confusion and misunderstanding surrounding the topic of power and management. And this misunderstanding is becoming increasingly burdensome because in today's large and com-

*John P. Kotter, "Power, Dependence, and Effective Management," *Harvard Business Review* (July-August 1977),

Author's note: This article is based on data from a clinical study of a highly diverse group of 26 organizations including large and small, public and private, manufacturing and service organizations. The study was funded by the Division of Research at the Harvard Business School. As part of the study process, the author interviewed about 250 managers.

[1]Charles A. Reich, *The Greening of America: How the Youth Revolution Is Trying to Make America Liveable* (New York: Random House, 1970).

plex organizations the effective performance of most managerial jobs requires one to be skilled at the acquisition and use of power.

From my own observations, I suspect that a large number of managers—especially the young, well-educated ones—perform significantly below their potential because they do not understand the dynamics of power and because they have not nurtured and developed the instincts needed to effectively acquire and use power.

In this article I hope to clear up some of the confusion regarding power and managerial work by providing tentative answers to three questions:

1. Why are the dynamics of power necessarily an important part of managerial processes?
2. How do effective managers acquire power?
3. How and for what purposes do effective managers use power?

I will not address questions related to the misuse of power, but not because I think they are unimportant. The fact that some managers, some of the time, acquire and use power mostly for their own aggrandizement is obviously a very important issue that deserves attention and careful study. But that is a complex topic unto itself and one that has already received more attention than the subject of this article.

RECOGNIZING DEPENDENCE IN THE MANAGER'S JOB

One of the distinguishing characteristics of a typical manager is how dependent he is on the activities of a variety of other people to perform his job effectively.[2] Unlike doctors and mathematicians, whose performance is more directly dependent on their own talents and efforts, a manager can be dependent in varying degrees on superiors, subordinates, peers in other parts of the organization, the subordinates of peers, outside suppliers, customers, competitors, unions, regulating agencies, and many others.

These dependency relationships are an inherent part of managerial jobs because of two organizational facts of life: division of labor and limited resources. Because the work in organizations is divided into specialized divisions, departments, and jobs, managers are made directly or indirectly dependent on many others for information, staff services, and cooperation in general. Because of their organization's limited resources, managers are also dependent on their external environments for support. Without some minimal cooperation from suppliers, competitors, unions, regulatory agencies, and cus-

[2]See Leonard R. Sayles, *Managerial Behavior: Administration in Complex Organization* (New York: McGraw-Hill, 1964) as well as Rosemary Stewart, *Managers and Their Jobs* (London: Macmillan, 1967) and *Contrasts in Management* (London: McGraw-Hill, 1976).

tomers, managers cannot help their organizations survive and achieve their objectives.

Dealing with these dependencies and the manager's subsequent vulnerability is an important and difficult part of a manager's job because, while it is theoretically possible that all of these people and organizations would automatically act in just the manner that a manager wants and needs, such is almost never the case in reality. All the people on whom a manager is dependent have limited time, energy, and talent, for which there are competing demands.

Some people may be uncooperative because they are too busy elsewhere, and some because they are not really capable of helping. Others may well have goals, values, and beliefs that are quite different and in conflict with the manager's and may therefore have no desire whatsoever to help or cooperate. This is obviously true of a competing company and sometimes of a union, but it can also apply to a boss who is feeling threatened by a manager's career progress or to a peer whose objectives clash with the manager's.

Indeed, managers often find themselves dependent on many people (and things) whom they do not directly control and who are not "cooperating." This is the key to one of the biggest frustrations managers feel in their jobs, even in the top ones, which the following example illustrates.

After nearly a year of rumors, it was finally announced in May 1974 that the president of ABC Corporation had been elected chairman of the board and that Jim Franklin, the vice president of finance, would replace him as president. While everyone at ABC was aware that a shift would take place soon, it was not at all clear before the announcement who would be the next president. Most people had guessed it would be Phil Cook, the marketing vice president.

Nine months into his job as chief executive officer, Franklin found that Phil Cook (still the marketing vice president) seemed to be fighting him in small subtle ways. There was never anything blatant, but Cook just did not cooperate with Franklin as the other vice presidents did. Shortly after being elected, Franklin had tried to bypass what he saw as a potential conflict with Cook by telling him that he would understand if Cook would prefer to move somewhere else where he could be a CEO also. Franklin said that it would be a big loss to the company but that he would be willing to help Cook in a number of ways if he wanted to look for a presidential opportunity elsewhere. Cook had thanked him but had said that family and community commitments would prevent him from relocating and all CEO opportunities were bound to be in a different city.

Since the situation did not improve after the tenth and eleventh months, Franklin seriously considered forcing Cook out. When he thought about the consequences of such a move, Franklin became more and more aware of just how dependent he was on Cook. Marketing and sales were generally the keys to success in their industry, and the company's sales force was one of the best, if not the best, in the industry. Cook had been with the company for 25 years. He had built a strong personal relationship with many of the people in the sales force and was universally popular. A mass exodus just might occur if Cook were fired. The loss of a large number of salesmen, or even a lot of turmoil in the department, could have a serious effect on the company's performance.

After one year as chief executive officer, Franklin found that the situation between Cook and himself had not improved and had become a constant source of frustration.

As a person gains more formal authority in an organization, the areas in which he or she is vulnerable increase and become more complex rather than the reverse. As the previous example suggests, it is not at all unusual for the president of an organization to be in a highly dependent position, a fact often not apparent to either the outsider or to the lower level manager who covets the president's job.

A considerable amount of the behavior of highly successful managers that seems inexplicable in light of what management texts usually tell us managers do becomes understandable when one considers a manager's need for, and efforts at, managing his or her relationships with others.[3] To be able to plan, organize, budget, staff, control, and evaluate, managers need some control over the many people on whom they are dependent. Trying to control others solely by directing them and on the basis of the power associated with one's position simply will not work—first, because managers are always dependent on some people over whom they have no formal authority, and second, because virtually no one in modern organizations will passively accept and completely obey a constant stream of orders from someone just because he or she is the "boss."

Trying to influence others by means of persuasion alone will not work either. Although it is very powerful and possibly the single most important method of influence, persuasion has some serious drawbacks too. To make it work requires time (often lots of it), skill, and information on the part of the persuader. And persuasion can fail simply because the other person chooses not to listen or does not listen carefully.

This is not to say that directing people on the basis of the formal power of one's position and persuasion are not important means by which successful managers cope. They obviously are. But, even taken together, they are not usually enough.

Successful managers cope with their dependence on others by being sensitive to it, by eliminating or avoiding unnecessary dependence, and by establishing power over those others. Good managers then use that power to help them plan, organize, staff, budget, evaluate, and so on. *In other words, it is primarily because of the dependence inherent in managerial jobs that the dynamics of power necessarily form an important part of a manager's processes.*

An argument that took place during a middle management training seminar I participated in a few years ago helps illustrate further this important relationship between a manager's need for power and the degree of his or her dependence on others.

---

[3]I am talking about the type of inexplicable differences that Henry Mintzberg has found; see his article "The Manager's Job: Folklore and Fact," HBR July-August 1975, p. 49.

Two participants, both managers in their thirties, got into a heated disagreement regarding the acquisition and use of power by managers. One took the position that power was absolutely central to managerial work, while the other argued that it was virtually irrelevant. In support of their positions, each described a very "successful" manager with whom he worked. In one of these examples, the manager seemed to be constantly developing and using power, while in the other, such behavior was rare. Subsequently, both seminar participants were asked to describe their successful managers' jobs in terms of the dependence *inherent* in those jobs.

The young manager who felt power was unimportant described a staff vice president in a small company who was dependent only on his immediate subordinates, his peers, and his boss. This person, Joe Phillips, had to depend on his subordinates to do their jobs appropriately, but, if necessary, he could fill in for any of them or secure replacement for them rather easily. He also had considerable formal authority over them; that is, he could give them raises and new assignments, recommend promotions, and fire them. He was moderately dependent on the other four vice presidents in the company for information and cooperation. They were likewise dependent on him. The president had considerable formal authority over Phillips but was also moderately dependent on him for help, expert advice, the service his staff performed, other information, and general cooperation.

The second young manager—the one who felt power was very important—described a service department manager, Sam Weller, in a large, complex, and growing company who was in quite a different position. Weller was dependent not only on his boss for rewards and information, but also on 30 other individuals who made up the divisional and corporate top management. And while his boss, like Phillips's was moderately dependent on him too, most of the top managers were not. Because Weller's subordinates, unlike Phillips's, had people reporting to them, Weller was dependent not only on his subordinates but also on his subordinates' subordinates. Because he could not himself easily replace or do most of their technical jobs, unlike Phillips, he was very dependent on all these people.

In addition, for critical supplies, Weller was dependent on two other department managers in the division. Without their timely help, it was impossible for his department to do its job. These departments, however, did not have similar needs for Weller's help and cooperation. Weller was also dependent on local labor union officials and on a federal agency that regulated the division's industry. Both could shut his division down if they wanted.

Finally, Weller was dependent on two outside suppliers of key materials. Because of the volume of his department's purchase relative to the size of these two companies, he had little power over them.

Under these circumstances, it is hardly surprising that Sam Weller had to spend considerable time and effort acquiring and using power to manage his many dependencies, while Joe Phillips did not.

As this example also illustrates, not all management jobs require an incumbent to be able to provide the same amount of successful power-oriented behavior. But most management jobs today are more like Weller's than Phillips's. And, perhaps more important, the trend over the past two or three decades is away from jobs like Phillips's and toward jobs like Weller's. So long as our technologies continue to become more complex, the average organization continues to grow larger, and the average industry continues to become more competitive and regulated, that trend will continue; as it does so, the effective acquisition and use of power by managers will become even more important.

ESTABLISHING POWER IN RELATIONSHIPS

To help cope with the dependency relationships inherent in their jobs, effective managers create, increase, or maintain four different types of power over others.[4] Having power based in these areas puts the manager in a position both to influence those people on whom he or she is dependent when necessary and to avoid being hurt by any of them.

Sense of obligation

One of the ways that successful managers generate power in their relationships with others is to create a sense of obligation in those others. When the manager is successful, the others feel that they should —rightly—allow the manager to influence them within certain limits.

Successful managers often go out of their way to do favors for people who they expect will feel an obligation to return those favors. As can be seen in the following description of a manager by one of his subordinates, some people are very skilled at identifying opportunities for doing favors that cost them very little but that others appreciate very much:

> "Most of the people here would walk over hot coals in their bare feet if my boss asked them to. He has an incredible capacity to do little things that mean a lot to people. Today, for example, in his junk mail he came across an advertisement for something that one of my subordinates had in passing once mentioned that he was shopping for. So my boss routed it to him. That probably took 15 seconds of his time, and yet my subordinate really appreciated it. To give you another example, two weeks ago he somehow learned that the purchasing manager's mother had died. On his way home that night, he stopped off at the funeral parlor. Our purchasing manager was, of course, there at the time. I bet he'll remember that brief visit for quite a while."

[4]These categories closely resemble the five developed by John R.P. French and Bertram Raven; see "The Bases of Social Power" in *Group Dynamics: Research and Theory*, Dorwin Cartwright and Alvin Zander, eds. (New York: Harper & Row, 1968), Chapter 20. Three of the categories are similar to the types of "authority"-based power described by Max Weber in *The Theory of Social and Economic Organization* (New York: Free Press, 1947).

Recognizing that most people believe that friendship carries with it certain obligations ("A friend in need . . . ."), successful managers often try to develop true friendships with those on whom they are dependent. They will also make formal and informal deals in which they give something up in exchange for certain future obligations.

Belief in a manager's expertise

A second way successful managers gain power is by building reputations as "experts" in certain matters. Believing in the manager's expertise, others will often defer to the manager on those matters. Managers usually establish this type of power through visible achievement. The larger the achievement and the more visible it is, the more power the manager tends to develop.

One of the reasons that managers display concern about their "professional reputations" and their "track records" is that they have an impact on others' beliefs about their expertise. These factors become particularly important in large settings, where most people have only secondhand information about most other people's professional competence, as the following shows:

Herb Randley and Bert Kline were both 35-year-old vice presidents in a large research and development organization. According to their closest associates, they were equally bright and competent in their technical fields and as managers. Yet Randley had a much stronger professional reputation in most parts of the company, and his ideas generally carried much more weight. Close friends and associates claim the reason that Randley is so much more powerful is related to a number of tactics that he has used more than Kline has.

Randley has published more scientific papers and managerial articles than Kline. Randley has been more selective in the assignments he has worked on, choosing those that are visible and that require his strong suits. He has given more speeches and presentations on projects that are his own achievements. And in meetings in general, he is allegedly forceful in areas where he has expertise and silent in those where he does not.

Identification with a manager

A third method by which managers gain power is by fostering others' unconscious identification with them or with ideas they "stand for." Sigmund Freud was the first to describe this phenomenon, which is most clearly seen in the way people look up to "charismatic" leaders. Generally, the more a person finds a manager both consciously and (more important) unconsciously an ideal person, the more he or she will defer to that manager.

Managers develop power based on others' idealized views of them in a number of ways. They try to look and behave in ways that others respect. They go out of their way to be visible to their employees and to give speeches about their organizational goals, values, and ideals. They even consider, while making hiring and promotion decisions, whether they will be able to develop this type of power over the candidates.

One vice president of sales in a moderate-size manufacturing company was reputed to be so much in control of his sales force that he could get them to respond to new and different marketing programs in a third of the time taken by the company's best competitors. His power over his employees was based primarily on their strong identification with him and what he stood for. Emigrating to the United States at age 17, this person worked his way up "from nothing." When made a sales manager in 1965, he began recruiting other young immigrants and sons of immigrants from his former country. When made vice president of sales in 1970, he continued to do so. In 1975, 85% of his sales force was made up of people whom he hired directly or who were hired by others he brought in.

Perceived dependence on a manager

The final way than an effective manager often gains power is by feeding others' beliefs that they are dependent on the manager either for help or for not being hurt. The more they perceive they are dependent, the more most people will be inclined to cooperate with such a manager.

There are two methods that successful managers often use to create perceived dependence.

Finding & acquiring resources

In the first, the manager identifies and secures (if necessary) resources that another person requires to perform his job, that he does not possess, and that are not readily available elsewhere. These resources include such things as authority to make certain decisions; control of money, equipment, and office space; access to important people; information and control of information channels; and subordinates. Then the manager takes action so that the other person correctly perceives that the manager has such resources and is willing and ready to use them to help (or hinder) the other person. Consider the following extreme—but true—example.

When young Tim Babcock was put in charge of a division of a large manufacturing company and told to "turn it around," he spent the first few weeks studying it from afar. He decided that the division was in disastrous shape and that he would need to take many large steps quickly to save it. To be able to do that, he realized he needed to develop considerable power fast over most of the division's management and staff. He did the following:

—He gave the division's management two hours' notice of his arrival.

—He arrived in a limousine with six assistants.

—He immediately called a meeting of the 40 top managers.

—He outlined briefly his assessment of the situation, his commitment to turn things around, and the basic direction he wanted things to move in.

—He then fired the four top managers in the room and told them that they had to be out of the building in two hours.

—He then said he would personally dedicate himself to sabotaging the career of anyone who tried to block his efforts to save the division.

—He ended the 60-minute meeting by announcing that his assistants would set up appointments for him with each of them starting at 7:00 A.M. the next morning.

Throughout the critical six-month period that followed, those who remained at the division generally cooperated energetically with Mr. Babcock.

Affecting perceptions of resources

A second way effective managers gain these types of power is by influencing other persons' perceptions of the manager's resources.[5] In settings where many people are involved and where the manager does not interact continuously with those he or she is dependent on, those people will seldom possess "hard facts" regarding what relevant resources the manager commands directly or indirectly (through others), what resources he will command in the future, or how prepared he is to use those resources to help or hinder them. They will be forced to make their own judgments.

Insofar as a manager can influence people's judgments, he can generate much more power than one would generally ascribe to him in light of the reality of his resources.

In trying to influence people's judgments, managers pay considerable attention to the "trappings" of power and to their own reputations and images. Among other actions, they sometimes carefully select, decorate, and arrange their offices in ways that give signs of power. They associate with people or organizations that are known to be powerful or that others perceive as powerful. Managers selectively foster rumors concerning their own power. Indeed, those who are particularly skilled at creating power in this way tend to be very sensitive to the impressions that all their actions might have on others.

Formal authority

Before discussing how managers use their power to influence others, it is useful to see how formal authority relates to power. By *formal authority,* I mean those elements that automatically come with a managerial job—perhaps a title, an office, a budget, the right to make

[5]For an excellent discussion of this method, see Richard E. Neustadt, *Presidential Power* (New York: John Wiley, 1960).

certain decisions, a set of subordinates, a reporting relationship, and so on.

Effective managers use the elements of formal authority as resources to help them develop any or all of the four types of power previously discussed, just as they use other resources (such as their education). Two managers with the same formal authority can have very different amounts of power entirely because of the way they have used that authority. For example:

—By sitting down with employees who are new or with people who are starting new projects and clearly specifying who has the formal authority to do what, one manager creates a strong sense of obligation in others to defer to his authority later.

—By selectively withholding or giving the high-quality service his department can provide other departments, one manager makes other managers clearly perceive that they are dependent on him.

On its own, then, formal authority does not guarantee a certain amount of power; it is only a resource that managers can use to generate power in their relationships.

EXERCISING POWER TO INFLUENCE OTHERS

Successful managers use the power they develop in their relationships, along with persuasion, to influence people on whom they are dependent to behave in ways that make it possible for the managers to get their jobs done effectively. They use their power to influence others directly, face to face, and in more indirect ways.

Face-to-face influence

The chief advantage of influencing others directly by exercising any of the types of power is speed. If the power exists and the manager correctly understands the nature and strength of it, he can influence the other person with nothing more than a brief request or command:

—Jones thinks Smith feels obliged to him for past favors. Furthermore, Jones thinks that his request to speed up a project by two days probably falls within a zone that Smith would consider legitimate in light of his own definition of his obligation to Jones. So Jones simply calls Smith and makes his request. Smith pauses for only a second and says yes, he'll do it.

—Manager Johnson has some power based on perceived dependence over manager Baker. When Johnson tells Baker that he wants a report done in 24 hours, Baker grudgingly considers the costs of compliance, of noncompliance, and of complaining to higher authorities. He decides that doing the report is the least costly action and tells Johnson he will do it.

TABLE 21-1 Methods of Influence

FACE-TO-FACE METHODS	WHAT THEY CAN INFLUENCE	ADVANTAGES	DRAWBACKS
Exercise obligation-based power.	Behavior within zone that the other perceives as legitimate in light of the obligation.	Quick. Requires no outlay of tangible resources.	If the request is outside the acceptable zone, it will fail; if it is too far outside, others might see it as illegitimate.
Exercise power based on perceived expertise.	Attitudes and behavior within the zone of perceived expertise.	Quick. Requires no outlay of tangible resources.	If the request is outside the acceptable zone, it will fail; if it is too far outside, others might see it as illegitimate.
Exercise power based on identification with a manager.	Attitudes and behavior that are not in conflict with the ideals that underlie the identification.	Quick. Requires no expenditure of limited resources.	Restricted to influence attempts that are not in conflict with the ideals that underlie the identification.
Exercise power based on perceived dependence.	Wide range of behavior that can be monitored.	Quick. Can often succeed when other methods fail.	Repeated influence attempts encourage the other to gain power over the influencer.
Coercively exercise power based on perceived dependence.	Wide range of behavior that can be easily monitored.	Quick. Can often succeed when other methods fail.	Invites retaliation. Very risky.
Use persuasion.	Very wide range of attitudes and behavior.	Can produce internalized motivation that does not require monitoring. Requires no power or outlay of scarce material resources.	Can be very time-consuming. Requires other person to listen.
Combine these methods.	Depends on the exact combination.	Can be more potent and less risky than using a single method.	More costly than using a single method.
INDIRECT METHODS	**WHAT THEY CAN INFLUENCE**	**ADVANTAGES**	**DRAWBACKS**
Manipulate the other's environment by using any or all of the face-to-face methods.	Wide range of behavior and attitudes.	Can succeed when face-to-face methods fail.	Can be time-consuming. Is complex to implement. Is very risky, especially if used frequently.
Change the forces that continuously act on the individual: Formal organizational arrangements. Informal social arrangements. Technology. Resources available. Statement of organizational goals.	Wide range of behavior and attitudes on a continuous basis.	Has continuous influence, not just a one-shot effect. Can have a very powerful impact.	Often requires a considerable power outlay to achieve.

—Young Porter identifies strongly with Marquette, an older manager who is not his boss. Porter thinks Marquette is the epitome of a great manager and tries to model himself after him. When Marquette asks Porter to work on a special project "that could be very valuable in improving the company's ability to meet new competitive products," Porter agrees without hesitation and works 15 hours per week above and beyond his normal hours to get the project done and done well.

When used to influence others, each of the four types of power has different advantages and drawbacks. For example, power based on perceived expertise or on identification with a manager can often be used to influence attitudes as well as someone's immediate behavior and thus can have a lasting impact. It is very difficult to influence attitudes by using power based on perceived dependence, but if it can be done, it usually has the advantage of being able to influence a much broader range of behavior than the other methods do. When exercising power based on perceived expertise, for example, one can only influence attitudes and behavior within that narrow zone defined by the "expertise."

The drawbacks associated with the use of power based on perceived dependence are particularly important to recognize. A person who feels dependent on a manager for rewards (or lack of punishments) might quickly agree to a request from the manager but then not follow through—especially if the manager cannot easily find out if the person has obeyed or not. Repeated influence attempts based on perceived dependence also seem to encourage the other person to try to gain some power to balance the manager's. And perhaps most important, using power based on perceived dependence in a coercive way is very risky. Coercion invites retaliation.

For instance, in the example in which Tim Babcock took such extreme steps to save the division he was assigned to "turn around," his development and use of power based on perceived dependence could have led to mass resignation and the collapse of the division. Babcock fully recognized this risk, however, and behaved as he did because he felt there was simply *no other way* that he could gain the very large amount of quick cooperation needed to save the division.

Effective managers will often draw on more than one form of power to influence someone, or they will combine power with persuasion. In general, they do so because a combination can be more potent and less risky than any single method, as the following description shows:

> "One of the best managers we have in the company has lots of power based on one thing or another over most people. But he seldom if ever just tells or asks someone to do something. He almost always takes a few minutes to try to persuade them. The power he has over people generally induces them to listen carefully and certainly disposes them to be influenced. That, of course, makes the persuasion process go quickly and easily. And he never risks getting the other person mad or upset by making what that person thinks is an unfair request or command."

It is also common for managers not to coercively exercise power based on perceived dependence by itself, but to combine it with other methods to reduce the risk of retaliation. In this way, managers are able to have a large impact without leaving the bitter aftertaste of punishment alone.

Indirect influence methods

Effective managers also rely on two types of less direct methods to influence those on whom they are dependent. In the first way, they use any or all of the face-to-face methods to influence other people, who in turn have some specific impact on a desired person.

Product manager Stein needed plant manager Billings to "sign off" on a new product idea (Product X) which Billings thought was terrible. Stein decided that there was no way he could logically persuade Billings because Billings just would not listen to him. With time, Stein felt, he could have broken through that barrier. But he did not have that time. Stein also realized that Billings would never, just because of some deal or favor, sign off on a product he did not believe in. Stein also felt it not worth the risk of trying to force Billings to sign off, so here is what he did:

—On Monday, Stein got Reynolds, a person Billings respected, to send Billings two market research studies that were very favorable to Product X, with a note attached saying, "Have you seen this? I found them rather surprising. I am not sure if I entirely believe them, but still . . . ."

—On Tuesday, Stein got a representative of one of the company's biggest customers to mention casually to Billings on the phone that he had heard a rumor about Product X being introduced soon and was "glad to see you guys are on your toes as usual."

—On Wednesday, Stein had two industrial engineers stand about three feet away from Billings as they were waiting for a meeting to begin and talk about the favorable test results on Product X.

—On Thursday, Stein set up a meeting to talk about Product X with Billings and invited only people whom Billings liked or respected and who also felt favorably about Product X.

—On Friday, Stein went to see Billings and asked him if he was willing to sign off on Product X. He was.

This type of manipulation of the environments of others can influence both behavior and attitudes and can often succeed when other influence methods fail. But it has a number of serious drawbacks. It takes considerable time and energy, and it is quite risky. Many people think it is wrong to try to influence others in this way, even people who, without consciously recognizing it, use this technique themselves. If they think someone is trying, or has tried, to manipulate them, they may retaliate. Furthermore, people who gain the reputation of being manipulators seriously undermine their own capacities for developing power and for influencing others. Almost no one, for example, will want to identify with a manipulator. And virtually no one accepts, at face value, a manipulator's sincere attempts at persuasion. In extreme cases, a reputation as a manipulator can completely ruin a manager's career.

A second way in which managers indirectly influence others is by making permanent changes in an individual's or a group's environment. They change job descriptions, the formal systems that measure performance, the extrinsic incentives available, the tools, people, and other resources that the people or groups work with, the architecture, the norms or values of work groups, and so on. If the manager is successful in making the changes, and the changes have the desired effect on the individual or group, that effect will be sustained over time.

Effective managers recognize that changes in the forces that surround a person can have great impact on that person's behavior. Unlike many of the other influence methods, this one doesn't require a large expenditure of limited resources or effort on the part of the manager on an ongoing basis. Once such a change has been successfully made, it works independently of the manager.

This method of influence is used by all managers to some degree. Many, however, use it sparingly simply because they do not have the power to change the forces acting on the person they wish to influence. In many organizations, only the top managers have the power to change the formal measurement systems, the extrinsic incentives available, the architecture, and so on.

GENERATING & USING POWER SUCCESSFULLY

Managers who are successful at acquiring considerable power and using it to manage their dependence on others tend to share a number of common characteristics:

1. They are sensitive to what others consider to be legitimate behavior in acquiring and using power. They recognize that the four types of power carry with them certain "obligations" regarding their acquisition and use. A person who gains a considerable amount of power based on his perceived expertise is generally expected to be an expert in certain areas. If it ever becomes publicly known that the person is clearly not an expert in those areas, such a person will probably be labeled a "fraud" and will not only lose his power but will suffer other reprimands too.

A person with whom a number of people identify is expected to act like an ideal leader. If he clearly lets people down, he will not only lose that power, he will also suffer the righteous anger of his ex-followers. Many managers who have created or used power based on perceived dependence in ways that their employees have felt unfair, such as in requesting overtime work, have ended up with unions.

2. They have good intuitive understanding of the various types of power and methods of influence. They are sensitive to what types of power are easiest to develop with different types of people. They recognize, for example, that professionals tend to be more influenced by perceived expertise than by other forms of power. They also have a grasp of all the various methods of influence and what each can accomplish, at what costs, and with what risks. (See Table 21-1) They are good at recognizing the specific conditions in any situation and then at selecting an influence method that is compatible with those conditions.

3. They tend to develop all the types of power, to some degree, and they use all the influence methods mentioned in the exhibit. Unlike managers who are not very good at influencing people, effective managers usually do not think that only some of the methods are useful or that only some of the methods are moral. They recognize that any of the methods, used under the right circumstances, can help contribute to organizational effectiveness with few dysfunctional consequences. At the same time, they generally try to avoid those methods that are more risky than others and those that may have dysfunctional consequences. For example, they manipulate the environment of others only when absolutely necessary.

4. They establish career goals and seek out managerial positions that allow them to successfully develop and use power. They look for jobs, for example, that use their backgrounds and skills to control or manage some critically important problem or environmental contingency that an organization faces. They recognize that success in that type of job makes others dependent on them and increases their own perceived expertise. They also seek jobs that do not demand a type or a volume of power that is inconsistent with their own skills.

5. They use all of their resources, formal authority, and power to develop still more power. To borrow Edward Banfield's metaphor, they actually look for ways to "invest" their power where they might secure a high positive return.[6] For example, by asking a person to do him two important favors, a manager might be able to finish his construction program one day ahead of schedule. That request may cost him most of the obligation-based power he has over that person, but in return he may significantly increase his perceived expertise as a manager of construction projects in the eyes of everyone in his organization.

Just as in investing money, there is always some risk involved in using power this way; it is possible to get a zero return for a sizable investment, even for the most powerful manager. Effective managers do not try to avoid risks. Instead, they look for prudent risks, just as they do when investing capital.

---

[6]See Edward C. Banfield, *Political Influence* (New York: Free Press, 1965), Chapter II.

6. Effective managers engage in power-oriented behavior in ways that are tempered by maturity and self-control.[7] They seldom, if ever, develop and use power in impulsive ways or for their own aggrandizement.

7. Finally, they also recognize and accept as legitimate that, in using these methods, they clearly influence other people's behavior and lives. Unlike many less effective managers, they are reasonably comfortable in using power to influence people. They recognize, often only intuitively, what this article is all about—that their attempts to establish power and use it are an absolutely necessary part of the successful fulfillment of their difficult managerial role.

DISCUSSION QUESTIONS

1. Earlier in this section, we listed five factors that seem to increase the probability of someone becoming a leader. Think of four leaders and indicate the extent to which you feel they possess each of those characteristics.

2. Think of two leaders you consider to be successful and two who are unsuccessful. Consider the six traits Ghiselli found to be most important for managerial success. Indicate the extent to which you think each of the four leaders possesses each of those traits. Discuss the extent to which your ratings of the successful and unsuccessful leaders are consistent with Ghiselli's findings.

3. Describe three cases you know of in which one person's behavior influenced the leader's behaviors. Specifically, how did the leader's behavior change? Relate this to the discussion of direction of causality in this section.

4. List and discuss five things you feel might serve as substitutes for leadership.

5. List three things a leader might do to influence his or her subordinates':

   a. valences of work related outcomes
   b. instrumentality perceptions
   c. expectancy perception

6. Do you agree more with Fiedler's approach or with House's? To what extent are the approaches similar? How do their implications differ? Could an organization try to use both approaches at the same time?

7. Do you feel that "the very existence of power is evil"? Why or why not?

8. Discuss the links between level of authority and vulnerability.

9. Think of someone you know—a parent, teacher, coworker, or

[7]See David C. McClelland and David H. Burnham, "Power Is the Great Motivator," HBR March-April 1976, p. 100.

whoever—who has somehow exerted power over you. To what extent did that person rely on the "trappings" of power? What bases of power were used? What were the consequences of such power usage?

10. Of the bases of power suggested by French and Raven, which do you think is most:

a. generally applicable?
b. ethical?
c. unethical?
d. useful in complex technologies?
e. costly?

11. Select three people in prominent positions of authority. To the greatest extent possible, specify your perceptions of their bases of power and the consequences of their reliance on those bases.

12. Are there any bases of power described in the previous chapters that you definitely would *not* use? Why or why not?

13. If you were to give a new subordinate three concrete tips concerning the acquisition and/or use of power, what would they be?

SECTION

Managing Work Groups

The purpose of this section is to describe characteristics of work groups and ways in which they might be more effectively managed. An important structural characteristic of any work group (or any organization) is its status system. Thus, the section opens with a discussion of the many dimensions and consequences of status. Next, we will offer a detailed discussion of wearing apparel as a symbol of status. Then, we will consider team spirit and how to manage it. Finally, ways to put team spirit into management by objectives (MBO) are described.

KEY TERMS

STATUS
STATUS SYMBOLS
ASCRIBED STATUS
ACHIEVED STATUS
STATUS INCONGRUENCE
UNIFORM CODE SYMBOLS
GROUP EVOLUTION
GROUP COHESIVENESS
NORMS

OBJECTIVES

1. To recognize symbols of status and their implications
2. To identify the determinants of status
3. To describe how to manage status systems
4. To describe how to use wearing apparel as a status symbol
5. To identify what work groups are and how they evolve
6. To describe how to build team spirit
7. To identify work group norms and how to influence them
8. To describe how to use management by group objectives

CHAPTER 22

Understanding The Role Of Status

John, a graduating senior from State University's College of Business Administration, has just returned from his first interview for a job in the banking industry. In trying to sort out the people he met during his interview with First National Bank, he recalls that the three people who interviewed him were assistant vice presidents: Mrs. Pearson, assistant vice president of personnel; Mr. Brown, assistant vice president of the Westside Branch office; and Mr. Cornback, assistant vice president of commercial banking. John is applying for the position of commercial loan officer trainee at the Westside Branch. He felt he got along well with Mrs. Pearson and Mr. Brown, but his feelings toward Mr. Cornback were pretty negative.

John asks himself, "Since they're all assistant vice presidents, who has the real clout in the bank?" John remembers that Mrs. Pearson's office was a twelve-by-twelve foot glassed-in cubicle with institutional-looking, drab, gray furniture. Mr. Brown's office was a bit bigger, with an attractive dark brown desk and matching chairs. Mr. Cornback's office was huge. His own personal secretary was parked out front; and his office was furnished with a couch and coffee table, in addition to a desk and chairs. John appropriately concludes that, with all those "status symbols," Mr. Cornback must be an awfully important person around First National. Thus, John decides that he had better continue his job search.

John exercised good common sense by being sensitive to the bank's status system. *Status* refers to the way people are ranked in a social system. Even though it is a simple concept, it is an important variable to consider in organizational behavior.

This chapter will begin by briefly addressing the trappings, or *status symbols*, associated with one's rank in the status system. Second, we will examine the causes of a person's status ranking in some detail. Third, we will assess the impact status has on an employee's job behavior. And, finally, we will introduce the topic of managing status systems.

STATUS SYMBOLS

One of the authors of this book previously was employed to clean the offices attached to a large manufacturing plant. In the plant, the foremen all wore gold jackets provided by the company. Presumably, the jackets helped employees identify their supervisors. (Of course, this assumes that an employee cannot readily recognize his or her boss with whom he spends at least forty hours a week.) Realistically, the jackets were provided to the foremen as a status symbol of their position of authority. When first employed to clean the offices, the author and his fellow janitorial personnel wore their street clothes to work; however, the plant security staff wanted to be able to identify us from a distance. So, one evening when we showed up for work, we

Clothing is often a status symbol.

found that white jackets had been supplied for us to wear over our street clothes. Apparently, the notion of lowly janitorial personnel being supplied with jackets like those the plant foremen wore greatly annoyed someone in the company. About a week after first enjoying our jackets, which helped to keep our clothes clean, we arrived at work to find the jackets radically altered: blue collars had been sewn on each and every one.

Types of status symbols

Clearly, organizational status symbols are important. One can identify a number of types of status symbols organizations use to denote a person's position in the pecking order. First, as we have already noted, clothing can be an obvious clue to someone's status. For instance, one large meat-packing firm provides different colored hard hats to plant employees to identify organizational level; and the vestments of a cardinal are certainly different from those worn by a parish priest in the Catholic Church. Recently, Betty Harragan (1977) wrote a book titled *Games Mother Never Taught You: Corporate Gamesmanship for Women.* The next chapter, an exerpt from her book, details the use of clothing as an organizational status symbol. As you can see from the title, Harragan's book is aimed at "corporate women," but the male reader also will find there are lessons to be learned.

A second type of status symbol frequently used is a title. What title would you prefer: the "personal secretary of the vice president of sales" or "administrative assistant to the vice president of sales"? Of course, this could be a case of the same jobs having two different titles, a common occurrence in many organizations. Vance Packard (1959) has noted that, from the organization's perspective, a title frequently serves as a no-cost reward to the titleholder.

A third status symbol is the office. The fewer the occupants, the more prime the location, the larger the size, and the greater the number of windows, the higher the status of an office's occupant(s). A private office located on the top floor in a corner of impressive size with a large number of windows clearly indicates that the office's occupant has "arrived."

A fourth status symbol is office furnishings. For example, Mound (1968) provides the following list of desks in ascending order of the status they symbolize:

1. a one-drawer steel table
2. a three-drawer steel desk
3. a full-sided oak desk
4. a pedestal steel desk
5. a walnut desk
6. a steel or walnut desk with a five-inch overhang

7. a mahogany desk
8. a teak desk

If you have ever examined advertisements for office furnishings, you know that manufacturers are marketing the status of their products as much as any other attribute. And you probably will find that as you move up the organizational ladder, you, too, will care about the carpet on your floor.

A fifth symbol of status usually reserved for members of top management is access to the executive washroom. In 1978, the Department of Energy moved into a building previously occupied by the Department of Defense. An interesting expense item in remodeling the building was the cost of three executive washrooms at $10,000 apiece. Even members of the federal bureaucracy are sensitive to the symbolism associated with even the most basic bodily functions.

A sixth status symbol many organizations use is which company dining facility an employee has access to. The assignment of company automobiles constitutes a seventh frequently used symbol of status. It would be most unusual to find a salesperson assigned a more prestigious company automobile than that assigned to the vice

FIGURE 22-1

"This is my executive suite and this is my executive vice-president, Ralph Anderson, and my executive secretary, Adele Eades, and my executive desk and my executive carpet and my executive wastebasket and my executive ashtray and my executive pen set and my . . ."

Drawing by H. Martin; ©1974 The New Yorker Magazine, Inc.

president of sales. An eighth symbol of organizational status is one's access to secretarial services. Low persons on the totem pole obtain their needed clerical services from a secretarial pool. And the ultimate in status is for one's personal secretary to have his or her own private secretary. A ninth organizational status symbol is the travel privileges afforded an employee. The employee who travels infrequently on organizational business and who is required to fly coach class on a restricted *per diem* budget is typically the low-status organizational member. At the other end of the continuum is the executive who chooses when and where he or she wants to travel, who is conveyed on the company jet, and who always stays at four-star hotels.

The list of organizational status symbols could go on and on, but the preceding examples clearly demonstrate that organizations do use status symbols and that organizational members pay a great deal of attention to those symbols. The lesson to be learned is that you, as an astute student of organizational behavior, should be sensitive to these clues to a person's position in an organization's social system.

DETERMINANTS OF STATUS

There are two distinct types of status: *ascribed* and *achieved*. Achieved status depends upon the person's own accomplishments and will be of central concern here. Ascribed status, however, also plays a role in organizational behavior. Ascribed status depends not upon one's accomplishments but rather, upon such factors as age, sex, and lineage. For example, being the son of the company's president clearly helps that individual's status in the organization; but a person's ascribed status essentially is beyond the control of the individual and the organization and is not as interesting as achieved status, which can be changed.

Litterer (1965) has identified seven possible determinants of the status a person can achieve in an organization setting. First, a person's occupation is a major influence on the level of status afforded him or her. The following health occupations are listed in ascending order of their status: therapist, dietitian, clinical laboratory technologist, registered nurse, and physician (Siegel, Rossi, and Hodge, in press). Thus, in a hospital setting, one would expect dietitians to be afforded more status and the symbols that go along with that status than are therapists; and, moving on up the status hierarchy, physicians would be afforded more status than any other hospital personnel. The same types of occupational comparisons can be made in banks, insurance firms, governmental agencies, manufacturing plants, and, for that matter, any work organization. Obviously, an individual's occupational choice determines much more in his or her life than merely what type of work he or she will perform.

A second determinant of status is the type of materials an employee works on. In general, the more costly the material an employee works on, the more status he or she has. The noted sociologist, William F. Whyte, (1948), provides a vivid example of this phenomenon. He found among cooks who work in the kitchens of large restaurants the following status hierarchy: Cooks who prepare fish have lower status than those who prepare chicken, and, in turn, chicken preparers have lower status than those cooks who prepare beef.

A third determinant of organizational status is the skill or knowledge required to perform one's assigned work. For instance, a small advertising agency employs three account executives. The firm acquires a new account that has had great difficulty in formulating an effective advertising campaign. Undoubtedly, the account executive assigned to this difficult new client will be afforded a higher level of status by his colleagues.

A fourth determinant of organizational status is the employee's rank in the organization's formal hierarchy. Admittedly, this is an obvious determinant of status but one that should not be overlooked. In a university, the president has more status than a dean, and a dean has more status than a department chairperson. Generally, the closer an employee is placed to the chief executive officer on a chart of the organization's structure, the higher his or her status.

A fifth and very important determinant of status is how much money the employee is paid by the organization. Highly paid persons are typically afforded more status than lower-paid employees. Employees frequently react very negatively to a pay raise just a few dollars below what they expected. From an economic perspective, the few dollars are unimportant; but, as a determinant of status, the small difference between an actual and expected pay increase may be significant.

A sixth determinant of organizational status is seniority. Seniority is a surprisingly dominant contributor to an employee's status and, not surprisingly, a major source of irritation to many organizational newcomers. It may be that, because organizational old-timers are commonly assumed to be in the know, they are accorded the high levels of status they typically receive. Rarely does one find a senior organizational member who does not enjoy a certain degree of status among his or her peers. The final determinant of status Litterer notes is the employee's associates. Two janitorial personnel may be the same in terms of each of the previously identified determinants; however, one is assigned to clean the offices of the chairman of the board and the other, the offices of the corporate comptroller. Invariably, the person cleaning the chairman's office will be granted a higher level of status.

The determinants depicted in figure 22-2 certainly are not exhaustive. The point is, though, that a number of factors can contribute to an employee's organizational status. Importantly, these factors may or may not necessarily be associated with an employee's level of job performance. Thus, a low-performing employee may well be afforded a higher level of status than a high-performing employee. And herein lies one of the many problems that an organization's status system can present to management.

FIGURE 22-2
Determinants of Organizational Status

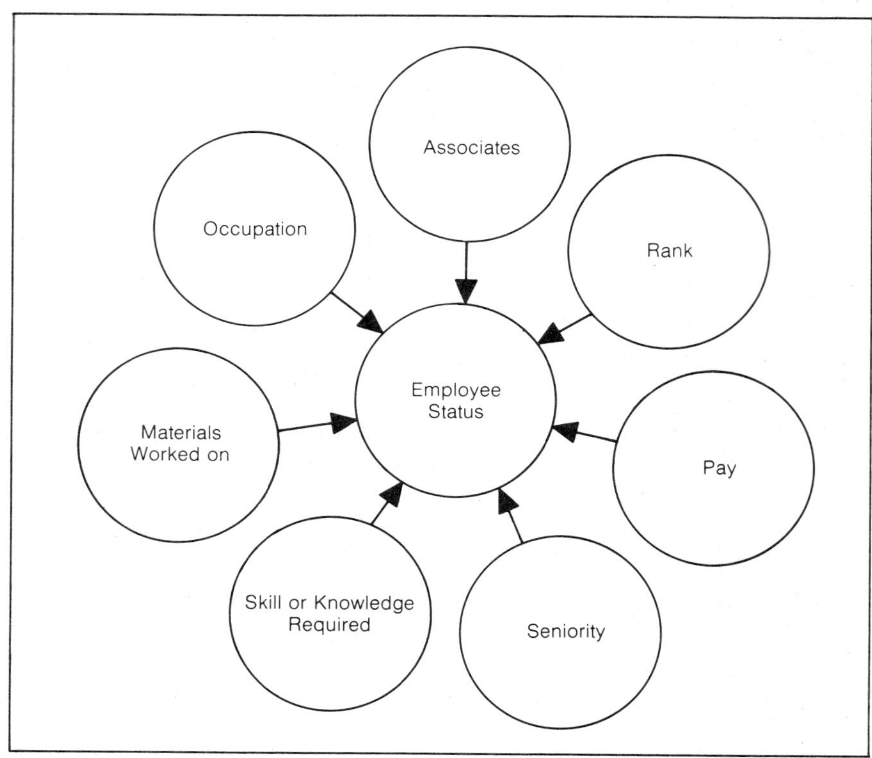

CONSEQUENCES OF STATUS

There are two major personal consequences of status for organizational members—one good and one not so good. First, high-status persons, as compared with low-status persons, have easier access to persons, information, and activities. For instance, the senior maintenance engineer assigned to service the most complex and costly equipment in a manufacturing plant is much more openly received by the plant manager than are his more junior colleagues. This access to the plant manager provides the senior engineer with more information about plant operations than his peers. Such information makes the senior engineer an even more central and powerful person in the plant's maintenance department. In other words, an employee's status can facilitate the acquisition of personal power within the organization. Simply put, status has a personal payoff for the organizational member.

The second personal consequence of status is not so good. An employee's status imposes certain limitations on his or her behavior. If the vice president of merchandising for a large chain of retail stores was seen at a local tavern of poor reputation wearing blue jeans and a tee-shirt and in the company of an attractive mail-room clerk, his organizational image might be shattered. Certain public behaviors are most assuredly considered off-limits for high-status organizational members. Thus, from a personal perspective, the acquisition of status is not a free good.

Some of the most important consequences of status involve the employee's immediate work group. That work group could be the organization's top management team or the three persons assigned to work the loading dock. *Norms* are the rules of conduct accepted by a group's members. High status group members generally conform more to the norms of the group than most group members. If this high-status group member has visibly contributed to the attainment of the group's goals in the past, he or she builds so-called *idiosyncrasy credits* with the group. These credits allow the high-status group member to deviate from the norms of the group without being sanctioned so long as the deviation contributes to group effectiveness. Take the case of Henry, a high-status middle manager in a major division of a food processing company. Henry is known to always wear the right clothes, say the right things, and be seen with the right people. The norm among the division managers with whom Henry works is to arrive at the office before 9:00 A.M. and to leave for home shortly after 6:00 P.M. In the past, Henry's ideas have contributed significantly to the earnings of his division. Henry, being a confirmed "night person," starts to arrive at work about 10:30 A.M. and leave well after 6:00 P.M. No one says a word to Henry about his deviation from the group's norm. But if any other manager had begun to show up at work as late as 10:30 A.M., he or she would have been the target of considerable resentment.

A second and third consequence of high status involves the communication patterns in the work group. High-status group members receive more communications than do low-status members. Again, we see the high-status person acquiring more information. There are at least two possible reasons why people direct more of their communications to high-status group members. First, if an employee for one reason or another does not personally enjoy a high level of status in the group, then talking with a high-status person may somehow compensate for this lack of status attainment. In other words, some employees substitute interpersonal interactions with a high-status person for their own status. Second, communicating with a high-status person may be one way of attempting to obtain a form of positive social reinforcement. Most of us would enjoy coming home from work and telling our spouse or friends that we had lunch with Marty, Marty being that distant, high-status person in our work group.

The content of the communications directed at high-status persons is considerably different from that which is directed at the low-status employee. In general, the communications directed at high-status persons are more positive. They rarely are aggressive and tend to be concerned with the tasks the work group is performing. This is probably true because low-status persons are afraid they will be rebuked or otherwise punished for acting aggressively toward the high-status group member. It is much less threatening and, therefore, easier to let out your hostilities against a fellow employee of the same or lower status than against the "kingpin" in your work group.

A final example of the consequences of status concerns the concept of *status incongruence.* There are many dimensions along which an organizational member's status can be determined; status incongruence occurs when all these dimensions are not consistent in indicating that person's status level. Clark (1958) provides an interesting example to demonstrate this point. He found that employees who check out purchases at the cash register in a supermarket have higher status than those employees who pack up the purchases. In addition, the check-out clerks typically are more senior and more experienced. He also found that when a more experienced checker is occasionally assigned to pack for a less experienced checker, tension is generated and productivity declines. Thus, status incongruence can have a negative impact on organizational functioning.

In total, employees' status influences how they behave, how their coworkers treat them, and how they react to their jobs. Such a conclusion clearly points to the need for managing an organization's status system.

MANAGING ORGANIZATIONAL STATUS SYSTEMS

The first task a manager must perform in managing a status system is to become familiar with both the *formal and informal status hierarchy.* An organization's formal hierarchy principally is determined by rank and, therefore, is the easiest to recognize. On the other hand, an organization's informal status hierarchy usually is determined by many factors, which are not codified (formally recognized by the organization's management). Thus, to become familiar with the organization's informal status system requires time and careful observation. The manager must observe how status symbols are distributed, the pattern of group communications, and other behaviors of a work group's members. Without being aware of the organization's pecking order, a manager will find himself or herself unknowingly making a host of social blunders. Such mistakes can and will, in most instances, adversely affect the job performance of the manager. For example, recall the pecking order in the restaurant kitchen—beef preparers, fowl preparers, then fish preparers. The newly employed graduate of a restaurant and hotel management program who inadvertently assigns a beef preparer to assist the fish preparer may find that he or she has generated a tense, unproductive work relationship.

Status symbols

Effective status system management requires that the distribution of organizational status symbols takes into account the status hierarchy that the members of the organization rely upon. In other words, managers should not, without forethought, award a symbol of high status to an employee who is commonly regarded as a low-status work-group member. This does not mean that, under no circumstance, should a symbol of high status be bestowed on a low-status employee. Rather, the manager should be aware of what he or she is doing and be prepared to defend and cope with the results of his or her actions.

In one midwestern university, offices with windows are reserved for faculty with rank and seniority. To occupy a smaller office with no windows is clearly a symbol of lower status. Recently, however, the dean decided to allocate office space on the basis of need. Thus, a new assistant professor with a demonstrable need for ample storage space was assigned to the large, exterior office of a retiring full professor. For months following this office assignment, many of the associate and full professors grumbled about this gaffe. Had the dean first announced his new policy and asked for reactions prior to assigning an exterior office to an assistant professor, he probably could have avoided some of the decrease in faculty morale and personal headaches he subsequently experienced. The lesson to be learned is, in distributing such status symbols as office space and furnishings, access to dining facilities, and automobiles, be conscious of how your distribution system meshes with the organization's intact status system. Unless it is your explicit intention to do so, don't rock the boat.

Learning the ropes

As we already implied, effective status system management requires learning the ropes of the organization's status hierarchy. Also, we noted that with high status come certain privileges and constraints on behavior. Employees who obtain positions of high status should know that definite behaviors will be expected of them. The employee occupying a high-status position who does not appreciate the access he or she has to people and information cannot and will not take advantage of this privilege. Further, the employee unfamiliar with the constraints his or her position of status places on personal behavior will undoubtedly spend many agonizing hours trying to decipher people's negative reactions to seemingly harmless blunders. Thus, to insure an employee's smooth transition to a position of higher status, the employee must be instructed in the rules of the game. Given that the privileges and constraints of status are not necessarily formally imposed by the organization, the recommended instruction typically will be informal. Probably the best way for such learning to take place is for the new role occupant to spend several days with his or her predecessor before assuming a position of high status. Many organizations, however, offer a formal course of training for newly hired or newly promoted employees who will be occupying high-status positions. These courses cover such topics as how to dress appropriately, personal grooming, and where the "right" places are to eat lunch. Whatever the approach, management should help prepare the individual adjust to a position of higher status. Such preparation will help the employee be more comfortable in his or her new role and better able to cope with the prerogatives and pressures of his or her position.

Communications

Effective status-system management also means effective management of the organization's communication systems. Since high-status persons receive more communications than low-status persons and since these communications are usually devoid of any negative information, managers must guard against several communication system disorders. First, high-status persons frequently find themselves overloaded with communications; it seems that everyone is trying to get his or her message through to the high-status person at once. When this occurs, there is a need to establish some sort of filtering mechanism, a set of procedures to screen out incoming communications that can best be handled elsewhere and to order incoming communications according to their urgency. High-status persons with personal secretaries often train and rely upon these subordinates to perform this filtering function. Without a person designated to act as a filter, the high-status employee must effectively manage his or her time. A fixed period of time each day should be set aside to answer incoming phone calls, to read incoming correspondence, and to meet with organizational personnel. If the timing of such activities is left to chance, the occupant of a high status position will spend his or her day decoding incoming messages. Unless specific time periods are set aside, little else will be accomplished.

The distribution of information is a second communications problem that must be dealt with. Too often, messages are sent to high-status persons with the assumption that the information will be passed on to lower-status work-group members. If a high-status person is, in fact, being used to channel information to other work-group members, the high-status person must be made aware of this responsibility. Possibly a better strategy is to communicate directly with those employees for whom the message is intended. This does not mean bypassing high-status work-group members; it means that the high-status employee will not be overburdened with the responsibility or being his or her work group's sole source of task-relevant information.

Finally, the high-status group member must recognize that the communications he or she receives from lower-status persons typically are incomplete or, at least, not perfectly accurate. For example, rarely will a low-status person freely communicate personally negative information about his or her job performance to a higher-status employee. There are two ways to overcome this communication roadblock. First, high-status persons must demonstrate to lower-status employees that they will appreciate and reward the communication of both positive *and* negative information. The high-status person demonstrates this appreciation by positively, verbally reinforcing the low-status employee when he or she communicates this negative information. The low-status person should be told the information is valued and that he or she is respected for being so honest and open. Second, when appropriate, high-status persons should establish formal reporting systems that periodically require lower-status employees to convey objectively both positive and negative task-relevant information. Such reporting systems encourage lower-status persons to be more candid. And the omission of negative information from a formal report will be considered a violation of one's job responsibilities.

Status incongruence

This last status-system management activity concerns the assignment of tasks to persons whose status suggests that the tasks will not be warmly received. For example, we consulted with a police department in which status was determined by only two factors: rank and seniority, with seniority being the major determinant of rank. One privilege of status was assignment to a desk job with a 9:00 A.M. to 5 P.M. work schedule. Thus, senior officers were rarely seen out on the streets and were virtually never seen after dark. The police chief, wanting to increase the amount of direct supervision given to patrolmen, reassigned three captains to be on the streets during the midnight shift. Two of the captains promptly threatened to resign from the force, because they felt that someone of their status shouldn't be assigned to a patrol car, particularly during the high-crime shift.

How do you, as managers, cope with such problems created by status incongruence? First, if it can be avoided, do not generate the incongruence; otherwise, morale and productivity may decline. Of course, effective organizational functioning occasionally mandates that high-status employees be assigned to perform relatively low-status tasks. When this occurs, you must do four things. First, tell the affected employees well in advance of the assignment. Second, tell them why the assignment is being made. Third, make clear to them that the assignment is not intended as a direct attack on their organizational status. And, finally, tell their coworkers of the circumstances under which the assignment is being made. Obviously, the assignment of high-status persons to lower-status tasks should not be made casually. If periodic pressures require reassignments of personnel, they should be planned well in advance, and these plans should be made available to the parties involved.

The preceding discussion illustrates that organizational status systems require managerial attention. Further, the management topics chosen for discussion were not meant to be exhaustive. As you gain managerial experience, you will become more aware of the importance of organizational status systems as well as their positive and negative consequences. The best piece of advice is: Think before you act. Take into consideration the impact of your actions on your organization's status system Only with such forethought can you effectively manage, rather than be managed, by your organization's status system.

SUMMARY

An employee's status (or ranking in the organization's social system) can be ascertained by the status symbols he or she enjoys. Some organizational status symbols are clothing, titles, office space, office furnishings, access to private washrooms and private dining facilities, automobiles, access to private secretarial services, and travel privileges. These symbols of an employee's organizational status receive a great deal of attention by most members of work organizations and, therefore, warrant close examination by management.

Many factors determine the level of an employee's achieved status. They include the employee's occupation, the materials the employee works on, the skill or knowledge required to perform the employee's assigned work, the employee's organizational rank, the employee's pay, the employee's seniority, and the employee's associates. Importantly, all these factors may not consistently indicate the same level of status. When this occurs, the employee experiences status incongruence. Other consequences of organizational status concern the behavioral privileges and constraints afforded high-status persons and the quantity and content of communications directed at such persons.

Each of these consequences frequently requires managerial action. Managers must guard against unintentionally assigning a symbol of high status to a low-status employee or, conversely, assigning a symbol of low status to a high-statue employee. To avoid undue stress, managers should inform employees about to occupy newly acquired high-status positions of the behavioral expectations inherent in such positions. Managers should insure that high-status persons are not overloaded with incoming communications and that these communications from lower-status persons are honest and open. Finally, managers must be cautious not to burden high-status persons with the responsibility of communicating all task-relevant information to the members of their work groups. In sum, effective managers must consider the impact of their actions on their organization's status system.

REFERENCES

Clark, J.U. "A Preliminary Investigation on Some Unconscious Assumptions Affecting Labor Efficiencies in Eight Supermarkets." Unpublished doctoral dissertation, Graduate School of Business Administration, Harvard University, 1958.

Harragan, B.L. *Games Mother Never Taught you: Corporate Gamesmanship for Women*. New York: Warner Brothers, 1977.

Litterer, J.A. *The Analysis of Organizations*. New York: Wiley, 1965.

Mound, M.C. "The Concept of Status As Practiced in Business Organizations." *MSU Business Topics 17* (1968): 7-19.

Packard, V. *The Status Seekers*. New York: David McKay Co., 1959.

Siegel, P.S.; Rossi, P.H.; and Hodge, R.W. *Social Standings of Occupations*. New York: Seminar Press, forthcoming.

Whyte, W.F. *Human Relations in the Restaurant Industry*. New York: McGraw-Hill , 1948.

CHAPTER

23

The Uniform: What To Wear As An Active Game Player*

If you were a comedian or cartoonist you'd probably have at least one sure-fire joke in your repertoire based on women's clothes. Unlimited mileage seems possible with variations on the "She didn't have a thing to wear" theme. Lampoons about women's indecisiveness and procrastination when it comes to selecting an appropriate costume for an important occasion are rampant, as are satires on women's flights into shopping expeditions to cure depression and loneliness. Masculine audiences are hugely entertained by visions of women making fools of themselves cavorting in ridiculous getups that are annually ordained by fashion moguls. Yet men never protest too violently except for expressing mock horror at the outrageous bills for these female fancies. As men see it, women's fashions are like trips through the fun house at the amusement park—harmless diversion for the fickle sex.

By alternately encouraging and disparaging women's interest in clothes, men gain a feeling of superiority, as much as to say, "What else can you expect of silly women? We men can't be bothered with such fashion frivolity; we have important things to do in this world." Let me tell you, nothing could be further from the truth. Men are *much more* attentive to their clothes than any woman. For centuries men have deluded women that clothing styles mean nothing to them. But if you look around you'll see that men can't pursue the most ordinary of their male-exclusive activities without just the right clothing. Look at policeman, garbagemen, doormen, clergymen, jockeys, firemen, Shriners, or the Ku Klux Klan to get a slight appreciation of the importance of clothes to male bonding.

---

*Abridged with permission of the publisher from *Games Mother Never Taught You* by B.L. Harragan, pp. 325-336. Copyright © 1977 by Rawson, Wade Publishers, Inc., New York, N.Y.

Business executives—the proprietors of the corporate hierarchies—are the most clothes-conscious of all. They are the acknowledged arbiters of men's fashions and they accept that responsibility with utmost seriousness. It is no accident that dressmaking is treated as an inferior craft to men's tailoring, nor that clerks who sell women's dresses are paid less than men's department clerks. The pay disparity is not solely due to sex discrimination; department store management insists that the items sold in women's dress departments are less prestigious and valuable than items in men's haberdashery (even though prices may be higher in the women's section).

MEN'S CLOTHES ARE IDENTIFYING UNIFORMS

For more than five years during my promotional career I plunged headlong into the Loch Ness of men's fashion hoping to disgorge the mythical monster of organization conformity. My client was a quality men's suit manufacturer who distributes under his own label but is also a private-label manufacturer for leading specialty and department stores across the country. (Private-label manufacturers produce the suits that are sold under designer or store names.) The effort was professionally fascinating (only two other women were connected with that field), highly educational (I'm just realizing how much of my business knowledge was gained during that stint), but thoroughly frustrating from a marketing viewpoint—the more things change in men's fashion, the more they remain the same.

The truth is, in the male business world there is not and can never be any serious interest in fashion as women understand it. That's because male business garb is nothing more than a standardized uniform. It is no more changeable as a matter of individual choice than the daily uniform of military personnel or the team garb of baseball, basketball, or football players. In every branch of the armed services, the team of officers is distinguishable from rank-and-file troops by the style and design of their uniforms; further gradations in rank and authority are visibly announced by tiny ornamentations added to the uniforms, the insignia. In business, men's clothing performs the same function. Your male boss's and colleagues' everyday work garments are loaded with symbolic and psychological import.

A young friend is one of two women management interns in the corporate headquarters of a large chemical company whose nonclerical employees are almost unanimously male. When riding the elevators with her fellow trainees she noticed that the men would occasionally stop talking business when certain other men were on the elevator. Mystified, she asked, "Who were they?" Her associates' response was, "Who cares? But they don't work for our company." To her the men were indistinguishable from the thousands of male company employees, so she suspected her co-workers were putting her on. It was possible to test their convictions because the company had sublet several floors to other business tenants. She was astounded to discover that the men her associates singled out invariably got off on one of the tenant floors. She is learning to spot the subtly different "look" about the strangers, but she can't articulate what makes the difference. Nevertheless, she is far ahead of other women in business, most of whom are oblivious to the panorama of class, job, and corporate distinctions passing before their eyes daily in the costumes worn by male business associates.

If you have any doubts that men's business suits are team uniforms, you can test for yourself. Follow my friend's system if you have a similar situation in your bank of elevators. The idea is to decide upon entering which men will exit on noncompany floors. This is not the easiest way to start off because departments within the same corporation can adopt subtle variations of the main uniform to distinguish local team groups. For instance, men in accounting might have a different "look" than men in advertising or sales. You will see many styles of men's dress, ranging from dark, conservative suits to well-tailored high-fashion outfits to loudly patterned noncoordinated sports jackets and flamboyant ties. Low-echelon or unambitious men are apt to be those who take a lax attitude toward their clothes symbols (as noted before, not all men are equally ambitious or intelligent). Executives, however, and perceptive junior executives will be noticeable for their neat, uniform look. Lobby-watching is a better exercise for beginners. You can try it in the morning when people are coming to work, any noontime when men are leaving for lunch, or after work when employees are going home. Stand or sit whenever you have an extensive view of the passing parade and watch how the men are dressed. Judging only from their wearing apparel and the impression it makes on you, try to guess what their job title or occupation might be.

What you'll discover after one or two sessions of lobby-watching is that you can quite easily distinguish top-level executives from lower-status men. You won't have to check your observation; you'll *know* you're right when you decide, "*That* man has a very important job." The status symbols will be pulsing loud and clear from his costume even though you don't know how to decipher the code. If you lobby-watch in a small office building which houses several companies in different industries, you may find yourself able to distinguish male employees of one company from those of another merely by scrutinizing their clothes. Should you be located in a suburban complex where all men obviously work for your company, you can try a sophisticated variation of the same exercise. Station yourself near the parking lot, and try to separate those men who work in one building or department from those who walk toward another building; which men work in the executive suites, and which in the test labs? A further refinement of this exercise is to scrutinze visitors in a main reception room and try to guess who in your company they have an appointment with. It may surprise you how perceptive you are. If you are familiar with your own executivés you're apt to find that their visitors "look" like them in costuming.

Now try any of the above exercises with passing women and see what happens if you try to guess job status and team affiliation from their clothing!

DECIPHERING THE UNIFORM CODE SYMBOLS

When you consider that the entire male sex wears the identical basic business outfit—suit, shirt, ties, shoes, socks—you can appreciate the exquisite care it takes to turn these stark modules into meaningful code symbols that spell out class, rank, team, and star status. Male players *must* pay inordinate attention to minuscule details, and successful men do! As a result, a male business outfit is a virtual hieroglyphic tablet composed of tiny picturegraphs, every one of which contributes to the overall message conveyed by dress. Seemingly innocuous details in a suit, such as a fractional narrowing of lapel width, a minute indentation in seam or dart tapering, an inch difference in vent height, a smidgen less shoulder padding, the stitching on buttonholes, a fingerbreadth variation in jacket or trouser length are enormously significant. Tremendous import is conveyed by color and fabric, each of which trumpet signals through almost imperceptible gradations of hue or shadowy suggestions of stripe or plaid designs. Proper fit is crucial, and men's suit manufacturers are graded for "quality" according to the amount of handtailoring they put into the finished garment which insures that the shaping will hold up. In effect, quality workmanship consists of sewing as many sacred hieroglyphs as possible into the business uniform. The suit is the master power symbol, but the rank message can be distorted if the caste marks are not painstakingly reinforced by matching emblems in shirts, ties, shoes, and socks. All five elements must be expertly coordinated to achieve the total symbolic effect. The wrong shirt or tie can make a disastrous mess of a perfect suit.

Women have been brought up in total ignorance of this male hieroglyphic dress code. Inasmuch as women were previously denied access to the realms of money and power, the only place where rank symbolism in clothing is used, their ignorance didn't matter. But, women who intend to move forward into the executive levels of business must be able to read the heraldic seals of the business knights and understand the role of clothing in the socioeconomic game. Fortunately for aspiring women, these secrets have recently been made public by John Molloy in a revealing book, *Dress for Success* (New York: Warner Books, Inc., 1976). Because this is a book by, for, and about aspiring men, it is a revealing distillation of business initiation rites in the male culture. It is a veritable dictionary of symbolic dress terminology translated into everyday lessons on how clothing emblems are displayed and manipulated. From it, women can learn how businessmen judge each other, and recognize equals, by their uniform dress insignia. It is noteworthy that one of the dress rules for success explicitly warns men: "Never wear any item that might be considered feminine." Under the male rules women have a long way to go to learn how to modify female fashion into an acceptable uniform for the corporate game table.

WOMEN'S APPAREL IS A BADGE OF SERVITUDE

Men's clothing is not unique in assigning attributes to its wearers; women's clothing is historically symbolic, too. As far as I know, no contemporary feminist has researched the subject (no nonfeminist would care), but women who are moving into the male world of work must begin to pay attention to the symbolism of clothing.

Why are men's and women's clothes so different? Why, as a woman, do you wear what you wear? What is your conscious or subconscious motivation each morning as you dress for work? Why not just wear your bathrobe?

The phenomenon of sex differential in wearing apparel intrigued Lawrence Langner, a prodigiously successful businessman who was also an erudite scholar, a popular playwright, and a perceptive social observer. His many-faceted talents led him to the theater where he founded the Theater Guild and the Shakespeare Festival at Stratford, Connecticut. The importance of costumes to theatrical productions and the social significance of costumes impelled him to study the meaning and psychology of clothing throughout history. In 1959 he published his remarkable psycho-history of clothing through the ages, *The Importance of Wearing Clothes* (New York: Hastings House). Several years before the current wave of feminism erupted, his studies led him to the following conclusion about the marked dissimilarity between men's and women's clothes:

> Contrary to established beliefs, the differentiation in clothing between men and women arose from the male's desire to assert superiority over the female and to hold her in his service. This he accomplished through the ages by means of special clothing which hampered or handicapped the female in her movements. Then men prohibited one sex from wearing the clothing of the other, in order to maintain this differentiation.

Langner traced his hypothesis as far back as Spanish Levant rock paintings, circa 10,000 B.C. and followed the evidence through subsequent ages, civilizations, and cultures. He found the primary purpose of women's dress throughout history was to prevent them from running away from their lords and masters. The ancient Chinese bound the feet of growing girls to hopelessly deform the adult woman's feet; African tribes weighted women's legs with up to fifty pounds of "beautifying" nonremovable brass coils or protruding metal disks; in Palestine women's ankles were connected with chains and tinkling bells; Moslems swathed women in heavy, opaque shrouds from head to toe; upper-class women in Venice and Spain had to be assisted by pages when they walked in their gorgeous gowns because of the fashionable chimpanies or stilts attached to their shoes—some as much as a yard high!

The only exception to foot crippling was found among nomadic tribes where women were forced to keep up with their men during the seasonal migrations. In these groups, the women were the beasts of burden, walking with the animals and loaded almost as heavily with household goods. They could walk but could not run far.

In Western societies the ubiquitous hobbling device for women has been skirts, usually accompanied by dysfunctional stilted shoes. Although skirt styles changed over time and in various societies, skirts of all kinds served to encumber women. Skirts that consisted of long robes reaching to or below the ankles hampered movement by entangling the legs in layers of heavy textiles. In more "modern" times straight fitted skirts effectively bound the knees or ankles together to impede free stride and enforce an awkward, staggering gait. Whatever the society, skirts for females were characterized by their impracticality, inefficiency, and uncomfortable designs. Not only walking but sitting, bending, stooping, and climbing were totally enjoined via "female" dress. Utility, comfort, ornamentation, or sexual attraction has nothing to do with why females wear skirts or other distinctively "female" articles of clothing. These garments were invented thousands of years ago by men to label females as dependents and to "keep them in their place." In consequence, "female" apparel carries a universal symbolism of servitude—the badge of subservience.

In contrast the exclusive male clothing in every society where women were constricted consisted of divided garments—trousers or knickerbockers—which permitted free, unrestricted movement while protecting the wearer's extremities. Men exerted superiority over women by laying exclusive claim to clothing which gives the greatest mobility, freedom for action, and self-protection.

At all times, from earliest societies, women were prohibited from wearing the clothing of males—and vice versa. The penalties for breaking the strict laws against transvestitism ("a morbid craving to dress in garments of the opposite sex") were (and are) severe. In Deuteronomy, the Old Testament thundered the "moral" imprecations which many women feel bound by even in the twentieth century. "A woman shall not wear that which pertaineth unto a man, neither shall a man put on a woman's garment."

Despite these savage laws and vicious punishments, women have periodically rebelled against their enforced clothing shackles, especially skirts. Early American feminists of the 1850s took up the issue of women's dress reform. Amelia Bloomer is the best known of the many who took to wearing short skirts or tunics over loose trousers gathered at the ankle. "Bloomers" became the derisive term for any divided skirt or knickerbocker dress. One optimistic feminist, Helen Marie Weber, told the Women's Rights Convention of 1850 in Worcester, Massachusetts that, "In ten years time male attire will be generally worn by women of most civilized countries." She was at least a hundred years off in her prediction; it has taken until the 1970s for women to dare to flout the age-old inventions of man to keep her inferior and immobile.

There are still corporations that issue edicts to keep women employees in their place by forbidding women to wear slacks or pants suits to work. Such a company policy is telling women employees that they are inferior beings whose only status in the corporate setup is to serve their male masters. The clothing symbolism says: "You have no mobility in this corporation." No woman who understands the significance of corporate status symbolism would be caught dead working for such a company. Displaying a blatant badge of servitude is no way to progress in the male corporate milieu, but that is exactly what "female" dress codes dictated by men set out to accomplish.

CHAPTER 24

Team Building

Work groups exist at all levels of an organization and are referred to by such labels as management teams, committees, task forces, and production units. Work groups either evolve naturally (or informally) or can be formally designated by an organization's managment. Regardless of the form of the work group, management wants group members to pull together as a team, a cooperating collective of employees with common organizational goals. The focus of this chapter is on building this *team spirit*. In other words, this chapter is concerned with how to create a work group whose members get along well, with a minimum of backbiting and infighting and a maximum of information sharing and integrated, goal-directed effort.

The first part of the chapter deals with identifying a work group and its development over time. Next, we will examine in detail the causes and consequences of team spirit (or *group cohesiveness*). Finally, we will discuss, from a managerial perspective, the impact of the rules that regulate group member behavior on group effectiveness.

WORK GROUP DEVELOPMENT

A *work group* is a social unit consisting of a number of individuals whose working relationships make them interdependent to some degree. A few examples may help to clarify this definition. First, a consumer goods firm is planning to introduce a new product, and the president of the firm appoints a task force to manage the product's introduction. The task force consists of a production planner, a packing design expert,. an advertising consultant, a retail distribution specialist, and the firm's vice president of marketing. Each person contributes to the introduction of the new product, and other members of the group support their efforts. Thus, the working relationships among these five persons are interdependent and, therefore, qualify them to be collectively labeled as a work group. Second, three members of the office services department of a brokerage firm are responsible for mailing the firm's promotional brochures. One person prints the brochures; a second person addresses and stamps the envelopes in which the brochures are to be mailed; and a third person folds the brochures, stuffs them into the envelopes, and seals the envelopes. Even though the department head has not formally designated these three persons as a production unit, they, too, meet our criteria as a work group, given the degree to which their jobs are interdependent. Finally, Mary is one of fifty sewing-machine operators employed by a small shirt manufacturer; and John is the maintenance person responsible for keeping Mary's machine in top operating condition. If Mary and the other operators did not use their machines, John would have no maintenance work to perform. If John did not keep Mary's machine in operating order, obviously Mary couldn't sew. Admittedly, we see a very different type of task interdependence between Mary and John than the previous two examples illustrated; but they also constitute a work group according to our definition.

Clues for identifying work groups

Given that many, if not most, work groups are not formally designated as such by management, how can you identify the formation of a work group? The following features of work groups should serve as clues in identifying whether or not a collection of employees does in fact function as a group: (1) the employees engage in frequent interaction either on or off the job; (2) the employees share a common set of rules governing their behavior, at least regarding matters of common interest; (3) the employees pursue interdependent goals; (4) the employees all perceive that they are members of the same group; and (5) the employees tend to act in a similar fashion towards their environment (Cartwright and Zander, 1968). If a manager notes that the same employees tend to eat lunch together, dress in a common style, talk about accomplishing the same types of goals, frequently refer to themselves as a group by using such terms as "us" and "we," and react to changes in organizational policies in the same way, then the manager should know that he or she is dealing with a social unit rather than a collective of autonomous individuals.

Group evolution

Assuming that a manager has designated or identified a number of employees as a group, what do we know about the formation and evolution of groups that can help the manager better understand the social unit he or she is responsible for managing? Muzafer Sherif (1968), a social scientist, has identified four essentials in the process of group formation. First, there must be some motivational base that causes repeated interpersonal interactions among the group members. From our perspective, the dominant motivation for interaction among work-group members is the need to perform interlocking organizational tasks. The employees' jobs are somehow interdependent, and, for a variety of motivational reasons, the employees feel compelled to perform their organizationally assigned tasks. Thus, two or more employees with totally independent jobs who do not interact on a periodic basis cannot be said to constitute a work group.

Second, the group evolves a structure of roles and statuses. A *role* is a set of behavioral expectations that members of the group apply to a group member. Stated somewhat differently, a role consists of those activities group members anticipate a person will engage in within the group. The simplist distinction between group members' roles is that between leaders and followers. For instance, in the previous example of the new-product task force, it became apparent during their first meeting that the vice president of marketing adopted the role of group leader, and the other four group members largely played the roles of followers. All groups develop a set of role expectations for their members; and the manager would benefit from knowing which members are playing which roles in the work group. In addition, groups evolve a pecking order among their members. In the previous two chapters. the causes, consequences, and symbols of such status systems were discussed.

A third essential in the process of group formation is the establishment of norms that govern the behavior of group members in matters of importance to the group. *Norms* are simply the rules of conduct a group member is expected to abide by. Later in the chapter, we will discuss the importance of work-group norms to the manager.

The final essential ingredient in the formation process is the exercise of control the group has over its members. Mere specification of rules of conduct is insufficient to influence a group member's behavior. The group must have available rewards and sanctions it can use to insure that a member conforms to its norms. For example, Sue is friendly with several of her coworkers in the billing department where she is employed. The group eats lunch together every day; and the members usually stop work ten minutes before their designated lunch period in order to get ready to go out to eat. For the last two days, due to a particularly heavy work load, Sue has stopped for lunch at the designated time and caught up with her friends at the local diner where they normally eat. When, for the third time in a row, Sue shows up "late" at lunch, her friends act coldly toward her and don't attempt to involve her in the group's conversation. Sue's work group members are sanctioning her for violating the group's norm of stopping work ten minutes prior to the company's official lunch period.

In total, a work group can be said to have evolved or reached a stage of maturity when some motivational base has been established that is conducive to repeated interactions; a structure of roles and statuses has evolved; rules of conduct have been formulated; and a degree of control is exerted over member behavior. Two additional points should be noted. First, the regulatory functions of work groups are the principal reason why the manager must become a serious student of group behavior. This work-group control over member behavior can be harnessed to further the attainment of organizational goals; or, if mismanaged, it can serve to inhibit the accomplishment of organizational objectives. Second, all four of the essentials in the process of group formation do not occur simultaneously. Bruce Tuchman (1965) has spelled out four sequential stages of development that groups go through. Persons initially orient themselves by testing what behaviors are acceptable in the group by observing the reactions of other group members to the behaviors they are trying out. In addition, persons early on become dependent on those group members who show signs of leadership and provide guidance and support. Following this orientation, testing, and dependence stage, intragroup conflict usually erupts. The conflict commonly focuses upon the roles and statuses established in the initial stage of group development. This conflict is overcome in the third stage of group development, when members begin to accept the existence of the group and show a desire to maintain and perpetuate it. At this point, group norms evolve, and harmony seems to be of maximum importance. In the final stage of group development, group members begin to focus their energies on the accomplishment of group goals, and member behavior is largely channeled in that direction. Now, the work group is a functional instrument that can work against or for the attainment of organizational goals. Again, it was shown that a collection of employees with the motivation to interact only can be labeled a work group when (1) a structure of roles and statuses has emerged; (2) norms have been established; and (3) available rewards and sanctions have been applied to insure conformity to norms. The management activities at this junction are described in the following section.

FIGURE 24-1

"Gentlemen, please! Let's move on to substantive issues."

CAUSES AND CONSEQUENCES OF TEAM SPIRIT

Team spirit or a sense of hanging together is called *group cohesiveness*, which is formally defined as the degree to which members are motivated to remain in the group (Shaw, 1976). Management can anticipate two general types of outcomes occurring due to a high level of cohesiveness within a work group. One of these clearly has *negative* consequences and indicates a degree of *mismanagement*. In general, highly cohesive groups are more effective in achieving their goals than are work groups that lack this sense of team spirit. Note that we have specified effectiveness in terms of the *group's goals*. Figure 24-2 shows four possible circumstances: (1) high cohesiveness, high congruence between group and organizational goals; (2) high cohesiveness, low congruence between group and organizational goals; (3) low cohesiveness, high congruence between group and organizational goals; and (4) low cohesiveness, low congruence between group and organizational goals. In the best possible circumstances, a manager is responsible for managing a work group that is highly cohesive *and* whose goals coincide precisely with those of the organization. Here, the manager will be dealing with a tightly knit group of employees pulling together to achieve the same objectives as the manager. Conversely, the worst possible situation is to manage a work group that is highly cohesive *but* whose goals are directly opposed to the goals of the organization. Some union-management relationships, where the union has a history of winning a number of bitter strikes against the organization, exemplify such a circumstance. Remember, highly cohesive groups are effective in terms of achieving *their goals*. Given a high level of cohesiveness, management must take every step possible to insure that the group's goals coincide with the goals of the organization. Chapter 25 offers some specific suggestions on how to encourage such goal agreement. At this point, note that group cohesiveness without member commitment to organizational goals spells trouble for the manager.

FIGURE 24-2
Cohesiveness and Goal Congruency*

	Group and Organizational Goals Congruent	Group and Organizational Goals Incongruent
High Cohesiveness		
Low Cohesiveness		

*Adapted from Kast and Rosenzweig (1970)

Sometimes a group may be highly cohesive but its goals may be contrary to those of the organization.

Let us, for the moment, ignore the issue of group commitment to organizational goals and examine in detail other consequences of cohesiveness. First, members of high-cohesive groups communicate with each other more than members of low-cohesive groups. Obviously, that's because people who are attracted to one another interact more than persons who do not like each other. Second, the content of communications among members of high-cohesive groups is more positively oriented than among members of low-cohesive groups. Taken together, these two consequences of group cohesiveness indicate that managers facing cohesive work groups will encounter collections of employees who talk frequently among themselves and act friendly and cooperatively toward one another. In addition, the manager can anticipate that cohesive work groups will structure activities that facilitate group interaction. For example, a cohesive committee may schedule an unusually large number of meetings; or a cohesive production unit may organize a Friday night poker game. On the other hand, managers facing work groups that lack cohesion will find that the members function as individuals rather than as a group and act aggressively and uncooperatively toward one another. Correspondingly, the members of uncohesive work groups will attempt to avoid interacting with one another even at the cost of organizational effectiveness.

Another consequence of group cohesiveness is member satisfaction. Members of high-cohesive work groups, as opposed to members of low-cohesive work groups, are more pleased with the group and its products. In the first place, this satisfaction with the group may influence the members' overall job satisfaction. In fact, one dimension of overall job satisfaction is the employee's satisfaction with coworkers. Satisfaction with the group production, however, may not always be as advantageous as member satisfaction with the work group *per se*. Member satisfaction with the group product could reflect an overemphasis on the work group's output. For instance, the long-range planning committee of one organization can be characterized as highly cohesive; and the members all seem to be exceedingly satisfied with the planning documents the committee has produced. Objectively, however, the plans the committee presented are incomplete and not very realistic. Thus, member satisfaction created by group cohesiveness may generate an awkward set of circumstances for the manager to deal with.

The final consequence of cohesiveness we will consider is the most important to the manager. As we said earlier, high-cohesive work groups exert greater control over their members than do low-cohesive groups. That's because one form of power is interpersonal attraction. Thus, highly cohesive work groups with members strongly attracted to one another have a considerable degree of power, which can be used to influence the opinions, judgments, and behaviors of their members. In other words, cohesive work groups are very effective in compelling their members to conform to the norms of the group.

Managing team spirit

The consequences of group cohesiveness that we have outlined clearly demonstrate that a sense of team spirit does influence the attitudes and behaviors of a work group's members; and this influence may or may not work to the manager's advantage. The question now becomes, "How can a manager manipulate the level of a work group's cohesiveness?" It can best be answered by examining the following managerial strategies. First, a manager wishing to develop team spirit must carefully compose the membership of the work group. He or she should follow three guidelines of group composition in order to lay the foundation for a highly cohesive unit: (a) the members should be as similar to one another as is feasible; (b) the members' personalities should be compatible; and, (c) the size of the group should be kept to a minimum. The specific dimensions of similarity the manager should consider are status, background, attitudes, and values. Persons who occupy relatively the same position in an organization's pecking order; who belong to the same religious, racial, ethnic, occupational, or age groups; who share the same general set of attitudes; and whose values are not in conflict are likely to get along well with one another. Conversely, it is much more difficult for a group of people with little or nothing in common to develop a strong attraction to one another. The compatibility of member personality traits refers to the fit between the distinct personalities that comprise the group. For example, authoritarian personality types are demanding, assertive, and dominating and *fit* with submissive personality types.

Based upon his or her observations of prior interactions, a manager can subjectively judge the personalities of potential group members and will want to avoid placing employees with obviously incompatible personalities in the same work group. The atmosphere of groups with such built-in sources of stress as incompatible personality types can typically be characterized by high levels of anxiety, tension, and dissatisfaction, which certainly are not conditions conducive to building cohesiveness. As the size of a group increases, several potentially dysfunctional consequences occur. The frequency and duration of interactions among group members decreases. Emotional ties among group members are more difficult to develop. And leadership, once centralized, becomes a dominant force in the group. Because all these consequences can make it more difficult for a sense of team spirit to evolve, large work groups (eight or more members) are to be avoided. In sum, small work groups composed of similar types of employees with compatible personalities are likely to exhibit team spirit. And, under many circumstances, managers are in control of a work group's composition.

The second important step a manager can take in building group cohesiveness is to create the right "climate" for group interactions. This climate should (a) allow members to communicate frequently with one another and to observe each other's behavior; (b) focus the energy of the group members on the achievement of some common goal whereby all members can share in the group output produced; (c) encourage group members to rely on democratic decision-making processes rather than being directed by one central and dominant power source; and (d) make it possible for the members to experience some measure of success. The manager who can create a work environment that encourages members to get to know one another, share a common objective, use participatory decision making, and feel a sense of group accomplishment is well on the way to building a cohesive work group.

These suggestions imply that a newly formed work group should be assigned an initial task that can be performed in a neutral and pleasant setting. Further, the task should capitalize on the common goals of the individual members and should not be so difficult as to put success out of easy reach. Finally, the task should be structured to ensure that each group member participates equally in its performance. For instance, the industrial relations director of a large firm recently appointed an employee welfare committee. She scheduled the first meeting of the committee to take place on Friday afternoon over lunch at the city's finest private club. The agenda for the first meeting included just two items: plan the company's annual picnic and schedule the committee's next meeting. As the strongest member of the committee, the industrial relations director chose not to attend.

These strategies assume that the manager is responsible for selecting the work group's members and staging the initial interactions of the group. If these assumptions are not true, what team-building strategies are left open to the manager? Actually, there are at least three options: create a "threatening" situation; make the work group more attractive by adding a "star" to the group; and directly increase the "merit" of group goal attainment. Groups that perceive a threat stemming from some source outside the group *and* that feel cooperative behavior can eliminate the threat typically will become more cohesive. A manager can create such a set of circumstances in several ways. For instance, the manager can demonstrate to the members of a work group that the organization in general and their work group in particular is being intimidated by a source in the organization's environment. Such an external source could be a competitor launching a new advertising campaign, a regulatory agency proposing a new set of governmental restrictions, or a major supplier of raw materials changing its price structure. Of course, the threat must be real, and the manager must be able to show the work group members how they might act together to overcome it. Another way of creating a common threat is for the manager to generate conflict between two or more work groups within the organization. This is most frequently done by placing similar production units in competition. The unit producing the most products in a given period of time is awarded some visible symbol of victory. The manager must be cautious, however, not to create a situation in which intergroup conflict produces largely negative rather than positive outcomes.

People are more highly attracted to successful persons that unsuccessful persons. So, adding a star performer to a work group may serve to increase the group's cohesiveness. In addition, if this star performer actually increases group effectiveness, the group's sense of team spirit will be even further enhanced due to the shared feelings of accomplishment derived from the group's higher level of performance. These stars should be carefully chosen to ensure that their prior track record is, in fact, outstanding and is clearly visible to the work group's members. In addition, the star and the work group members should thoroughly understand the star's role in the group *before* the newcomer joins the group.

A final team-building strategy open to the manager is to create a reward structure whereby successful cooperative behavior *and* group performance lead to positively valent outcomes for all the work group's members. We discussed this approach in chapter 12, "Using the Carrot or the Stick?," and we will say more about it in the following section on norms.

WORK GROUP NORMS

As previously defined, *norms* are the rules of conduct a group member is expected to abide by, and their establishment is an essential ingredient in the process of group formation. Work group norms are important to the manager because they are the principal vehicle the group employs to control a member's behavior. Violation of group norms generally produces a group reaction that tends to correct the deviant group member's behavior. Herein lie the regulatory properties associated with norms. Remember, for example, Sue, the billing clerk, who violated the group norm of stopping for lunch ten minutes early and whose fellow group members reacted coldly to this deviation? Her exclusion from participating in the group's luncheon conversation quickly compelled Sue to again conform to her work group's norm.

A work group does not develop a norm to govern every possible behavior. Rather, norms evolve to regulate behaviors that most members of the work group feel are important to either the maintenance of the group or the task effectiveness of the group. *Group maintenance* refers to the continuation of the group as a social unit, and task effectiveness here refers only to the performance of group-defined tasks. Casual observation of a variety of types of work groups indicates that most groups develop norms regarding such things as (1) the level of member contribution to organizational effectiveness and (2) publicly stated attitudes toward the organization and authority figures within the organization. Some work groups establish norms that encourage members to maximize their contributions to the organization, while other work groups' norms cause members to restrict their level of output. Further, the norm in some work groups supports the organization and its management; while in other work groups, norms compel the members to voice negative attitudes toward the organization and its management. Again, the social influence a work group exerts can serve to enhance or diminish organizational effectiveness.

As implied, norms govern stated attitudes as well as the behavior of group members. Norms do *not* regulate the private thoughts and feelings of work group members, because the private opinions of group members are not observable. In other words, for a norm to influence a member's behavior, the group must be able to observe the member's violation of that norm. In addition, for norms to be effective regulators of behavior, (1) the member must be aware of the norms, and (2) the group must be able to reward conformity to the norms and/or be able to punish deviation from them. In sum, *without observability, member awareness, and group power to reward or punish, conformity to work group norms will not occur.*

We noted in chapter 22, "Understanding the Role of Status," that, in certain situations, high-status group members are allowed to deviate from group norms more than low-status group members. More generally, not all norms apply equally to all members of a work group. Norms that hold for one or a few members of a group help to define the roles of those group members. This is how norms can be said to partially determine the structure of work groups.

Conformity

Now that we have pointed out some, but by no means all, of the characteristics of norms, we will focus on three principal factors that influence member conformity to these potentially important regulators of employee behavior. First, employees conform more to work-group norms when they are personally unsure of what behaviors they should engage in. For example, Bill, a newly hired construction worker, notes that the fellows he works with are always borrowing tools from the company for fix-up projects at their homes. Either the supervisor isn't aware of what's going on or ignores the behavior. So Bill joins in with the group and becomes a frequent borrower. If Bill's boss had made it perfectly clear to him and the other members of the work group that using company tools after working hours is against company policy and will not be tolerated, it is unlikely that Bill would have so readily developed the borrowing habit. Thus, the more a manager can reduce the ambiguity about what are and are not appropriate job behaviors, the lower the level of employee conformity to work group norms.

Second, conformity to a given norm increases as the members in the work group agree upon the appropriateness and importance of those norms. If the members of a work group unanimously agree that compliance with a particular norm is of utmost importance to the attainment of group goals, rarely will a group member deviate from that norm.

The third factor influencing conformity to group norms concerns the nature of the communication patterns within the work group. In groups with decentralized communication networks, where members talk freely to one another rather than receiving most messages from one central source (say, the group leader), conformity to group norms is at its highest. That's because decentralized communication networks encourage group members to have direct contact with each other; and these direct contacts allow the group to exert pressure on the individual member to conform.

In sum, *employees who are inwardly unsure of what behavior to engage in, who face a norm unanimously agreed upon by their work group, and whose fellow group members can freely communicate with them, are not likely to engage in any behaviors perceived to be deviant.* Of course, this assumes that the employees are aware of the norm, that each employee's norm-relevant behaviors can be observed by the work group, and that the group has the power to reward or punish its members. This last point warrants more attention.

Rejection is a type of reinforcement work groups employ to keep their members in line. Rejection can take one of two forms. The group can generally ignore the deviant group member and reduce their communications to him or her. Or the group can communicate mostly negative messages to the deviant. A work group is more likely to employ the second form of rejection because it doesn't want to cut off the deviant totally from the group for fear of completely losing that person—unless, of course, that is the group's intention. Employees can respond to rejection from their work group in three ways: (a) conform to the group's norms, (b) convince the group that their deviant behavior is appropriate under the circumstances, or (c) leave the group. Typically, only high-status group members will attempt to convince the group of the appropriateness of their behavior, and only persons with little attraction to the group will choose to leave. Thus, most group members will tend to conform, with the degree of their conformity varying as a function of the factors previously discussed.

From an organizational effectiveness perspective, managers will want to encourage member conformity to work group norms when those norms are supportive of organizational goal attainment. Again, this will occur only when group and organizational goals are congruent. Under such a circumstance, the preceding material should help the manager encourage work-group members to conform to those norms that are supportive of the organization.

SUMMARY

A work group is a social unit consisting of a number of individuals whose working relationship makes them interdependent to a degree. Work-group members frequently interact, share a common set of rules governing their behavior, pursue interdependent goals, think of themselves as members of the same group, and act in a similar fashion toward their environment. Thus, for a work group to form, there must be some motivational base that causes repeated interactions among the group members; a structure of roles and statuses must evolve; rules of group member conduct must be established; and the group must acquire the power to reward and or sanction its members. The group formation process moves from a stage of member orientation, testing, and dependency to the point where the members are able to focus their energies on the accomplishment of group goals.

Group cohesiveness, or team spirit, is the degree to which members are motivated to remain in the group. Members of high-cohesive groups communicate more with each other than do members of low-cohesive groups, and the content of these communications is more positive. In addition, members of high-cohesive groups are more satisfied and exert a greater degree of control over each other's behavior than low-cohesive groups.

Small work groups with members sharing similar statuses, backgrounds, attitudes, and values and whose members' personalities are compatible tend to be more cohesive than large groups composed of dissimilar persons with incompatible personalities. In addition, a work environment that encourages members to get to know one another, share a common objective, use participatory decision making, and feel a sense of group accomplishment also is conducive of team building. Finally, three managerial strategies for developing cohesiveness with intact work groups are: creating a "threatening" situation, adding a "star" to the work group, and increasing the "merit" of group goal attainment.

Norms are the rules of conduct members are to abide by. Norms are not developed to govern every possible behavior. Nor do norms regulate the private thoughts and feelings of work-group members. Not all norms apply equally to all members of a work group. Employees who are inwardly unsure of what behaviors to engage in, who face a norm unanimously agreed upon by their work group, and whose fellow group members can freely communicate to them are not likely to engage in any behaviors perceived to be deviant. Of course, this statement assumes that the employees are aware of the norm; that the employees' norm-relevant behaviors can be observed by the work group; and that the group has the power to reward or punish its members. From an organizational effectiveness perspective, managers will want to encourage member conformity to work-group norms when those norms are supportive of organizational goal attainment. This will occur only when group and organizational goals are congruent.

One strategy for directly obtaining congruence between group and organizational goals is *management by group objectives*, a spin-off from the more traditional management-by-objectives approach. The following chapter by the noted organizational scientist, Rensis Likert, and one of his colleagues, M. Scott Fisher, offers a sound introduction to this new and seemingly promising managerial approach. Taken together, this chapter and the one that follows should help the manager develop his or her own philosophy of work-group management.

REFERENCES

Cartwright, D.C., and Zander, A., eds. *Group Dynamics: Research and Theory*. New York: Harper and Row, 1968.

Kast, F.E., and Rosenzweig, J.E. *Organization and Management: A Systems Approach*. New York: McGraw-Hill, 1970.

Likert, R., and Fisher, M.S. "MBGO: Putting Some Team Spirit into MBO." *Personnel* 54 (1977): 40-47.

Sherif, M. "Group Formation." In *International Encyclopedia of the Social Sciences*, edited by D.L. Silles. New York: Macmillan, 1968, 276-84.

Tuchman, B.W. "Developmental Sequence in Small Groups." *Psychological Bulletin* 63 (1965): 384-99.

SUGGESTIONS FOR ADVANCED READINGS

Barnard, C.I. "Functions and Pathology of Status Systems in Formal Organizations." In *Industry and Society*, edited by W.F. Whyte. New York: McGraw-Hill, 1946.

Blau, P., and Duncan, O.D. *The American Occupational Structure*. New York: Wiley, 1967.

Cartwright, D.C., and Zander, A., eds. *Group Dynamics: Research and Theory*. New York: Harper and Row, 1968.

Hackman, J.R. "Group Influences on Individuals." In *Handbook of Industrial and Organizational Psychology*, edited by M.D. Dunnette. Chicago: Rand McNally, 1976.

Hollander, E.P., and Willis, R.H. "Some Current Issues in the Psychology of Conformity and Nonconformity." *Psychological Bulletin* 68 (1967): 62-76.

Likert, R. *New Patterns of Management*. New York: McGraw-Hill, 1961.

Lott, A.J., and Lott, B.E. "Group Cohesiveness As Interpersonal Attraction: A Review of Relationships with Antecedent and Consequent Variables." *Psychological Bulletin* 64 (1965): 259-302.

Shaw, M.E. *Group Dynamics: The Psychology of Small Group Behavior*. New York: McGraw-Hill, 1976.

CHAPTER

25

MBGO: Putting Some Team Spirit Into MBO*

Management by objectives (MBO), when properly used, can be an effective procedure for improving performance. However, with modification, MBO can be made into a much more potent management instrument—management by group objectives (MBGO).

MBO VS. MBGO

With MBO, managers relate to each of their subordinates as individuals. All interaction is *person to person*. Consequently, subordinates frequently strive to achieve their own objectives while disregarding whether their colleagues achieve theirs. Even worse, the evaluation and reward processes of MBO can cause each work group member to avoid cooperating with, and giving help to, other group members. Because each person's achievement if compared with the relative success of the other members, if they do well, his work is likely to be seen less favorably. If they do poorly, his work will be seen more favorably.

Thus work group members may even act so as to contribute to the poor performance of their colleagues. This kind of behavior is clearly contrary to the best interests of the firm and adversely affects its success. In fact, many firms have found peer competition among work group members so costly that they have abandoned MBO.

With MBGO, managers and their subordinates act as teams in setting objectives and evaluating performance in achieving them. Thus

*From Rensis Likert and M. Scott Fisher, "MBGO: Putting Some Team Spirit into MBO," *Personnel* (Jan.-Feb., 1977) pp. 40-47. Reprinted by permission of the publisher interaction is between the manager and all the subordinates who report to him or her in *group* problem-solving sessions.

In addition, with MBGO, managers and their subordinates not only set overall objectives but also set the particular goals that the manager and the group expect each member to achieve. Each member therefore knows what is expected of him or her and what is expected of the others and why. Each knows how these various objectives are interrelated and is aware of how failure to accomplish any one of them will adversely affect the capability of the others to accomplish their objectives and thus the objectives of the group.

Consequently, the expectations of peers and the desire not to let down one's colleagues make MBGO a more potent motivational technique than MBO. They also help to create an atmosphere of cooperative teamwork. Work group members are motivated to help each other by sharing the workload and by sharing new insights and better strategies for accomplishing desired results. If one member of the work group is temporarily overloaded, a colleague can easily pick up part of the load to ensure organizational success and avoid breakdowns. There is no need for precise definitions of responsibility, which eliminates fear and the desire to protect one's "turf" from encroachment by others. Only broad, general assignments are required because of the cooperative relationships among work group members. Moreover, each cycle of objective setting and evaluation reaffirms the area of individual responsibility of each member of the group and reemphasizes the need for each to feel responsible for the success of the entire group's efforts.

HOW MBGO WORKS

In setting objectives with MBGO, the manager and his work group use the same information as with MBO. Past results are available for each relevant performance variable showing the level achieved in relation to the objectives set for that variable. If data on the human organization variables are available, such as measurements of leadership, organizational climate, motivation, and communication, objectives are set for them as well as for performance results.

Objectives are also set for appropriate time periods. Specific goals may be set for short time periods such as three to six months or for one year. More general objectives are set for longer time periods such as three, five, or ten years.

The manager's performance expectations are an important force in the group problem-solving sessions in which objectives are set. Managers who attain impressive results with MBGO have high-performance, no-nonsense goals for themselves and for their organizational units. This orientation of the manager provides a pervasive atmosphere that encourages the group to set objectives that they can achieve and at the same time work hard to do so. In other words, the objectives are possible but they stretch the organization to achieve them and yield great satisfaction as they are met.

The evaluation of achievement is, of course, also a group problem-solving process. At the end of each period, the manager and his or her work group examine all relevant data and assess how well the specific goals and overall objectives have been achieved. In addition, they consider how well each member has achieved the objectives that were the responsibilities of a particular individual. New goals and objectives are then set for the next period. Again, each member of the work group knows what is expected both over all and from each group member.

MBGO AND SYSTEM 4

For MBGO to make full use of the powerful motivational forces that a team effort can develop, managers must be skilled in the use of group

HOW SYSTEM 4 MANAGEMENT WORKS

System 4 combines a method for measuring the characteristics of an organization with a prescription for the ideal state of the organization and a formula for moving the organization from its actual state to the ideal state.

First, how do you measure an organization? Likert, together with his colleagues, developed a questionnaire; typically, it ranges from 50 to 100 items, the responses describing what he calls the management system—a cluster of factors that includes organizational climate, leadership behavior, and the perceptions of the employees regarding such things as decision making, communication, and satisfaction. Everyone in the organization or unit of the organization being studied completes the questionnaire.

On the basis of this information, it's possible to prepare a profile of organizational characteristics and to identify the organization as being System 1, Exploitative-Authoritative; System 2, Benevolent-Authoritative; System 3, Consultative; System 4, Participative Group; or somewhere in between.

The ideal state of the organization—at least, it's the most nearly ideal of the four—is System 4. By ideal, Likert means organizational performance or effectiveness defined in both humanistic terms —maximum employee satisfaction and morale—and the traditional business criteria of performance—maximum output and earnings, the latter variables being measured by standards independent of the questionnaire, are optimized. Specifically, System 4 appears to be consistently associated with the most effective performance and System 1 with the least effective performance in every kind of organization Likert has studied. System 2 was more effective than System 1 but less effective than System 3, and so forth.

(For a more detailed description of how System 4 was successfully implemented, see "At General Motors: System 4 Builds Performance and Profits," *Organizational Dynamics*, Winter 1975.)

problem solving and train their work groups to use it well. This, again, is an important difference between MBO and MBGO. MBO is described as being equally useful by authoritarian managers as by those using more participative management styles. MBGO requires the manager to use an effective form of participative management such as System 4.

The work group is most likely to become proficient in group problem solving if the manager has regular meetings with the work group and uses group problem solving routinely. This will develop the group's skill in problem solving and create high team loyalty among its members.

In some organizations, there has been a "creeping change." They are now using MBGO and are getting good results. MBGO, consequently, does not represent for them a radical change from MBO, but a sound further development. Since the change is gradual and incomplete, such firms are not yet deriving the full benefit from a complete application of MBGO. These firms would gain more if they made a deliberate effort to apply in a coordinated manner all the steps required for the effective use of MBGO.

MBGO IN A RETAIL SALES DIVISION

A retail sales division of a firm making consumer products began using MBGO about two years ago, following the division's shift to a System 4 management style. The result has been an improvement in both group goal setting and group effectiveness.

Local managers meet quarterly with their regional sales managers. Distances prevent more frequent meetings. The meetings are used for information sharing and training and for goal setting and problem solving.

Each group sets goals for the next quarter and at a subsequent meeting three months later evaluates the results. They discuss problems, share ideas, make plans, and revise goals for the next quarter.

The groups have tended to set conservative goals, especially at first. The regional managers have responded supportively, as have group members, and they have offered ideas that help the groups improve their performance. Charts mailed monthly show the average for the region and for each of the groups.

The sharing of data, which all requested and agreed to, helped team members set progressively higher standards for themselves. No punitive action resulted from failure to achieve goals. Praise and a modest commission—together with the satisfaction of group goal achievement—have been the rewards.

Participants have reported having a positive experience with group goal setting and problem solving. Regional managers have found that the group activity enabled them to play more of a supportive role than they had experienced previously with their groups.

The results were also good for the business. During the first year, the retail groups contributed $292,000 to corporate profits above plan,

FIGURE 25-1 MBGO Linkage in an Automotive Plant

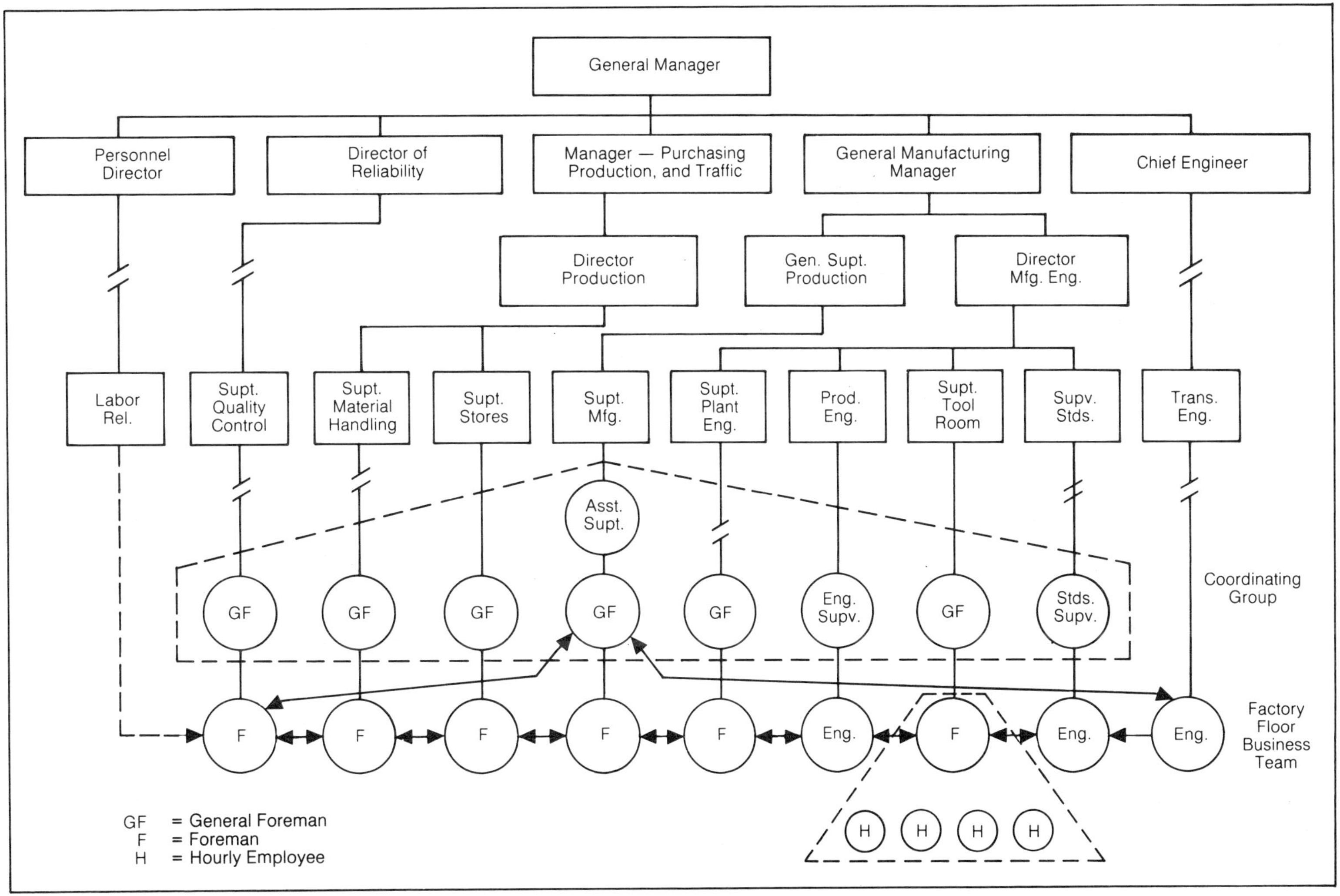

a 27 percent increase over the previous year. Equally impressive results were reported by other regions involved in MBGO activity.

This improvement was achieved in the 1974-1975 fiscal year—a period of general economic recession. Factors such as growth in personnel or additional territory did not contribute to the improvement. One factor, however, that may have contributed to the increase was an improved relationship with manufacturing. There was greater confidence in the quality of manufacturing and speed of delivery—both of which increased markedly. The manufacturing segment of the business had been involved in System 4 management development, including MBGO, over the previous two years. Direct labor productivity in manufacturing increased by 22 percent over the two-year period of development and 69 percent since the beginning of the project four years ago.

For the period ending the first quarter of the 1976 fiscal year, sales for the division ($13 million) were 26 percent greater than for the same period in 1975.

MBGO IN AN AUTOMOTIVE PLANT

An assembly plant in an automobile company adopted MBGO principles by organizing teams of foremen on each shift. The foremen meet weekly and sometimes twice weekly to discuss mutual problems and manage the daily activity at the floor level. Team members represent all key functions—production, quality control, maintenance, material handling, stores, and engineering (see figure 25-1).

The foremen, through their cross-functional teams and group goal-setting activities, have been able to improve coordination significantly and improve the effectiveness of their operation. Communication among the foremen improved dramatically, and productivity rose by 15 percent in some areas during the program's first year. Scrap savings were $108,000 (25 percent) under budget for the period.

The following year the foremen teams attempted to reduce the number of rejects at the final assembly operation. Over a one-year period, rejects were reduced from 14 to 7 percent, and efforts to increase the hourly rate on each machine met with equally impressive success.

SUMMARY

With MBGO, participation in setting the work group's objectives heightens the motivation of each member to achieve both his or her own objectives and the objectives of other members of the group. Loyalty to other members is added to loyalty to the superior as a source of motivation. MBGO, consequently, surpasses MBO in achieving better understanding among group members of their interdependent objectives and relationships, in mobilizing greater motivation among a manager's subordinates to reach objectives, and in establishing better teamwork and coordination.

DISCUSSION QUESTIONS

1. Think about the last job interview you had for either a full or part-time position. What did the interviewer's office tell you about his or her status in the work organization?

2. What is the difference between ascribed and achieved status? Describe a person you know whose ascribed status is incongruent with his or her achieved status.

3. Identify the four persons of your same age and sex with whom you are most friendly. Including yourself, rank these persons from low to high in terms of their status. Based upon your experience with this group of friends, does the person you identified as the highest-status group member receive more communications from the other group members than does any other person? Why?

4. Formulate at least three guidelines for the management of an organization's status system.

5. In the *male* business world, why can it be said that "there is not and can never be any serious interest in fashion as women understand it"?

6. Explain why women's apparel is a "badge of servitude."

7. If you were going for a job interview at a bank, what would you ideally want to wear? Be specific as to style, color, and so on. Why did you select the outfit you did?

8. Describe the process a collection of employees goes through in being a functional work group.

9. When can high levels of group cohesiveness become organizationally dysfunctional?

10. Assume you were asked to compose the long-range planning committee of your community's United Way Fund. What team-building variables would you consider in composing the group? How might consideration of these variables affect the technical quality of the plans the committee produced and their political acceptability within the community?

11. What is a norm? What can managers do to facilitate conformity to work-group norms?

12. Do norms govern private thoughts and feelings? Why?

13. What are the differences between MBO and MBGO?

14. Explain how MBGO works.

15. What is "System 4 Management?" How does it relate to MBGO?

16. How might a group's status structure affect the use of MBGO?

SECTION VIII

Maintaining Organizational Vitality

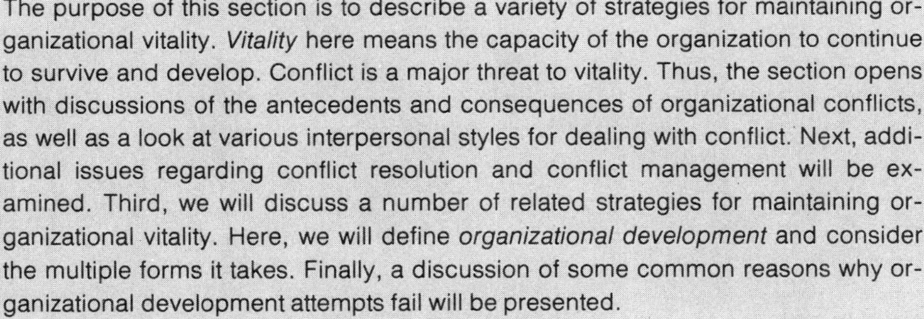

The purpose of this section is to describe a variety of strategies for maintaining organizational vitality. *Vitality* here means the capacity of the organization to continue to survive and develop. Conflict is a major threat to vitality. Thus, the section opens with discussions of the antecedents and consequences of organizational conflicts, as well as a look at various interpersonal styles for dealing with conflict. Next, additional issues regarding conflict resolution and conflict management will be examined. Third, we will discuss a number of related strategies for maintaining organizational vitality. Here, we will define *organizational development* and consider the multiple forms it takes. Finally, a discussion of some common reasons why organizational development attempts fail will be presented.

KEY TERMS

STYLES OF CONFLICT RESOLUTION
- Tough battler
- Friendly helper
- Runaway
- Problem solver

PROBLEM-SOLVING METHODS

POWER-ORIENTED METHODS

ORGANIZATIONAL DEVELOPMENT

ORGANIZATIONAL CLIMATE
- Autonomy
- Structure
- Reward orientation
- Warmth and support

OBJECTIVES

1. To identify structural sources of organizational conflict
2. To describe various styles of dealing with conflict
3. To identify the positive *and* negative consequences of conflict
4. To describe the differences between power-oriented and problem-solving methods of dealing with conflict

5. To define organizational development and describe some of its more popular forms
6. To describe how alternating an organization's climate may be viewed as an organizational development intervention
7. To identify common reasons why organizational development attempts fail

CHAPTER 26

Conflict Resolution*

Conflict, whether in the form of open hostility or quiet dissension, has been with us since the beginning of mankind. Even though conflict between persons can be thought of as a naturally occurring event, we are all well aware that conflict can be a destructive force. For example, conflict between a superior and subordinate can lead to one or both parties having their feelings hurt, the subordinate quitting his or her job, or the subordinate somehow attempting to sabotage the plans of the superior. As we will show later in this chapter, however, conflict also can serve to enhance the effectiveness of an organization. Since we can safely assume that conflict will be present but not always as a destructive force, the central question becomes: "How does one effectively manage conflict and its resolution to insure that the organization benefits rather than suffers from the occasional clashes between persons, groups, and departments? The purpose of this chapter is to offer some answers to this question.

The first part of the chapter focuses on the antecedents of organizational conflict. Next we will examine in detail various styles of dealing with conflict. Finally, we will discuss the positive and negative consequences of organizational conflict and identify various managerial strategies for successfully coping with conflict.

ANTECEDENTS OF CONFLICT

Sam and John are staff physicians in a large metropolitan hospital. Their distaste for one another is common knowledge throughout the hospital. Behind each other's back, they continuously criticize one

*Portions of the material for this chapter are drawn from Filley (1975).

another's work and personal mannerisms. The only time they speak directly to each other is during the weekly staff meeting; any position Sam takes, John will attack and *vice versa*. Everyone dreads attending these meetings because they quickly degenerate into a battle between Sam and John. Most people explain the conflict between the two physicians in terms of a clash between dominant personalities or in terms of professional jealousy.

Admittedly, conflict does erupt in work organizations because of the inability of two or more persons to get along and work well together. In most instances, however, there are a number of situational factors that have helped set the stage for conflict. A manager concerned with reducing the potential for organizational conflict can search out these sources of tension and attempt to remedy the situation before disaster strikes. In the remainder of this section, we will identify several situational factors that are conducive to outbreaks of organizational conflict.

Situational factors

When two or more persons, groups, or departments are unclear as to which party is responsible for performing a set of activities, the potential for conflict is heightened. Imagine, for example, one party accusing another party of not performing the activities assigned to it, while the accused party is thinking, "I didn't know that was my responsibility." Also typical of this source of conflict would be two parties finding out after the fact that they have both performed the same set of activities, thus duplicating each other's work. The major reason these *jurisdictional disputes* occur is that the manager in charge has failed to define clearly the boundaries of each of his or her subordinates' areas of responsibility. The astute manager will determine who is responsible for performing which tasks and communicate this information to all involved parties. Such structuring of the work environment will undoubtedly reduce the potential for conflict among members of a work group, be they production-line employees, committee members, or department heads.

Competition for scarce resources may be the principal cause behind many, if not most, organizational conflicts. The scarce resource in contention can be any number of things—a pay raise, a promotion, additional personnel, an office with a window, a new piece of office equipment, or the use of a secretary's time. Whenever the wants and desires of two or more parties total *more than* the available pool of resources, conflict will occur. Thus, when a manager faces the responsibility of allocating scarce resources that two or more parties desire, he or she should plan ahead and not make a last-minute allocation decision. This planning involves determining the basis for allocating the resource, assessing the needs and wants of the parties competing for the resource, making the allocation decision, and communicating to the parties what the decision is *and* how and why it was made. Such careful attention to the allocation of seemingly unimportant resources will lessen the chances of people's feelings being hurt and hostilities rising to the surface. The manager who haphazardly makes allocation decisions without considering the thoughts and feelings of the involved parties and adequately justifying his or her decision to those parties is looking for trouble.

Barriers to open and honest communications between parties are a frequent cause of organizational conflicts. Many times these barriers are not due to lack of trust between the parties or any other interpersonal reason; rather, communication barriers are often physical in nature. For example, Jane manages a small satellite plant that supplies parts to her firm's major assembly plant twenty miles away. Jim, the manager of the assembly plant, and Jane are always at each other's throats. Either Jim is upset with Jane for not supplying promptly the appropriate parts as called for by his production schedule, or Jane is annoyed with Jim for not notifying her early enough what his production plans are. If Jane and Jim were not separated by twenty miles and were able to see one another on a daily basis, their conflict-generating communication problem probably never would have occurred.

Another communication barrier often exists when parties are separated by time rather than distance. The best example of this source of irritation is the failure of the day- and night-shift supervisors in an organization to communicate with one another. Frequently, the night supervisor is angry because he or she is responsible for "cleaning up" after the day-shift employees; and the day-shift supervisor is furious with the night-shift supervisor for not completing a job. If there were an hour or two overlap between the shifts of the two supervisors, the communication barrier between them would be broken down and the likelihood of conflict reduced.

The lesson to be learned by the manager supervising employees who are separated by time or distance and whose job responsibilities are interrelated is to be aware of the potential communication barrier and to ensure that all parties have sufficient opportunities to communicate openly. This show of managerial sensitivity should prevent the development of a conflict situation.

Parties that are dependent upon one another are more likely to engage in conflict than parties whose jobs are independent from one another. If, in order to complete his or her own work, one employee must rely upon the abilities of others to complete their work, the potential for conflict is present. Thus, one way to reduce the level of conflict between two organizational members whose jobs are interdependent is to reduce the dependency between the parties. This can be done by restructuring the employees' jobs or by reassigning the employees to noninterdependent jobs. Either one of these strategies is frequently used when the employees involved are considered valuable assets to the organization, and the level of conflict between them has become intolerable.

The level of conflict in an organization increases as the organization becomes more differentiated. *Differentiation* increases as the number of levels in the organization's hierarchy increases and as the number of distinct departments at the same level increases. Exactly why organizational differentiation leads to conflict is unknown. It may be that the compartmentalization of people caused by differentiation gives rise to a number of vested-interest groups within the organization; the differing views these groups hold may lead to the greater levels of conflict seen in highly differentiated organizations. Whatever the case, the manager in a highly differentiated organization must somehow integrate the disparate parts of the organization and overcome the increased potential for unmanagable levels of conflict. A number of *integration* strategies are available. For example, permanent or temporary teams composed of personnel from various organizational levels and/or various departments can be established for the purpose of maximizing the level of cooperative behavior.

When a boss says to two of his or her employees, "I want the two of you to decide together what to do about this issue," he or she is setting the stage for conflict between the two employees. In general, when parties are required to make joint decisions, the probability for conflict occurring increases. As noted in chapter 18, groups frequently produce better and more acceptable decisions than do individuals; therefore, managers are often required to encourage their employees to engage in joint decision making. The solution to reducing the conflict potential generated by joint decision making is *not* to prevent employees from participating in those decision contexts where they can make a contribution. Rather, when relying on a group to make a decision, managers should channel the conflict that will be present in the group in a productive direction. To do this, the manager can use one of a number of structured group decision-making techniques, such as those presented in chapters 18 and 19. The point is, joint decision making is often necessary, even though it frequently leads to conflict; and, it is the manager's responsibility to cope effectively with that conflict rather than despairing of it.

Once the manager decides to rely upon a group rather than an individual decision, the worst possible thing he or she can do in terms of generating conflict is to require everyone in the group to agree publicly with the decision. In other words, requiring the members of a group to reach *consensus* is conflict producing. Disagreement between parties is natural, so, in most instances, it makes sense to rely on a majority rather than a consensus group decision. In fact, even though a manager requires a consensus decision, he or she probably won't get one. The disgruntled employee dissatisfied with the group's decision may publicly raise his or her hand in support of the group's decision—and then leave the group meeting with no intention at all of helping to implement the decision. Managers, therefore, should have a solid reason for imposing a consensus decision rule on a group and should not do so unless they are fairly certain that their reason is worth the inevitable conflict.

Standardized procedures, rules, and policies that are not consistently enforced are resisted, and this employee resistance to authority leads to conflict. For example, Ann and Morris both work in the window-display department of a large retail store. The company policy regarding tardiness states that if an employee is more than five minutes late to work, the employee's wages will be docked for the time absent from work. Ann, who happens to be a close friend of her supervisor, comes to work ten or fifteen minutes late at least once a week, but her wages have never been docked. On the other hand, Morris, who is usually prompt, shows up to work about ten minutes late on two consecutive days, and *his* wages are adjusted. Morris and his friends in the department are outraged at how inequitably Morris has been treated. They begin to agitate and plot a confrontation with their supervisor. Organizational regulations that are consistently and fairly enforced serve to control employee behavior and can, in fact, reduce the likelihood of conflict. But managers who *arbitrarily* enforce their organization's regulations will inevitably find themselves embroiled in a conflict.

Another source of conflict is the failure to agree about ends prior to discussing means. Let's look at the case of Kay and Laura, two nursing administrators, who meet to discuss the strategy they will use to recruit a new employee. The two administrators violently disagree: Kay wants to recruit on the campuses of four-year universities, and Laura wants to recruit on the campuses of two-year community colleges. Kay and Laura will never agree on a recruitment strategy because Kay is interested in hiring a staff nurse who can ultimately be promoted to a head-nurse position, which requires a four-year degree, and Laura is interested in hiring a staff nurse with no aspirations of being promoted. Thus, Kay and Laura have failed to agree upon their recruiting objectives (ends) before discussing a recruiting strategy (means). Managers must make every attempt possible to ensure that the parties involved in any sort of planning process agree on their objective *before* the parties begin planning how to achieve those objectives. Without such a preventive step, unmanageable conflict is bound to erupt.

The final structural source of conflict we will discuss is probably the most obvious—unresolved prior conflicts. Poorly managed conflicts that aren't resolved to the satisfaction of all parties involved tend to fester over time and explode at a later date with an even greater degree of force. The conflict-resolution styles managers use should generate sufficient levels of commitment to the chosen solution to allow all the parties involved to recognize that the matter is closed. Typically, the manager who relies solely on the power of his or her office to resolve organizational conflicts will not generate those sufficient levels of commitment.

Figure 26-1 depicts those factors frequently found to be associated with high levels of organizational conflict. When jurisdictional boundaries are unclear, resources are scarce, communication barriers exist, parties are dependent on one another, the organization is highly differentiated, parties make joint decisions with a consensus rule, regulations are enforced arbitrarily, means are discussed prior to agreeing on ends, and prior conflicts are unresolved, conditions are ripe for major organizational conflicts. We hope that our brief discussion of these factors will one day help you reduce the potential

FIGURE 26-1
Sources of Conflict

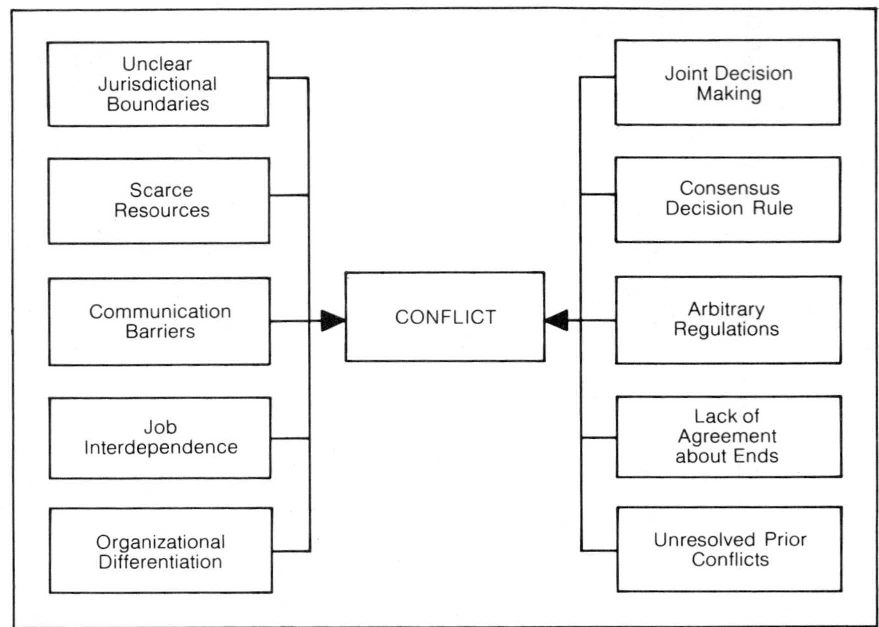

for disruptive conflicts in your organization. The following material should also help you meet that objective.

STYLES OF CONFLICT RESOLUTION[1]

As you all know, not everyone reacts the same to conflict situations or behaves the same when in conflict with another person. A manager's style of resolving conflicts will both influence his or her personal success and have a long-term impact on organizational effectiveness. So being aware of your conflict resolution style and, if necessary, modifying that style are important managerial functions. What follows are descriptions of five general styles of resolving conflicts.

1. *Tough battler.* These persons care little about what other people think of them. Tough Battlers think conflict occurs only when others are too stupid, stubborn, or misinformed to see that their position is the right one. Confronted with such an "inferior" person who openly disagrees with their position, Tough Battlers attack viciously. Winning a conflict exhilarates Tough Battlers, while losing reduces their sense of self-worth. Because they consider winning so important, Tough Battlers frequently show signs of anger, frustration, and outrage during a conflict. When they fail to prove that their opponents are wrong with "facts," Tough Battlers behave much like spoiled children who are told they can't have any more candy.

[1]Material for this section is drawn, in part, from Blake and Mouton (1970) and Hall (1969).

2. *Friendly helper.* Winning the acceptance and friendship of others tends to be the dominant need of Friendly Helpers. In a conflict situation, they are likely to say, "If that's what you really want and it will make you happy, I'll go along with it." Friendly Helpers think that harmony and cooperation are the natural order of things. They view conflict as unnatural and something that occurs because someone's ego was hurt. In a conflict situation, Friendly Helpers rarely if ever show anger; more typically, they crack jokes to inject some humor in an attempt to cool things off. Also, they frequently suggest that the parties in conflict engage in some other activity (for example, breaking for lunch or taking up some new business), anything to avoid confrontation. In the end, however, Friendly Helpers usually yield to their opponents and lose rather than taking the chance of hurting someone's feelings.

3. *Runaway.* These persons see the probability of winning a conflict as near zero and, therefore, feel conflict is a personally punishing experience. In the face of conflict, Runaways flee. This flight can either be psychological or physical. Psychologically, Runaways ignore the presence of conflict and will not take sides in a disagreement even if their interests are to be affected by the outcome. Thus, they feel little or no commitment to a decision reached through conflict. The obvious physical reaction of Runaways is to leave the scene of the conflict by not showing up at a meeting, requesting a transfer, resigning from the organization, or engaging in some other form of escape behavior. In general, Runaways tend to keep interpersonal involvements at a minimum.

4. *Compromiser.* Compromisers actually enjoy the political maneuvering involved in a conflict, and they are not above showing their anger or their charm, depending on the demands of the situation. In the face of conflict, Compromisers seek a middle ground that they feel will satisfy all the parties involved. If that doesn't work, they will fall back on such tactics as voting, trading, and making side payments (that is, bribery). Compromisers value the quick settlement of a conflict. Frequently, mediators of labor-management disputes are described as Compromisers.

5. *Problem solver.* These persons feel that conflict is natural and that conflicts can be resolved to the satisfaction of all parties involved without sacrificing anyone's goals. Unfortunately, true Problem Solvers are exceedingly rare individuals. In a conflict situation, Problem Solvers create trust by being honest and open while, at the same time, being sensitive to people's feelings. In addition, they encourage everyone to participate in the resolution process and to express their true thoughts, feelings, and positions. In total, Problem Solvers seek to fulfill their own needs without ignoring the needs of others.

It is important to note that the boundaries between the conflict resolution styles identified are not hard and fast, and the styles people use are not totally consistent in all situations. In other words, a person's dominant conflict resolution style, for example, can reflect a combination of Tough Battler and Compromiser, Compromiser and Problem Solver, or Friendly Helper and Runaway. Further, a person may rely principally on one conflict resolution style at work and another style at home. Nevertheless, the five styles presented offer a useful way of thinking about how different people deal with conflict.

The research provides some clues about the outcomes of conflicts with parties relying on the various styles (Cummings, Harnett, & Stevens, 1971). For example, the Tough Battler usually will win against the Friendly Helper but will stalemate when opposing another Tough Battler. A Problem Solver also usually will win against a Friendly Helper but will more often than not lose when facing a Tough Battler. These outcomes refer to the win-lose status of the individual and not necessarily to the well-being of the organization. In general, the health of the organization is enhanced when all the parties involved in an organizational conflict can say they have won. Win-win outcomes, however, tend to occur only when a Problem Solver faces a Problem Solver. We will now describe the characteristics of this optimum type of conflict situation.

MANAGING CONFLICT

When two parties are in conflict, the confrontation is usually resolved with one party feeling it has won and the other party feeling it has lost. Another common outcome is for both parties to feel they have lost. As we previously noted, however, it is possible to obtain a win-win outcome with both parties feeling like winners. It may seem far-fetched to think that both parties in a conflict could walk away winners. Admittedly, the vast majority of conflicts do not result in a win-win outcome. However, if a manager can convince the parties to stick to the following guidelines, the chances for obtaining a win-win outcome are greatly enhanced.

1. Focus on defeating the mutual problem rather than each other. Try not to personalize the conflict; instead, view the *problem* as a *depersonalized objective* to be mutually achieved through joint problem solving.

2. Avoid voting, averaging, or trading to reach a solution. Talk things out.

3. Seek facts to resolve points of disagreement. Don't make decisions based on pure speculation.

4. Recognize that conflict can be helpful. Avoid making conflict a threatening or defense-invoking process.

5. Don't fail to recognize others' needs and positions. Avoid acting solely on behalf of your own interest.

If, prior to the onset of conflict, you can demonstrate to the parties involved that adherence to these guidelines will benefit both individuals *and* the organization, then they probably will adopt the guidelines. Alan Filley's (1975) highly readable book, *Interpersonal Conflict Resolution*, does much to convince the reader that the Problem Solver approach is viable and that it offers a sound basis for training in effective conflict management. In the following chapter, Filley describes his own approach to conflict management.

Win-win outcomes

Assuming a win-win outcome is obtained, what benefits can the organization anticipate? First, the probability of future, more serious conflicts erupting is reduced because the current conflict has been resolved. Second, the resolution probably reflects a quality decision because the process of obtaining a win-win outcome has tapped the creative potential of the parties involved. Finally, group cohesiveness and performance are generally enhanced because the parties have demonstrated to themselves that they can work successfully together.

Win-lose and lose-lose outcomes

Obviously, the preceding guidelines can't or won't be strictly followed in all conflict situations. So let's reconsider those win-lose and lose-lose outcomes. The characteristics of conflict associated with win-lose and lose-lose outcomes include seeing issues only from your own point of view; an "us versus them" way of thinking; the personalization of issues and positions; and emphasizing the immediate resolution of the conflict rather than allowing time to talk things out. In addition, win-lose outcomes frequently occur when a dominant party exercises his or her power or authority or when a majority voting rule is used. Lose-lose outcomes frequently occur when parties "split the difference," use bribery, or call in a third-party neutral. From the organization's perspective, inevitable costs associated with win-lose and lose-lose outcomes include a desire on the part of losers to get even, low levels of commitment and support by the losers for the chosen solution, and a reduced attachment to the organization by the losers. The totality of these negative consequences is likely to reduce job performance and ultimately affect organizational effectiveness adversely.

The manager who faces a conflict situation has a major problem. The circumstances surrounding the given situation, as well as the personalities of the parties involved, often make it impossible for the parties to use that style of conflict resolution that leads to a win-win outcome. Also, the use of certain tactics—for example, relying on managerial authority, using a majority voting rule, splitting the difference, bribery, or employing a neutral—creates one or more losers, and the reactions of these losers produce largely negative consequences. So what do managers do when they can't convince all the parties involved in a conflict situation to adopt a Problem Solver approach? One thing they can do is use a negotiated decision-making strategy described by three organizational behaviorists, Fremont Shull, Andre' Delbecq, and Larry Cummings (1970). Their strategy accepts open conflict, provides for a due process between conflicting parties and proportional representation of each party, allows for compromise, and treats negotiation as a legitimate means of evolving organizational policies.

Negotiated decision making

The negotiated decision-making strategy requires that the manager compose a group of several representatives from each party. The number of representatives per party should be proportional to the size or power of that party—with one exception: if it can be avoided, a minority party should never be represented by fewer than two persons. It is difficult for one person to reflect adequately the possibly diverse opinions represented in his or her group; and it is doubtful that one person standing in isolation will have the opportunity or courage to exert any meaningful level of influence in the resolution process. Then the manager should appoint an impartial person, acceptable to all the involved parties, to chair the negotiated decision-making group. Once the group has been established, the representatives must be informed of the roles they are expected to play in the decision-making process. Essentially, each representative is instructed to articulate clearly and to protect the dominant concerns of his or her party and not to speak on behalf of his or her own narrow interests. In addition, each representative is told to seek a compromise solution that will be acceptable to his or her party.

There are three actual processes used in negotiated decision-making:

1. The chair ensures orderly communication and thus allows each party the opportunity to be heard while not allowing any one party to dominate the discussion.

2. Disputes are formally resolved through voting, with each party possessing veto power.

3. The use of "brute force" to obtain a compromise is avoided; instead, participants rely upon a variety of analytic, factually oriented procedures. The style of the representatives engaged in the negotiation process should be characterized as honest and open, accepting of due process, willing to allow the chair to mediate, and devoid of emotional hostility and personal aggression.

Finally, the negotiated decision-making group should desire, above all, to reach agreement. Further, it should share the opinion that conflict is natural and that individuals have the freedom to disagree. The group also should be open to new analytical approaches and recognize that *partial* agreement is realistic, legitimate, and acceptable. For the negotiated decision-making strategy to be successful, management and participating parties must adhere to the structure, roles, processes, and style, and norms just outlined. A well-accepted, skillful chairperson is, therefore, essential. Such persons most frequently are found outside the organization and have a reputation for successfully playing the role of Compromiser. In the industrial relations area, these types of people assume the role of a professional neutral and act as fact-finders, mediators, and arbitrators in the process of resolving labor-management disputes. But managers should not ignore the talents of these persons for resolving disputes other than labor-management conflicts.

In spite of its advantages, the negotiated decision-making strategy does not provide an ideal solution (win-win) to a conflict situation; therefore, it should be used only when all the parties involved cannot adopt the Problem Solver style. The negotiated decision-making strategy provides the manager with *one means* of resolving conflict when there is no other reasonable option.

One other managerial strategy for resolving conflict also warrants our attention. Virtually every manager will, on occasion, resort to the legitimate authority invested in his or her position by the organization to resolve a conflict. This is only natural and right and should occur most frequently under three circumstances: there is pressure to make a quick decision, the point at issue appears to be relatively unimportant, and the manager involved has a reputation for being fair and just. The point is, managers should not feel guilty about exercising the power of their office. In fact, it is their responsibility to the organization to do so.

SUMMARY

Conditions are ripe for the outbreak of major organization conflicts when (a) jurisdictional boundaries are unclear, (b) resources are scarce, (c) communication barriers exist, (d) parties are dependent on one another, (e) the organization is highly differentiated, (f) parties make joint decisions with a consensus rule, (g) regulations are enforced arbitrarily, (h) means are discussed prior to agreeing on ends, and (i) prior conflicts are unresolved. Managers can and should take steps to reduce each of these sources of tension.

There are five general styles of conflict resolution: Tough Battler, Friendly Helper, Runaway, Compriser, and Problem Solver. If all parties involved in a conflict adopt the Problem Solver style, a win-win outcome is obtainable.

Win-win outcomes result when the parties focus on defeating a mutual problem; avoid voting, averaging, or trading; seek facts to resolve points of disagreement; recognize that conflict can be helpful; and recognize others' needs and positions. Win-win outcomes lead to the reduction of future conflicts, quality decisions, and increased group cohesiveness and performance. But practical considerations often prohibit win-win outcomes. When this occurs, managers may want to rely upon negotiated decision making. This conflict resolution strategy accepts open conflict; provides for a due process between parties and proportional representation of each party; allows for compromise; and treats negotiation as a legitimate means of evolving organizational policies.

REFERENCES

Blake, R.R., and Mouton, J.S. "The Fifth Achievement." *Journal of Applied Behavioral Science* 6 (1970): 413-26.

Cummings, L.L.; Harnett, D.L.; and Stevens, O.J. "Risk, Fate, Conciliation and Trust: An International Study of Attitudinal Differences among Executives." *Academy of Management Journal* 14 (1971): 285-304.

Filley, A.C. *Interpersonal Conflict Resolution.* Glenview, Ill.: Scott, Foresman, 1975.

Hall, J. *Conflict Management Survey.* Conroe, Texas: Teleometrics, 1969.

Shull, F.A.; Delbecq, A.L., and Cummings, L.L. *Organizational Decision-Making.* New York: McGraw-Hill, 1970.

SUGGESTIONS FOR ADVANCED READINGS

Maier, N.R.F. *Problem Solving Discussions and Conferences: Leadership Methods and Skills.* New York: McGraw-Hill, 1963.

Thomas, K. "Conflict and Conflict Management." In *Handbook of Industrial and Organizational Psychology,* edited by M.D. Dunnette. Chicago: Rand McNally, 1976.

Walton, R.E., and McKersie, R.B. *A Behavioral Theory of Labor Negotiations: An Analysis of a Social Interaction System.* New York: McGraw-Hill, 1965.

CHAPTER 27

Some Normative Issues In Conflict Management*

This article addresses several issues related to conflict resolution and conflict management. It will consider the causes and consequences of conflict resolution methods by discussing three major premises. In discussing these premises, it will suggest why power-oriented methods such as bargaining and domination are popular for the resolution of conflicts and why methods of joint problem solving may be underutilized.[1] It will also consider possible consequences of these approaches, and it will suggest changes to precondition the use of problem solving in conflict management.

The thesis presented here is somewhat one-sided, though I hope not naively so. It suggests that problem solving and collaborative methods can, and generally should, be used in situations where parties are mutually dependent, where support for and implementation of agreement is required, and where the use of creative resources by the parties involved is important. It does not deny that power-oriented methods of conflict resolution are popular, that people use different methods for different kinds of conflicts, that there are some positive consequences to be gained from conflict, or that there are some situations where problem solving may prove too costly to use.[2] Ultimately, a contingency model of conflict resolution methods will be developed. Until then, the positive consequences of problem solving as a resolution strategy seem sufficiently documented to emphasize its use.

KNOWLEDGE VERSUS PERCEPTIONS

The first premise may help one to understand the relative frequency with which power-oriented rather than problem-solving methods are used for conflict resolution. The premise states that *knowledge is unlimited, but our perceptions are very limited.* In the present context, this suggests that there is a way to resolve a conflict to the mutual satisfaction and benefit of the parties but that perceptions of the situation encourage power-oriented behavior. Reference to Figure 27-1 will help clarify this; the figure shows the possible payoffs to two parties involved in a disagreement. The parties may be individuals or groups; the payoff may be satisfaction with the outcome, objective accomplishment, or a combination of satisfaction and objective attainment.[3]

Any point on the line labeled Power-Oriented Methods divides a fixed pie of 100 percent, or what is otherwise called a "zero-sum" situation (so named because when the amount won by one party and the amount lost by the other party are totaled, the sum is zero). Movement along the line changes the proportions of the shares, and one party's gain is the other party's loss. Most conflicts occur because the people involved perceive the situation in this way. For example, conflicts frequently occur about two solutions with no discussion or identification of the goals involved. This "my-way-versus-your-way" leads naturally to power-oriented behavior. If Person and Other both want an orange, they may fight until one gains all and the other loses all. If Person wins, then he gets 100 percent of the orange (Point A) and Other gets nothing.

Perceptions of fixed-sum situations also induce bargaining and compromise. Person and Other in Figure 1 may decide that the way to solve the dispute is to split the orange. In so doing, Person may try to

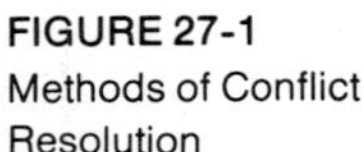

FIGURE 27-1
Methods of Conflict Resolution

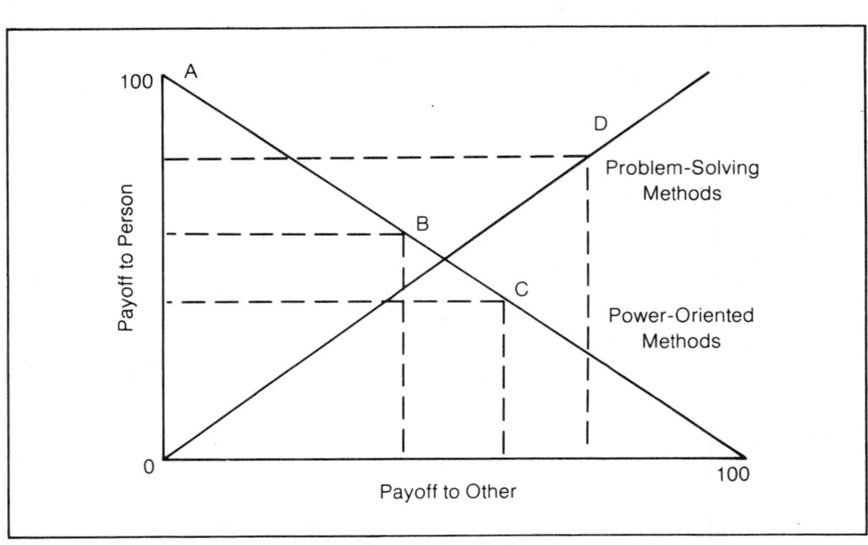

Adapted from K. Thomas, "Conflict and Conflict Management," in M. Dunnette, *Handbook of Industrial and Organizational Psychology* (Chicago: Rand-McNally, 1976), p. 899.

move from Point C, a smaller share, to Point B, a larger share. Other will try to do the opposite. Thus, bargaining is another power strategy created in part by the assumption of a zero-sum situation. The actual bargaining behavior by the parties and their effectiveness will depend upon such conditions as personality of the bargainers,[4] status differences,[5] and knowledge of bargaining strategies and tactics. Bargaining methods themselves may be readily learned through social models and courses or books on the subject.

THE PROBLEM-SOLVING ALTERNATIVE

In contrast with power-oriented methods, problem-solving methods assume that it is possible to find a solution to the conflict that will benefit both parties. As shown in Figure 27-1, they do not assume a zero-sum situation, since the gain of one party is equal to the loss of the other; instead, both parties may gain with the outcome. At point D, for example, both Person and Other each receive nearly 100 percent of possible payoff.

Their use of problem solving is encouraged when the parties take a we-versus-the-problem focus and seek to maximize the payoff to both parties. There is no great mystery to this process. It involves identifying the goals or values that each party wants to achieve with the present preferred alternatives, and then an exhaustive search for solutions that meet such combined goals. In the conflict about the orange, such discussion may indicate that one party wants the orange peel to bake a cake, while the other wants the pulp for its juice.

Problem-solving methods involve the application of facts and logic to solving problems that are created by conflictive situations. They evoke intellectual intensity rather than emotional intensity or power. Where a conflict is present and the perceptions, attitudes, feelings, situation, and process produce power-oriented relations between the parties, *conflict management* may alter these conditions, allowing the use of problem-solving methods.

To be illustrative rather than exhaustive, the following are possible changes in conditions which might allow problem-solving methods of conflict resolution to replace power-oriented methods.

Perceptual—identifying the problem in terms of goals rather than two solutions;[6] identifying the existence of mutually beneficial solutions;[7] changing the focus of attention to the problem rather than the other party;[8] identifying the costs of not agreeing; identifying the costs of self-sacrifice or domination.[9]

Attitudinal—enhancing desirability of mutually acceptable solutions by demonstrating the negative effects of losing on self-esteem and pointing out the unwillingness of the loser to support the agreement;[10] enhancing trust between parties by increasing mutuality of influence and by sharing relevant information.[11]

Affective—establishing positive feelings by each party about themselves and others[12] through clinical or fact-gathering methods;

minimizing feelings of anger, threat, or defensiveness by depersonalizing the problem and by using neutral language.

Situational—reducing time pressure;[13] providing neutral spatial arrangements;[14] increasing proximity and interaction of the parties;[15] equalizing or ignoring power differences.[16]

In addition, changes may be made in the process. Communication between parties can be clarified to insure common meaning;[17] issues can be stated specifically and not generalized;[18] problems may be jointly defined by the parties;[19] feedback can be made descriptive;[20] process stages of problem identification, solution generation, and evaluation may be separated;[21] problem statements may be redefined in terms of needs rather than solutions;[22] and process rules may proscribe forcing, acquiescing, or avoiding behaviors.[23]

The items stated above should suggest that it is possible to manage the resolution of conflictive situations so that problem-solving rather than power-oriented methods are used. Limited perceptions by the parties of both the process and the content considerations involved may be altered to more fully utilize their creative capacities. Such alteration may benefit from the use of a third party who can help manage conflict more effectively.

PRACTICE REINFORCES BEHAVIORS

The second major premise underlying the use of conflict resolution methods is that *practiced behaviors are self-reinforcing*. Behavior is a function of its consequences, and behaving in a familiar way is generally more comfortable than behaving in an unfamiliar way. Given a choice between new behavior which has the possibility of high payoff and practiced behavior that has a guaranteed payoff, people will often choose the latter. There are inherent rewards in the tried and true.

This premise may account for the fact that individuals use relatively stable patterns of conflict-resolving behaviors.[24] The tendency to use force or power in one situation predicts the use of that style in other situations as well—likewise compromising, acquiescing, problem solving, or other forms of conflict resolution. Thus, if people use methods of conflict resolution that are relatively dysfunctional when compared with other available methods, the anomaly may be explained by the development of such patterns of behavior before their consequences are known or by justifying relatively poor patterns when others are not known.

Power-oriented methods of dominance, submission, and bargaining are learned and practiced in a variety of socializing processes, while problem-solving methods appear to be underlearned as they apply to social interaction. Children, students, and employees learn to obey, and parents, teachers, and bosses learn to direct and control. Individuals learn to bargain and compete. In contrast, the methods of problem solving seem to be less well articulated and modeled.

The use of power-oriented methods is further justified by what might be called the "ethic of the good loser." This ethic may be expressed with the following logic:

—In a disagreement, there must be a winner and loser.

—The loser is not going to be me.

—So, you will have to lose.

—But losers can make trouble.

—So, I'll tell you that you are bad (or evil) if you complain about your loss.

As with the power-oriented behavior which accompanies it, the ethic of the good loser is learned in various socializing experiences. In a family, the child may be told to follow orders without question or that the parent is boss. In a classroom, the student may be told to obey the teacher, accepting information and authority without question. In a job, the employee may be told to accept orders and not challenge authority. The justification for such power-oriented relationships is often that the recipient will be a parent, teacher, or boss someday and take his turn at being a winner with his own set of good losers.

While one might wish to criticize such behavior on moral grounds, it is eminently susceptible to criticism on economic grounds as well. To the extent that the ethic of the good loser succeeds in making a person feel like a loser and lowers the person's self-esteem, the consequences may be a reduction of his intellectual and physical resources. When self-esteem is reduced, the result may be passive behavior, fatigue, less creativity, and even less measured intelligence. Organizations that seek "resourceful" members should attempt to raise, not lower, the self-esteem of those members.

OVERCOMING ENTRENCHED BEHAVIOR

If practiced behavior is self-rewarding, and if problem-solving methods are preferred over power-oriented methods, then there is value to be gained by giving people successful experiences in using problem-solving methods. In addition, by clearly identifying the processes of problem solving as well as those of power-oriented methods, parties might well elect to use the method shown to have the highest payoff under the particular circumstances at hand. Once a repertoire of conflict resolution methods is available, objective attainment rather than a limited range of behavior can become the determinant of method choice.

In this vein, even such traditionally power-laden situations as labor-management relations have begun to differentiate between situations that are best handled by problem solving between the union and company management and those that are perceived to require traditional bargaining.[25] Experiences in problem solving are being provided in other social units as well. In some families, children are included as equal participants in family meetings, where norms are set and decisions are made by consensus. In addition, models for training parents to deal with children as equal participants in decision making are becoming popular.[26]

In educational institutions at all levels, various forms of experimental programs have been established to enhance the self-esteem as well as the learning of participants. These include learning communities in which members agree on learning goals, individual learning contracts between student and teacher, and systems in which students share in the evaluation of their educational experience.

Finally, several problem-solving methods are being established and practiced in work organizations. Some examples include the use of joint problem-solving meetings between organizational units;[27] joint agreements between managers and employees about expected performance; group decision making on matters affecting different member needs; and various forms of work teams.

It is difficult to dismiss such developments in the use of problem-solving methods as trivial. Nor are they likely to be justified on the grounds of altruism. Instead, they seem to be based on the self-interest of parties who want resourceful people, productive energy expenditure, and viable organizations.

CHOOSING BETWEEN ALTERNATIVE BEHAVIORS

The third major premise in this discussion is that *in the same conflictive situation, the parties may choose to engage in conflict behavior or in problem-solving behavior.* In other words, conflict resolution may take the form of an exercise in power or an exercise in collaboration. These are two entirely different methods for dealing with the same situation. Either may be chosen, providing one sees the availability of both and knows how to perform both. Where one wants to defeat an opponent, define the objective from one's own point of view, or seek the exhilaration of the fight, then conflict behavior may be the better choice. On the other hand, where one wants to defeat the problem, arrive at a mutually beneficial outcome, or forego the emotion of the fight, problem solving may be preferred.

Neither form of resolution presupposes that conflicts do not or should not occur in organizations. Conflicts can have positive value. Minor conflicts seem to diffuse the number of major incidents[28] and can stimulate the search for new facts and creative solutions. The issue is not whether conflicts occur, but rather how they are resolved.

WHEN PROBLEM SOLVING IS PREFERRED

Previously, the professional literature on management and organization seemed to suggest that the ideal organization would have no conflict or that conflict should be eliminated. Now the literature more accurately is concerned with the forms and consequences of conflict behavior and, of interest here, the forms and consequences of conflict resolution.

It seems reasonable to suggest that where parties in an organization are dependent upon each other, cooperation is functional and desirable. Where conflicts occur, it seems that problem solving is a preferred strategy over force or compromise, since it will evoke greater cooperation between the parties in the end.

There is nothing startling in this view. It suggests why, even though individuals have fixed patterns of resolution behavior, problem solving is the most frequently used resolution strategy between superiors and subordinates.[29] It suggests why managers reporting incidents of effective and ineffective conflict resolution mention problem solving as a major type of effective resolution and forcing as a major type of ineffective resolution.[30] Or, it explains why people engaged in group decisions who disagree openly and then resolve their differences by problem solving make better decisions than the average or the best member of the group.[31]

Problem-solving methods are also preferred where commitment and implementation of an agreement by the parties are desired. Capitulation or compromise of personal goals engendered through forcing strategies is not likely to generate high levels of support for an agreement. Problem-solving methods, which provide for achievement of each party's goals, will generate higher levels of support.[32] Thus, as suggested previously, where cooperation between parties is necessary because of their mutual dependency, where the use of creative resources by the parties is important, and where support for and implementation of the agreement is necessary, problem-solving methods of conflict resolution appear to have advantages over power-oriented methods.

SUMMARY

This article has reviewed normative issues involved in conflict resolution in the context of three premises: (1) knowledge is unlimited but perceptions of knowledge create unwarranted outcomes; (2) practiced behaviors are self-rewarding, inducing power-oriented outcomes where parties have established those as patterns of behavior; and (3) power-oriented and problem-solving methods are alternate ways for solving a conflict. The means for establishing outcomes to conflict which are mutually beneficial are presently available and can be implemented through proper conflict management.

REFERENCES

1. As used here, power-oriented methods include such resolution strategies as forcing, bargaining, and appeasement or acquiescence. Problem-solving methods include integrative decision making and consensus. Labels such as confrontation, collaboration, and creative problem solving refer to the latter methods.

2. For more detailed discussion, see A.C. Filley, *Interpersonal Conflict Resolution* (Glenview, Ill.: Scott, Foreman and Co., 1975); and K. Thomas, "Conflict and Conflict Management," in M. Dunnette, ed., *Handbook of Industrial and Organizational Psychology* (Chicago: Rand-McNally, 1976), pp. 889-935.

3. N.R.F. Maier, *Problem Solving Discussions and Conferences: Leadership Methods and Skills* (New York: McGraw-Hill, 1963).

4. D.L. Harnett, L.L. Cummings, and W.C. Hamner, "Personality, Bargaining Style, and Payoff in Bilateral Monopoly Bargaining Among European Managers," *Sociometry* (1973), pp. 325-345.

5. P.A. Renwick, "Perception and Management of Superior-Subordinate Conflict," *Organizational Behavior and Human Performance* (1975), pp. 444-456.

6. Filley, op. cit., pp. 108-109

7. R.R. Blake and J.S. Mouton, "The Intergroup Dynamics of Win-Lose Conflict and Problem-Solving Collaboration in Union Management Relations," in M. Sherif, ed., *Intergroup Relations and Leadership* (New York: Wiley, 1962), pp. 94-104; and R.J. Burke, "Methods of Resolving Superior-Subordinate Conflict: The Constructive Use of Subordinate Differences and Disagreements," *Organizational Behavior and Human Performance* (1970), pp. 393-411.

8. Blake and Mouton, op. cit.

9. R.R. Blake, H.A. Shepard, and J.S. Mouton, *Managing Intergroup Conflict in Industry* (Houston: Gulf Publishing Co., 1964); and M. Deutsch and R.M. Krause, "The Effect of Threat Upon Interpersonal Bargaining," *Journal of Abnormal and Social Psychology* (1960), pp. 181-189.

10. Deutsch and Krause, op. cit.; M. Deutsch, *The Resolution of Conflict* (New Haven: Yale University Press, 1973); Burke, op. cit.; N.R.F. Maier, *Problem Solving and Creativity in Individuals and Groups* (Belmont, Calif.: Brooks-Cole Publishing Co., 1970); V.H. Vroom and P.W. Yetton, *Leadership and Decision-Making* (Pittsburgh: University of Pittsburgh Press, 1973).

11. D.E. Zand, "Trust and Managerial Problem Solving," *Administrative Science Quarterly* (June 1972), pp. 229-239; W.A. Haythorn, E.H. Couch, D. Haefner, P. Langham, and L. Carter, "The Behavior of Authoritarian and Equalitarian Personalities in Groups," *Human Relations* (1956), pp. 57-74; Deutsch, op. cit.

12. Blake, Shepard, and Mouton, op. cit., 1964; I. Janis, "Personality Correlates of Susceptibility to Persuasion," *Journal of Personality* (1954), pp. 504-518; J. Kagen and P.H. Mussen, "Dependency Themes on the TAT and Group Conformity," *Journal of Consultive Psychology* (156), pp. 29-32; A.R. Cohen, "The Effects of Individual Self-Esteem and Situational Structure on Threat-Oriented Reactions to Power," *Dissertation Abstracts* (154), pp. 727-728.

13. R.L. Hamblin, "Leadership and Crises," *Sociometry* (1959), pp. 322-335.

14. R. Sommer, *Personal Space: The Behavioral Basis of Design* (Englewood Cliffs, N.J.: Prentice-Hall, 1959).

15. W.M. Evan and J.A. MacDougall, "Interorganizational Conflict: A Labor-Management Bargaining Experiment," *Journal of Conflict Resolution* (December 1967), pp. 398-413; A.J. Lott and B.E. Lott, "Group Cohesiveness as Interpersonal Attraction: A Review of Relationships with Antecedent and Consequent Variables," *Psychological Bulletin* (1964), pp. 259-302.

16. G.H. Shure, R.J. Meeker, and E.A. Hansford, "The Effectiveness of Pacifist Strategies in Bargaining Games," *The Journal of Conflict Res-*

olution (1965), pp. 106-117; A. Rapoport, "Experiments in Dyadic Conflict and Cooperation," *Bulletin of the Menninger Clinic* (1966), pp. 284-291.

17. Deutsch, op. cit., 1973.

18. M. Deutsch, "Conflict and Its Resolution," in C.G. Smith, ed., *Conflict Resolution: Contributions of the Behavioral Sciences* (Notre Dame University Press, 1971), pp. 36-57.

19. R.E. Walton and R.B. McKersie, "Behavioral Dilemmas in Mixed-Motive Decision Making," *Behavioral Science* (1966), pp. 370-384; D. Druckman, "Prenegotiation Experience and Dyadic Conflict Resolution in a Bargaining Situation," *Journal of Experimental Social Psychology* (1968), pp. 367-383; J.J. Miller, B. Brehmer, and K.R. Hammond, "Communication and Conflict Reduction: A Cross-Cultural Study," *Journal International de Psychologie* (1970), pp. 75-87.

20. Filley, op. cit., pp. 35-47; Walton and McKersie, op. cit.

21. N.R.F. Maier and A.R. Solem, "Improving Solutions by Turning Choice Situations into Problems," *Personnel Psychology* (1962), pp. 151-157; G. Nadler, *Work Systems Design: The IDEALS Concept* (Homewood, Ill.: Irwin, 1967).

22. Maier, op. cit.; Nadler, op. cit.

23. J. Hall, "Decisions, Decisions, Decisions," *Psychology Today* (November 1971), pp. 51-54.

24. P.A. Renwick, "Impact of Topic and Source of Disagreement on Conflict Management," *Organizational Behavior and Human Performance* (1975), pp. 416-425.

25. R.E. Walton and R.B. McKersie, *A Behavioral Theory of Labor Negotiations: An Analysis of a Social Interaction System* (New York: McGraw-Hill, 1965). For an example of union training in problem solving, see I. Stern and R.F. Pearse, "Collective Bargaining: A Union's Program for Reducing Conflict," *Personnel* (May-June 1968), pp. 61-72.

26. T. Gordon, *Parent Effectiveness Training* (New York: Wyden, 1970).

27. P.R. Lawrence and J.W. Lorsch, *Organization and Environment: Managing Differentiation and Integration* (Boston, Mass.: Division of Research, Graduate School of Business Administration, Harvard University, 1967); A. Delbecq and A.C. Filley, "A Study of the Weather Satellite Program Management and Organizational Systems," in *Multidisciplinary Studies of the Social, Economic, and Political Impact Resulting from Recent Advances in Satellite Meteorology* (Space Science and Engineering Center, University of Wisconsin—Madison), Vol. 4, pp. 1-174.

28. R.G. Corwin, "Patterns of Organizational Conflict," *Administrative Science Quarterly* (1969), pp. 507-521. For a discussion of possible advantages of conflict, see Thomas, op. cit., p. 891.

29. Burke, op. cit.; Renwick, op. cit.

30. Burke, op. cit.

31. Hall, op. cit, p. 88. For related evidence, see L.R. Hoffman and N.R.F. Maier, "Quality and Acceptance of Problem Solving Solutions by Members of Homogeneous and Heterogeneous Groups." *Journal of Abnormal and Social Psychology* (March 1962), pp. 401-407.

32. Blake, Shepard, and Mouton, op. cit., Vroom and Yetton, op. cit.

CHAPTER 28

Developing Effective Organizations

As occasional patients, we all are familiar with the "medical model" of problem solving. Let's imagine, for example, that your stomach has been hurting for three or four days. You decide it may be serious, so you begrudgingly make an appointment to visit a physician. The physician attempts to diagnose the source of the stomach ache. He or she takes an oral medical history, physically examines you, and runs a number of diagnostic tests. Based upon the physician's analysis of these data, a course of treatment is prescribed. The treatment can take such forms as an alteration in your diet, medication, or, in more serious instances, surgery. The conscientious physician will follow up on the prescribed plan of treatment to make sure that you are on the road back to health. If he or she finds that you are not progressing satisfactorily, a different form of medical intervention will be tested out. This process continues until, ideally, you have recovered.

A large number of organizational practitioners have adopted this medical model and used it in an attempt to keep organizations healthy. This collection of techniques has been labeled *organizational development* or OD. In this chapter, we will introduce the OD phenomenon by first offering a definition of the concept and a general discussion of the stages that constitute the process. Next, we will identify various types of OD interventions. Finally, we will present a somewhat detailed discussion of OD interventions aimed at altering the organization's "personality." The following chapter presents a thorough analysis of actual OD interventions.

WHAT IS OD?

Organization development is a planned, organization-wide effort managed from the top to increase organization effectiveness through interventions in the organization's processes using behavioral science knowledge (Beckhard, 1969). Let's pick apart this seemingly abstruse definition and try to gain a deeper understanding of what OD is all about. First, OD is a planned change effort aimed at the aggregate organization rather than at particular individuals within the organization. Thus, an OD intervention, as is the case with a medical intervention, does not just happen. Diagnosis precedes prescription; and the utility of the prescribed intervention is tested out and not merely accepted as a cure-all. OD incorporates a design component with identifiable, sequential steps. The notion of change implies that the intermediary outcome of an OD intervention is the establishment of new actions, beliefs, and attitudes among a substantial portion of the organization's membership.

In other words, the process of OD leads, in part, to changes in employee behavior, and these changes in behavior are typically accompanied by an alteration in the structure and functioning of the organization. Interestingly, many behavioral scientists believe that people are naturally resistant to change: people avoid giving up the comfortable, familiar, and secure for the unknown. Most OD processes, therefore, explicitly incorporate some attempt to overcome this resistance to change. Frequently, OD relies upon a form of the general change process formulated by the noted psychologist, Kurt Lewin (1958). As figure 28-1 shows, the process consists of three steps: (1) unfreezing-awareness and development of the need to change, (2) moving-diagnosis and establishment of action elements, and (3) refreezing-evaluation and stabilization of the change.

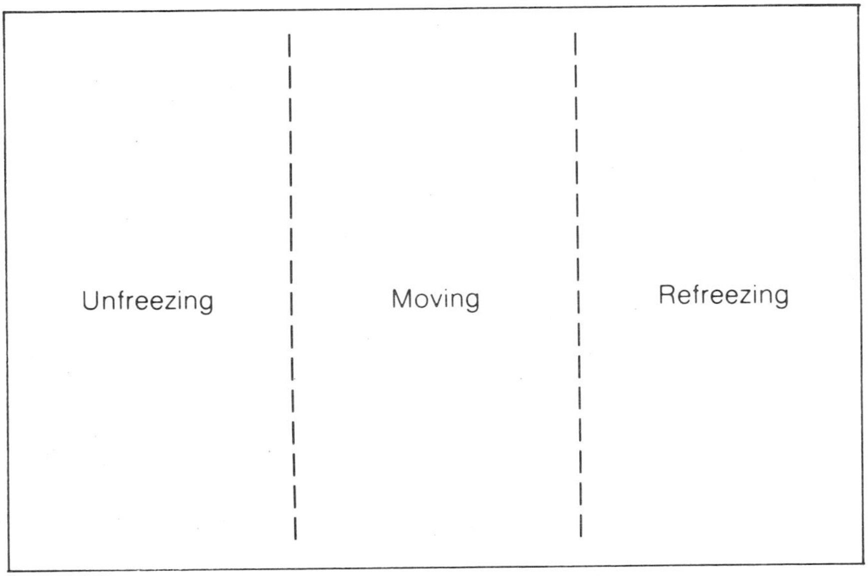

Unfreezing	Moving	Refreezing

FIGURE 28-1
Lewin's Model of the Change Process

Leadership for the OD process is drawn from the top of the organization and not from the middle or bottom. This means that, through the management of the OD program, the organization's leaders make a personal investment in seeing that the process works. The organization's top management, therefore, is both knowledgeable about and committed to the methods and goals of the OD program. Without this active top-management support, the so-called OD program becomes a wolf in sheep's clothing, a technique most assuredly doomed to failure. Unfortunately, it is not uncommon for a personnel director or some person other than the chief executive officer to retain an OD consultant. Due to the time pressures on the executive and the poor judgment of the consultant, the executive does not become intimately involved in the OD process. When a proposed intervention ultimately is presented to the executive for approval, the executive may say, "I don't think this behavioral science stuff is worth its weight in salt. Anyway, we don't need to change our way of doing things around here so drastically. I've been CEO for eight years, and we've turned a profit each of those years. I appreciate your efforts, but I'm just not ready to move on the proposal."

Another component of the definition of OD concerns its ultimate goal, the increased effectiveness of the organization. From an OD perspective, organizational effectiveness is viewed in terms of the organization's "health status." In general, a *healthy organization* is one that successfully copes with and adapts to changes both within and without its task environment, rather than becoming stagnant and failing to respond to the new demands placed on it. More specifically, a healthy organization is one that is self-renewing in the sense that it recruits and develops talented organizational members; offers a hospitable home to the individual organizational member; has built-in provisions for self-criticism; is flexible in terms of altering its internal structure; and has some means for combating the process by which people become prisoners of their procedures (Garder, 1965). In other words, a manager becomes interested in an OD intervention because the changes in actions, beliefs, and attitudes brought about by that intervention will facilitate the continued achievement of the organization's goals. Without this goal, OD degenerates into a grab bag of human relations gimmicks aimed at making employees happy. Admittedly, this is an important objective, but it certainly does not represent the dominant responsibility of management.

The final component of the definition of OD is the concept of an intervention. According to Chris Argyris (1970), a principal developer of intervention theory, an *intervention* can best be thought of as the act of entering into an organization's ongoing system of relationships to alter the interactions between and among persons, groups, and objects with the intent of somehow improving the system's functioning. OD interventions share several common characteristics: (1) they are freely chosen by the members of the organization and not some external party; (2) the choice process relies upon valid information rather than unfounded speculation; (3) the members of the organization exhibit a high level of internal commitment to them; and (4) their foundations can be traced to one of the behavioral sciences, such as organizational behavior. An intervention that is not characterized by free choice, valid information, internal commitment, and the behavioral sciences is *not*, by definition, an OD intervention.

By now, you are probably curious about what forms these OD interventions might take. Actually, the known forms of OD interventions are unbelievably varied and, as a group, are difficult to characterize beyond what we have said thus far. Before considering these specific OD interventions, however, we will draw upon the previous discussion and outline a general model of the stages comprising the OD process.

A model of the OD process

There are at least four sequentially ordered components of the OD process: problem recognition by top management, data gathering and solution development, intervention, and evaluation. Larry Greiner (1970), a noted OD specialist on the faculty of the University of Southern California, has formulated a more detailed description of the stages that constitute the OD process. His formulation, as shown in figure 28-2, consists of six distinct stages.

1. *Pressure and arousal.* Such events as lower sales, stockholder discontent, competitor breakthroughs, union strikes, low productivity, high cost, or interdepartmental conflicts exert pressure on organization's top management, which arouses them to try to alleviate the perceived threat.

2. *Entry and reorientation.* A newcomer respected for his or her skills at improving organizational practices enters at the top of the organization. This newcomer (typically an internal or external OD consultant) helps to reorient top management to its own internal problems.

3. *Diagnosis and recognition.* Here the newcomer joins the power structure of the organization from top to bottom to collect information for the purpose of collaboratively identifying the location and causes of problems. This process demonstrates to organizational members at all levels that (a) top management is willing to change, (b) important problems are being confronted, and (c) ideas from lower levels are being recognized by upper levels.

4. *Invention and commitment.* Widespread and intensive searches are undertaken to identify creative, new problem solutions. This process yields a proposed intervention of high technical quality, with parties at all organizational levels committed to its success.

5. *Experimentation and evaluation.* Before it is adopted on an organization-wide basis, the intervention is reality tested in one or

FIGURE 28-2 A Model of Organization Change

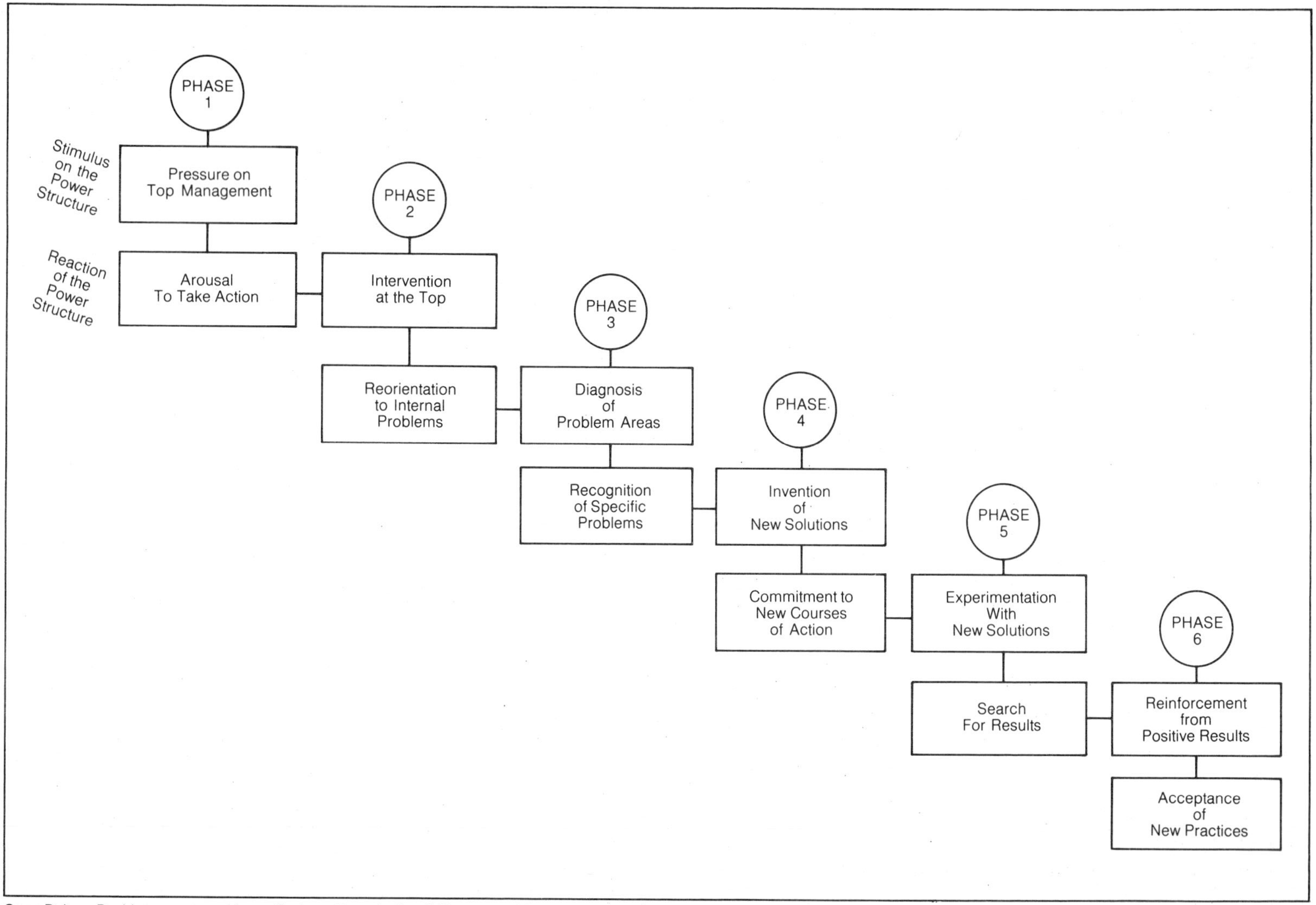

PHASE 1
Stimulus on the Power Structure
Pressure on Top Management
Reaction of the Power Structure
Arousal To Take Action

PHASE 2
Intervention at the Top
Reorientation to Internal Problems

PHASE 3
Diagnosis of Problem Areas
Recognition of Specific Problems

PHASE 4
Invention of New Solutions
Commitment to New Courses of Action

PHASE 5
Experimentation With New Solutions
Search For Results

PHASE 6
Reinforcement from Positive Results
Acceptance of New Practices

Gene Dalton, Paul Lawrence, and Larry Greiner, *Organizational Change and Development* (Homewood, Ill.: Richard D. Irwin, 1970), p. 222. © 1970 by Richard D. Irwin, Inc.

more subunits of the organization, and the results of these organizational experiments are rigorously evaluated.

6. *Reinforcement and acceptance.* Favorable results from the experimentation and evaluation stage serve as a source of positive reinforcement to all those organizational members involved in the OD process. This reinforcement leads to widespread acceptance of the usefulness of the proposed intervention and its subsequent successful diffusion throughout the organization.

Even though OD is sometimes considered a fuzzy concept, we hope you now have some feel for what OD is and how the process works—*at least in its ideal state.* At a minimum, you should now recognize what OD is *not:* it is not a process that happens haphazardly; it does not proceed without top management commitment; it does not leave important organizational relationships intact; and it does not reinforce the *status quo* of the organization. Again, the following material about specific OD intervention techniques will help to further clarify your understanding of this important and potentially elusive managerial tool.

INTERVENTION TECHNIQUES

Parts of the material presented in virtually every one of the preceding chapters can, under certain circumstances, be labeled an OD intervention strategy or technique. In table 28-1, we list and briefly describe a number of more popular OD approaches. Several of these approaches are discussed in considerably more detail elsewhere in the book.

This list is by no means comprehensive. We could have listed numerous other approaches, but we felt these represent some of the most popular interventions currently being used and provide you with an appreciation of the variety of forms OD can assume. Also, many of the presented approaches overlap in activities and purposes and cover somewhat different stages of the OD process model presented. Finally, we give no real indication of when to use which intervention approach or how effective the different approaches are. One reason for this lack of information is that, beyond attempting to fit diagnosed problems with the stated purposes of a particular intervention strategy, there are no good guidelines to help in the choice of an OD intervention. Furthermore, little research has been done to determine the relative effectiveness of the interventions listed. In practice, it seems that managers largely rely on whatever intervention strategy their OD consultant advocates. In other words, they accept the utility of a particular intervention approach on blind faith. Because we do not believe this approach represents good managerial practice, we advise the manager who contemplates retaining an OD consultant to do some comparison shopping and to maintain a "show me" attitude. The following chapter, by Richard Walton (1975), ex-

TABLE 28-1
Popular OD Approaches

APPROACH	DESCRIPTION
1. Confrontation/ Third-Party Consultation	Typical of this approach is the "confrontation meeting" advocated by Richard Beckhard (1967). Here, the entire management group of an organization is involved, with the top manager first communicating his or her goals, interests, and concerns to the group. Next, each individual manager systematically contributes his or her perspective on organizational problems and prospects. Following this sharing of information, subgroups are formed and mandated to set priorities and develop action plans. These subgroup plans then are integrated by the total management group into an organization action plan. Immediate follow-up by top management and periodic progress reviews conclude the process. The confrontation meeting approach most typically is facilitated by the involvement of an external consultant. The role of this third party essentially is to regulate interactions, sharpen issues, and diagnose relationships.
2. Gestalt Orientation	This approach relies heavily on a psychoanalytic perspective that advocates that the OD consultant should encourage both individuals in the superior and subordinate dyad to recognize where they are now and to help them find their own unique paths to growth and change. This is largely accomplished by emphasizing that parties fully recognize their negative feelings toward each other and the organization by staying with transactions until *both* parties have completed their business with one another. In this process, the consultant serves as a role model through his or her own clear and explicit statement of what he or she wants and how he or she feels.
3. Job Enrichment/ Job Redesign	An example of this form of intervention is the sociotechnical approach to job design. Basically, the approach involves reconstituting the content of organizational jobs and experimenting with these new configurations. This process follows a number of principles, such as ensuring an optimum variety of tasks in the job, making each job seem to constitute a single overall task, and establishing an optimum length of work cycle. Chapter 14 deals in detail with this intervention strategy.
4. Laboratory/ Sensitivity Training	The best-known form of this intervention technique is the "T-group," where a face-to-face, largely unstructured group of organizational members serves as the primary vehicle for learning. The group leader or trainer emphasizes that members should

(Table 28-1 continued)

APPROACH	DESCRIPTION
4. Laboratory/ Sensitivity Training (cont.)	freely express themselves and openly react to these free expressions and that a general orientation of trust and interpersonal risk taking is present. The organizationally relevant outcomes of this process purportedly are numerous, including the removal of interpersonal obstacles to increased job performance through the development and testing of new social skills.
5. Life Planning	This approach involves the organization assisting its members in reviewing, evaluating, and examining their life plans. According to Gordon Lippitt (1970), a well-known OD consultant, the organization endorses such an intervention to demonstrate its social responsibility, to show that it cares for its employees as individuals, to effectively release the potential of the individual on behalf of the organization, to help the individual prepare for change, to strengthen the psychological contract between the individual and the organization, to plan more effective learning experiences, and to recognize the total life of the individual, including its nonwork components. Life planning, which is usually conducted within a group context, supposedly helps organizational members decide what is important to them and to develop projects for the future, as well as facilitating trusting and helping behaviors.
6. Grid Organizational Development	Robert Blake and Jane Mouton's (1975) popular approach focuses on individual learning, team development, strengthening intergroup relationships, and structuring the organization. The approach revolves around altering the leadership styles used in the organization. Some of the goals of Blake's and Mouton's intervention strategy include improving the skills of executives and supervisors to work together and to encourage all managers to plan and introduce improvements.
7. Organizational Renewal Process	As formulated by Gordon Lippett (1975), this intervention technique relies upon films, instruments and group learning to help leaders of an organization confront various aspects of organizational life. More specifically, the approach helps managers examine the forces in their organization's environment; optimize organizational human resources; analyze, initiate, and cope with change; and spread, reinforce, and secure multiple commitments to planned change efforts. The approach attempts to recognize the uniqueness of an organization's situation and to respond to these situational constraints and opportunities.

(Table 28-1 continued)

APPROACH	DESCRIPTION
8. Process Consultation	Edgar Schein (1969), the best-known advocate of process consultation, defines the approach as a set of OD activities that help organizational members perceive, understand, and act upon process events that occur in the members' environment. The essential forms of the OD consultant's interventions include such things as asking questions that direct attention to interpersonal issues and holding meetings about these issues; feeding back observations to organizational members; coaching or counseling individuals or groups; and suggesting changes in organizational structure.
9. Survey-Guided Development	This approach was largely developed at the University of Michigan's Institute for Social Research. Survey data are collected and tabulated for each and every work group in the organization, as well as for each combination of groups that represent an area of responsibility, including the total organization. These data are then fed back to each supervisor and manager. The survey data describe current organizational practices, as well as the outcomes of these practices. Thus, the data can be used to identify needed areas of change and serve as an impetus for implementing these changes.
10. Transactional Analysis	TA (Transactional Analysis) is a system of psychotherapy based on the examination of social interactions (or transactions). It stresses the impact of one's early experiences on the formation of lifestyles and resultant behaviors; it acknowledges unconscious motives. The purpose of TA is to improve the quality of human interactions within the organization. TA is usually used in conjunction with other OD approaches and is commonly presented in the form of a supervisory training program. The purpose of the training is to make supervisors more sensitive and aware of the dynamics of interactions and to demonstrate the options available to them when they find themselves in futile transactions.
11. Team Development	Team development activities can take many forms. Richard Beckhard (1972) suggests one approach: within the context of a work group meeting, the leader and members of the group, with the assistance of an OD consultant, jointly establish goals or priorities; analyze and distribute work; examine the group's procedures, processes, and norms; and examine the relationships among group members as they work.

amines the issue of OD failures; Walton methodically zeros in on the failure of a proposed job redesign intervention to be adopted and highlights a number of potential causes for this lack of success.

ORGANIZATIONAL CLIMATE AND OD

Earlier, we talked about how a warm and supportive organizational climate leads to employee loyalty. Now we will examine more thoroughly the concept of climate and how it relates to organizational development. An organization's climate can be thought of as the personality of the organization as seen by its members. More formally defined, climate is a set of attributes specific to a particular organization that describes how that organization deals with its members. The weather (or climate) of a particular geographic region can be described in terms of specific attributes—for example, temperature, wind velocity, and precipitation; the winter climate in Duluth, Minnesota, generally can be described as freezing cold, gusty, and snowy, while the winter climate of Miami Beach, Florida is warm, calm, and relatively dry.

What, then, are the specific climatic dimensions that can be used to describe how an organization deals with its members? A number of different organizational behavioralists (cf. Campbell, Dunnette, Lawler, and Weick, 1970) have found that the following attributes encompass most of these dimensions.

1. *Autonomy*—the degree to which the organization allows its members to be their own bosses and to exercise considerable decision-making power and initiative

2. *Structure*—the degree to which an organization defines for its members the objectives of their jobs *and* the methods to be used in obtaining those objectives

3. *Reward orientation*—the degree to which an organization actively promotes its members' job performance by rewarding high performance with pay increases, advances, and other positively valent outcomes

4. *Warmth and support*—the degree to which an organization, through its leadership practices, fosters a sense of fellowship and helpfulness among its members

To see how organizational climates can differ, let's consider the jobs of Betty and Jane, both reference librarians employed in two different municipal libraries. Betty is allowed a great deal of autonomy in her library. For example, she works under a "flexitime" system, which essentially allows her to determine when she arrives at work, when she breaks for lunch, and when she leaves for home. Betty's job is loosely structured. She determines how best to deal with the many different types of requests for information she receives and relies on no set pattern of work methods. All employees in Betty's library receive the same percentage annual pay increase, and promotions generally are granted on the basis of seniority. Betty's boss is a considerate person who helps Betty out when she is overloaded; in turn, Betty helps her fellow reference librarians when they are in need. Conversely, Jane works on a rigid nine-to-five schedule, and her boss is continually checking to make sure that she returns promptly from her forty-five-minute lunch break. On Jane's desk sits a rules and procedures manual to which she refers in determining the library's policy for dealing with a particular type of information request. Jane's boss periodically evaluates the job performance of each reference librarian and relies solely on those evaluations in making recommendations for pay increases and promotions. Because Jane's boss expects each employee to carry his or her own weight, everyone operates quite independently. In total, the climate of the library Jane works in can be described as low in terms of autonomy and warmth and consideration and high in terms of structure and reward orientation. Conversely, the climate of the library Betty works in can be described as high in terms of autonomy and warmth and consideration, and low in terms of structure and reward orientation. Thus, you can see how the four attributes provided can be used to describe an organization's climate just as temperature, wind velocity, and precipitation describe the climate of a geographical region.

Some people prefer living in a region with one season all year long, and others enjoy the changing of the seasons. The same is true with organizational climate. Not all people respond the same way to the same organizational climate. Most people, however, do enjoy warm, sunny weather, and certain dimensions of organizational climate have been found to be fairly consistently related to job satisfaction. For instance, in most organizations there is a positive association between the warmth and support dimension of climate and employee satisfaction. In general, though, it is safest to conclude that there is no one best climate. Just as different forms of plant life flourish best in different atmospheric climates, the health status of an organization also depends, to a degree, on its climatic condition. Although we cannot manipulate weather conditions, it is possible to alter an organization's climate to fit the needs of its members as well as its dominant mission. Herein lies the link between climate and OD. Diagnosing the fit between an organization's climate and its needs for certain climatic conditions and adjusting the climate to meet those needs is what OD is all about. Given the comprehensive degree to which an organization's internal environment can be described by the four dimensions of climate, the concept of organization climate provides a reasonably exhaustive way of thinking about OD interventions.

The work of Fritz Steele and Stephen Jenks (1977), OD consultants, offers an example of the relationship between climate and the OD process. Their recommended strategy for starting and implementing organizational change consists of three steps, which are shown in figure 28-3. First, describe the climate as it currently exists. To do

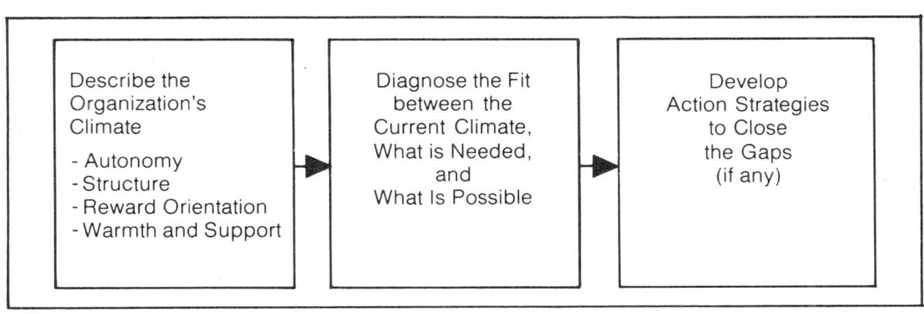

FIGURE 28-3
Improving an Organization's Climate

this, they suggest conducting an employee attitude survey, moving around the organization and observing the physical setting and how people use it, venturing behind the scenes in other organizations to get a feel for the kinds of climates that have evolved elsewhere, and relying upon new observers to offer their frequently more objective insights. The second step, after describing the climate, is to make a diagnosis based on the collected information. This involves analyzing the discrepancy (if any) between what is needed and what is possible. Steele and Jenks provide a framework to expedite such an analysis. For example, they suggest that extreme pressure for results and a high level of structure will produce stifling conditions; but where there is little pressure for results, structure produces predictability and stability. Thus, Jane, the librarian who works in a highly structured climate, may flourish, assuming the requests for information she receives are neither too numerous nor too complex. Conversely, if Jane is under a lot of pressure and is receiving numerous, sophisticated requests, the constraints imposed by the high level of structure may cause her to become ineffectual. The third step Steele and Jenks prescribe, assuming a need for change has been detected, is to develop various strategies for action to close the gap between desired and actual climate. Some of the possible targets they identify for these plans of action include reward systems, norms, disclosure patterns, goals and goal-setting processes, managerial style, decision-making processes, career development systems, physical structures, problem-solving skills, intergroup relations, and formal policies.

In sum, Steele's and Jenk's treatment of organization climate from an OD perspective offers a conceptual framework that helps us see how OD can become an operational tool for management. Their work recognizes that OD is a planned change process that relies on a problem-oriented research philosophy; the end goal is the assimilation and utilization of knowledge as a means of solving organizational problems.

SUMMARY

Organization development is a planned, organization-wide effort managed from the top to increase organization effectiveness through interventions in the organization's processes using behavioral science knowledge. The six stages of a successful OD program are: (1) pressure and arousal, (2) entry and reorientation, (3) diagnosis and recognition, (4) invention and commitment, (5) experimentation and evaluation, and (6) reinforcement and acceptance.

The more popular forms of OD intervention strategies that organizations use include confrontation/third party consultation, Gestalt orientation, job enrichment/job redesign, laboratory/sensitivity training, life planning, grid organizational development, organizational renewal process, process consultation, survey guided development, transactional analysis, and team development. There exists no grand conceptual framework to ensure the selection of an appropriate OD intervention, and very little research has been done to determine the relative effectiveness of the interventions listed.

Organizational climate is a set of attributes (for example, autonomy, structure, reward orientation, and warmth and support) specific to a particular organization that describes the way that organization deals with its members. The process of diagnosing and altering an organization's climate offers a conceptual framework that shows us how OD can become an operational tool for management. This perspective recognizes that OD is a planned change process that relies on a problem-oriented research philosophy; the end goal is the absorption and use of knowledge to solve organizational problems.

REFERENCES

Argyris, C. *Intervention Theory and Method: A Behavioral Science View.* Reading, Mass.: Addison-Wesley, 1970.

Beckhard, R. "The Confrontation Meeting." *Harvard Business Review* 45 (1967): 149-55.

Beckhard, R. *Organization Development: Strategies and Models.* Reading, Mass.: Addison-Wesley, 1969.

Beckhard, R. "Optimizing Team-building Efforts." *Journal of Contemporary Business* (1972): 23-27 and 30-32.

Blake, R.R., and Mouton, J.J. "An Overview of the Grid." *Training and Development Journal* 12 (1975): 29-37.

Campbell, J.P.; Dunnette, M.D.; Lawler, E.E.; and Weick, K.E. *Managerial Behavior, Performance, and Effectiveness.* New York: McGraw-Hill, 1970.

Garder, J.W. "How to Prevent Organizational Dry Rot." *Harpers*, 1965.

Greiner, L.E. "Patterns of Organizational Change." In *Organizational Development and Change*, edited by G.W. Dalton, P.R. Lawrence, and L.E. Greiner. Homewood, Ill.: Irwin, 1970.

Lewin, K."Group Decision and Social Change." In *Readings in Social Psychology*, edited by T.N. Newcomb and E.L. Hartley. New York: Holt, Rinehart, and Winston, 1958.

Lippitt, G.L. "Developing Life Plans: A New Concept and Design for Training and Development." *Training and Development Journal* 7 (1970): 2-7.

Lippitt, G.L. "Implementing the Organizational Renewal Process (ITORP)—A Situational Approach to OD." In *New Technologies in Organizational Development*, edited by

W.W. Burke. La Jolla, Ca.: University Associates, 1975.

Schein, E.H. *Process Consultation: Its Role in Organization Development.* Reading, Mass.: Addison-Wesley, 1969.

Steele, F., and Jenks, S. *The Feel of the Workplace: Understanding and Improving Organization Climate.* Reading, Mass.: Addison-Wesley, 1977.

Walton, R.E. "The Diffusion of New Work Structures: Explaining Why Success Didn't Take." *Organizational Dynamics* 3 (1975): 3-21.

SUGGESTIONS FOR ADVANCED READINGS

French, W.L.; Bell, C.H.; and Zawacki, R.A., eds. *Organizational Development: Theory, Practice, and Research.* Dallas: Business Publications, 1978.

Margulies, N., and Raia, A.P., eds. *Conceptual Foundation of Organizational Development.* New York: McGraw-Hill, 1978.

Mirvis, P.H., and Berg, D.N., eds. *Failures in Organizational Development and Change: Cases and Essays for Learning.* New York: Wiley, 1977.

CHAPTER

29

Explaining Why Success Didn't Take*

When organizations engage in experimental projects in work restructuring, an underlying assumption is that if the innovation is effective, it will be adapted and used by other units in the organization. Most of us would expect that an organizational pattern that is working better than the one it replaced will be recommended by superiors and emulated by peers. Experience, however, shows this to be not necessarily true: The assumed tendencies are sometimes nullified and offset by competing organizational dynamics.

I have studied a sample of organizations that made early efforts at the comprehensive redesign of work, asking: How much diffusion has occurred, particularly within the same firm? What are the vehicles for diffusion? What barriers are encountered? How does the character of the innovation affect the rate of its diffusion? Answers to questions such as these can help us formulate better diffusion strategies and tactics.

EIGHT EXPERIMENTS

The eight firms included in the study had the following characteristics: All started their research on work redesign in the 1960s; their early experiments involved relatively comprehensive work restructuring; these experiments were all judged initially successful; the firms had a number of physically separate facilities, usually geographically dispersed; the change efforts of all the firms received substantial publicity.

*From Richard E. Walton, "Explaining Why Success Didn't Take," *Organizational Dynamics*, (Winter 1975), pp. 3-22. Reprinted, by permission of the publisher,

Of the eight firms, two are in the U.S., two in Canada, one in Great Britain, two in Norway, and one in Sweden. The firms in the U.S. are Corning Glass, which initiated a study in its Medfield, Mass., assembly plant in 1965, and the General Foods Corporation, which initiated an experiment in its pet food plant in Topeka, Kansas, in January 1971, although it had begun planning for change in 1968. The Canadian organizations are the Sales and Fabrication Division of Alcan and the Advanced Devices Center, a division of Northern Electric Company, subsequently renamed Microsystems International, Ltd. In 1964, a group of Alcan managers launched a project in one plant in the works at Kingston, Ontario; over time the innovations developed in the first effort at Kingston were extended to other existing Sales and Fabrication Division plants and eventually to a new cold rolling mill. The Northern Electric unit designed a radically different organization for a new semiconductor facility that was occupied in January 1966.

The European companies form the remainder of the sample. Shell U.K. introduced change in several locations in the mid-1960s, including a new refinery at Teesport, which came on stream in 1968. Several Norwegian projects were carried out in different industries under the Industrial Democracy Project, an action research program sponsored jointly by the Norwegian Federation of Employers and the Trades Union Council of Norway and guided by social scientists associated with the Work Research Institute in Oslo. The two projects included in this study were the fertilizer plants at Norsk Hydro in Porsgrunn and a department in the Hunsfos pulp and paper complex near Kristiansand. They were initiated in the mid-1960s.

A Swedish experiment in Volvo's truck assembly plant in Lundby, begun in 1969, has been followed by similar changes in a neighboring auto assembly plant, the design of a revolutionary car plant at Kalmar that went on stream in 1974, and a commitment to an advanced form of work structuring in a new Volvo plant in the U.S. planned for 1975.

An important similarity existed in the change strategies employed by seven of these eight firms. An early experiment in one unit of the firm was regarded as a pilot project from which the larger organization could learn. The positive results, if any, could demonstrate the value of work restructuring. Lessons gained from the experiment then could be made available to other units. The eighth, Shell U.K., by contrast followed a change strategy in which the demonstration projects were not the point of departure.

The extent of diffusion that has occurred within these eight firms has varied widely. In four companies (Corning, Northern Electric, Hunsfos, and Norsk Hydro) diffusion has been nonexistent or small. In three companies (General Foods, Shell U.K., and Alcan) somewhat more diffusion has occurred; however, the rate either has been slow or it has not been sustained. Only in one company in my sample, namely Volvo, was diffusion truly impressive. Managers involved in all the changes, including those at Volvo, clearly had expected more rapid and extensive change.

GENERAL MODEL

Before exploring the diffusion of "work restructuring" or the lack of diffusion, let us clarify what we mean by the term. The work restructuring approach pursued in the eight cases studied embraces many aspects of work, including the content of the job, compensation schemes, scope of worker responsibility for supervision and decision making, social structure, status hierarchy, and so on. The design of each element is intended to contribute to an internally consistent work culture—one that *appropriately* enlarges workers' scope for self-management, enhances their opportunity for learning new abilities, strengthens their sense of connectedness with co-workers, increases their identification with the product and manufacturing process, and promotes their sense of dignity and self-worth. The word "appropriately" is used in the preceding sentence to signify that the extent to which work structures can realistically depart from today's conventional work organization depends upon many situational factors, especially the type of technology involved, composition of the work force (Is it educated and skilled?), and economic forces (Do they favor the expenditures of time and money involved in a comprehensive attempt at job restructuring?).

Each diffusion effort had its own unique characteristics, but they all also shared many points. A generalized model of the change efforts, containing seven aspects or steps, will highlight both the similarities and the differences. Although I have viewed the early experiments as the first of a number of steps in transforming work throughout the larger corporation, they were not necessarily so conceived at the time they were initiated, either by direct participants or by corporate officials.

Step 1: Initiation of the pilot experiment. Although perhaps similarly inspired, pilot experiments took a variety of forms. Some were in new plants—GF's Topeka, Corning's Medfield, Alcan's Center Plant at the Kingston Works, and Northern Electric's plant at Montreal. Others were in established plants—Hunsfos' pulp and paper mill and Volvo's Lundby truck plant. At Norsk Hydro, experiments were initiated simultaneously in an existing and a new fertilizer facility. The Shell U.K. demonstration projects occurred as a later step in the process of restructuring work, but they too embraced both existing and new facilities.

Some experiments involved relatively radical and comprehensive work restructuring at the outset—especially GF's pet food plant, Norsk Hydro's fertilizer plants, Hunsfos' chemical pulp department, and Shell U.K.'s new Teesport refinery. Significantly, each of these four facilities is relatively small, employing fewer than 100 workers, and involves a continuous-processing technology. Also, the way work was restructured in these continuous-processing plants is remarkably similar: Self-managing teams were formed to take responsibilty for large segments of the process. Job rotation among team members was encouraged both to improve control of the technology and to provide intrinsically satisfying learning experiences for workers. Support activities, such as maintenance, quality control, and cleaning were incorporated into operating team responsibilities. Because of the diverse abilities required to manage, operate, and maintain these technologies, team members received heavy doses of skills training. Pay was based on the relevant skills and knowledge a worker had acquired rather than on the particular job he was performing. New information and measurement systems were developed to enable teams to keep on top of their enlarged responsibilities.

Northern Electric's Advanced Devices Center, because it focused mostly on professional and managerial personnel, differed from the four continuous-processing facilities. The Advanced Devices Center featured a matrix organization, functional and business teams, elaborate communication schemes, open office layouts, and nontraditional titles and reporting relationships.

Other experiments—in the new plants at Alcan and Corning and the existing facilities at Volvo and Shell U.K.—involved more moderate change. Significantly, two of these, Corning and Volvo, are assembly plants where the nature of the tasks and technology provided relatively little opportunity for upgrading the abilities of the work teams. Thus in these plants emphasis was placed on freeing workers from the tedium of short repetitive work cycles and on steps that would improve communication. Within those constraints, both were bold efforts at work restructuring. The changes that evolved over several years were rotation among and/or enlargement of assembly tasks, the formation of teams, and mechanisms for worker participation or consultation.

An incremental approach to work restructuring in the initial projects in both the Alcan plants and Shell's existing refineries was necessary in part because of constraints related to collective bargaining.

The initial experiment in a majority of cases occurred at the urging of a middle-level line manager, typically a plant manager, or with his active participation. Staff people and outside consultants or researchers also played an active role in designing and implementing most of the initial experiments. In the Norwegian projects, the researchers actually sought out the companies and persuaded them to collaborate in undertaking the projects. Similarly, in the Corning experiment, a corporate consultant began by stimulating interest among supervisors to try their own mini-experiments, which, if successful, could lead to plantwide work restructuring. Interestingly, although the management and worker members of the Norwegian and the Corning experiments subsequently came to "own" the projects, dependency upon outside experts long remained a factor in these cases, each of which resulted in little intracompany diffusion.

Step 2: Pilot experiment declared early success. The study included only those experiments that were judged successful after a year or two, when participants had had significant experience with the new work structures and when operating results could be assessed.

Spokesmen for these projects claimed that they had produced improved performance, increased worker knowledge and skills, and resulted in a generally more responsible and motivating work culture. In no case were there wholly independent performance audits or measurements that would persuade the most ardent skeptics of work restructuring. While my own field visits led me to conclude that in most cases some discounting of claims seemed to be required, I accept the original judgments of early success.

Results claimed on both the hard and soft sides of the benefits ledger varied: Only about 25 percent of the Northern Electric workers said they experienced a relatively large gain in the quality of their working life; among General Foods workers it was 80 percent. The balance, at least during the initial periods, would fall somewhere between. Six cases reported quality improvement and more efficient production due to decreased scrap, less down-time, or more efficient methods. Also, most companies reported reduced turnover and absentee rates. A case in point: The pet food plant after 18 months reported an overhead rate that was 33 percent lower than in the old plant. The absentee rate was 9 percent below the industry norm, and turnover was far below average.

Step 3: Recognition and resources provided for further work restructuring. After becoming acquainted with the results of the pilot experiment, top management typically gave its blessing to the approach. In several cases, notably GF, Alcan, and Norsk Hydro, it became company or division policy to diffuse work restructuring throughout the various facilities. In Hunsfos, it became company policy to spread work restructing to other departments in the mill complex. In the case of Volvo, the recognition of work restructuring became very strong. The new president took a special interest in the subject and had made a dramatic commitment to the program in existing plants in the early 1970s. He personally had pressed for and contributed to a revolutionary approach to the designing of a new auto assembly plant in Kalmar that involved a 10 percent higher capital investment to accommodate the desired work structure. This action gave work restructuring a high priority in other plants. Exceptions should be noted in the cases of Corning and Northern Electric, where apparently no strong encouragement of diffusion came from the corporate level other than from organizational development groups.

In Northern Electric, in fact, the reverse was true. A new manager who took over in the third year of the experiment terminated it before it could have reached the diffusion stage. The new organization was regarded as a success at its home base, but corporate management took a different view.

In a few cases, recognition eventually took the form of a management philosophy hammered out by a group of line managers with the assistance of staff consultants more familiar with work restructuring. A General Foods statement, for example, emerged shortly after other corporate measures had been taken to promote diffusion.

Another diffusion measure was the assignment of specific responsibility for promoting work restructuring. For example, in General Foods, the line manager responsible for pet food operations at the divisional level was transferred to the corporate level and made an internal consultant to several dozen plants.

Step 4: More general interest in work restructuring aroused. In every case, these experiments have been the subject of widely circulated written reports in the news media, oral presentations to other groups, and visits by interested parties to the experimental site. Dissemination activities often helped the project leaders secure top-management recognition and approval, but they had other objectives as well. They were intended to interest and inform managers and union officials of sister units within the same firm and those outside the firm. The visibility and favorable acclaim, of course, were gratifying to the participants, who were proud of the work culture they had created and the performance results they had achieved.

Step 5: Change agent's interventions extend throughout the corporate system. We have already noted the tendency to designate some individuals or committees to help initiate projects and monitor their development. The change interventions led by the internal consultant at General Foods will help illustrate this aspect of a diffusion effort, although the activities are more elaborate than in other cases, except Shell U.K.

In late 1971, the newly appointed GF internal consultant, Lyman Ketchum, addressed a group of 150 top managers from operations, engineering, quality assurance, and personnel, together with several corporation group vice-presidents. Forms of work restructuring and their rationale were discussed. The chairman of GF and a key vice-president were present and sanctioned the role of the new change agent.

A steering committee comprised of the division operating managers was formed to guide the change activities. As a committee the managers assessed the progress of diffusion, and as individuals they were expected to collaborate with the change agent in his work in their divisions.

Change initiatives occurred at the plant level. Priority was given to new and recent plants over existing plants because more progress could be made with less effort. Further priority was given to larger plants because of their greater importance. Recognizing these priorities, the change agent began working with plant managers who manifested the most interest in change.

The change agent's initial work with plants involved a three-day meeting with the plant manager and his staff, who were encouraged to explore their own values and the connections between values and work structures.

These initial three-day meetings by themselves seldom produced much action. After a month or so had elapsed, the change agent usually scheduled another meeting with a group drawn from the next level below the plant manager's staff.

As a parallel activity, the corporate change agent organized three-day seminars on the techniques of work analysis and design; these were attended largely by staff personnel such as engineers.

Where a commitment to work restructuring developed, the change agent helped form a plant steering committee comprised of key line and staff managers, and union officials where appropriate. Subordinate action committees were formed to explore and recommend specific projects within a limited area of the plant. The change agent himself and other consulting resources were made available to the plant committees to assist them in the actual work restructuring.

Diffusion interventions at Norsk Hydro took a somewhat different form: The first major event was a policy clinic where managers and their union counterparts could discuss the ideas and techniques of achieving employee participation at the shop floor in the planning and introduction of change. These discussions were somewhat inhibited by managers who believed that the area manager was authoritarian and unsympathetic. The area manager discovered the content of these policy discussions and stopped them.

In 1971, a second effort was made with the responsibility for work restructuring initiatives assigned to the Joint Consultation Board. A supervisory training program was also introduced. Some new initiatives worked out; others did not.

By 1972 top management concluded that the diffusion policy still was not working. Middle managers were told to "get cracking," and a training program was devised to better equip them to play their role. In the meantime the area manager had been replaced, in part because he had not helped implement the work restructuring project. This development was offset by the departure of an influential union official who was interested in diffusing the work structures pioneered in the fertilizer plants.

A supplementary vehicle for diffusion was the conversion of the ten-man professional staff of the firm's industrial engineering methods group "from MTM engineers to socio-technical consultants." The head of this department understood the need for reshaping the role of the department and began in 1971 to reeducate the staff. Over time this development may greatly facilitate diffusion of the work restructuring ideas pioneered in the fertilizer plants.

Step 6: Facilitative networks develop. This is a step taken in only a few of the change programs studied. An interunit network of personnel involved in work restructuring is created to exchange ideas, to provide a supportive reference group for its members, and to build a constitutency for change in corporate policies and procedures more favorable to work restructuring. In GF, networks of plant managers and their personnel managers are evolving to a point where many of their members can serve others, generally as outside consultants.

Step 7: Personnel movement occurs. The transfer of experienced personnel from an innovative unit is a way of exporting the knowledge, values, and skills at the heart of work restructuring. The innovative unit then can educate the new managers who transfer into the unit.

A few favorable moves can be cited to illustrate the possibilities. In a strategic move at Norsk Hydro, the person who had been personnel manager in the Porsgrunn area was promoted to corporate headquarters. He was intimately familiar with the fertilizer project and an articulate proponent of the underlying philosophy. He moved to a better position to advise top management on the diffusion of work restructuring. Not surprisingly, the advantage of this move to headquarters was partly offset by the loss felt in the local area.

The manager at Alcan's Kingston Works was promoted to a division-level position after the program was well under way at Kingston. Later, however, he reportedly lost touch with the innovations and became less supportive.

In Shell U.K., the transfer of key personnel was disruptive of the program under way in the U.K., but some moves seeded other parts of the Shell International organization—for example, the Australian unit—with managers who were committed to finding better ways of organizing work.

THE SHELL U.K. APPROACH

A major variation on the procedure in the other seven firms—that of starting small with a single experiment—is provided by Shell U.K. From the outset, the approach was conceived as companywide, comprehensive in its effect on the work situation, and planned to last from five to ten years.

The first step was not a demonstration project. Work redesign was undertaken only after large amounts of organizational time had been spent in sessions developing and affirming a supportive managerial philosophy.

Attitudes, in short, were changed before structure. Tavistock social scientists worked closely with an internal staff resource group to design the activities in this and subsequent phases, beginning in 1965 with the development of a philosophy to which senior managers could commit themselves.

The second phase was intended to ensure that the operating philosophy was freely accepted by all 6,000 members of the organization from senior managers to hourly workers. To accomplish this dissemination—involving active testing and consensus building—required 18 months, from fall 1965 to spring 1967—and a cascade of conferences.

The implementation phase was launched in March 1966 by a third top-management conference. The first strategic approach to implementation was to set up pilot projects that "could act as centers of organizational learning." These projects, set up in one refinery, did not go well. Moreover, the concentration of attention on a few groups at one site created resentment among many others who had been through the philosophy discussions, and who were emotionally and intellectually primed to implement the philosophy.

Next, the implementation strategy was altered, and responsibility for change was placed on the department-manager level across the company—an approach made possible by the massive dissemination process. To enable department managers to initiate their own change projects, short training courses were provided to teach them techniques of work analysis and principles of work restructuring.

A network of committees representing both management and unions helped to change work rules that otherwise would prevent many types of restructuring, such as flexible manning patterns and paying workers for multiple job skills.

Although pilot projects as centers for organization learning no longer formed the primary foundation for implementation, it was decided to apply the concepts to a new refinery at Teesport, where construction began in 1965 and which came on stream in April 1968.

Evaluation conferences were held in March 1967 on the previous two major sites covered, Stanlow and Shell Haven. Shortly thereafter, a number of changes took place that served to arrest the diffusion process and tended to demoralize the innovative systems already introduced.

PROBLEM AREAS IN DIFFUSION

My investigation attempted to find out why diffusion was not more rapid and extensive. The reasons ranged from defects in the design of the original experiment to unanticipated consequences of the success of the initial pilot project.

Regression in the pilot project

Because diffusion typically occurs over a significant period of time, the sustained success of early experiments can help build momentum for companywide change; conversely, emergent weaknesses in the pilot projects can erode initial support for change.

A clear correlation between the continued success of initial projects and the rate of diffusion is found in several extreme cases. Volvo's truck plant experiment has continued to be effective and has been followed by relatively high diffusion. The Northern Electric experiment was discontinued, and also produced no significant diffusion within the company. A similar consistency is found in the demoralization of Corning's Medfield experiment, after a period of effectiveness, and the lack of diffusion throughout the firm.

Both Shell U.K. and Alcan experienced moderate effectiveness in their early experiments and have shown moderate amounts of diffusion, although causal connections are not indicated. Shell U.K. achieved its diffusion soon after its change program was undertaken; the initial projects subsequently became somewhat demoralized and no further diffusion has occurred. Alcan has recently diffused the ideas of the earlier experiments into a new mill, although there has been a decline in management and worker involvement in the plants in which the earlier innovations were established.

There is not always a correlation between initial project success and diffusion. The strong success of the Topeka plant in GF is not matched so far by a high amount of diffusion, and in the cases of Norsk Hydro and Hunsfos, there is even less correlation. Continued success of initial change projects appears to be only one of many influences on diffusion.

What can cause a successful early experiment to deteriorate later on? I have noted several factors: (1) internal inconsistencies in the original design; (2) loss of support from levels of management above the experimental unit; (3) premature turnover of leaders, operators, or consultants directly associated with a project; (4) stress and crises that lead to more authoritarian management, which in turn demoralizes the innovative unit; (5) tension in the innovative unit's relations with other parties—peer units, staff groups, superiors, labor unions; (6) letdown in participant's involvement after initial success with its attendant publicity; (7) lack of diffusion to other parts of the organization, which isolates the original experiment and its leaders.

The seventh factor or principle, succinctly stated, is "diffuse or die"; it suggests that a circular relationship exists whereby lack of diffusion can *eventually* undermine the viability of the initial project, just as weaknesses that develop in the initial project can undermine the diffusion effort. The converse of this circular relationship is not strong; as I have noted above, continued success in the initial project does not necessarily lead to diffusion throughout the larger organization.

Poor model for change

Even if the pilot project remains viable over time, it may be an ineffective model for diffusion in the firm because it lacks either visibility or credibility. These deficiencies may reflect the behavior of leaders of the experiment, or they may relate to the way policy is formulated by higher officials. Also, many characteristics inherent in the site of the initial experiment affect its ability to stimulate further change. Consider the many conditions of the GF pet food plant that enhanced the success of that project: The Topeka plant was new, was located in a favorable labor market, required few workers, and was geographically separate from headquarters and other existing facilities of GF. Since it was a new plant with a new work force, no union agreement was required to establish the new work structure. Many of these conditions, of course, did not exist elsewhere in GF, and many managers asked, "Is work restructuring possible in other situations—for example, in a large, established, unionized plant?"

The credibility of the Corning and Northern Electric projects suffered not only for similar reasons but also from an additional site characteristic: The technology involved in the experimental plant was significantly different from that employed in other plants in the system.

In terms of site characteristics, Volvo, Alcan, and Shell U.K. appear to have presented relatively good prospects for further diffusion of a successful experiment. They were initiated in large, established, unionized facilities and involved technologies typical of the larger systems of which they were a part.

The prospects for diffusion of the work restructuring innovations at the Norsk Hydro fertilizer plants would have to be regarded as even more favorable. By 1973 a dozen different plants were adjacent to each other in the Porsgrunn area, each producing a different product—ammonia, nitric acid, urea, formic acid, magnesium, plastics, and so on. They were similar in ways that made the fertilizer work organization generally relevant: They employed continuous-process technologies, and large pieces of capital were manned by relatively small work forces. In addition, Norsk Hydro had operations in a number of other locations, and in fact was the largest industrial undertaking in Norway. Thus, one could project the spread of demonstrably successful ideas throughout the Porsgrunn works and other parts of the firm, and because of the firm's prominence in Norway, to other industrial firms in this small country. Obviously, for an explanation of why much diffusion did not occur, we will have to look elsewhere than to site characteristics.

The way the project leaders present the experiment to others in the firm will influence its visibility and credibility. One basic choice is whether to maintain a low profile or to seek visibility in the corporate environment.

A low profile reduces the career risks associated with failure, and less publicity also minimizes the risk of creating a "showcase" complex with longer-run adverse effects on the work climate. However, in the cases studied, the incentive to publicize the experiments increased substantially once they appeared to be successfully established. Visibility, it was felt, was essential if diffusion were to occur, and the natural pride in the innovation was accompanied by a desire for wider recognition—inside the company and beyond. Some favorable publicity often created an appetite for more. The project leaders sometimes lost control of publicity to other corporate officials and the media.

Except possibly for Corning's Medfield and Northern Electric's Advanced Devices Center, the initial experiments in my sample achieved sufficient visibility throughout their corporate organizations.

Confusion over what is to be diffused

Even if the initial site is favorable for eventual diffusion and the project leaders manage the publicity effectively, higher management can botch up the process in the way they formulate and communicate the diffusion policy.

If the form of work structure indicated by company policy is stated too conceptually, the policy may be dismissed as abstract and platitudinous or action may be delayed because managers don't know how to translate the concepts.

On the other hand, if the ideas about the desired forms of work structure are stated too operationally, then they may be rejected as inappropriate by managers whose units have different types of work forces, different technologies, or different economic conditions.

Norsk Hydro presents an interesting case in point. Six years after the initiation of the fertilizer experiment and many years after it had become official company policy to diffuse this type of work innovation, managers still complained about the lack of clarity. Was the policy to diffuse "job enrichment," "autonomous groups," "organizational development," "socio-technical systems," or something more general that underlies all of these?

There was general agreement that diffusion would have proceeded more rapidly if it had been clear that the policy was for managers to pursue certain *aims* (such as making better use of the talents of employees and allowing for more day-to-day influence by employees over their work) rather than to employ particular *techniques*.

Inappropriateness of concepts employed

The long-run diffusion of work restructuring is affected by another issue: While the concepts should be inspiring, they must also be realistic.

"Autonomous groups" was the key concept employed in the Norwegian experiments to characterize the work restructuring innovations. The term, which many found inspiring, was later dropped because it was not feasible for many groups to become truly autonomous.

"Equal status" was a concept in the design of Shell U.K.'s Teesport work system. The term captured the imagination of the workers as well as the originators, but overstated what higher management was prepared to do. Differences persisted between blue- and white-collar workers, although all employees were placed on salary. The differences remaining were especially resented because of the expectations aroused by the "equal status" concept.

Deficient implementation

The initial project may be viable in itself, but the follow-through may be inadequate, in terms of locating accountability for the change and providing "how-to" knowledge.

The first point has already been illustrated. Norsk Hydro unsuccessfully attempted to place the responsibility for diffusion with Joint Consultation Boards and then shifted it to middle management. Shell U.K. started implementation by selecting a few projects with heavy reliance upon a few staff people but then shifted to a policy in which all department heads become accountable for change in their units. Accountability for work restructuring in Volvo was clearest—it was an essential part of the plant managers' responsibility period!

As is true with many types of change in organizations, "how-to" knowledge must be provided through training, consulting, or both. Resources for this seemed to have been a limiting factor at one time or another in GF, Corning, and Alcan.

Lack of top management commitment

A period of sustained priority for work restructuring is important in achieving diffusion. The continuing interest and commitment of Volvo's president is a prime case in point. By contrast, the shifting priority given work restructuring in several other firms' studies hindered diffusion. An illustrative case is Norsk Hydro, where the work restructuring objective received lower priority during 1970-73 than it did in the period 1967-69.

Priority declined for several reasons. First, when the initial experiment was launched there was a high sense of urgency about improving industrial relations and productivity. But with a general improvement in industrial relations and the competitiveness of the business, the sense of urgency declined.

Second, according to the middle-level managers, they have come under increasing pressure to meet demanding volume and cost objectives, making it risky in the short run to start any major projects. One manager said, "I have the freedom to innovate but not the time."

Third, the company has been transformed by rapid expansion and revolutionary change in the raw materials and processes used in much of its business. The changes absorbed the attention of top management and the director-general became more formal and less accessible to members of the organization—at least to those who wanted to lobby for work restructuring.

The Shell U.K. managers perceived a similar set of changes as weakening their work restructuring program. In 1971, Hill reported that after mid-1967 there was a lack of continuing visible commitment at the top. In 1967, the U.K. company was reorganized to include North Sea exploration and production as well as U.K. refining activities, and a new chief executive was appointed. The refineries repeatedly requested assurances that the top management of the enlarged company endorsed and supported the philosophy behind the work restructuring program. When the new management team became absorbed in supply problems created by the 1967 Middle East War and failed to formally endorse an amended statement of philosophy tailored to the company's enlarged role, managers in the refineries became less willing to embark on change.

In many cases, including those just mentioned, inconsistencies in higher-management behavior weakened diffusion efforts. Even before they perceived that the program was down-graded, Shell U.K. managers were concerned that although they were asked to protect and develop their human resources, they were being assessed mainly on their handling of the technical system alone.

In the latter part of the 1960s, Alcan division management reportedly shifted toward a more directive, top-down type of leadership and away from a consultative, problem-oriented management pattern. This directly contradicted and undermined the innovative work structure that had been developed at the Kingston works and had an inhibiting effect on further diffusion of work restructuring in the division.

Union opposition

Like sustained top-management commitment, union support or acceptance is a necessary condition for any significant diffusion of work restructuring. In some cases, union support has been, on balance, a positive factor. In other cases, perceived opposition by the union has been a reason for not trying to diffuse work restructuring into unionized plants. Mostly, unions have had more complicated effects—on the process of introducing change, the nature of the work structures introduced, and the work climate.

The Scandinavian union movement has been more positive toward work restructuring than trade unions in the U.K. and North America. Clearly, joint union-management sponsorship of the Norwegian experiments served to legitimize the program for workers. However, the actual effects of the union officials on diffusion within Norsk Hydro and Hunsfos were mixed, just as the effects on the management side were mixed.

In Norsk Hydro a particularly key union official had moved from the area and the loss of his support hurt the diffusion effort. In Hunsfos, where the chief shop steward and the company president were strongly committed to the diffusion program, local effort received no backing from the trade union movement. Although the trade union movement as a whole was not averse to the changes pioneered at Hunsfos, the chief shop steward reported criticism from other quarters. He said he took risks with his own constituency every time he "stuck his neck out" (for example, on a change that resulted in a crew reduction). Also, radical sociologists accused him of selling out to management, increasing company efficiency at the expense of workers.

At Volvo, the unions have played an active and positive role in the work restructuring program. Management had initiated the job redesign aspects of the program and the union the consultative aspects. Both parties, moreover, claim joint ownership of the total program.

In the case of the Shell U.K. program, the union deliberately slowed down the rate of diffusion of work restructuring during 1965-68 until productivity bargaining had progressed to the point where they had been able to establish the economic quid pro quo for certain changes.

The union had played its role in the recent demoralization of the Shell U.K. change program. Management negotiated wage increases in 1971 and 1972 that were below the national pattern, and then in 1973 the government constraints prevented the parties from making up the difference. The union has reflected and perhaps amplified worker resentment.

Another factor at Shell is tension around manning. Top management continues to put pressure on refinery managers to reduce the work force. When we recall that guarantees against dismissal and provisions for extra pay were a quid pro quo in the initial change program, we can see how reviving the issue has led to poorer union-management relations and inhibited the further diffusion of work restructuring.

Three projects started in nonunion plants of firms whose other plants were mostly unionized. Unions representing these other plants were expected to oppose or otherwise complicate work restructuring in them. The three firms were General Foods, Corning, and Northern Electric. In the case of GF, where work restructuring efforts have actually been undertaken in unionized plants, the collective bargaining relationship complicated change in the early steps but has not prevented it. With Corning and Northern Electric little or no attempt was made to diffuse change to union plants.

To summarize, unions' effect has taken many forms:

First, unions have influenced the basic climate for change. Sometimes the effect was positive, helping to legitimize work restructuring or entering into an informal problem-solving pattern consistent with the work culture sought by the work restructuring experiment. Sometimes the effect of unions was negative, inhibiting management from trying to diffuse change or formalizing and politicizing relations contradictory to the spirit of the work culture being diffused.

Second, unions have complicated the change process by requiring additional consensus-seeking efforts.

Third, unions have affected the preconditions for change or limited the nature of the change itself. Sometimes they have obtained assurances on job security and earnings maintenance and have bargained for workers to obtain a share of the increased productivity that resulted from more flexibility and reduced work crews. Sometimes they have prevented certain changes, e.g., modifications in job content that affect union jurisdictional boundaries or historical patterns.

Bureaucratic barriers

The importance of this issue belies the simplicity with which it can be stated. Diffusion efforts are frustrated by vested interests and existing organizational routines that limit local autonomy.

Innovative plant managements have often felt harassed by staff groups, who for their part have often become irritated and impatient with many of the plants' demands for self-sufficiency and exemption from uniform company policies. These tensions may be present during the establishment of the initial experiment, and they are escalated when serious diffusion begins."Experiments," by definition, minimize the scope and duration of the effects of the change involved. However, when the changes are declared enduring or an attempt is made to spread them, the stakes are raised for groups affected.

Bureaucratic barriers can be illustrated from the experience of one company, where managers themselves introduced the term. One problem relates to the level at which decisions are made in the line organization. In 1973, workers were operating informally without supervisors on two of the four shifts, but formalization of this arrangement and extension to a third and fourth shift was not within the authority of the manager of the innovative plant.

Another example involved the method for judging operator qualification for increased pay in the innovative plant. Central personnel insisted that the "theoretical" tests of knowledge appropriate for each job had to be mastered before "practical" knowledge could be compensated. Previously, theoretical knowledge could be learned and compensated *after* a person had shown he could perform the day-to-day operations associated with a particular job and had received an adjustment for that practical mastery. These events not only demoralized the participants of the project, but also discouraged other managers from initiating projects.

The experience of General Foods, Shell U.K., and other firms in which an ambitious diffusion effort has been undertaken are rich with similar illustrations, involving such issues as whether quality assurance procedures at plant level must be uniform throughout the corporation, whether a common job evaluation scheme should be applied to plants with radically different work structures, what should be the respective roles of central engineering and local staff in plant expansion programs, how much local autonomy should exist in creating and filling plant management positions, and whether reporting requirements must be applied uniformly throughout the system.

Threatened obsolescence

A restructured work situation requires new roles and new skills and makes others obsolete. We have already mentioned the resistance of staff groups who may have to acquire new knowledge, develop new consultative patterns for imparting their expertise, and see some of their functions being performed by nonspecialists.

However, the greatest threat was to first-line supervision. The number of first-line supervisors was often decreased. Sometimes the position was even eliminated. Where the position was retained, the role was changed in the ways that required new attitudes and greater interpersonal and group skills.

Supervisors individually and as a group are weak compared with other groups potentially affected by new work structures. They themselves have not mounted much effective opposition to the diffusion or tried to shape the form of work restructuring, with one exception —Volvo, where within the past year the supervisors' union has taken an active role to protect its members' interests. In at least one case, Hunsfos, concern by workers about the effect of work restructuring on their supervisors created a major snag in the diffusion process. In many other cases, management's uncertainty about how to handle the potential obsolescence of existing foremen has been a factor inhibiting diffusion.

In some cases the resistance of supervisors and other salaried personnel was not due to a direct threat to their existing roles; rather, they felt neglected by comparison with blue-collar workers. They resented the fact that the blue-collar worker's job was enriched and his status and influence upgraded, while their lot had not improved.

Self-limiting dynamics

In companies that employed the most comprehensive diffusion strategy, there was a tendency for pilot projects to be self-limiting or "self-sealing." The tendency was strongest in instances like Norsk Hydro, Hunsfos, and General Foods, where a single small unit was involved in the original experiment and where serious efforts to introduce work restructuring into other units came only after widespread publicity on the success of the experimental unit.

One dynamic involved a "star-envy" phenomenon, which can be illustrated by Norsk Hydro. The original experiment in the fertilizer plants received an enormous amount of publicity within Norway and outside. The fertilizer plants became the object of innumerable visits by managers, trade union officials, social scientists, and schoolchildren. Top management looked approvingly on the project and made it company policy for others to follow the lead of the fertilizer project. Not surprisingly, the attention given the fertilizer groups engendered resentment and envy among the other persons who were asked to adopt the innovation in their own operations. The resentment was accompanied by resistance to the work restructuring program. The experience of the Topeka plant in General Foods was strikingly similar.

A second dynamic involved a shift in the reward structure. Payoffs for pioneers and those who followed them in the same organization differed in important respects, providing a much less favorable benefit-risk picture for the subsequent users of organizational innovations. Managers who adapted the innovation and succeeded received less credit than the pioneer received, and if they had failed, they probably would have lost more standing in management than the pioneer would have if he had failed. Managers who did not utilize the innovation often figured that while they might be prodded and goaded for not taking any organizational initiatives, ultimately they would be judged on the basis of production and profit performance. In short, they felt that they could afford to resist pressure.

A third dynamic involved the tendency for participants to feel special and to regard their experimental work system as superior. On the one hand, this feeling reinforced their commitment to the group and was a positive factor in helping to establish a new form of social organization. On the other hand, this tended to lead outsiders to conclude that the culture created was unique and to discount the general applicability of the experiment.

A fourth dynamic came into play at a later date. Rivalry sometimes developed among those engaged in work restructuring. They stressed minor differences in their approaches, while ignoring the similarity in underlying values and assumptions. One effect of this form of rivalry among change agents and among innovative units was to weaken their ability to form the collegial networks described as part of the general diffusion model.

A fifth dynamic also came into play at a later stage in those cases where diffusion did not occur fairly rapidly. It was a secondary consequence of two factors related above: the bureaucratic barriers and the special self-image developed by experimental units. The leaders of some innovative units had engaged in so many skirmishes with superiors and staff groups over corporate practices and were so aggressive in asserting the correctness of their positions that they hurt their careers. Observing this, some peers resolved not to get similarly burned.

OTHER INFLUENTIAL FACTORS

After having studied the diffusion process in eight companies and after having analyzed the situational factors that seemed to account for a generally slower-than-expected rate of diffusion, I became interested in assessing how inherently difficult or easy these new structures are to diffuse.

The early classic studies of diffusion traced the adoption of improved agricultural practices. More recent studies have covered other innovations, including farm practices, medical drugs, educational techniques, machinery, management control techniques, and so on. Should we expect diffusion of work restructuring to be relatively slower or faster than diffusion of innovations in these other fields?

Recent reviews of the literature on diffusion consistently concurred on a number of attributes of innovations that influenced their adoption rate. Most are plausible, at least on the surface.

1. *Relative advantage.* This is an obvious attribute that enhances the rate of diffusion. The cost-benefit analysis implied in this attribute includes not only financial but also perceived social costs and benefits. The problem with work restructuring is that there is a singular lack of agreement among its proponents over the benefits derived. Some stress tangible impacts on such factors as productivity and turnover; others choose to emphasize the psychic dividends paid to workers.

2. *Communicability.* Diffusion will be enhanced if the innovation can be explained easily and if its effects are easily separable from other influences in the environment. Work restructuring innovations rate low on this attribute compared with all other types of innovations cited. Volvo may be an exception. The changes were straight-

forward and readily grasped. Well-established production norms permitted an easy assessment of any loss of efficiency, and the desired decrease in turnover was quickly measured (although not always persuasively explained). Thus communicability may help explain why Volvo's relatively simple changes on the existing assembly lines were diffused relatively rapidly.

3. *Compatability.* Diffusion is aided if the innovation is perceived as being congruent with existing norms, values, and structures. Again, work restructuring innovations must be rated low because by definition they call for important structural and normative changes in the existing industrial organizations. (Work restructuring threatens what many managers in the United States continue to regard as their prerogatives.) However, the same innovations would rate higher in compatability in Scandinavia than in the U.S.

4. *Pervasiveness.* This term refers to the number of aspects of the system affected by the innovation. Less pervasiveness permits more rapid diffusion. By definition, what we refer to as "work restructuring" strives to be comprehensive, embracing division of labor, rewards, supervision, status systems, and power relations. This factor, too, makes diffusing work restructuring inherently difficult.

5. *Reversibility.* Can an innovation be adopted on an experimental basis and reversed without serious consequences? If the status quo ante cannot be readily restored, diffusion will be inhibited. Many managers believe that work restructuring creates expectations that will become a liability if the innovation must be abandoned. My limited observations support that belief. Thus work restructuring may rate moderate to low on the reversibility factor.

6. *Number of gatekeepers.* Numerous approval channels that must be satisfied before an innovation can be adopted will tend to inhibit the rate of diffusion. In work restructuring, top management, departmental or plant managers, staff groups, supervisors, unions, and the workers themselves all have some gatekeeping role to perform. One could hardly imagine gatekeeping conditions less favorable for diffusion of new work structures.

Finally, a major difficulty in diffusing work restructuring is that frequently it's not literally a matter of "adoption." Because work forces, technologies, and economics affect the appropriate work structure, tailored application of the general principles of work restructuring is required rather than adoption of a predetermined model.

CONCLUSION

One important reason for the unimpressive rate of diffusion in the eight companies studied is that, especially in their more comprehensive form, these innovations have many attributes that make their diffusion inherently slow. Even if they offer relative advantages over existing work structures, their character and results are not highly communicable; they are not congruent with existing norms and values; their potential effect in a given work situation is pervasive rather than fractional; they are not readily reversed without incurring social costs; and too many affected parties serve as gatekeepers for the effective implementation of the innovations.

Another set of explanations for the actual diffusion observed in the eight companies relates to the barriers the diffusion efforts encountered and the efficacy of companies' strategies and tactics.

Many key areas are readily identifiable: Does the experiment continue to show good results? Is the experiment sufficiently visible and sufficiently convincing? Is organizational accountability for initiating change clear, and is know-how for implementation available? Is there sustained support for diffusion from powerful groups such as top management and union officials? Careful planning is required to ensure that the answers to these questions are positive.

Two problem areas deal with organizational dilemmas generated by the nature of the innovations. Work restructuring requires an increase in local autonomy, thereby threatening the power of central staff groups and some managers. It also threatens to make some roles obsolete or to eliminate the positions of some staff specialists and first-line supervisors. These problems are not easily resolved and require imaginative solutions—solutions not yet obvious to me.

Last, perhaps the most interesting type of barrier to diffusion is the self-limiting dynamics of pilot projects. Ironically, several of these are unexpected consequences of the success of the project: The greater the attention given pilot units, the more likely are managers of peer units to be "turned off" by the example. The more successful the pioneer, the less favorable are the payoffs and the greater the risks for those who follow. The more esprit de corps and sense of being special that develops in the unit, the less generalizable it appears to others.

Some of the implications of our analysis of these and other self-limiting tendencies are apparent once the dynamics are understood: There is an advantage in (1) introducing a number of projects at the same time in the same firm, (2) avoiding over-exposure and glorification of particular change efforts, and (3) having the innovative program identified with top management at the initial project stage.

As the examples of work restructuring in the larger society become more numerous, however, the self-limiting tendencies should pose less of a problem.

In conclusion, I expect relatively little diffusion of potentially significant restructuring in the work place—over the short run. Hopefully the long run may tell a different story.

Increasingly, what many employees expect from their jobs is different from what organizations are prepared to offer them. Work restructuring is the preeminent answer to closing the gap. I would expect the latent dissatisfactions of workers to be activated and pressure for work restructuring to increase as the issues receive more public attention and as more successful examples of comprehensive work restructuring raise the general level of worker expectations. I would also be surprised if future experiments did not profit from the pioneering efforts. Together, these factors should generate an increase in the number of diffusions and a hastening of the pace of diffusion. But how many diffusions and how fast the pace, I can't even begin to guess.

SELECTED BIBLIOGRAPHY

A useful volume of papers on the problems associated with work is *The Worker and the Job: Coping with Change*, edited by Jerome M. Rosow (Prentice-Hall, Inc., 1974).

Included in that volume is a paper of mine, "Innovative Restructuring of Work," which reports on other aspects of the study on which the present article is based. It describes the rationale for, nature of, and results, achieved by a dozen pilot projects in work restructuring. It also analyzes the viability of these projects over time.

Two recent reviews of the factors influencing diffusion of innovations in a wide range of fields are Gerald Zaltman, Robert Duncan, and Jonny Holbek's *Innovations and Organizations* (John Wiley & Sons, 1973) and John Kimberly's "Policies for Innovation in the Service Sector," prepared for the OECD Directorate for Scientific Affairs, October 1973.

The studies at the Work Research Institute in Oslo, Norway have also noted what Philip Herbst has called the "self-encapsulating" effects of experimental changes in work design. See Herbst's "Some Reflections on the Work Democratized Project —1974. I: The Process of Diffusion," Work Research Institutes, Oslo, Document 13/1974.

I wish to acknowledge the helpful comments of Chris Argyris on an earlier draft of this paper and the support for this research provided by the Ford Foundation and the Division of Research, Harvard Graduate School of Business Administration.

DISCUSSION QUESTIONS

1. Do you think it is possible to design a conflict-free organization? Why? Assuming it is possible, is a conflict-free organization desirable?

2. If you were in conflict with a Tough Battler, how would you react? Why?

3. Describe the guidelines you would follow in attempting to obtain a win-win outcome.

4. Explain the following statement and discuss its implications: "Knowledge is limited; but perceptions of knowledge create unwarranted outcomes."

5. What are the basic differences between power-oriented and problem-solving methods of resolving conflicts?

6. What are the essential characteristics of an OD intervention?

7. Select one of the classes you are currently enrolled in. Write a one-paragraph description for each of the following dimensions of that class's climate: autonomy, structure, reward orientation, and warmth and support. Is there a gap between how you described the climate and how you would like the climate to be? If so, select an OD intervention to close the gap. How would you evaluate the success of your chosen intervention?

8. Why is there an advantage to introducing a number of work restructuring projects at the same time in the same firm?

9. Why is it important that top management identifies with an innovative program at the initial project stage?

SECTION IX

Managing Careers In Organizations

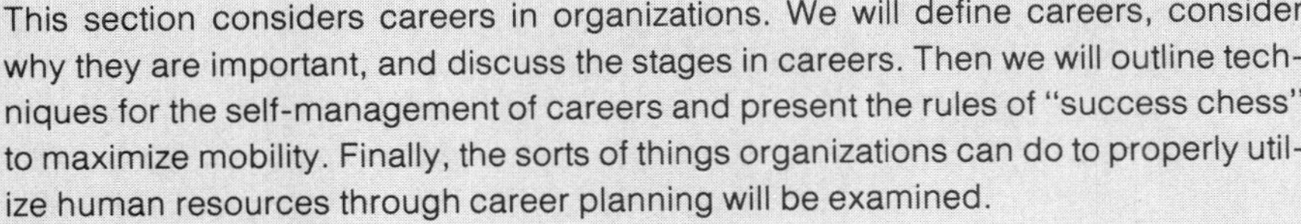

This section considers careers in organizations. We will define careers, consider why they are important, and discuss the stages in careers. Then we will outline techniques for the self-management of careers and present the rules of "success chess" to maximize mobility. Finally, the sorts of things organizations can do to properly utilize human resources through career planning will be examined.

KEY TERMS

CAREER
PROTEAN CAREER
CAREER STAGES
SUCCESS CHESS
CRUCIAL SUBORDINATE
EXPOSURE
VISIBILITY
MOBILOGRAPHY
CAREER IDENTITY
CAREER ATTITUDES
CAREER ADAPTABILITY
PSYCHOLOGICAL SUCCESS
ASSESSMENT CENTER
JOB PATHING
DUAL CAREERS
CAREER-GROWTH CYCLE

OBJECTIVES

1. To consider what is meant by a career
2. To recognize why careers are important
3. To identify career stages
4. To describe how to manage one's own career
5. To point out things that influence career mobility
6. To show how to maximize one's own career mobility
7. To identify career outcomes besides measures of performance
8. To suggest what organizations can do to utilize human resources through career planning

CHAPTER 30

Career Management[1]

Back in chapter 3, we discussed how people choose jobs. We concluded by saying that we hoped the chapter would one day help you develop a highly successful career. That seems like a reasonable hope. After all, we all have some idea of what a career is. And, certainly, a successful career is better than one that is unsuccessful. In a sense, though, our comment left a lot unsaid. First, of course, there is much more to a career than choice of a job. Further, it is perhaps not clear exactly what a career really is. Nor, for that matter, is success so easy to pin down.

Consider, for example, the case of Mary. After graduating from high school, Mary took a job as a baker at Better Bagels, Inc. Following her marriage to Bill, she left her baking job to become a housewife. Years later, with her family grown, Mary decided to pursue an interest she had recently developed. She started a handicraft business, first selling from her home, then opening a small shop, and finally running a chain of four stores in town. Did Mary's marriage interrupt her career, or was it part of her career?

Or consider the Smith brothers. Identical twins in all ways except their desires for upward mobility, each took an entry-level job with a national pet-store chain, Animals Amalgamated. Shortly after they began work, the brothers were each offered similar significant promotions. However, the promotions would require moves to Alabaster, Alaska, home of the whistling seal. Bob, the ambitious brother, jumped at the chance without even bothering to consult his wife. Sam considered the effects on his family of making the move, weighed the pros and cons of the promotion, and decided that upward mobility really was not that important to him. Years later, Sam

[1]Much of this chapter is based on Hall (1976).

was in the same position in the organization, spending most of his day changing papers in parakeets' cages. Still, his family was happy, he was satisfied with his lot in life, and he often enjoyed reading the papers as he changed them. In the meantime, Bob had been a shooting star in the business, rising in just ten years to the presidency of the firm, with high status, astronomical salary and bonuses, and free Chameleon Chow. However, Bob's marriage had broken up because of the strains associated with his career, and his struggle to the top had alienated his friends. Who had the most successful career, Bob or Sam?

THE DEFINITION OF A CAREER

What is a career? One definition, given by Douglas T. Hall, is that "the career is the individually perceived sequence of attitudes and behaviors associated with work-related experiences and activities over the span of the person's life" (1976, p. 4). Hall put together this definition on basis of the following four assumptions about careers.

1. Career per se doesn't imply success or failure, fast or slow advancement. There is more to a career than movements "up" and "down" between jobs.

2. The career is individually perceived, so career success or failure is best assessed by the person whose career is being considered.

3. The career is made up of both attitudes and behaviors. While we tend to think of careers in terms of moves from one job to another and of related behaviors, they also involve changes in values, attitudes, and motivation.

4. Because the career is a sequence of work-related experiences, all sorts of work—volunteer, homemaking, political activities, as well as on-the-job work—fit this definition of a career.

This definition and the related assumptions should make it clear that there is more to a career than movement up a hierarchy. Like beauty, career success is in the eye of the beholder. The definition also emphasizes that many things besides organizational level change during a career. Even our basic values change.

This definition of a career suggests a shift in the locus of control from things external to the individual to the individual himself or herself. Individuals are seen as being less passive, as formulating their own definition of success, and as seeing many factors besides upward mobility as important.

Hall refers to this approach as the *protean career*. Proteus, according to Greek mythology, was able to change his shape easily in any way he wanted—from fire to lion to dragon to tree. Only when he was held against his will would he finally assume a single form. As Hall describes it:

The protean career is a process which the person, not the organization, is managing. It consists of all of the person's varied experiences in education, training, work in several organizations, changes in occupational field, etc. The protean career is *not* what happens to the person in any one organization. The protean person's own personal career choices and search for self-fulfillment are the unifying or integrative elements in his or her life. The criterion of success is internal (psychological success), not external. (1976, p. 201)

This view of career calls for a fundamental change in values, sense of personal control, definition of performance, and other important variables. Table 30-1 summarizes some key differences between the traditional and the protean career.

THE IMPORTANCE OF CAREERS

It may be useful to point out specifically some of the reasons why people are concerned about careers. Hall (1976) provides the following six.

1. The career represents the person's entire *life* in the work setting. Also, work is generally a key factor in determining the quality of life. Work has the potential for directly or indirectly satisfying almost all human needs. Faced with retirement, many people fantasize about dying, and, in fact, mortality rates do seem to rise sharply immediately after retirement.

TABLE 30-1
Differences Between the Traditional Career and the Protean Career*

ISSUE	PROTEAN CAREER	TRADITIONAL CAREER
Who's in charge?	Person	Organization
Core values	Freedom; Growth	Advancement; Power
Degree of mobility	High	Lower
Important performance dimensions	Psychological success	Position level; Salary
Important attitude dimensions	Work satisfaction; Professional commitment	Work satisfaction Organizational commitment
Important identity dimensions	Do I respect myself? (self-esteem) What do I want to do? (self-awareness)	Am I respected in this organization? (esteem from others) What should I do? (organizational awareness)
Important adaptability dimensions	Work-related flexibility Current competence (Measure: marketability)	Organization-related flexibility (Measure: organizational survival)

*From *Careers in Organizations*, by Douglas T. Hall, p. 202. Copyright © 1976 by Goodyear Publishing Co. reprinted by permission.

2. Work is one way to achieve social equality and social liberation. Since the work career is becoming a primary target in the politics of social change, organizations will have to place increasing emphasis on the career opportunities they give their employees.

3. With a growing emphasis in our society on "doing your own thing," people who are dissatisfied with their jobs are more likely to change jobs and even occupations than in the past. Such mobility is no longer necessarily frowned upon. In a related vein, many people are now refusing to let their careers unduly interfere with their personal lives. Thus, they probably won't passively accept transfers and other disrupting moves. It will become more and more necessary for organizations to recognize this growing emphasis on personal freedom and plan accordingly.

4. Because they have a better grasp of what motivates subordinates, managers who understand career interests and career dynamics are likely to manage people more effectively.

5. Changes in the job or organization affect employees' careers. Managers who are sensitive to their subordinates' career interests and aspirations will be best able to realize change.

6. Understanding career processes can aid in self-awareness and self-control, resulting in better management of one's own career.

CAREER STAGES

In chapter 3, when we discussed how people choose jobs, we reviewed three stages of occupational aspirations—the fantasy stage, the tentative stage, and the realistic stage. There are other descriptions of the stages that people go through, both in choosing and in experiencing a career.

For example, Delbert Miller and William Form (1964) described five occupational stages based on job behaviors. The *preparatory work period* consists of early experiences and adjustments in the home, school, and community as the individual develops mental and physical maturity. The *initial work period* begins when the individual seeks a first job while still in school; jobs accepted during this period are part-time and occasional. The *trial work period* starts with the first regular full-time job and continues until the individual—usually in his or her late twenties or early thirties—settles into a stable field of work. The *stable work period*, is followed by *retirement*. Table 30-2 presents characteristics of the three periods of active work life. People differ in the extent to which they stay in each of these stages; in fact, they may never enter some of them at all. Some jump directly from school to the stable work period. Others go through all the stages. Still others, for one reason or another, never reach a stable work period.

Another theory of career stages is based on life stages. Donald Super and his colleagues use a model of five developmental stages: (1)

PERIODS OF WORK ADJUSTMENT	INITIAL PERIOD	TRIAL PERIOD	STABLE PERIOD
NATURE OF JOB	Part-time and summer employment	Full-time employment	Full-time employment
MOBILITY	High occupational and work plant mobility	High occupational and work plant mobility	Low occupational and work plant mobility
WORKER'S OCCUPATIONAL HISTORY IS CHARACTERIZED BY:	Job impermanence	Job transition	Job persistence
PSYCHOLOGICAL COMPONENTS: I. Feelings of the worker	Worker feels that he is only working temporarily and that his performance on the job is secondary to his school life.	Worker feels that he is working at a job (1) in preparation for a more responsible job or (2) to find out if he wants to remain at his present job or work plant, or is merely (3) holding on until he can make a change.	Worker feels that he has found the job and the work plant in which he intends to remain, or finds himself unable to move from the job or the work plant.
II. Attitudes of worker and observers as described by common folk expressions	"Making some spending money" "Preparing himself" "Helping out" "Working temporarily"	"Getting started" "Moving around" "Trying to find out what he likes" "Staying until the first of the year" "It's a living for a while"	"A fixture" "Old-timer" "Intends to stick here" "He likes his job" "He's stuck in that rut"

*Figure 13.2 "Periods of Active Work Life," from *Industrial Sociology,* 2nd Edition by Delbert C. Miller and William H. Form. Copyright © 1964 by Delbert C. Miller and William H. Form. Reprinted by permission of Harper & Row, Publishers, Inc.

TABLE 30-2
Periods of Active Work Life*

childhood, (2) adolescence, (3) young adulthood, (4) maturity, and (5) old age (Super and Bohn, 1970). The primary tasks in these five stages are, respectively, growth, exploration of career interests and opportunities, establishment in a particular field, maintenance of position, and decline and disengagement. These vocational life stages are presented in more detail in table 30-3.

Douglas T. Hall and Khalil Nougaim (1968) have presented evidence that supports the idea of career stages. Hall and Nougaim followed young managers at American Telephone and Telegraph Company through the first five years of their careers. They were interested in part in testing whether Maslow's need hierarchy was valid. While their results indicated that Maslow's arguments don't hold up very well under empirical testing, they did discover some interesting patterns. For example, in the first year of employment, there were strong concerns for safety—that is, needs to become recognized, established members of the organization. These safety needs declined in importance until, by the fifth year, they were the least important of the four needs measured. On the other hand, needs for

TABLE 30-3
Vocational Life Stages*

1. *Growth Stage* (Birth-14)

   Self-concept develops through identification with key figures in family and in school, needs and fantasy are dominant early in this stage; interest and capacity become more important in this stage with increasing social participation and reality testing. Substages of the growth stage are:

   Fantasy (4-10). Needs are dominant, role playing in fantasy is important.

   Interests (11-12). Likes are the major determinant of aspirations and activities.

   Capacity (13-14). Abilities are given more weight, and job requirements (including training) are considered.

2. *Exploration Stage* (Age 15-24)

   Self-examination, role tryouts, and occupational exploration take place in school, leisure activities, and part-time work. Substages of the exploration stage are:

   Tentative (15-17). Needs, interests, capacities, values, and opportunities are all considered. Tentative choices are made and tried out in fantasy, discussion, courses, work, etc.

   Transition (18-21). Reality considerations are given more weight as the youth enters labor market or professional training and attempts to implement a self-concept.

   Trial (22-24). A seemingly appropriate field having been located, a beginning job in it is found and is tried out as a life work.

3. *Establishment Stage* (Age 25-44)

   Having found an appropriate field, effort is put forth to make a permanent place in it. There may be some trial early in this stage, with consequent shifting, but establishment may begin without trial, especially in the professions. Substages of the establishment stage are:

   Trial (25-30). The field of work presumed to be suitable may prove unsatisfactory, resulting in one or two changes before the life work is found or before it becomes clear that the life work will be a succession of unrelated jobs.

   Stabilization (31-44). As the career pattern becomes clear, effort is put forth to stabilize, to make a secure place, in the world of work. For most persons these are the creative years.

4. *Maintenance Stage* (Age 45-64)

   Having made a place in the world of work, the concern is now to hold it. Little new ground is broken, but there is continuation along established lines.

5. *Decline Stage* (Age 65 on)

   As physical and mental powers decline, work activity changes and in due course ceases. New roles must be developed, first that of selective participant and then that of observer rather than participant. Substages of this stage are:

   Deceleration (65-70). Sometimes at the time of official retirement, sometimes late in the maintenance stage, the pace of work slackens, duties are shifted, or the nature of the work is changed to suit declining capacities. Many men find part-time jobs to replace their full-time occupations.

   Retirement (71 on). As with all the specified age limits, there are great variations from person to person. But complete cessation of occupation comes for all in due course, to some easily and pleasantly, to others with difficulty and disappointment, and to some only with death.

*Reprinted with permission of the publisher from *Vocational Development: A Framework for Research* by Super et al, pp. 40-41. Copyright © 1954 by Teachers' College Press, New York, N.Y.

esteem and achievement became increasingly important over the five years. During those five years, the managers seemed to move from Super's establishment stage into a period of advancement, perhaps a part of the stabilization segment of Super's stages.

Although they could only speculate beyond the five-year period they considered, Hall and Nougaim felt that, once managers in their sample sensed they were nearing the limit of their advancement, their careers probably would level off, and the need to compete would decrease. Recognizing they were on a terminal plateau, they would find means other than hierarchical advancement to achieve gratification. Such a description fits Super's maintenance stage. Hall (1976) notes that stabilization apparently occurs earlier in managerial careers than in careers in general as described by Super. Advancement takes up the remainder of the years Super includes under stabilization.

The various career stages place substantially different demands on the individual, in terms both of job requirements and of socio-emotional needs. Hall's summary of developmental needs is presented in table 30-4.[2]

TABLE 30-4
Developmental Needs in Early, Middle, and Late Career*

STAGE	TASK NEEDS	SOCIO-EMOTIONAL NEEDS
EARLY CAREER	1. Develop action skills 2. Develop a specialty 3. Develop creativity, innovation. 4. Rotate into new area after 3-5 years.	1. Support 2. Autonomy 3. Deal with feelings of rivalry, competition.
MIDDLE CAREER	1. Develop skills in training and coaching others (younger employees). 2. Training for updating and integrating skills. 3. Develop broader view of work and organization. 4. Job rotation into new job requiring new skills.	1. Opportunity to express feelings about mid-life (anguish, defeat, limited time, restlessness). 2. Reorganize thinking about self (mortality, values, family, work). 3. Reduce self-indulgence and competitiveness. 4. Support and mutual problem solving for coping with mid-career stress.
LATE CAREER	1. Shift from power role to one of consultation, guidance, wisdom. 2. Begin to establish self in activities outside the organization (start on part-time basis).	1. Support and counseling to help see integrated life experiences as a platform for others. 2. Acceptance of one's one and only life cycle. 3. Gradual detachment from organization.

*From *Careers in Organizations,* by Douglas T. Hall, (p. 90). Copyright © 1976 by Goodyear Publishing Co. reprinted by permission.

[2]For another model of career development in organizations, see Schein (1971).

SELF-MANAGEMENT OF CAREERS

Douglas T. Hall (1976) presents the following useful set of guidelines for career planning.

1. *Develop basic career competencies.* John Crites (1973) has identified five such competencies: self-appraisal, occupational information, goal selection, planning, and problem solving. Each of these competencies can be developed.

a. *Self-appraisal.* Mature career development requires self-awareness. The counseling, guidance, career planning, or personnel offices on most campuses can help at this stage. Counseling interviews, aptitude and interest tests, and career-planning exercises may all be helpful. Also, just asking others, such as an instructor or boss, to give you feedback about your performance can be enlightening.

b. *Occupational information.* Career development requires a fit between you and your job. So it's important to learn about potential jobs. Some sources that provide information about types of work, skill requirements, occupational developments, worker trait requirements, or other relevant factors include the *Dictionary of Occupational Titles,* the U.S. Department of Labor's *Occupational Outlook Handbook,* and the *Occupational Outlook Quarterly.* Also, some interactive computer methods for providing career information are now available.

c. *Goal Selection.* Career success, according to the approach taken in this chapter, means achieving one's goals, so the process of properly setting goals is crucial. Chris Argyris (1964) argues that goals leading to growth are challenging, relevant to the person's self-image, set by the person (alone or in collaboration with another), and implemented by the person's independent effort. Proper goal setting depends upon a prior awareness of one's self and of occupations. That is, goals must be set that are consistent with career capabilities. Counselors, supervisors, or one's own work experiences may be useful in defining appropriate goals. Also, some useful career planning exercises are now available.

d. *Planning.* Once a goal is set, plans must be made for its achievement. That is, it's necessary to specify the steps to be taken to meet that goal and to determine the order of those steps. Both counseling and career planning exercises may help at the planning stage.[3]

e. *Problem solving.* Because problems constantly arise during careers, competence in problem solving can be crucial to the successful movement through a career. Many of the techniques discussed in chapter 16 could readily be applied to career problems.

[3]For example, see Hall, Bowen, Lewicki, and Hall (1975).

2. *Choose an organization carefully.* Your choice of an organization to work for is extremely important. The organization will control many important rewards, may determine where you live, and may even influence the sorts of competencies you develop and the kinds of skills you exercise. Also, your initial choice of an employer may have lasting consequences in terms of the possibilities of future moves to other organizations. For example, in a university setting, it is unlikely that someone seeking to fill a position at a high-status institution, such as Stanford or Yale, would seriously consider the application of someone from what they feel to be a low-status institution, despite that individual's impressive credentials.

3. *Get a challenging initial job.* In choosing a first job, such short-run considerations as salary and location should generally be given less weight than challenge and potential for career growth. If you do take a job that offers little challenge, you should probably either try to make a subsequent job change or try to redefine your job to assume greater responsibility.

4. *Be an outstanding performer.* Good performance enhances your esteem both in the eyes of others, such as your boss, and in your own eyes. Ask your boss to help set challenging goals, to give feedback, and to coach you.

5. *Develop professional mobility.* As is generally the case, more options are better than fewer. So mobility and potential mobility are

Most colleges and universities have placement offices to help students find jobs after they've finished their education.

crucial to career success. A set of rules for the development of mobility is detailed in the next section.

6. *Plan your own and your spouse's careers collaboratively.* If both spouses are working, or may work, severe strains can result unless there is careful career planning. It is unrealistic and unfair to assume that one partner will passively go along when the other takes a job.

7. *Get help in career management.* Seek advice from experts in your school or organization. Consider using professional job counselors or placement specialists.

8. *Anticipate chance events.* No matter how precisely you plan, chance will play a role. Develop contingency plans that specify what you will do if various things—good or bad—take place.

9. *Continually reassess your career.* Mid-course corrections may be needed. Career choices have to be made all through life, not just when you leave school. Continually ask where you are, where you want to be, and how to get there.

CAREER MOBILITY

One reason career mobility is important is that mobility and its potential increase available options. Also, Eugene Jennings has argued that mobility is valued in itself. Here he writes about *mobicentric man*, someone for whom mobility is an end rather than a means.

> The mobicentric man values motion and action not because they lead to change but because they are change, and change is his ultimate value . . . Freedom to him is a form of movement. He frequently changes positions, sometimes within just one company (though never within just one department) and sometimes between companies. . . For him, success is represented less by position, title, salary or performance than by moving and movement. (1970, p. 35)

Mobility rates

Many types of people reach the tops of organizations—sons or daughters of owners, those who entered at the top from another organization, and those who worked their way up from within the same organization where they started their careers. Those in the latter category are called *pure hierarchs*. According to Jennings, the majority of pure hierarchs move through the organizational hierarchy in a predictable pattern of three distinct stages:

1. The technical level, which is nonmanagerial and includes salespeople, engineers, scientists, accountants, and so on;
2. The managerial level;

3. The executive level, made up of the president, his or her immediate subordinates, and those who report directly to those immediate subordinates.

Jennings calls the technical phase an entrance stage to a managerial career. The second stage in the mobility cycle of the pure hierarch is called developmental; there, rapid mobility, both lateral and upward, somewhat resembles an upward spiral. The final stage of the journey to the top is called arrival; an individual is at the arrival stage when he or she assists an individual who sits on the executive committee. Table 30-5 indicates the average times of "supermobiles," "normal mobiles," and "submobiles" in each of the stages.

Findings concerning mobility

Jennings (1967) presents the following findings about mobility.

1. Mobility and corporate strategy are related. The routes and rates of mobility change with the strategy of the corporation. As a particcular functional area—such as marketing or manufacturing or accounting—gains emphasis, the number of managers in those areas moving to the top of the organization increases.

2. Mobility rates of men at the top are strengthened by them. The top executives bring along their crucial subordinates, who have similar mobility patterns. The routes become strengthened through the successes of the managers who created them.

3. There is a strong relationship between mobility and competency. The requirements of most jobs can probably be learned in eighteen months or less. The manager who can move into a position, grasp its uniqueness, master new responsibilities and assignments, and move to another job is likely to gain more competency than others. "Overlearning" a job—that is, spending time on a job after you've mastered its essentials—results in lost career time.

4. Mobility is closely related to organization growth. Firms with high growth rates have high rates of mobility of all kinds —geographical, between divisions, across functional areas, as well as up the hierarchy.

TABLE 30-5
Average Relative Times (in Years) for Career Stages*

	SUPERMOBILE	NORMAL MOBILE	SUBMOBILE
Entrance Stage	0-2	2-3	3-4
Developmental Stage	11	14	15
Arrival Stage	8	10	17
Average Age When Made President	47	50	54

*Adapted from Jennings (1967, p. 9)

5. Mobility is largely the result of a relationship between two or more people. Most managers who arrive at the top were sponsored by someone who had the power to promote or recommend promotion.

6. Mobility is related to entrance age. The chances of making thirty thousand dollars a year while in one's thirties are four times as great for individuals who get out of the technical or entrance stage in two years than for those who stay five years or more.

7. Mobility is related to leverage. When mobile managers see that their upward mobility is being blocked by a slow-moving superior, they may leave the corporation and join another. Permanent identification with one organization hampers mobility. However, using leverage without carefully considering the characteristics of the corporation to be joined often leads to another leverage—and to wasted time.

8. Mobility is creating mobicentric managers. As noted earlier, managers are beginning to desire mobility itself. Movement, whether upward or lateral, is gratifying. Position, title, and salary may all be important, but getting and leaving positions are, to many managers, what really count.

Success chess

Based on these observations and others, Jennings (1971) has set down nine rules to maximize mobility. Briefly summarized, his rules of "success chess" are as follows:

Rule No. 1. Maintain the widest set of options possible. Don't remain too long in technical work. Don't become stereotyped. And, while staff experience may be imperative, it's also necessary to get a good line reputation.

Rule No.2. Observe the penalty of loss of career time. Try not to work for an immobile superior, one who doesn't move in over three years. Check to see if there are open routes upward. If there are not, try to get out of the situation somehow.

Rule No.3. Become a *crucial subordinate* to a mobile superior. A crucial subordinate is one whom the boss needs as much as he or she needs the boss. A crucial subordinate will move as the boss moves.

Rule No. 4. Always favor increased *exposure* and *visibility*. Exposure is the frequency with which you are seen by those above you. Visibility is the frequency with which you can see those above you. Decades ago, people were advised that the best way to get to the top was to get a desk near the boss's door. There's probably still some merit to that advice. In some cases, lateral moves or even moves downward may be necessary to get into an exposed position in an open route.

Rule No. 5. Be prepared to practice self-nomination. Take an active rather than a passive role. Let people in power know when you want a job. Generally, at least two moves in a career span are by self-nomination. Don't just wait for your immediate superior to determine your options. Of course, you have to be careful that your actions aren't so aggressive as to suggest that you're power hungry.

Rule No. 6. If you decide to leave the company, do it at your own convenience. Leave on the best of terms. Don't wait for the situation to deteriorate or a face-off to occur. Quit while you are ahead.

Rule No. 7. Quitting requires the benefit of a rehearsal. Don't leave in a state of high emotion. To see whether you can really act on your desire to quit, write out your resignation and wait a week. Act out what would happen if you quit: tell your family, take a week-long vacation, and bring your biographical data sheet up to date. After a week, decide whether or not to quit. But don't keep rehearsing. One way or the other, make up your mind.

Rule No. 8. Define the corporation as a market. The corporation represents a marketplace for skill that brings high performance. It's important to recognize which specific skills are in demand in a given company or industry at a particular time. By reading business periodicals such as the *Wall Street Journal* or *Business Week,* try to learn which industries need, or will need, your skills.

Rule No. 9. Don't let success cut off your options. People who are successful in one area can often succeed in another. Consider multiple careers. "Repotters," people who change their careers rather than just their job locations, may find themselves more satisfied than those who have grown in the same spot. Roots are comforting and often necessary, but if you remain too long in the same place, it's easy to become root-bound.

Mobilography

To determine the career progress of managers, Jennings has developed an interesting approach called *mobilography.* Mobilography tries to evaluate the career moves made by a manager in order to arrive at a score that is useful in assessing career progress to date and in predicting future progress. Some mobilographic terms are presented in table 30-6.

TABLE 30-6
Selected Mobilographic Terms*

T (Technical). Nonmanagerial position of any kind. The individual is positioned as a salesperson, engineer, or accountant.

U (Up). Promotion to a position of higher authority, responsibility, or difficulty. A U means line promotion to a line job, and U means promotion to staff job. U' refers to the first-level management position.

L (Lateral). Transfer to a job of similar magnitude and nature, carrying the same degrees of authority and responsibility.

S (Stay). Staying in a position and not receiving a promotion. T and S are the only nondirectional terms.

D (Demotion). Movement to a position of reduced authority, responsibility, or difficulty.

X (Exit). The manager has left the organization.

*Reprinted with permission of the publisher from *The Mobile Manager: Study of the New Generation of Top Executives* by E.E. Jennings, p. 9). Copyright © 1967 by the Graduate School of Business Administration, University of Michigan, Ann Arbor, MI, 48109.

Based upon the sequence and number of each of these categories, mobility points are assigned to indicate the manager's career potential. Table 30-7 shows some examples of mobility points.

The pattern of occurrence of career moves is considered relevant. For example, while a lateral move (L) receives three points, a second consecutive lateral move is awarded only two points. While lateral moves give the manager a broader basis for developing his or her management style, two consecutive L's may suggest that the manager wasn't felt to be ready for a promotion. Also, while a stay is awarded two points (based on the logic that one stay may show that the manager has mastered his or her job and may be marking time), a second consecutive stay is penalized two points, canceling those added by the first stay. Additional consecutive stays each result in subtracting three points from the manager's score since they suggest he or she is losing time, opportunity, and experience.[4]

TABLE 30-7
Selected Mobility Points*

TU (T followed by U)	=	15
L	=	3
S	=	2
U	=	5
D	=	—10
X	=	0
LL	=	5
SS	=	0
SSS	=	—3

*Reprinted with permission of the publisher from *The Mobile Manager: Study of the New Generation of Top Executives* by E.E. Jennings, p. 9. Copyright © 1967 by the Graduate School of Business Administration, University of Michigan, Ann Arbor, MI, 48109.

[4]For a full discussion of "mobilogic," see Jennings (1967).

Jennings classifies managers on the basis of their mobility patterns. Table 30-8 presents some common patterns and their names.

Jennings presents many other mobilographic terms—mobility audit, career age, mobility quotient, penalty rate, mobility channels, and others—we lack the space to discuss them here. We suggest you read his books for a fuller understanding of mobilography.

Is mobility out of our control?

This discussion of career mobility suggests that the sorts of things we do should make a difference in achieving our goals, whatever those goals may be. Hard work, careful planning, personality, perseverence, and other characteristics and behaviors of the individual are seen as important. However, we should point out that many things outside our control also may influence some aspects of our careers. For instance, Miller and Form (1964) provide data showing that our chances for career mobility are affected by:

1. Father's occupation (Children of business leaders, small businessmen, or professional men are more likely than others to become chief executives.)
2. Historical circumstances
3. Father's income and education (These play a major role in determining the children's education.)
4. Financial aids and influential contacts
5. Social and economic conditions

Some evidence suggests, however, that these factors may be less important than they were in, say, the 1920s and 1930s. Even as early

TABLE 30-8
Selected Mobility Patterns*

GAMMA—A manager at any level who draws two or more consecutive S's (Such people are "shelf sitters.")

ZETA—A manager at any level who has used two or more laterals dispersed among four or more U's (This is determined when the manager has four U's and not before.)

MU—A manager who has had a demotion

CHI—A manager who quit the company to get promotions sooner than he or she could draw a U in the company (This is called "leveraging.")

PSI—Executives who are the president's immediate subordinates or one position removed (They are in the arrival stage.)

OMEGA—Executives who have become presidents

*Reprinted with permission of the publisher from *The Mobile Manager: Study of the New Generation of Top Executives* by E.E. Jennings, p. 9. Copyright © 1967 by the Graduate School of Business Administration, University of Michigan, Ann Arbour, MI, 48109.

as 1955, W. Lloyd Warner and James Abegglen reported, "The sons of men from the wrong side of the tracks are finding their ways increasingly to the places of power and prestige." (1955, p. 36) Also, evidence now suggests that the real impact of family's position on educational and occupational attainment is through the development of status aspirations and the encouragement of others to carry out those aspirations. Once status aspirations and their encouragement are controlled, a family's position does not play much of a role.[5] If you have high aspirations and the persistence to pursue them, a disadvantaged family background, while certainly not helpful, may be less detrimental than was previously assumed.

OTHER CAREER OUTCOMES[6]

When we think of career outcomes, we tend to focus primarily on some measure of performance—number of promotions, sizes of salary increases, number of subordinates, level of responsibility, performance ratings by superiors and others, and so on. However, Hall (1976) stresses that at least three other outcomes are important: *career identity, career attitudes,* and *career adaptability.*

Career identity

Hall points out the close link in our society between solving our personal identity problems and establishing an occupational identity.

> We find, therefore, that the age at which people generally work through their personal identity "crises" (late teens, early twenties) is also the age at which individuals in our society are expected to choose occupational identities as well. The question, "What do you do?" is often a more acceptable way of asking, "Who are you?" (1976, p. 135)

This view suggests that career development involves an integration of the person with the requirements of his or her work environment.

Background factors help determine identity development. For example, membership in various ethnic, racial, or sex groups may influence the possibilities of entry into, and mobility within, certain occupations. The presence or absence of such possibilities may influence the individual's feelings of helplessness, apathy, self-control over destiny, and so on. Also, minority-group members may have to resolve two identity questions—that of personal identity and that of identity as a group member.

Events in the process of the person's career also influence identity changes. Three major passages through which an individual moves during a career are 1) *separation* of the person from his or her customary environment, 2) *initiation* from the old role to a new one, and

[5]For example, see Haller and Portes (1973).
[6]This section is drawn from Hall (1978).

3) *incorporation* or *reintegration* into the original or a new environment.

During the initiation phase, people who are currently in the desired role test the newcomer to see if he or she is acceptable. If so, they certify—sometimes publicly, sometimes in more subtle ways—that he or she is one of them. Certification could range from formal initiation, as in a fraternity, to the boss's indication of confidence in a newcomer. Because of that certification, the individual begins to feel like part of the group. In general, the more difficult it is to gain certification, the more the individual will identify with the role.

Movement between roles also results in identity change. New expectations associated with a role cause new feelings of responsibility and self-perceptions. In fact, attitudes and self-perceptions may begin to change in anticipation of a move.[7] For example, studies have shown that medical students, Ph.D. candidates, and assistant pastors all developed more favorable self-perceptions as they anticipated adopting more advanced roles.

Career attitudes

It seems that attitudes are shaped by the climate and dominant attitudes in the work environment. For example, one longitudinal study showed graduate business students initially holding a set of attitudes between those of senior business executives and professors. After two years of study, the students' attitudes had shifted toward those of the faculty. Then, after a year or so on the job, their attitudes had become more similar to those of the senior business executives.[8]

Other attitudes also change after some time on the job. For instance, satisfaction with work generally declines during the first years on the job, perhaps reflecting a dampening of unrealistically high expectations. However, despite reduced satisfaction with work, employees' job involvement appears to increase over time.

Also, successful managers hold more favorable attitudes and expectations regarding the organization and occupation than do others. This may reflect the relatively high self-esteem of successful managers as well as the fact that they probably receive relatively high rewards.

A final important set of career attitudes relates to *organizational commitment*, a reflection of willingness to remain in the organization and to exert effort to accomplish its goals, and *organizational identification*, a feeling of being a part of the organization. In general, we are most likely to identify with, and be committed to, an organization if it gives us the opportunity to achieve valued goals. Thus, challenging work and the opportunity to obtain organizational rewards are both likely to increase commitment and identification. Also, the longer we remain in an organization and the farther we move up its hier-

[7]See Hall (1976) for a fuller discussion of this *anticipatory socialization* process.
[8]Schein (1967).

archy, the more we'll generally identify with it, especially if the organization has a policy of promoting from within.

Career adaptability

We often hear such terms as "job burn-out" and "managerial obsolescence," which suggest that, after a while on the job, managers may become inflexible in their attitudes, outdated in their knowledge, and less intrinsically motivated by the job. To some extent, periodic training in technical aspects of the job and interpersonal skills may help. Also, actively working with new, young employees may keep the manager in tune with new concepts. And, of course, it may be possible to fit managers to jobs that better mesh with their current competencies and interests. Many issues relating to career outcomes are discussed in the following reading, "What's New in Career Management."

SUMMARY

An understanding of career interests and dynamics is important both to individuals who hope to manage others successfully and to those wishing to maximize their own career success.

A "successful" career is one that meets the goals of the individual. For some people, success may mean rapid upward mobility. For others, stability or some other criterion may define success.

Individuals go through a number of career stages, each with its own unique characteristics and demands. We reviewed a variety of approaches to the specification of career stages. And we presented the following guidelines to help you manage your career: develop basic career competencies, carefully choose an initial employing organization and job, develop mobility potential, anticipate chance events, and regularly reassess your career.

Mobility and its potential increase available options. Also, for many managers mobility has come to be valued in itself. We reviewed a number of findings concerning mobility and saw how it is related to such variables as organization strategy and growth, competency, sponsorship, entrance age, and leverage. We also summarized the rules of "success chess," specifying the sorts of actions that would maximize mobility, and we discussed mobilography.

While many external factors, such as our family's position in society, influence the probability that we can reach high-level positions in an organization, some of those factors are apparently not as important as they once were. Also, there is now reason to believe that if individuals develop high aspirations and stick to them, their family's position may not be crucial.

Finally, there are many outcomes of careers in addition to measures of performance. Among those outcomes are career identity, career attitudes, and career adaptability. We reviewed the factors influencing the development of each of these sets of outcomes.

In this chapter, we considered what careers are, why they are important, the characteristics and demands of various career stages, and what *individuals* can do to manage their careers. The following reading, by Douglas T. Hall and Francine S. Hall, discusses new issues in career management and points out what *organizations* can do to better utilize human resources through career planning.

So, we'll once again wish you success in your future career, however you define it.

REFERENCES

Argyris, C. *Integrating the Individual and the Organization.* New York: Wiley, 1964.

Crites, J.O. *Theory and Research Handbook, Career Maturity Inventory.* Monterey, Cal.: McGraw-Hill, 1973.

Hall, D.T. *Careers in Organizations* Pacific Palisades, Cal.: Goodyear Pub. Co., 1976.

Hall, D.T.; Bowen, D.D.; Lewicki, R.J.; And Hall, F.S. *Experiences in Management and Organizational Behavior.* Chicago: St. Clair Press, 1975.

Hall, D.T., and Nougaim, K. "An examination of Maslow's Need Hierarchy in an Organization Setting." *Organizational Behavior and Human Performance 3* (1968): 12-35.

Haller, A.O., and Portes, A. "Status Attainment Processes." *Sociology of Education 46* (1973): 51-91.

Jennings, E.E. *The Mobile Manager: Study of the New Generation of Top Executives.* Ann Arbor, Mich.: Bureau of Industrial Relations, Graduate School of Business Administration, The University of Michigan, 1967.

Jennings, E.E. "Mobicentric Man." *Psychology Today,* July 1970, 35-40.

Jennings, E.E. *Routes to the Executive Suite.* New York: McGraw-Hill, 1971.

Miller, D.C., and Form, W.H. *Industrial Sociology.* 2nd Ed. New York: Harper and Row, 1964.

Schein, E.H. "Attitude Change During Management Education: A Study of Organizational Influences on Student Attitudes. *Administrative Science Quarterly 11* (1967): 601-28.

Schein, E.H. "The Individual, the Organization, and the Career: A Conceptual Scheme." *Journal of Applied Behavioral Science 7* (1971): 401-26.

Super, D.E., and Bohn, M.J., Jr. *Occupational Psychology.* Belmont, Cal.: Wadsworth, 1970.

Super, D.E.; Crites, J.; Moser, H.; Overstreet, P.; and Warnath, C. *Vocational Development: A Framework for Research.* New York: Teachers College Press, 1957.

Warner, W.L., and Abegglen, J. *Occupational Mobility in American Business and Industry.* Minneapolis, Minn.: University of Minnesota Press, 1955.

SUGGESTIONS FOR ADVANCED READINGS

Bolles, R.N. *What Color Is Your Parachute? A Practical Manual for Job Hunters and Career Changers.* Berkeley, Cal.: Ten Speed Press, 1975.

Hall, D.T. *Careers in Organizations.* Pacific Palisades, Cal.: Goodyear Pub. Co., 1976.

Hall, D.T., and Nougaim, K. "An Examination of Maslow's Need Hierarchy in an Organizational Setting." *Organizational Behavior and Human Performance 3* (1968): 12-35.

Jennings, E.E. *Routes to the Executive Suite*. New York, McGraw-Hill, 1971.

Livingston, J.S. "Pygmalion in Management." *Harvard Business Review* 47 (1969): 81-89.

CHAPTER 31

What's New In Career Management*

In many organizations, the largest item in the corporate budget consists of wages and salaries. For this reason, financial problems that dictate cost reductions and increased efficiency usually boil down to problems of personnel and human resource management. Therefore, more creative, flexible, and efficient utilization of human resources through better corporate career planning can be a powerful means of dealing with some of the current headaches of managing a stable or shrinking organization in a stagnant economy. In this article, we will review some current (and probably all-too-familiar) human-resource management problems and report on how some organizations are coping with them through creative techniques for career management. We will also point out what is being neglected in the area of career development. And we will conclude with some general principles about how to make corporate career planning more effective.

PROBLEM 1: HOW CAN WE REDUCE TURNOVER AMONG RECENTLY HIRED EMPLOYEES?

Students often graduate from college or business school with unrealistically high expectations about the amount of challenge and responsibility they will find in their first job. Then they are put through a job-rotation training program or into a fairly undemanding en-

*From Douglas T. Hall and Francis S. Hall, "What's New in Career Management," *Organizational Dynamics*, Vol. 5, No. 1, (Summer 1976), pp. 17-33. Reprinted by permission of the publisher try-level job, and they get turned off. They experience "reality shock." The result is low morale, low productivity, and high turnover. Some companies lose as many as one-third or one-half of their new recruits in the first year or two of employment. One company was hiring 130 people at one time in order to have 30 at the end of the first year!

The cost of turnover is tremendous, especially among professionals and management candidates. Michael Alexander, of Touche, Ross & Co., calculated in 1973 that the total cost (including recruiting expenses, training, reduced performance during orientation, and so on) of replacing a manager was $25,000 to $30,000. After three years of inflation, that figure might be closer to $40,000. Therefore, if your company hires 100 new MBAs this year and loses 25 of them in the first year, that first year of "reality shock" may be adding $1,000,000 annually to your operating expenses.

Obviously, then, you can save a lot of money by managing the entry and first year of new employees in a more satisfying way. As companies like AT&T and General Electric have found, making initial jobs more challenging and "stretching" not only decreases turnover, but also improves long-term career performance. In one study of two AT&T operating companies, David E. Berlew and Douglas T. Hall (1966) found that management trainees who received the most challenging first-year jobs were the most successful performers five to seven years later.

Select a challenging first job. Granted, then, that one answer to Problem One is to make the first job more challenging. Just how do you go about it? First, instead of simply putting the new employee into any open job, give the matter more careful thought. If more than one job assignment is available, purposely slot the new employee into the most demanding one. "But," you ask, "how can I be sure he or she can handle it?" Good question; obviously, you can't be sure. However, our research shows that managers are quite conservative on this issue and usually err in the direction of making the first assignment too easy. This may eliminate the possibility of failure, but it also prevents the employee from achieving *psychological success*, the exhilarating sense of accomplishment that results only from achieving a task that entailed a reasonable probability of failure. More likely than not, the new recruit will perform well in a tough assignment —especially if you are available to provide help and support when needed.

Provide job enrichment. A second way of enhancing the first job is to provide a measure of job enrichment. How? Add more responsibility to the job, give the new employee increased authority, and let the new person deal directly with clients and customers (not through you); if new employees are doing special projects and making recommendations to you, let them follow through and implement these ideas. AT&T is currently training supervisors of certain new employees in the skills of job enrichment as a way of making initial jobs more of a "stretching" experience.

Assign the new recruit to demanding bosses. A third way of improving the first job is to give more care and thought to selecting the supervisor to whom you assign the new recruit. As J. Sterling Livingston has shown, there is a "Pygmalion effect" in the relationships between a new employee and his or her boss. The more the boss expects and the more confident and supportive the boss is of the new employee, the better the recruit will perform. So don't assign a new employee to a "dead wood," undemanding, or unsupportive supervisor. Choose high-performing supervisors who will set high standards for the new employee during the critical, formative first year.

Give realistic job previews. If it's not possible to upgrade the first job experience, the opposite strategy is to provide the employee with realistic expectations during the recruiting process. Several organizations (Prudential Insurance Company, Texas Instruments, the Southern New England Telephone Company, and the U.S. Military Academy) have employed *realistic job previews* (RJPs) in the formof booklets, films, visits, or talks that convey not only the positive side of organizational life, but some of the problems and frustrations as well (example: the close supervision, lack of variety, limited socializing opportunities, and criticism experienced by telephone operators).

"But we'll never be able to hire anyone if we tell them the bad news about the job," you may be thinking. Research by John Wanous and others has shown, however, that these fears are unjustified. The recruitment rate is the same for people receiving RJPs as for those who get the more traditional one-sided information.

The big return comes later, after the person starts work. Among the recipients of RJPs, turnover and dissatisfaction are significantly lower than for people on the receiving end of traditional previews. So to retain more of your new recruits, as the (now somewhat dated) saying goes, "Tell it like it really is."

A somewhat different form of the RJP has been experimentally introduced into management classrooms at the University of Wisconsin-Parkside in cooperation with the Goodyear Tire and Rubber Company's North Chicago Hose Plant. When a new recruit reacted to his first job with, "We never learned this in a classroom!" training manager Ernie LaBrecque gradually began to bring supervisors into Parkside's classes on a regular basis. The purpose is quite simple: to provide tomorrow's hires with first-hand knowledge of what to expect.

While the Parkside-Goodyear efforts have been limited, the model has significant potential for companies that recruit on a regular basis at particular universities. Not only are business leaders generally welcome in classes, but the opportunity to establish an ongoing relationship has obvious mutual benefits.

PROBLEM 2: HOW CAN WE QUICKLY DEVELOP HIGH-POTENTIAL CANDIDATES FOR MANAGEMENT POSITIONS?

The problem of identifying and selecting high-potential management candidates has been well researched over the years and is pretty well understood. Job sampling and other ways of simulating management jobs, such as assessment centers, have been shown to be effective though expensive ways of identifying managerial talent. The real problem is how we can best *train and develop* these promising candidates once they are identified.

Assessment centers for development. Assessment centers were originally developed for selection purposes, to identify high-potential candidates for hiring or promotion. When used for selection purposes, the results of the assessment process are used by managers responsible for these personnel decisions and are often not fed back to the employee. More recently, however, assessment centers have also been used successfully for employee development. When they are used in this way, the emphasis is on feedback of results to the employee following the assessment experience. In a feedback session, a trained staff member points out the candidate's strong and weak points, illustrating them with examples of the candidate's behavior in the assessment activities. After the employee understands and accepts the feedback, the discussion turns to counseling and planning for future training experiences and developmental assignments that would lead to a particular target job in management.

Many companies, viewing the results of the assessment center experience as classified information, are reluctant to feed back this information to the employee. This secrecy represents a waste of extremely valuable developmental input, particularly in view of the high cost of putting the employee through the two- or three-day experience. Such secrecy also probably leads the candidate to develop unrealistically high expectations (as in the first job). If, on the other hand, assessment results are used for feedback and career counseling, several benefits are reaped: (1) The candidate's expectations are more realistic; (2) the candidate is helped in overcoming weaknesses; (3) the candidate has a specific career plan; and (4) the company is viewed as a partner rather than an adversary in career planning, something better calculated to result in career satisfaction.

Job pathing. The AT&T research cited earlier showed the impact the first job can have on the employee's development. A logical extension of this idea is that a *sequence of jobs* can have even greater effects on the person's career growth. In fact, we would argue that *carefully sequenced job assignments have greater impact on a person's development than any other kind of training experience.* Job requirements demand that a person learn certain job-related skills. Training programs, by contrast, by and large do not demand learning. Job activities and job-related learning are by definition integrated into the ongoing work environment, whereas off-the-job training programs are often hard to reconcile with the "back home" job environment.

The critical factors in using jobs for developmental purposes are to identify (1) the skills and experience a person needs to reach a certain target job and (2) which jobs, in what sequence, will provide these skills and experiences in small enough increments so the person will not be overwhelmed, but in large enough jumps so that the person is always being stretched—thus minimizing career time to reach the target job.

One large retailing organization, for example, is undertaking just such a job-pathing program in an attempt to reduce the amount of time it takes to "grow" a store manager. Conventional wisdom in the organization is that it takes around fifteen years, but initial experiences with careful job plotting indicate that it can probably be done in five. Another widely held belief in this organization is that there are one or two main paths to the store manager's positon. Yet examination of several alternative paths, which are quite feasible but for some reason never used, indicates that the company has more flexibility in plotting career paths than it is currently using. Plotting paths through several different functions makes it possible to grow "broader" managers.

Talent development among hourly employees. Several existing methods of developing managerial talent among hourly workers may need to be reexamined in light of the need to comply with legislation on equal employment opportunity. Companies are beginning to address the question: "How can we attract a substantial number of women and minorities into these presupervisory programs?" To answer this question, some have begun to assess employee *perceptions* of upward mobility opportunities, organizational barriers to or support mechanisms for upward mobility, and the self-perceptions and role perceptions held by women and minorities. When, for example, a plant manager in a brewing company queried a woman on the reasons she *resisted* the opportunity to move into management, she replied, " I thought a production supervisor had to be a 'Two-Ton Tony.' " Obviously, this woman's resistance stemmed at least in part from the discrepancy between her perception of the role requirements and her self-image.

Another approach has been the use of in-service training institutes conducted by professional or trade organizations. While these are common in manufacturing (the Midwest Manufacturing Association, for example, has sponsored numerous "certificate" programs), organizations such as the National Association of Banking Women are also seeking ways of developing their numbers. Frequently, women and minorities view the opportunity for training through these associations as being less competitive and more supportive than company-sponsored programs.

PROBLEM 3: HOW CAN WE INCREASE PROMOTION OPPORTUNITIES IN A STABLE OR CONTRACTING ORGANIZATION?

For many organizations, the current push for career development, especially for women and minority candidates, comes in an economic period when career growth is hardest to provide: a period of corporate slow-down or retrenchment. When many new management positions are opening up in an organization, career opportunities abound; when they dry up, career advancement requires more careful planning. How can we make the most of these declining opportunities?

Cross-functional moves. One developmental method is the cross-functional or lateral transfer. Such rotational transfers may occur often at the beginning of a person's career. After a certain point, however, organizations tend to keep people in a particular functional area in which they can become highly trained and specialized and spend enough time to pay off the company's investment. In the long run, this policy leads to obsolescence; the person who is not forced to learn about new areas from time to time ends up stale, bored, and increasingly less creative and productive. Cross-functional transfers throughout the career keep a person fresh and open to new learning and give him or her a broader perspective on the company as a whole.

An example of this sort of transfer occurred at Union Carbide, where three executive vice-presidents traded jobs. The reason for the move was to give each one a better "big picture" view of the total organization and prepare them better for the presidency. One of the men, Warren M. Anderson, explained the value of the move in an article in *Business Week* (July 14, 1975, pp. 82, 84):

> We were a holding company until the mid-1950's, and you could count on your fingers the number of people who moved from division to division. You grow up in a division, and you get about four miles tall but not very broad. . . . Everybody had sneered at lateral transfers. Now, they can point to us. I feel this gives me a chance to see the whole business.

Job pathing enables us to identify jobs *at the same organizational level* that demand more skills in certain areas than do other jobs. Thus the great potential of lateral moves for development is more effectively tapped. After two people trade jobs, as one retailing organization found, it is possible for each to end up in a more demanding position!

A critical issue in any kind of lateral move is how the transfer decision is made. When personnel staff specialists make the decisions, the moves may make good, sound technical sense—but may be unacceptable to the bosses of the people to be moved. Also, this kind of decision-making process implies that career planning is purely a staff function, and not the manager's job.

Management-personnel committees. One way of getting managers more involved in career planning is through the mechanism of management-personnel committees. In this structure, which is employed by the Southern New England Telephone Company (SNET), each personnel committee is made up of managers from all the functions at the same level of management. Each committee meets once every week or two to decide what transfers will be made between their departments among people who report to them. They also make recommendations on promotions. Employees are assessed in terms of their management potential, ranging from Category 1 (high-level potential) to Category 6 (not promotable even if the company is on the verge of going out of business).

According to Robert Neal, director of human resources development for SNET, this process results in a high quality of personnel decisions and in personnel actions that generally are well accepted by those affected—both the bosses and the transferred employees. The process does deal with tough issues of bargaining ("I'll take one from your Category 5, but let's agree in writing that you'll take him back in two years"). Actual contracts are written and signed, in much the way that "player swaps" are handled in professional sports. Another benefit of this system, according to Neal, is that a "Cat. 5" in one department—say, marketing—may blossom into a "Cat. 2" in traffic. Employees are periodically reassessed in light of *recent* performance, since these transfers enable an employee to demonstrate potential that might otherwise have been hidden forever if he or she had stayed in one function or department.

One disadvantage of this process, of course, is that like most committee structures, it takes a fair amount of time. However, the benefits seem to justify the time invested. Another management "plus" of this system is that the the managers who serve on personnel committees develop a greater identification with the company as a whole. The decision process involved forces them to rise above their own department loyalties and look at decisions from a broader perspective. The rate of interfunctional movement has increased from 5 percent of all transfers in 1968 to 50 percent now.

Whenever we discuss development lateral moves with executives, the response is usually surprisingly strong, either pro or con. Some people see it as a radical, impractical idea because the need for retraining would be great, as would the organizational risk of having managers who are inexperienced in their new function or department. Lateral moves also buck a common norm in many organizations —namely that the only good move is a promotion. Other managers report that they are beginning to experiment with cross-functional moves, and their experiences are generally favorable. Still others report they have never really thought abut cross-functional moves, but they get very excited about this "creative new idea." There is nothing new or creative about lateral moves, however; the fact is that in many companies promotion policies are simply taken for granted, like "organizational wallpaper," when they might quite easily and profitably be changed.

Fallback positions. One risk of a cross-functional transfer or promotion, especially when it occurs at a senior level, is that the person may fail in the new job simply because it's too demanding. Because many organizations are reluctant to move people down a level, there is some risk that the cross-functional transferee may become stuck in a position beyond his or her level of competence—the Peter Principle in action.

A novel way of reducing this risk in a high-level job move is to identify a fallback position into which the person can move if he or she is not successful after promotion or transfer. The fallback position assures the person of a position equal in status and pay to his and her original job if things don't work out in the new one. Establishing a fallback position in advance lets everyone involved know that (1) there is some risk in the promotion or transfer, (2) the company is willing to accept some of the responsibility for it, and (3) moving into the fallback position does not constitute failure. As a result, the ratchet effect of upward-only movement is partially eliminated, and the organization's degree of freedom in manpower planning is substantially increased.

Consider this illustration of the fallback-position concept. In the Heublein organization, one management-information systems expert was moved to finance, and a human-resources specialist was transferred to a job in production management. Without the fallback position, neither person might have been willing to take the risk. With it, people who have become highly specialized (perhaps overspecialized) can be helped to work their way back into general management. Among the other companies that have employed fallback positions are Procter and Gamble, Continental Can, and Lehman Brothers (*Business Week*, September 28, 1974).

Downward transfers. More dramatic than the establishment of fallback positions is the policy of legitimizing downward transfers (demotions). Being able to move people down as well as up introduces considerably more flexibility in manpower planning. As organizational growth decreases, and as more people elect to "stay put" in their present job (or are compelled to), the result could be corporate stagnation—with few people entering or leaving the organization. To maintain flexibility, therefore, new ways of creating internal mobility become critical. For every person moved downward, a shot at a promotion is created for numerous people below this level. Where there is a policy against moving people down, the only way a vacancy could open up would be through retirement or death (assuming no organizational growth or turnover).

The problem with downward transfers, obviously, is the strong norm in our society against moving down. Moving up is good, moving laterally is suspect, and moving down spells *failure*.

The upward-mobility norm is a tough one to buck, but it is being challenged on several fronts.

1. As concern over the quality of life increases, more people are turning down promotions or accepting lower-level jobs in order to move to or to stay in such desirable geographical areas as San Diego, Minneapolis, Atlanta, and Seattle. When, for example, the department of psychology at San Diego State University advertised an opening for an assistant professor (a position generally filled by someone fresh out of graduate school), the department received many applications from full professors and department chairmen who were willing to move down in order to live in San Diego.

2. Realizing that growth opportunities are becoming more limited, people are willing to move down into a new area or company as a possible base from which to move up later on.

3. Given the option of being terminated or being demoted, people are often willing to accept a move down. As with many decisions in life, the attractiveness of a demotion often depends upon the nature of the alternatives. In recent cuts of technical personnel, companies such as General Electric and Chrysler first tried to place as many employees as possible in lower-level jobs rather than terminate them. Those who were moved down rather than out were viewed as being quite fortunate.

4. As the economy settles into a period of slower growth, expectations of rapid advancement may diminish and the upward-mobility norm may weaken. There is already evidence that the American success ethic is moving away from advancement and money as success symbols, toward self-fulfillment. As Daniel Yankelovich put it:

> Since World War II most Americans have shaped their ideas of success around money, occupational status, possessions, and the social mobility of their children. Now, ideas about success are beginning to revolve around various forms of self fulfillment. If the key motif of the past was "keeping up with the Joneses," today it is, "I have my own life to live, let Jones shift for himself."

As part of this quest for personal self-fulfillment (which does not necessarily have to occur on the job), people may be more likely to take a lower-level job that gives them more autonomy or challenge or simply more freedom to pursue fulfillment off the job.

Other organizations are using downward transfers to open up management training and mobility options that otherwise would not exist. One large Canadian oil company has been experimenting with downward transfers at senior executive levels. This company has learned certain principles that increase the success of downward transfers. First, the people who are chosen to be moved down should be people who are known (by themselves and other employees) to be outstanding performers. This helps dissociate downward movement from failure (and, it is to be hoped, may even associate it with success). Over time, if enough obviously competent people are moved down, the norm of promotion-as-a-sign-of-success may be replaced with movement-as-a-sign-of-success. People to be moved down should be informed well in advance and told that they may be moved back to their present levels later.

Why are outstanding performers moved down? First, because even if a person is performing successfully at his or her job, there are still many equally promising people at the next level down, waiting for a higher-level challenge. Moving one person down temporarily gives many more people a good opportunity for development. The obviously successful person would be more secure and more effective in a downward move than would a less outstanding performer. Second, there may be "hot spots" at a lower level in the organization that call for the temporary trouble-shooting services of a successful higher-level person. Perhaps a tough marketing problem needs to be solved or maybe a department needs reorganizing. A key executive could come in on a one-year assignment, clean things up, and then move back to his previous level or to a new "hot spot."

A second principle is that important ground rules must be established: (1) No one will suffer a cut in pay as a result of a downward move, and (2) no one moved down will be terminated (to make it clear that the next move after moving down isn't out the door). People moved down thus received a sort of "tenure" that gave them more security than most other employers.

What are some of the preliminary results of the downward-transfer system in this firm? The most obvious is that intra-organizational mobility and flexibility have increased. More young people can move up into high-responsibility positions faster than before. They can also move back down and into other functional areas more easily.

What about the effects on the people moved down? According to the personnel director, the first few people (as one might anticipate) had mixed emotions about it. After several months, however, they began to appreciate the freedom from higher-level responsibilities and pressures. They appreciated having a bit more time to spend with their families, getting to know their grandchildren, and so on. They also enjoyed the stimulation of working with younger managers —learning new ideas and techniques from them and transmitting wisdom and experience to them.

An unintended consequence of these downward transfers has been an improvement in two-way communication, especially in the upward direction.

Corporate tenure

Some of the career-management policies we have just discussed, such as cross-functional transfers and downward moves, are often difficult to implement because of the threats they may pose to the person's security in the organization. One way to increase employees' sense of security, and at the same time to establish tougher performance standards and feedback, is through a system of corporate tenure.

Such a novel system has been used in a medium-sized Pennsylvania manufacturing firm. The president of this firm, Robert Seidel, took a look at how various types of organizations develop personnel. He decided that universities, for all their problems, did have one promising feature: the tenure system. The tenure system forces the university to take a good hard look at a person's performance and to give him or her straight feedback: "up or out."

Seidel modified the tenure system in this way. When a new employee is hired, he or she is put on a short-term probation period, a customary procedure in many organizations. At the end of the period, the employee's immediate superior and a personnel expert carefully appraise the person's performance. If it has been satisfactory, the employee is encouraged to stay on.

At this point, however, a novel twist occurs. The two evaluators make a second judgment: If there were to be a economic downturn and we had to make a 20 percent staff cut, would this person be in the 20 percent we would terminate? The answer to this question, which is fed back to the employee, gives him a realistic idea of where he stands with the company. People who are not in this 20 percent marginal group are thus granted a form of organizational tenure. Knowing that their jobs are secure, they feel freer to assume the risks of interdepartmental transfer, promotion, or demotion. Interestingly, this tenure does not result in "slacking off," perhaps because of clear standards of high performance in the organization.

What about the effect on the people in the 20 percent group? Often they elect to remain in the organization. In some cases, the feedback results in improved performance. One major advantage of this tenure system is that it forces the organization to appraise new employees all the time, not just on a "crash" basis when a personnel cut is necessary.

The need for internal mobility

The common theme in all these methods of providing for better career development in a slower growth economy is increased intra-organizational mobility. If job changes are not going to be facilitated so much by the entrance or departure of people or by the opening up of new positions, we will have to find new ways to move people around within the organization.

We know from the work of Paul Lawrence and Jay Lorsch and others that organizations have to become more flexible if they are to adapt to changes and uncertainty in the external environment. The methods we have been discussing (downward transfers, cross-functional moves, and so on) are all specific ways in which the organization can increase its own flexibility and that of its human resources.

Executives are rethinking their norms about what kind of movement is appropriate. Both employees and the organization have to plan career moves more carefully and work harder at career development, because the economy is no longer doing the job for us. In an ironic twist, a slow growth economy is giving (or forcing upon) individuals and organizations more control over the way careers unfold.

WHAT IS NOT BEING DONE ABOUT CAREER DEVELOPMENT?

So much for the good news; now let's see where less progress is being made.

Integrating career development and manpower planning

Work on organizational careers has a schizophrenic aspect. On the one hand, there are attempts to facilitate the careers of individual employees through career counseling, goal setting, and so forth (the micro approach). At the other extreme, manpower planners chart the moves of large numbers of people through various positions in the organization—identifying future staffing gaps, "fast tracks," and the like (the macro approach). But these two types of career planning are rarely integrated.

Most organizations, in fact, use only one of these approaches—an unfortunate practice no matter which one they choose. The company that focuses on individuals, for example, may well do a good job of developing people—but if overall corporate manpower needs are ignored, these individuals may be "all developed with no place to go" or find themselves being routed into dead-end jobs.

On the other hand, the organization that develops corporate manpower plans without adequately developing and training people to move through various positions (or to move through a different sequence of positions) is not really managing and planning careers, but merely monitoring them. Even in the organization that is doing both micro and macro career planning, most of the potential of each approach is lost if (as is often the case) the micro and macro people don't talk to each other.

It seems almost trite to suggest that the micro and macro facets of career management be integrated because it seems so straightforward and reasonable. One wonders why this integration does not occur more often. One reason is that organizations large enough to need systematic career management generally have career counseling and manpower planning in different departments. Practitioners in each area often come out of different professional disciplines —counselors from psychology, and manpower planners from economic or systems analysis. And it is difficult to integrate the two—to undertake sound manpower forecasts and then to translate them into specific training and development activities.

Dealing with second-generation EEO problems

Many organizations are now into what we might call Phase II of affirmative action. The main need in Phase I, which concerned recruitment and selection, was to get more women and minority employees to enter managerial and professional positions. Now that more women and minorities *are* entering these positions, other problems arise—such as the need for training and development, meeting new needs of new kinds of employees, and coping with the reactions of white male employees.

The problem of providing organizational support. A subtle pattern seems to be evolving, in which some executives subvert EEO goals while apparently implementing them. The equation for this process is "Equal opportunity + low support = discrimination." If a woman or minority employee is hired for a position traditionally occupied by white males, the new person will probably need some technical training as well as informal advice, coaching, and support. In fact, most of us need—and receive—all kinds of informal help and support in any new job. However, when female or minority employees are placed in a nontraditional position (that is, given equal employment opportunity), they are often socially isolated from peers and senior colleagues who could give them words of wisdom, feedback, prodding, encouragement, "Dutch uncle" talks, and the like; these new employees are simply left alone to do their job—and frequently to fail. One young woman, for example, was hired by a high-prestige (and high-pressure) university despite the concern some people felt about her lack of experience and confidence in dealing with the demanding students she would encounter. A senior faculty member assured the others that he would take her "under his wing" and help her cope with her environment. So she was hired—the first woman in her department—and all eyes were on her. And the senior professor left for a sabbatical as soon as she arrived! No one else was willing to act as a substitute sponsor in his absence. Without support or counsel, she floundered in the classroom. She spent so much time working on her teaching that she didn't spend much time on research—and no one "bugged" her to do any publishing. Now the reaction of her colleagues is, "Well, we tried giving a woman a chance; I guess we'd better not make *that* mistake again." Thus with equal opportunity and low support, low initial expectations for the person's success can create a vicious self-fulfilling prophecy.

The problem of meeting the needs of the white male. Because of the slow economy, promotions are harder to come by these days—and those that *are* available are often used to advance women and minority employees. Consequently, the white male often feels frustrated and demotivated. It is no consolation to him to say that this reverse discrimination is a temporary corrective measure to make up for past generations of discrimination in favor of white males. After all, he wasn't responsible for what happened earlier, so why should he suffer now?

The group being hurt most is white males of average competence. Outstanding performers will always have corresponding career opportunities. And poor performers are likely always to have problems —but right now, EEO activity is giving them a handy scapegoat. It is the average white male who is most likely to lose out in competition with women and minorities who show equal performance and qualifications.

Most companies seem aware of this problem, but see little they can do about it. They often handle the issue by cloaking promotion data in great secrecy—perhaps in the hope that if white males aren't told they're not getting anywhere, maybe they won't notice it! The irony here is that in many companies white males tend to overestimate their relative disadvantage. More open information would probably show that white males are moving faster than their perceptions would suggest.

One way to deal with this issue is to be sure that white males receive at least as much career counseling and assistance in career planning as do women and minorities, because the former group may need to plan their career moves more carefully. The white male may have a greater need for occupational information inside and outside the company than do other, higher-priority groups. In fact, many companies started career-planning programs for women and minorities only and then opened them up to all employees. In these organizations, white males have more career-planning services now available than they ever would have had without EEO pressures.

Another strategy—a high-risk, but high-potential one—would be to hold career workshops in which male and female employees, black and white, meet to discuss their feelings about career opportunities and explore methods of aiding their career development. Such group sessions could meet employees' need for: (1) ventilating feelings, (2) being counseled, (3) getting career information, (4) doing some self-assessment, and (5) solving career problems.

Managing dual careers

As more women embark upon full-time work careers, more dual-career families come into existence. When both husband and wife have full-time careers, their personal career flexibility decreases (if they want to live together), so career planning becomes more difficult and necessary. It is, of course, more difficult to transfer a dual-career employee to a different city or, if the spouse is transferred by his or her firm, to attempt to make a similar move for the partner who works for you. You may find yourself losing good people because of a spouse's career. Alternatively, you might find it difficult to attract someone whose spouse could not find good career opportunities in your organization's geographical area.

The best way for organizations to deal with dual careers is not clear. Many executives do not yet see the problem as an important one. The first step, therefore, is to demonstrate to managers the ways in which dual careers can affect their organization. Our preliminary research indicates that the main problem caused by dual careers comes in making personnel transfers. Recruitment and hiring do not seem to be so strongly affected, although again managers may just be less aware of the dual-career people they lose in the hiring process than of the ones they hire and can't transfer.

Companies seem to be dealing with the transfer problem by adopting a more flexible attitude toward people who turn down transfers. An employee is now informally granted more transfer refusals without prejudice to future promotions than in the past. There also seems to be more effort to find developmental moves within the same geographic location. This is another reason why cross functional moves may become more common.

Another corporate response to dual careers is an increasing awareness that the organization has some stake in the spouse's career, even if the spouse works elsewhere. Thus various supportive services, mainly informal, are being extended to unemployed spouses (for example, help in setting up job interviews with other organizations.) Nepotism rules are also being relaxed, making it easier for husband and wife to work for the same organization or even in the same department. (The emerging norm in many organization is that spouses can work in the same department as long as one is not supervising the other.) Flexible workhours are helpful, too.

Some organizations are finding that attracting dual-career people requires dual recruiting, or helping to find a job for the spouse as well as the primary candidate. This may require cooperative interorganizational recruiting. Dealing with another organization's personnel executives, over whom you have no control, can be a real test of managerial and persuasive skills. The fact is, however, that the spouse's career opportunities have became a bargaining point in recruiting and retaining dual-career employees. This issue is just beginning to show up with younger, more junior people. In time, these will become key people and then the problem will be critical. The executive who responds that this is the couple's problem, not the organization's, will lose many good employees. The issue, we feel, is a real organizational "time bomb."

GENERAL PRINCIPLES OF EFFECTIVE CAREER PLANNING

So far, we've examined what novel ideas are being tried and what isn't being done. Let's conclude with a few general guidelines about what *should* be done in developing employee careers.

Utilize the career-growth cycle

First, let's consider just how career growth occurs. This process, shown in Figure 31-1, is triggered by a job that provides challenging, stretching goals. The clearer and more challenging the goals, the more effort the person will exert—and the more effort exerted, the more likely it is that good performance will result. If the person does a good job and receives positive feedback, he or she will feel successful (psychologically successful). Feelings of success increase a

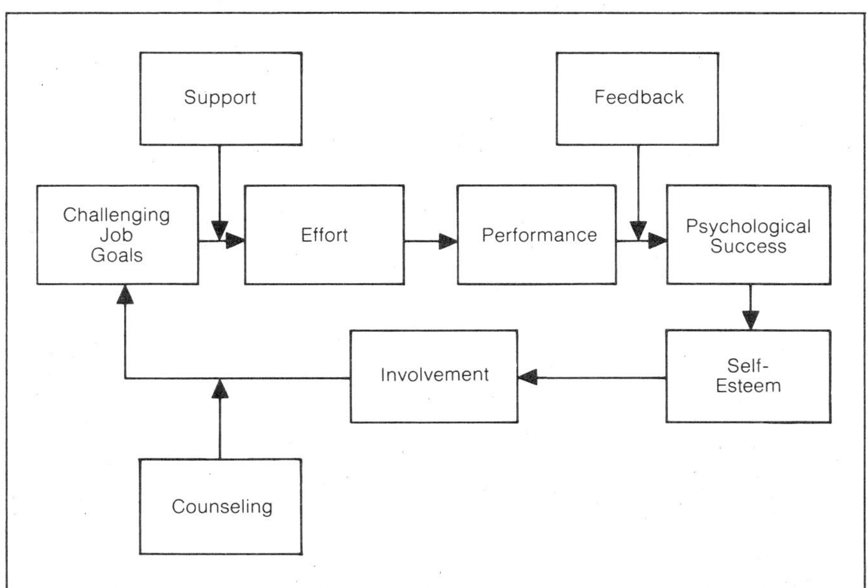

FIGURE 31-1
The Career-Growth Cycle

person's feelings of confidence, self-worth, or self-esteem. This internal gratification leads the person to become more involved in work, which in turn leads to the setting of future stretching goals. Let us consider more specifically how a company might use this growth cycle.

Plan and utilize the job itself

Since the career-growth cycle is triggered by challenging work goals, the person's job should be made as challenging as possible (as we explained earlier). Too many companies see career development only as something done by "those people in personnel." Each job should represent a challenge, and the sequence of jobs should be planned to provide a systematic and continuing growth of career skills.

Goal setting. In general, people tend not to set work goals for themselves. But when they do, the results can be dramatic. This doesn't mean that you need a formal MBO system—just mutual agreement between you, your boss, and your subordinate on a few specific objectives over the next few months that will help the employee focus his or her efforts.

Frequent performance review and feedback. Although most organizations have formal policies regarding performance appraisals, few performance appraisals are actually handled properly for the benefit of employees. People need feedback to help assess how well they have performed and where changes should be made. Such feedback can be given informally, on a continuing basis, instead of in a stressful, formal, once-a-year ordeal. It is also easier to provide feedback if specific goals have been set; then you can talk not only about how well activities were carried out, but also about whether certain ones where carried out at all.

Counseling and support from the boss. When building the conditions for career success into the job, don't forget the boss. As a source of support (in translating goals into action) and counseling and planning (for translating involvement into future goals), supervisors can be far more influential than any personnel or career specialist. The supervisor is also the best person to provide goal-setting stimulation and performance feedback.

Train and reward supervisors for career-planning skills

If the supervisor is to be expected to provide support, feedback, and counseling, don't think this will happen easily. One reason supervisors don't do more along these lines now is that they don't feel comfortable doing it. And they feel uncomfortable for a number of reasons. One is that they often lack the necessary skills. A second reason is that they often experience role conflict between being a "boss" and being a "helper." A two- or three-day training program would be an enormous aid for supervisors, enabling them to learn both how to conduct good performance appraisals and how to be good informal agents of career planning. This approach to career planning is already being taken in one of the major auto manufacturers, with good results.

Tying employee development specifically into the supervisor's own performance appraisal is another good way to reward these activities. This is a simple idea, but it is rarely practiced. General Electric has been successful in including managers' affirmative action progress in their performance appraisals. The result has been a great increase in EEO attainments. A large Canadian computer company requires each manager to pick and develop a successor before the manager will be considered for promotion. This is a very clear and powerful way of linking the career development of subordinates to the career progress of the manager.

Personnel specialists as monitors. Tying career development into the everyday work environment of supervisors frees personnel specialists to act in an indirect, support role (which is what a staff function is intended to be, anyway). Personnel people can work in two ways: (1) They can train the supervisors in the career-developing skills just discussed, and (2) they can monitor the process to make sure that periodic goal setting, feedback, and career planning are discussed. The following application of these ideas gives more details.

An illustrative example: AT&T. Several of these principles are illustrated in career programs being used at AT&T. Joel Moses, a personnel specialist, cites one early identification program—the Initial Management Development Program—for noncollege employees being considered for management positions. The employees first go through a one-day assessment program. Then they are given feedback by a trained person (either in personnel or in the person's own department), who then continues to function as the employee's *career counselor.* Explicit career plans are made. Then the person and the boss jointly set work targets to help achieve the career plan. Although most of the planning is done within the employee's department, the personnel specialist functions as monitor of the process. The third-party career counselor is useful because of the high turnover in superior-subordinate relationships.

Another program is a successor to the Initial Management Development Program, but is more "user oriented" than IMDP. The stress is on *boss training* in the areas of job design, joint target setting, and appraisal skills. At the end of the first year of employment, the person goes through a two-day assessment program. Following this is a meeting with the person's boss, a member of the assessment center, and a personnel coordinator. One of three decisions is made. Terminate, don't promote, or prepare for middle management. A feedback meeting is held with the employee to discuss the results of the assessment process. Then in the second year a career plan is drawn up—entailing a target job, the training needed, interim assignments, and a time frame. The three parties review this plan and the progress made every six months.

The following principles are reflected in these AT&T programs:

1. Emphasize the development of high-potential people. Don't try to change people who lack management potential.

2. Set specific development objectives. Identify specific job experiences and skills the person needs (for example, "ability to supervise a central office PBX group.")

3. Train the supervisor to provide the day-to-day job experiences (for example, challenging goals and feedback) that facilitate career development.

4. Give personnel experts the responsibilty for structuring and monitoring the development *process,* but reserve for the employee and the supervisor the responsibilty for its actual content.

CONCLUSION

The more we use the job itself and the superior-subordinate relationship for career development and call upon the personnel department for outside resources and process monitors, the better use we are making of the respective resources of each.

We hope that the new process of career development will not be accepted or implemented without careful thought and planning, since it could become just another management fad. Rather, career development, the enhancement of human talent, should be viewed as a management function that has always been performed in effective organizations—yet one that can benefit from being conceptualized and practiced in new ways.

REFERENCE

Berlow, D.E. and Hall, D.T. "The Socialization of Managers." *Administrative Science Quarterly* 11(1966): 207-223.

DISCUSSION QUESTIONS

1. List the five main goals you hope to achieve during your career. Rank them from most important to least important. What do you realistically feel are the probabilities that you will be able to achieve each of those goals? What do you feel will be the key barriers to their attainment? Is there anything you can do in anticipation of surmounting those barriers?

2. List the actions you have already taken to plan your career. Have you utilized counseling services or career-planning exercises? Have you seriously weighed the extent to which each of your goals is likely to be met? Did you consciously choose a career direction, or did you "drift" into it?

3. Try to present as realistic a picture as you can of the sort of position you expect (rather than hope) to be in fifteen years from now. Indicate how each of the following factors might be relevant:

   a. Your spouse's career

   b. How well you got along with your first boss

   c. Your desire for a stable education for your children

   d. Trade-offs between upward mobility and job security

   e. Preferences for a particular city or geographical area

   f. Wishes of your spouse and children

   g. Severe unanticipated financial problems

4. Determine the mobility points associated with each of the following patterns—TUD, TUSS, TUSX, TULULULU—and indicate the name Jennings has given to patterns of each type. (Note: Refer to tables 30-6 & 30-7 of chapter 30 to answer the questions. Actual scoring of the last pattern is really slightly more complicated than table 30-7 suggests, but your answer will be a good approximation.)

5. Do you see any ethical questions that might arise as organizations more actively manage their employees' careers?

6. What disadvantages do you see to the idea of "corporate tenure"?

7. What links do you see between Jennings' mobilography and the logic of job pathing?

8. Do you agree with Hall and Hall that white males should "receive at least as much as career counseling and assistance in career planning as. . . women and minorities?" Why or why not?

Index

H

I

J

L

M

N

O

P

Q

R

S

T

U

V

W

†